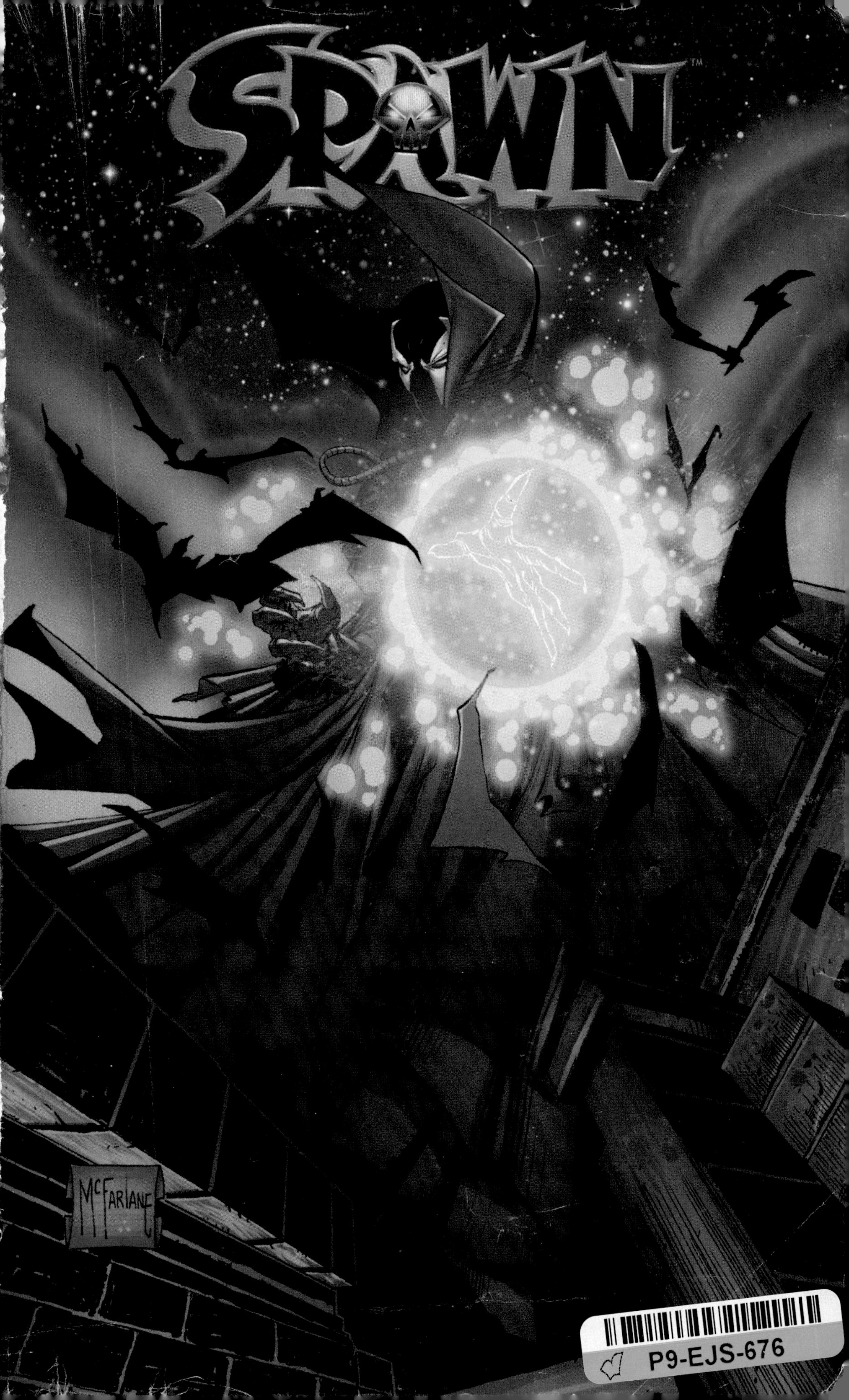
SPAWN™
McFARLANE

Spawn / Al Simmons
Once the U.S. Government's best operative and highest deco-rated soldier, Al Simmons was murdered by his own men and sent to Hell. There, he agreed to lead Hell's army in the upcoming Armageddon in order to return to see his beloved wife. The flawed agreement sent Simmons to earth five years later to find his widow happily married to his best friend with a child he could never give her. Stripped of his life and identity, he is now known as Spawn and lives in the shadows of the New York City alleys where he struggles to understand his twisted circumstances.

Clown / Violator
A demon who appears as a clown to serve as a guide to the earth-bound Hell Spawn. When he is angered or becomes jealous of the special treatment the Hell Spawn receives, he returns to his lizard-like form to vent his rage.

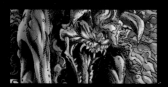

Malebolgia
The supreme master of the dark netherworld who gathers souls in preparation for Armageddon. He set up the agreement with Al Simmons in return for his services as the General of Hell's army.

Terry Fitzgerald and his wife Wanda Blake
While Al Simmons was alive and working for the government, Terry Fitzgerald was his partner and best friend. Today, Terry is married to Al's widow, Wanda Blake, and although Wanda loves Terry, she misses Al greatly and thinks of him often.

Jason Wynn
Head of the United States Security Group and probably the most powerful man alive. He has overseen projects from secret assassinations to interference in other nations' internal affairs. He is the man who recruited, manipulated, and disposed of Al Simmons.

Sam Burke and Twitch Williams
New York City Police Department detective partners who are complete opposites. Sam Burke is a single, gruff, heavy-handed ex-military officer dedicated to finding the truth, while Twitch Williams is a sharp-shooting, cool-headed, college-edu-cated family man. Together, they form an effective crime-fight-ing partnership on the streets and in the alleys of New York City.

Billy Kincaid
A murderous pedophile who drives an ice cream truck to attract the children he preys upon.

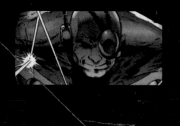

Overt-Kill
A man meshed with bionics, a successful experiment funded by the Mafia to create a super hit man.

ORIGINAL SERIES

STORY AND ART
Todd McFarlane

STORY FOR ISSUE 11
Frank Miller

COLORING
Steve Oliff
Reuben Rude
and Olyoptics

COVER
Todd McFarlane

LETTERING
Tom Orzechowski

EDITOR
Wanda Kolomyjec

SPAWN: COLLECTED EDITION

EDITOR
Brian Haberlin

DESIGN
Brian Haberlin
and Francis Takenaga

Editor-in-Chief
Brian Haberlin

President of Entertainment
Terry Fitzgerald

President of McFarlane Toys
Larry Marder

Executive Director of
Spawn.com
Tyler Jeffers

Art Director
Ben Timmreck

Graphic Designer
Jason Gonzalez

Manager of International
Publishing for TMP
Suzy Thomas

Publisher for Image Comics
Erik Larsen

Spawn created by
Todd McFarlane

TODD McFARLANE
PRODUCTIONS
www.spawn.com

SPAWN COLLECTION, VOL. 1. June 2007. Fourth Printing. Published by IMAGE COMICS, 1942 University Ave. Berkeley, CA 94704, Spawn, its logo and its symbol are registered trademarks © 2007 Todd McFarlane Productions, Inc. All other related characters are TM and © 2007 Todd McFarlane Productions, Inc. All rights reserved. The characters, events and stories in this publication are entirely fictional. With exception of artwork used for review purposes, none of the contents of this publication may be reprinted without the permission of Todd McFarlane Productions, Inc. PRINTED IN CANADA

INTRODUCTION

I read Spawn every month it actually comes out, I like Spawn a whole lot. Spawn is a berserker, balls-out journey through territories fun, sick, often preposterous and sometimes poignant. But enough about Spawn. There's few things more annoying than picking up a comic book collection and having to wade through an introduction that tells you how cool it is when you've already got it in your hands. When you can already make your own judgments about the story and artwork. There's few things more annoying than that, but I can't name more than four, off the top of my head. The last thing you need is some pretentious clown tossing in references to Great Art and Great Literature and telling you that boy, you'dd better appreciate this. So enough about Spawn. At least in terms of what you're about to read. Instead, let me tell you why Spawn pisses so many people off.

Spawn isn't just a trip through the inventive, somewhat demented imagination of author and artist Todd McFarlane, although it is most certainly that. Spawn is a chunk of comics history, and an important one. Spawn is a Boston Tea Party, a loud, rude act of defiance against a bad, broken system built on abusing its finest.

"SPAWN IS A BOLD GAMBL
COMIC BOOKS A BETTER FIELD FOR ANY

Spawn is a bold gamble that paid off and made comic books a better field for anybody with talent and a fresh idea. Todd McFarlane didn't invent creator's rights, nor is he some lonely, sole champion who transformed our field single-handedly, but he's done his bit big time. And he had damn good reasons for doing so.

The creators of childhood myths like Superman, Spiderman, Captain America, and all the rest were, to say the least, treated abominably by publishers who reaped millions from their work. Many of these creators died in poverty. Virtually all were denied proper credit, any compensation beyond slave-wage page rates, even the possession of the physical artwork they drew with their own hands. As a generation of comic book fans came of age, filled with a passion to follow in the paths of Jack Kirby, Steve Ditko, and so many other brilliant cartoonists, some of us struggled from within the existing system to change the way things were done at the old publishing houses, and certain progress was made. Original artwork was returned. Royalties (of a sort) began to be paid. It became possible to make a decent living writing and drawing comic books.

My generation of cartoonists had little reason for complaint on our own behalf-unless the editor had a buddy who wanted our job, or he wanted it himself, or worse, unless we made the stupid mistake of creating anything new. This much remained intact of the old system, and it was its central mechanism that made any true and meaningful reform impossible: the publisher maintained absolute control over everything it published by seizing the trademarks and copyrights, thereby denying the cartoonist the legal authorship of what he created with his own mind and hands.

To create a new character was an exercise in self-abuse. Inevitably, desperate to prove their unprovable authorship, the old publishers would, sooner or later, get around to firing artists from their own creations. Add to this the humiliation of seeing your work turned into million-dollar lines of toys and big budget movies without a nickel or a credit line tossed your way, and the conclusion to draw is obvious.

You content yourself to doing the old stuff, to strip-mining the work of your predecessors, or you leave. Leave we did. As years passed, feeling restless, wishing sincerely to break the old cycle of resentment and bitterness, hungry to put behind us the increasingly distasteful job of defibrillating tired old heroes, eager as hell as we were to pump some new blood, some of our own blood, into a once-vital artform gone catatonic, many of us turned our backs on the old publishers. We found new publishers, ready to do business as equals, ready to swim into the uncertain waters ahead rather than drown in the stagnant pool we'd all inherited. The result was not revolutionary. Not for years, it wasn't.

Not till Spawn.

Things stayed more or less the same, for quite some time. The new comics were tolerated as marginal items, charity cases. They were branded with that most sales-quelching term, "alternative," by retailers, readers, and even the people who published them. The "mainstream" of the comics field consisted almost entirely of characters created before the readership was born. Brand loyalty fed by misguided nostalgia enabled old publishers to keep comics frozen in time. True, the ice was melting, the "mainstream" was being steadily redefined, but slowly, ever so slowly…

They never should've given an inch, those old publishers. Not if they wanted the old order to continue unthreatened. They never should've allowed the talent any semblance of dignity. Getting our artwork back gave us the opportunity to find out that it was worth something to the fans, that they were willing to pay hard cash for it. Paying us royalties gave us a sense of exactly how much money our efforts were making out there. But the most critical error of all was the one earliest made, and that error was giving us credit.

THAT PAID OFF AND MADE
DY WITH TALENT AND A FRESH IDEA."

Just as my generation grew up knowing that Jack Kirby drew the coolest comics, so the next generation of readers had names to attach to their favorite comics. A "star system" emerged. Artists and writers became "hot." "Hot" translated into sales, and increased power for the talent.

The old machinery tried to re-tool. There was no stopping this trend. The fans wouldn't allow it. So the old machinery built up popular artists into comics superstars, using their names as proof their "product" wasn't obsolete, gambling that, with a steady stream of wide-eyed wannabe cogs ready to replace any of us who turned into monkey wrenches, the dear old works could keep clunking along and appear hip at the same time. Then along came one big, mean spanner by the name of Todd.

With superb timing, expert strategy, and palpable arrogance, Todd McFarlane, the hottest artist of the day, rallied his fellow comics superstars to abandon sad old Marvel Comics all at once, and just as their popularity hit a fever pitch. With slick production, artwork that rippled with enthusiasm, and stories slapped together with euphoric abandon, Todd and his buddies formed Image Comics and competed jaw to jaw with Marvel, and won.

The kids went with them.

While Marvel staggers on, still an industry giant, its roar has gone hollow, and its feet of clay are visible to all.

Whether Image Comics will continue to make creator owned comics its mainstay, or will succumb to the temptations of the robber-baron policies that have enervated the field since its inception, remains to be seen. In the meantime, it's good news indeed for artists, and for readers, that for the time the best-selling comic book in America, Spawn, is wholly owned and controlled by the talent who made it up. Our future looks bright. Now, at last, free of the sorry restraints of the past and having no excuse to be slackers, it's up to us to prove that we can cut the mustard.

Frank Miller
Los Angeles, 1995*

*reprinted from original Spawn Trade

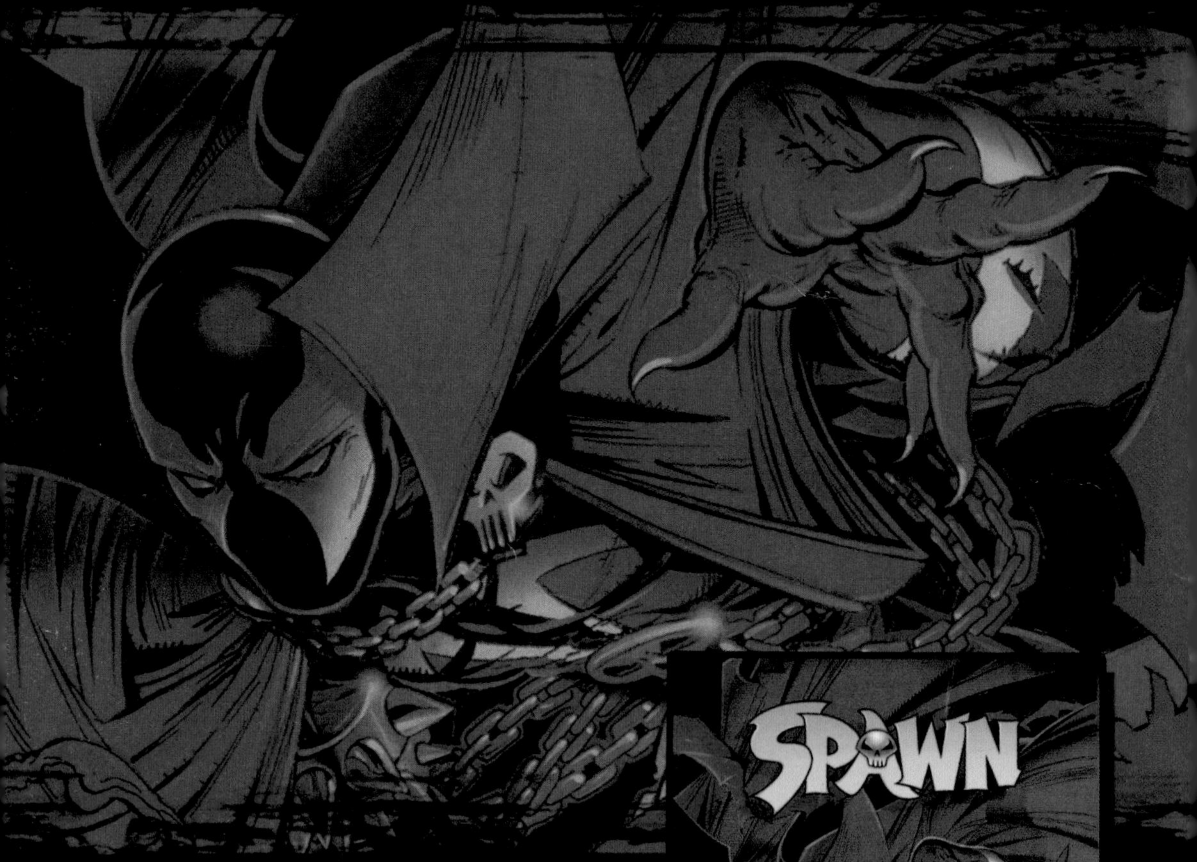

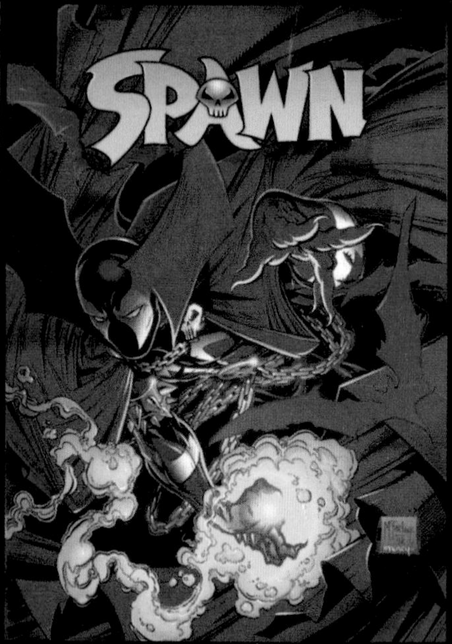
SPAWN

ISSUE ONE

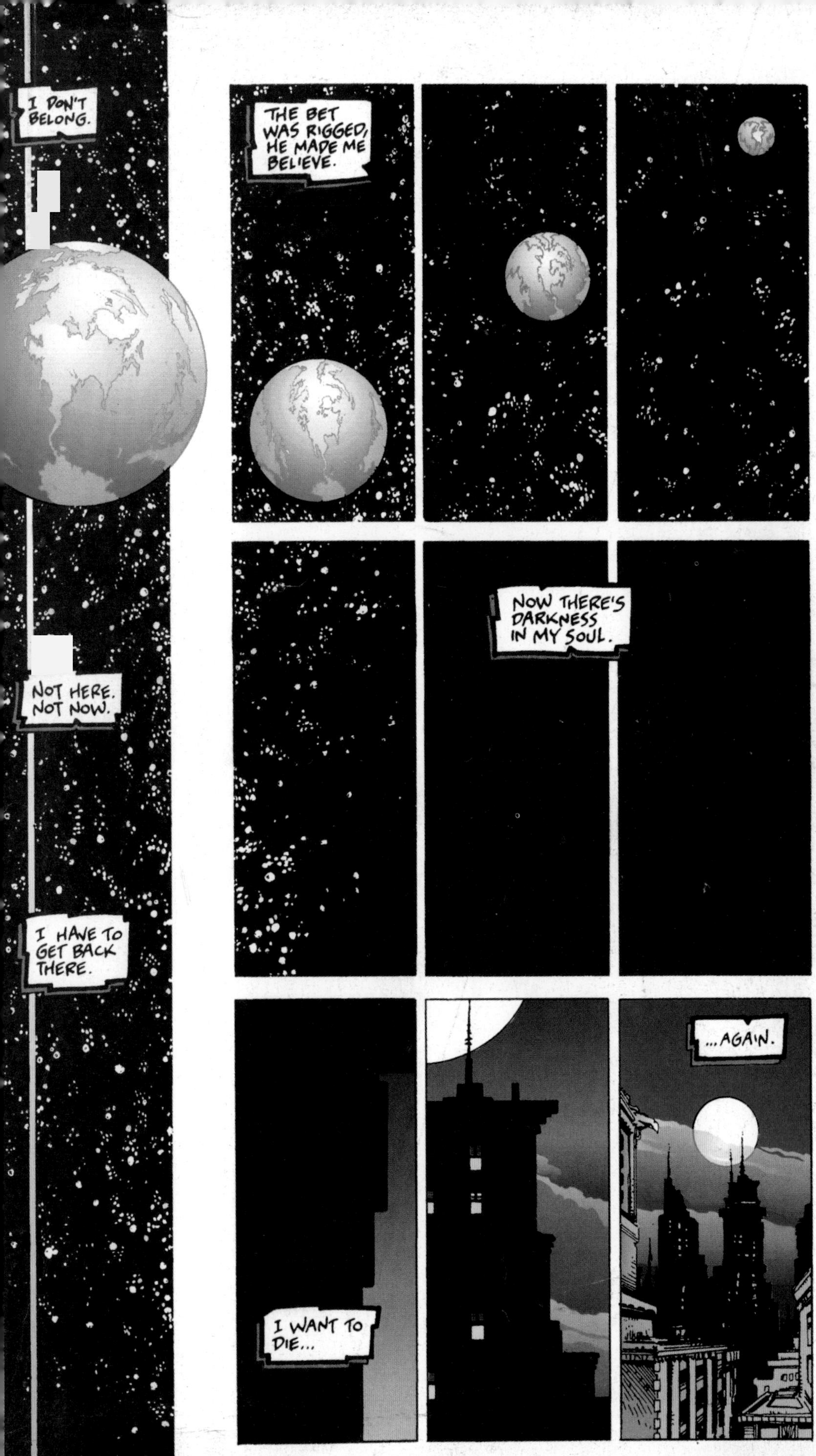
I DON'T BELONG.
NOT HERE. NOT NOW.
I HAVE TO GET BACK THERE.
THE BET WAS RIGGED, HE MADE ME BELIEVE.
NOW THERE'S DARKNESS IN MY SOUL.
I WANT TO DIE...
...AGAIN.

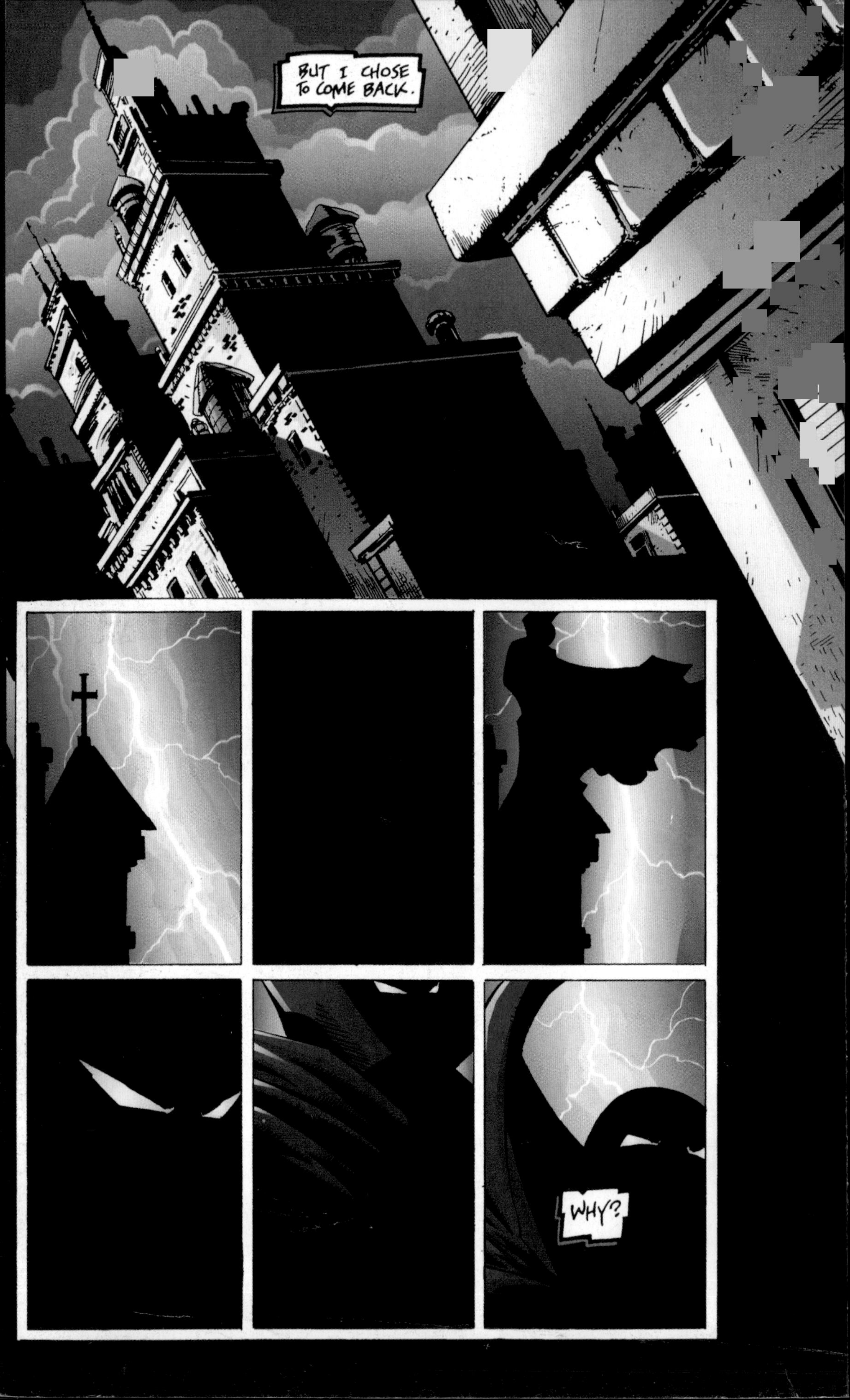
BUT I CHOSE
TO COME BACK.
WHY?

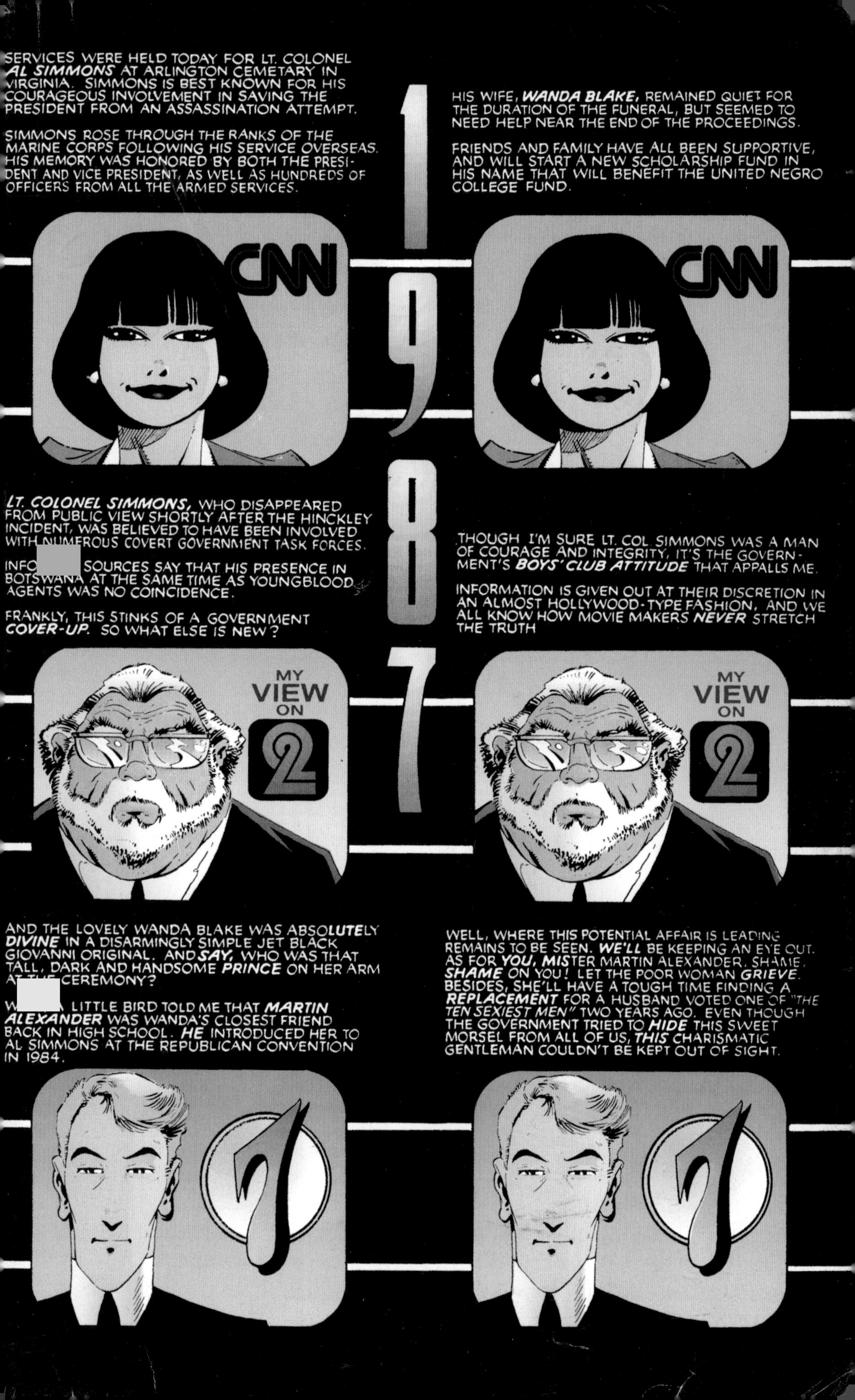
SERVICES WERE HELD TODAY FOR LT. COLONEL AL SIMMONS AT ARLINGTON CEMETARY IN VIRGINIA. SIMMONS IS BEST KNOWN FOR HIS COURAGEOUS INVOLVEMENT IN SAVING THE PRESIDENT FROM AN ASSASSINATION ATTEMPT.
SIMMONS ROSE THROUGH THE RANKS OF THE MARINE CORPS FOLLOWING HIS SERVICE OVERSEAS. HIS MEMORY WAS HONORED BY BOTH THE PRESIDENT AND VICE PRESIDENT, AS WELL AS HUNDREDS OF OFFICERS FROM ALL THE ARMED SERVICES.
1987
HIS WIFE, WANDA BLAKE, REMAINED QUIET FOR THE DURATION OF THE FUNERAL, BUT SEEMED TO NEED HELP NEAR THE END OF THE PROCEEDINGS.
FRIENDS AND FAMILY HAVE ALL BEEN SUPPORTIVE, AND WILL START A NEW SCHOLARSHIP FUND IN HIS NAME THAT WILL BENEFIT THE UNITED NEGRO COLLEGE FUND.
CNN
CNN
LT. COLONEL SIMMONS, WHO DISAPPEARED FROM PUBLIC VIEW SHORTLY AFTER THE HINCKLEY INCIDENT, WAS BELIEVED TO HAVE BEEN INVOLVED WITH NUMEROUS COVERT GOVERNMENT TASK FORCES.
INFO SOURCES SAY THAT HIS PRESENCE IN BOTSWANA AT THE SAME TIME AS YOUNGBLOOD AGENTS WAS NO COINCIDENCE.
FRANKLY, THIS STINKS OF A GOVERNMENT COVER-UP. SO WHAT ELSE IS NEW?
THOUGH I'M SURE LT. COL. SIMMONS WAS A MAN OF COURAGE AND INTEGRITY, IT'S THE GOVERNMENT'S BOYS' CLUB ATTITUDE THAT APPALLS ME.
INFORMATION IS GIVEN OUT AT THEIR DISCRETION IN AN ALMOST HOLLYWOOD-TYPE FASHION, AND WE ALL KNOW HOW MOVIE MAKERS NEVER STRETCH THE TRUTH
MY VIEW ON 2
MY VIEW ON 2
AND THE LOVELY WANDA BLAKE WAS ABSOLUTELY DIVINE IN A DISARMINGLY SIMPLE JET BLACK GIOVANNI ORIGINAL. AND SAY, WHO WAS THAT TALL, DARK AND HANDSOME PRINCE ON HER ARM AT THE CEREMONY?
W A LITTLE BIRD TOLD ME THAT MARTIN ALEXANDER WAS WANDA'S CLOSEST FRIEND BACK IN HIGH SCHOOL. HE INTRODUCED HER TO AL SIMMONS AT THE REPUBLICAN CONVENTION IN 1984.
WELL, WHERE THIS POTENTIAL AFFAIR IS LEADING REMAINS TO BE SEEN. WE'LL BE KEEPING AN EYE OUT. AS FOR YOU, MISTER MARTIN ALEXANDER, SHAME, SHAME ON YOU! LET THE POOR WOMAN GRIEVE. BESIDES, SHE'LL HAVE A TOUGH TIME FINDING A REPLACEMENT FOR A HUSBAND VOTED ONE OF "THE TEN SEXIEST MEN" TWO YEARS AGO. EVEN THOUGH THE GOVERNMENT TRIED TO HIDE THIS SWEET MORSEL FROM ALL OF US, THIS CHARISMATIC GENTLEMAN COULDN'T BE KEPT OUT OF SIGHT.

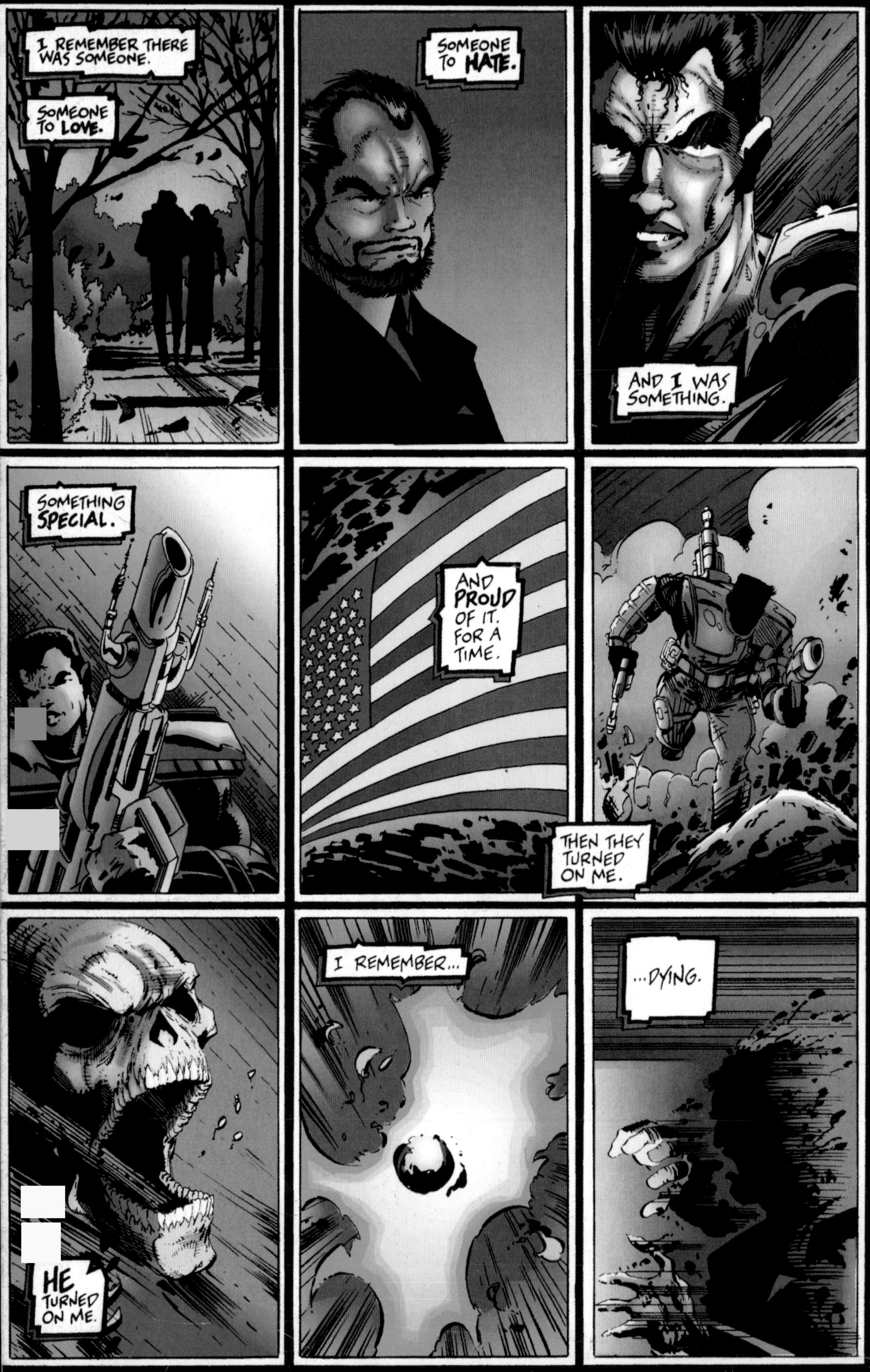
I REMEMBER THERE WAS SOMEONE.
SOMEONE TO LOVE.
SOMEONE TO HATE.
AND I WAS SOMETHING.
SOMETHING SPECIAL.
AND PROUD OF IT. FOR A TIME.
THEN THEY TURNED ON ME.
HE TURNED ON ME.
I REMEMBER...
...DYING.

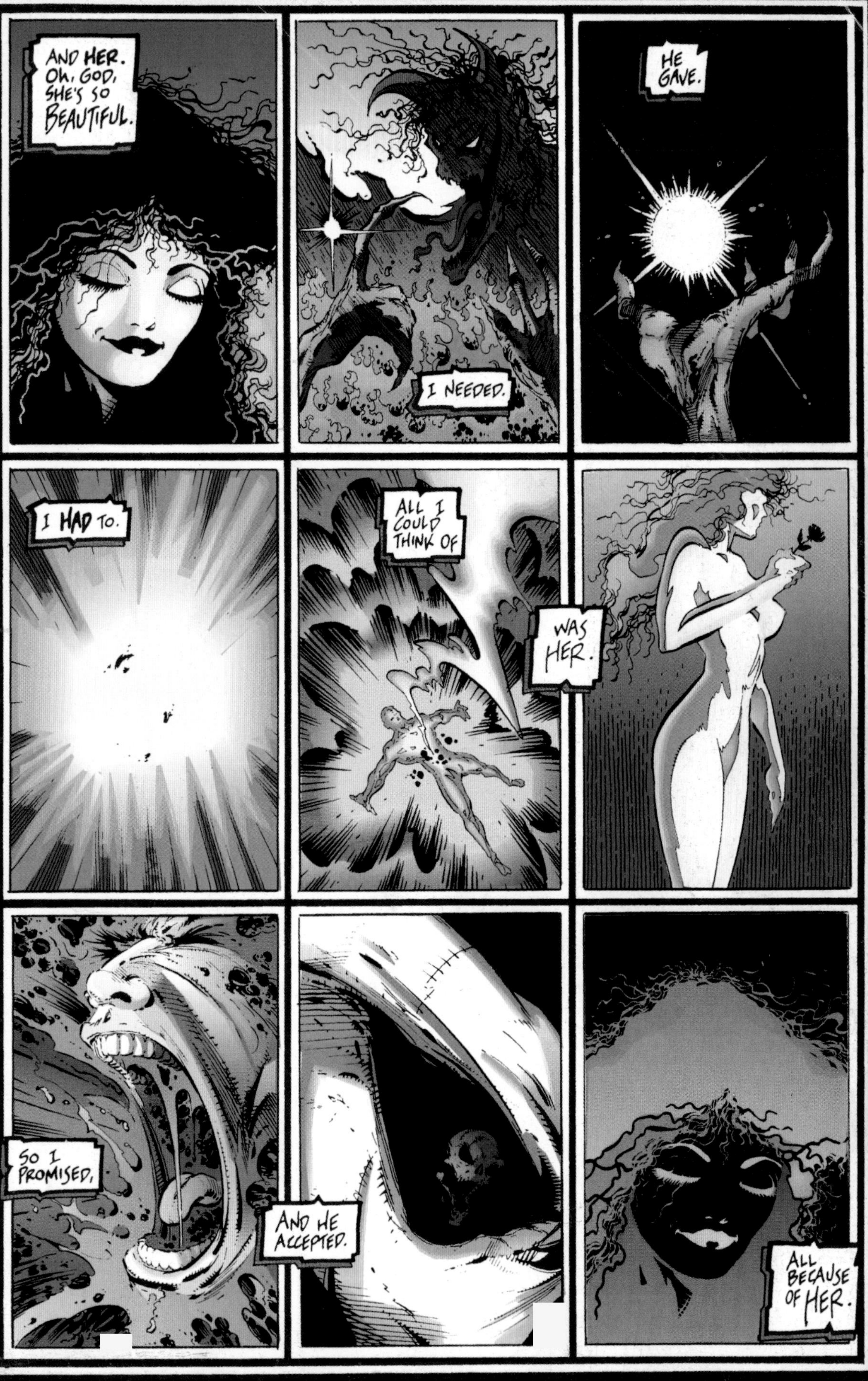
AND HER. Oh, GOD, SHE'S SO BEAUTIFUL.
I NEEDED.
HE GAVE.
I HAD TO.
ALL I COULD THINK OF
WAS HER.
SO I PROMISED,
AND HE ACCEPTED.
ALL BECAUSE OF HER.

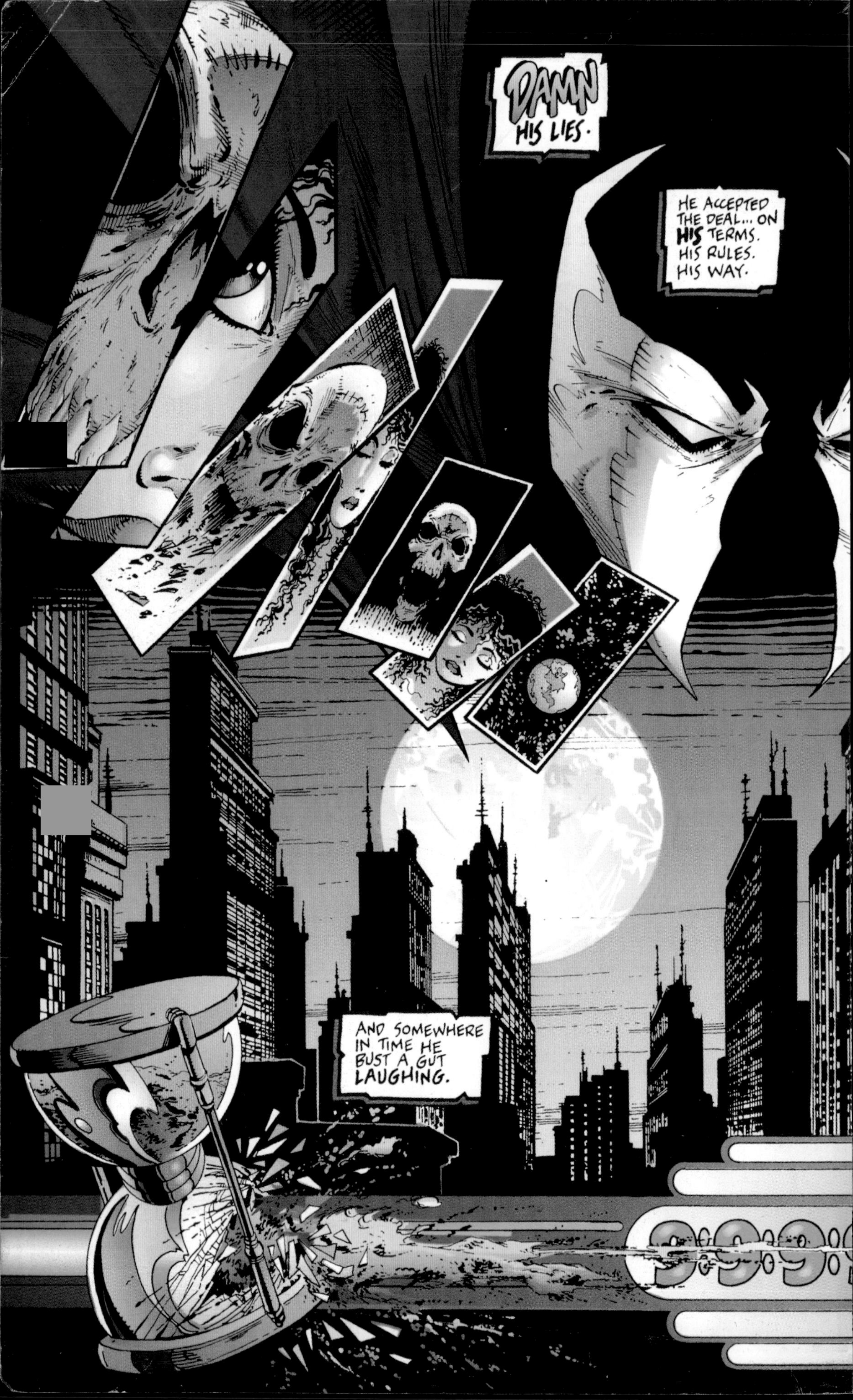
DAMN HIS LIES.
HE ACCEPTED THE DEAL... ON HIS TERMS. HIS RULES. HIS WAY.
AND SOMEWHERE IN TIME HE BUST A GUT LAUGHING.

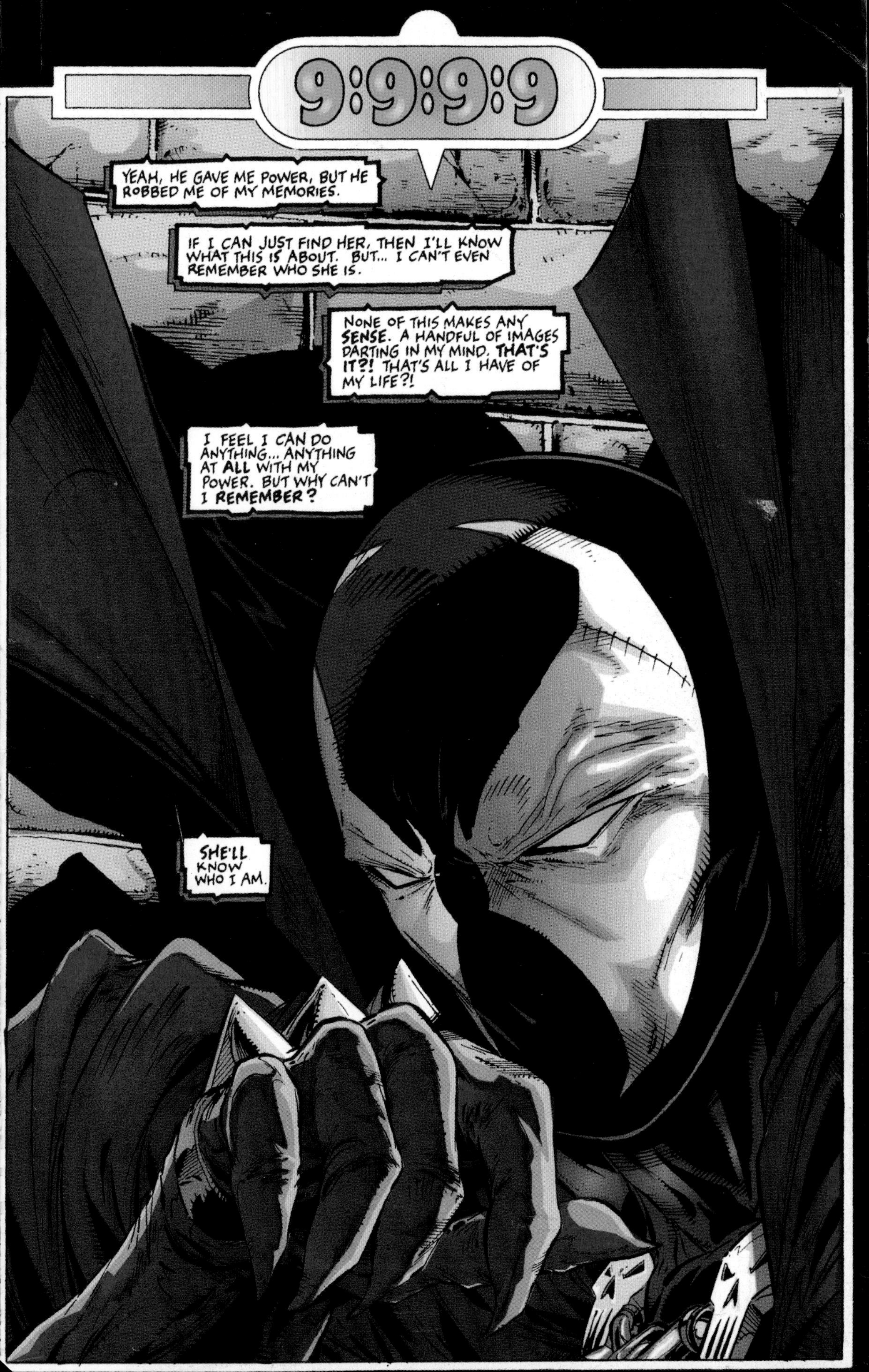
9:9:9:9
YEAH, HE GAVE ME POWER, BUT HE ROBBED ME OF MY MEMORIES.
IF I CAN JUST FIND HER, THEN I'LL KNOW WHAT THIS IS ABOUT. BUT... I CAN'T EVEN REMEMBER WHO SHE IS.
NONE OF THIS MAKES ANY SENSE. A HANDFUL OF IMAGES DARTING IN MY MIND. THAT'S IT?! THAT'S ALL I HAVE OF MY LIFE?!
I FEEL I CAN DO ANYTHING... ANYTHING AT ALL WITH MY POWER. BUT WHY CAN'T I REMEMBER?
SHE'LL KNOW WHO I AM.

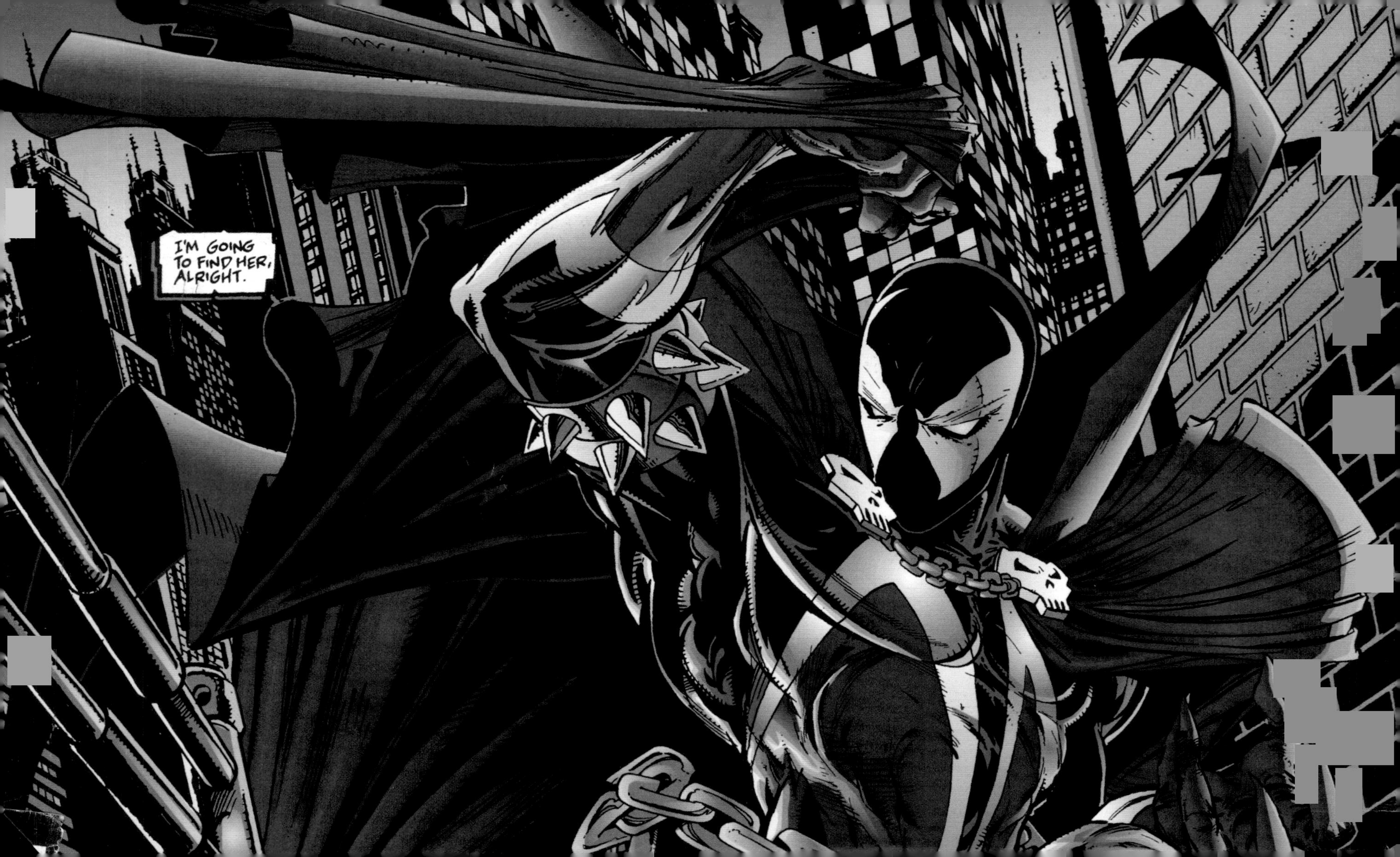
I'M GOING TO FIND HER, ALRIGHT.

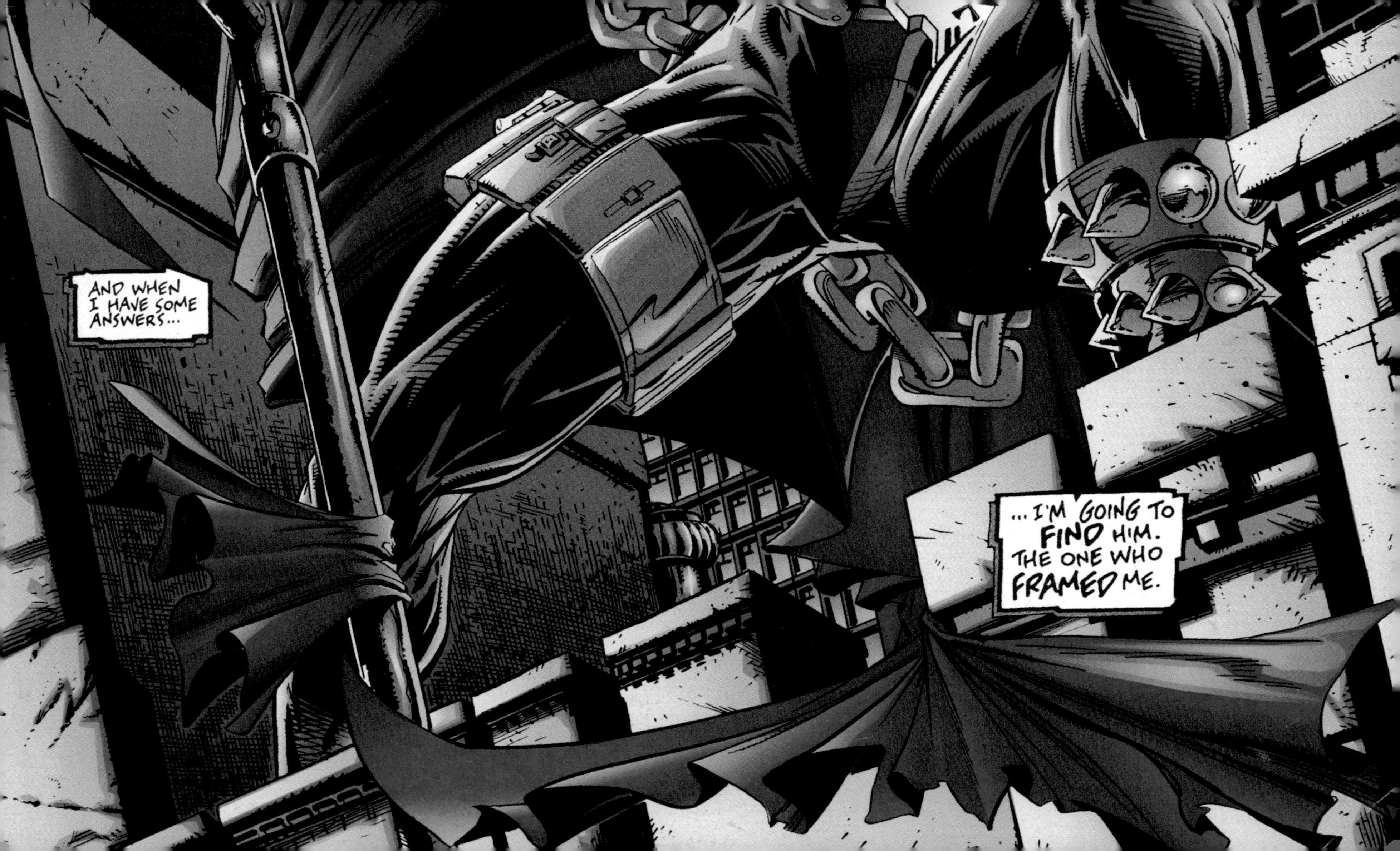
AND WHEN I HAVE SOME ANSWERS...
...I'M GOING TO FIND HIM. THE ONE WHO FRAMED ME.

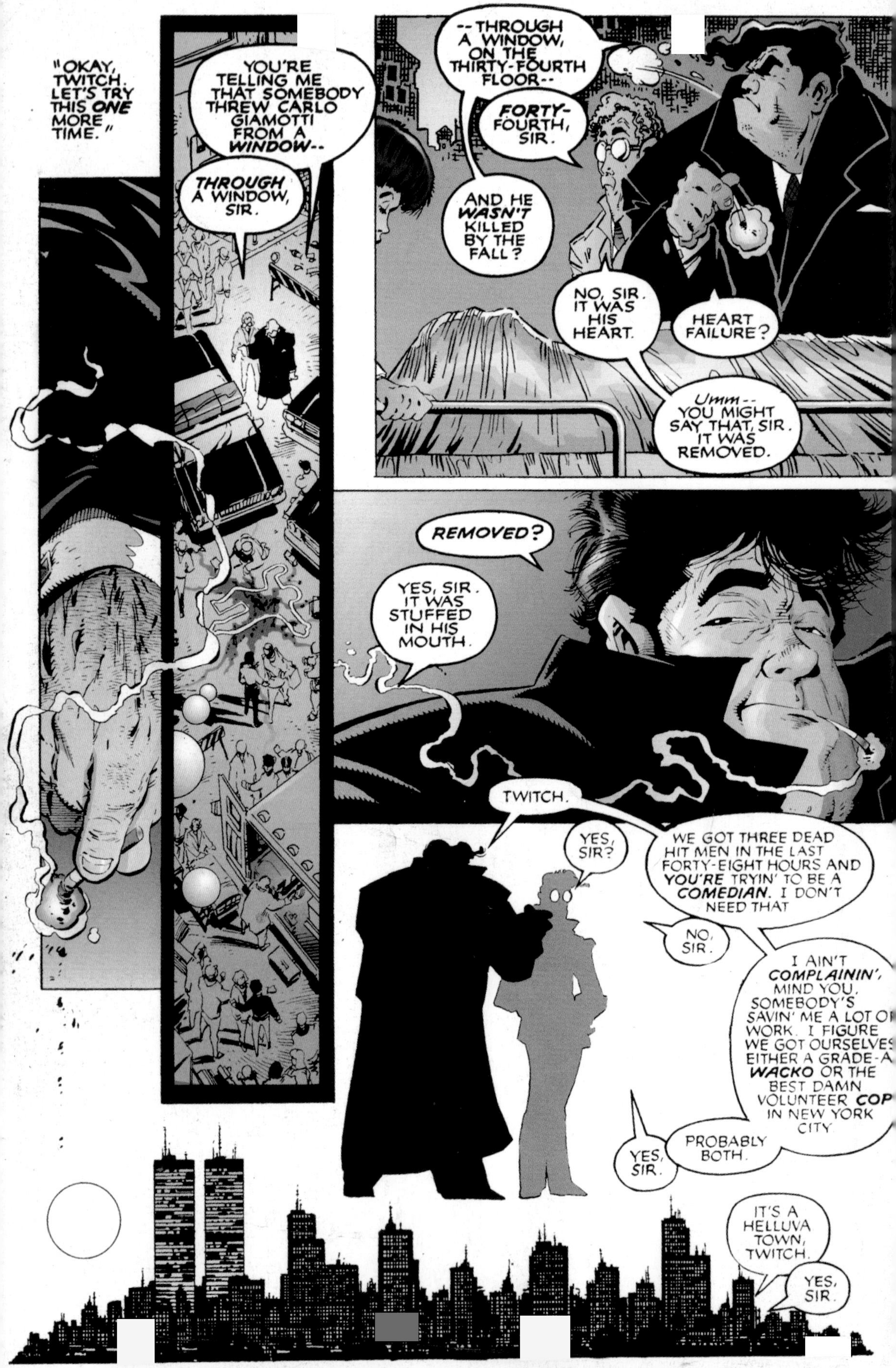
"OKAY, TWITCH. LET'S TRY THIS *ONE* MORE TIME."
YOU'RE TELLING ME THAT SOMEBODY THREW CARLO GIAMOTTI FROM A *WINDOW*--
THROUGH A WINDOW, SIR.
--THROUGH A WINDOW, ON THE THIRTY-FOURTH FLOOR--
FORTY-FOURTH, SIR.
AND HE *WASN'T* KILLED BY THE FALL?
NO, SIR. IT WAS HIS HEART.
HEART FAILURE?
Umm-- YOU MIGHT SAY THAT, SIR. IT WAS REMOVED.
REMOVED?
YES, SIR. IT WAS STUFFED IN HIS MOUTH.
TWITCH.
YES, SIR?
WE GOT THREE DEAD HIT MEN IN THE LAST FORTY-EIGHT HOURS AND *YOU'RE* TRYIN' TO BE A *COMEDIAN*. I DON'T NEED THAT
NO, SIR.
I AIN'T *COMPLAININ'*, MIND YOU. SOMEBODY'S SAVIN' ME A LOT O WORK. I FIGURE WE GOT OURSELVES EITHER A GRADE-A *WACKO* OR THE BEST DAMN VOLUNTEER *COP* IN NEW YORK CITY.
YES, SIR.
PROBABLY BOTH.
IT'S A HELLUVA TOWN, TWITCH.
YES, SIR.

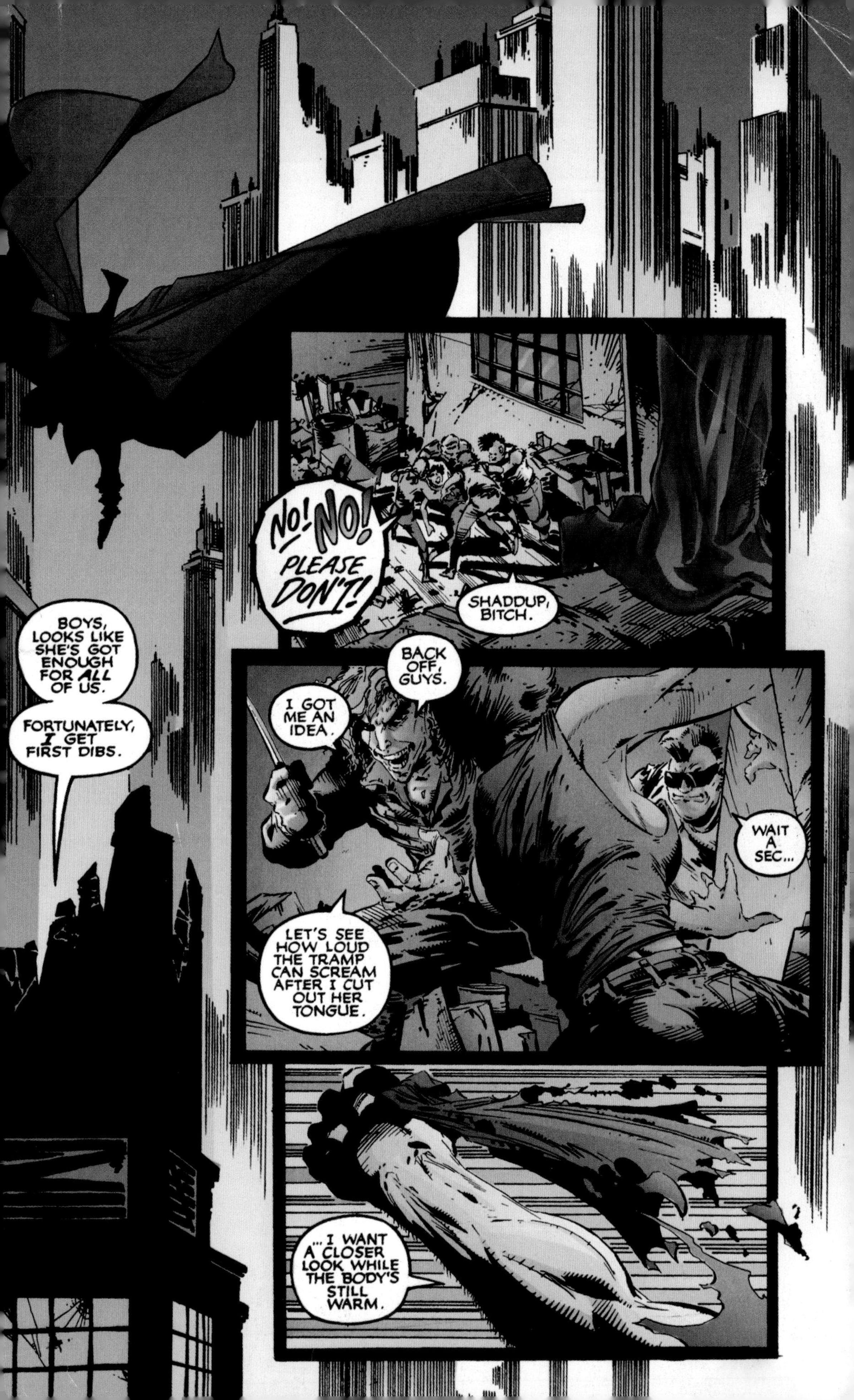
NO! NO! PLEASE DON'T!
SHADDUP, BITCH.
BOYS, LOOKS LIKE SHE'S GOT ENOUGH FOR ALL OF US.
FORTUNATELY, I GET FIRST DIBS.
BACK OFF, GUYS.
I GOT ME AN IDEA.
LET'S SEE HOW LOUD THE TRAMP CAN SCREAM AFTER I CUT OUT HER TONGUE.
WAIT A SEC...
...I WANT A CLOSER LOOK WHILE THE BODY'S STILL WARM.

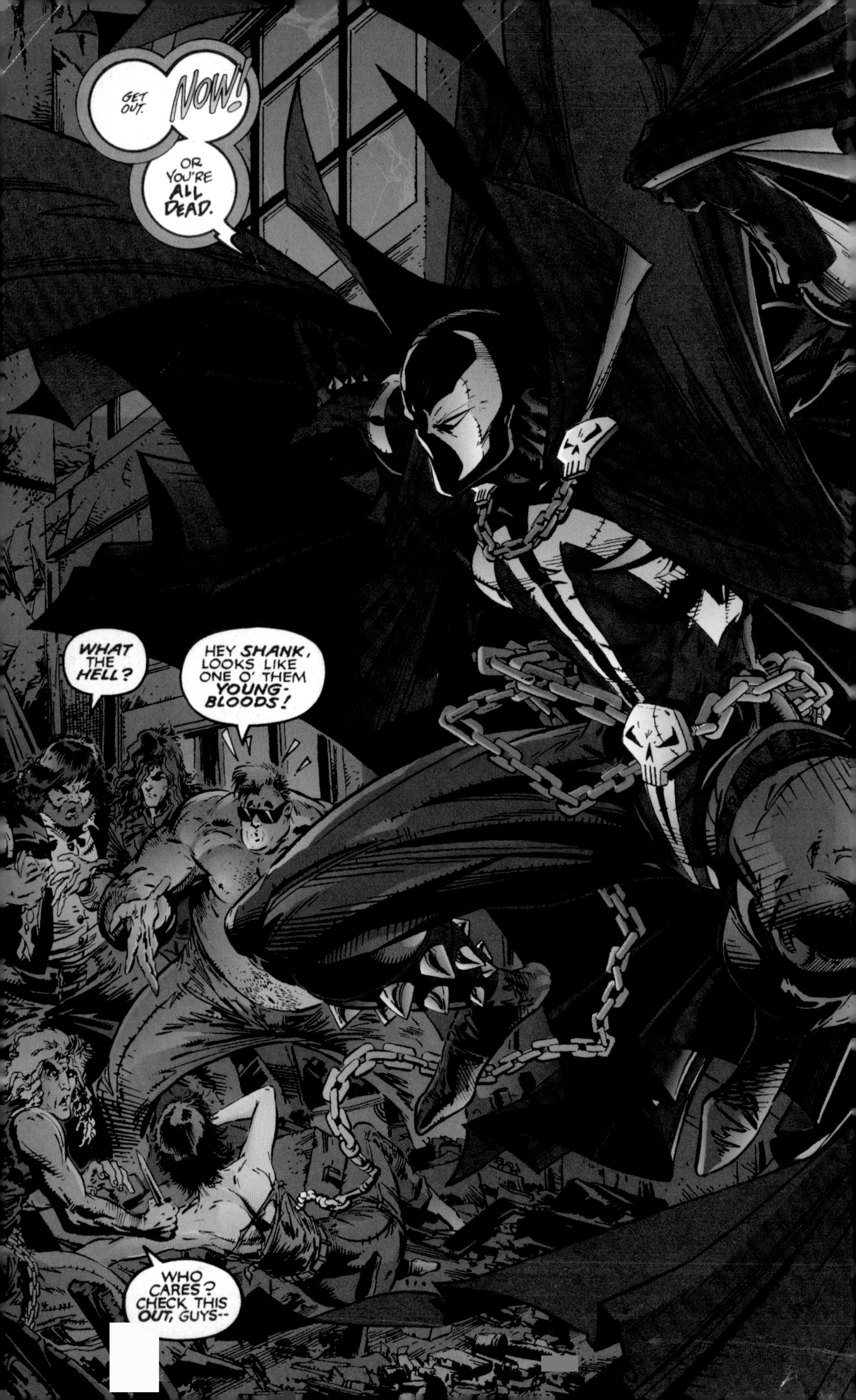
GET OUT. NOW!
OR YOU'RE ALL DEAD.
WHAT THE HELL?
HEY SHANK, LOOKS LIKE ONE O' THEM YOUNG-BLOODS!
WHO CARES? CHECK THIS OUT, GUYS--

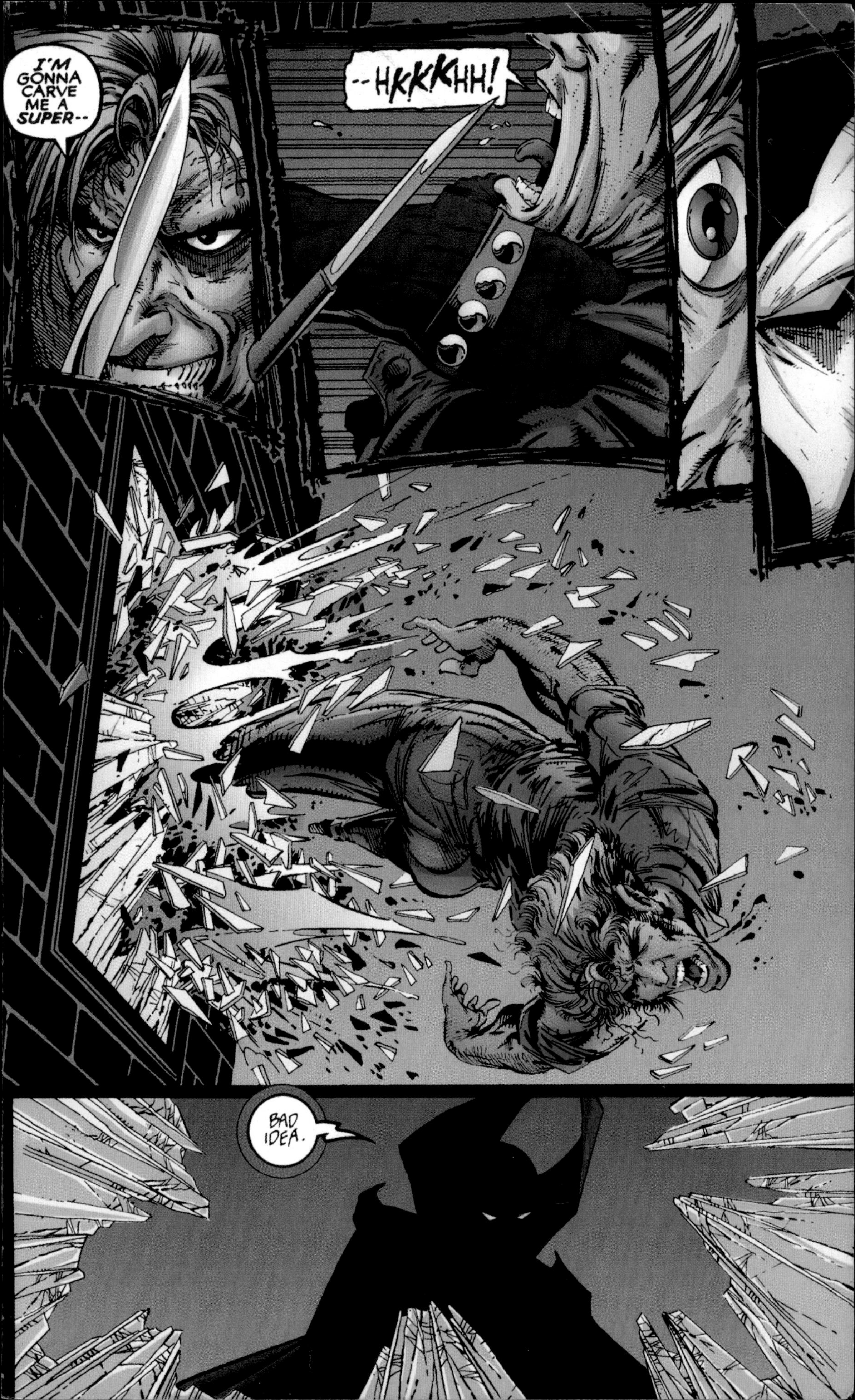
I'M GONNA CARVE ME A SUPER--
--HKKKHH!
BAD IDEA.

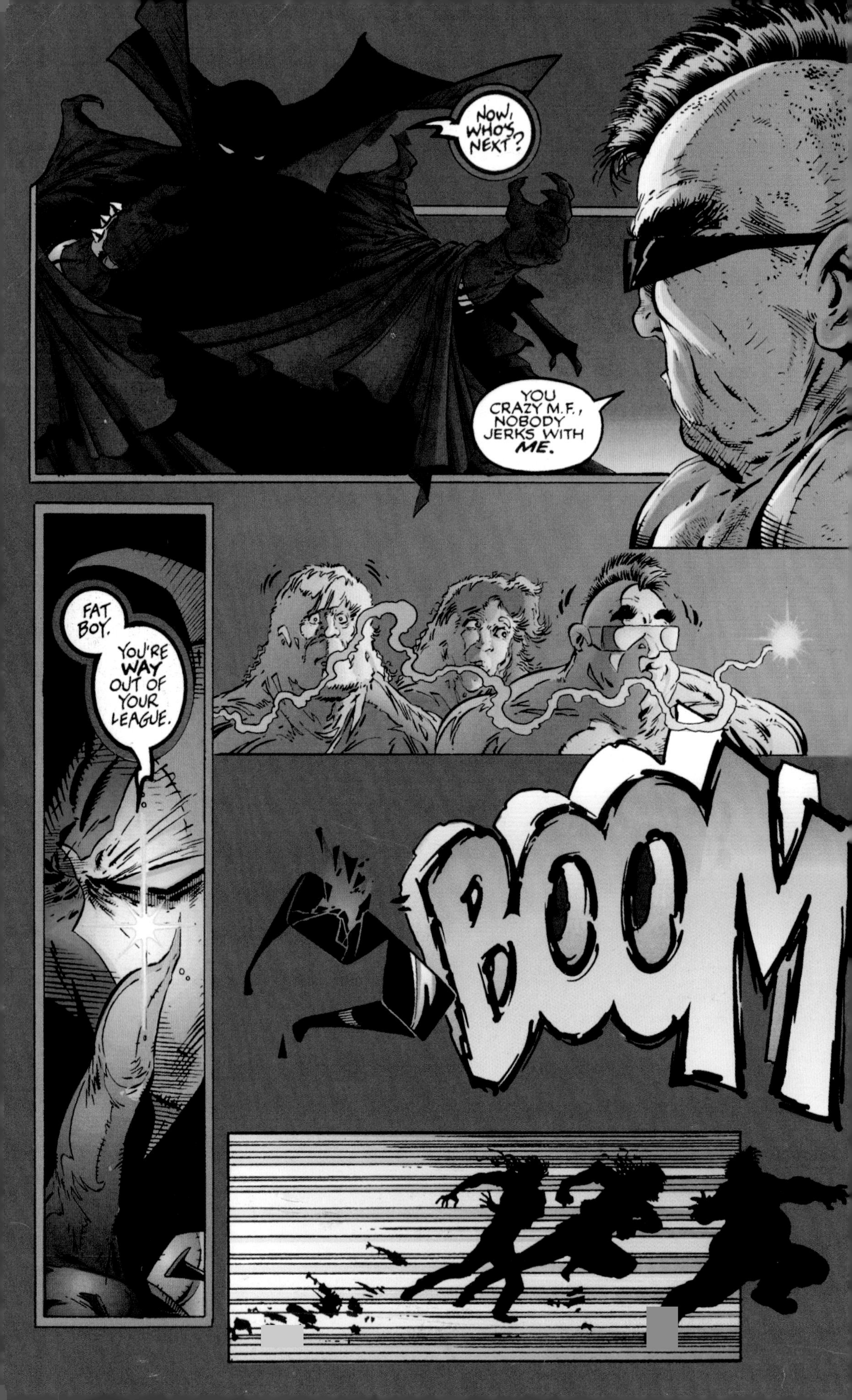
NOW, WHO'S NEXT?
YOU CRAZY M.F., NOBODY JERKS WITH ME.
FAT BOY.
YOU'RE WAY OUT OF YOUR LEAGUE.
BOOM

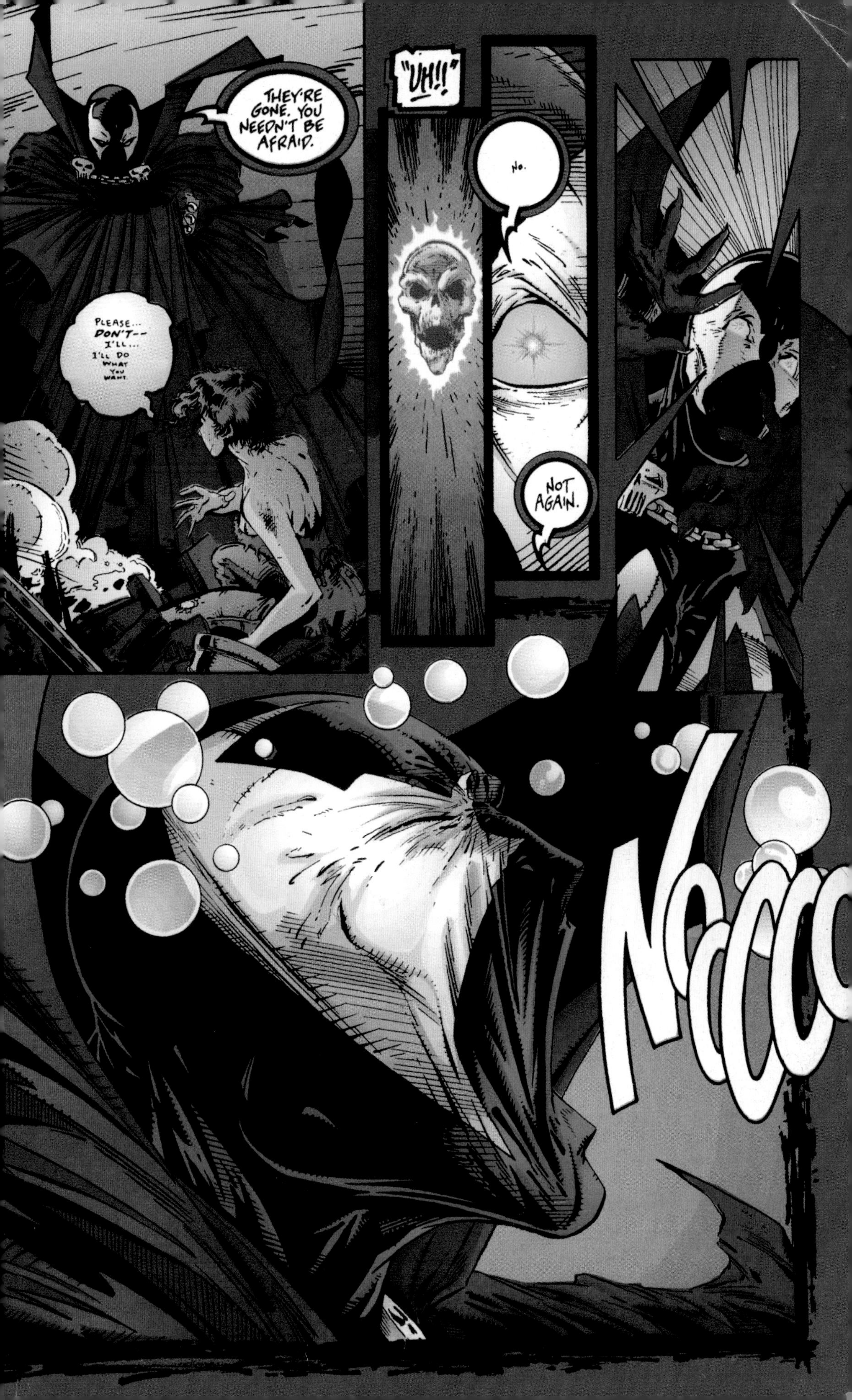
THEY'RE GONE. YOU NEEDN'T BE AFRAID.
PLEASE... DON'T-- I'LL... I'LL DO WHAT YOU WANT.
"UH!!"
NO.
NOT AGAIN.
NOOOOO

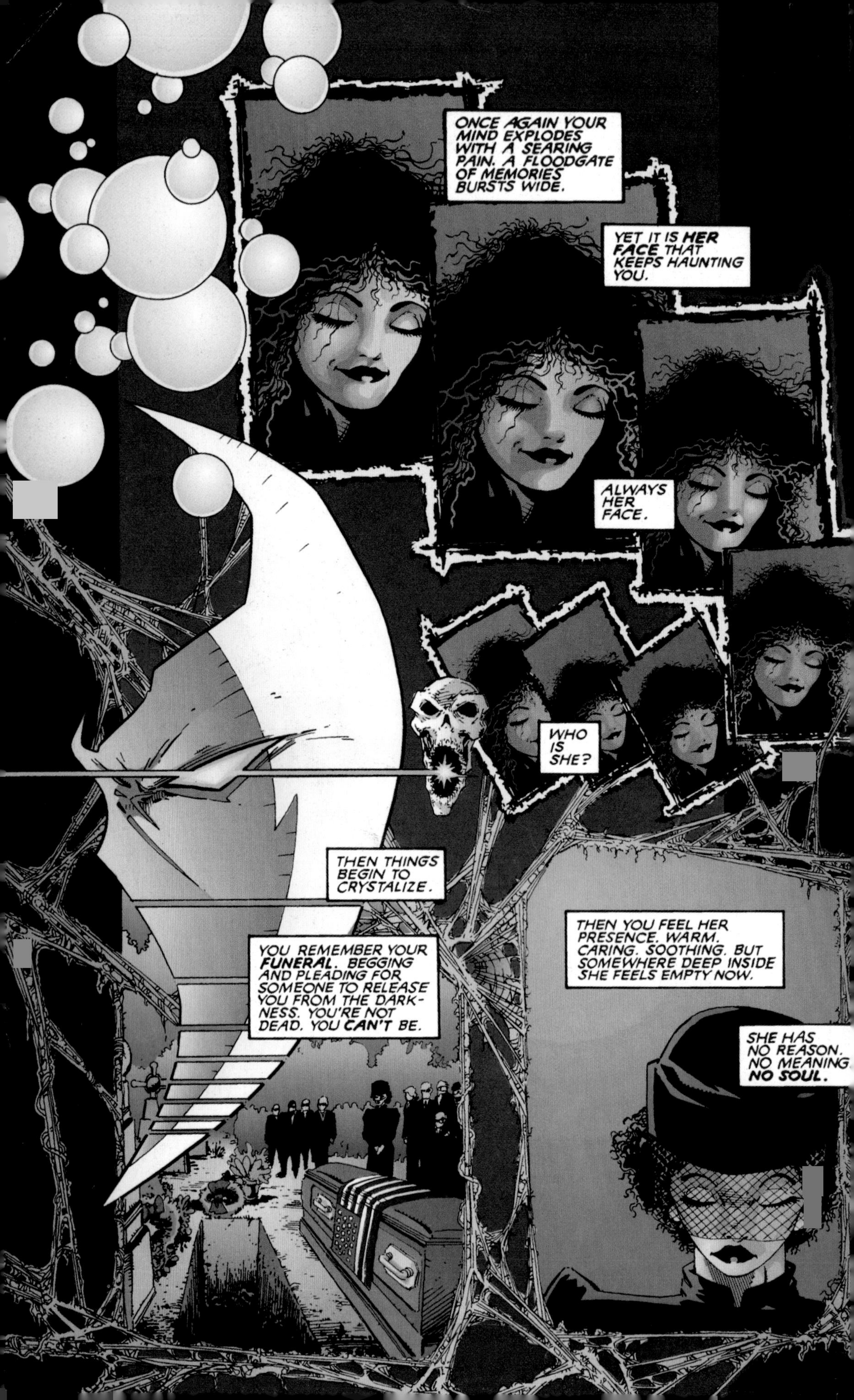
ONCE AGAIN YOUR MIND EXPLODES WITH A SEARING PAIN. A FLOODGATE OF MEMORIES BURSTS WIDE.
YET IT IS HER FACE THAT KEEPS HAUNTING YOU.
ALWAYS HER FACE.
WHO IS SHE?
THEN THINGS BEGIN TO CRYSTALIZE.
YOU REMEMBER YOUR FUNERAL. BEGGING AND PLEADING FOR SOMEONE TO RELEASE YOU FROM THE DARK-NESS. YOU'RE NOT DEAD. YOU CAN'T BE.
THEN YOU FEEL HER PRESENCE. WARM. CARING. SOOTHING. BUT SOMEWHERE DEEP INSIDE SHE FEELS EMPTY NOW.
SHE HAS NO REASON. NO MEANING. NO SOUL.

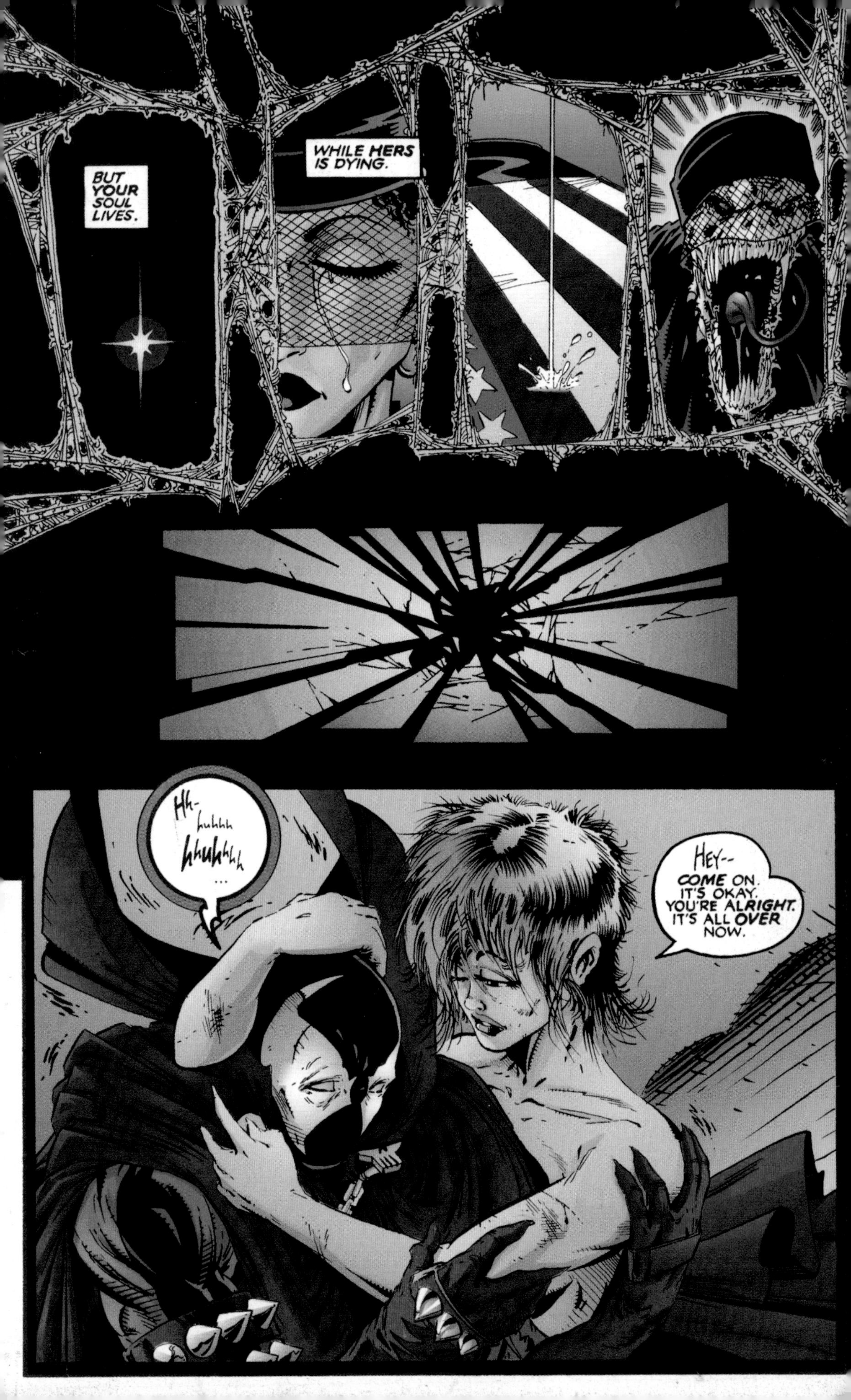
BUT YOUR SOUL LIVES.
WHILE HERS IS DYING.
Hh-huhhh hhuhhhh ...
HEY-- COME ON. IT'S OKAY. YOU'RE ALRIGHT. IT'S ALL OVER NOW.

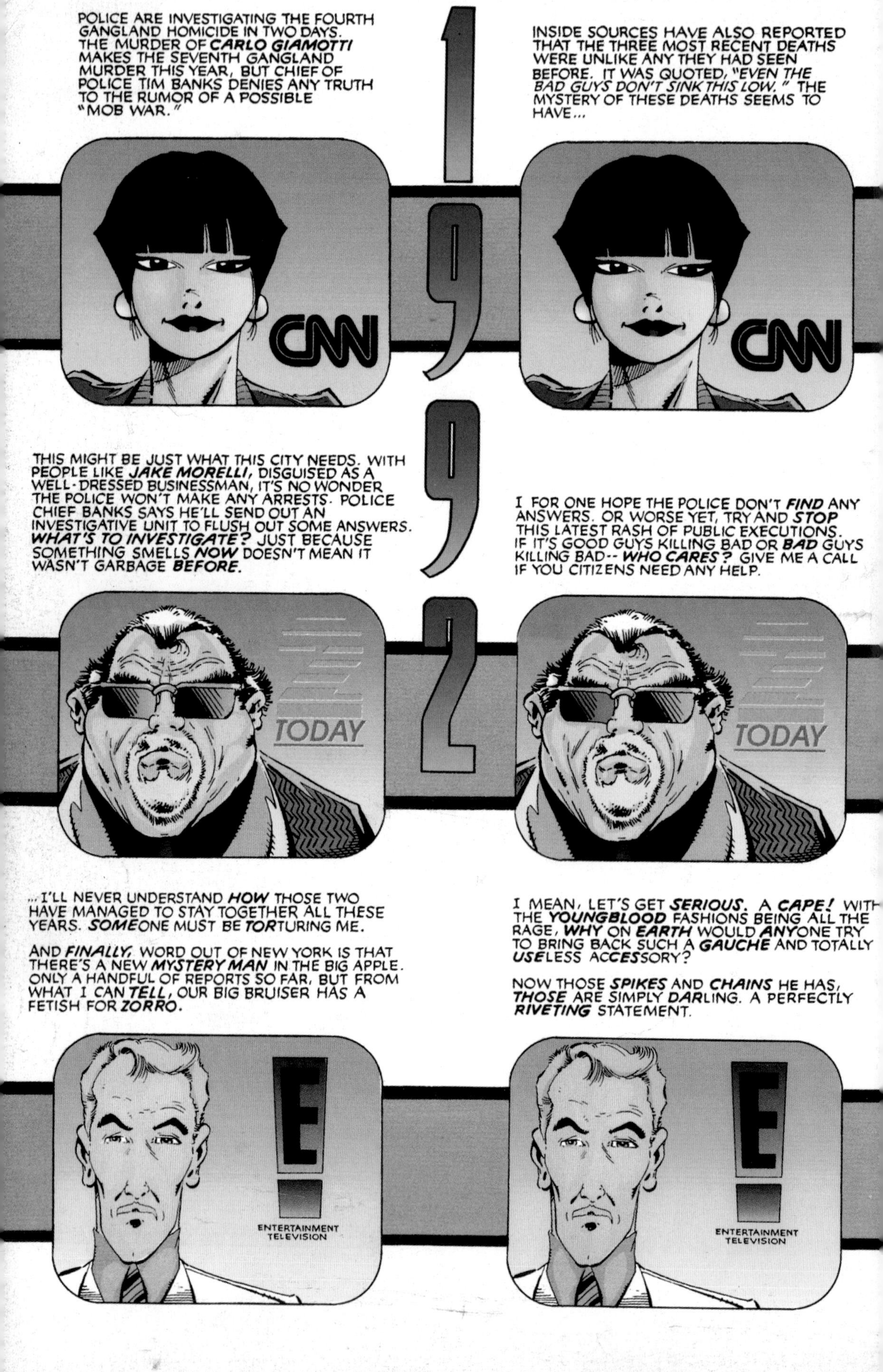
POLICE ARE INVESTIGATING THE FOURTH GANGLAND HOMICIDE IN TWO DAYS. THE MURDER OF CARLO GIAMOTTI MAKES THE SEVENTH GANGLAND MURDER THIS YEAR, BUT CHIEF OF POLICE TIM BANKS DENIES ANY TRUTH TO THE RUMOR OF A POSSIBLE "MOB WAR."
INSIDE SOURCES HAVE ALSO REPORTED THAT THE THREE MOST RECENT DEATHS WERE UNLIKE ANY THEY HAD SEEN BEFORE. IT WAS QUOTED, "EVEN THE BAD GUYS DON'T SINK THIS LOW." THE MYSTERY OF THESE DEATHS SEEMS TO HAVE...
1992
CNN
CNN
THIS MIGHT BE JUST WHAT THIS CITY NEEDS. WITH PEOPLE LIKE JAKE MORELLI, DISGUISED AS A WELL-DRESSED BUSINESSMAN, IT'S NO WONDER THE POLICE WON'T MAKE ANY ARRESTS. POLICE CHIEF BANKS SAYS HE'LL SEND OUT AN INVESTIGATIVE UNIT TO FLUSH OUT SOME ANSWERS. WHAT'S TO INVESTIGATE? JUST BECAUSE SOMETHING SMELLS NOW DOESN'T MEAN IT WASN'T GARBAGE BEFORE.
I FOR ONE HOPE THE POLICE DON'T FIND ANY ANSWERS. OR WORSE YET, TRY AND STOP THIS LATEST RASH OF PUBLIC EXECUTIONS. IF IT'S GOOD GUYS KILLING BAD OR BAD GUYS KILLING BAD-- WHO CARES? GIVE ME A CALL IF YOU CITIZENS NEED ANY HELP.
TODAY
TODAY
...I'LL NEVER UNDERSTAND HOW THOSE TWO HAVE MANAGED TO STAY TOGETHER ALL THESE YEARS. SOMEONE MUST BE TORTURING ME.
AND FINALLY, WORD OUT OF NEW YORK IS THAT THERE'S A NEW MYSTERY MAN IN THE BIG APPLE. ONLY A HANDFUL OF REPORTS SO FAR, BUT FROM WHAT I CAN TELL, OUR BIG BRUISER HAS A FETISH FOR ZORRO.
I MEAN, LET'S GET SERIOUS. A CAPE! WITH THE YOUNGBLOOD FASHIONS BEING ALL THE RAGE, WHY ON EARTH WOULD ANYONE TRY TO BRING BACK SUCH A GAUCHE AND TOTALLY USELESS ACCESSORY?
NOW THOSE SPIKES AND CHAINS HE HAS, THOSE ARE SIMPLY DARLING. A PERFECTLY RIVETING STATEMENT.
E! ENTERTAINMENT TELEVISION
E! ENTERTAINMENT TELEVISION

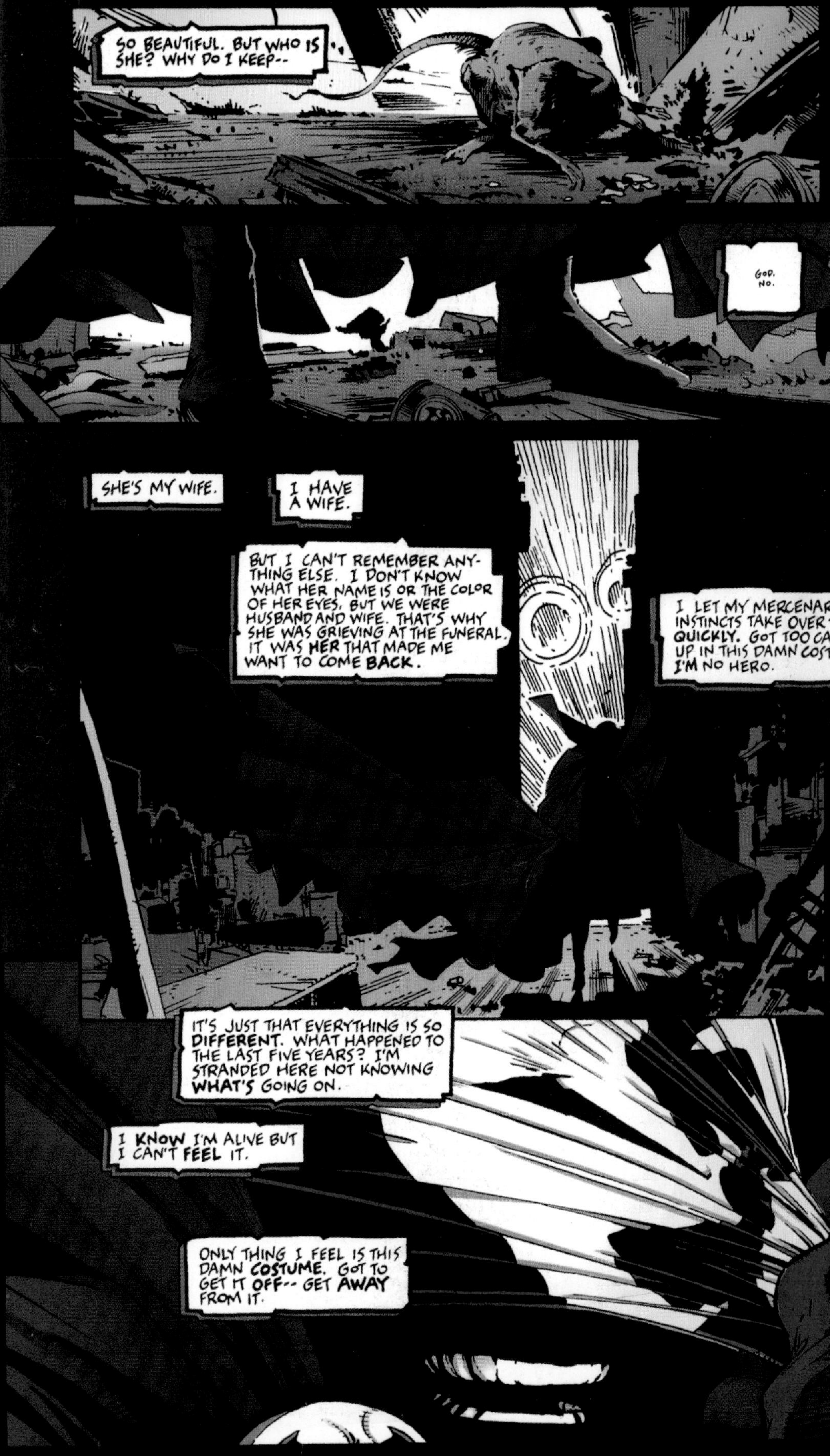
SO BEAUTIFUL. BUT WHO IS SHE? WHY DO I KEEP--
GOD. NO.
SHE'S MY WIFE.
I HAVE A WIFE.
BUT I CAN'T REMEMBER ANYTHING ELSE. I DON'T KNOW WHAT HER NAME IS OR THE COLOR OF HER EYES, BUT WE WERE HUSBAND AND WIFE. THAT'S WHY SHE WAS GRIEVING AT THE FUNERAL. IT WAS HER THAT MADE ME WANT TO COME BACK.
I LET MY MERCENARY INSTINCTS TAKE OVER TOO QUICKLY. GOT TOO CAUGHT UP IN THIS DAMN COSTUME. I'M NO HERO.
IT'S JUST THAT EVERYTHING IS SO DIFFERENT. WHAT HAPPENED TO THE LAST FIVE YEARS? I'M STRANDED HERE NOT KNOWING WHAT'S GOING ON.
I KNOW I'M ALIVE BUT I CAN'T FEEL IT.
ONLY THING I FEEL IS THIS DAMN COSTUME. GOT TO GET IT OFF-- GET AWAY FROM IT.

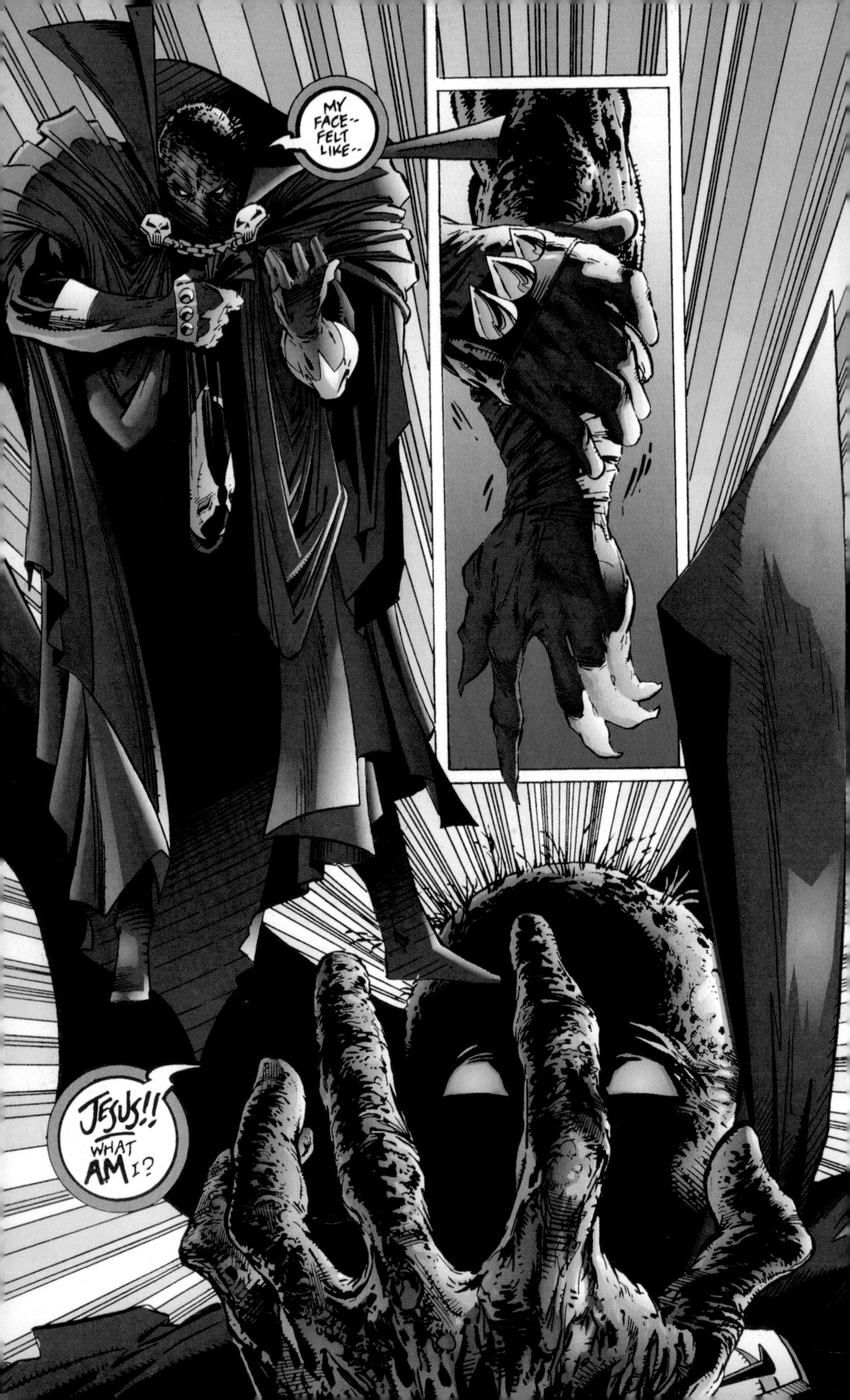
MY FACE-- FELT LIKE--
JESUS!! WHAT AM I?

WHAT AM I?

I DUNNO, TWITCH...

IF IT REALLY *IS* SOME GOVERNMENT HERO GONE WACKO, THEM WASHINGTON STIFFS AIN'T GONNA LET US GET CLOSE. THEM TIGHT ASSES. BUT IF THIS GUY DECIDES HE WANTS TO START SNUFFING OUT "JOE AVERAGE," THEN WE GOT OURSELVES A *SERIOUS* PROBLEM.

AND THE DAMAGE THIS GUY HAS DONE TO THOSE THREE BODIES IS FRIGGIN' *UNREAL*. WONDER HOW MUCH *POWER* THIS GUY HAS IN HIM?

9:9:9:5
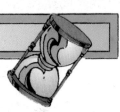

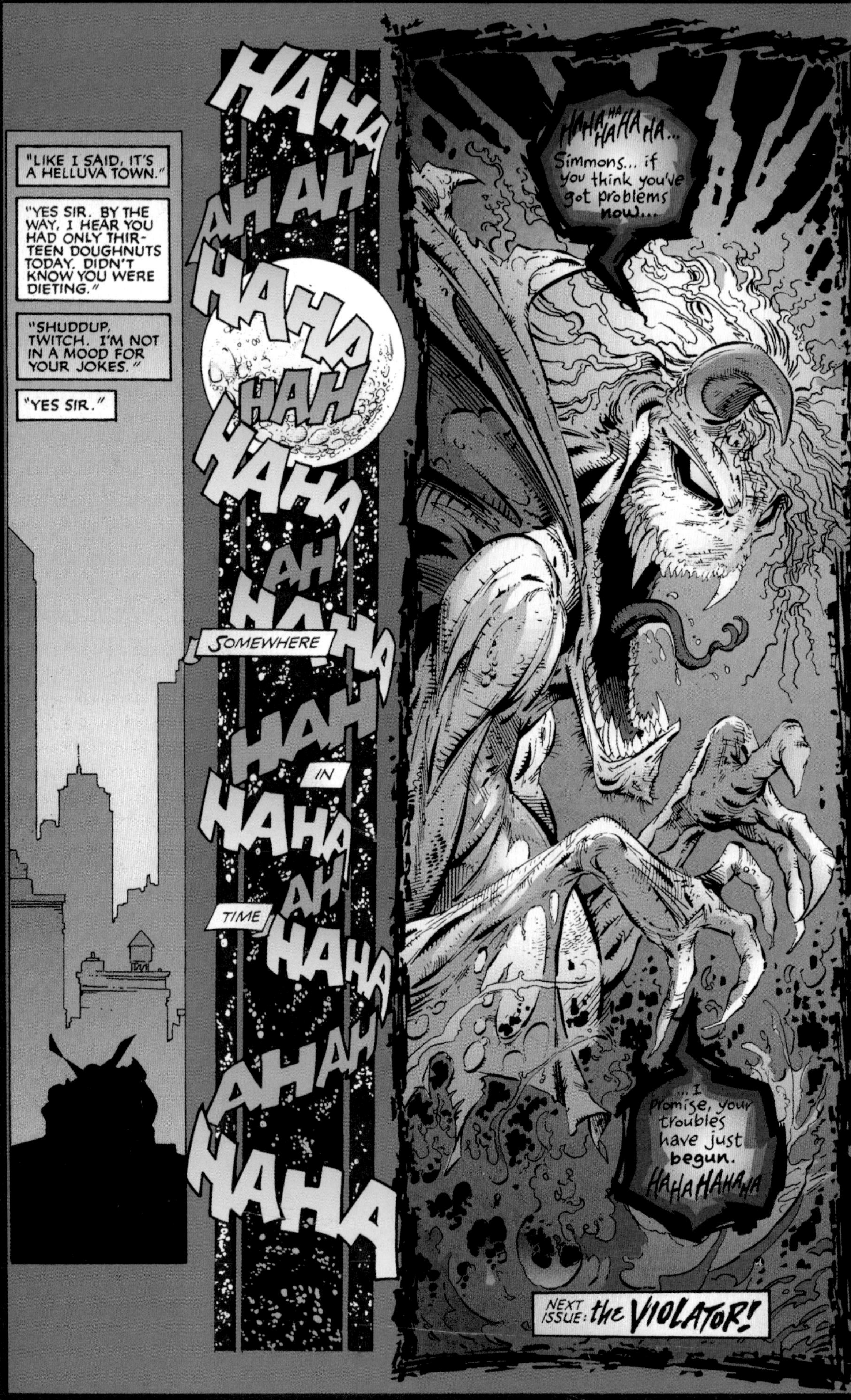
"LIKE I SAID, IT'S A HELLUVA TOWN."
"YES SIR. BY THE WAY, I HEAR YOU HAD ONLY THIRTEEN DOUGHNUTS TODAY. DIDN'T KNOW YOU WERE DIETING."
"SHUDDUP, TWITCH. I'M NOT IN A MOOD FOR YOUR JOKES."
"YES SIR."
HAHAHAHAHAHAHAHAHAHAHAHAHAHAHAHAHAHAHAHAHAHAHAHA
SOMEWHERE
IN
TIME
HAHAHAHAHAHA... Simmons... if you think you've got problems now...
...I promise, your troubles have just begun. HAHAHAHAHAHA
NEXT ISSUE: the VIOLATOR!

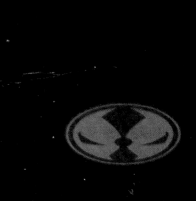

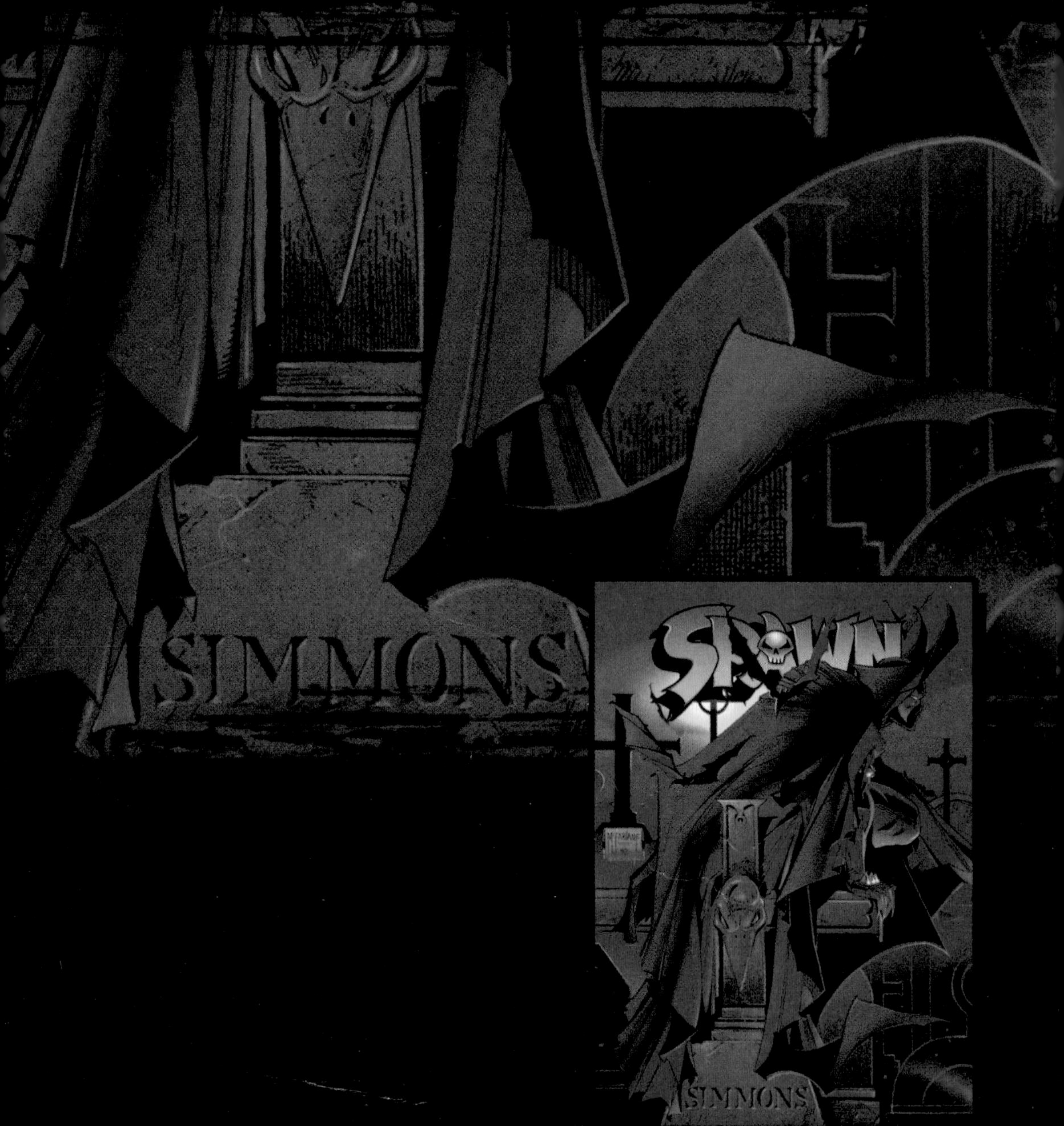
SIMMONS
SPAWN
SIMMONS

ISSUE TWO

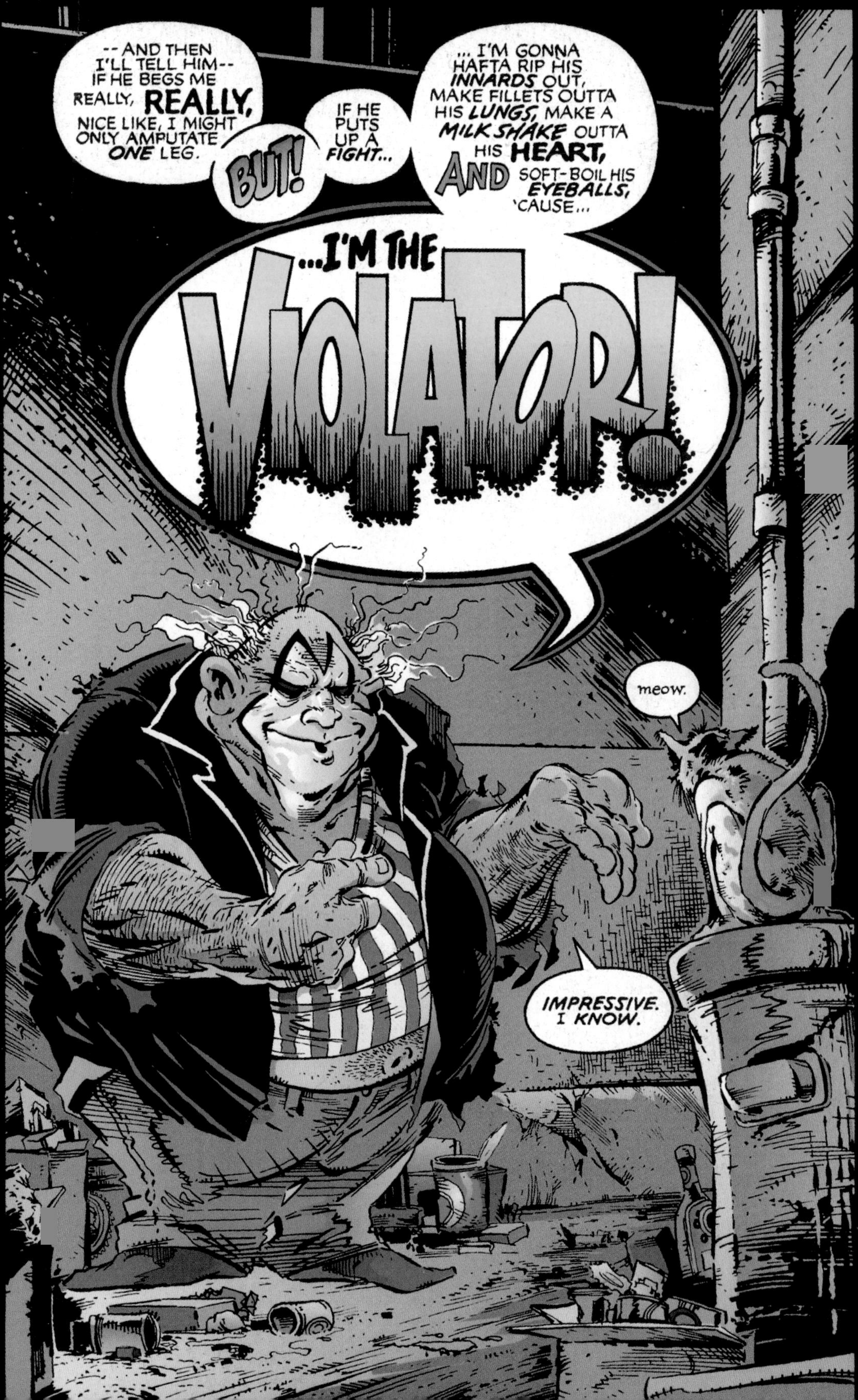
-- AND THEN I'LL TELL HIM-- IF HE BEGS ME REALLY, REALLY, NICE LIKE, I MIGHT ONLY AMPUTATE ONE LEG.
BUT!
IF HE PUTS UP A FIGHT...
... I'M GONNA HAFTA RIP HIS INNARDS OUT, MAKE FILLETS OUTTA HIS LUNGS, MAKE A MILKSHAKE OUTTA HIS HEART, AND SOFT-BOIL HIS EYEBALLS, 'CAUSE...
...I'M THE VIOLATOR!
meow.
IMPRESSIVE. I KNOW.

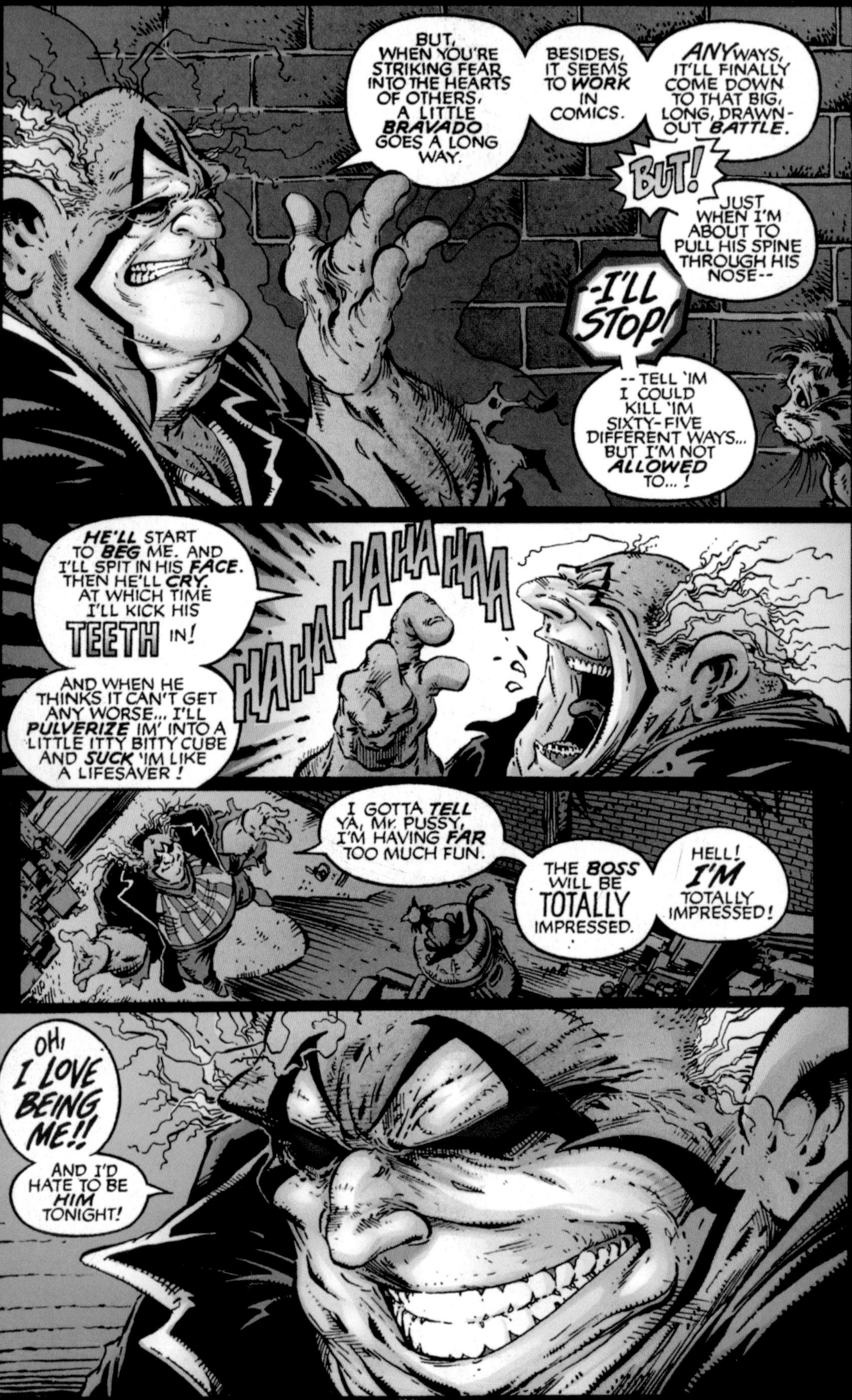
BUT, WHEN YOU'RE STRIKING FEAR INTO THE HEARTS OF OTHERS, A LITTLE BRAVADO GOES A LONG WAY.
BESIDES, IT SEEMS TO WORK IN COMICS.
ANYWAYS, IT'LL FINALLY COME DOWN TO THAT BIG, LONG, DRAWN-OUT BATTLE.
BUT!
JUST WHEN I'M ABOUT TO PULL HIS SPINE THROUGH HIS NOSE--
-I'LL STOP!
--TELL 'IM I COULD KILL 'IM SIXTY-FIVE DIFFERENT WAYS... BUT I'M NOT ALLOWED TO...!
HE'LL START TO BEG ME. AND I'LL SPIT IN HIS FACE. THEN HE'LL CRY. AT WHICH TIME I'LL KICK HIS TEETH IN!
AND WHEN HE THINKS IT CAN'T GET ANY WORSE... I'LL PULVERIZE IM' INTO A LITTLE ITTY BITTY CUBE AND SUCK 'IM LIKE A LIFESAVER!
HAHAHAHAHAHAA
I GOTTA TELL YA, MR. PUSSY, I'M HAVING FAR TOO MUCH FUN.
THE BOSS WILL BE TOTALLY IMPRESSED.
HELL! I'M TOTALLY IMPRESSED!
OH, I LOVE BEING ME!!
AND I'D HATE TO BE HIM TONIGHT!

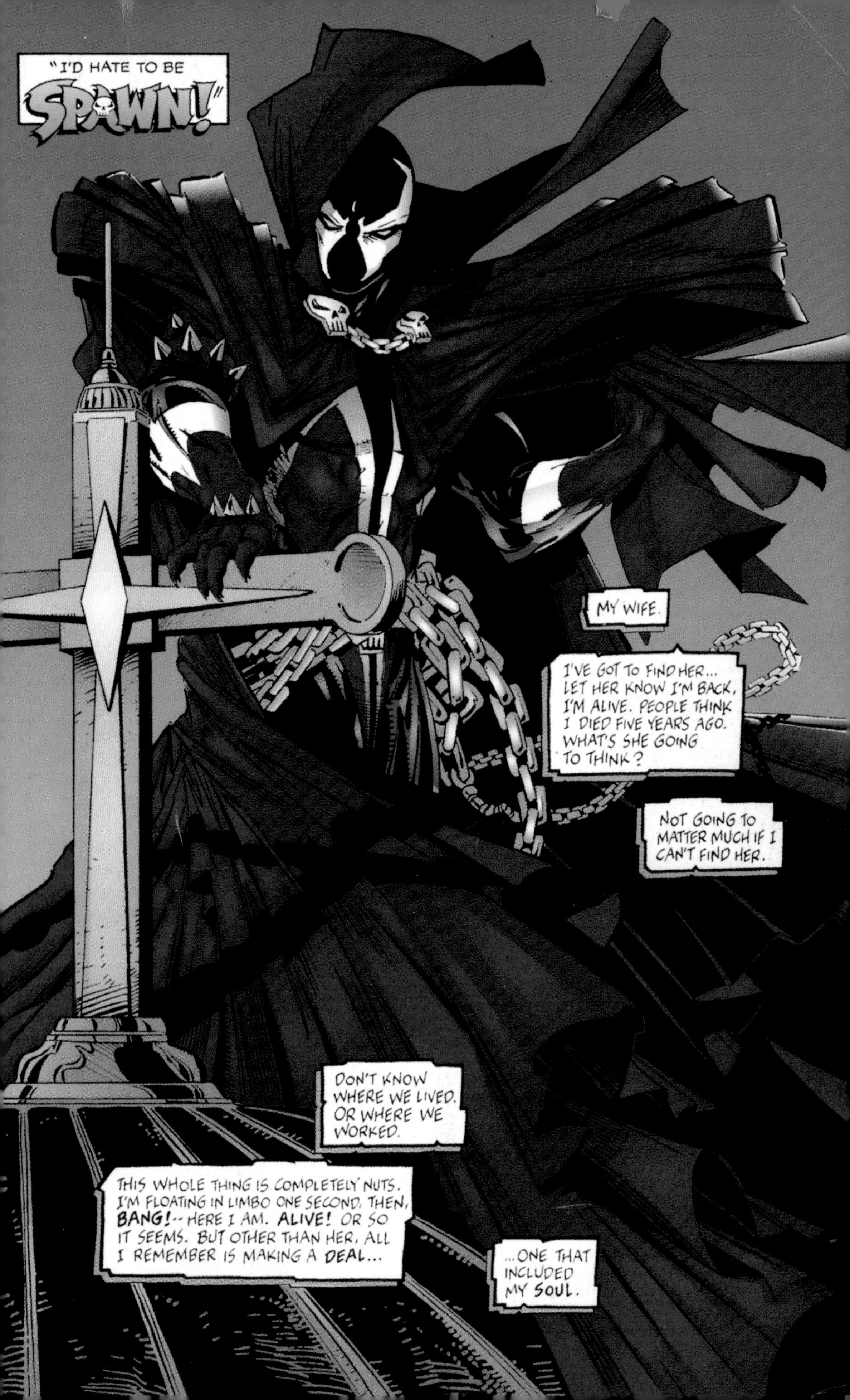
"I'D HATE TO BE SPAWN!"
MY WIFE.
I'VE GOT TO FIND HER... LET HER KNOW I'M BACK, I'M ALIVE. PEOPLE THINK I DIED FIVE YEARS AGO. WHAT'S SHE GOING TO THINK?
NOT GOING TO MATTER MUCH IF I CAN'T FIND HER.
DON'T KNOW WHERE WE LIVED. OR WHERE WE WORKED.
THIS WHOLE THING IS COMPLETELY NUTS. I'M FLOATING IN LIMBO ONE SECOND, THEN, BANG!-- HERE I AM. ALIVE! OR SO IT SEEMS. BUT OTHER THAN HER, ALL I REMEMBER IS MAKING A DEAL...
...ONE THAT INCLUDED MY SOUL.

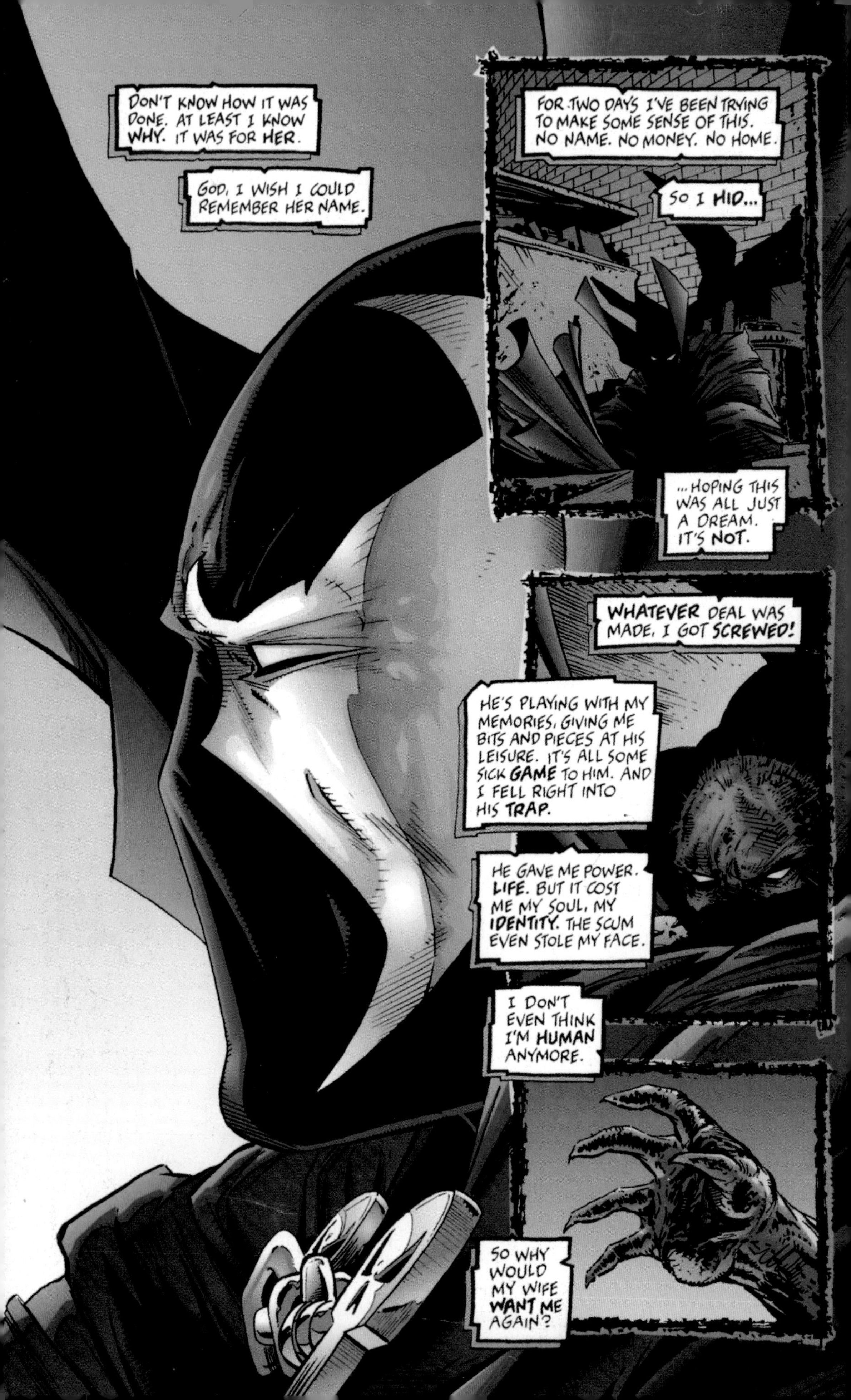

DON'T KNOW HOW IT WAS DONE. AT LEAST I KNOW WHY. IT WAS FOR HER.
GOD, I WISH I COULD REMEMBER HER NAME.
FOR TWO DAYS I'VE BEEN TRYING TO MAKE SOME SENSE OF THIS. NO NAME. NO MONEY. NO HOME.
SO I HID...
...HOPING THIS WAS ALL JUST A DREAM. IT'S NOT.
WHATEVER DEAL WAS MADE, I GOT SCREWED!
HE'S PLAYING WITH MY MEMORIES, GIVING ME BITS AND PIECES AT HIS LEISURE. IT'S ALL SOME SICK GAME TO HIM. AND I FELL RIGHT INTO HIS TRAP.
HE GAVE ME POWER. LIFE. BUT IT COST ME MY SOUL, MY IDENTITY. THE SCUM EVEN STOLE MY FACE.
I DON'T EVEN THINK I'M HUMAN ANYMORE.
SO WHY WOULD MY WIFE WANT ME AGAIN?

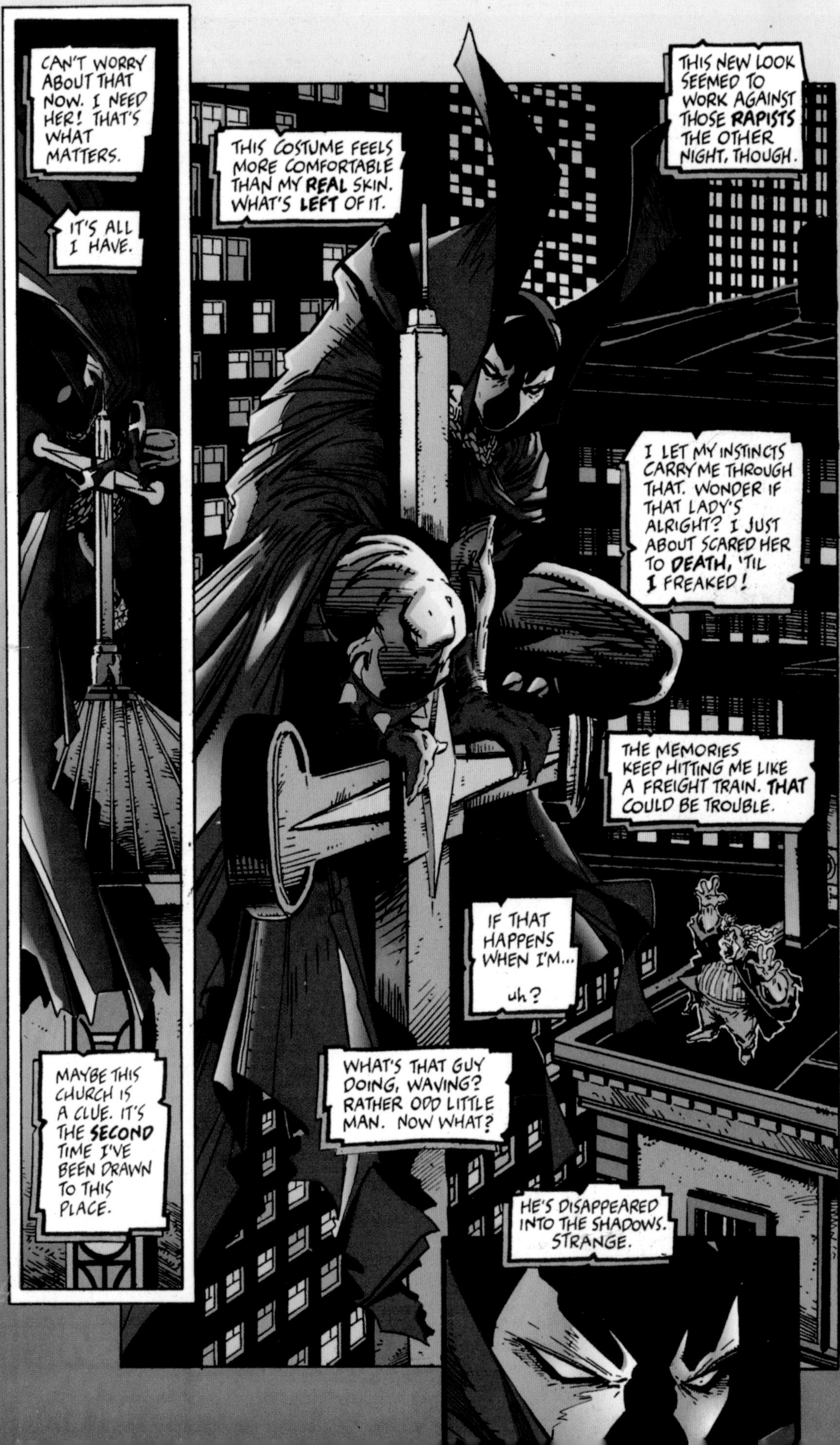
CAN'T WORRY ABOUT THAT NOW. I NEED HER! THAT'S WHAT MATTERS.
IT'S ALL I HAVE.
THIS COSTUME FEELS MORE COMFORTABLE THAN MY REAL SKIN. WHAT'S LEFT OF IT.
THIS NEW LOOK SEEMED TO WORK AGAINST THOSE RAPISTS THE OTHER NIGHT, THOUGH.
I LET MY INSTINCTS CARRY ME THROUGH THAT. WONDER IF THAT LADY'S ALRIGHT? I JUST ABOUT SCARED HER TO DEATH, 'TIL I FREAKED!
THE MEMORIES KEEP HITTING ME LIKE A FREIGHT TRAIN. THAT COULD BE TROUBLE.
IF THAT HAPPENS WHEN I'M...
uh?
MAYBE THIS CHURCH IS A CLUE. IT'S THE SECOND TIME I'VE BEEN DRAWN TO THIS PLACE.
WHAT'S THAT GUY DOING, WAVING? RATHER ODD LITTLE MAN. NOW WHAT?
HE'S DISAPPEARED INTO THE SHADOWS. STRANGE.

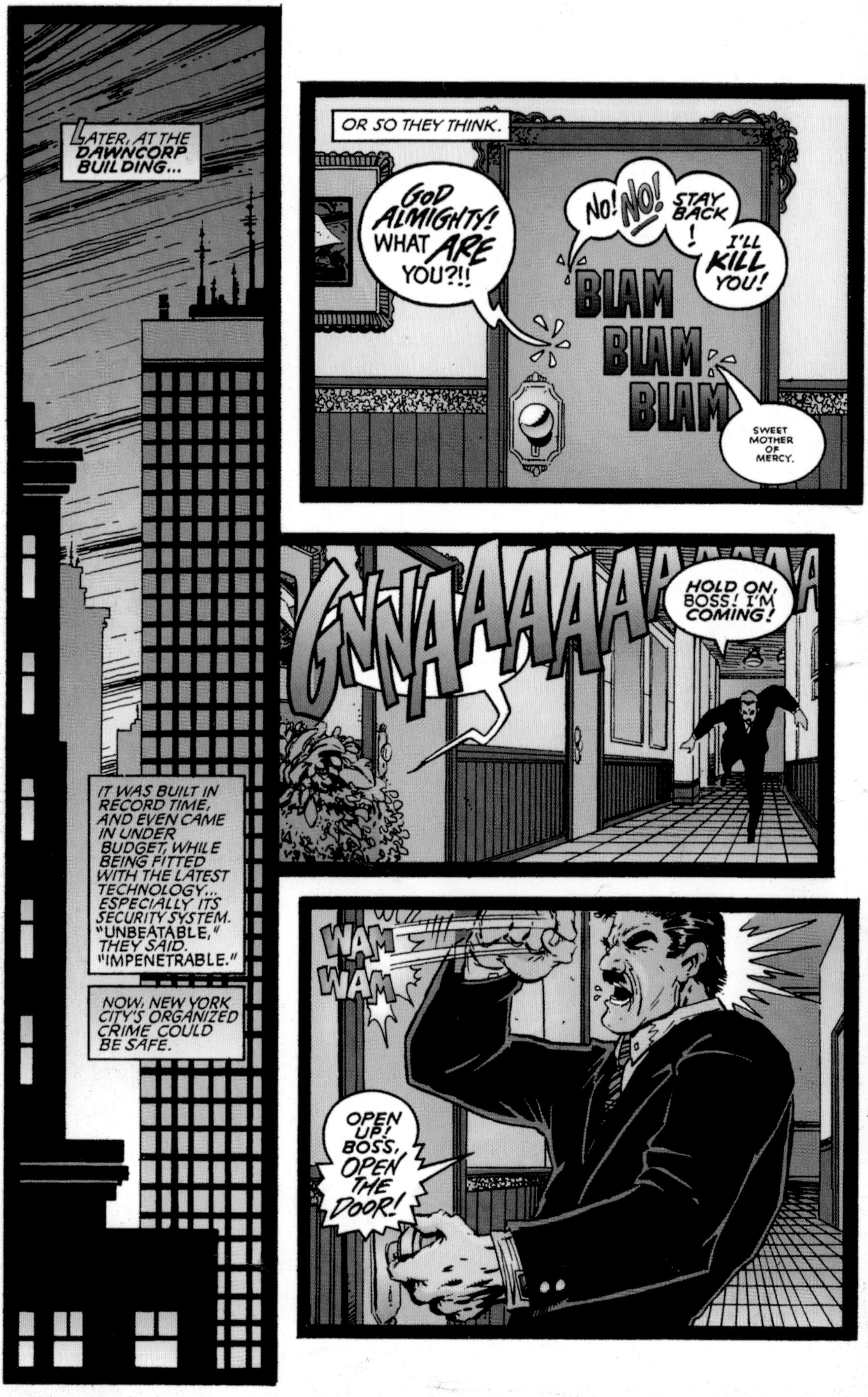

LATER, AT THE DAWNCORP BUILDING...
IT WAS BUILT IN RECORD TIME, AND EVEN CAME IN UNDER BUDGET, WHILE BEING FITTED WITH THE LATEST TECHNOLOGY... ESPECIALLY ITS SECURITY SYSTEM. "UNBEATABLE," THEY SAID. "IMPENETRABLE."
NOW, NEW YORK CITY'S ORGANIZED CRIME COULD BE SAFE.
OR SO THEY THINK.
GOD ALMIGHTY! WHAT ARE YOU?!!
No! NO! STAY BACK! I'LL KILL YOU!
BLAM BLAM BLAM
SWEET MOTHER OF MERCY.
GNNAAAAAAAAA
HOLD ON, BOSS! I'M COMING!
WAM WAM
OPEN UP! BOSS, OPEN THE DOOR!

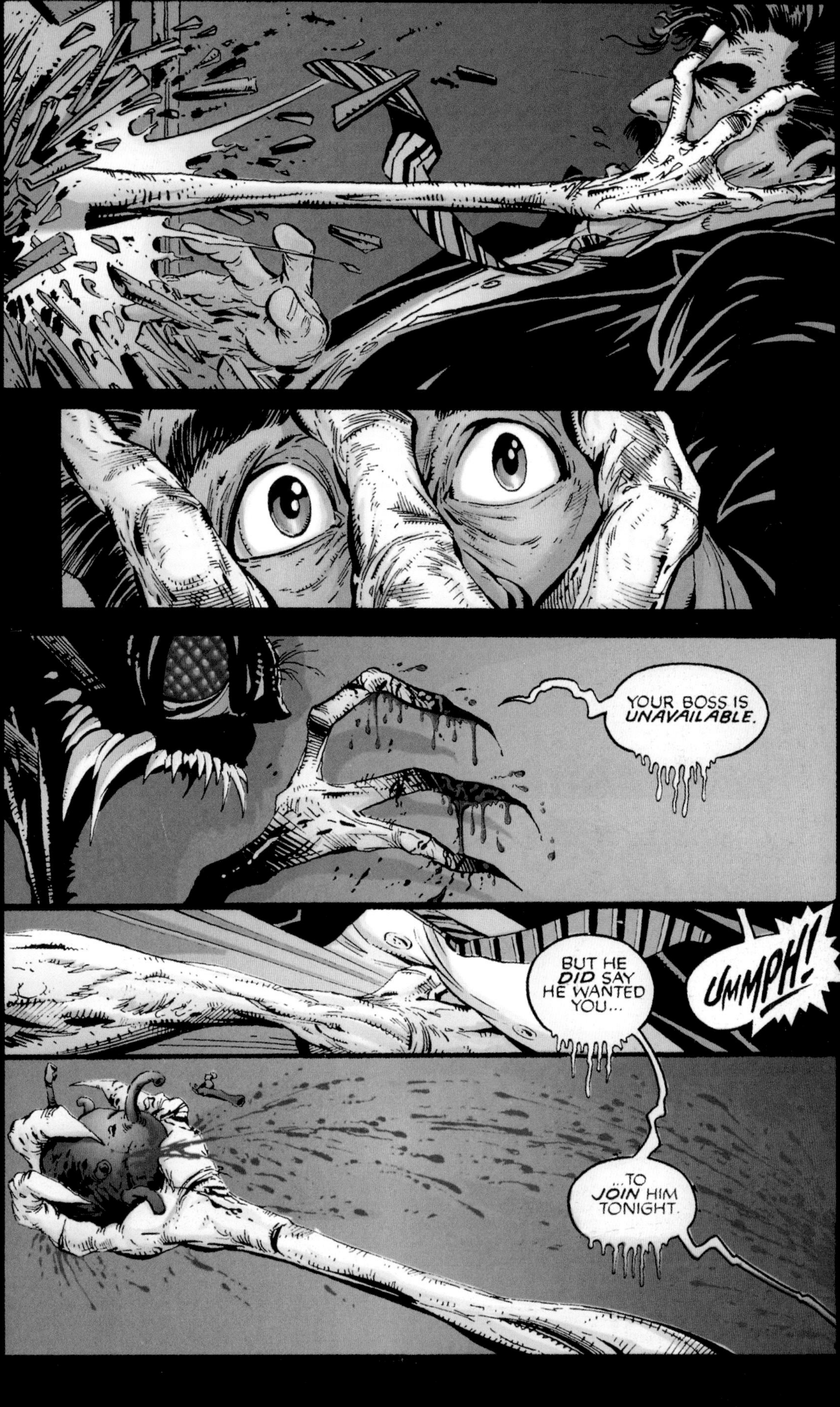
YOUR BOSS IS *UNAVAILABLE.*
BUT HE *DID* SAY HE WANTED YOU...
UMMPH!
...TO *JOIN* HIM TONIGHT.

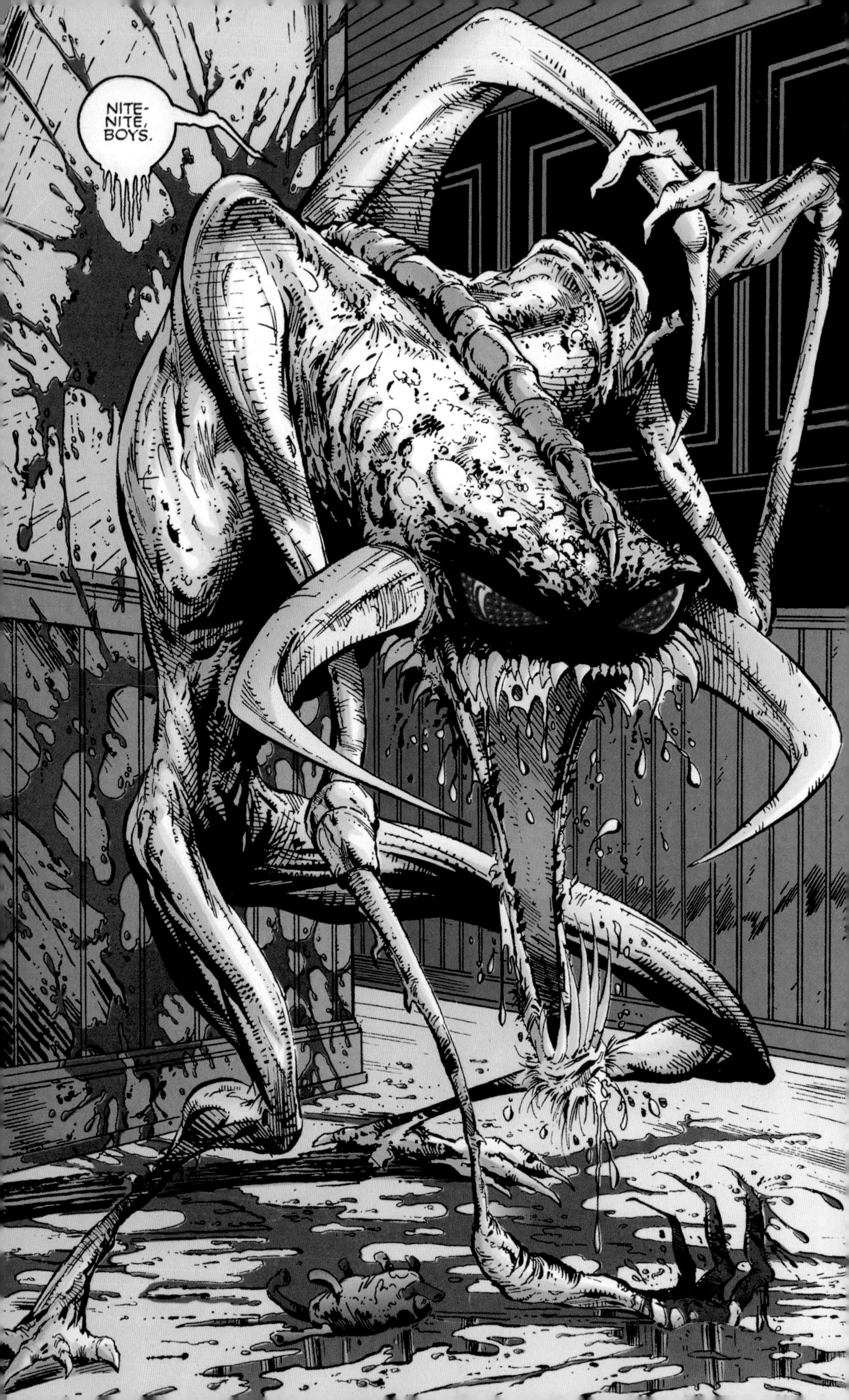
NITE-NITE, BOYS.

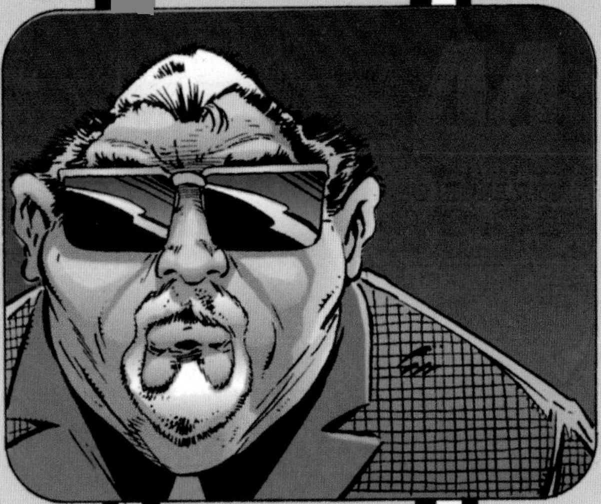

WELL, WELL, WELL. IT BREAKS MY HEART TO REPORT ANOTHER COUPLE OF MAFIA KILLINGS. IT LOOKS LIKE OUR BOY THE "HEART SURGEON" IS AT IT AGAIN. THOUGH THE POLICE HAVEN'T CONFIRMED ANY CONNECTION TO THE ***OTHER*** DEATHS, ONLY THOSE OF US WHO ARE BRAIN-DEAD CAN'T FIGURE ***THIS*** ONE OUT.

THE POLICE ALSO REPORT THAT THEY'VE DOUBLED THE TASK FORCE INVESTIGATING THESE VEG-O-MATIC KILLINGS. MY ONLY QUESTION:

WHY?!! LAST TIME I CHECKED, ***ALL*** SIX OF THEM WERE 'LEG-BREAKERS.

WHAT'S TO INVESTIGATE? AM I THE ONLY ONE ASKING THIS QUESTION?

I'VE GOT A BETTER IDEA-- LET ME HELP DIG THE GRAVES.

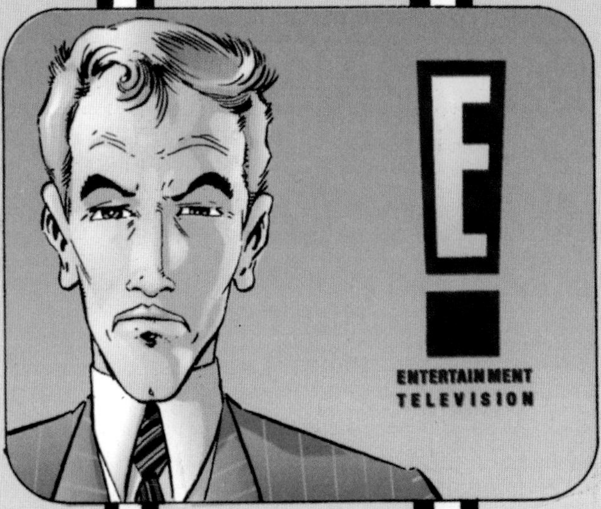
E!
ENTERTAINMENT
TELEVISION

AS I'VE STATED BEFORE, RUMORS ARE THE UGLY SIDE OF SHOW BIZ.

THE YOUNGBLOODS, CHANGING THEIR COSTUMES FOR ONE UNIFIED LOOK? ***C'MON***, IT'S THE MYRIAD COLORS AND ENSEMBLES THAT ***TOOK*** THEM TO THE TOP, ***WHY*** IN HEAVEN'S NAME WOULD THEY WANT TO ALIENATE THEIR FANS ***NOW?***

SEX APPEAL HAS ***AL***WAYS BEEN A BIG PRIORITY TO THE MARKETING GENIUSES BEHIND OUR HEROES IN TIGHTS. 'BLOOD MERCHANDISE IS OVER THE $2.2 ***BIL***LION MARK AL***READY.*** I JUST ***KNEW*** THERE'D BE A DAY THEY'D TOPPLE THOSE PIZZA-EATING TURTLES.

AND ***SPEAKING*** OF GREEN GUYS, CHICAGO IS REPORTING THE APPEARANCE OF A ***DRAGON***, FIN AND ***ALL***. NOW WOULDN'T ***THAT*** MAKE A GREAT TICKLER.

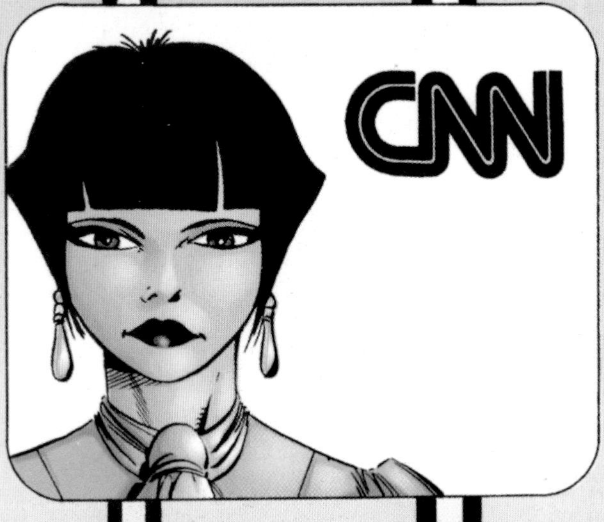
CNN

... SOURCES ALSO INDICATE THAT SINCE TONIGHT'S MURDERS, OVER A DOZEN OF NEW YORK'S MOST POWERFUL MEN HAVE ASKED FOR POLICE PROTECTION. ALL OF THESE MEN HAVE 'ALLEGED' CONNECTIONS TO CRIMINAL AFFAIRS.

ON A MORE POSITIVE NOTE, ***WANDA BLAKE***, WIDOW OF ***LT. COL. AL SIMMONS***, HELPED OPEN ANOTHER CARE CLINIC FOR DISABLED CHILDREN.

MONEY GENERATED BY HER LATE HUSBAND'S MEMORIAL FUND HELPED FINISH THE CENTER, WHICH HAD BEEN ON HOLD. THE CURRENT RECESSION IS BLAMED.

THIS IS THE THIRD SUCH PROJECT THAT Ms. BLAKE HAS BEEN INVOLVED WITH.

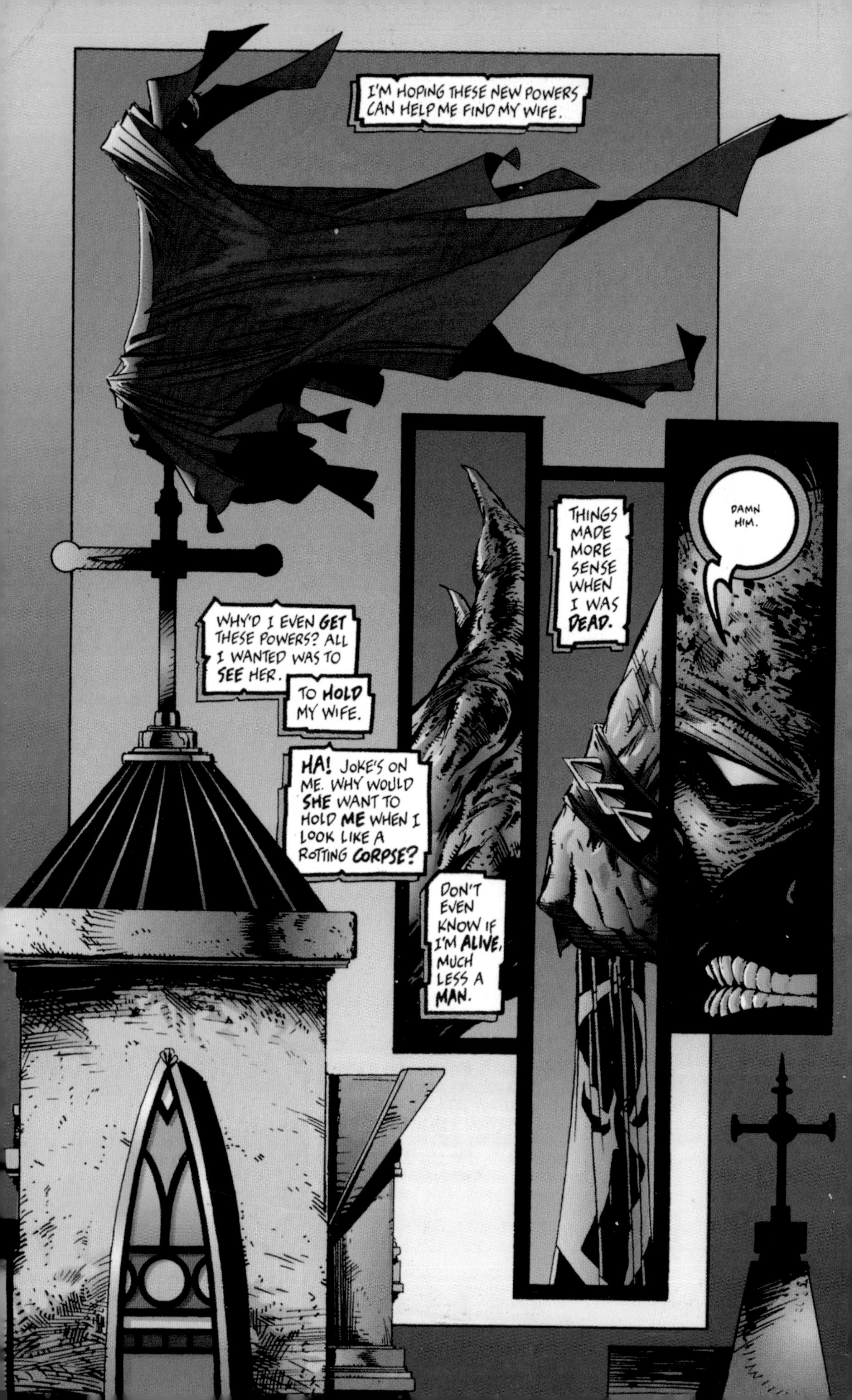
I'M HOPING THESE NEW POWERS CAN HELP ME FIND MY WIFE.
WHY'D I EVEN GET THESE POWERS? ALL I WANTED WAS TO SEE HER.
TO HOLD MY WIFE.
HA! JOKE'S ON ME. WHY WOULD SHE WANT TO HOLD ME WHEN I LOOK LIKE A ROTTING CORPSE?
DON'T EVEN KNOW IF I'M ALIVE, MUCH LESS A MAN.
THINGS MADE MORE SENSE WHEN I WAS DEAD.
DAMN HIM.

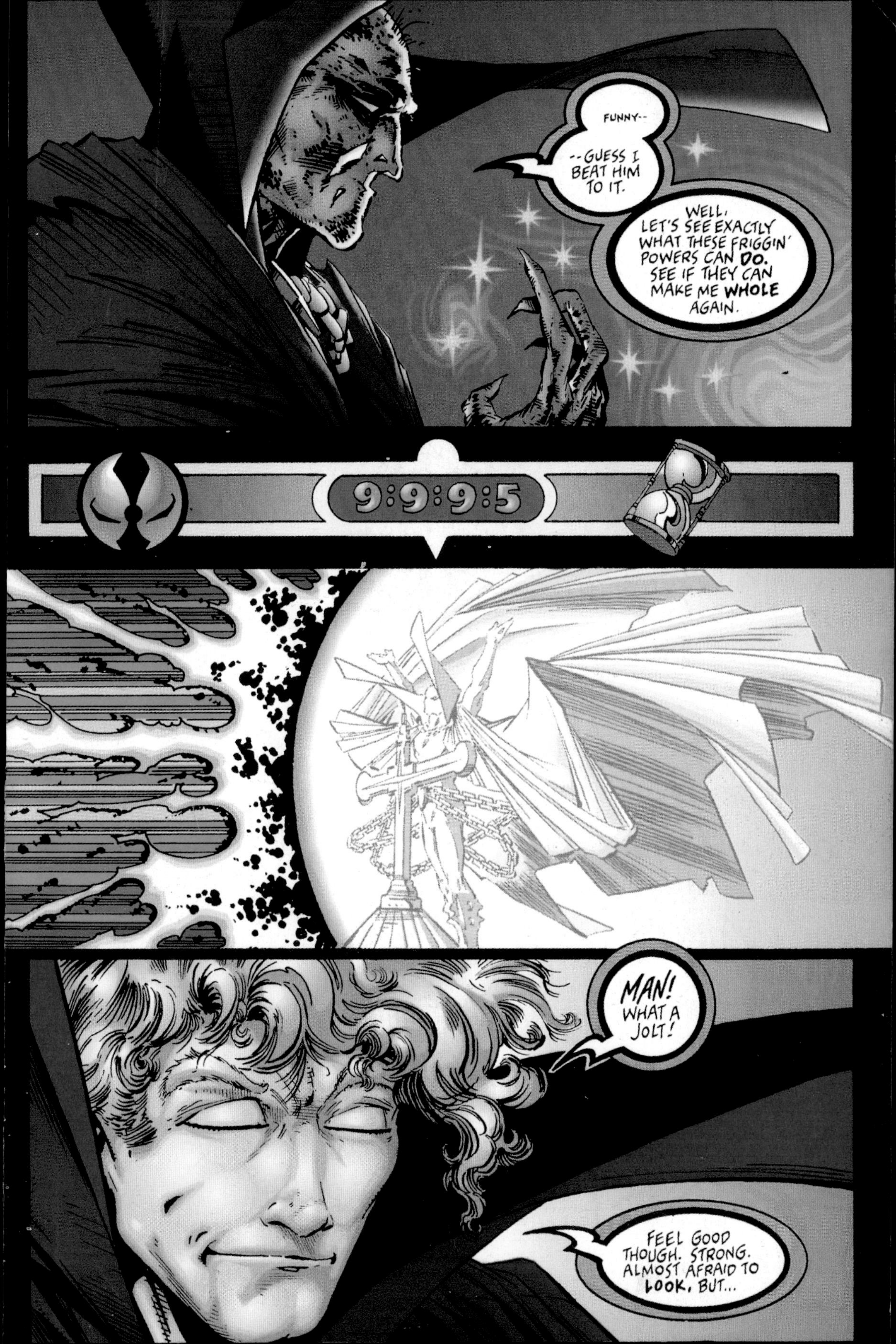
FUNNY--
--GUESS I BEAT HIM TO IT.
WELL, LET'S SEE EXACTLY WHAT THESE FRIGGIN' POWERS CAN **DO.** SEE IF THEY CAN MAKE ME **WHOLE** AGAIN.
9:9:9:5
MAN! WHAT A JOLT!
FEEL GOOD THOUGH. STRONG. ALMOST AFRAID TO **LOOK,** BUT...

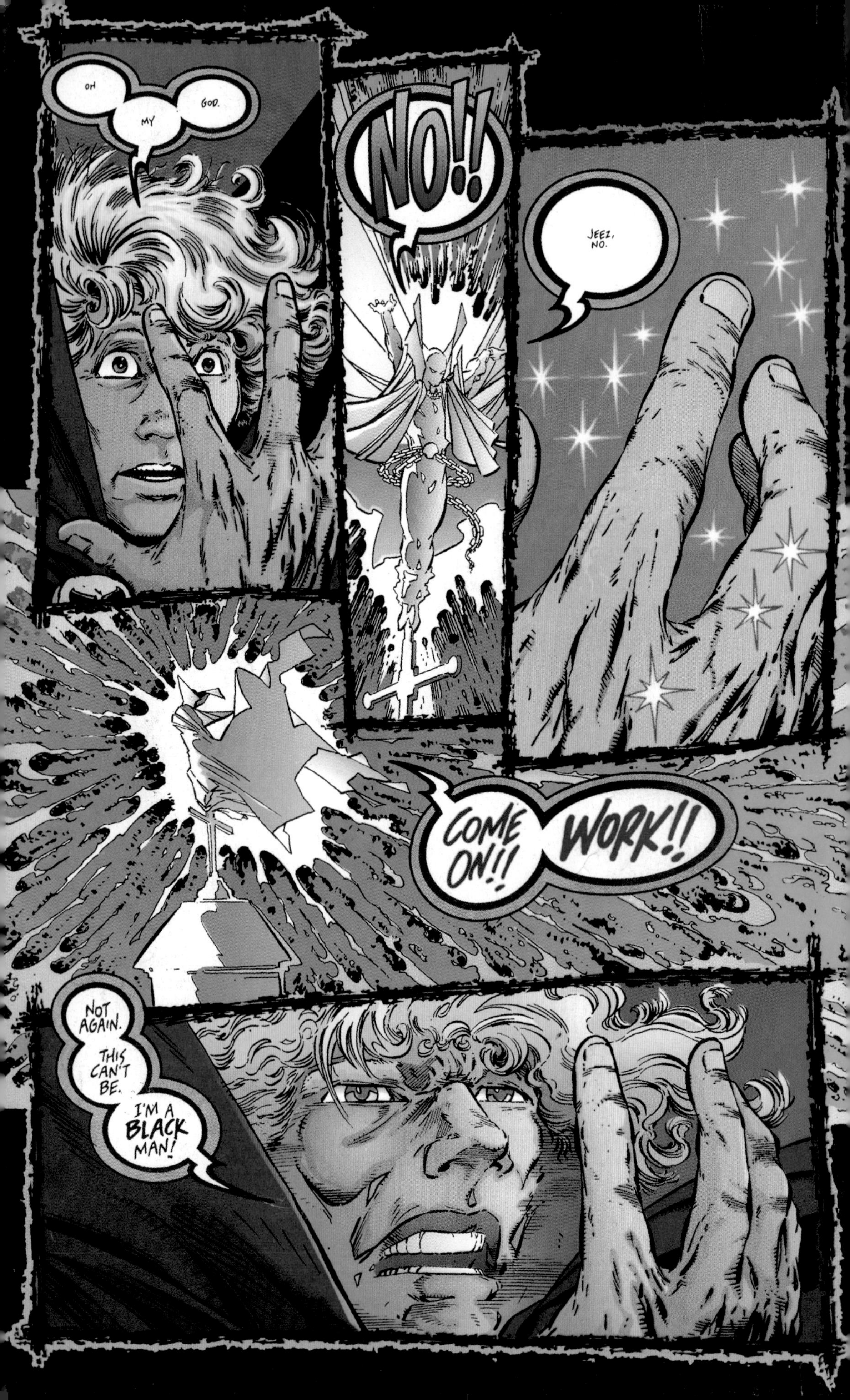
OH
MY
GOD.
NO!!
JEEZ, NO.
COME ON!!
WORK!!
NOT AGAIN.
THIS CAN'T BE.
I'M A BLACK MAN!

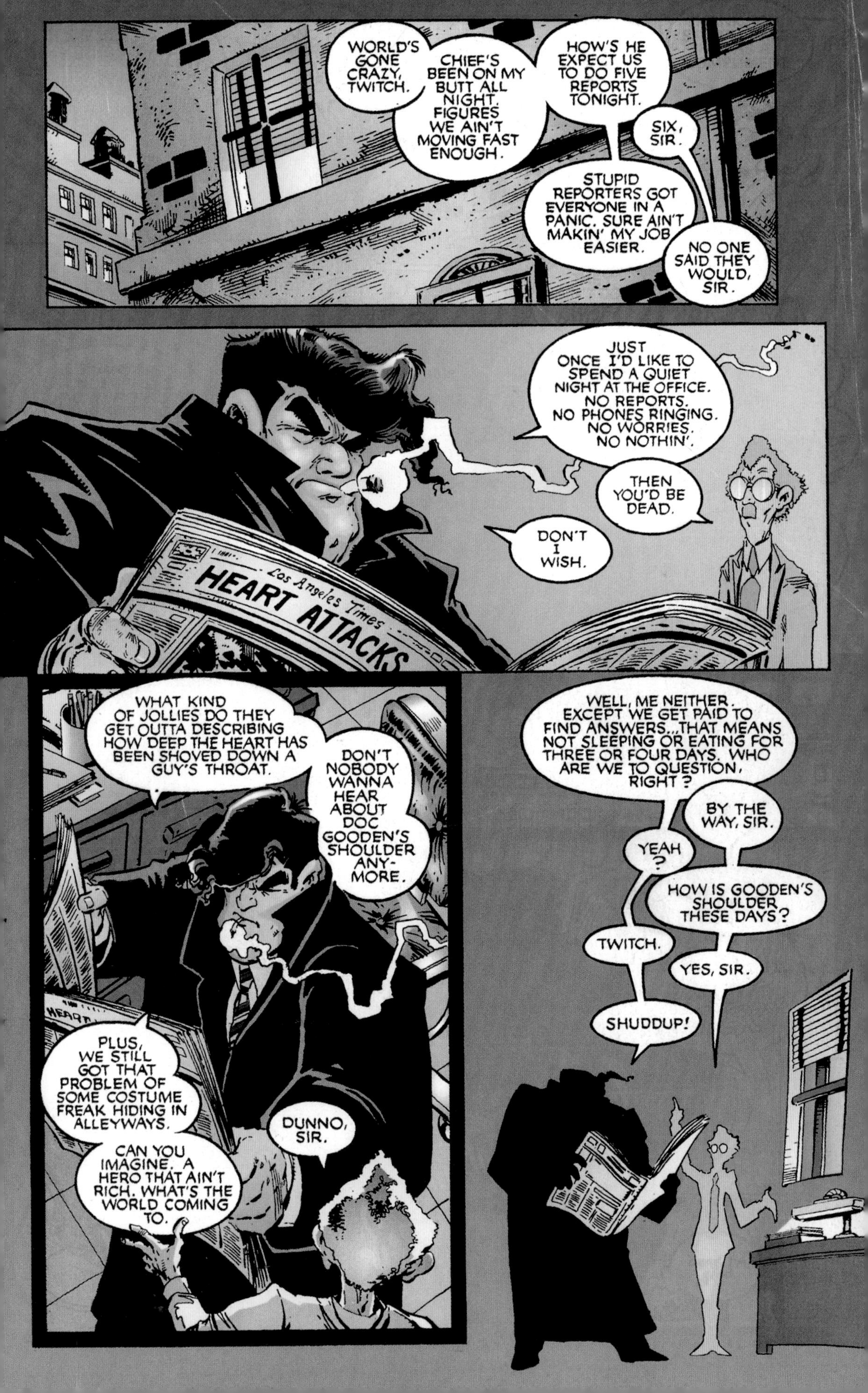
WORLD'S GONE CRAZY, TWITCH.
CHIEF'S BEEN ON MY BUTT ALL NIGHT. FIGURES WE AIN'T MOVING FAST ENOUGH.
HOW'S HE EXPECT US TO DO FIVE REPORTS TONIGHT.
SIX, SIR.
STUPID REPORTERS GOT EVERYONE IN A PANIC. SURE AIN'T MAKIN' MY JOB EASIER.
NO ONE SAID THEY WOULD, SIR.
JUST ONCE I'D LIKE TO SPEND A QUIET NIGHT AT THE OFFICE. NO REPORTS. NO PHONES RINGING. NO WORRIES. NO NOTHIN'.
THEN YOU'D BE DEAD.
DON'T I WISH.
Los Angeles Times
HEART ATTACKS
WHAT KIND OF JOLLIES DO THEY GET OUTTA DESCRIBING HOW DEEP THE HEART HAS BEEN SHOVED DOWN A GUY'S THROAT.
DON'T NOBODY WANNA HEAR ABOUT DOC GOODEN'S SHOULDER ANY-MORE.
PLUS, WE STILL GOT THAT PROBLEM OF SOME COSTUME FREAK HIDING IN ALLEYWAYS.
CAN YOU IMAGINE. A HERO THAT AIN'T RICH. WHAT'S THE WORLD COMING TO.
DUNNO, SIR.
WELL, ME NEITHER. EXCEPT WE GET PAID TO FIND ANSWERS...THAT MEANS NOT SLEEPING OR EATING FOR THREE OR FOUR DAYS. WHO ARE WE TO QUESTION, RIGHT?
BY THE WAY, SIR.
YEAH?
HOW IS GOODEN'S SHOULDER THESE DAYS?
TWITCH.
YES, SIR.
SHUDDUP!

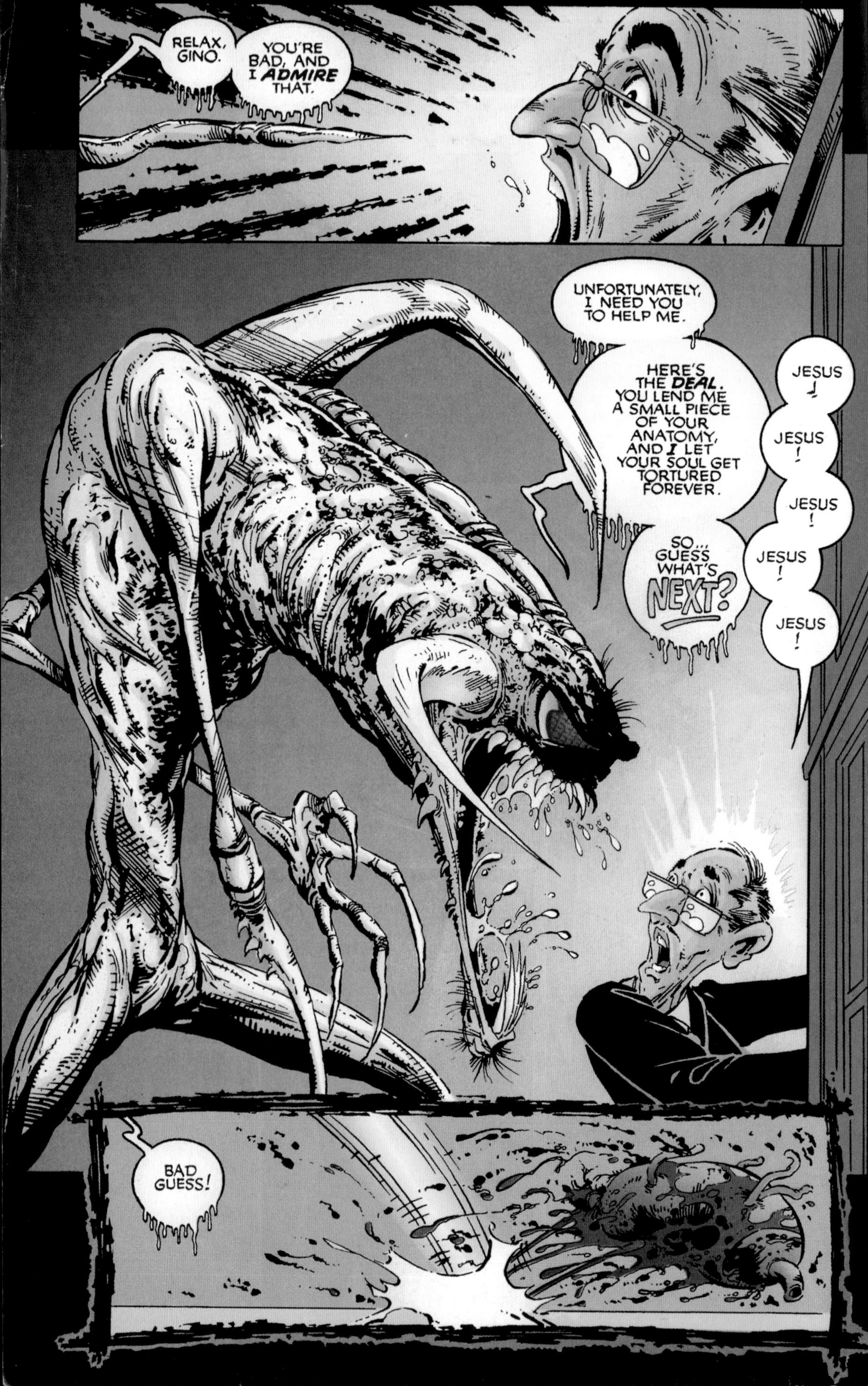
RELAX, GINO.
YOU'RE BAD, AND I ADMIRE THAT.
UNFORTUNATELY, I NEED YOU TO HELP ME.
HERE'S THE DEAL. YOU LEND ME A SMALL PIECE OF YOUR ANATOMY, AND I LET YOUR SOUL GET TORTURED FOREVER.
SO... GUESS WHAT'S NEXT?
JESUS!
JESUS!
JESUS!
JESUS!
JESUS!
BAD GUESS!

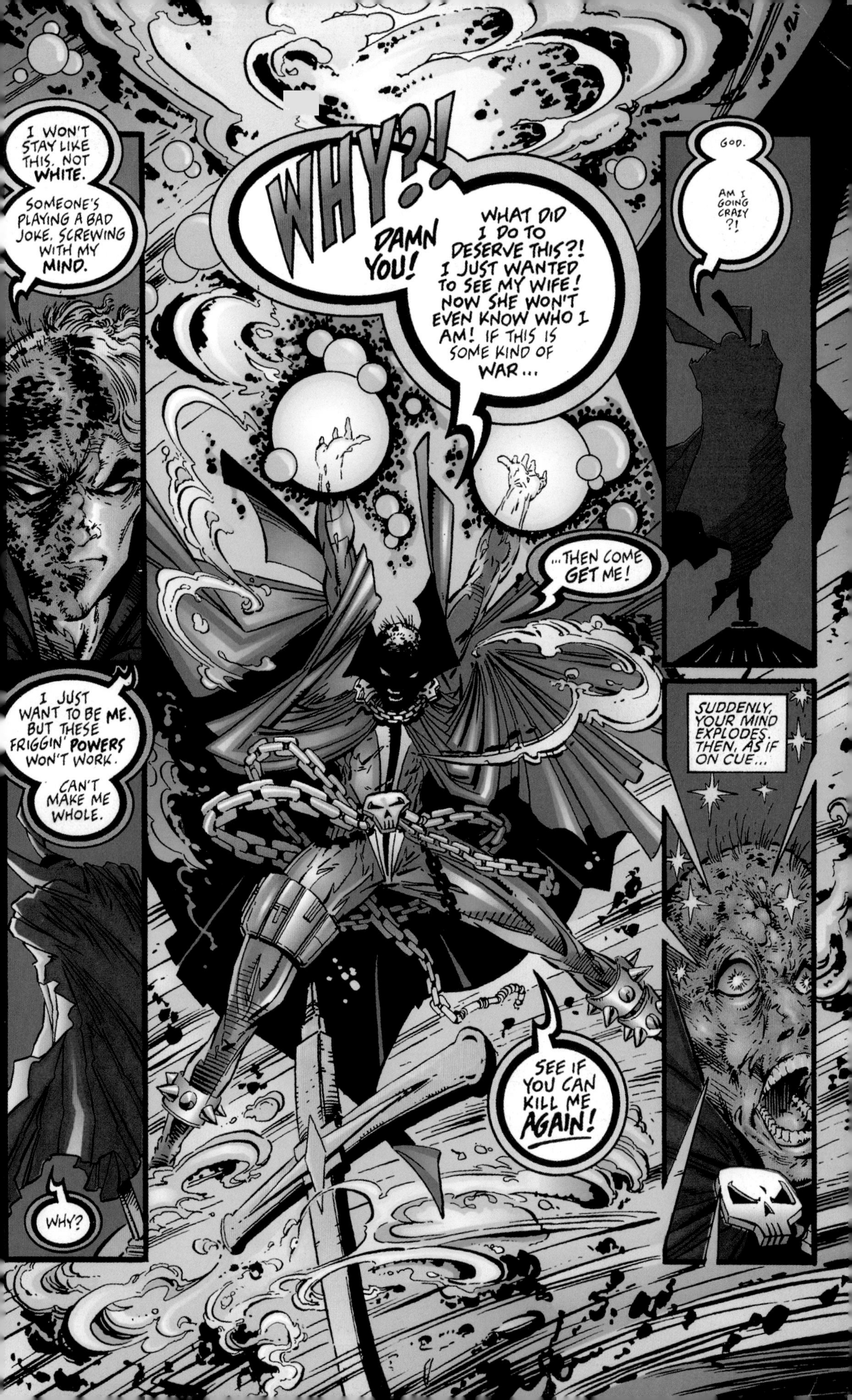
I WON'T STAY LIKE THIS. NOT WHITE.
SOMEONE'S PLAYING A BAD JOKE. SCREWING WITH MY MIND.
WHY?!
DAMN YOU!
WHAT DID I DO TO DESERVE THIS?! I JUST WANTED TO SEE MY WIFE! NOW SHE WON'T EVEN KNOW WHO I AM! IF THIS IS SOME KIND OF WAR...
GOD.
AM I GOING CRAZY ?!
...THEN COME GET ME!
I JUST WANT TO BE ME. BUT THESE FRIGGIN' POWERS WON'T WORK.
CAN'T MAKE ME WHOLE.
WHY?
SEE IF YOU CAN KILL ME AGAIN!
SUDDENLY, YOUR MIND EXPLODES. THEN, AS IF ON CUE...

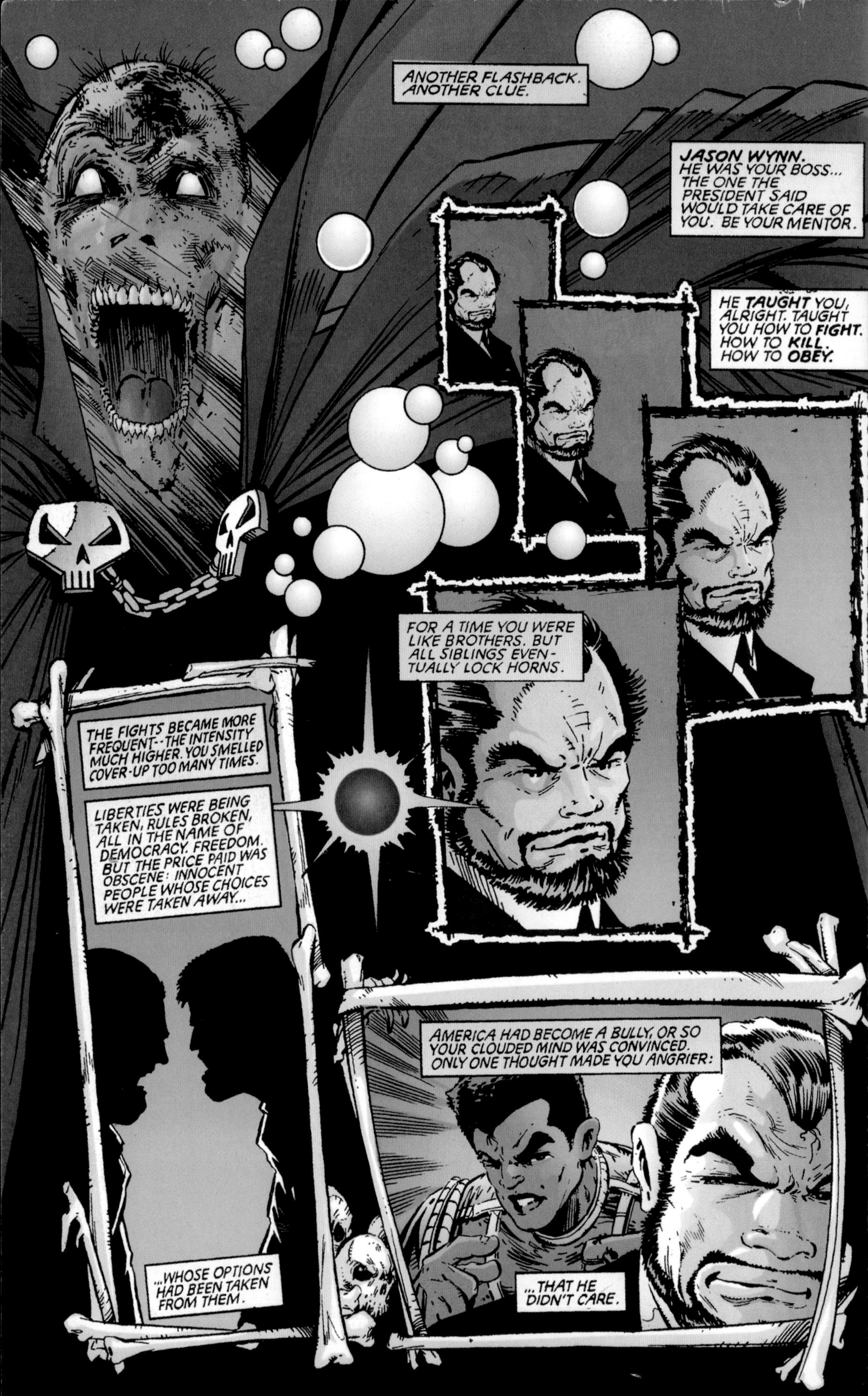
ANOTHER FLASHBACK. ANOTHER CLUE.
JASON WYNN. HE WAS YOUR BOSS... THE ONE THE PRESIDENT SAID WOULD TAKE CARE OF YOU. BE YOUR MENTOR.
HE TAUGHT YOU, ALRIGHT. TAUGHT YOU HOW TO FIGHT. HOW TO KILL. HOW TO OBEY.
FOR A TIME YOU WERE LIKE BROTHERS. BUT ALL SIBLINGS EVEN-TUALLY LOCK HORNS.
THE FIGHTS BECAME MORE FREQUENT--THE INTENSITY MUCH HIGHER. YOU SMELLED COVER-UP TOO MANY TIMES.
LIBERTIES WERE BEING TAKEN, RULES BROKEN, ALL IN THE NAME OF DEMOCRACY. FREEDOM. BUT THE PRICE PAID WAS OBSCENE: INNOCENT PEOPLE WHOSE CHOICES WERE TAKEN AWAY...
...WHOSE OPTIONS HAD BEEN TAKEN FROM THEM.
AMERICA HAD BECOME A BULLY, OR SO YOUR CLOUDED MIND WAS CONVINCED. ONLY ONE THOUGHT MADE YOU ANGRIER:
...THAT HE DIDN'T CARE.

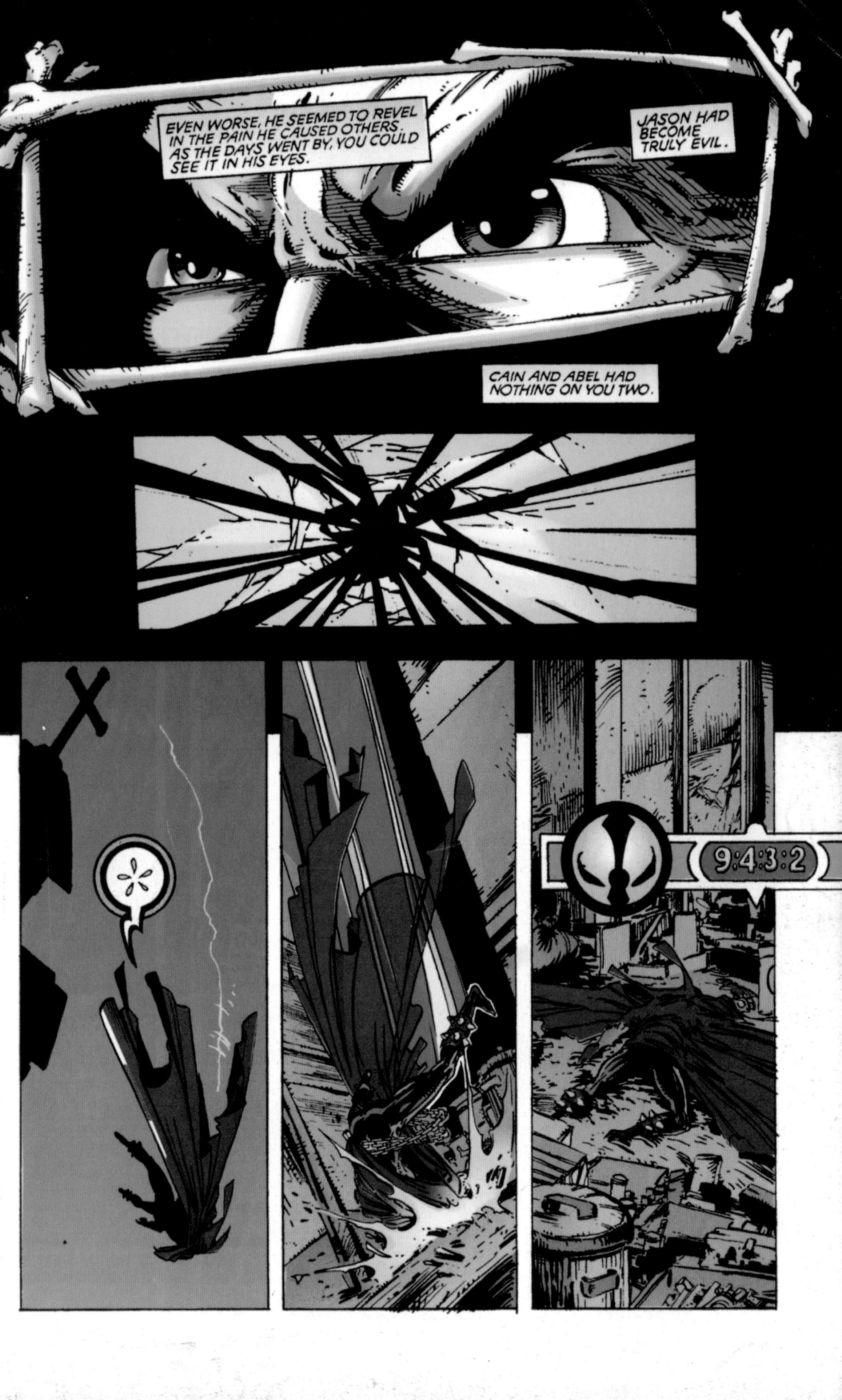
EVEN WORSE, HE SEEMED TO REVEL IN THE PAIN HE CAUSED OTHERS. AS THE DAYS WENT BY, YOU COULD SEE IT IN HIS EYES.
JASON HAD BECOME TRULY EVIL.
CAIN AND ABEL HAD NOTHING ON YOU TWO.
9:4:3:2

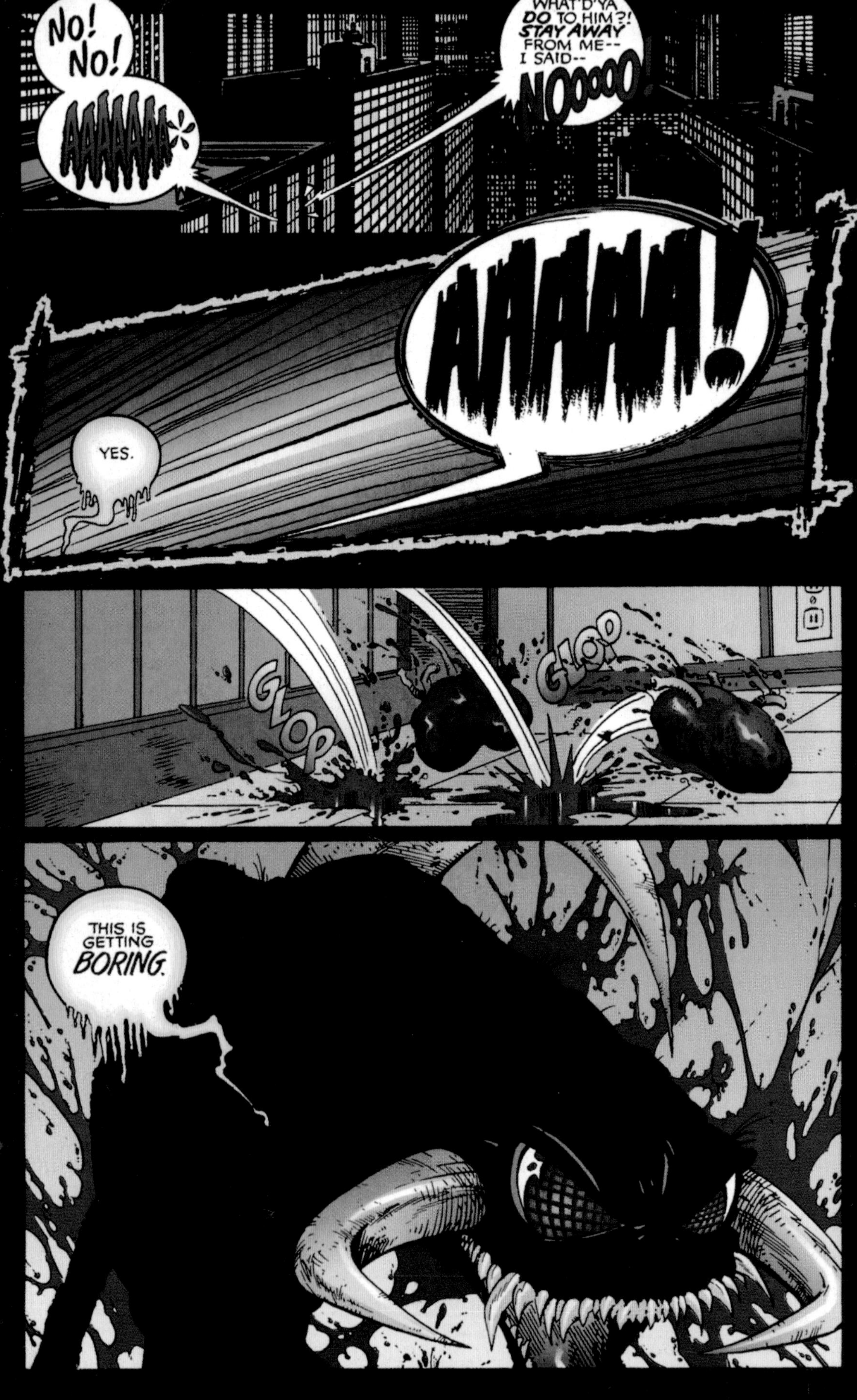
No! No!
AAAAAAA!
WHAT'D'YA DO TO HIM?! STAY AWAY FROM ME-- I SAID--
NOOOOO
AAAAAA!
YES.
GLOP
GLOP
THIS IS GETTING BORING.

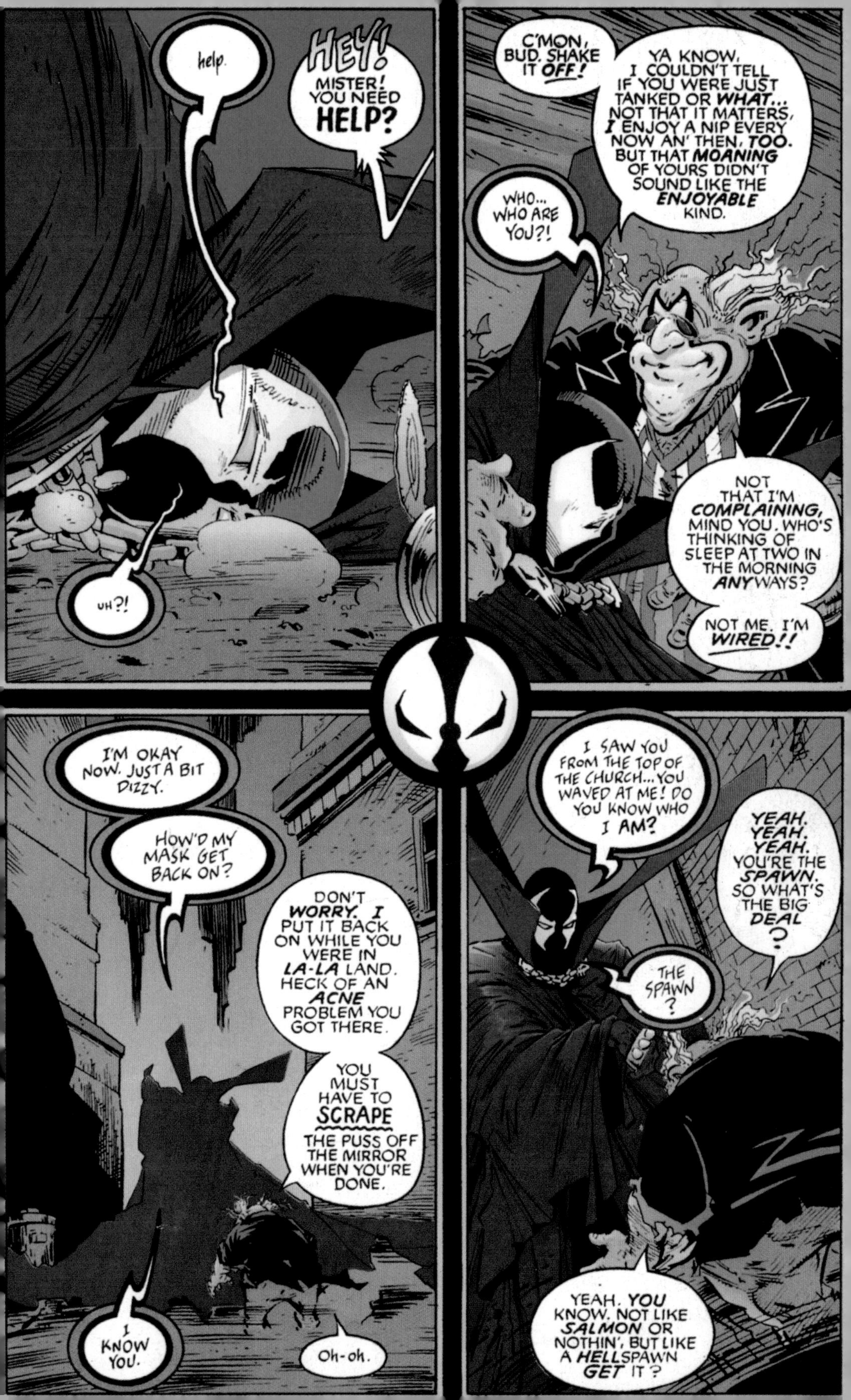
help.
HEY! MISTER! YOU NEED HELP?
UH?!
C'MON, BUD. SHAKE IT OFF!
YA KNOW, I COULDN'T TELL IF YOU WERE JUST TANKED OR WHAT... NOT THAT IT MATTERS, I ENJOY A NIP EVERY NOW AN' THEN, TOO. BUT THAT MOANING OF YOURS DIDN'T SOUND LIKE THE ENJOYABLE KIND.
WHO... WHO ARE YOU?!
NOT THAT I'M COMPLAINING, MIND YOU. WHO'S THINKING OF SLEEP AT TWO IN THE MORNING ANYWAYS?
NOT ME. I'M WIRED!!
I'M OKAY NOW. JUST A BIT DIZZY.
HOW'D MY MASK GET BACK ON?
DON'T WORRY. I PUT IT BACK ON WHILE YOU WERE IN LA-LA LAND. HECK OF AN ACNE PROBLEM YOU GOT THERE.
YOU MUST HAVE TO SCRAPE THE PUSS OFF THE MIRROR WHEN YOU'RE DONE.
I KNOW YOU.
Oh-oh.
I SAW YOU FROM THE TOP OF THE CHURCH... YOU WAVED AT ME! DO YOU KNOW WHO I AM?
YEAH. YEAH. YEAH. YOU'RE THE SPAWN. SO WHAT'S THE BIG DEAL?
THE SPAWN?
YEAH. YOU KNOW. NOT LIKE SALMON OR NOTHIN', BUT LIKE A HELLSPAWN GET IT?

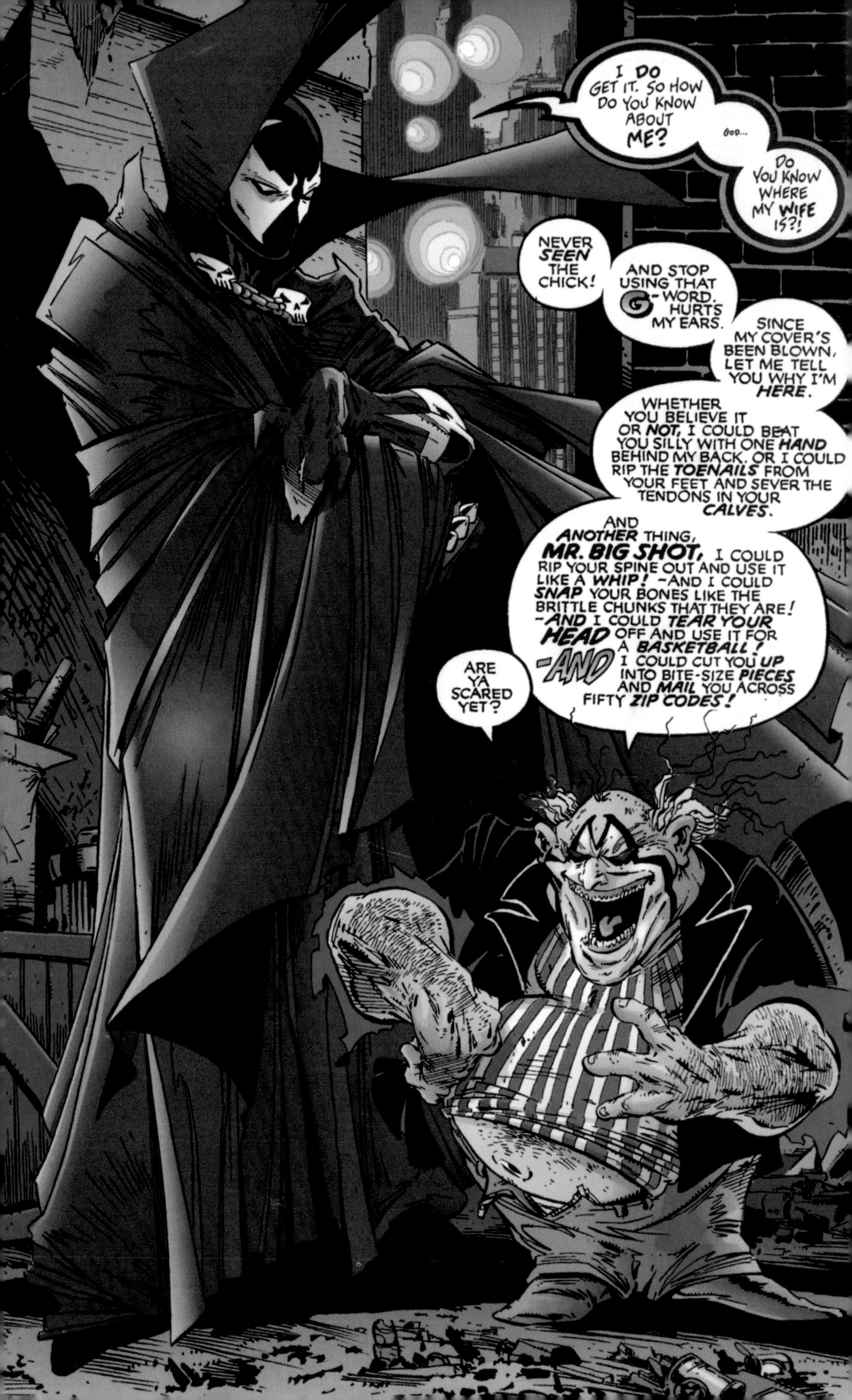

I DO GET IT. SO HOW DO YOU KNOW ABOUT ME?
GOD...
DO YOU KNOW WHERE MY WIFE IS?!
NEVER SEEN THE CHICK!
AND STOP USING THAT G-WORD. HURTS MY EARS.
SINCE MY COVER'S BEEN BLOWN, LET ME TELL YOU WHY I'M HERE.
WHETHER YOU BELIEVE IT OR NOT, I COULD BEAT YOU SILLY WITH ONE HAND BEHIND MY BACK. OR I COULD RIP THE TOENAILS FROM YOUR FEET AND SEVER THE TENDONS IN YOUR CALVES.
AND ANOTHER THING, MR. BIG SHOT, I COULD RIP YOUR SPINE OUT AND USE IT LIKE A WHIP! -AND I COULD SNAP YOUR BONES LIKE THE BRITTLE CHUNKS THAT THEY ARE! -AND I COULD TEAR YOUR HEAD OFF AND USE IT FOR A BASKETBALL! -AND I COULD CUT YOU UP INTO BITE-SIZE PIECES AND MAIL YOU ACROSS FIFTY ZIP CODES!
ARE YA SCARED YET?

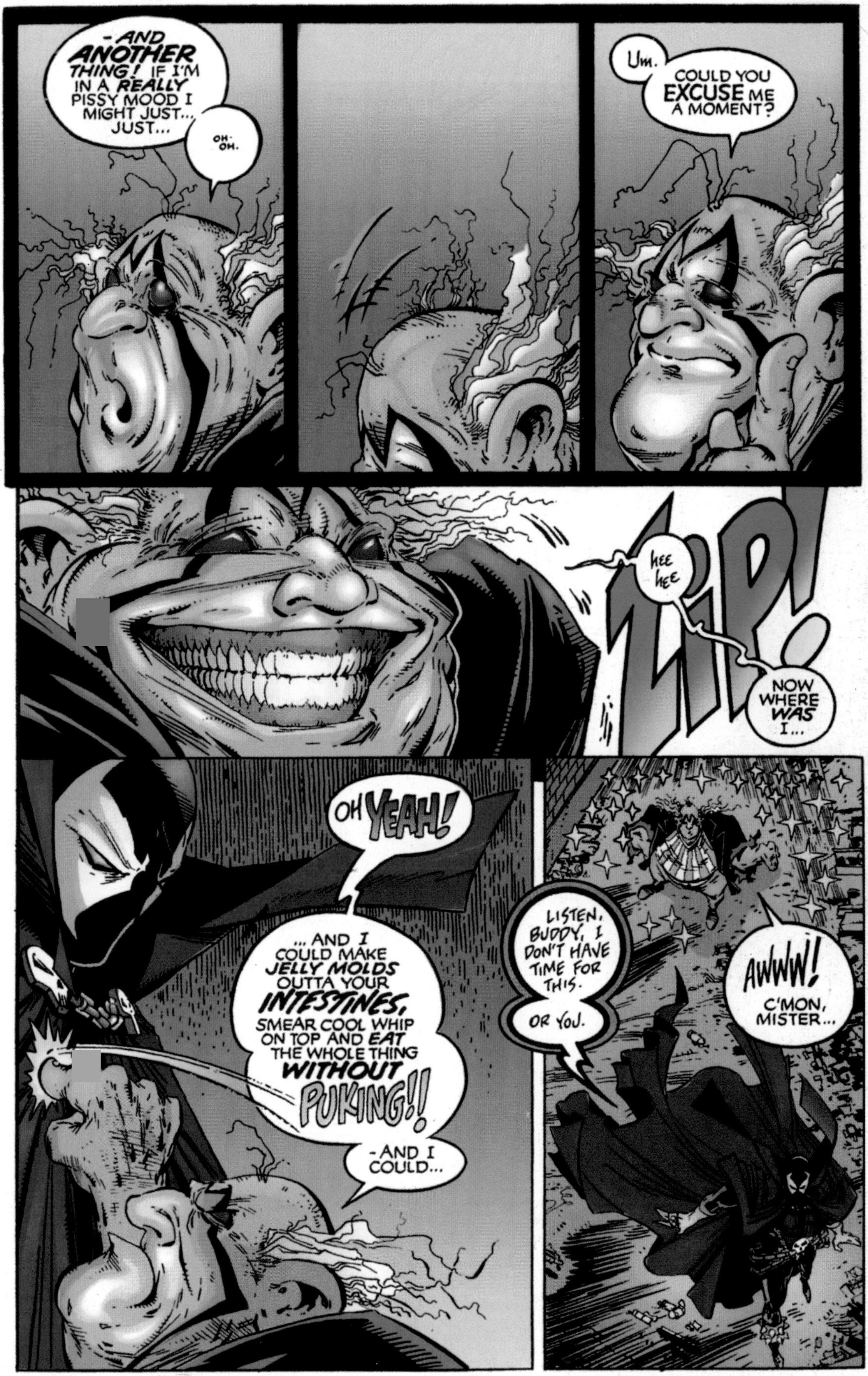
-AND ANOTHER THING! IF I'M IN A REALLY PISSY MOOD I MIGHT JUST... JUST...
OH-OH.
Um.
COULD YOU EXCUSE ME A MOMENT?
hee hee
ZIP!
NOW WHERE WAS I...
OH YEAH!
...AND I COULD MAKE JELLY MOLDS OUTTA YOUR INTESTINES, SMEAR COOL WHIP ON TOP AND EAT THE WHOLE THING WITHOUT PUKING!!
-AND I COULD...
LISTEN, BUDDY, I DON'T HAVE TIME FOR THIS.
OR YOU.
AWWW! C'MON, MISTER...

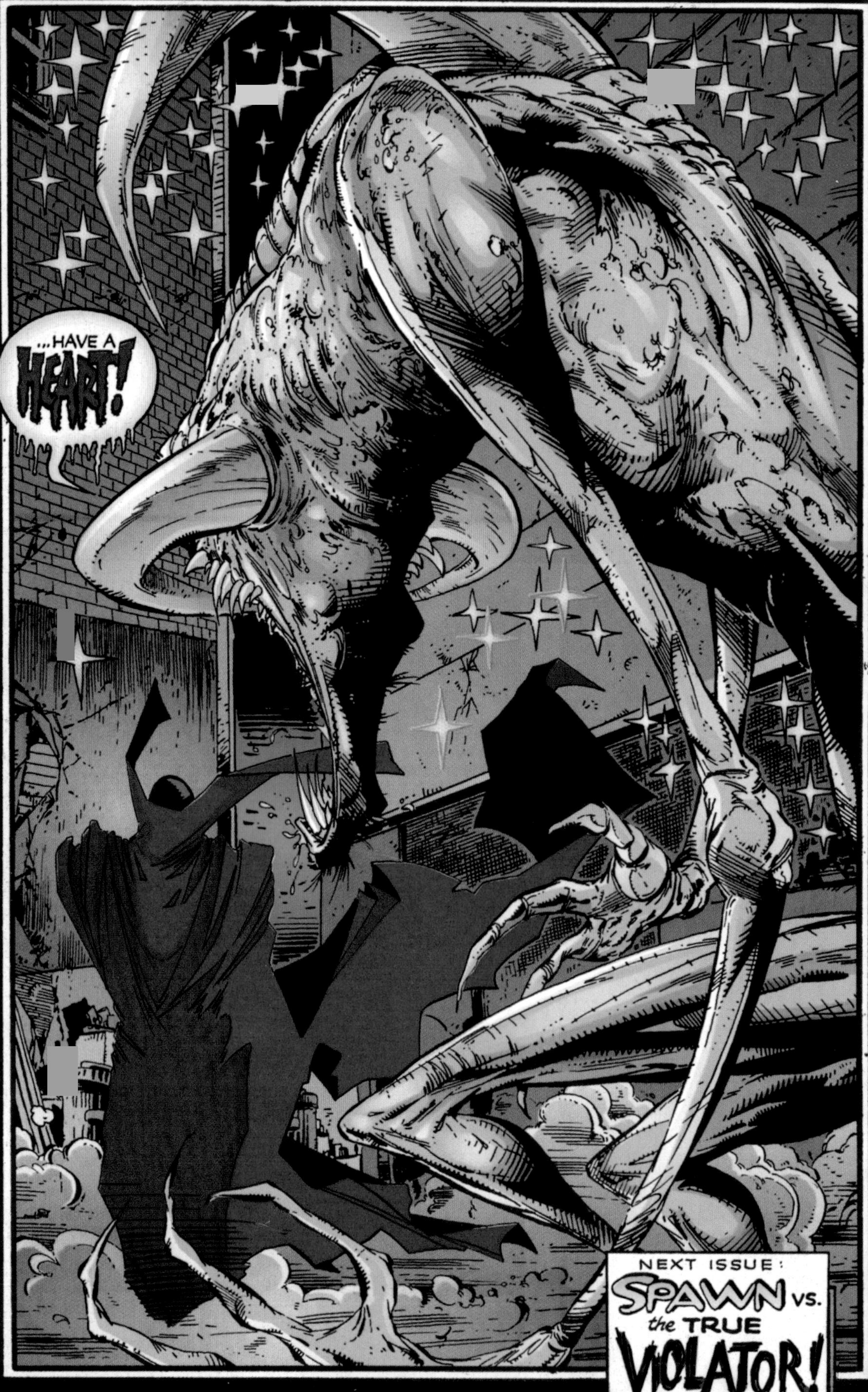
...HAVE A HEART!
NEXT ISSUE: SPAWN VS. the TRUE VIOLATOR!

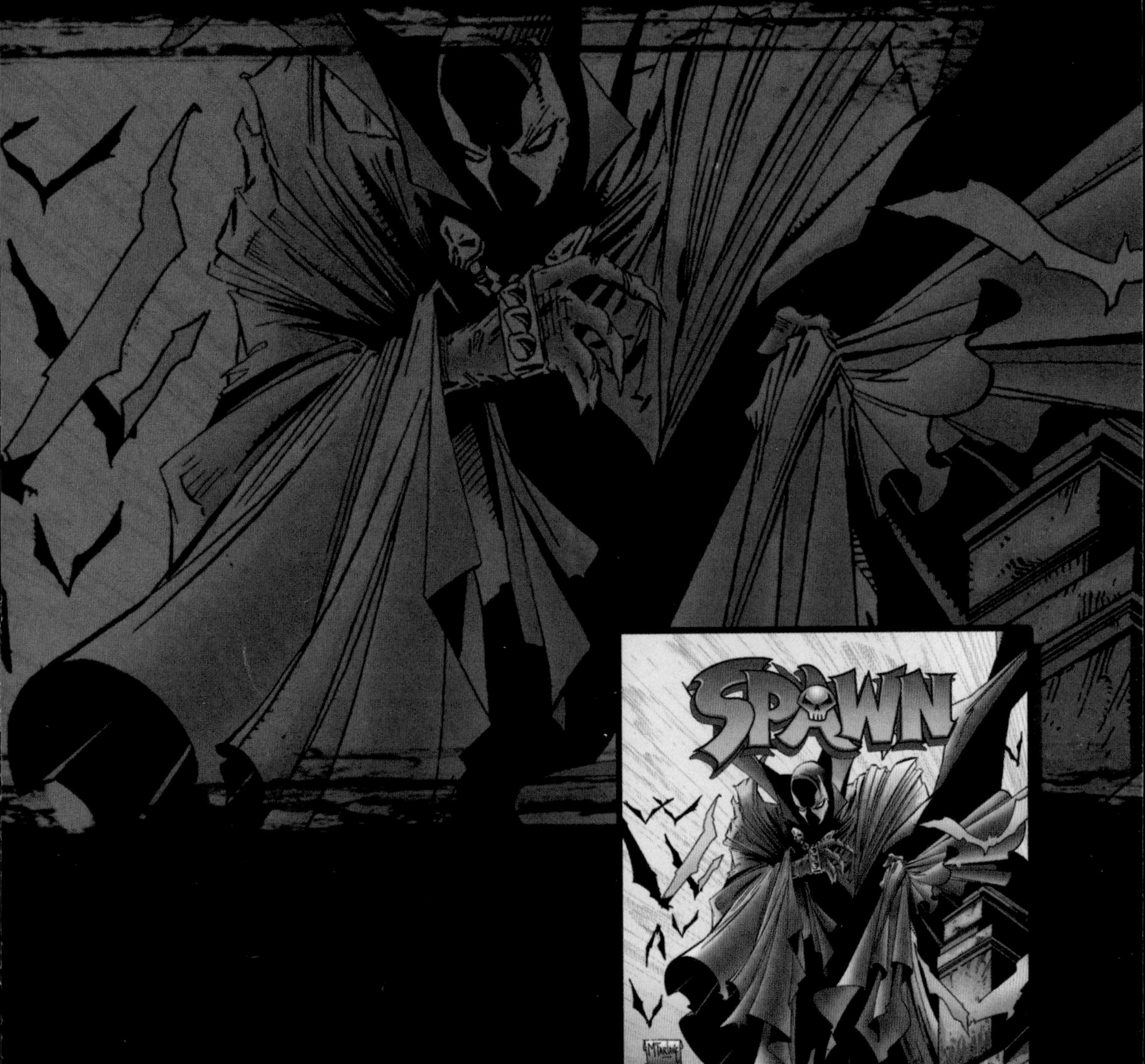
SPAWN

ISSUE THREE

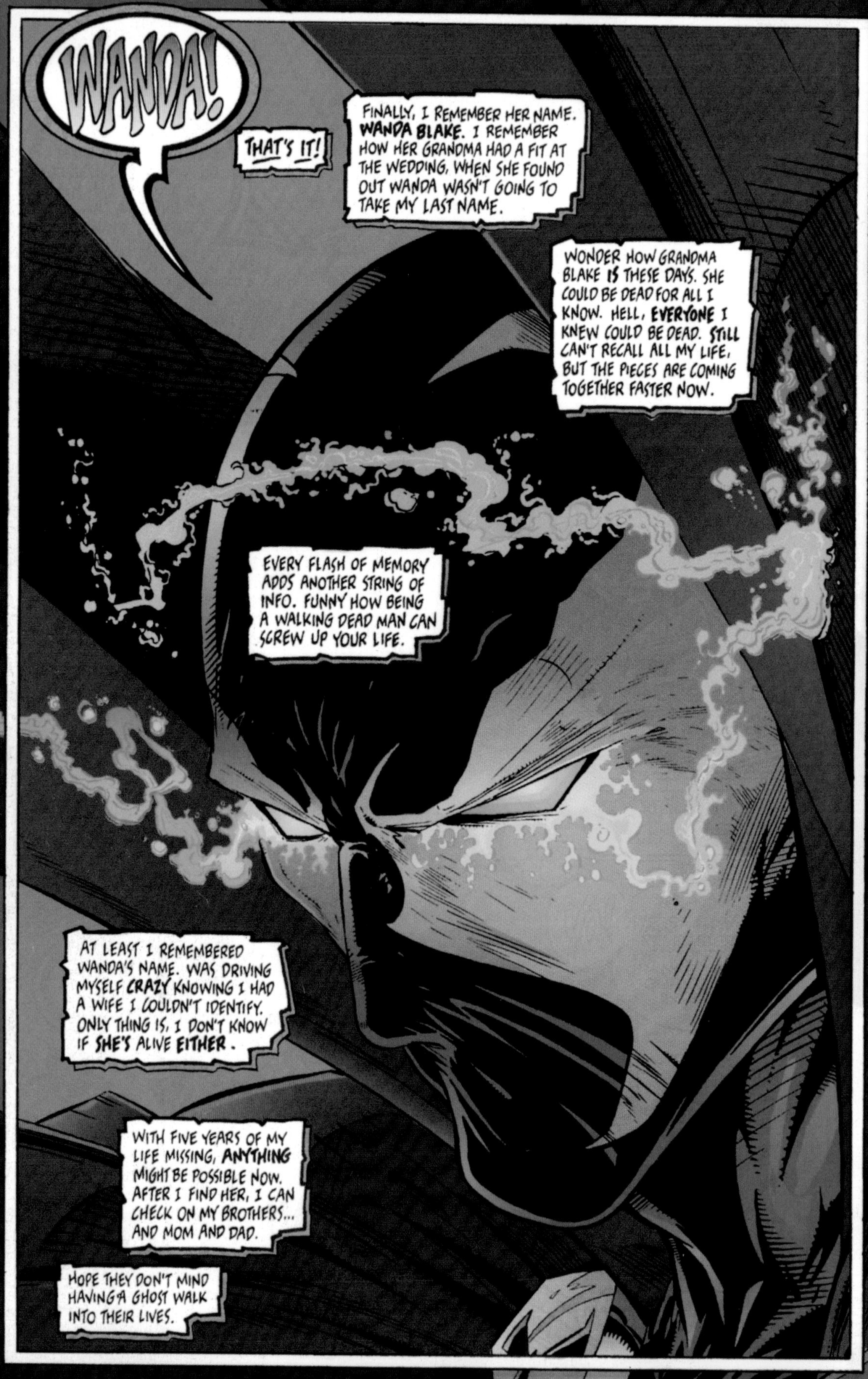
WANDA!
THAT'S IT!
FINALLY, I REMEMBER HER NAME. WANDA BLAKE. I REMEMBER HOW HER GRANDMA HAD A FIT AT THE WEDDING, WHEN SHE FOUND OUT WANDA WASN'T GOING TO TAKE MY LAST NAME.
WONDER HOW GRANDMA BLAKE IS THESE DAYS. SHE COULD BE DEAD FOR ALL I KNOW. HELL, EVERYONE I KNEW COULD BE DEAD. STILL CAN'T RECALL ALL MY LIFE, BUT THE PIECES ARE COMING TOGETHER FASTER NOW.
EVERY FLASH OF MEMORY ADDS ANOTHER STRING OF INFO. FUNNY HOW BEING A WALKING DEAD MAN CAN SCREW UP YOUR LIFE.
AT LEAST I REMEMBERED WANDA'S NAME. WAS DRIVING MYSELF CRAZY KNOWING I HAD A WIFE I COULDN'T IDENTIFY. ONLY THING IS, I DON'T KNOW IF SHE'S ALIVE EITHER.
WITH FIVE YEARS OF MY LIFE MISSING, ANYTHING MIGHT BE POSSIBLE NOW. AFTER I FIND HER, I CAN CHECK ON MY BROTHERS... AND MOM AND DAD.
HOPE THEY DON'T MIND HAVING A GHOST WALK INTO THEIR LIVES.

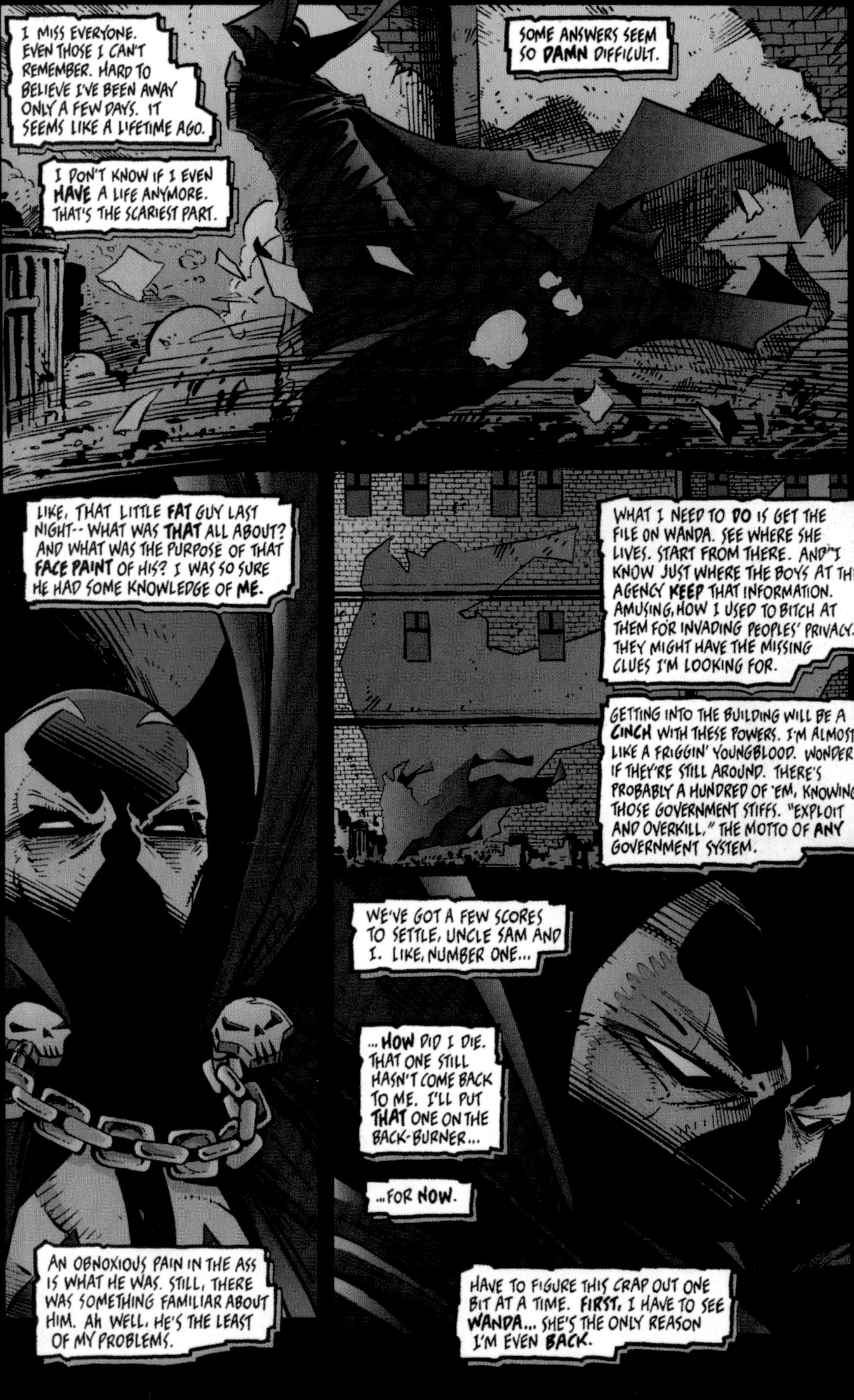

I MISS EVERYONE. EVEN THOSE I CAN'T REMEMBER. HARD TO BELIEVE I'VE BEEN AWAY ONLY A FEW DAYS. IT SEEMS LIKE A LIFETIME AGO.
I DON'T KNOW IF I EVEN HAVE A LIFE ANYMORE. THAT'S THE SCARIEST PART.
SOME ANSWERS SEEM SO DAMN DIFFICULT.
LIKE, THAT LITTLE FAT GUY LAST NIGHT-- WHAT WAS THAT ALL ABOUT? AND WHAT WAS THE PURPOSE OF THAT FACE PAINT OF HIS? I WAS SO SURE HE HAD SOME KNOWLEDGE OF ME.
AN OBNOXIOUS PAIN IN THE ASS IS WHAT HE WAS. STILL, THERE WAS SOMETHING FAMILIAR ABOUT HIM. AH WELL, HE'S THE LEAST OF MY PROBLEMS.
WHAT I NEED TO DO IS GET THE FILE ON WANDA. SEE WHERE SHE LIVES. START FROM THERE. AND I KNOW JUST WHERE THE BOYS AT THE AGENCY KEEP THAT INFORMATION. AMUSING, HOW I USED TO BITCH AT THEM FOR INVADING PEOPLES' PRIVACY... THEY MIGHT HAVE THE MISSING CLUES I'M LOOKING FOR.
GETTING INTO THE BUILDING WILL BE A CINCH WITH THESE POWERS. I'M ALMOST LIKE A FRIGGIN' YOUNGBLOOD. WONDER IF THEY'RE STILL AROUND. THERE'S PROBABLY A HUNDRED OF 'EM, KNOWING THOSE GOVERNMENT STIFFS. "EXPLOIT AND OVERKILL," THE MOTTO OF ANY GOVERNMENT SYSTEM.
WE'VE GOT A FEW SCORES TO SETTLE, UNCLE SAM AND I. LIKE, NUMBER ONE...
...HOW DID I DIE. THAT ONE STILL HASN'T COME BACK TO ME. I'LL PUT THAT ONE ON THE BACK-BURNER...
...FOR NOW.
HAVE TO FIGURE THIS CRAP OUT ONE BIT AT A TIME. FIRST, I HAVE TO SEE WANDA... SHE'S THE ONLY REASON I'M EVEN BACK.

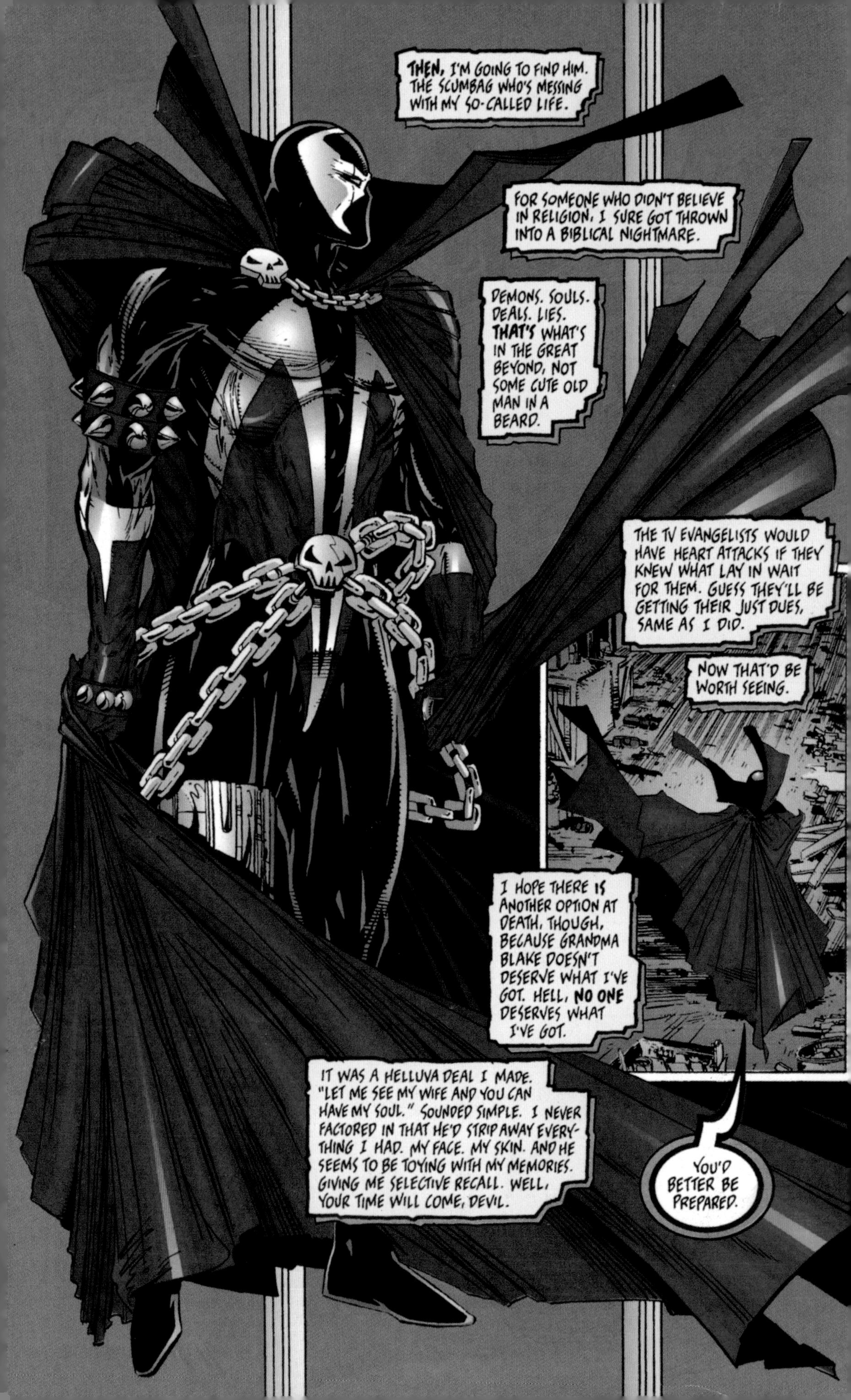
THEN, I'M GOING TO FIND HIM. THE SCUMBAG WHO'S MESSING WITH MY SO-CALLED LIFE.
FOR SOMEONE WHO DIDN'T BELIEVE IN RELIGION, I SURE GOT THROWN INTO A BIBLICAL NIGHTMARE.
DEMONS. SOULS. DEALS. LIES. THAT'S WHAT'S IN THE GREAT BEYOND, NOT SOME CUTE OLD MAN IN A BEARD.
THE TV EVANGELISTS WOULD HAVE HEART ATTACKS IF THEY KNEW WHAT LAY IN WAIT FOR THEM. GUESS THEY'LL BE GETTING THEIR JUST DUES, SAME AS I DID.
NOW THAT'D BE WORTH SEEING.
I HOPE THERE IS ANOTHER OPTION AT DEATH, THOUGH, BECAUSE GRANDMA BLAKE DOESN'T DESERVE WHAT I'VE GOT. HELL, NO ONE DESERVES WHAT I'VE GOT.
IT WAS A HELLUVA DEAL I MADE. "LET ME SEE MY WIFE AND YOU CAN HAVE MY SOUL." SOUNDED SIMPLE. I NEVER FACTORED IN THAT HE'D STRIP AWAY EVERYTHING I HAD. MY FACE. MY SKIN. AND HE SEEMS TO BE TOYING WITH MY MEMORIES. GIVING ME SELECTIVE RECALL. WELL, YOUR TIME WILL COME, DEVIL.
YOU'D BETTER BE PREPARED.

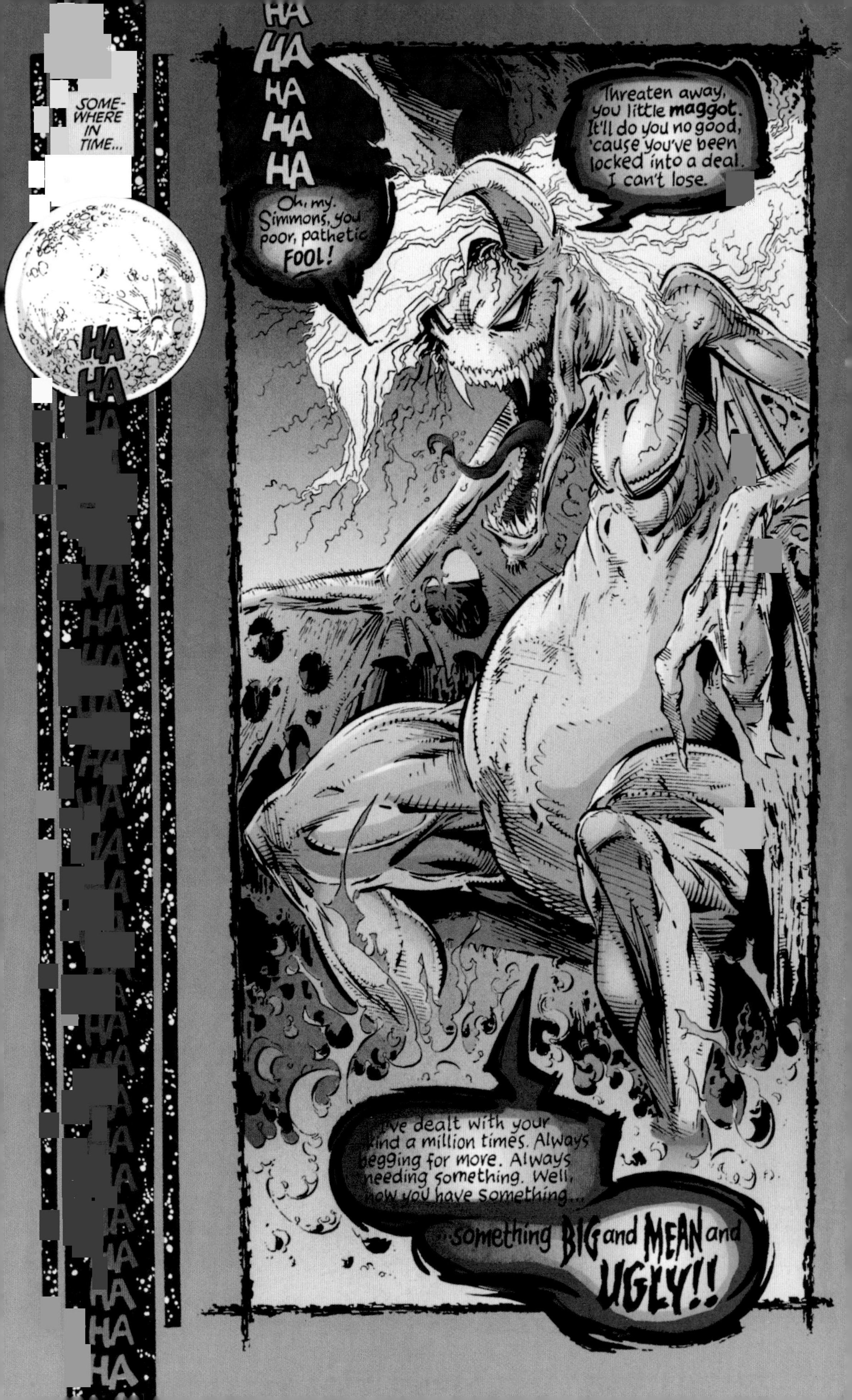

SOME-WHERE IN TIME...
HA HA HA HA HA
Oh, my. Simmons, you poor, pathetic FOOL!
Threaten away, you little maggot. It'll do you no good, 'cause you've been locked into a deal I can't lose.
HA HA
HA HA HA HA HA HA HA HA HA HA HA HA HA HA HA HA
've dealt with your ind a million times. Always egging for more. Always eeding something. Well, now you have something...
...something BIG and MEAN and UGLY!!

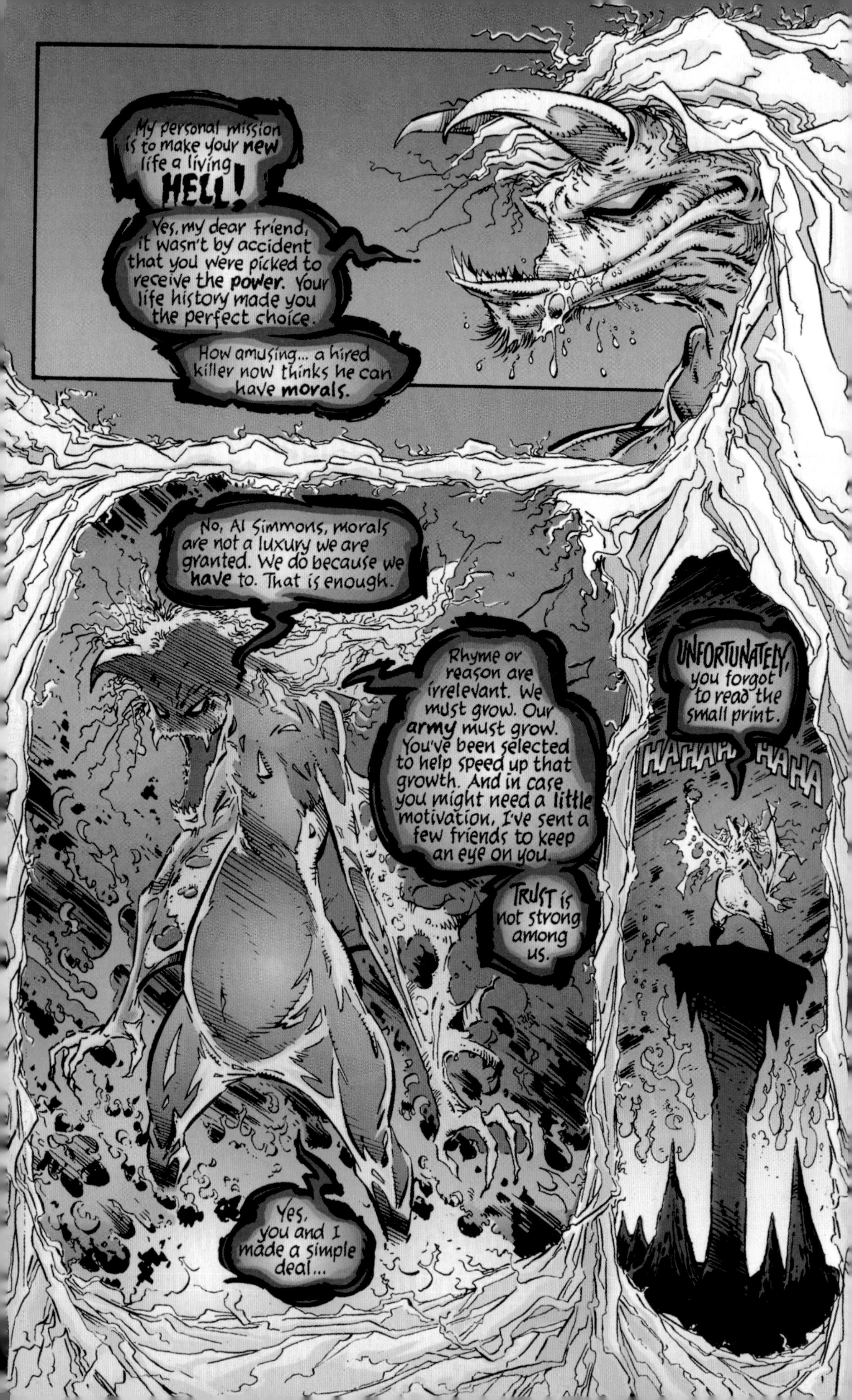
My personal mission is to make your new life a living HELL!
Yes, my dear friend, it wasn't by accident that you were picked to receive the power. Your life history made you the perfect choice.
How amusing... a hired killer now thinks he can have morals.
No, Al Simmons, morals are not a luxury we are granted. We do because we have to. That is enough.
Rhyme or reason are irrelevant. We must grow. Our army must grow. You've been selected to help speed up that growth. And in case you might need a little motivation, I've sent a few friends to keep an eye on you.
TRUST is not strong among us.
Yes, you and I made a simple deal...
UNFORTUNATELY, you forgot to read the small print.
HAHAH HAHA

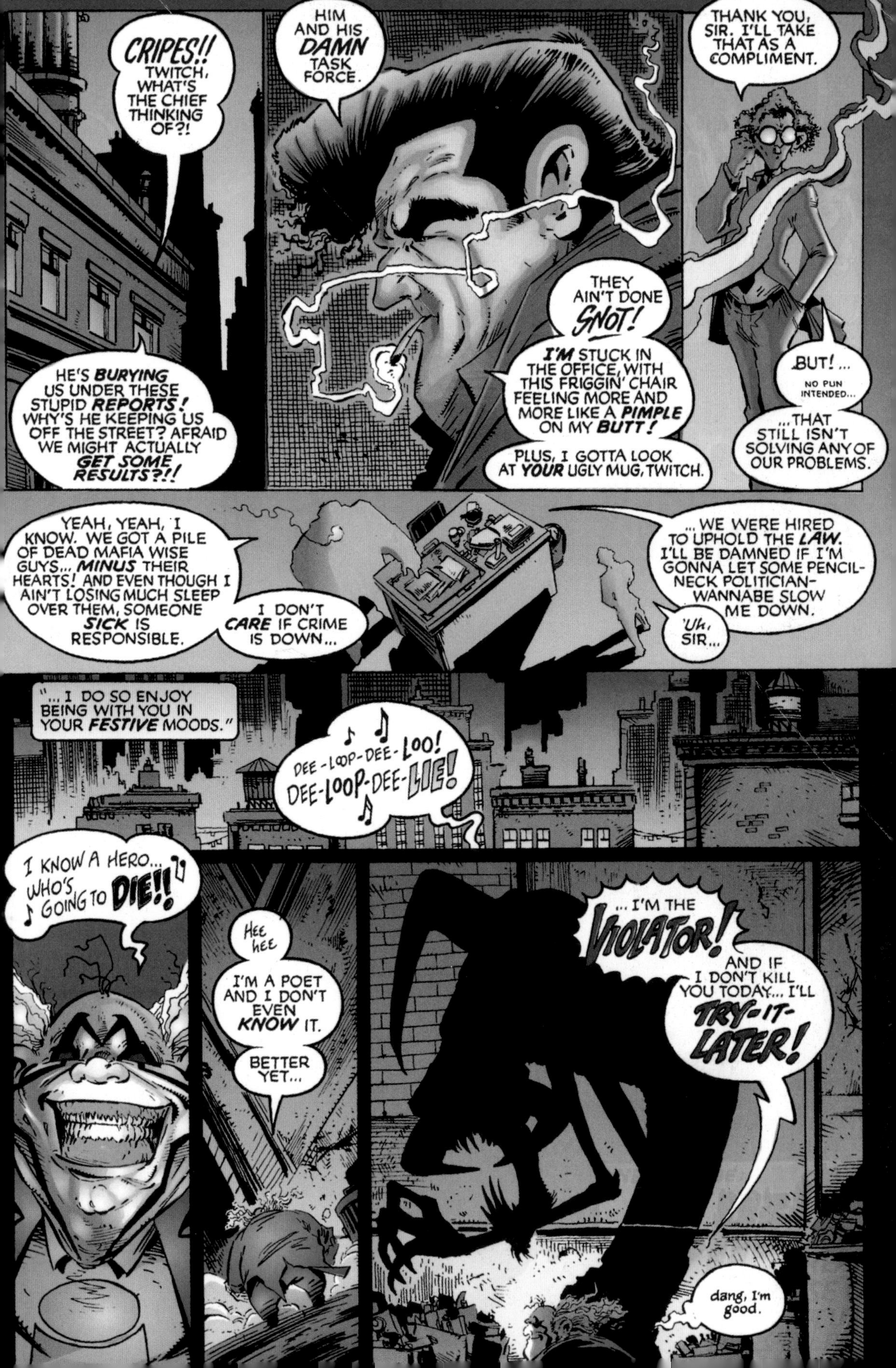
CRIPES!! TWITCH, WHAT'S THE CHIEF THINKING OF?!
HE'S BURYING US UNDER THESE STUPID REPORTS! WHY'S HE KEEPING US OFF THE STREET? AFRAID WE MIGHT ACTUALLY GET SOME RESULTS?!!
HIM AND HIS DAMN TASK FORCE.
THEY AIN'T DONE SNOT!
I'M STUCK IN THE OFFICE, WITH THIS FRIGGIN' CHAIR FEELING MORE AND MORE LIKE A PIMPLE ON MY BUTT!
PLUS, I GOTTA LOOK AT YOUR UGLY MUG, TWITCH.
THANK YOU, SIR. I'LL TAKE THAT AS A COMPLIMENT.
BUT! ...
NO PUN INTENDED...
...THAT STILL ISN'T SOLVING ANY OF OUR PROBLEMS.
YEAH, YEAH, I KNOW. WE GOT A PILE OF DEAD MAFIA WISE GUYS... MINUS THEIR HEARTS! AND EVEN THOUGH I AIN'T LOSING MUCH SLEEP OVER THEM, SOMEONE SICK IS RESPONSIBLE.
I DON'T CARE IF CRIME IS DOWN...
...WE WERE HIRED TO UPHOLD THE LAW. I'LL BE DAMNED IF I'M GONNA LET SOME PENCIL-NECK POLITICIAN-WANNABE SLOW ME DOWN.
'Uh, SIR...
"... I DO SO ENJOY BEING WITH YOU IN YOUR FESTIVE MOODS."
DEE-LOOP-DEE-LOO! DEE-LOOP-DEE-LIE!
I KNOW A HERO... WHO'S GOING TO DIE!!
Hee hee
I'M A POET AND I DON'T EVEN KNOW IT.
BETTER YET...
...I'M THE VIOLATOR!
AND IF I DON'T KILL YOU TODAY... I'LL TRY-IT-LATER!
dang, I'm good.

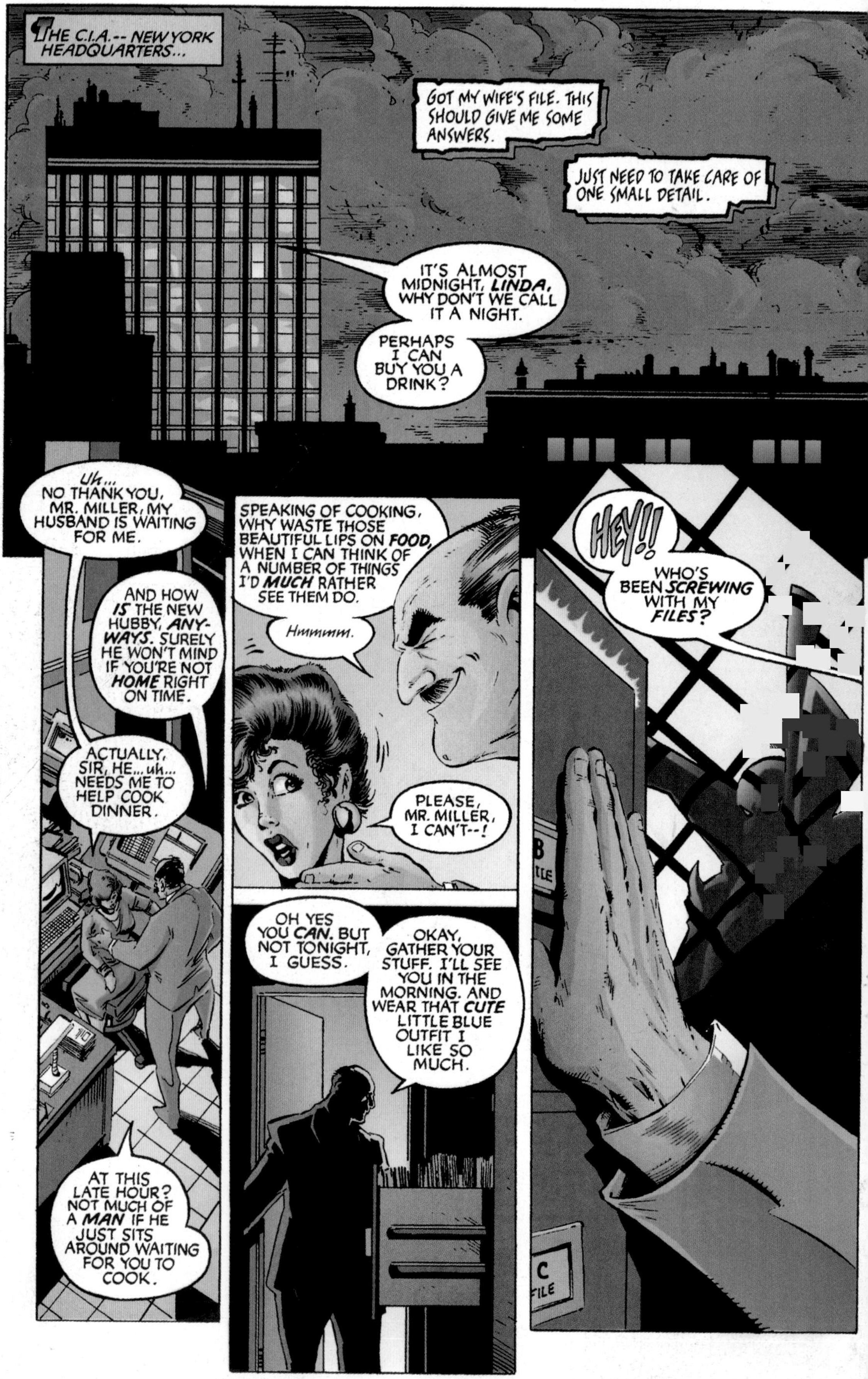
THE C.I.A.-- NEW YORK HEADQUARTERS...
GOT MY WIFE'S FILE. THIS SHOULD GIVE ME SOME ANSWERS.
JUST NEED TO TAKE CARE OF ONE SMALL DETAIL.
IT'S ALMOST MIDNIGHT, LINDA, WHY DON'T WE CALL IT A NIGHT.
PERHAPS I CAN BUY YOU A DRINK?
UH... NO THANK YOU, MR. MILLER, MY HUSBAND IS WAITING FOR ME.
AND HOW IS THE NEW HUBBY, ANYWAYS. SURELY HE WON'T MIND IF YOU'RE NOT HOME RIGHT ON TIME.
ACTUALLY, SIR, HE... UH... NEEDS ME TO HELP COOK DINNER.
AT THIS LATE HOUR? NOT MUCH OF A MAN IF HE JUST SITS AROUND WAITING FOR YOU TO COOK.
SPEAKING OF COOKING, WHY WASTE THOSE BEAUTIFUL LIPS ON FOOD, WHEN I CAN THINK OF A NUMBER OF THINGS I'D MUCH RATHER SEE THEM DO.
Hmmmm.
PLEASE, MR. MILLER, I CAN'T--!
OH YES YOU CAN. BUT NOT TONIGHT, I GUESS.
OKAY, GATHER YOUR STUFF. I'LL SEE YOU IN THE MORNING. AND WEAR THAT CUTE LITTLE BLUE OUTFIT I LIKE SO MUCH.
HEY!!
WHO'S BEEN SCREWING WITH MY FILES?
B
C
FILE

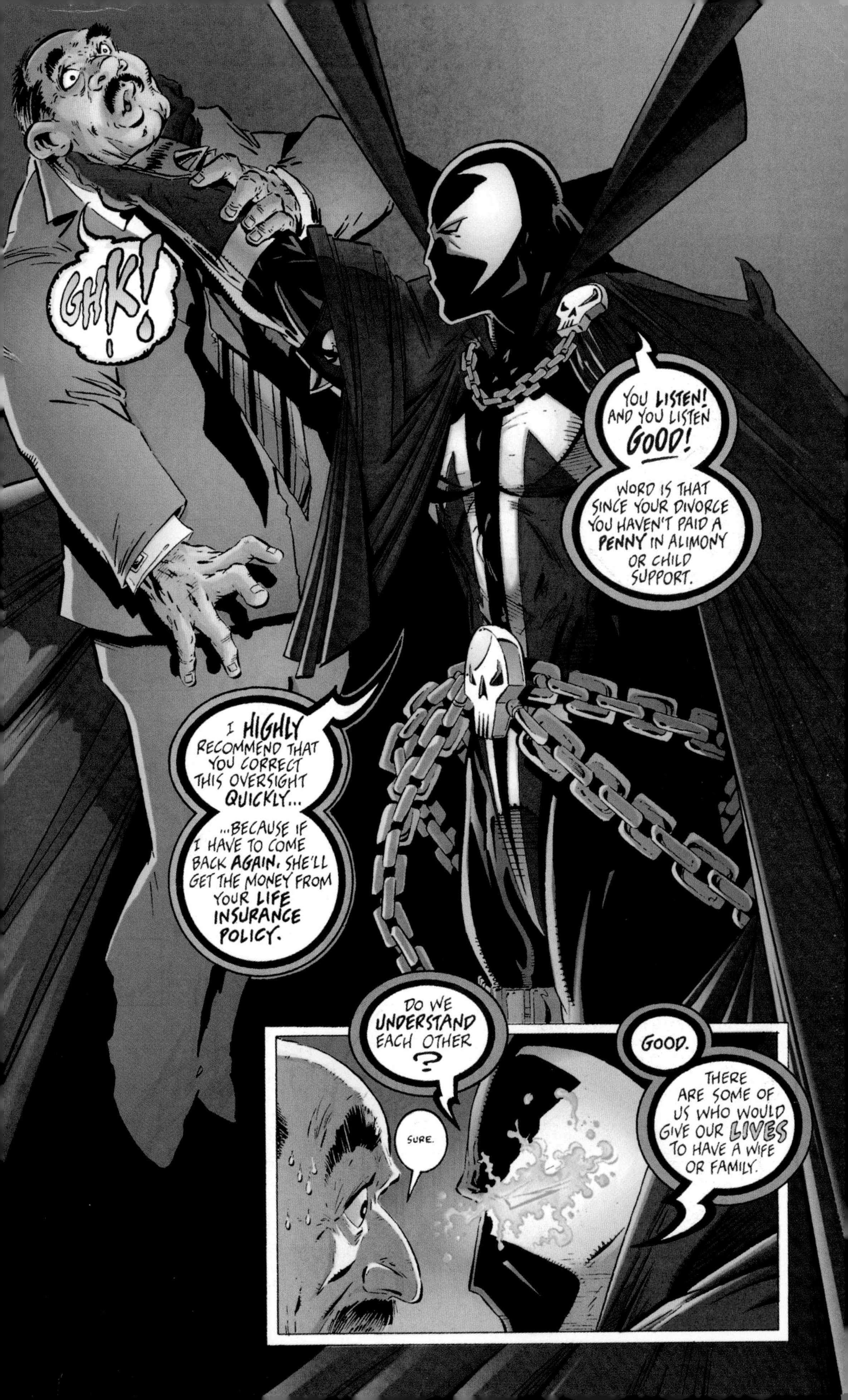
GHK!
YOU LISTEN! AND YOU LISTEN GOOD!
WORD IS THAT SINCE YOUR DIVORCE YOU HAVEN'T PAID A PENNY IN ALIMONY OR CHILD SUPPORT.
I HIGHLY RECOMMEND THAT YOU CORRECT THIS OVERSIGHT QUICKLY...
...BECAUSE IF I HAVE TO COME BACK AGAIN, SHE'LL GET THE MONEY FROM YOUR LIFE INSURANCE POLICY.
DO WE UNDERSTAND EACH OTHER?
SURE.
GOOD.
THERE ARE SOME OF US WHO WOULD GIVE OUR LIVES TO HAVE A WIFE OR FAMILY.

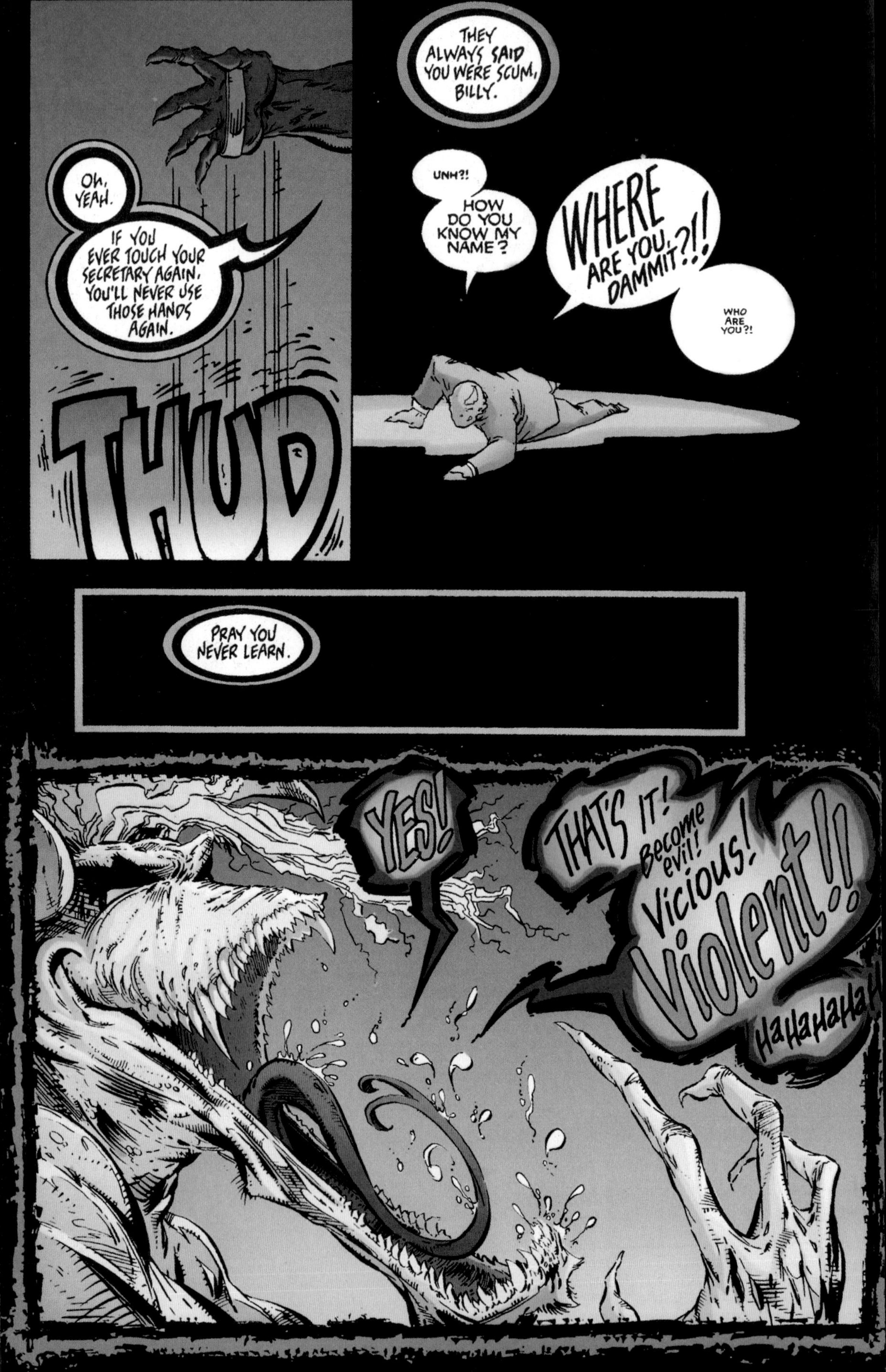
THEY ALWAYS SAID YOU WERE SCUM, BILLY.
Oh, YEAH.
IF YOU EVER TOUCH YOUR SECRETARY AGAIN, YOU'LL NEVER USE THOSE HANDS AGAIN.
THUD
UNH?!
HOW DO YOU KNOW MY NAME?
WHERE ARE YOU, DAMMIT?!!
WHO ARE YOU?!
PRAY YOU NEVER LEARN.
YES!
THAT'S IT! Become evil! Vicious! Violent!!
HaHaHaHaH

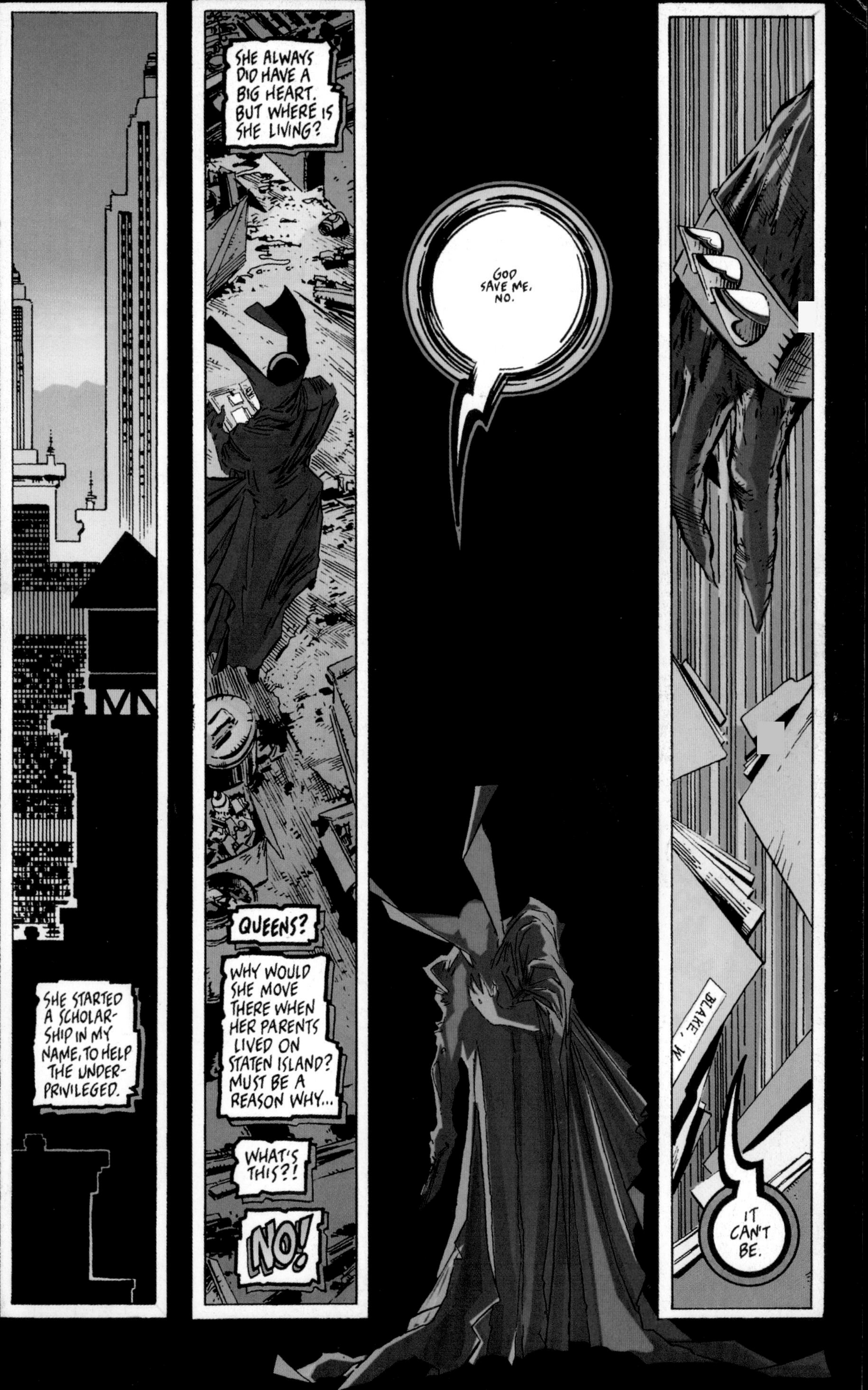
SHE STARTED A SCHOLAR-SHIP IN MY NAME, TO HELP THE UNDER-PRIVILEGED.
SHE ALWAYS DID HAVE A BIG HEART. BUT WHERE IS SHE LIVING?
QUEENS?
WHY WOULD SHE MOVE THERE WHEN HER PARENTS LIVED ON STATEN ISLAND? MUST BE A REASON WHY...
WHAT'S THIS?!
NO!
GOD SAVE ME, NO.
BLAKE, W
IT CAN'T BE.

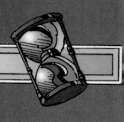

QUEENS, THE NEXT DAY...

A TWENTY-FIVE MINUTE COMMUTE FROM MANHATTAN STANDS A NONDESCRIPT HOUSE. WHITE FENCE. PORCH. THE PERFECT LITTLE HIDEWAY--

--AND THE HOME OF WANDA BLAKE, WIDOW OF LT. COL. AL SIMMONS.

...I LOOK LIKE SOME CALIFORNIA BEACH BUM.

AND OF ALL THE HAIR COLORS-- WHY BLONDE?!

TIME TO CHANGE INTO HUMAN FLESH AGAIN. WISH I COULD LOOK LIKE MYSELF, BUT THESE POWERS SEEM TO HAVE A MIND OF THEIR OWN SOMETIMES.

I CAN'T EVEN CHANGE MY APPEARANCE. KEEP TURNING INTO THIS DAMN WHITE GUY.

WORSE YET...

FEEL LIKE SOME STUPID SCHOOL KID GOING OUT ON HIS FIRST DATE. NOW THERE'S A JOKE, WE DATED THREE YEARS AND WERE MARRIED FIVE...

THAT'S IT, KEEP JOKING. THEN MAYBE YOUR NERVES WILL SETTLE DOWN.

OR AT LEAST YOUR HANDS WILL STOP SHAKING.

HAVE TO GO SLOW. FEELS LIKE I'VE BEEN GONE ONLY A FEW DAYS, BUT FIVE YEARS HAVE PASSED FOR HER. HOPE SHE'LL REMEMBER.

HOPE I CAN COUNT ON HER.

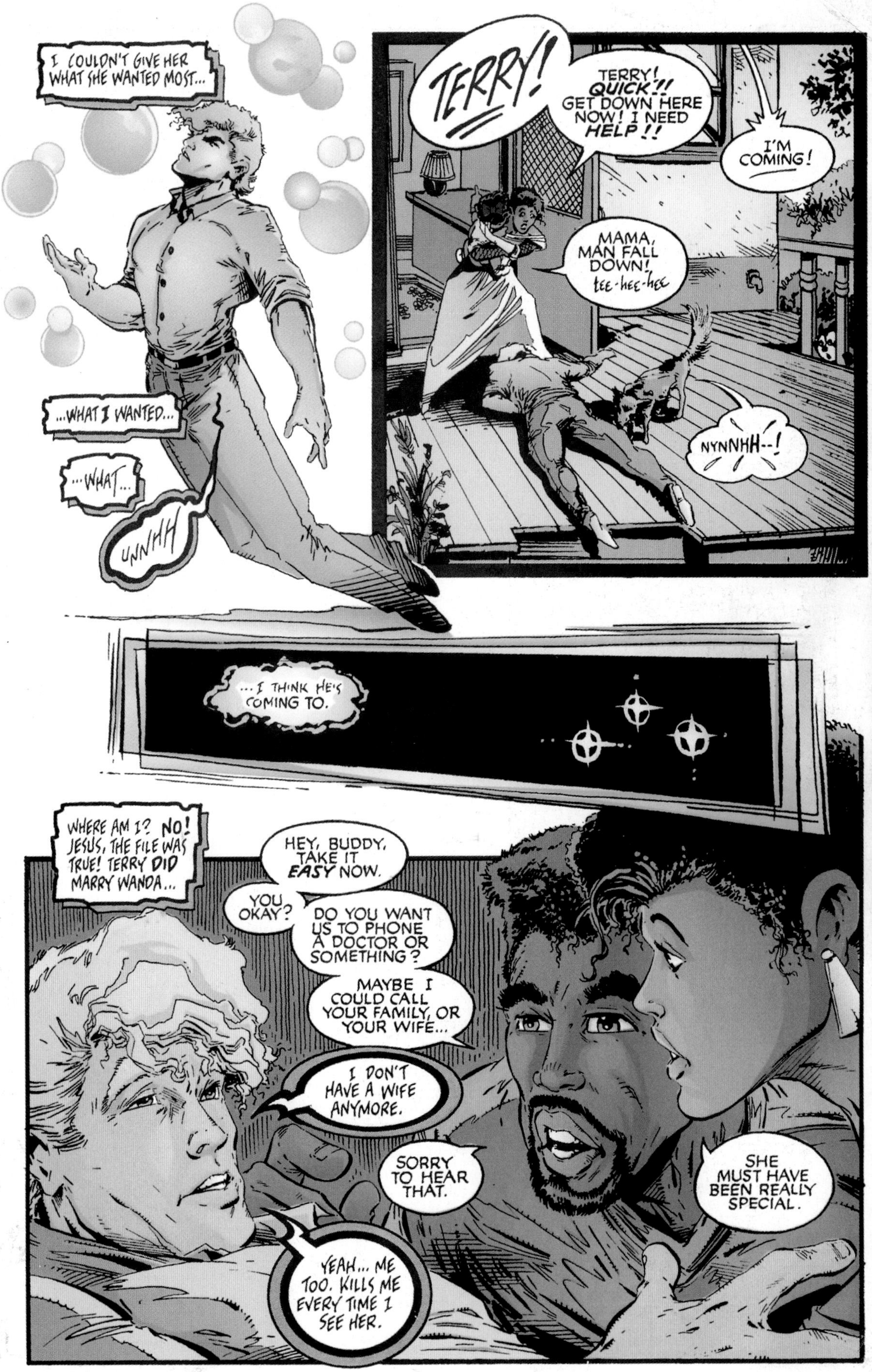
I COULDN'T GIVE HER WHAT SHE WANTED MOST...
TERRY!
TERRY! QUICK!! GET DOWN HERE NOW! I NEED HELP!!
I'M COMING!
MAMA, MAN FALL DOWN! tee-hee-hee
...WHAT I WANTED...
...WHAT...
UNNHH
NYNNHH--!
...I THINK HE'S COMING TO.
WHERE AM I? NO! JESUS, THE FILE WAS TRUE! TERRY DID MARRY WANDA...
HEY, BUDDY, TAKE IT EASY NOW.
YOU OKAY?
DO YOU WANT US TO PHONE A DOCTOR OR SOMETHING?
MAYBE I COULD CALL YOUR FAMILY, OR YOUR WIFE...
I DON'T HAVE A WIFE ANYMORE.
SORRY TO HEAR THAT.
SHE MUST HAVE BEEN REALLY SPECIAL.
YEAH... ME TOO. KILLS ME EVERY TIME I SEE HER.

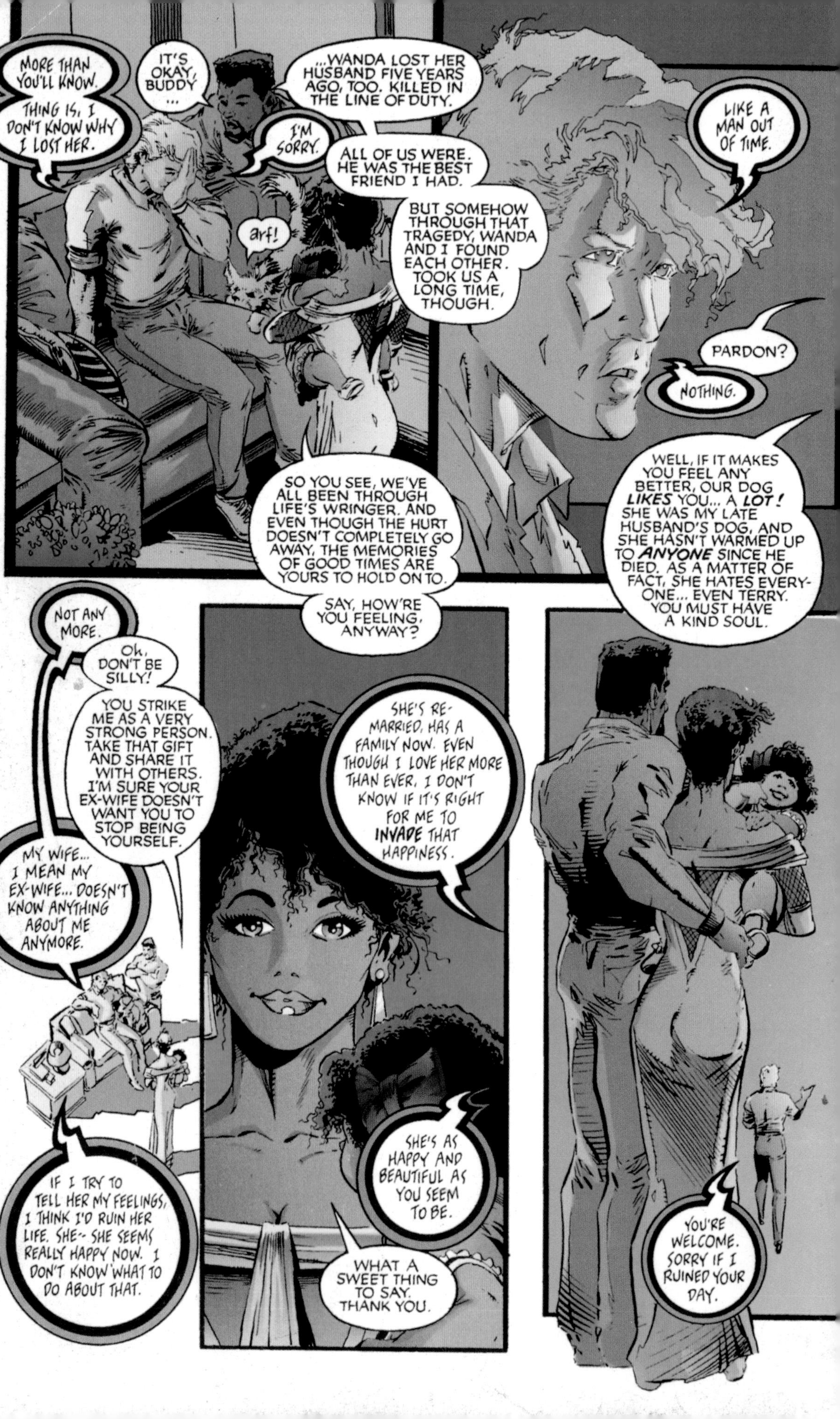

MORE THAN YOU'LL KNOW.
THING IS, I DON'T KNOW WHY I LOST HER.
IT'S OKAY, BUDDY ...
...WANDA LOST HER HUSBAND FIVE YEARS AGO, TOO. KILLED IN THE LINE OF DUTY.
I'M SORRY.
ALL OF US WERE. HE WAS THE BEST FRIEND I HAD.
arf!
BUT SOMEHOW THROUGH THAT TRAGEDY, WANDA AND I FOUND EACH OTHER. TOOK US A LONG TIME, THOUGH.
LIKE A MAN OUT OF TIME.
PARDON?
NOTHING.
SO YOU SEE, WE'VE ALL BEEN THROUGH LIFE'S WRINGER. AND EVEN THOUGH THE HURT DOESN'T COMPLETELY GO AWAY, THE MEMORIES OF GOOD TIMES ARE YOURS TO HOLD ON TO.
SAY, HOW'RE YOU FEELING, ANYWAY?
WELL, IF IT MAKES YOU FEEL ANY BETTER, OUR DOG LIKES YOU... A LOT! SHE WAS MY LATE HUSBAND'S DOG, AND SHE HASN'T WARMED UP TO ANYONE SINCE HE DIED. AS A MATTER OF FACT, SHE HATES EVERY-ONE... EVEN TERRY. YOU MUST HAVE A KIND SOUL.
NOT ANY MORE.
Oh, DON'T BE SILLY!
YOU STRIKE ME AS A VERY STRONG PERSON. TAKE THAT GIFT AND SHARE IT WITH OTHERS. I'M SURE YOUR EX-WIFE DOESN'T WANT YOU TO STOP BEING YOURSELF.
MY WIFE... I MEAN MY EX-WIFE... DOESN'T KNOW ANYTHING ABOUT ME ANYMORE.
IF I TRY TO TELL HER MY FEELINGS, I THINK I'D RUIN HER LIFE. SHE-- SHE SEEMS REALLY HAPPY NOW. I DON'T KNOW WHAT TO DO ABOUT THAT.
SHE'S RE-MARRIED, HAS A FAMILY NOW. EVEN THOUGH I LOVE HER MORE THAN EVER, I DON'T KNOW IF IT'S RIGHT FOR ME TO INVADE THAT HAPPINESS.
SHE'S AS HAPPY AND BEAUTIFUL AS YOU SEEM TO BE.
WHAT A SWEET THING TO SAY. THANK YOU.
YOU'RE WELCOME. SORRY IF I RUINED YOUR DAY.

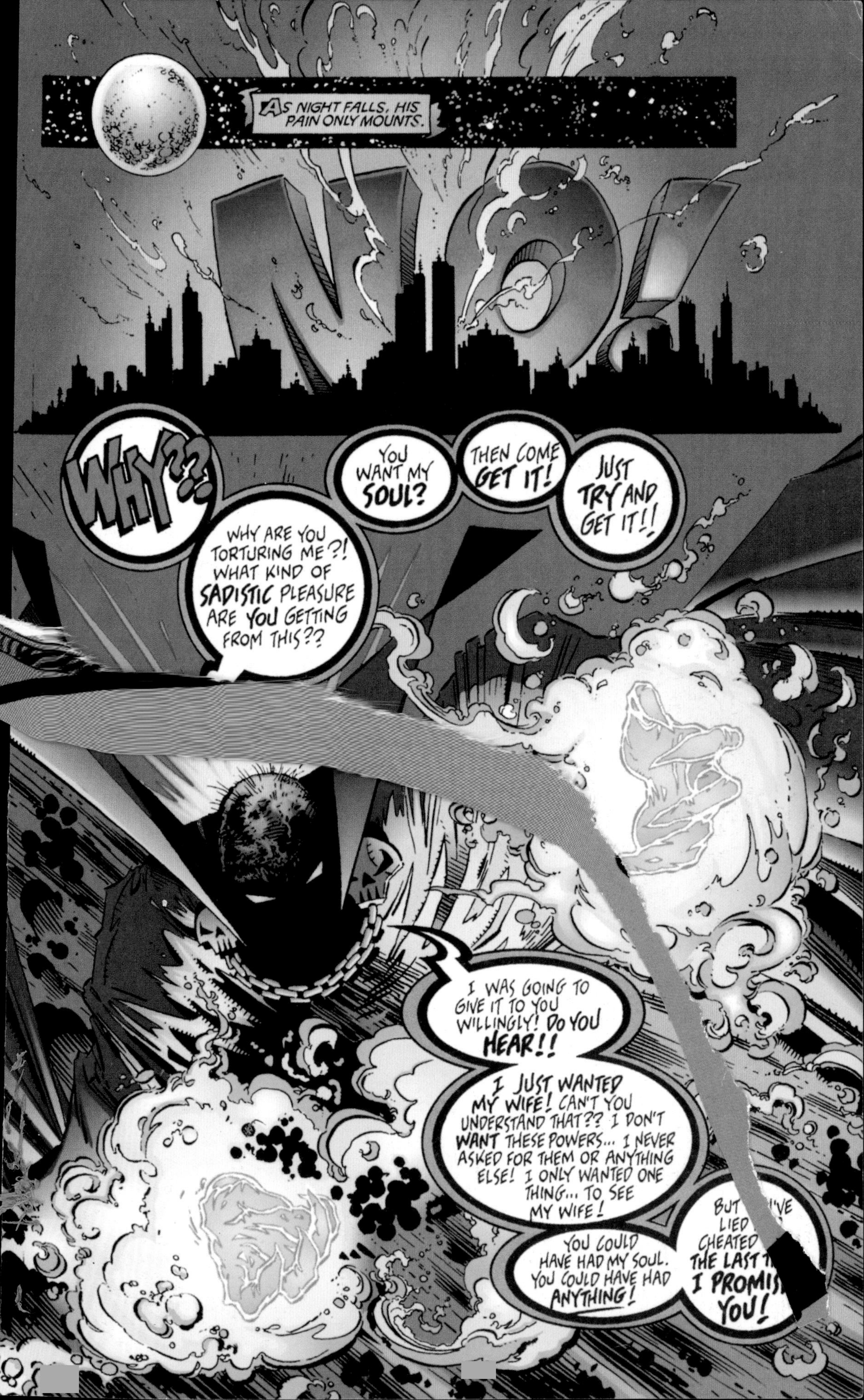

AS NIGHT FALLS, HIS PAIN ONLY MOUNTS.
NO!
WHY??
WHY ARE YOU TORTURING ME?! WHAT KIND OF SADISTIC PLEASURE ARE YOU GETTING FROM THIS??
YOU WANT MY SOUL?
THEN COME GET IT!
JUST TRY AND GET IT!!
I WAS GOING TO GIVE IT TO YOU WILLINGLY! DO YOU HEAR!!
I JUST WANTED MY WIFE! CAN'T YOU UNDERSTAND THAT?? I DON'T WANT THESE POWERS... I NEVER ASKED FOR THEM OR ANYTHING ELSE! I ONLY WANTED ONE THING... TO SEE MY WIFE!
YOU COULD HAVE HAD MY SOUL. YOU COULD HAVE HAD ANYTHING!
BUT 'VE LIED CHEATED THE LAST T I PROMIS YOU!

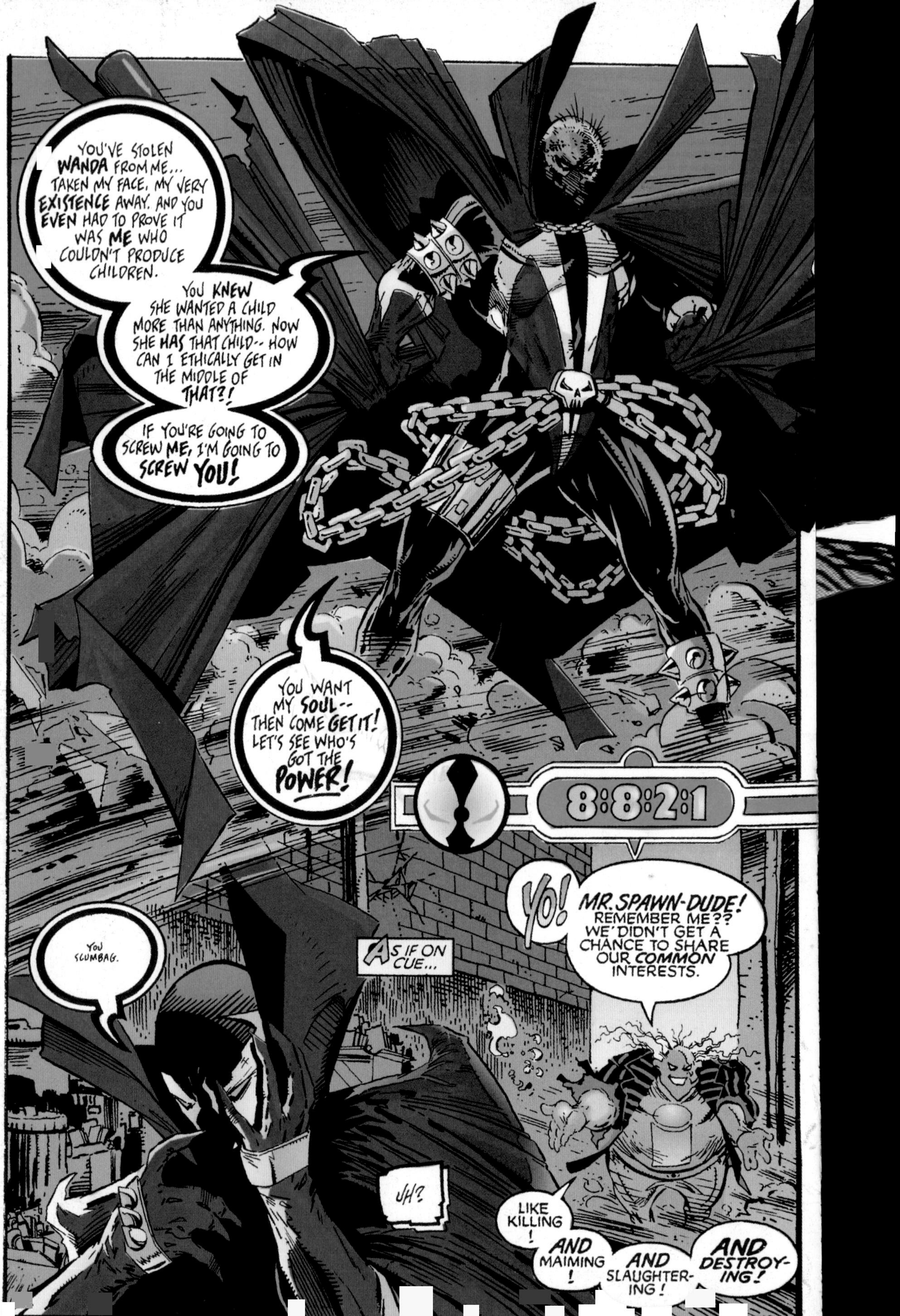
YOU'VE STOLEN WANDA FROM ME... TAKEN MY FACE, MY VERY EXISTENCE AWAY. AND YOU EVEN HAD TO PROVE IT WAS ME WHO COULDN'T PRODUCE CHILDREN.
YOU KNEW SHE WANTED A CHILD MORE THAN ANYTHING. NOW SHE HAS THAT CHILD-- HOW CAN I ETHICALLY GET IN THE MIDDLE OF THAT?!
IF YOU'RE GOING TO SCREW ME, I'M GOING TO SCREW YOU!
YOU WANT MY SOUL-- THEN COME GET IT! LET'S SEE WHO'S GOT THE POWER!
8:8:2:1
YOU SCUMBAG.
AS IF ON CUE...
YO! MR. SPAWN-DUDE! REMEMBER ME?? WE DIDN'T GET A CHANCE TO SHARE OUR COMMON INTERESTS.
UH?
LIKE KILLING!
AND MAIMING!
AND SLAUGHTERING!
AND DESTROYING!

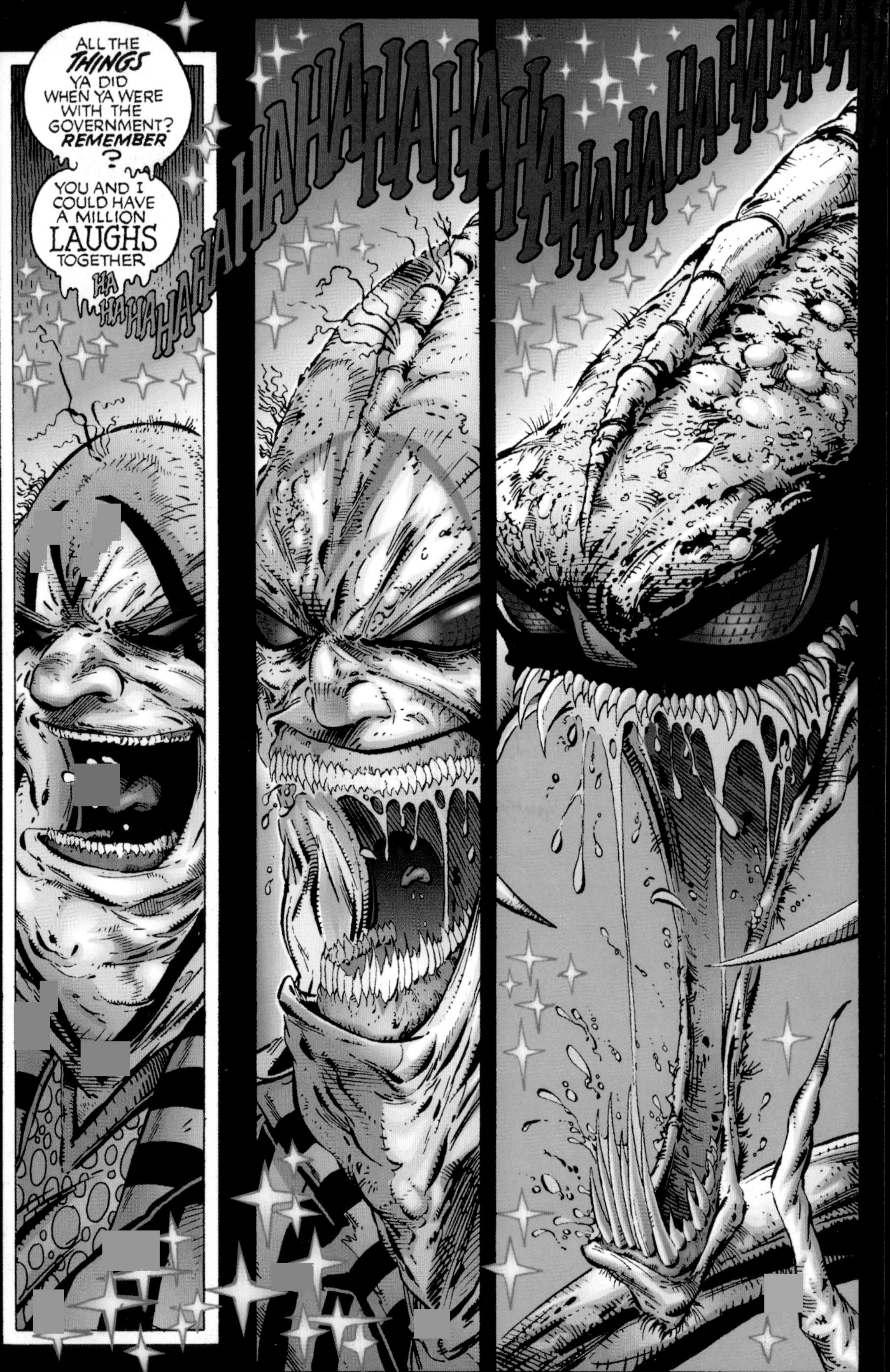
ALL THE THINGS YA DID WHEN YA WERE WITH THE GOVERNMENT? REMEMBER?
YOU AND I COULD HAVE A MILLION LAUGHS TOGETHER

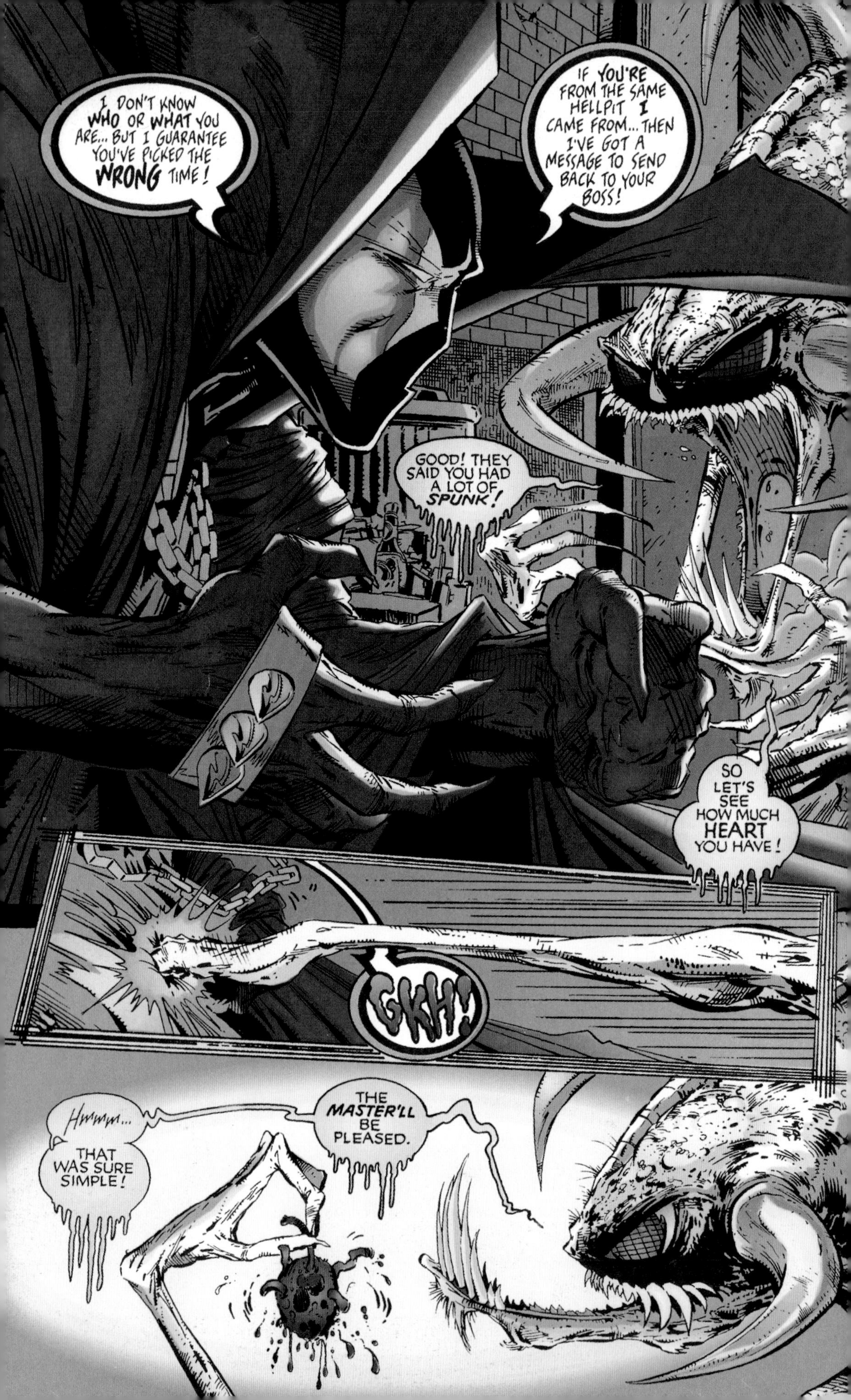

I DON'T KNOW WHO OR WHAT YOU ARE... BUT I GUARANTEE YOU'VE PICKED THE WRONG TIME!
IF YOU'RE FROM THE SAME HELLPIT I CAME FROM... THEN I'VE GOT A MESSAGE TO SEND BACK TO YOUR BOSS!
GOOD! THEY SAID YOU HAD A LOT OF SPUNK!
SO LET'S SEE HOW MUCH HEART YOU HAVE!
GKH!
Hmmm... THAT WAS SURE SIMPLE!
THE MASTER'LL BE PLEASED.

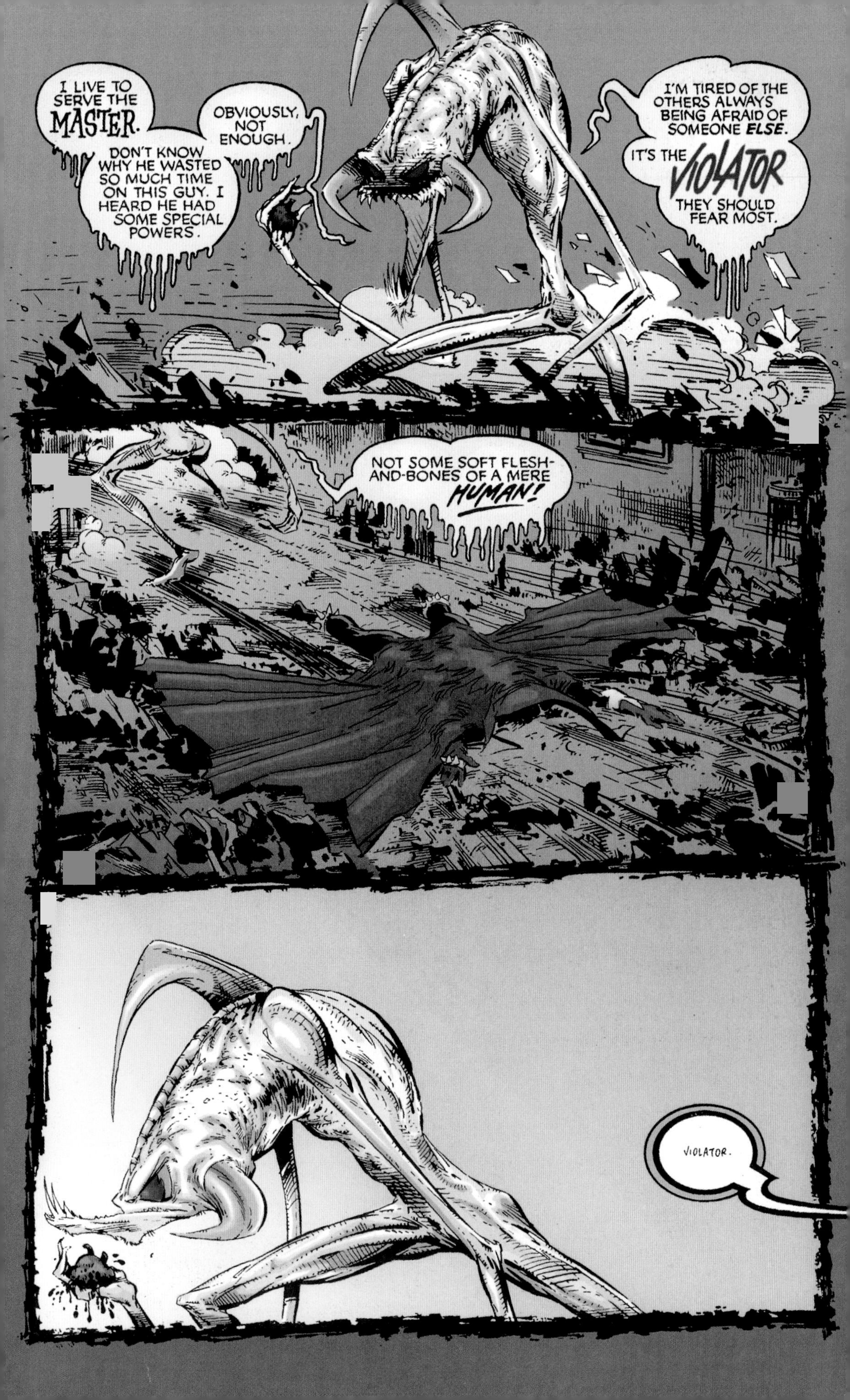
I LIVE TO SERVE THE MASTER.
DON'T KNOW WHY HE WASTED SO MUCH TIME ON THIS GUY. I HEARD HE HAD SOME SPECIAL POWERS.
OBVIOUSLY, NOT ENOUGH.
I'M TIRED OF THE OTHERS ALWAYS BEING AFRAID OF SOMEONE ELSE.
IT'S THE VIOLATOR THEY SHOULD FEAR MOST.
NOT SOME SOFT FLESH-AND-BONES OF A MERE HUMAN!
VIOLATOR.

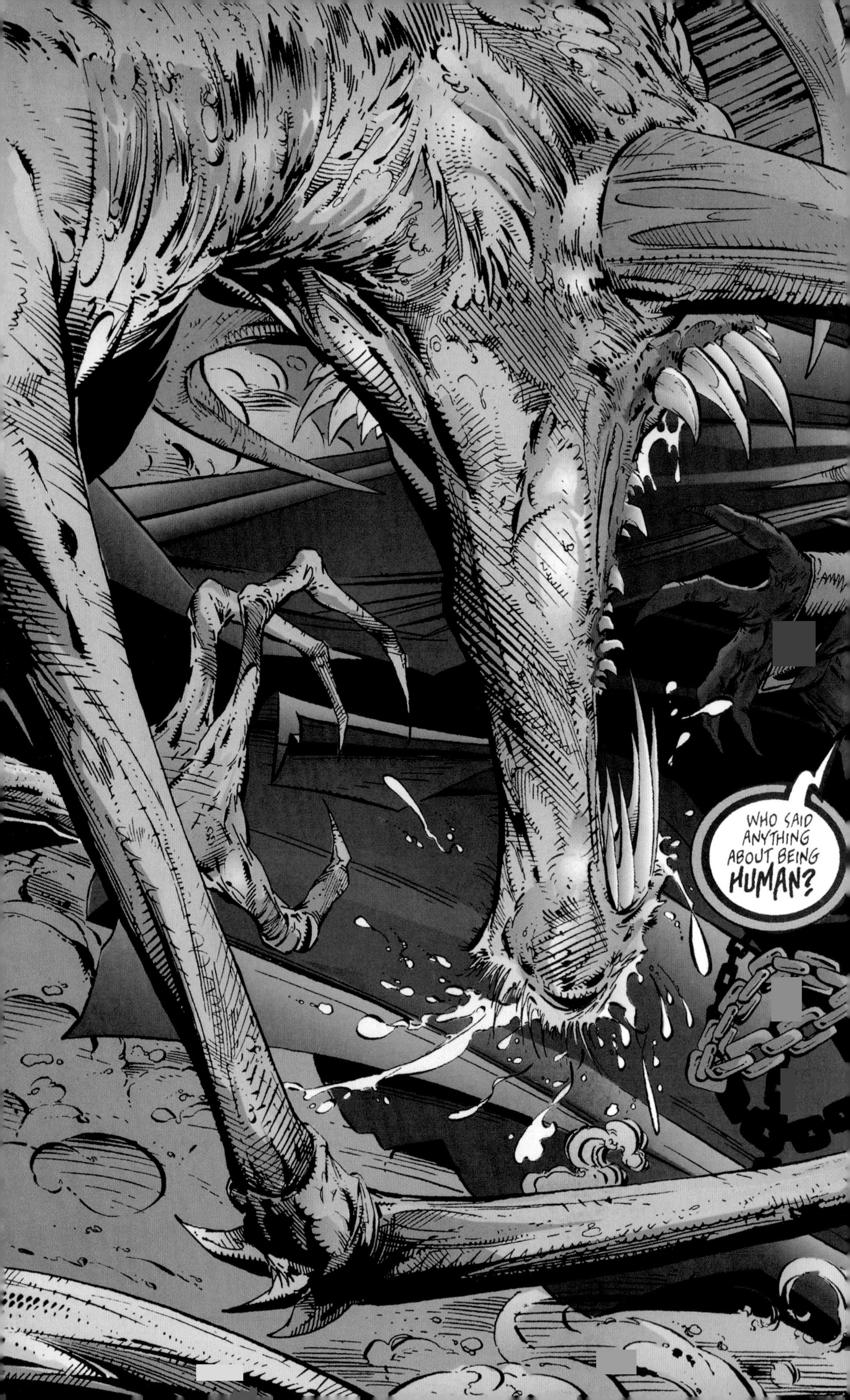
WHO SAID ANYTHING ABOUT BEING HUMAN?

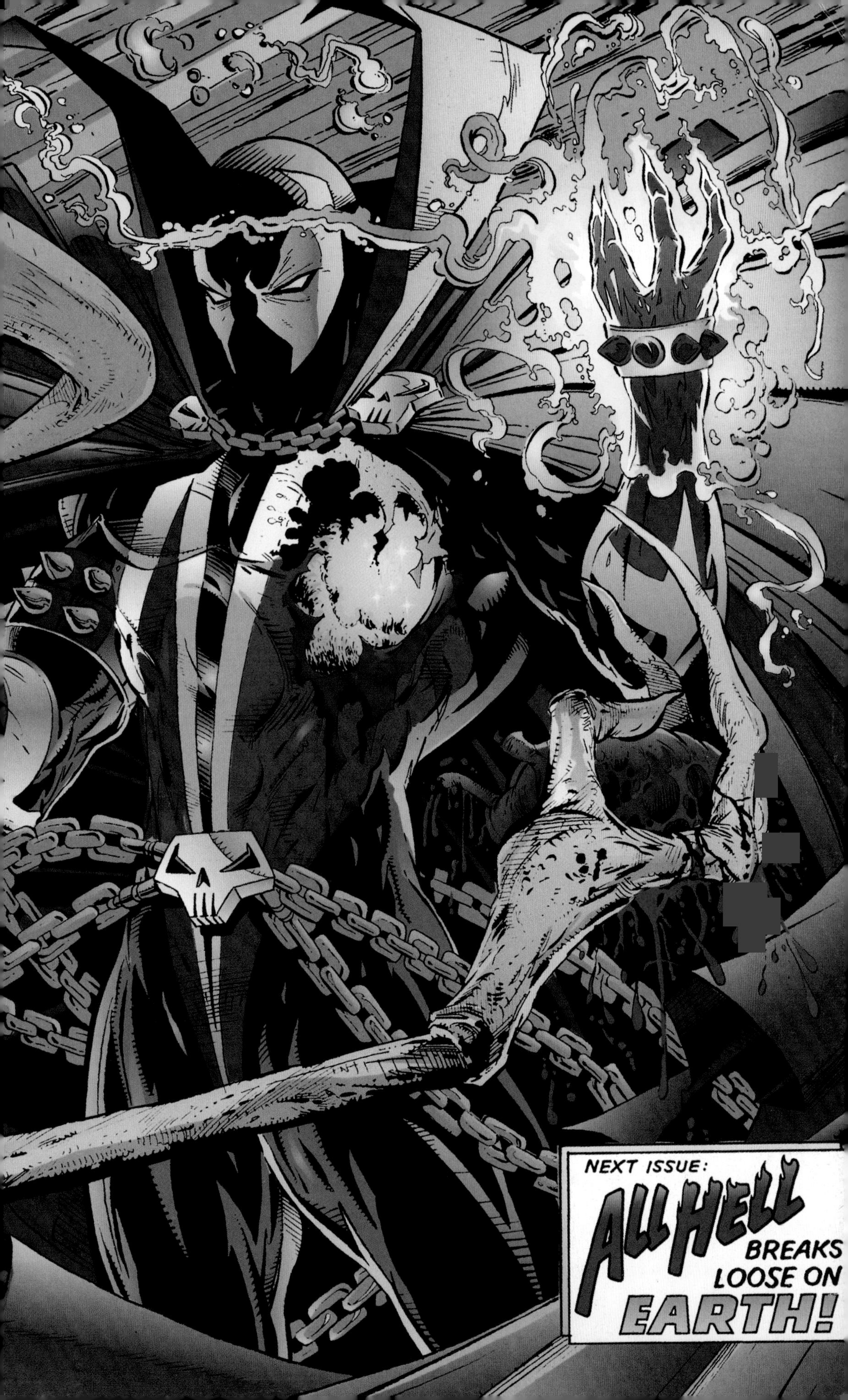
NEXT ISSUE:
ALL HELL BREAKS LOOSE ON EARTH!

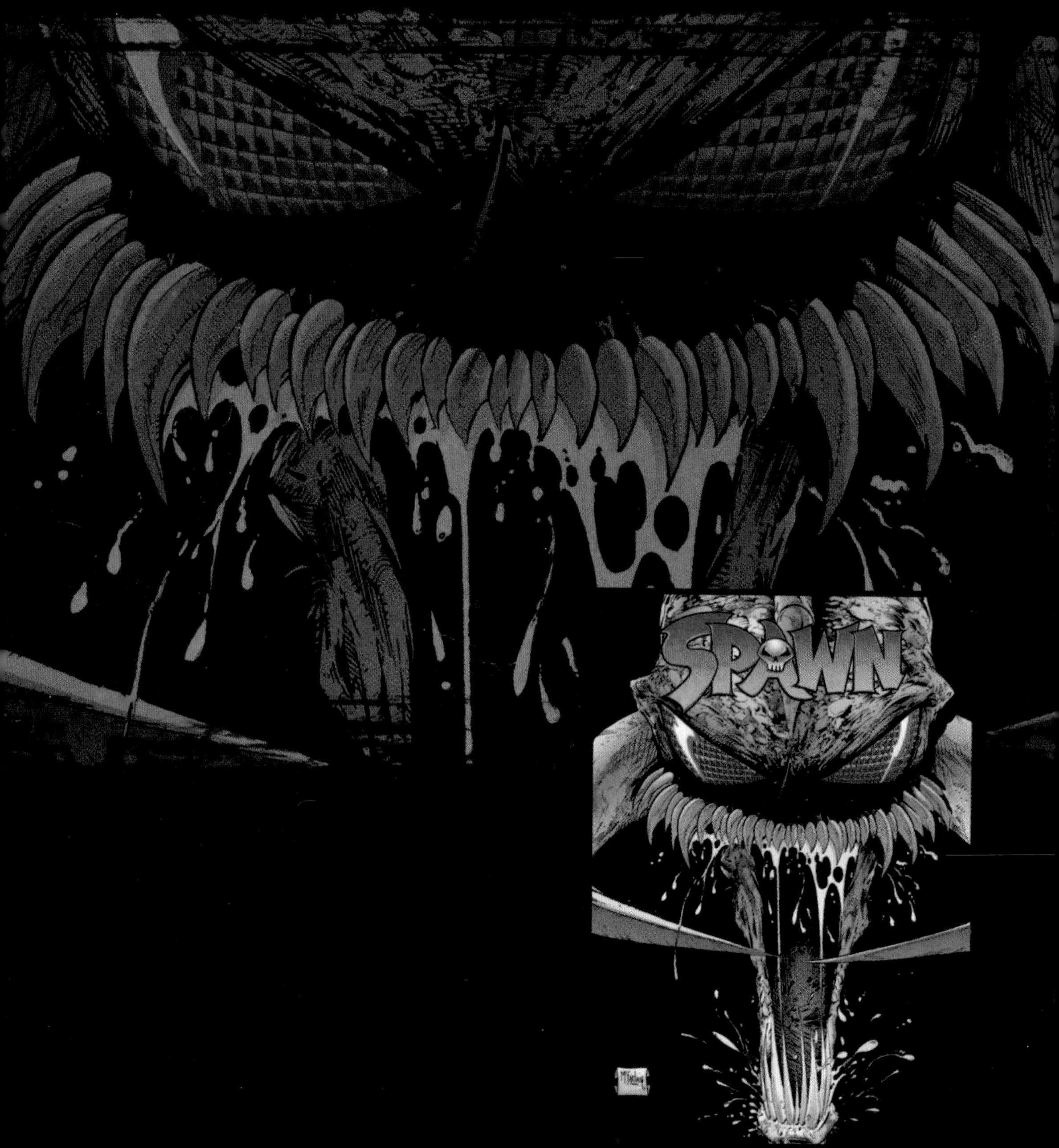
SPAWN

ISSUE FOUR

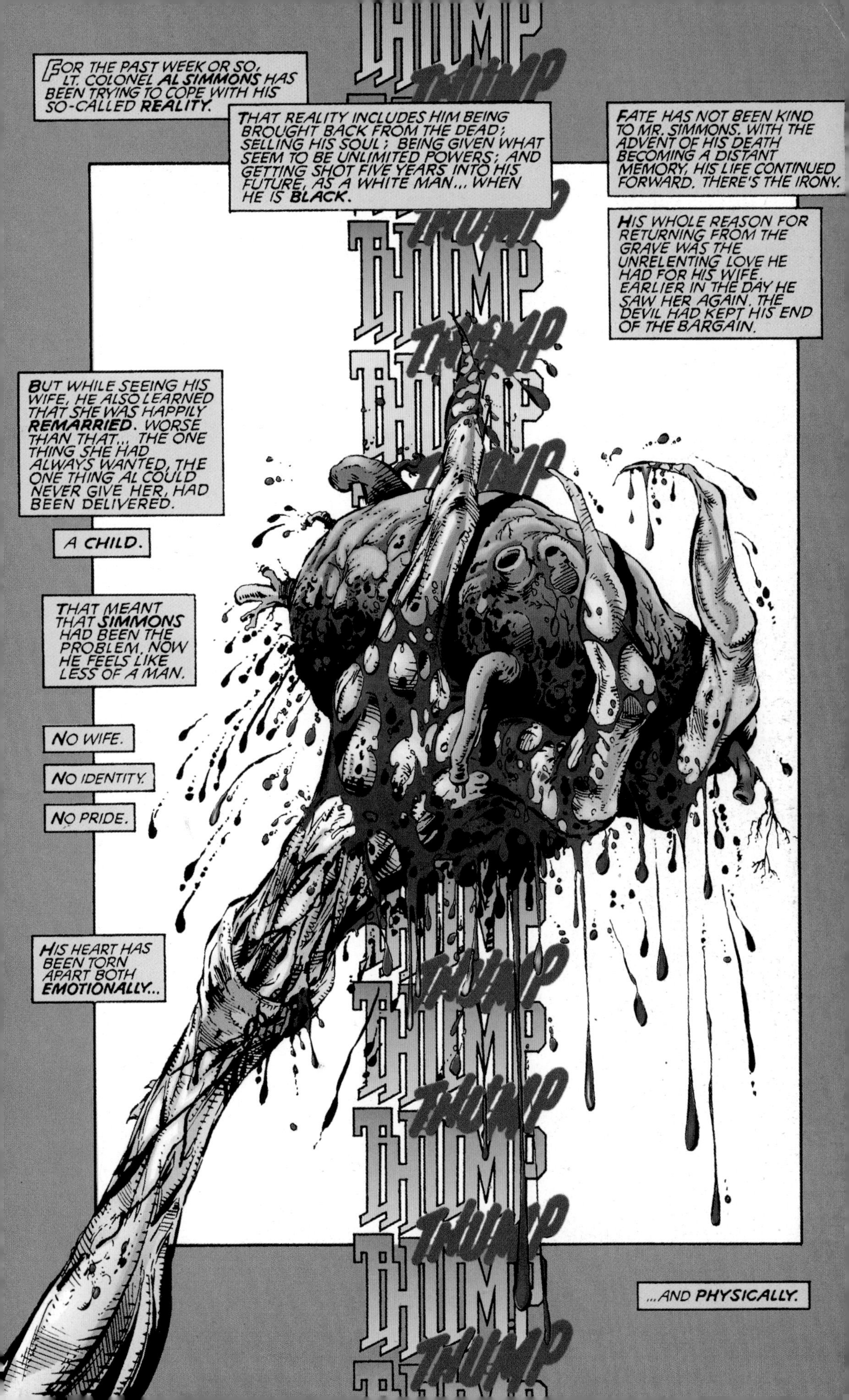
FOR THE PAST WEEK OR SO, LT. COLONEL AL SIMMONS HAS BEEN TRYING TO COPE WITH HIS SO-CALLED REALITY.
THAT REALITY INCLUDES HIM BEING BROUGHT BACK FROM THE DEAD; SELLING HIS SOUL; BEING GIVEN WHAT SEEM TO BE UNLIMITED POWERS; AND GETTING SHOT FIVE YEARS INTO HIS FUTURE, AS A WHITE MAN... WHEN HE IS BLACK.
FATE HAS NOT BEEN KIND TO MR. SIMMONS. WITH THE ADVENT OF HIS DEATH BECOMING A DISTANT MEMORY, HIS LIFE CONTINUED FORWARD. THERE'S THE IRONY.
HIS WHOLE REASON FOR RETURNING FROM THE GRAVE WAS THE UNRELENTING LOVE HE HAD FOR HIS WIFE. EARLIER IN THE DAY HE SAW HER AGAIN. THE DEVIL HAD KEPT HIS END OF THE BARGAIN.
BUT WHILE SEEING HIS WIFE, HE ALSO LEARNED THAT SHE WAS HAPPILY REMARRIED. WORSE THAN THAT... THE ONE THING SHE HAD ALWAYS WANTED, THE ONE THING AL COULD NEVER GIVE HER, HAD BEEN DELIVERED.
A CHILD.
THAT MEANT THAT SIMMONS HAD BEEN THE PROBLEM. NOW HE FEELS LIKE LESS OF A MAN.
NO WIFE.
NO IDENTITY.
NO PRIDE.
HIS HEART HAS BEEN TORN APART BOTH EMOTIONALLY...
...AND PHYSICALLY.
THUMP THUMP THUMP THUMP THUMP THUMP THUMP THUMP THUMP THUMP THUMP THUMP

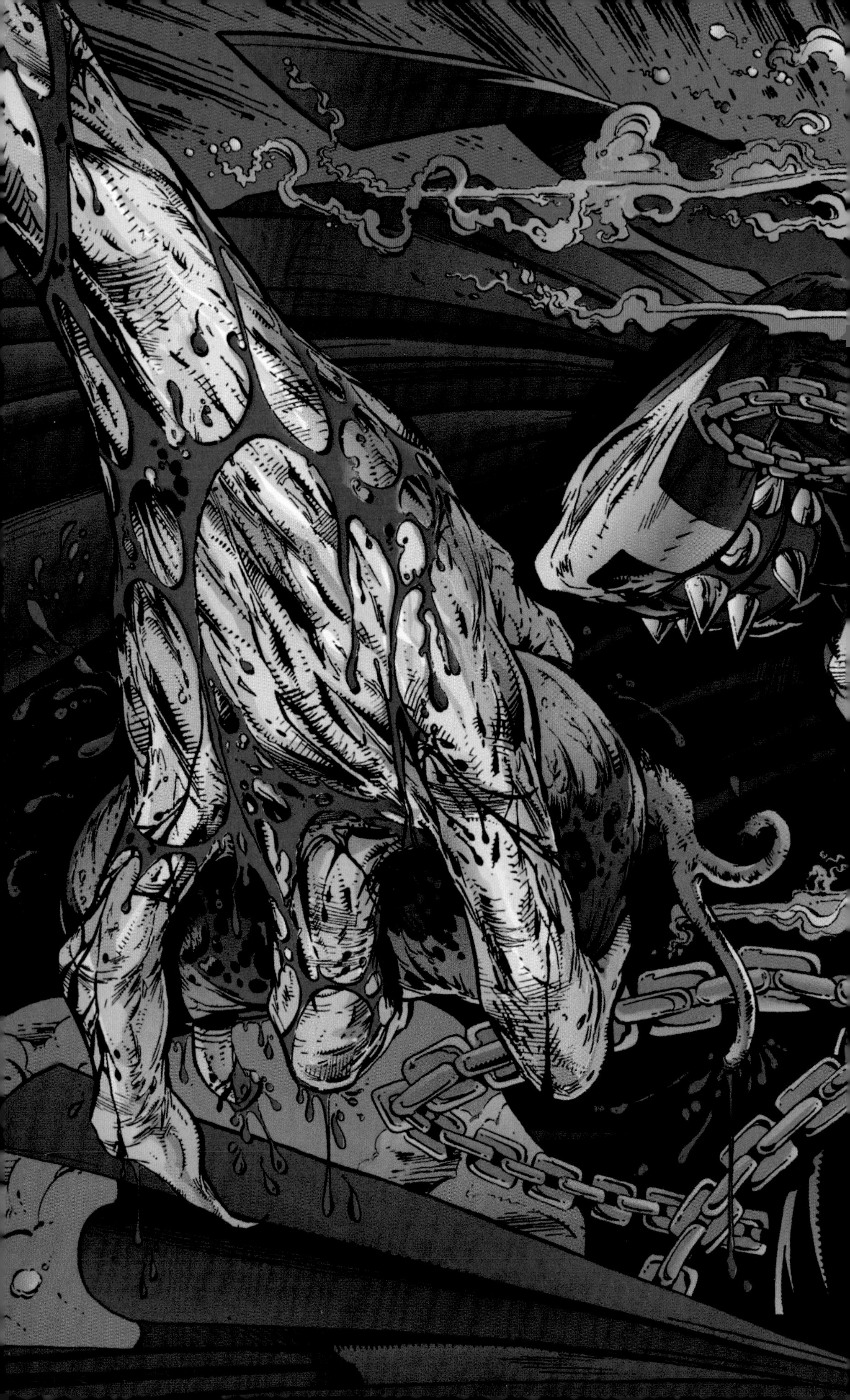

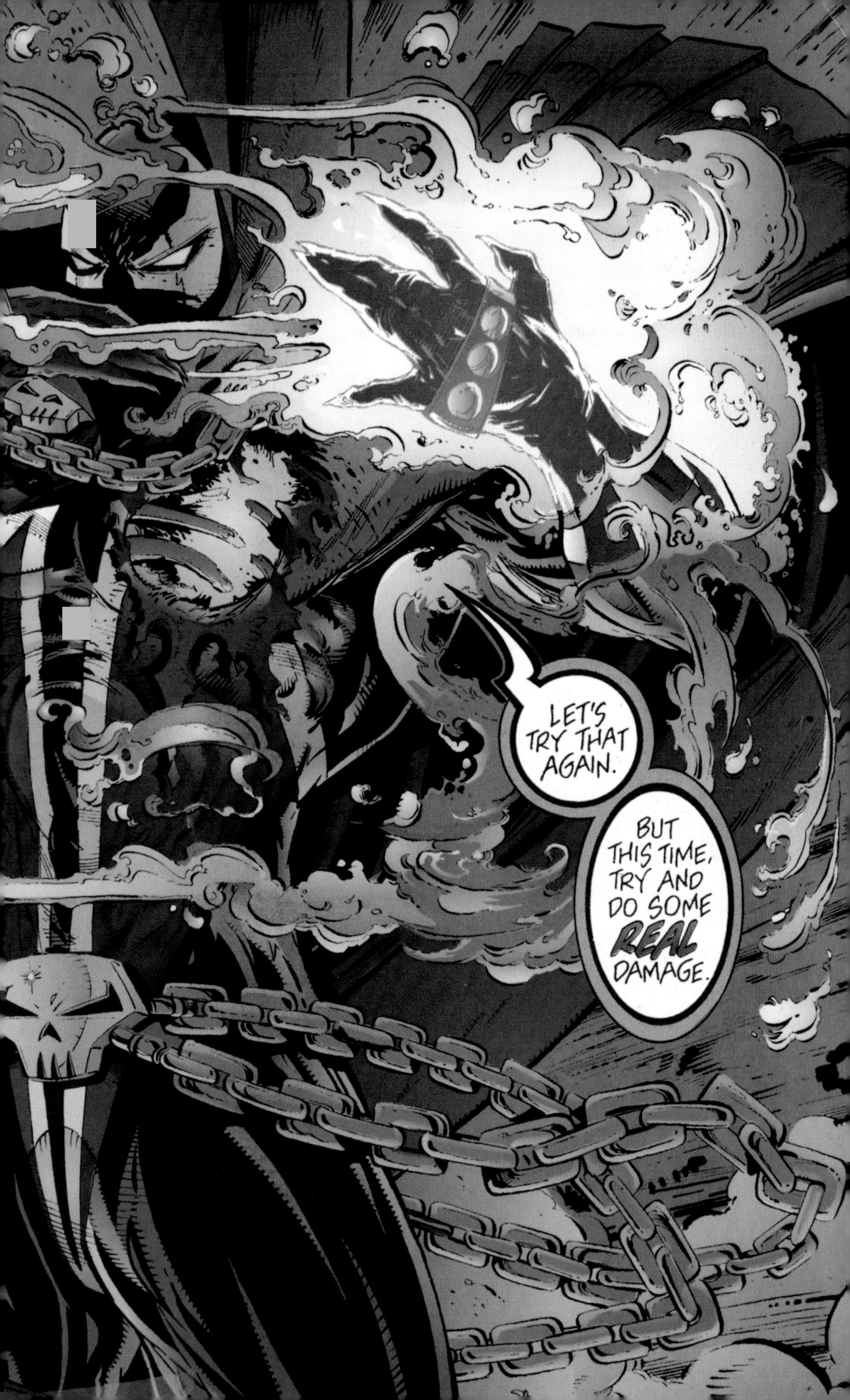
LET'S TRY THAT AGAIN.
BUT THIS TIME, TRY AND DO SOME REAL DAMAGE.

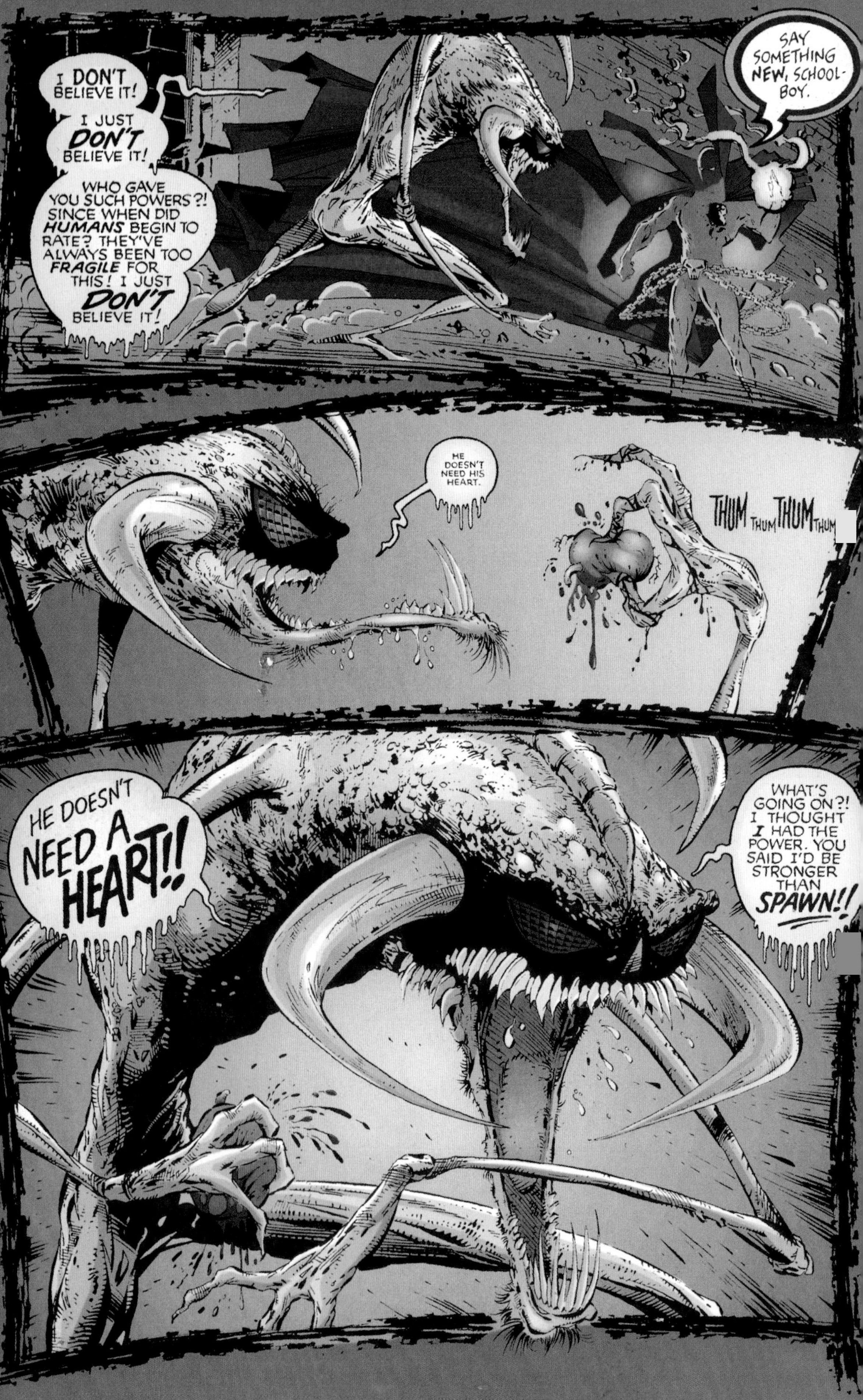

I DON'T BELIEVE IT!
I JUST DON'T BELIEVE IT!
WHO GAVE YOU SUCH POWERS?! SINCE WHEN DID HUMANS BEGIN TO RATE? THEY'VE ALWAYS BEEN TOO FRAGILE FOR THIS! I JUST DON'T BELIEVE IT!
SAY SOMETHING NEW, SCHOOL-BOY.
HE DOESN'T NEED HIS HEART.
THUM THUM THUM THUM
HE DOESN'T NEED A HEART!!
WHAT'S GOING ON?! I THOUGHT I HAD THE POWER. YOU SAID I'D BE STRONGER THAN SPAWN!!

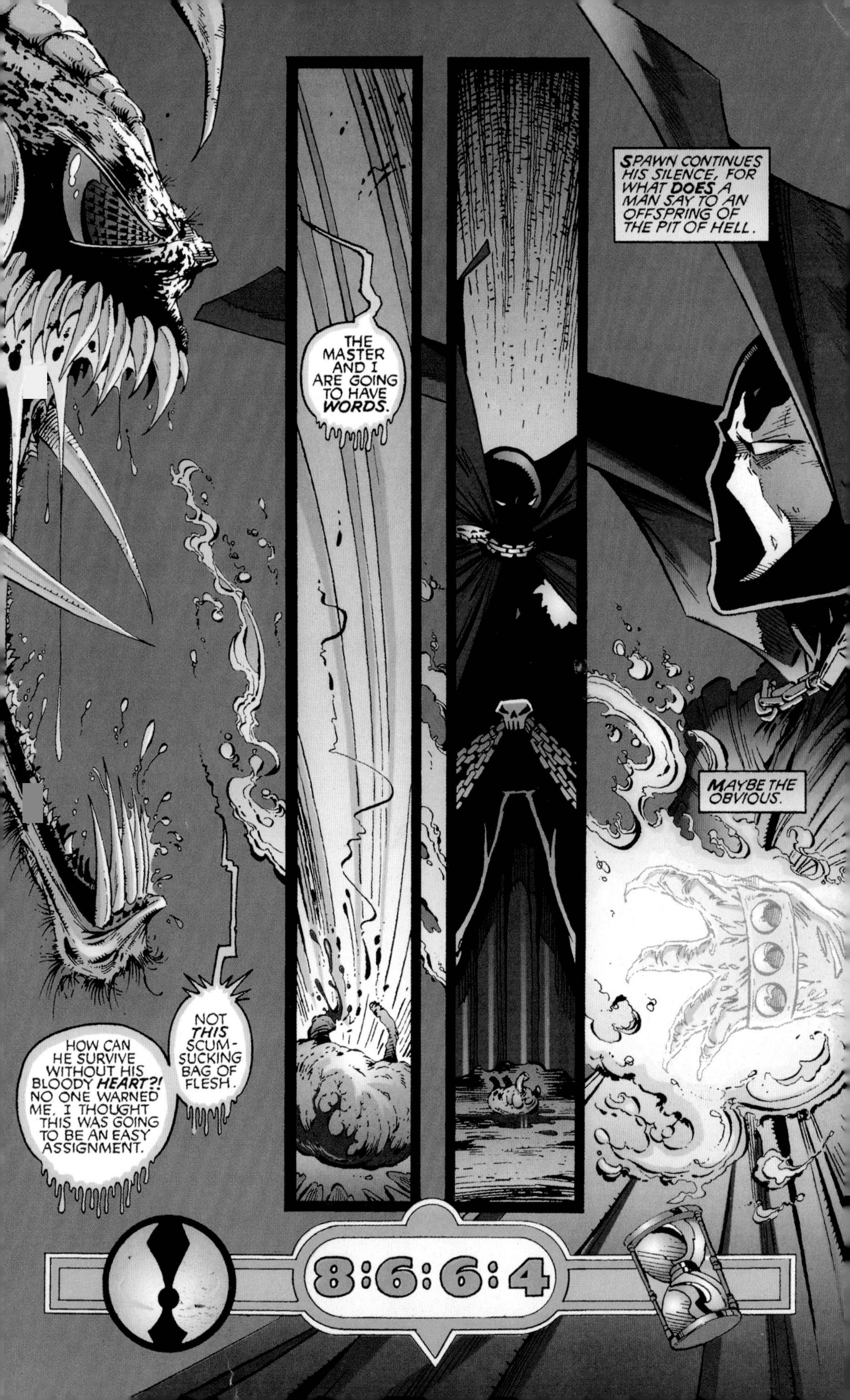
SPAWN CONTINUES HIS SILENCE, FOR WHAT DOES A MAN SAY TO AN OFFSPRING OF THE PIT OF HELL.
THE MASTER AND I ARE GOING TO HAVE WORDS.
NOT THIS SCUM-SUCKING BAG OF FLESH.
HOW CAN HE SURVIVE WITHOUT HIS BLOODY HEART?! NO ONE WARNED ME. I THOUGHT THIS WAS GOING TO BE AN EASY ASSIGNMENT.
MAYBE THE OBVIOUS.
8:6:6:4

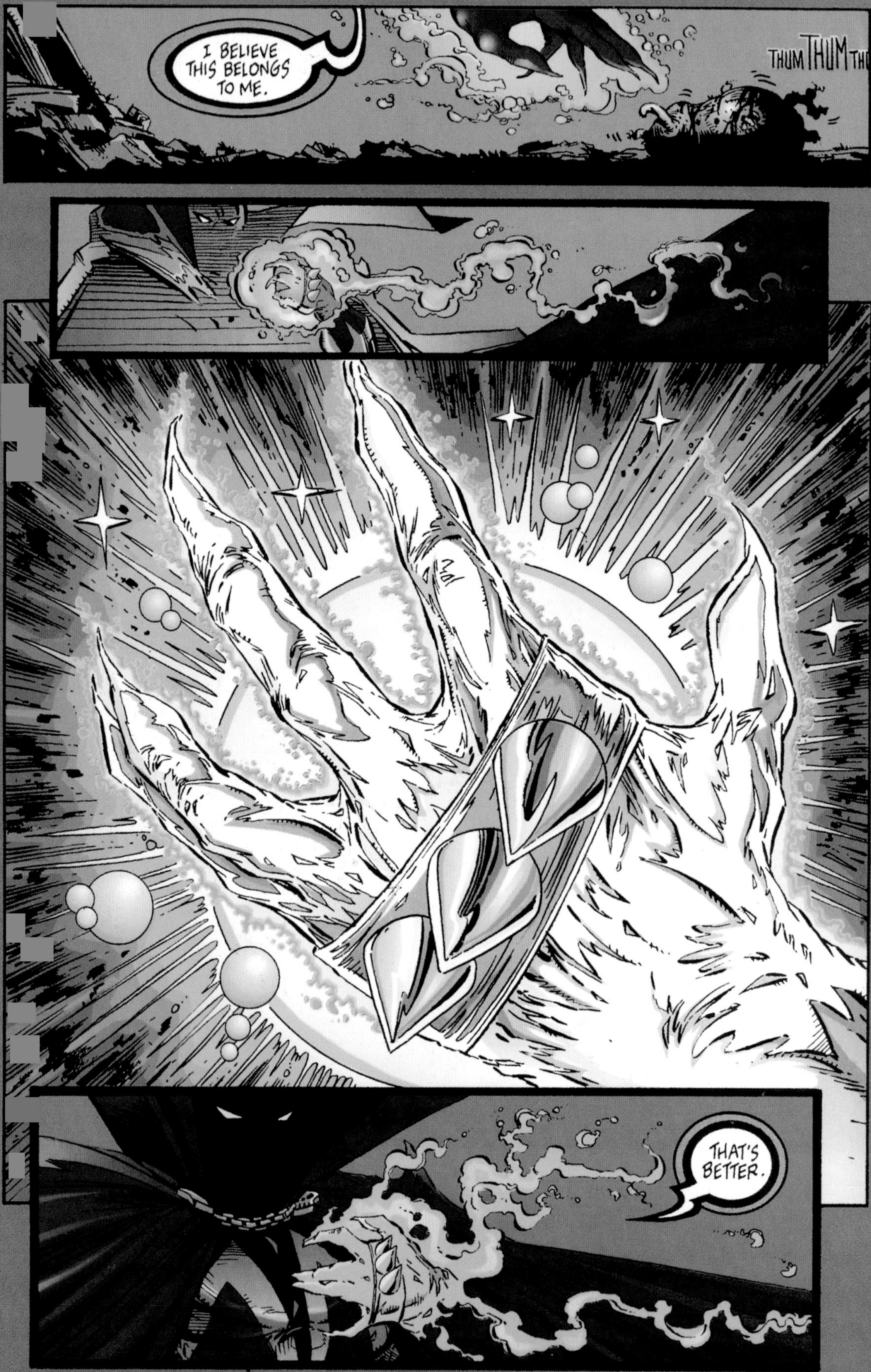
I BELIEVE THIS BELONGS TO ME.
THUM THUM THU
THAT'S BETTER.

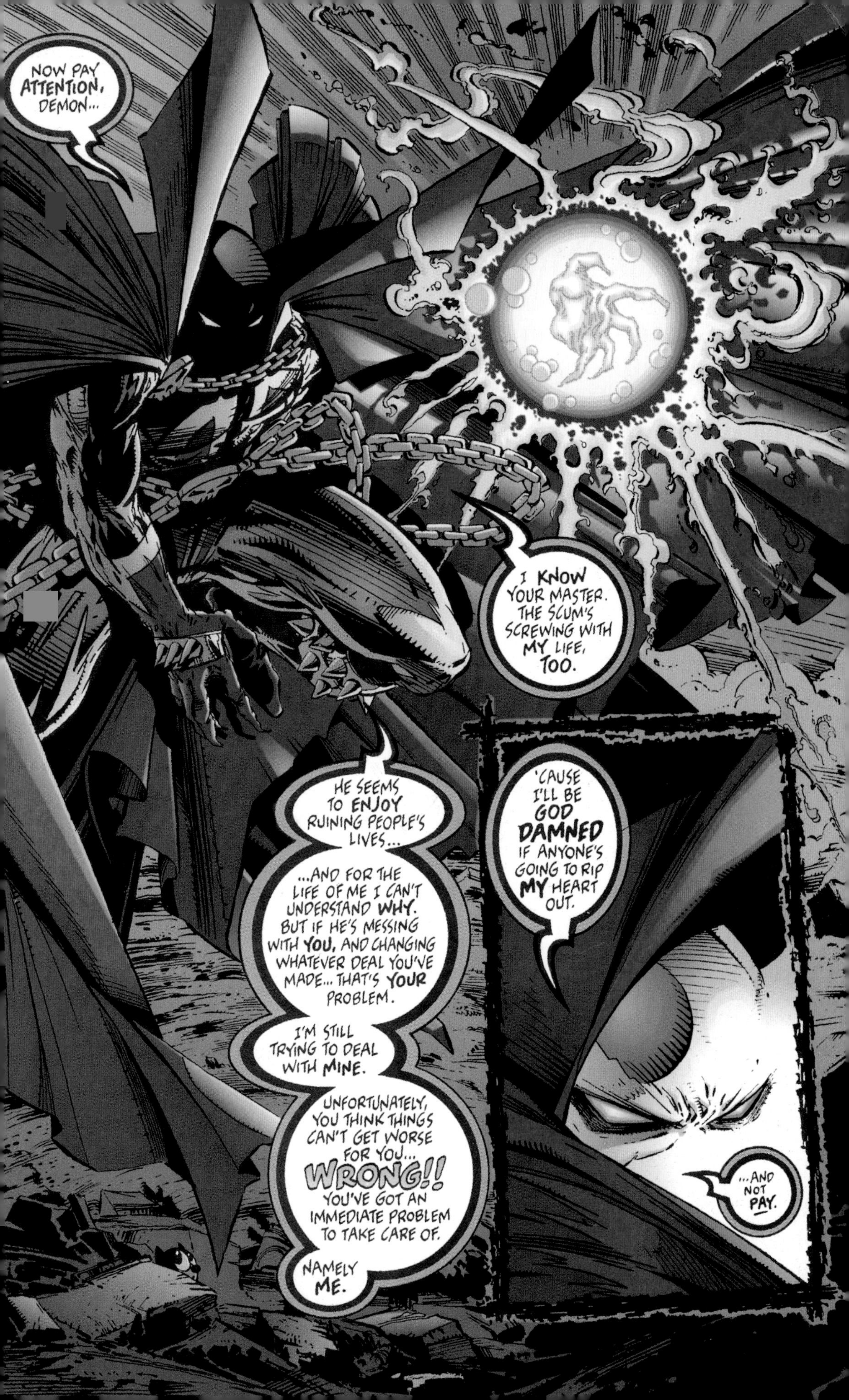
NOW PAY ATTENTION, DEMON...
I KNOW YOUR MASTER. THE SCUM'S SCREWING WITH MY LIFE, TOO.
HE SEEMS TO ENJOY RUINING PEOPLE'S LIVES...
...AND FOR THE LIFE OF ME I CAN'T UNDERSTAND WHY. BUT IF HE'S MESSING WITH YOU, AND CHANGING WHATEVER DEAL YOU'VE MADE... THAT'S YOUR PROBLEM.
I'M STILL TRYING TO DEAL WITH MINE.
UNFORTUNATELY, YOU THINK THINGS CAN'T GET WORSE FOR YOU... WRONG!! YOU'VE GOT AN IMMEDIATE PROBLEM TO TAKE CARE OF.
NAMELY ME.
'CAUSE I'LL BE GOD DAMNED IF ANYONE'S GOING TO RIP MY HEART OUT.
...AND NOT PAY.

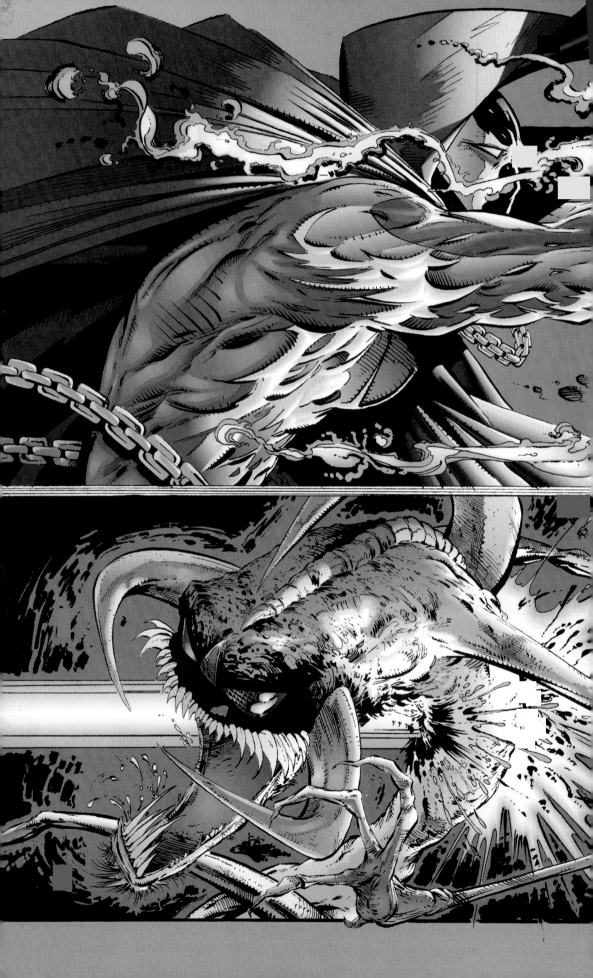

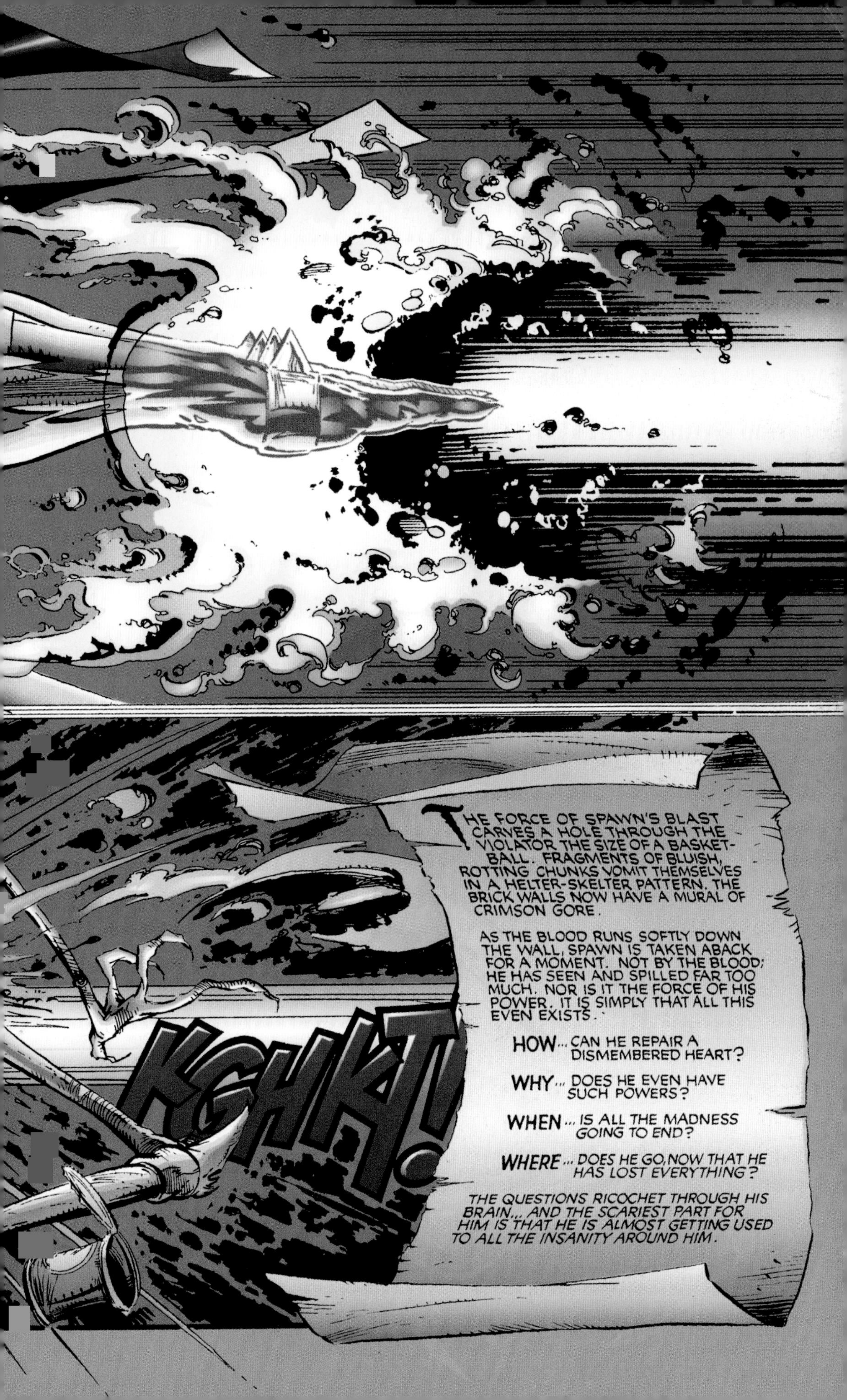
THE FORCE OF SPAWN'S BLAST CARVES A HOLE THROUGH THE VIOLATOR THE SIZE OF A BASKETBALL. FRAGMENTS OF BLUISH, ROTTING CHUNKS VOMIT THEMSELVES IN A HELTER-SKELTER PATTERN. THE BRICK WALLS NOW HAVE A MURAL OF CRIMSON GORE.
AS THE BLOOD RUNS SOFTLY DOWN THE WALL, SPAWN IS TAKEN ABACK FOR A MOMENT. NOT BY THE BLOOD; HE HAS SEEN AND SPILLED FAR TOO MUCH. NOR IS IT THE FORCE OF HIS POWER. IT IS SIMPLY THAT ALL THIS EVEN EXISTS.
HOW... CAN HE REPAIR A DISMEMBERED HEART?
WHY... DOES HE EVEN HAVE SUCH POWERS?
WHEN... IS ALL THE MADNESS GOING TO END?
WHERE... DOES HE GO, NOW THAT HE HAS LOST EVERYTHING?
THE QUESTIONS RICOCHET THROUGH HIS BRAIN... AND THE SCARIEST PART FOR HIM IS THAT HE IS ALMOST GETTING USED TO ALL THE INSANITY AROUND HIM.
KCHKT!

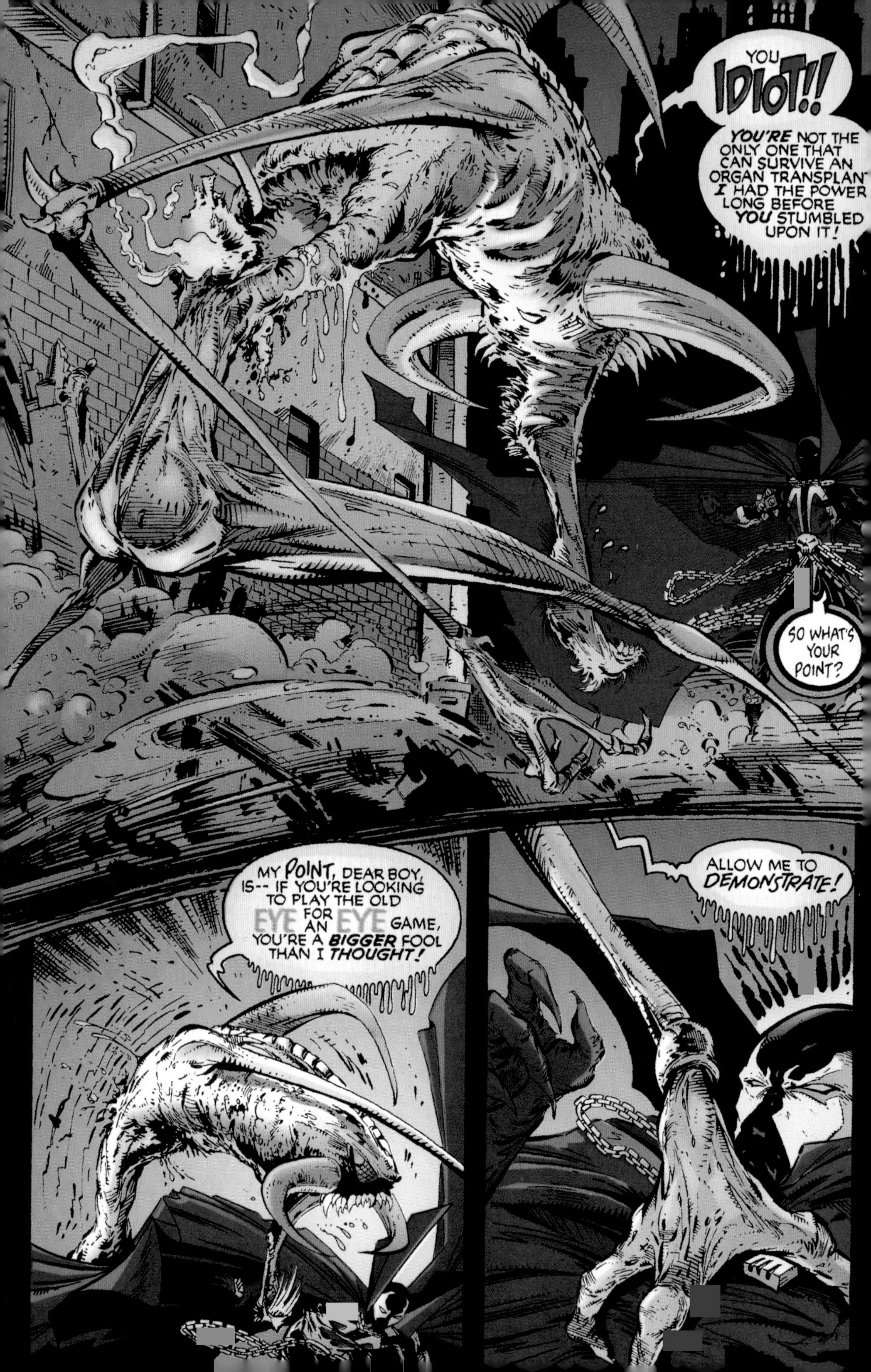
YOU IDIOT!! YOU'RE NOT THE ONLY ONE THAT CAN SURVIVE AN ORGAN TRANSPLAN I HAD THE POWER LONG BEFORE YOU STUMBLED UPON IT!
SO WHAT'S YOUR POINT?
MY POINT, DEAR BOY, IS-- IF YOU'RE LOOKING TO PLAY THE OLD EYE FOR AN EYE GAME, YOU'RE A BIGGER FOOL THAN I THOUGHT!
ALLOW ME TO DEMONSTRATE!

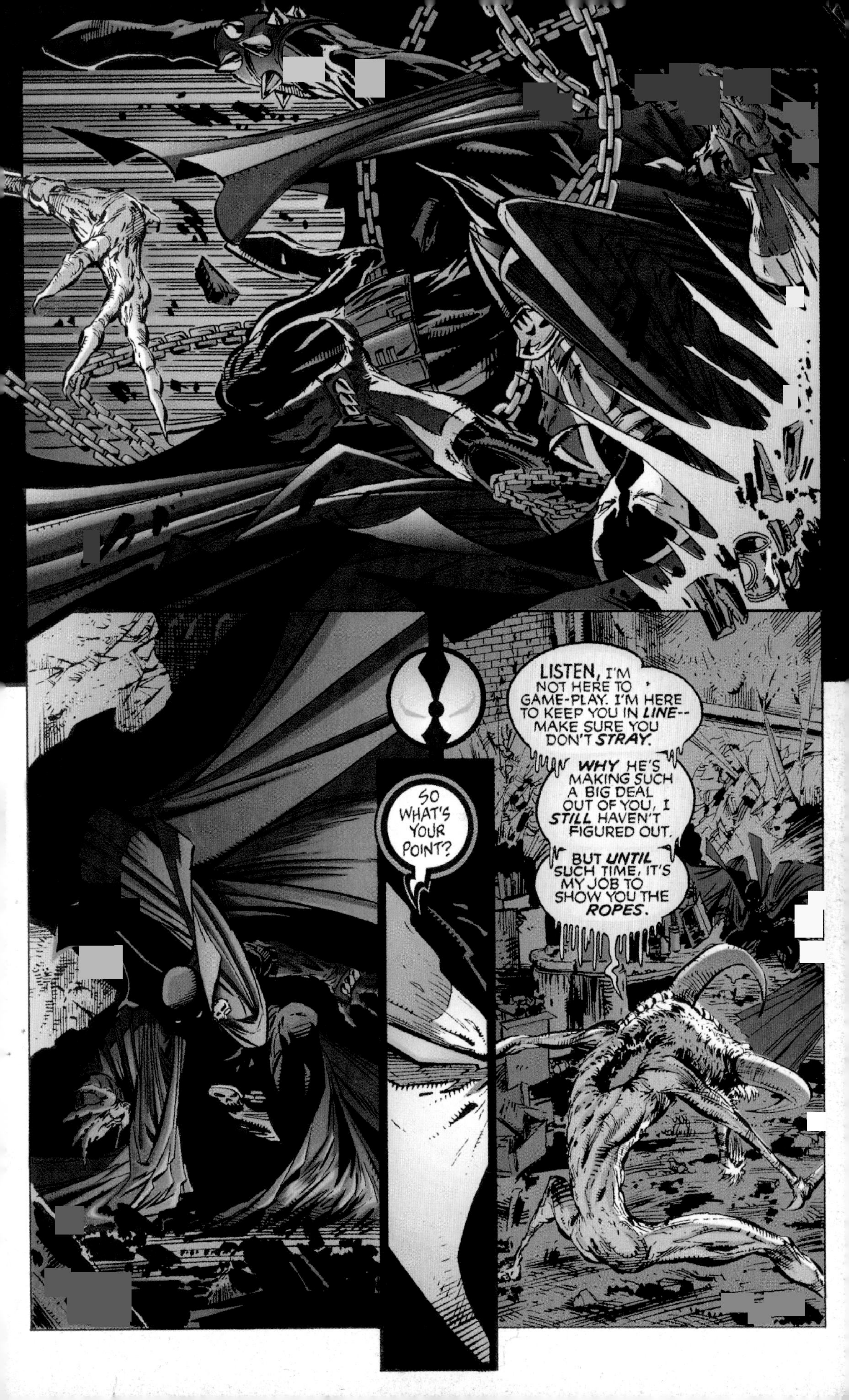
LISTEN, I'M NOT HERE TO GAME-PLAY. I'M HERE TO KEEP YOU IN LINE-- MAKE SURE YOU DON'T STRAY.
SO WHAT'S YOUR POINT?
WHY HE'S MAKING SUCH A BIG DEAL OUT OF YOU, I STILL HAVEN'T FIGURED OUT.
BUT UNTIL SUCH TIME, IT'S MY JOB TO SHOW YOU THE ROPES.

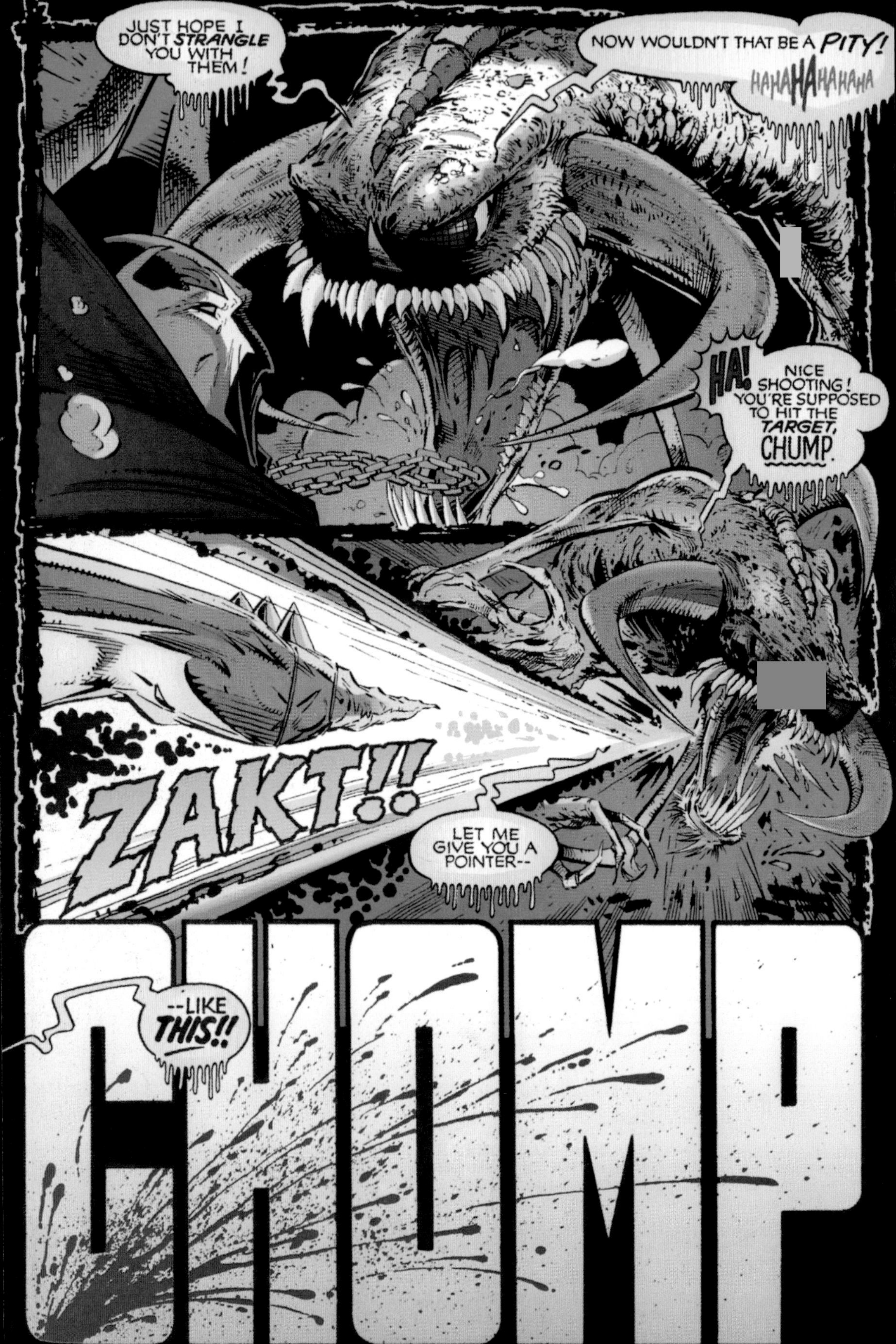
JUST HOPE I DON'T STRANGLE YOU WITH THEM!
NOW WOULDN'T THAT BE A PITY!
HAHAHAHAHAHAHA
HA! NICE SHOOTING! YOU'RE SUPPOSED TO HIT THE TARGET, CHUMP.
ZAKT!!
LET ME GIVE YOU A POINTER--
CHOMP
--LIKE THIS!!

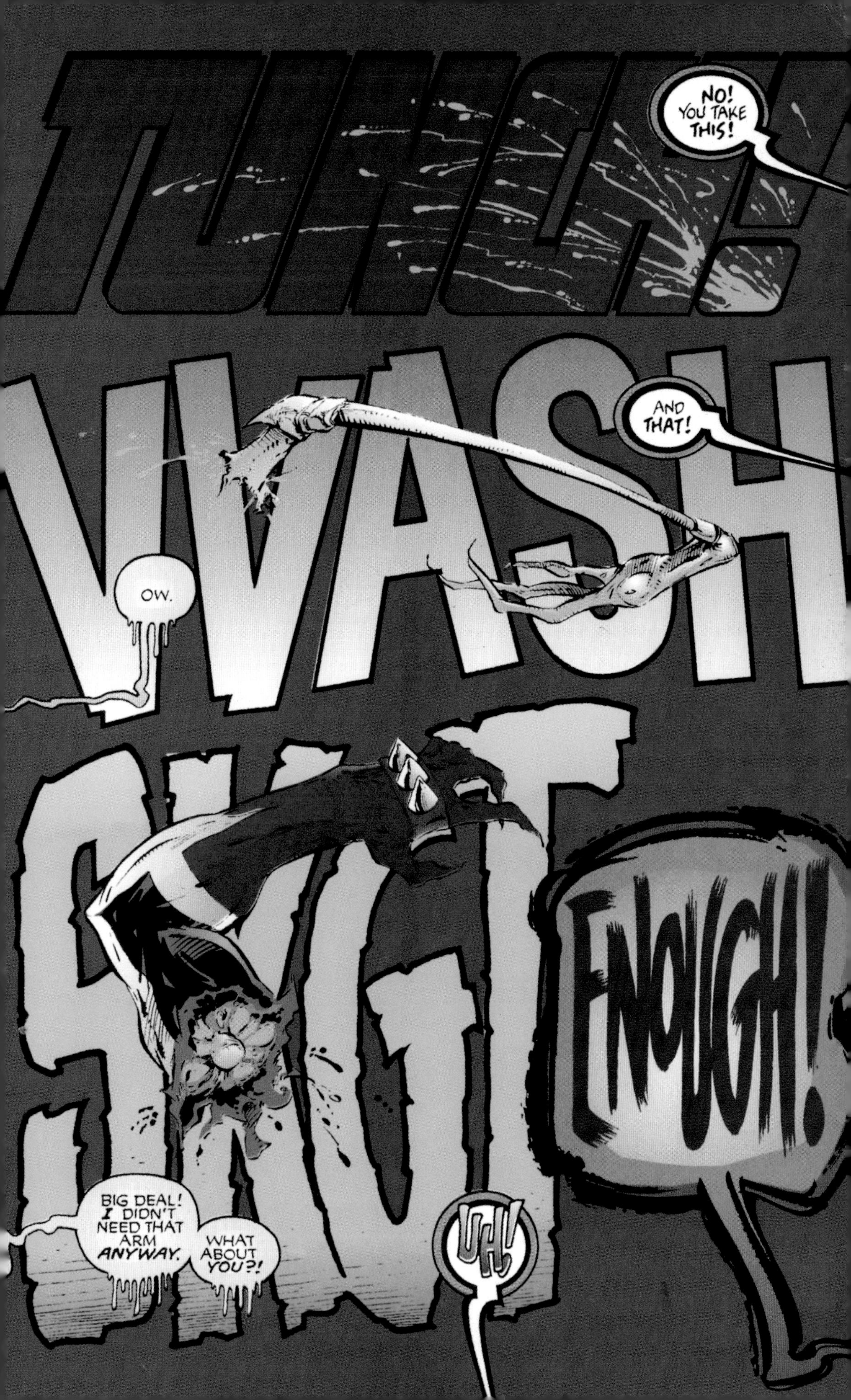
NO! YOU TAKE THIS!
AND THAT!
OW.
ENOUGH!
BIG DEAL! I DIDN'T NEED THAT ARM ANYWAY.
WHAT ABOUT YOU?!
UH!

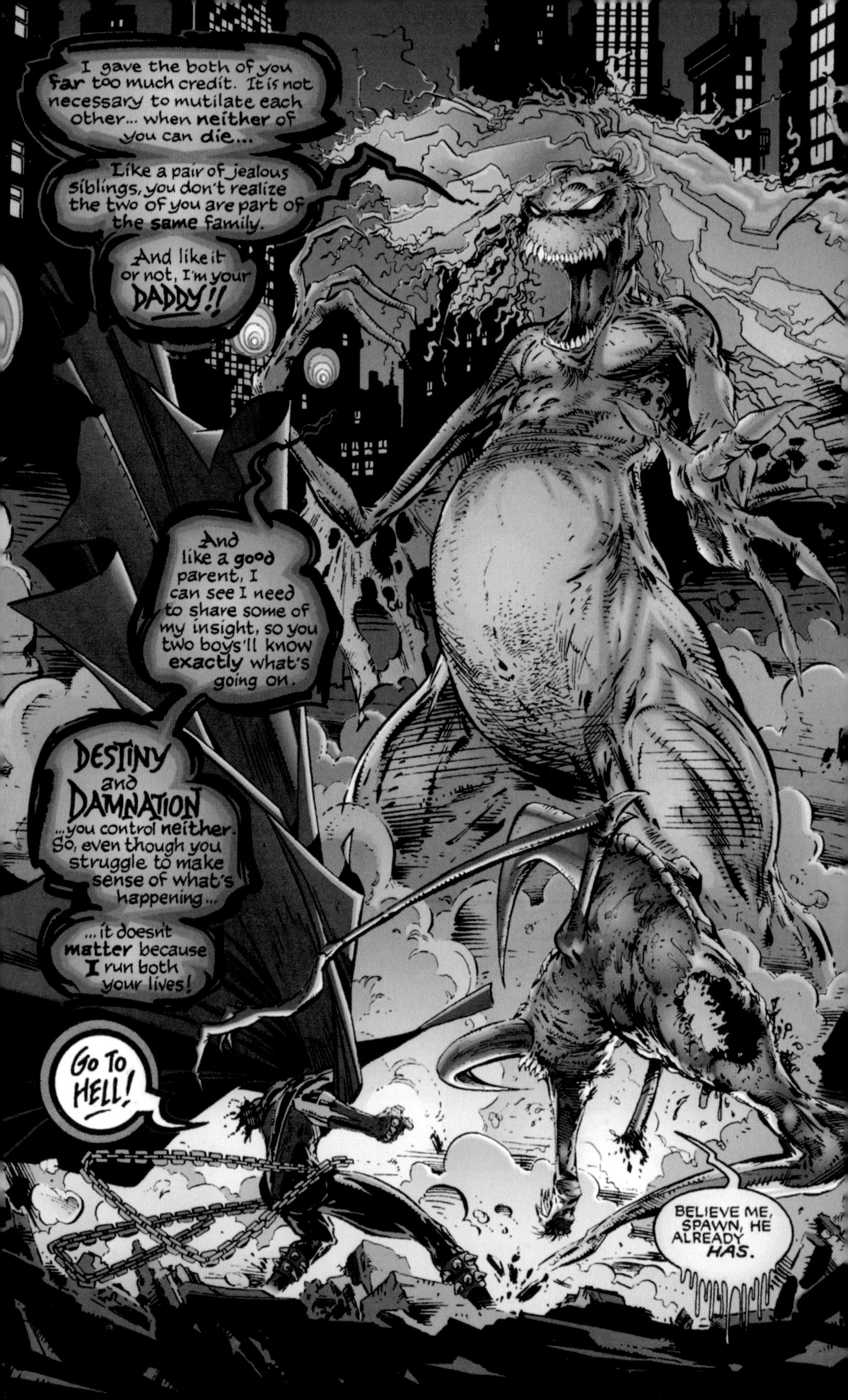
I gave the both of you far too much credit. It is not necessary to mutilate each other... when neither of you can die...
Like a pair of jealous siblings, you don't realize the two of you are part of the same family.
And like it or not, I'm your DADDY!!
And like a good parent, I can see I need to share some of my insight, so you two boys'll know exactly what's going on.
DESTINY and DAMNATION ...you control neither. So, even though you struggle to make sense of what's happening...
...it doesn't matter because I run both your lives!
GO TO HELL!
BELIEVE ME, SPAWN, HE ALREADY HAS.

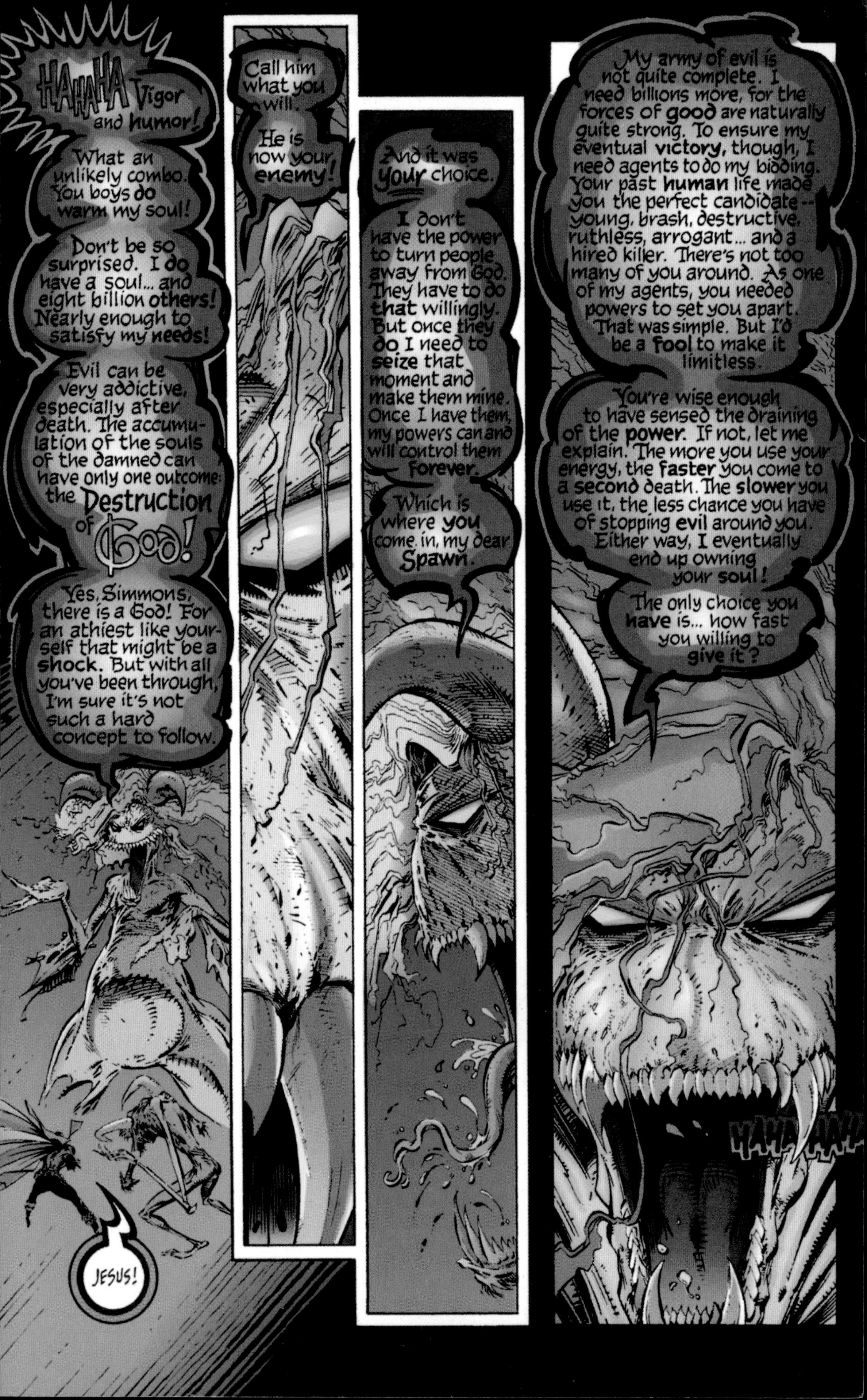
HAHAHA Vigor and humor!
What an unlikely combo. You boys do warm my soul!
Don't be so surprised. I do have a soul... and eight billion others! Nearly enough to satisfy my needs!
Evil can be very addictive, especially after death. The accumulation of the souls of the damned can have only one outcome: the Destruction of God!
Yes, Simmons, there is a God! For an athiest like yourself that might be a shock. But with all you've been through, I'm sure it's not such a hard concept to follow.
JESUS!
Call him what you will.
He is now your enemy!
And it was your choice.
I don't have the power to turn people away from God. They have to do that willingly. But once they do I need to seize that moment and make them mine. Once I have them, my powers can and will control them forever.
Which is where you come in, my dear Spawn.
My army of evil is not quite complete. I need billions more, for the forces of good are naturally quite strong. To ensure my eventual victory, though, I need agents to do my bidding. Your past human life made you the perfect candidate -- young, brash, destructive, ruthless, arrogant... and a hired killer. There's not too many of you around. As one of my agents, you needed powers to set you apart. That was simple. But I'd be a fool to make it limitless.
You're wise enough to have sensed the draining of the power. If not, let me explain. The more you use your energy, the faster you come to a second death. The slower you use it, the less chance you have of stopping evil around you. Either way, I eventually end up owning your soul!
The only choice you have is... how fast you willing to give it?
HAHAHAHA

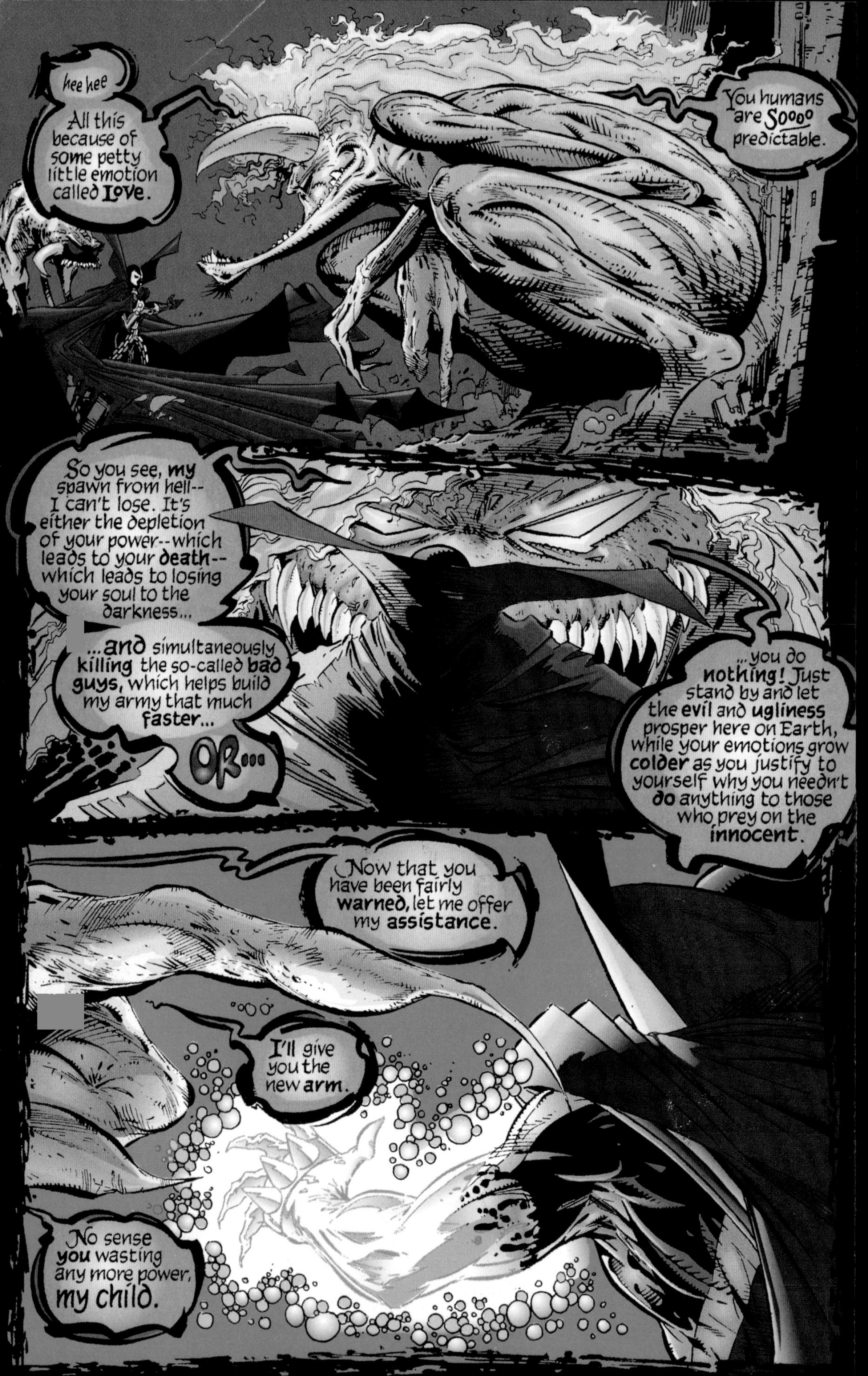
hee hee
All this because of some petty little emotion called Love.
You humans are Soooo predictable.
So you see, my spawn from hell-- I can't lose. It's either the depletion of your power--which leads to your death--which leads to losing your soul to the darkness...
...and simultaneously killing the so-called bad guys, which helps build my army that much faster...
OR...
...you do nothing! Just stand by and let the evil and ugliness prosper here on Earth, while your emotions grow colder as you justify to yourself why you needn't do anything to those who prey on the innocent.
Now that you have been fairly warned, let me offer my assistance.
I'll give you the new arm.
No sense you wasting any more power, my child.

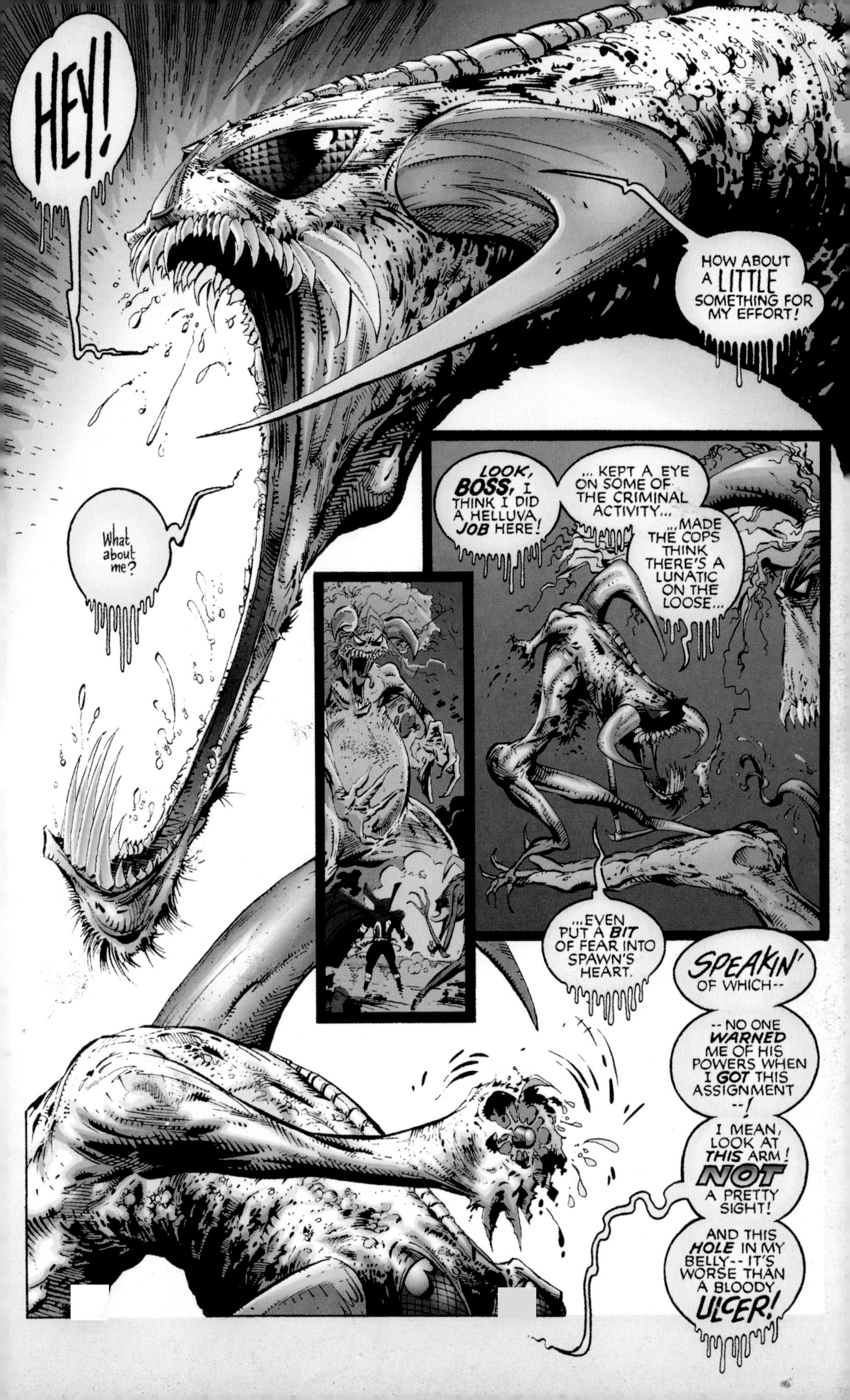

HEY!
HOW ABOUT A LITTLE SOMETHING FOR MY EFFORT!
What about me?
LOOK, BOSS, I THINK I DID A HELLUVA JOB HERE!
... KEPT A EYE ON SOME OF THE CRIMINAL ACTIVITY...
...MADE THE COPS THINK THERE'S A LUNATIC ON THE LOOSE...
...EVEN PUT A BIT OF FEAR INTO SPAWN'S HEART.
SPEAKIN' OF WHICH--
--NO ONE WARNED ME OF HIS POWERS WHEN I GOT THIS ASSIGNMENT--!
I MEAN, LOOK AT THIS ARM! NOT A PRETTY SIGHT!
AND THIS HOLE IN MY BELLY--IT'S WORSE THAN A BLOODY ULCER!

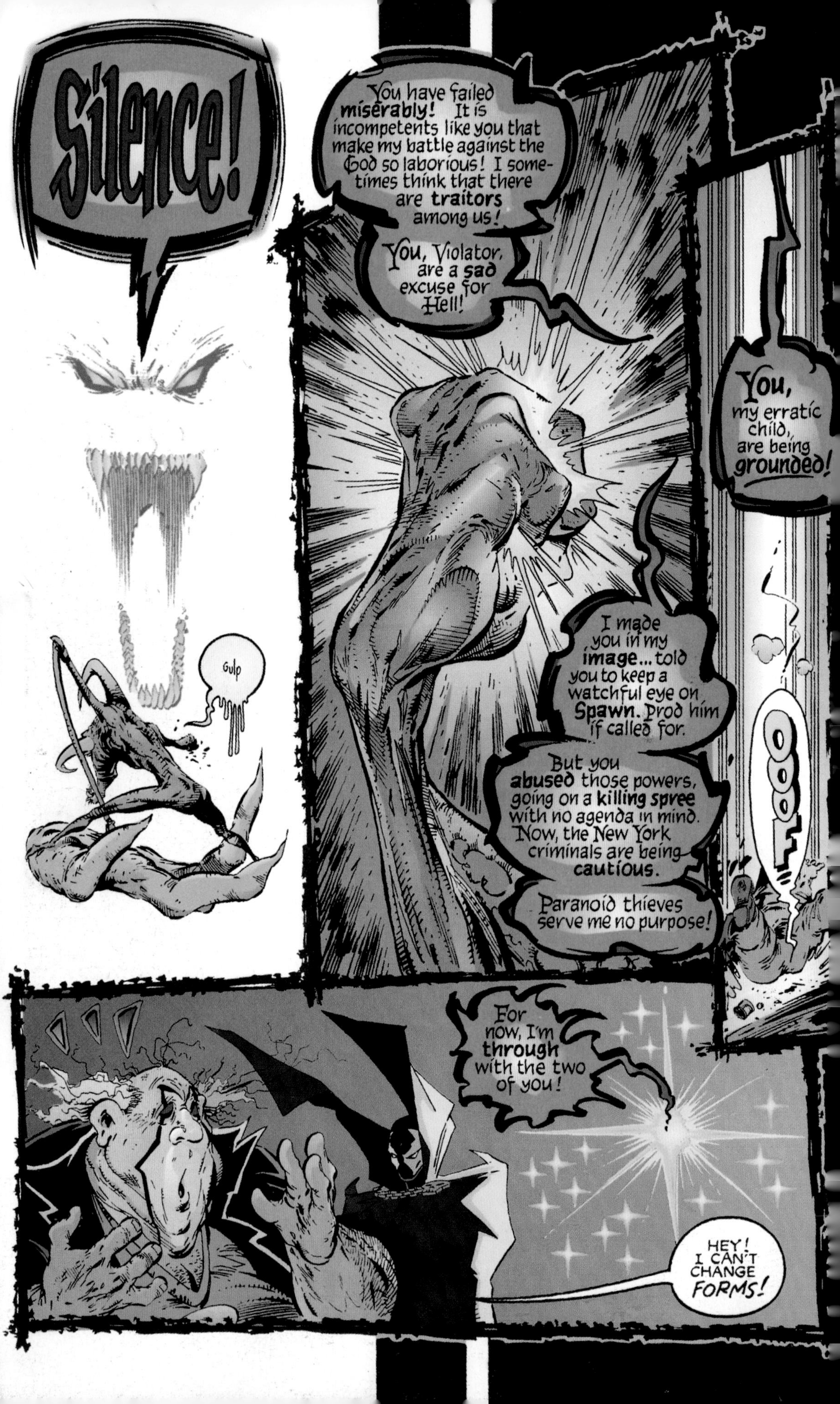

Silence!
You have failed miserably! It is incompetents like you that make my battle against the God so laborious! I sometimes think that there are traitors among us!
You, Violator, are a sad excuse for Hell!
Gulp
You, my erratic child, are being grounded!
I made you in my image... told you to keep a watchful eye on Spawn. Prod him if called for.
But you abused those powers, going on a killing spree with no agenda in mind. Now, the New York criminals are being cautious.
Paranoid thieves serve me no purpose!
OOOF!
For now, I'm through with the two of you!
HEY! I CAN'T CHANGE FORMS!

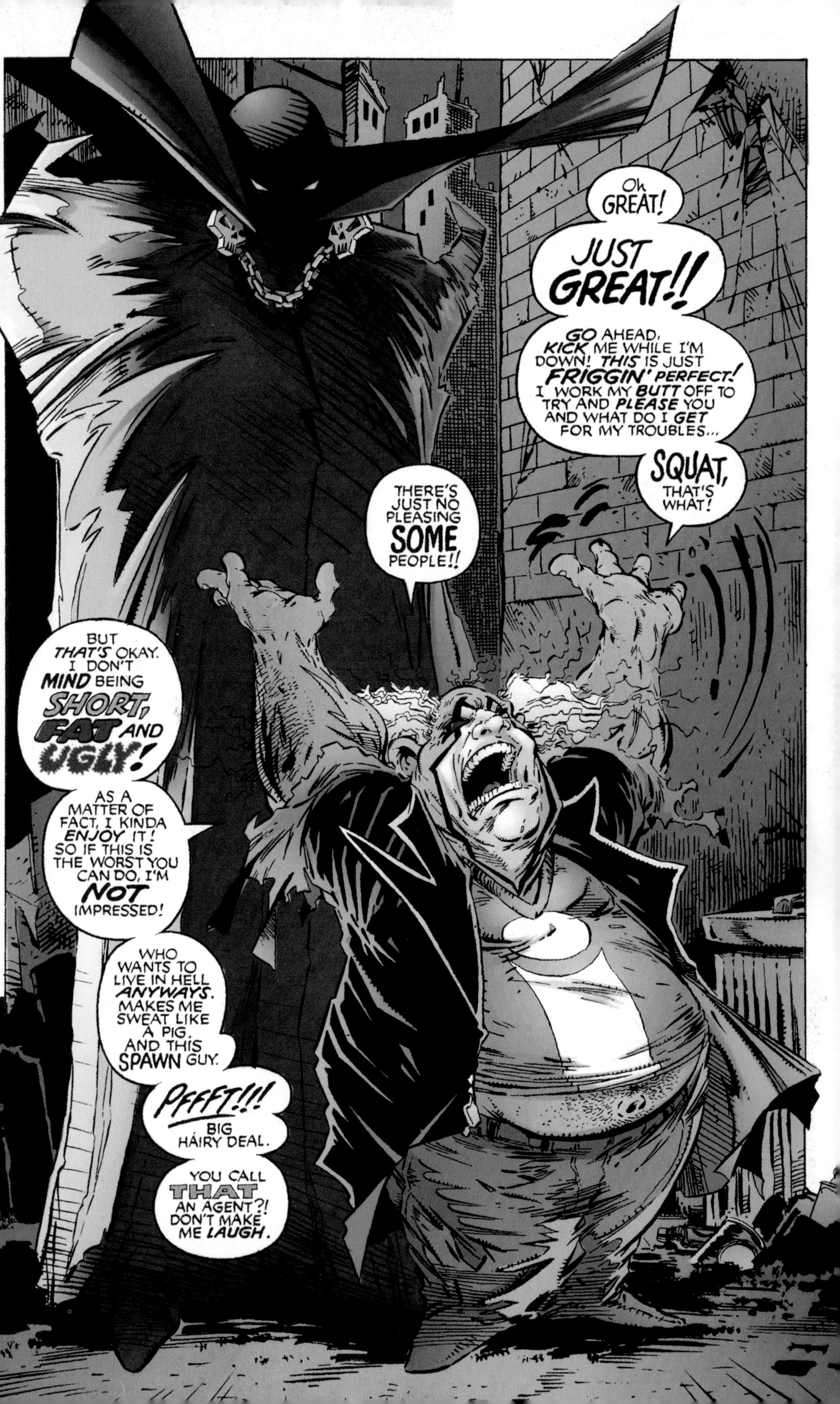

Oh GREAT!
JUST GREAT!!
GO AHEAD, KICK ME WHILE I'M DOWN! THIS IS JUST FRIGGIN' PERFECT! I WORK MY BUTT OFF TO TRY AND PLEASE YOU AND WHAT DO I GET FOR MY TROUBLES...
SQUAT, THAT'S WHAT!
THERE'S JUST NO PLEASING SOME PEOPLE!!
BUT THAT'S OKAY. I DON'T MIND BEING SHORT, FAT AND UGLY!
AS A MATTER OF FACT, I KINDA ENJOY IT! SO IF THIS IS THE WORST YOU CAN DO, I'M NOT IMPRESSED!
WHO WANTS TO LIVE IN HELL ANYWAYS. MAKES ME SWEAT LIKE A PIG. AND THIS SPAWN GUY.
PFFFT!!! BIG HAIRY DEAL.
YOU CALL THAT AN AGENT?! DON'T MAKE ME LAUGH.

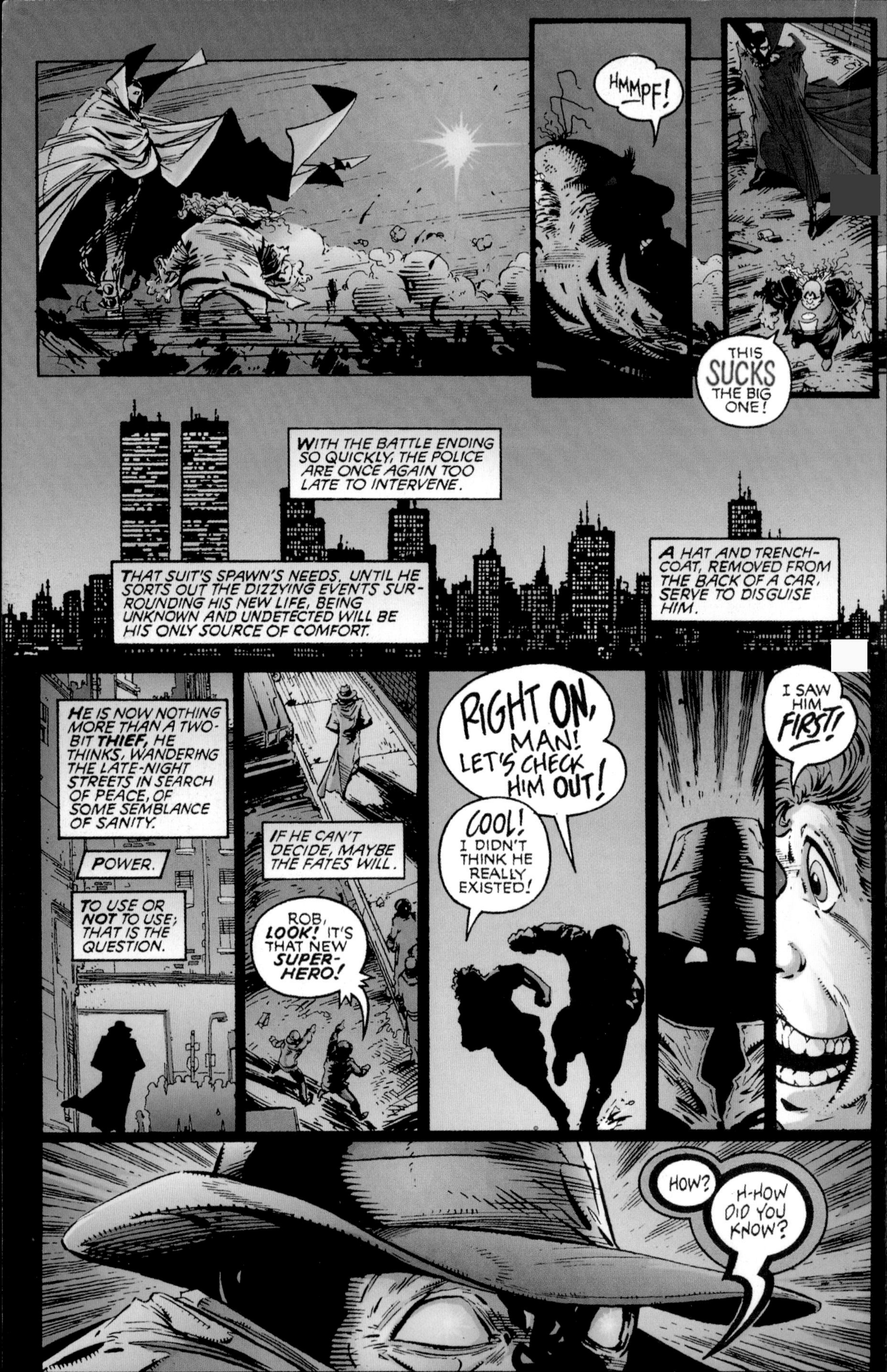
HMMPF!
THIS SUCKS THE BIG ONE!
WITH THE BATTLE ENDING SO QUICKLY, THE POLICE ARE ONCE AGAIN TOO LATE TO INTERVENE.
THAT SUIT'S SPAWN'S NEEDS. UNTIL HE SORTS OUT THE DIZZYING EVENTS SURROUNDING HIS NEW LIFE, BEING UNKNOWN AND UNDETECTED WILL BE HIS ONLY SOURCE OF COMFORT.
A HAT AND TRENCH-COAT, REMOVED FROM THE BACK OF A CAR, SERVE TO DISGUISE HIM.
HE IS NOW NOTHING MORE THAN A TWO-BIT THIEF, HE THINKS, WANDERING THE LATE-NIGHT STREETS IN SEARCH OF PEACE, OF SOME SEMBLANCE OF SANITY.
POWER.
TO USE OR NOT TO USE; THAT IS THE QUESTION.
IF HE CAN'T DECIDE, MAYBE THE FATES WILL.
ROB, LOOK! IT'S THAT NEW SUPER-HERO!
RIGHT ON, MAN! LET'S CHECK HIM OUT!
COOL! I DIDN'T THINK HE REALLY EXISTED!
I SAW HIM FIRST!
HOW?
H-HOW DID YOU KNOW?

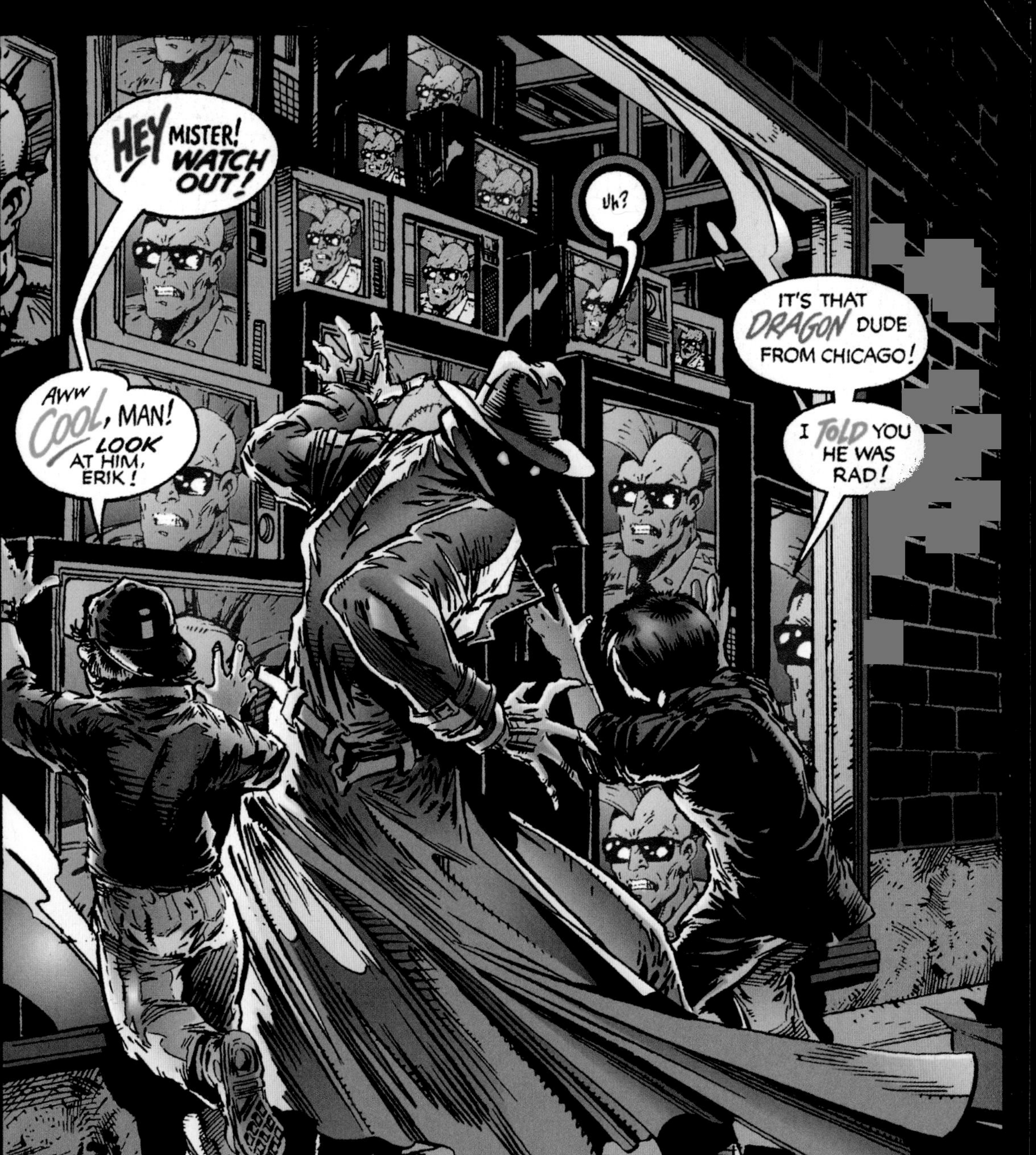
HEY MISTER! WATCH OUT!
UH?
AWW COOL, MAN! LOOK AT HIM, ERIK!
IT'S THAT DRAGON DUDE FROM CHICAGO!
I TOLD YOU HE WAS RAD!

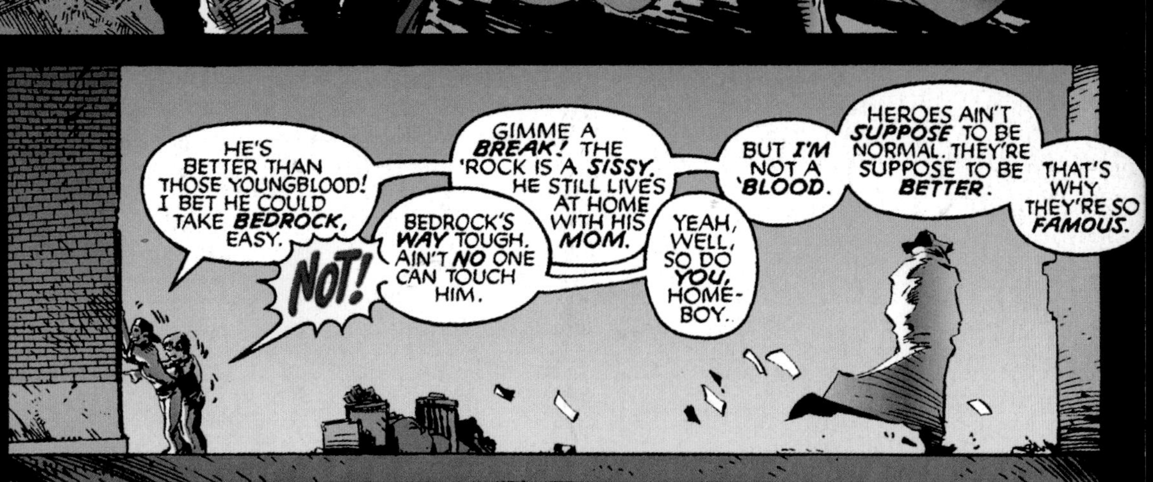
HE'S BETTER THAN THOSE YOUNGBLOOD! I BET HE COULD TAKE BEDROCK, EASY.
NOT!
BEDROCK'S WAY TOUGH. AIN'T NO ONE CAN TOUCH HIM.
GIMME A BREAK! THE 'ROCK IS A SISSY. HE STILL LIVES AT HOME WITH HIS MOM.
YEAH, WELL, SO DO YOU, HOME-BOY.
BUT I'M NOT A 'BLOOD.
HEROES AIN'T SUPPOSE TO BE NORMAL. THEY'RE SUPPOSE TO BE BETTER.
THAT'S WHY THEY'RE SO FAMOUS.

NOOO!

"BESIDES, WHO WANTS TO BE *NORMAL* ANYWAY."

2:36 A.M. THE CALM SILENCE OF SLEEP IS SHATTERED AS THE SOUL OF ANOTHER POOR VICTIM IS DRAWN FURTHER INTO PLAY.

WANDA, WHAT *IS* IT?! A DREAM?

AL! IT WAS **AL!** I SAW HIM ALIVE, B-BUT HE WAS *DIFFERENT* SOME-HOW-- *CHANGED.* HE WAS CALLING TO ME, ASKING FOR HELP-- *BEGGING* FOR IT!

IT WAS ALMOST AS IF-- AS *IF*--

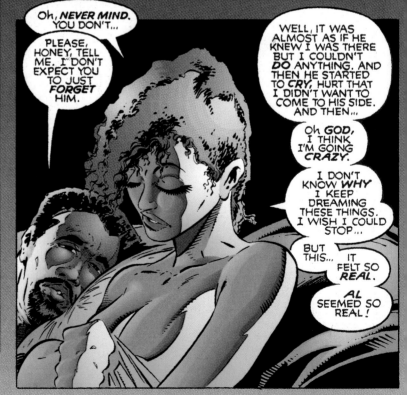

Oh, *NEVER MIND.* YOU DON'T...

PLEASE, HONEY, TELL ME. I DON'T EXPECT YOU TO JUST *FORGET* HIM.

WELL, IT WAS ALMOST AS IF HE KNEW I WAS THERE BUT I COULDN'T *DO* ANYTHING. AND THEN HE STARTED TO *CRY,* HURT THAT I DIDN'T WANT TO COME TO HIS SIDE. AND THEN...

Oh *GOD,* I THINK I'M GOING *CRAZY.*

I DON'T KNOW *WHY* I KEEP DREAMING THESE THINGS. I WISH I COULD STOP...

BUT THIS... IT FELT SO *REAL.*

AL SEEMED SO *REAL!*

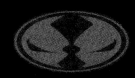

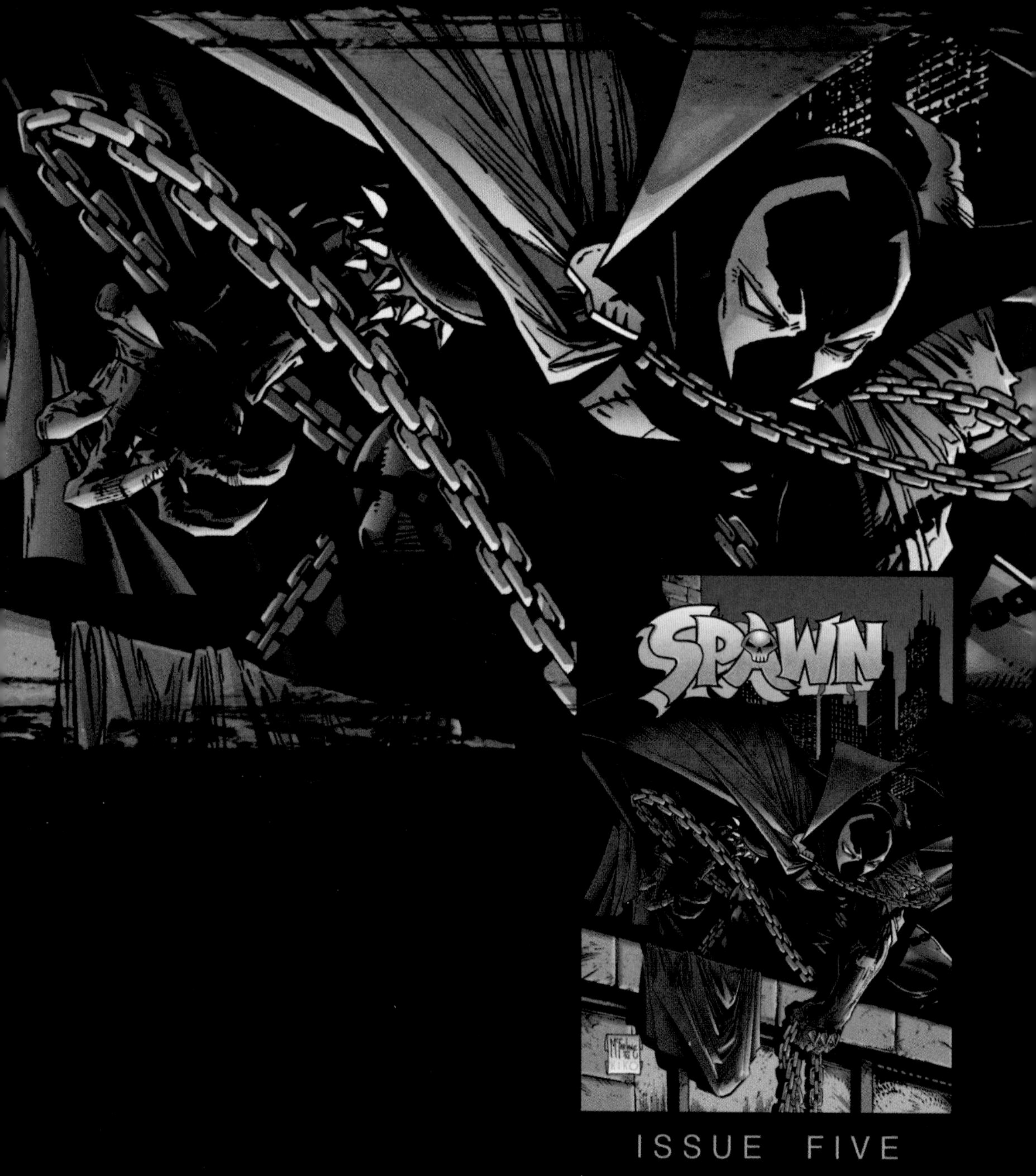
SPAWN

ISSUE FIVE

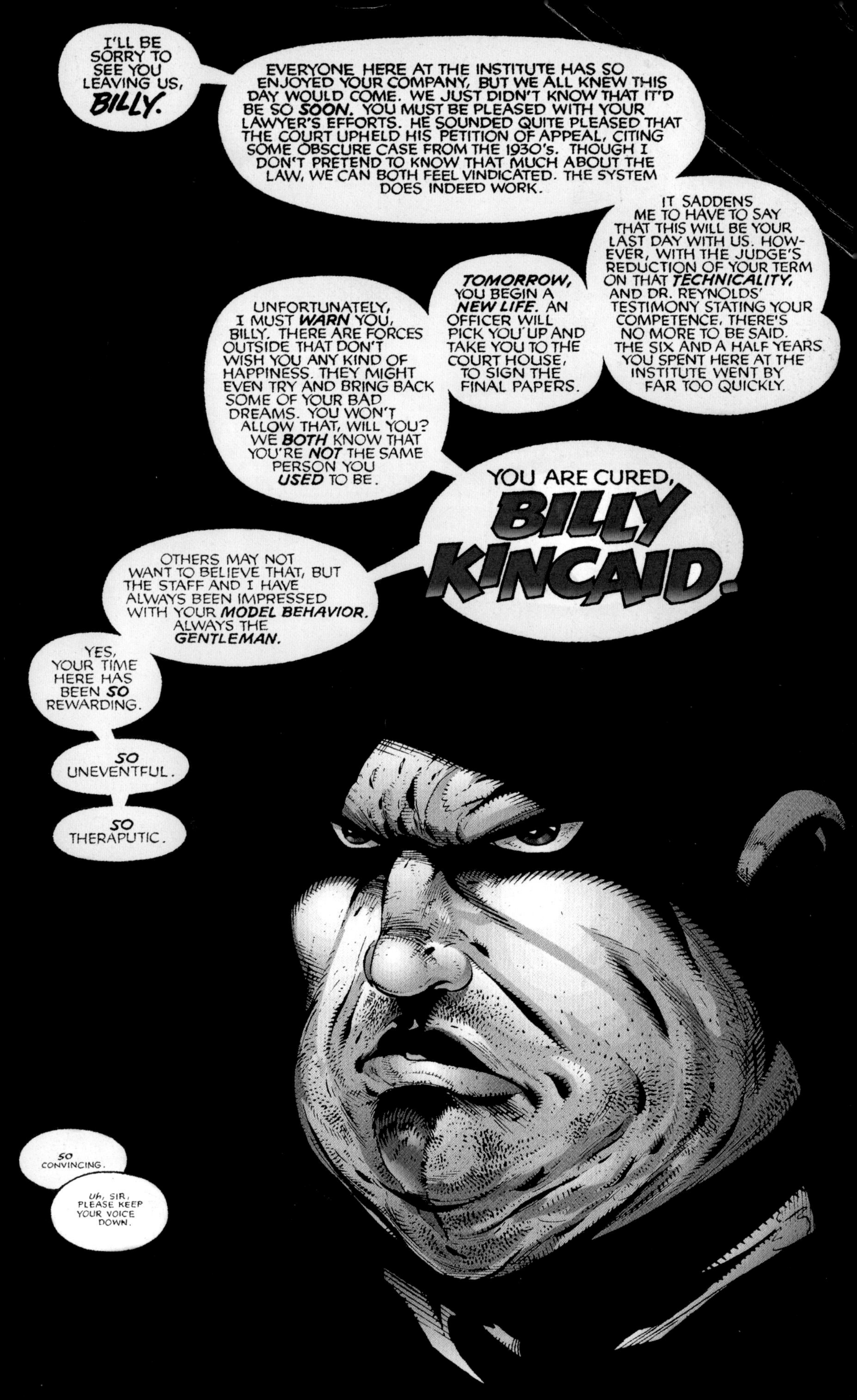
I'LL BE SORRY TO SEE YOU LEAVING US, BILLY.
EVERYONE HERE AT THE INSTITUTE HAS SO ENJOYED YOUR COMPANY, BUT WE ALL KNEW THIS DAY WOULD COME. WE JUST DIDN'T KNOW THAT IT'D BE SO SOON. YOU MUST BE PLEASED WITH YOUR LAWYER'S EFFORTS. HE SOUNDED QUITE PLEASED THAT THE COURT UPHELD HIS PETITION OF APPEAL, CITING SOME OBSCURE CASE FROM THE 1930's. THOUGH I DON'T PRETEND TO KNOW THAT MUCH ABOUT THE LAW, WE CAN BOTH FEEL VINDICATED. THE SYSTEM DOES INDEED WORK.
IT SADDENS ME TO HAVE TO SAY THAT THIS WILL BE YOUR LAST DAY WITH US. HOWEVER, WITH THE JUDGE'S REDUCTION OF YOUR TERM ON THAT TECHNICALITY, AND DR. REYNOLDS' TESTIMONY STATING YOUR COMPETENCE, THERE'S NO MORE TO BE SAID. THE SIX AND A HALF YEARS YOU SPENT HERE AT THE INSTITUTE WENT BY FAR TOO QUICKLY.
TOMORROW, YOU BEGIN A NEW LIFE. AN OFFICER WILL PICK YOU UP AND TAKE YOU TO THE COURT HOUSE, TO SIGN THE FINAL PAPERS.
UNFORTUNATELY, I MUST WARN YOU, BILLY. THERE ARE FORCES OUTSIDE THAT DON'T WISH YOU ANY KIND OF HAPPINESS. THEY MIGHT EVEN TRY AND BRING BACK SOME OF YOUR BAD DREAMS. YOU WON'T ALLOW THAT, WILL YOU? WE BOTH KNOW THAT YOU'RE NOT THE SAME PERSON YOU USED TO BE.
YOU ARE CURED, BILLY KINCAID.
OTHERS MAY NOT WANT TO BELIEVE THAT, BUT THE STAFF AND I HAVE ALWAYS BEEN IMPRESSED WITH YOUR MODEL BEHAVIOR. ALWAYS THE GENTLEMAN.
YES, YOUR TIME HERE HAS BEEN SO REWARDING.
SO UNEVENTFUL.
SO THERAPUTIC.
SO CONVINCING.
Uh, SIR, PLEASE KEEP YOUR VOICE DOWN.

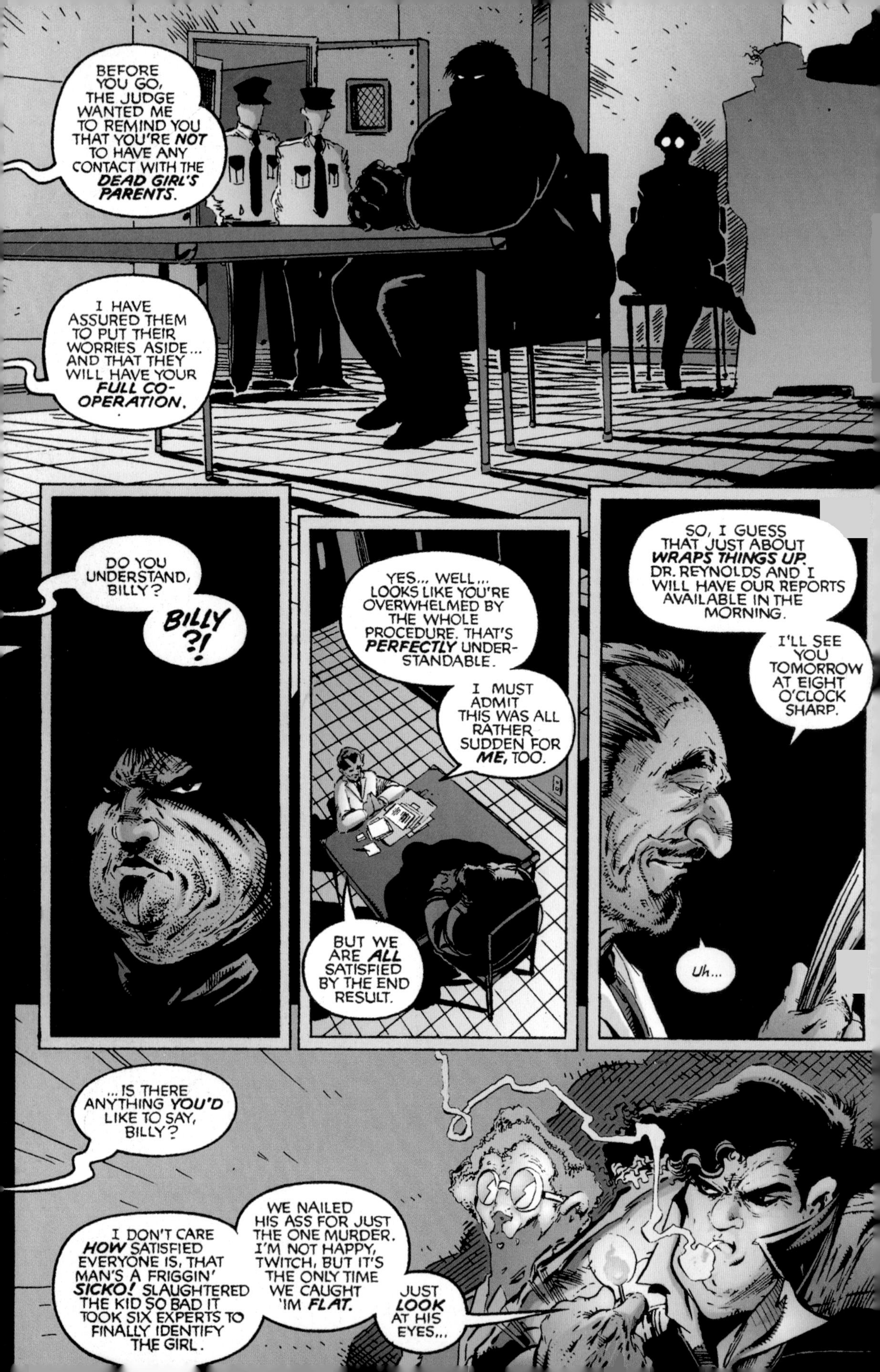
BEFORE YOU GO, THE JUDGE WANTED ME TO REMIND YOU THAT YOU'RE NOT TO HAVE ANY CONTACT WITH THE DEAD GIRL'S PARENTS.
I HAVE ASSURED THEM TO PUT THEIR WORRIES ASIDE... AND THAT THEY WILL HAVE YOUR FULL CO-OPERATION.
DO YOU UNDERSTAND, BILLY?
BILLY ?!
YES.., WELL... LOOKS LIKE YOU'RE OVERWHELMED BY THE WHOLE PROCEDURE. THAT'S PERFECTLY UNDER-STANDABLE.
I MUST ADMIT THIS WAS ALL RATHER SUDDEN FOR ME, TOO.
BUT WE ARE ALL SATISFIED BY THE END RESULT.
SO, I GUESS THAT JUST ABOUT WRAPS THINGS UP. DR. REYNOLDS AND I WILL HAVE OUR REPORTS AVAILABLE IN THE MORNING.
I'LL SEE YOU TOMORROW AT EIGHT O'CLOCK SHARP.
Uh...
...IS THERE ANYTHING YOU'D LIKE TO SAY, BILLY?
I DON'T CARE HOW SATISFIED EVERYONE IS, THAT MAN'S A FRIGGIN' SICKO! SLAUGHTERED THE KID SO BAD IT TOOK SIX EXPERTS TO FINALLY IDENTIFY THE GIRL.
WE NAILED HIS ASS FOR JUST THE ONE MURDER. I'M NOT HAPPY, TWITCH, BUT IT'S THE ONLY TIME WE CAUGHT 'IM FLAT.
JUST LOOK AT HIS EYES...

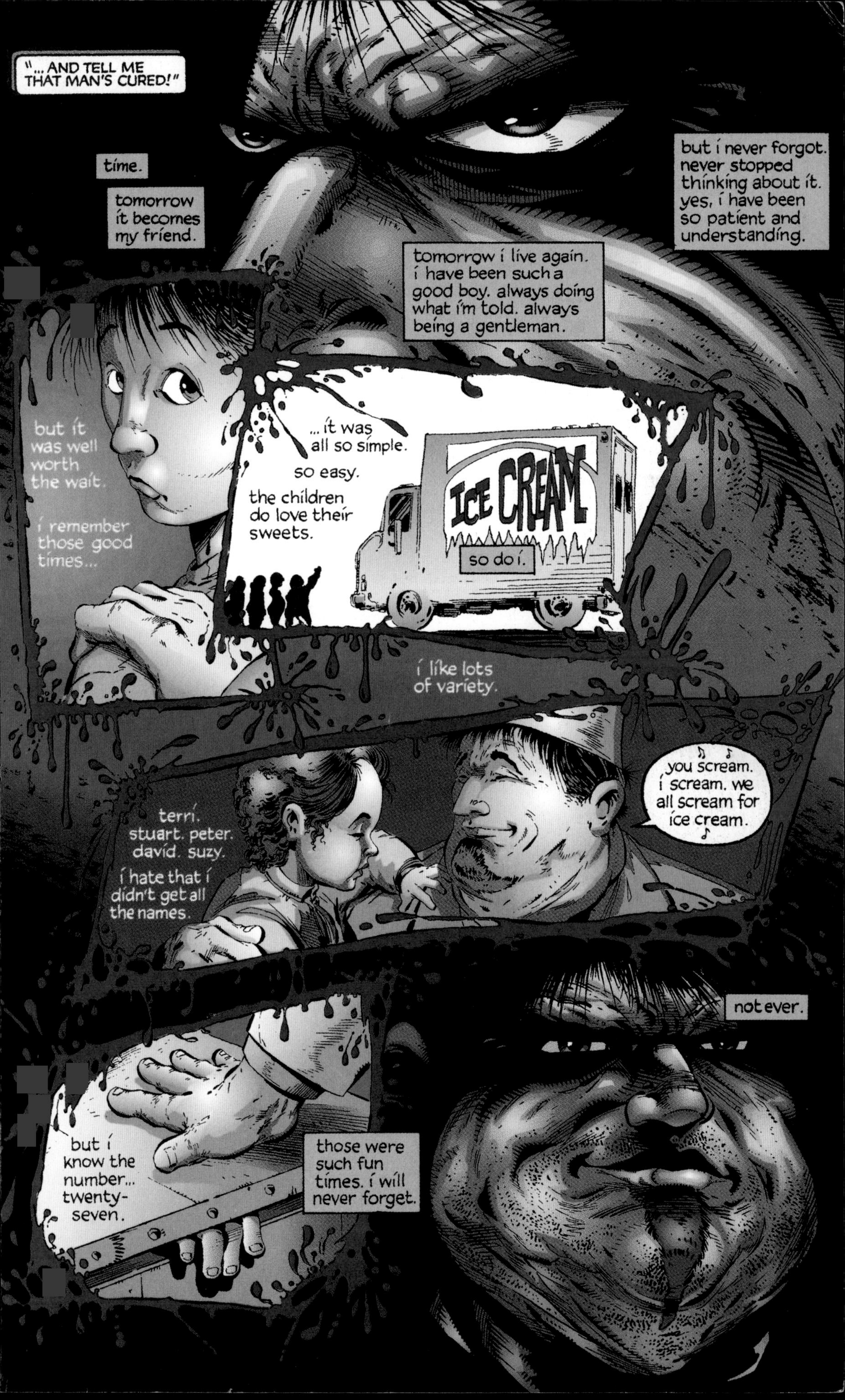
"... AND TELL ME THAT MAN'S CURED!"
time.
tomorrow it becomes my friend.
tomorrow i live again. i have been such a good boy. always doing what i'm told. always being a gentleman.
but i never forgot. never stopped thinking about it. yes, i have been so patient and understanding.
but it was well worth the wait.
i remember those good times...
... it was all so simple.
so easy.
the children do love their sweets.
ICE CREAM
so do i.
i like lots of variety.
terri. stuart. peter. david. suzy.
i hate that i didn't get all the names.
you scream. i scream. we all scream for ice cream.
but i know the number... twenty-seven.
those were such fun times. i will never forget.
not ever.

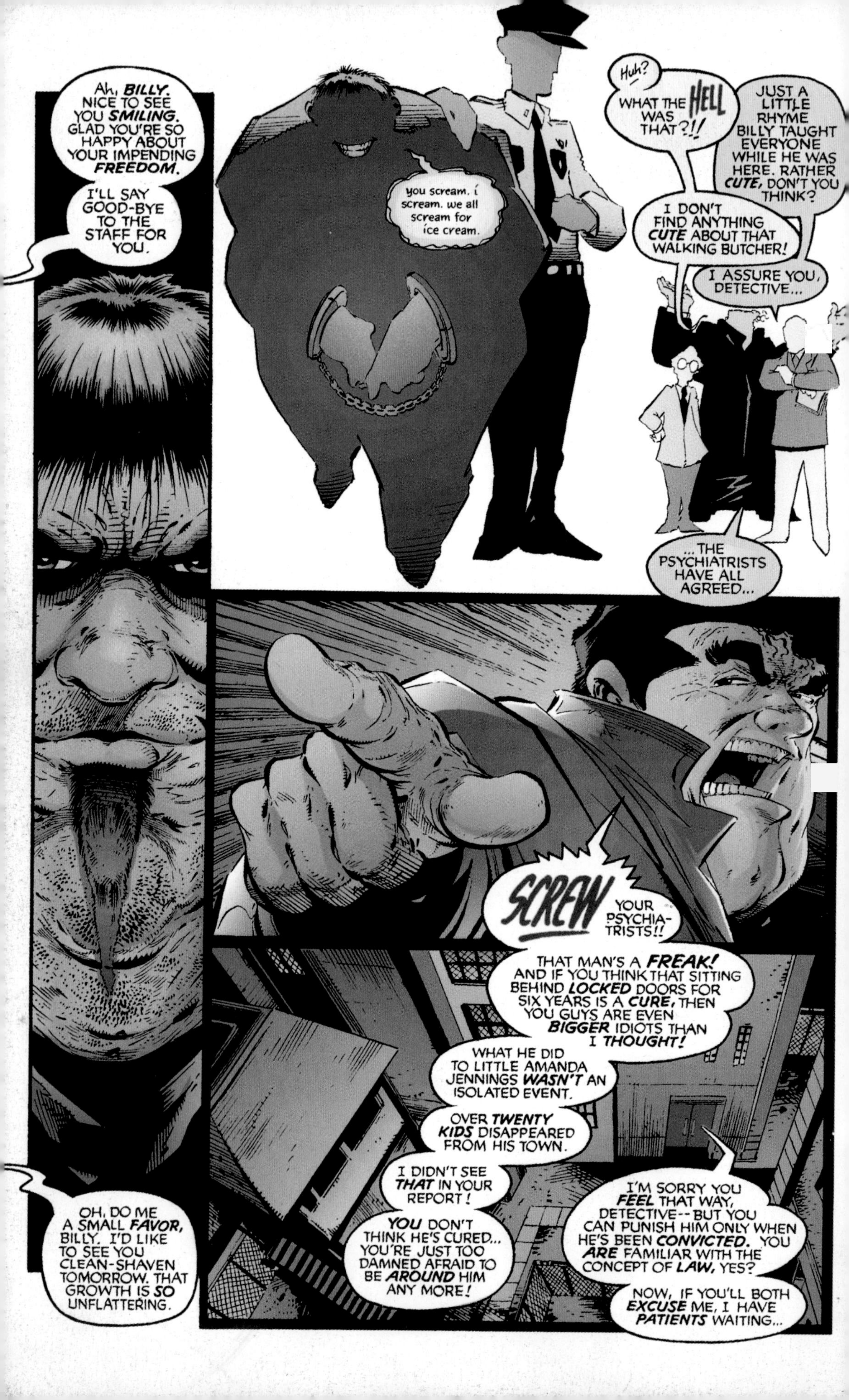
Ah, BILLY. NICE TO SEE YOU SMILING. GLAD YOU'RE SO HAPPY ABOUT YOUR IMPENDING FREEDOM.
I'LL SAY GOOD-BYE TO THE STAFF FOR YOU.
you scream. i scream. we all scream for ice cream.
Huh?
WHAT THE HELL WAS THAT?!!
JUST A LITTLE RHYME BILLY TAUGHT EVERYONE WHILE HE WAS HERE. RATHER CUTE, DON'T YOU THINK?
I DON'T FIND ANYTHING CUTE ABOUT THAT WALKING BUTCHER!
I ASSURE YOU, DETECTIVE...
...THE PSYCHIATRISTS HAVE ALL AGREED...
SCREW YOUR PSYCHIATRISTS!!
THAT MAN'S A FREAK! AND IF YOU THINK THAT SITTING BEHIND LOCKED DOORS FOR SIX YEARS IS A CURE, THEN YOU GUYS ARE EVEN BIGGER IDIOTS THAN I THOUGHT!
WHAT HE DID TO LITTLE AMANDA JENNINGS WASN'T AN ISOLATED EVENT.
OVER TWENTY KIDS DISAPPEARED FROM HIS TOWN.
I DIDN'T SEE THAT IN YOUR REPORT!
YOU DON'T THINK HE'S CURED... YOU'RE JUST TOO DAMNED AFRAID TO BE AROUND HIM ANY MORE!
I'M SORRY YOU FEEL THAT WAY, DETECTIVE-- BUT YOU CAN PUNISH HIM ONLY WHEN HE'S BEEN CONVICTED. YOU ARE FAMILIAR WITH THE CONCEPT OF LAW, YES?
NOW, IF YOU'LL BOTH EXCUSE ME, I HAVE PATIENTS WAITING...
OH, DO ME A SMALL FAVOR, BILLY. I'D LIKE TO SEE YOU CLEAN-SHAVEN TOMORROW. THAT GROWTH IS SO UNFLATTERING.

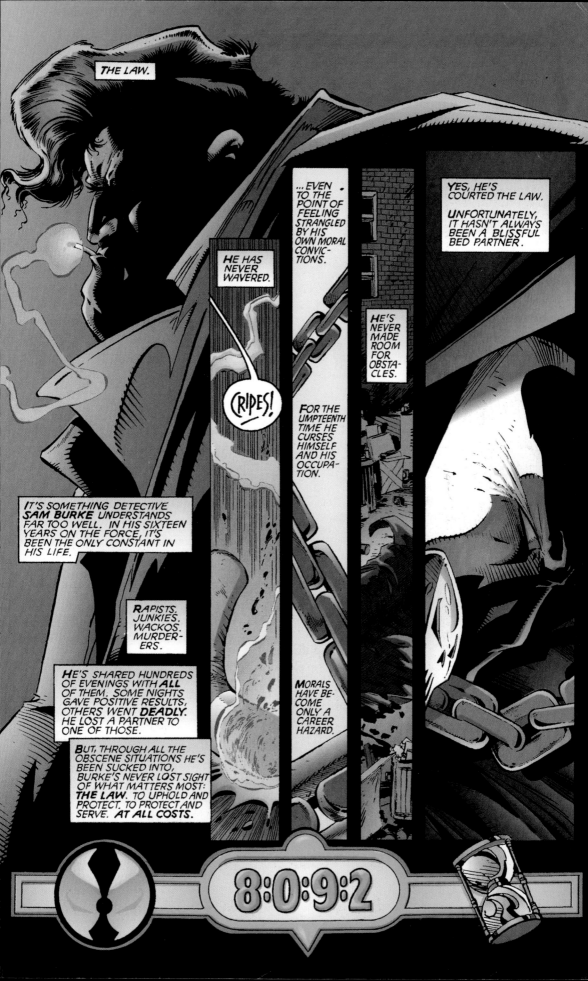

THE LAW.

...EVEN TO THE POINT OF FEELING STRANGLED BY HIS OWN MORAL CONVICTIONS.

HE HAS NEVER WAVERED.

CRIPES!

FOR THE UMPTEENTH TIME HE CURSES HIMSELF AND HIS OCCUPATION.

HE'S NEVER MADE ROOM FOR OBSTACLES.

YES, HE'S COURTED THE LAW.

UNFORTUNATELY, IT HASN'T ALWAYS BEEN A BLISSFUL BED PARTNER.

IT'S SOMETHING DETECTIVE *SAM BURKE* UNDERSTANDS FAR TOO WELL. IN HIS SIXTEEN YEARS ON THE FORCE, IT'S BEEN THE ONLY CONSTANT IN HIS LIFE.

RAPISTS. JUNKIES. WACKOS. MURDERERS.

HE'S SHARED HUNDREDS OF EVENINGS WITH *ALL* OF THEM. SOME NIGHTS GAVE POSITIVE RESULTS, OTHERS WENT *DEADLY.* HE LOST A PARTNER TO ONE OF THOSE.

MORALS HAVE BECOME ONLY A CAREER HAZARD.

BUT, THROUGH ALL THE OBSCENE SITUATIONS HE'S BEEN SUCKED INTO, BURKE'S NEVER LOST SIGHT OF WHAT MATTERS MOST: *THE LAW.* TO UPHOLD AND PROTECT. TO PROTECT AND SERVE. *AT ALL COSTS.*

8:0:9:2

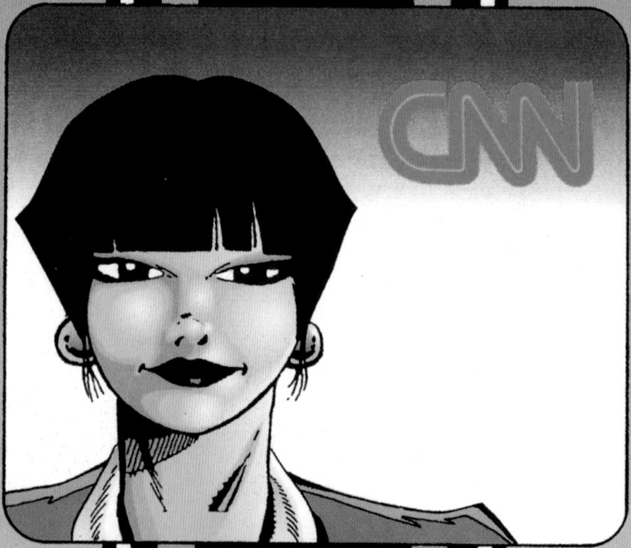
CNN

AND IN NEW YORK, JEFF PITMAN, ATTORNEY FOR CONVICTED CHILD KILLER BILL KINCAID, WAS FINALLY SUCCESSFUL IN HIS ATTEMPTS TO MITIGATE KINCAID'S SENTENCE. THE ORIGINAL TWENTY-TWO YEAR TERM WAS REDUCED TO TEN YEARS. THAT, COMBINED WITH TIME OFF FOR GOOD BEHAVIOR AND TIME SERVED, MAKE BILL KINCAID A FREE MAN TOMORROW.

IT WAS NEARLY EIGHT YEARS AGO THAT A JOGGER IN NEW YORK CITY FOUND AMANDA JENNINGS' BODY UNDER THE GEORGE WASHINGTON BRIDGE. THE EIGHT YEAR OLD GIRL WAS THE DAUGHTER OF FORMER SENATOR PAUL JENNINGS.

JENNINGS' HIGH-PROFILE EXTRA-MARITAL AFFAIR TARNISHED HIS RE-ELECTION BID A YEAR EARLIER. SOME SOURCES FELT THAT HIS MORE TRADITIONALLY-ORIENTED FORMER SUPPORTERS IN LAW ENFORCEMENT GAVE THE MATTER LESS ATTENTION THAN IT WARRANTED.

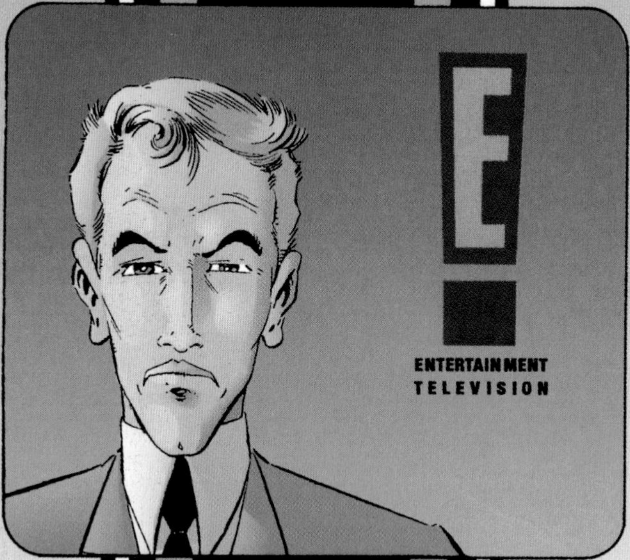
E!
ENTERTAINMENT TELEVISION

BELIEVE ME, IT WAS ***ONE*** TORRID LOVE AFFAIR. SENATOR JENNINGS AND ***MARLA FLEET*** WERE THE TALK OF THE TOWN DURING HIS RE-ELECTION CAMPAIGN. VOTERS DIDN'T WANT TO HEAR ABOUT BUDGETS OR TAXES. THEY WERE MORE INTERESTED IN THE ***STEAMY DETAILS*** OF HOW SENATOR JENNINGS SWEPT THE FORMER ***MISS UNIVERSE*** OFF HER FEET. MIX IN AN ***EXTREMELY*** VENGEFUL WIFE AND THE MEDIA HAD ITSELF A FEAST FOR ***MONTHS***.

THE STORY THAT MADE THE ROUNDS AT THE TIME-- THAT THE ***FORMER*** SENATOR'S ***RAGING*** HORMONES LED TO LESS OF AN INVESTIGATION OF HIS DAUGHTER'S DEATH-- IS TRULY DISTURBING. THESE WAGS IMPLY THAT WHILE JENNINGS WASN'T MUCH LOVED WHILE ***IN*** OFFICE, THE TAWDRY TRUTH BEHIND HIS DOWNFALL MAY HAVE LED TO INADEQUATE INFORMATION REACHING THE INTERESTED PARTIES.

AS A RESULT, BILLY KINCAID RECEIVED A TWENTY-TWO YEAR STRETCH INSTEAD OF THE LIFE SENTENCE WITHOUT PAROLE THAT THE PUBLIC SO DEARLY WANTED.

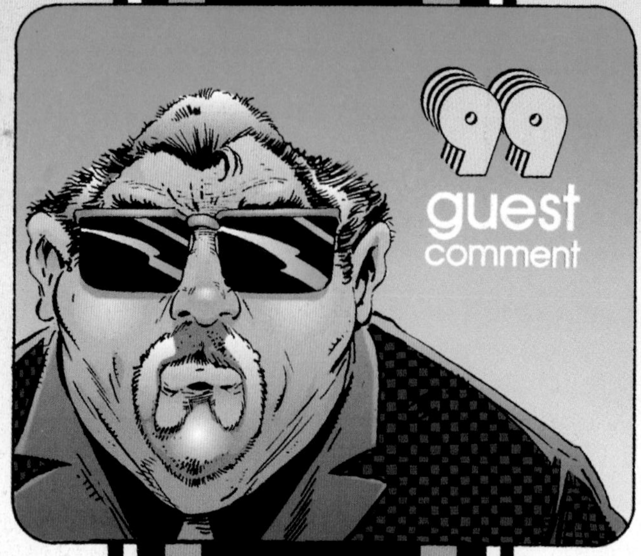
99
guest
comment

SURPRISE! SURPRISE!

KIDDIE KILLER KINCAID, FREE TO WALK THE STREETS OF THE BIG APPLE! WE'VE BEEN FAVORED WITH YET ***ANOTHER*** AWE-INSPIRING RULING AS THE COURTS ALLOW THIS CHILD-MURDERER HIS FREEDOM. AFTER PESTERING THE JUDICIAL SYSTEM WITH HIS ***WHINING*** AND ***APPEALS*** THESE PAST FIVE YEARS, KINCAID'S LAWYER FINALLY GOT WHAT HE WANTED-- ANOTHER ***PSYCHO*** READY TO ROAM CENTRAL PARK. OH JOY! OH RAPTURE! I FEEL SAFER ALREADY.

C'MON, FOLKS! I HATE REPEATING MYSELF BUT I'M NOT SURE ANYONE'S ***LISTENING.*** LOOKIT, THE WAY ***I*** SEE IT, KINCAID'S LAWYER DID US ***ALL*** A FAVOR. FOR THE PAST SIX YEARS, BILLY'S BEEN ***HIDDEN*** FROM US, BUT NOW WE HAVE AN OPEN ***OPPORTUNITY.*** I GUARANTEE THAT HE WAS A LOT ***SAFER*** ON THE ***INSIDE***.

MY ONLY WISH IS THAT SOMEONE BREAKS HIS BACK. ***HELLO!*** ARE YOU LISTENING, ***MR. SHADOWHAWK?***

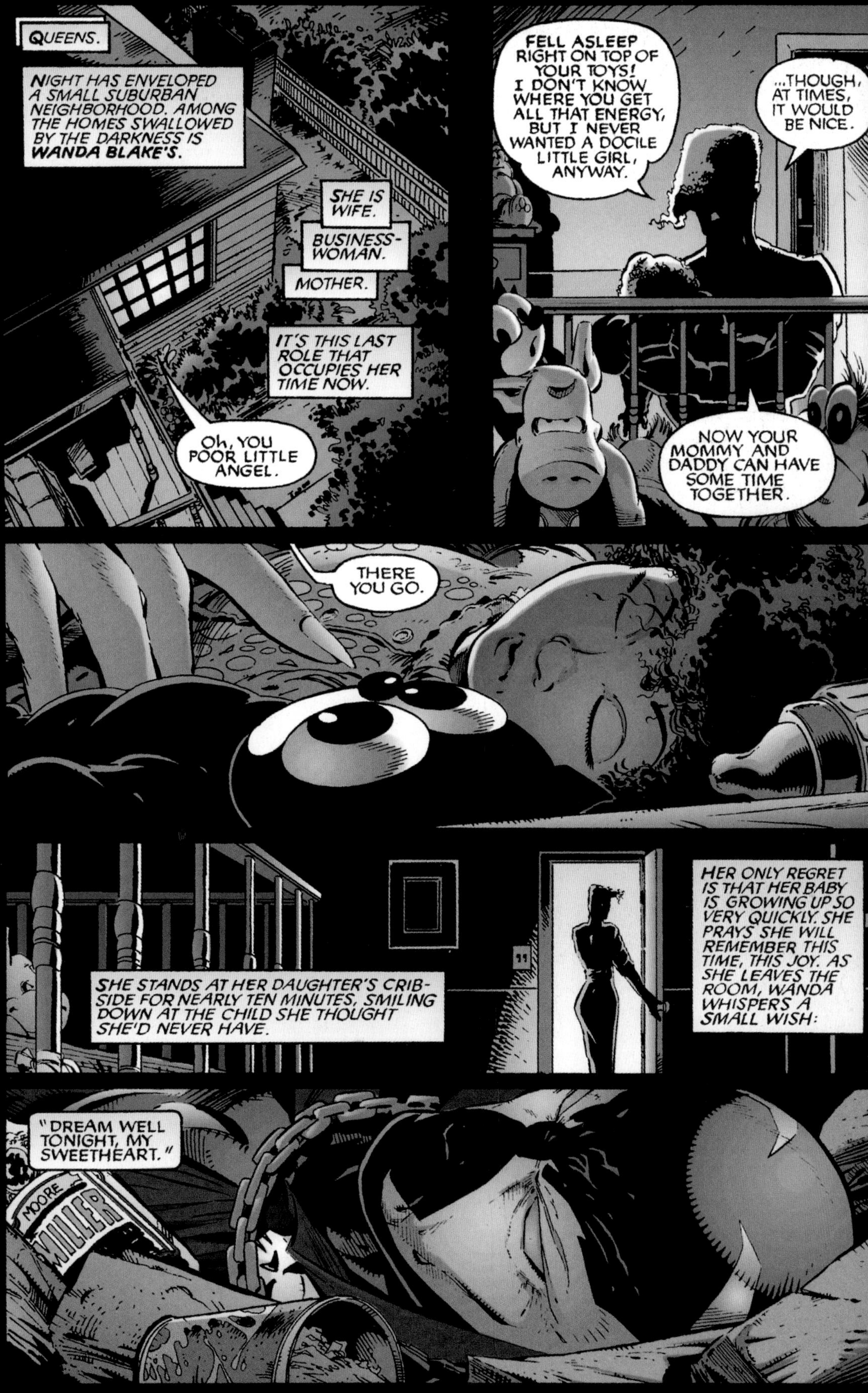
QUEENS.
NIGHT HAS ENVELOPED A SMALL SUBURBAN NEIGHBORHOOD. AMONG THE HOMES SWALLOWED BY THE DARKNESS IS WANDA BLAKE'S.
SHE IS WIFE.
BUSINESS-WOMAN.
MOTHER.
IT'S THIS LAST ROLE THAT OCCUPIES HER TIME NOW.
Oh, YOU POOR LITTLE ANGEL.
FELL ASLEEP RIGHT ON TOP OF YOUR TOYS! I DON'T KNOW WHERE YOU GET ALL THAT ENERGY, BUT I NEVER WANTED A DOCILE LITTLE GIRL, ANYWAY.
...THOUGH, AT TIMES, IT WOULD BE NICE.
NOW YOUR MOMMY AND DADDY CAN HAVE SOME TIME TOGETHER.
THERE YOU GO.
SHE STANDS AT HER DAUGHTER'S CRIB-SIDE FOR NEARLY TEN MINUTES, SMILING DOWN AT THE CHILD SHE THOUGHT SHE'D NEVER HAVE.
HER ONLY REGRET IS THAT HER BABY IS GROWING UP SO VERY QUICKLY. SHE PRAYS SHE WILL REMEMBER THIS TIME, THIS JOY. AS SHE LEAVES THE ROOM, WANDA WHISPERS A SMALL WISH:
"DREAM WELL TONIGHT, MY SWEETHEART."
MOORE
MILLER

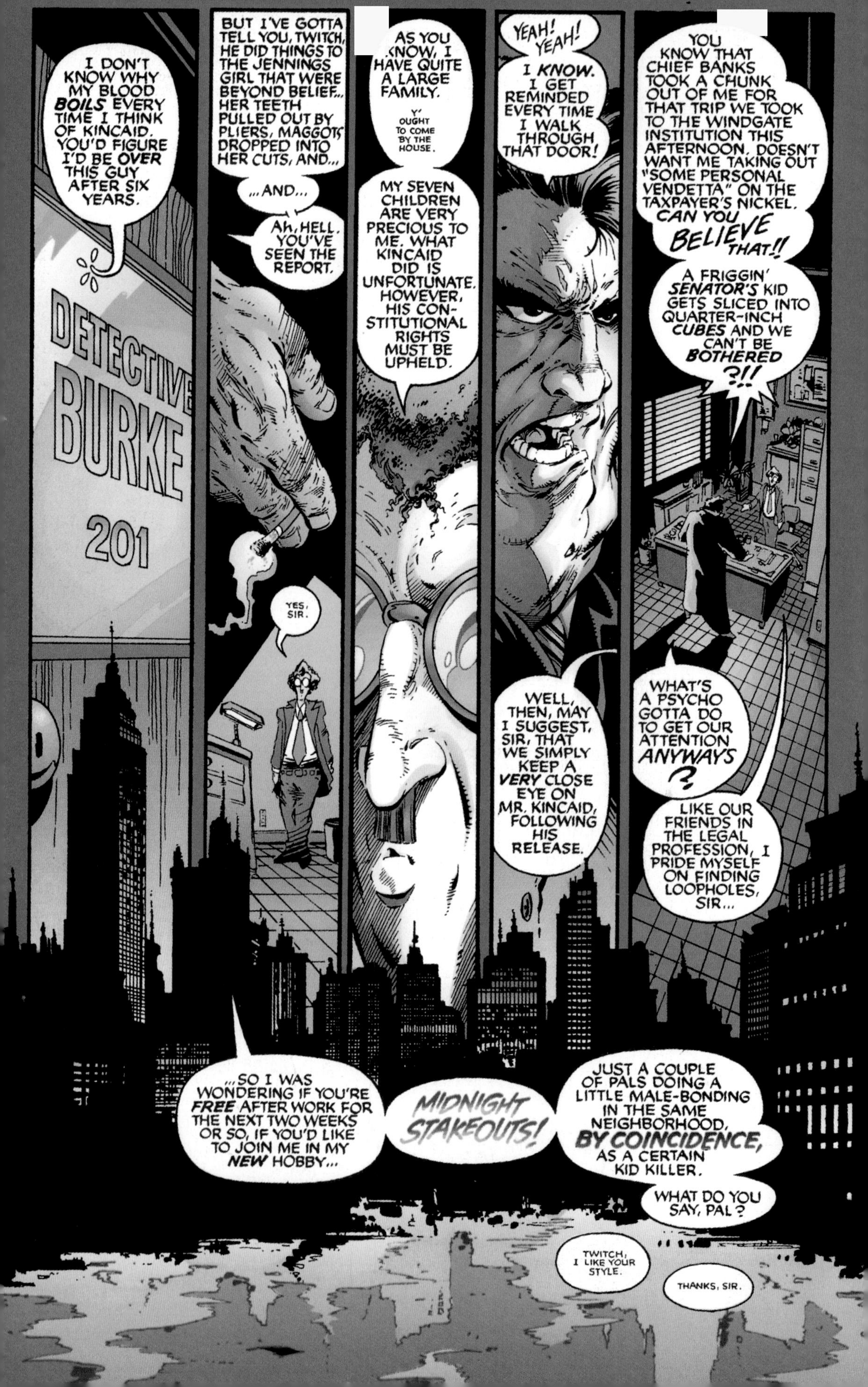
I DON'T KNOW WHY MY BLOOD BOILS EVERY TIME I THINK OF KINCAID. YOU'D FIGURE I'D BE OVER THIS GUY AFTER SIX YEARS.
DETECTIVE BURKE 201
BUT I'VE GOTTA TELL YOU, TWITCH, HE DID THINGS TO THE JENNINGS GIRL THAT WERE BEYOND BELIEF... HER TEETH PULLED OUT BY PLIERS, MAGGOTS DROPPED INTO HER CUTS, AND...
...AND...
Ah, HELL. YOU'VE SEEN THE REPORT.
YES, SIR.
AS YOU KNOW, I HAVE QUITE A LARGE FAMILY.
Y' OUGHT TO COME BY THE HOUSE.
MY SEVEN CHILDREN ARE VERY PRECIOUS TO ME. WHAT KINCAID DID IS UNFORTUNATE. HOWEVER, HIS CONSTITUTIONAL RIGHTS MUST BE UPHELD.
YEAH! YEAH!
I KNOW. I GET REMINDED EVERY TIME I WALK THROUGH THAT DOOR!
WELL, THEN, MAY I SUGGEST, SIR, THAT WE SIMPLY KEEP A VERY CLOSE EYE ON MR. KINCAID, FOLLOWING HIS RELEASE.
YOU KNOW THAT CHIEF BANKS TOOK A CHUNK OUT OF ME FOR THAT TRIP WE TOOK TO THE WINDGATE INSTITUTION THIS AFTERNOON. DOESN'T WANT ME TAKING OUT "SOME PERSONAL VENDETTA" ON THE TAXPAYER'S NICKEL. CAN YOU BELIEVE THAT!!
A FRIGGIN' SENATOR'S KID GETS SLICED INTO QUARTER-INCH CUBES AND WE CAN'T BE BOTHERED ?!!
WHAT'S A PSYCHO GOTTA DO TO GET OUR ATTENTION ANYWAYS ?
LIKE OUR FRIENDS IN THE LEGAL PROFESSION, I PRIDE MYSELF ON FINDING LOOPHOLES, SIR...
...SO I WAS WONDERING IF YOU'RE FREE AFTER WORK FOR THE NEXT TWO WEEKS OR SO, IF YOU'D LIKE TO JOIN ME IN MY NEW HOBBY...
MIDNIGHT STAKEOUTS!
JUST A COUPLE OF PALS DOING A LITTLE MALE-BONDING IN THE SAME NEIGHBORHOOD, BY COINCIDENCE, AS A CERTAIN KID KILLER.
WHAT DO YOU SAY, PAL?
TWITCH, I LIKE YOUR STYLE.
THANKS, SIR.

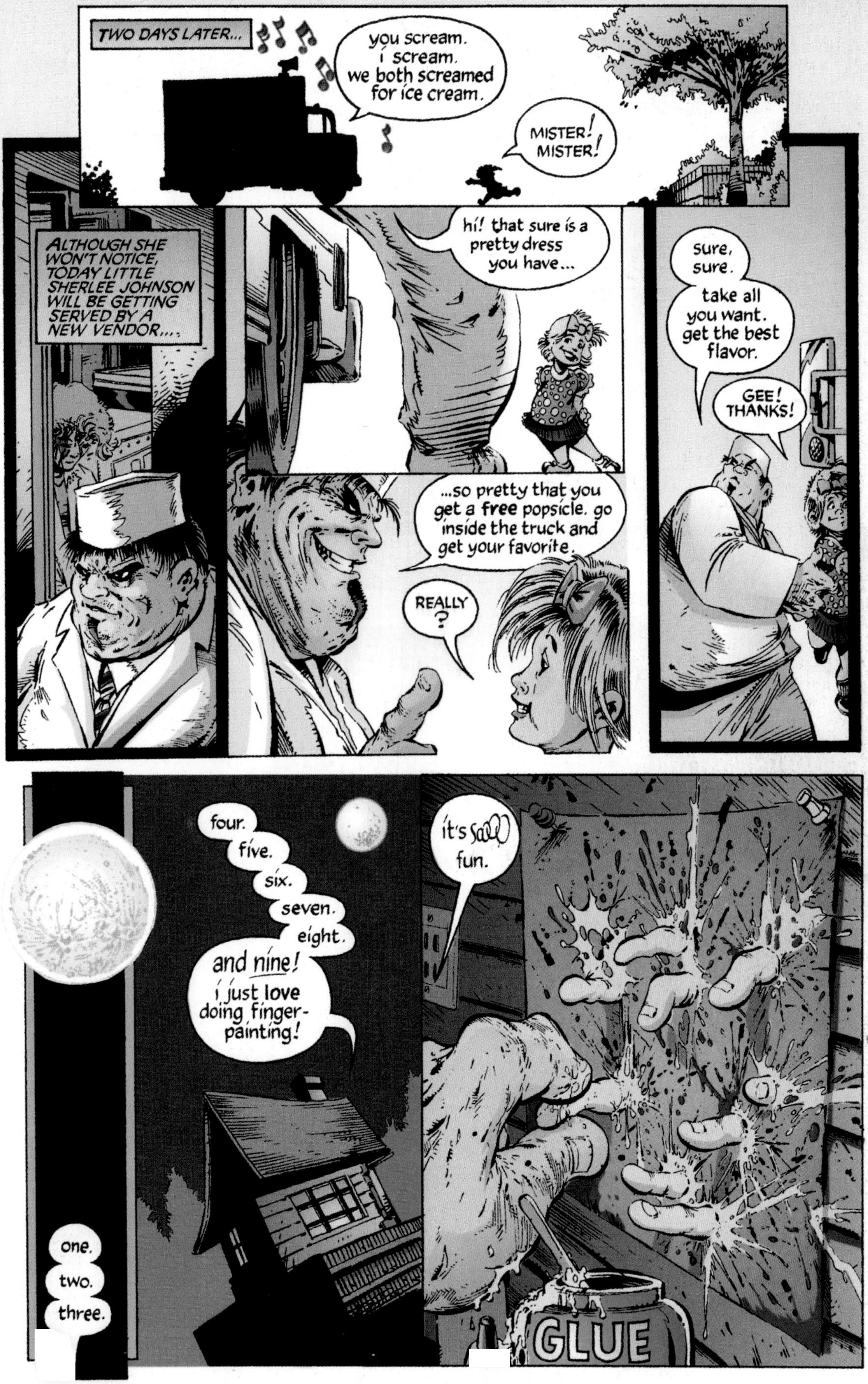
TWO DAYS LATER...
you scream. i scream. we both screamed for ice cream.
MISTER! MISTER!
ALTHOUGH SHE WON'T NOTICE, TODAY LITTLE SHERLEE JOHNSON WILL BE GETTING SERVED BY A NEW VENDOR...
hi! that sure is a pretty dress you have...
...so pretty that you get a free popsicle. go inside the truck and get your favorite.
REALLY?
sure, sure.
take all you want. get the best flavor.
GEE! THANKS!
one.
two.
three.
four.
five.
six.
seven.
eight.
and nine!
i just love doing finger-painting!
it's sooo fun.
GLUE

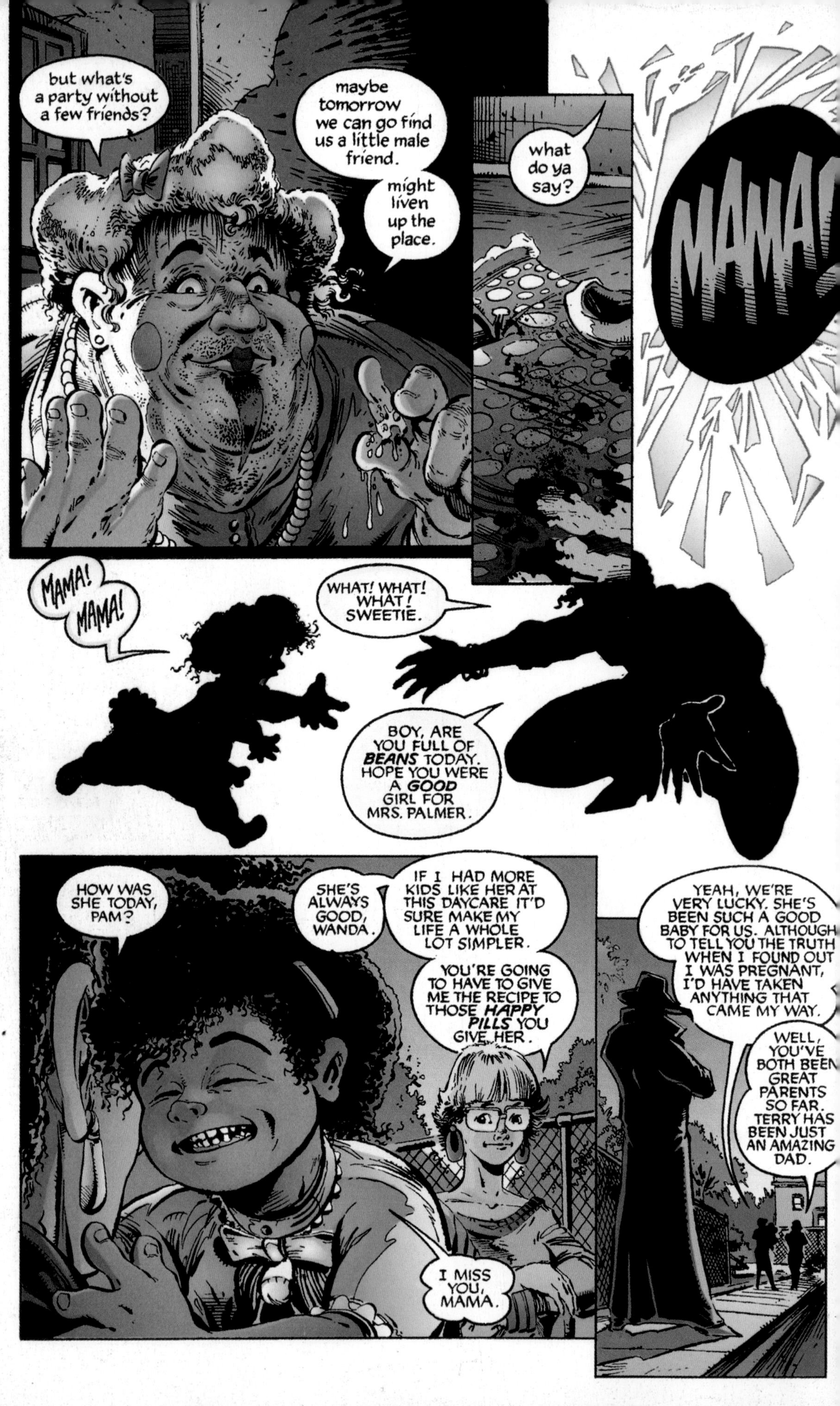
but what's a party without a few friends?
maybe tomorrow we can go find us a little male friend.
might liven up the place.
what do ya say?
MAMA!
MAMA! MAMA!
WHAT! WHAT! WHAT! SWEETIE.
BOY, ARE YOU FULL OF BEANS TODAY. HOPE YOU WERE A GOOD GIRL FOR MRS. PALMER.
HOW WAS SHE TODAY, PAM?
SHE'S ALWAYS GOOD, WANDA.
IF I HAD MORE KIDS LIKE HER AT THIS DAYCARE IT'D SURE MAKE MY LIFE A WHOLE LOT SIMPLER.
YOU'RE GOING TO HAVE TO GIVE ME THE RECIPE TO THOSE HAPPY PILLS YOU GIVE HER.
I MISS YOU, MAMA.
YEAH, WE'RE VERY LUCKY. SHE'S BEEN SUCH A GOOD BABY FOR US. ALTHOUGH TO TELL YOU THE TRUTH WHEN I FOUND OUT I WAS PREGNANT, I'D HAVE TAKEN ANYTHING THAT CAME MY WAY.
WELL, YOU'VE BOTH BEEN GREAT PARENTS SO FAR. TERRY HAS BEEN JUST AN AMAZING DAD.

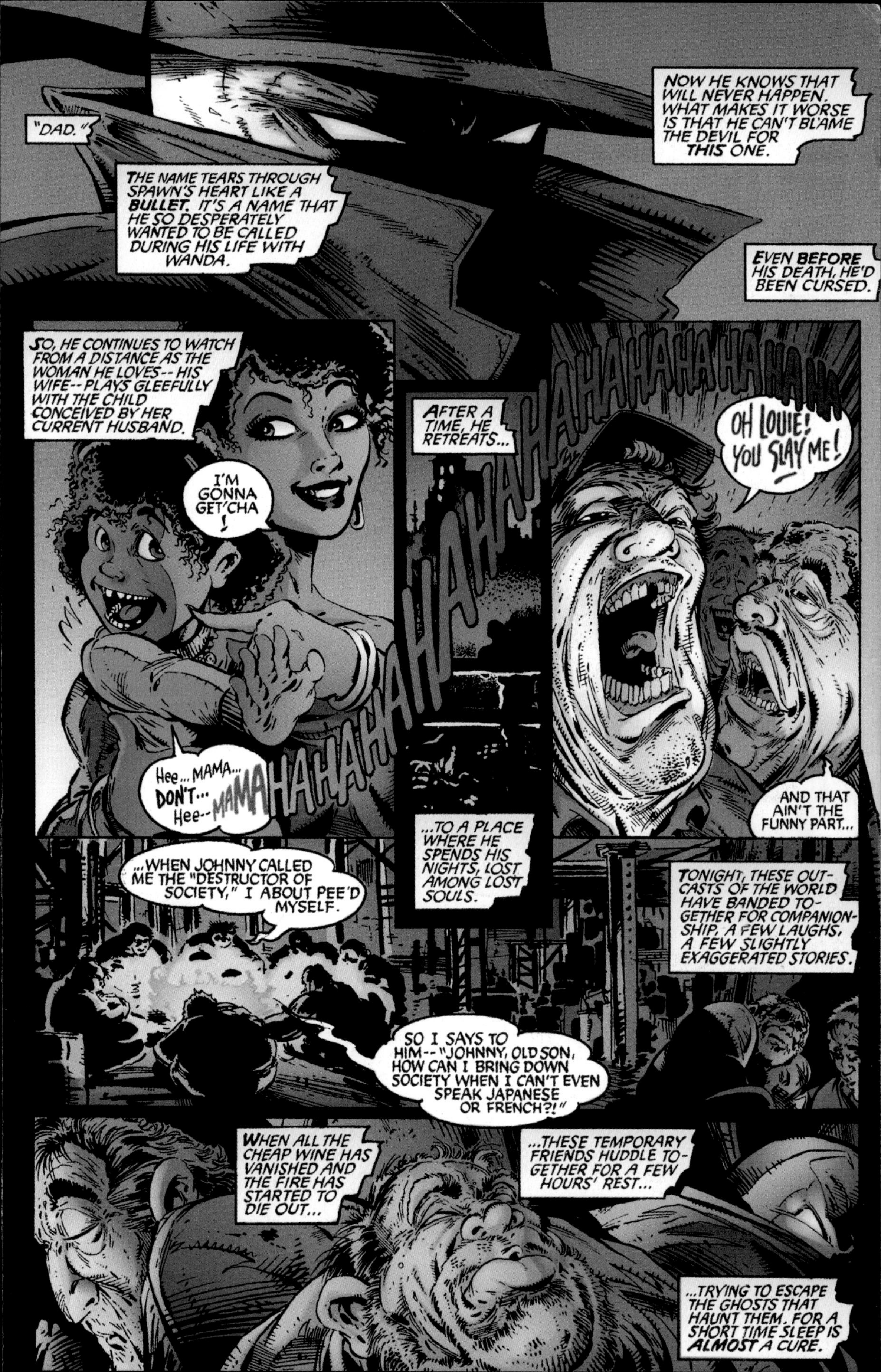
"DAD."
THE NAME TEARS THROUGH SPAWN'S HEART LIKE A BULLET. IT'S A NAME THAT HE SO DESPERATELY WANTED TO BE CALLED DURING HIS LIFE WITH WANDA.
NOW HE KNOWS THAT WILL NEVER HAPPEN. WHAT MAKES IT WORSE IS THAT HE CAN'T BLAME THE DEVIL FOR THIS ONE.
EVEN BEFORE HIS DEATH, HE'D BEEN CURSED.
SO, HE CONTINUES TO WATCH FROM A DISTANCE AS THE WOMAN HE LOVES-- HIS WIFE-- PLAYS GLEEFULLY WITH THE CHILD CONCEIVED BY HER CURRENT HUSBAND.
I'M GONNA GET'CHA!
Hee... MAMA... DON'T... Hee-- MAMA
AFTER A TIME, HE RETREATS...
HAHAHAHAHAHAHAHAHAHAHAHAHA
OH LOUIE! YOU SLAY ME!
AND THAT AIN'T THE FUNNY PART...
...TO A PLACE WHERE HE SPENDS HIS NIGHTS, LOST AMONG LOST SOULS.
...WHEN JOHNNY CALLED ME THE "DESTRUCTOR OF SOCIETY," I ABOUT PEE'D MYSELF.
TONIGHT, THESE OUTCASTS OF THE WORLD HAVE BANDED TOGETHER FOR COMPANIONSHIP, A FEW LAUGHS, A FEW SLIGHTLY EXAGGERATED STORIES.
SO I SAYS TO HIM-- "JOHNNY, OLD SON, HOW CAN I BRING DOWN SOCIETY WHEN I CAN'T EVEN SPEAK JAPANESE OR FRENCH?!"
WHEN ALL THE CHEAP WINE HAS VANISHED AND THE FIRE HAS STARTED TO DIE OUT...
...THESE TEMPORARY FRIENDS HUDDLE TOGETHER FOR A FEW HOURS' REST...
...TRYING TO ESCAPE THE GHOSTS THAT HAUNT THEM. FOR A SHORT TIME SLEEP IS ALMOST A CURE.

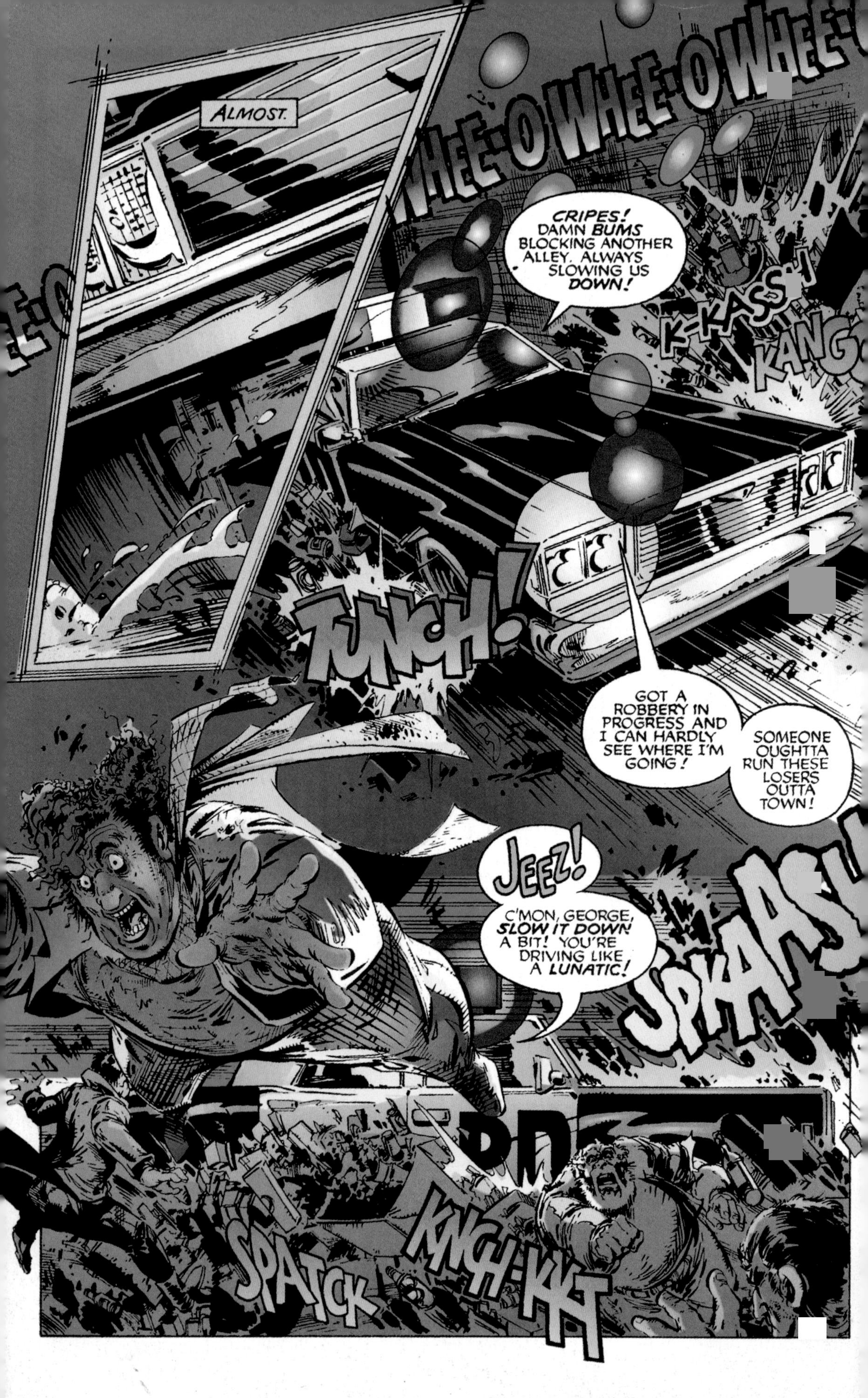
ALMOST.
WHEE-O WHEE-O WHEE-O WHEE-O
CRIPES! DAMN BUMS BLOCKING ANOTHER ALLEY. ALWAYS SLOWING US DOWN!
K-KASS-H
KANG
TUNCH!
GOT A ROBBERY IN PROGRESS AND I CAN HARDLY SEE WHERE I'M GOING!
SOMEONE OUGHTTA RUN THESE LOSERS OUTTA TOWN!
JEEZ!
C'MON, GEORGE, SLOW IT DOWN A BIT! YOU'RE DRIVING LIKE A LUNATIC!
SPKASH
SPATCK
KNCH-KKT

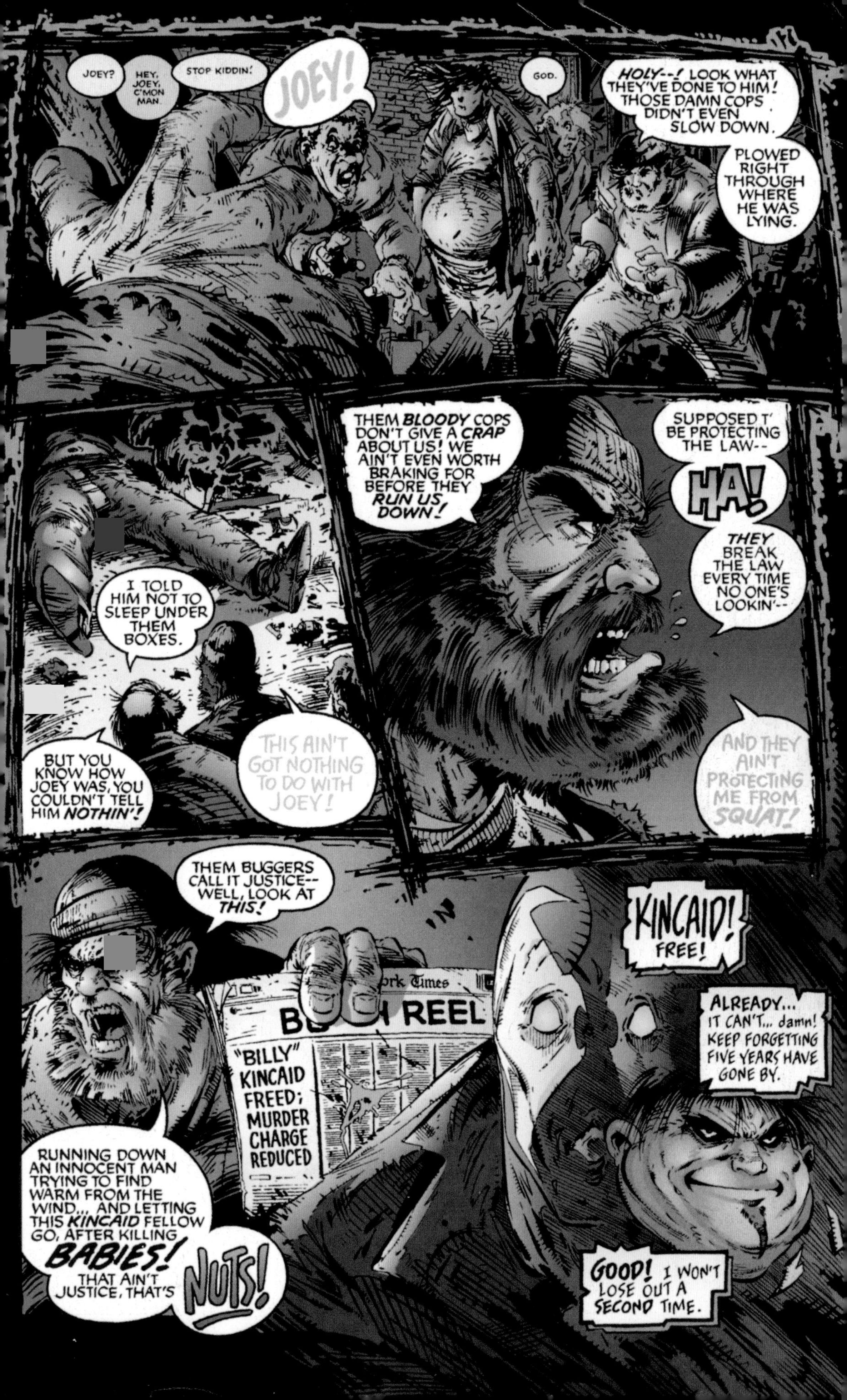

JOEY?
HEY, JOEY, C'MON MAN.
STOP KIDDIN'!
JOEY!
GOD.
HOLY--! LOOK WHAT THEY'VE DONE TO HIM! THOSE DAMN COPS DIDN'T EVEN SLOW DOWN.
PLOWED RIGHT THROUGH WHERE HE WAS LYING.
I TOLD HIM NOT TO SLEEP UNDER THEM BOXES.
BUT YOU KNOW HOW JOEY WAS, YOU COULDN'T TELL HIM NOTHIN'!
THIS AIN'T GOT NOTHING TO DO WITH JOEY!
THEM BLOODY COPS DON'T GIVE A CRAP ABOUT US! WE AIN'T EVEN WORTH BRAKING FOR BEFORE THEY RUN US DOWN!
SUPPOSED T' BE PROTECTING THE LAW--
HA!
THEY BREAK THE LAW EVERY TIME NO ONE'S LOOKIN'--
AND THEY AIN'T PROTECTING ME FROM SQUAT!
THEM BUGGERS CALL IT JUSTICE-- WELL, LOOK AT THIS!
"BILLY" KINCAID FREED; MURDER CHARGE REDUCED
RUNNING DOWN AN INNOCENT MAN TRYING TO FIND WARM FROM THE WIND... AND LETTING THIS KINCAID FELLOW GO, AFTER KILLING BABIES!
THAT AIN'T JUSTICE, THAT'S NUTS!
KINCAID! FREE!
ALREADY... IT CAN'T... damn! KEEP FORGETTING FIVE YEARS HAVE GONE BY.
GOOD! I WON'T LOSE OUT A SECOND TIME.

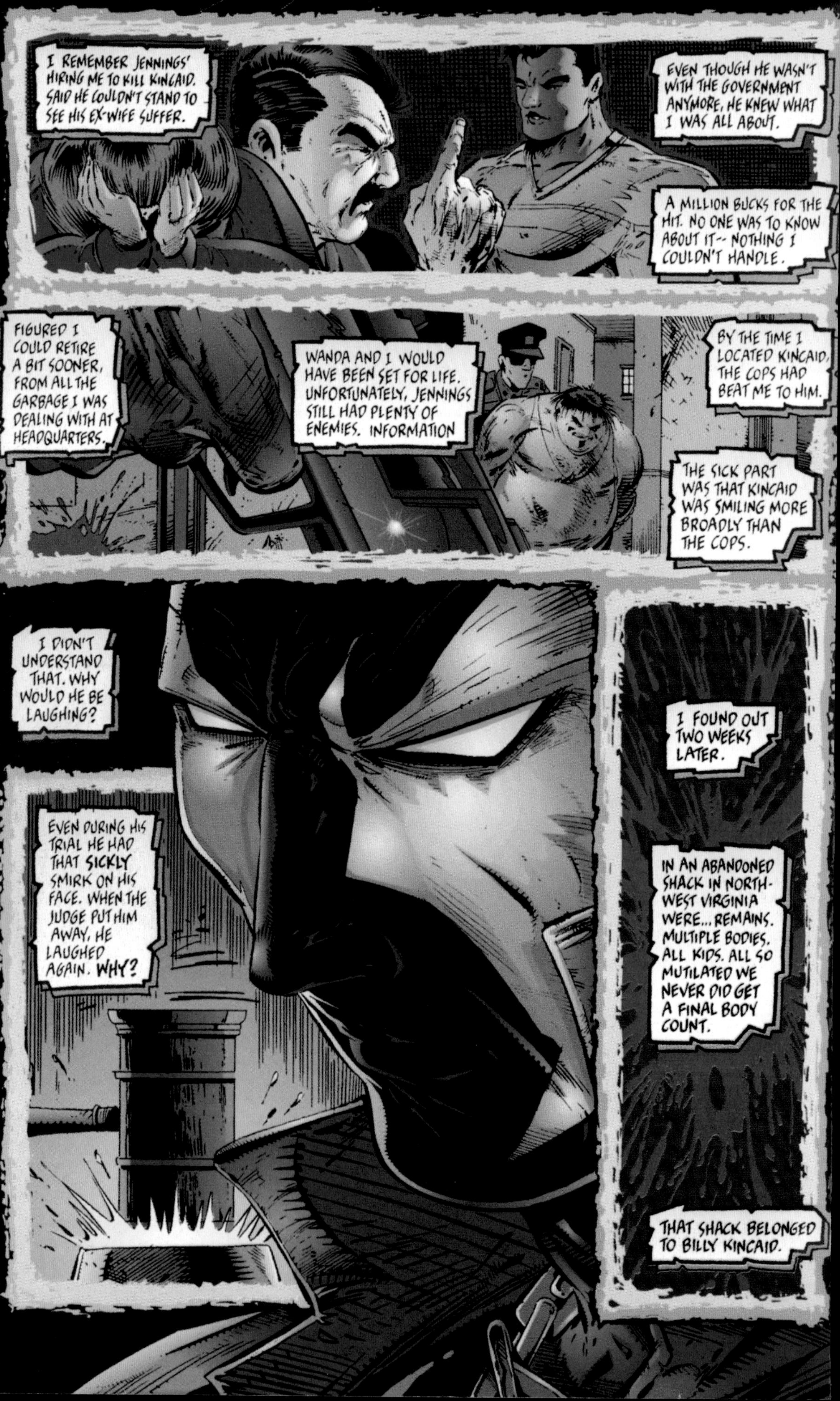
I REMEMBER JENNINGS' HIRING ME TO KILL KINCAID. SAID HE COULDN'T STAND TO SEE HIS EX-WIFE SUFFER.
EVEN THOUGH HE WASN'T WITH THE GOVERNMENT ANYMORE, HE KNEW WHAT I WAS ALL ABOUT.
A MILLION BUCKS FOR THE HIT. NO ONE WAS TO KNOW ABOUT IT-- NOTHING I COULDN'T HANDLE.
FIGURED I COULD RETIRE A BIT SOONER, FROM ALL THE GARBAGE I WAS DEALING WITH AT HEADQUARTERS.
WANDA AND I WOULD HAVE BEEN SET FOR LIFE. UNFORTUNATELY, JENNINGS STILL HAD PLENTY OF ENEMIES. INFORMATION
BY THE TIME I LOCATED KINCAID, THE COPS HAD BEAT ME TO HIM.
THE SICK PART WAS THAT KINCAID WAS SMILING MORE BROADLY THAN THE COPS.
I DIDN'T UNDERSTAND THAT. WHY WOULD HE BE LAUGHING?
EVEN DURING HIS TRIAL HE HAD THAT SICKLY SMIRK ON HIS FACE. WHEN THE JUDGE PUT HIM AWAY, HE LAUGHED AGAIN. WHY?
I FOUND OUT TWO WEEKS LATER.
IN AN ABANDONED SHACK IN NORTH-WEST VIRGINIA WERE... REMAINS. MULTIPLE BODIES. ALL KIDS. ALL SO MUTILATED WE NEVER DID GET A FINAL BODY COUNT.
THAT SHACK BELONGED TO BILLY KINCAID.

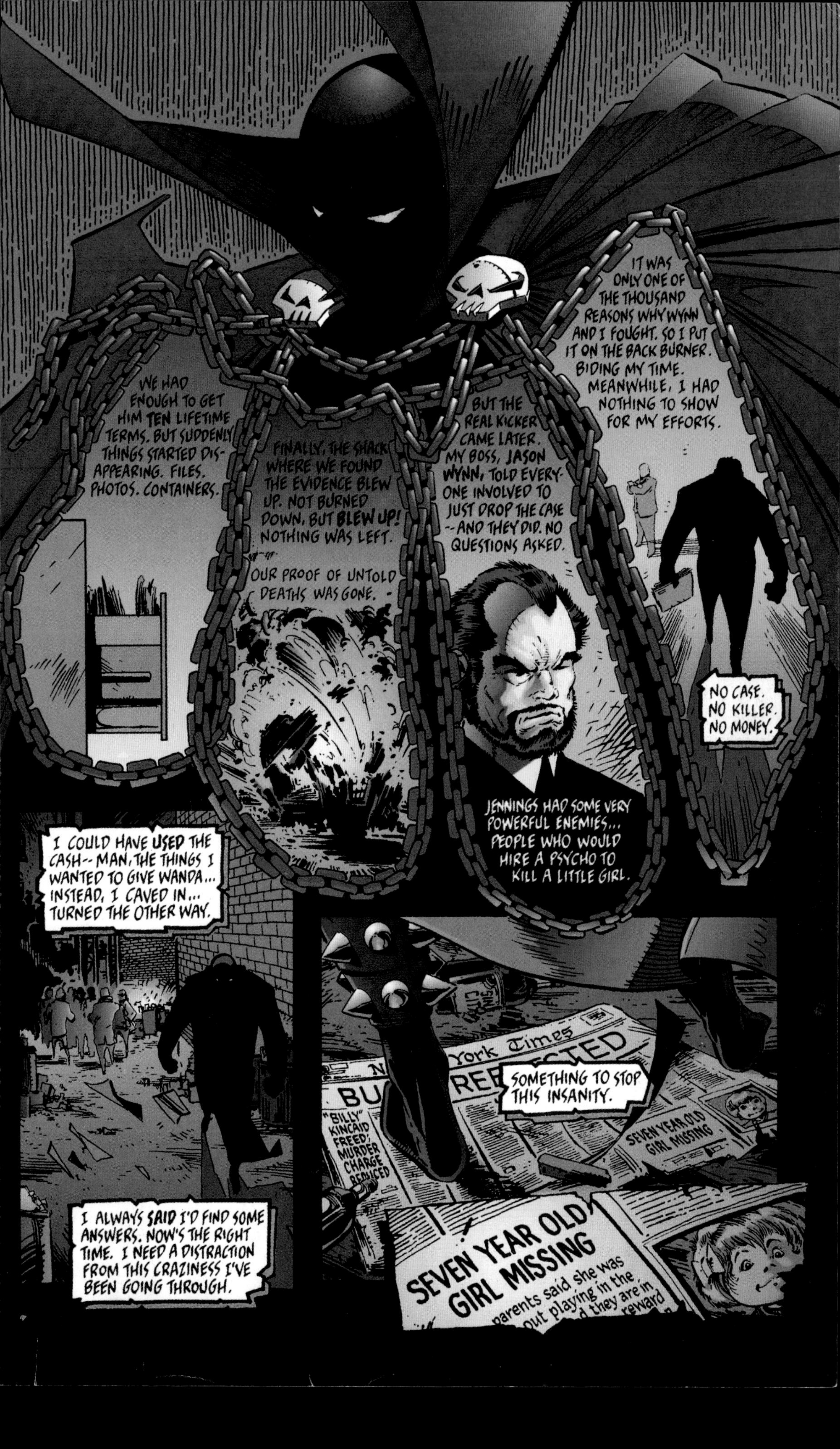

WE HAD ENOUGH TO GET HIM TEN LIFETIME TERMS. BUT SUDDENLY THINGS STARTED DIS-APPEARING. FILES. PHOTOS. CONTAINERS.
FINALLY, THE SHACK WHERE WE FOUND THE EVIDENCE BLEW UP. NOT BURNED DOWN, BUT BLEW UP! NOTHING WAS LEFT.
OUR PROOF OF UNTOLD DEATHS WAS GONE.
BUT THE REAL KICKER CAME LATER. MY BOSS, JASON WYNN, TOLD EVERY-ONE INVOLVED TO JUST DROP THE CASE --AND THEY DID. NO QUESTIONS ASKED.
JENNINGS HAD SOME VERY POWERFUL ENEMIES... PEOPLE WHO WOULD HIRE A PSYCHO TO KILL A LITTLE GIRL.
IT WAS ONLY ONE OF THE THOUSAND REASONS WHY WYNN AND I FOUGHT. SO I PUT IT ON THE BACK BURNER. BIDING MY TIME. MEANWHILE, I HAD NOTHING TO SHOW FOR MY EFFORTS.
NO CASE. NO KILLER. NO MONEY.
I COULD HAVE USED THE CASH-- MAN, THE THINGS I WANTED TO GIVE WANDA... INSTEAD, I CAVED IN... TURNED THE OTHER WAY.
I ALWAYS SAID I'D FIND SOME ANSWERS. NOW'S THE RIGHT TIME. I NEED A DISTRACTION FROM THIS CRAZINESS I'VE BEEN GOING THROUGH.
SOMETHING TO STOP THIS INSANITY.
York Times
"BILLY" KINCAID FREED; MURDER CHARGE REDUCED
SEVEN YEAR OLD GIRL MISSING
SEVEN YEAR OLD GIRL MISSING
parents said she was out playing in the

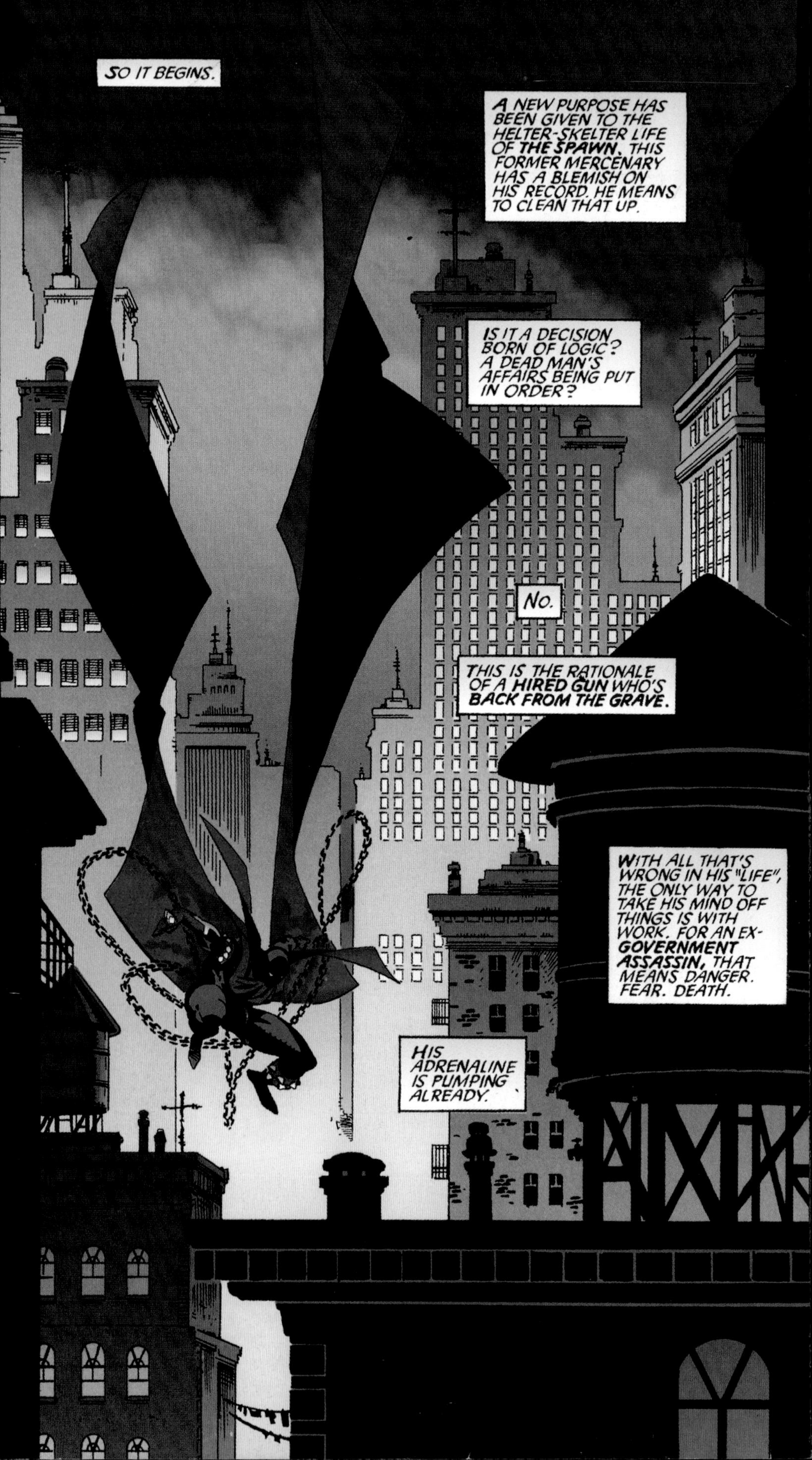
SO IT BEGINS.
A NEW PURPOSE HAS BEEN GIVEN TO THE HELTER-SKELTER LIFE OF THE SPAWN. THIS FORMER MERCENARY HAS A BLEMISH ON HIS RECORD. HE MEANS TO CLEAN THAT UP.
IS IT A DECISION BORN OF LOGIC? A DEAD MAN'S AFFAIRS BEING PUT IN ORDER?
No.
THIS IS THE RATIONALE OF A HIRED GUN WHO'S BACK FROM THE GRAVE.
WITH ALL THAT'S WRONG IN HIS "LIFE", THE ONLY WAY TO TAKE HIS MIND OFF THINGS IS WITH WORK. FOR AN EX-GOVERNMENT ASSASSIN, THAT MEANS DANGER. FEAR. DEATH.
HIS ADRENALINE IS PUMPING ALREADY.

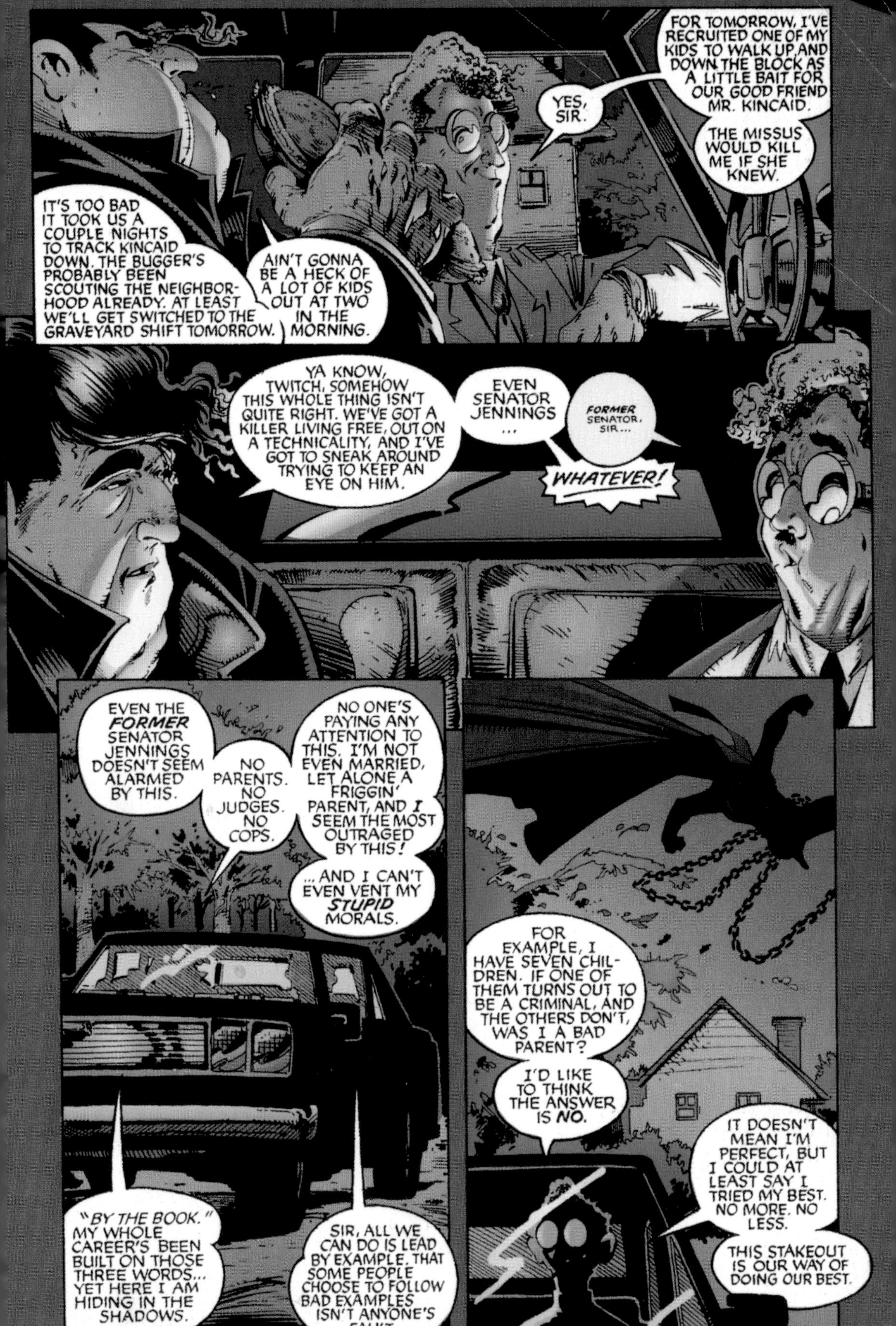

FOR TOMORROW, I'VE RECRUITED ONE OF MY KIDS TO WALK UP AND DOWN THE BLOCK AS A LITTLE BAIT FOR OUR GOOD FRIEND MR. KINCAID.
YES, SIR.
THE MISSUS WOULD KILL ME IF SHE KNEW.
IT'S TOO BAD IT TOOK US A COUPLE NIGHTS TO TRACK KINCAID DOWN. THE BUGGER'S PROBABLY BEEN SCOUTING THE NEIGHBORHOOD ALREADY. AT LEAST WE'LL GET SWITCHED TO THE GRAVEYARD SHIFT TOMORROW.
AIN'T GONNA BE A HECK OF A LOT OF KIDS OUT AT TWO IN THE MORNING.
YA KNOW, TWITCH, SOMEHOW THIS WHOLE THING ISN'T QUITE RIGHT. WE'VE GOT A KILLER LIVING FREE, OUT ON A TECHNICALITY, AND I'VE GOT TO SNEAK AROUND TRYING TO KEEP AN EYE ON HIM.
EVEN SENATOR JENNINGS ...
FORMER SENATOR, SIR...
WHATEVER!
EVEN THE FORMER SENATOR JENNINGS DOESN'T SEEM ALARMED BY THIS.
NO PARENTS. NO JUDGES. NO COPS.
NO ONE'S PAYING ANY ATTENTION TO THIS. I'M NOT EVEN MARRIED, LET ALONE A FRIGGIN' PARENT, AND I SEEM THE MOST OUTRAGED BY THIS!
...AND I CAN'T EVEN VENT MY STUPID MORALS.
"BY THE BOOK." MY WHOLE CAREER'S BEEN BUILT ON THOSE THREE WORDS... YET HERE I AM HIDING IN THE SHADOWS.
SIR, ALL WE CAN DO IS LEAD BY EXAMPLE. THAT SOME PEOPLE CHOOSE TO FOLLOW BAD EXAMPLES ISN'T ANYONE'S FAULT.
FOR EXAMPLE, I HAVE SEVEN CHILDREN. IF ONE OF THEM TURNS OUT TO BE A CRIMINAL, AND THE OTHERS DON'T, WAS I A BAD PARENT?
I'D LIKE TO THINK THE ANSWER IS NO.
IT DOESN'T MEAN I'M PERFECT, BUT I COULD AT LEAST SAY I TRIED MY BEST. NO MORE. NO LESS.
THIS STAKEOUT IS OUR WAY OF DOING OUR BEST.

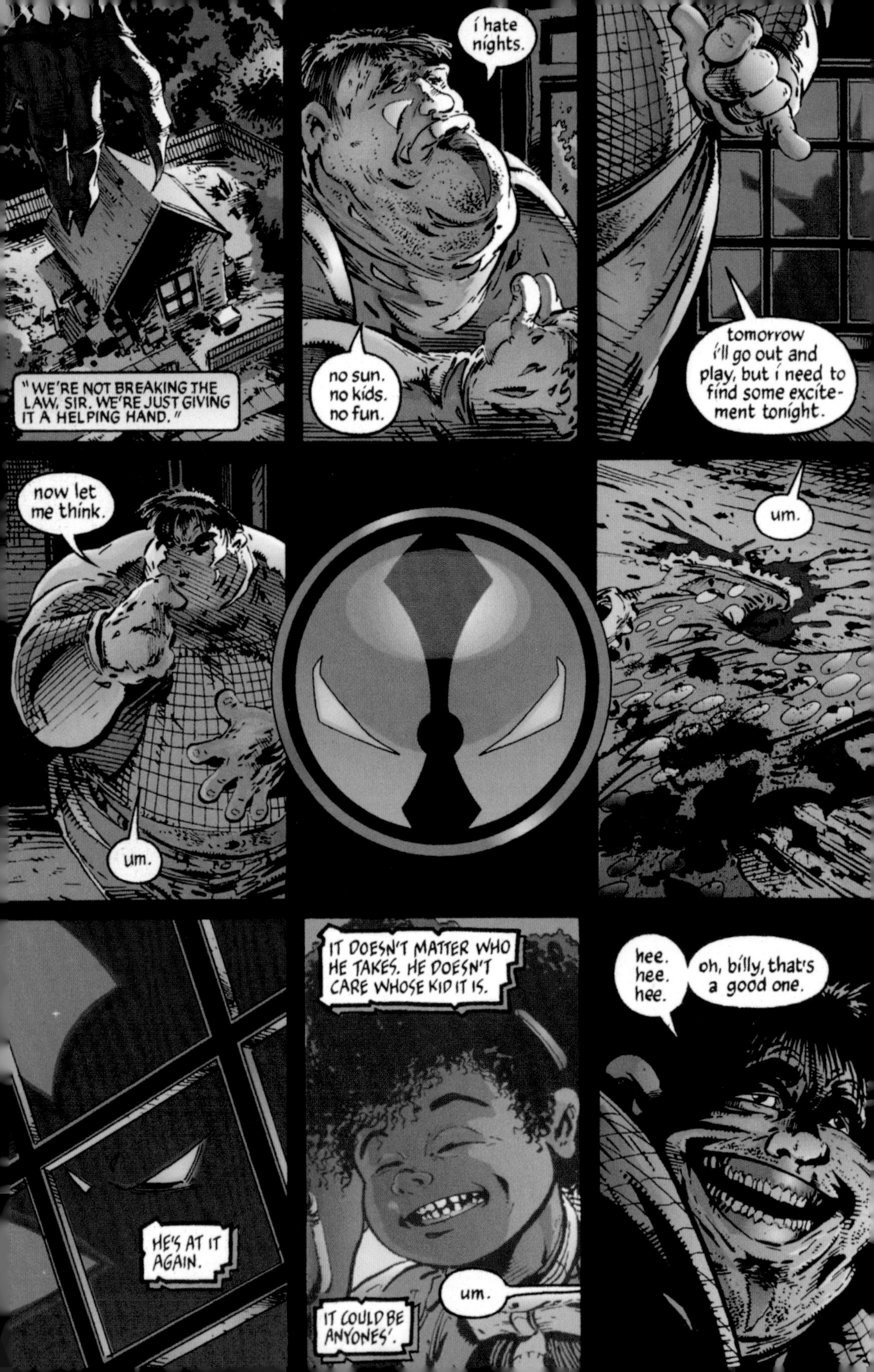
"WE'RE NOT BREAKING THE LAW, SIR. WE'RE JUST GIVING IT A HELPING HAND."
i hate nights.
no sun. no kids. no fun.
tomorrow i'll go out and play, but i need to find some excite-ment tonight.
now let me think.
um.
um.
IT DOESN'T MATTER WHO HE TAKES. HE DOESN'T CARE WHOSE KID IT IS.
HE'S AT IT AGAIN.
um.
IT COULD BE ANYONES'.
hee. hee. hee.
oh, billy, that's a good one.

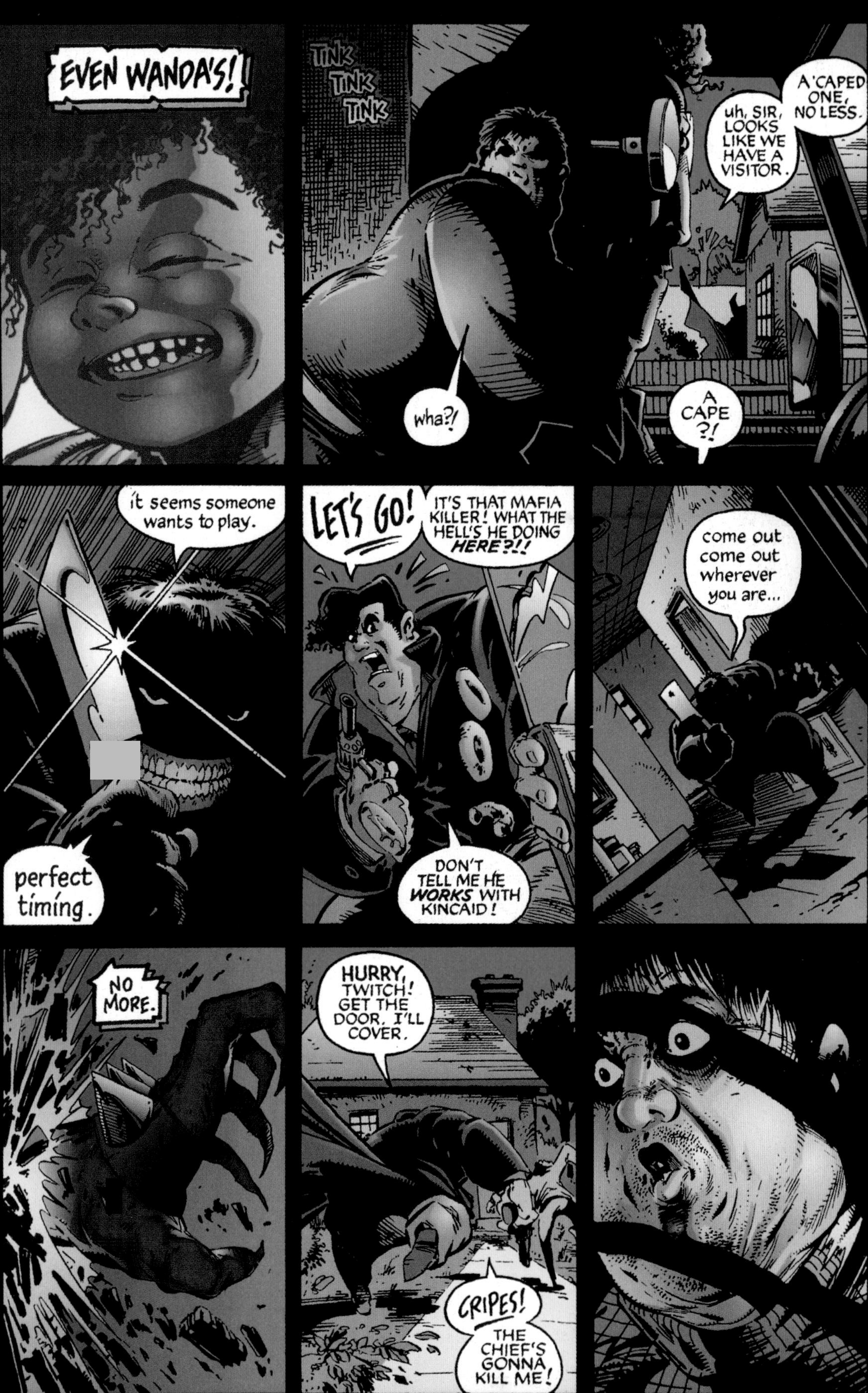
EVEN WANDA'S!
TINK TINK TINK
wha?!
uh, SIR, LOOKS LIKE WE HAVE A VISITOR.
A CAPED ONE, NO LESS.
A CAPE ?!
it seems someone wants to play.
perfect timing.
LET'S GO!
IT'S THAT MAFIA KILLER! WHAT THE HELL'S HE DOING HERE?!!
DON'T TELL ME HE WORKS WITH KINCAID!
come out come out wherever you are...
NO MORE.
HURRY, TWITCH! GET THE DOOR. I'LL COVER.
CRIPES!
THE CHIEF'S GONNA KILL ME!

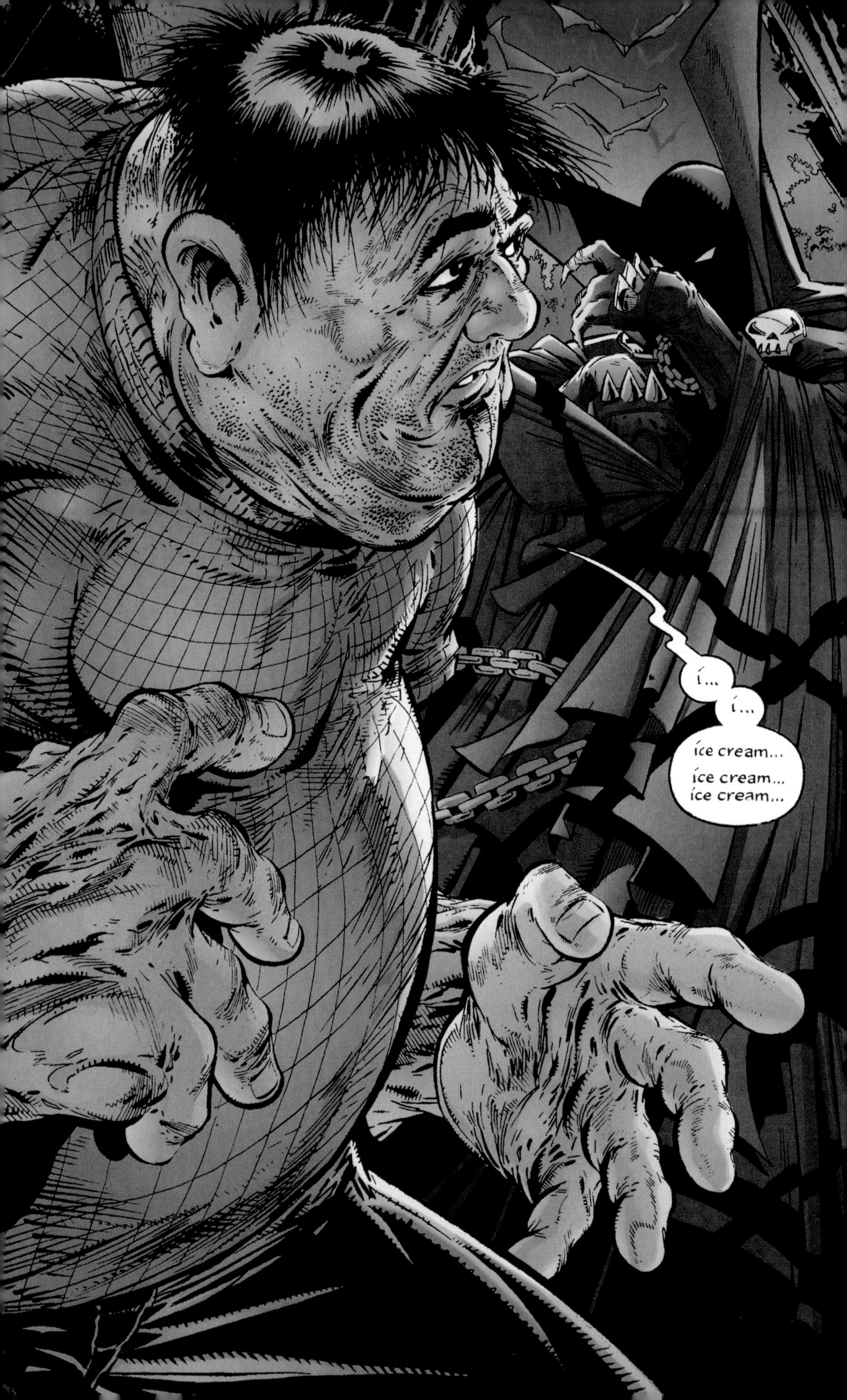
I...
I...
ice cream...
ice cream...
ice cream...

WHAT THE...!

SWEET MOTHER! WHAT'S HAPPENING *HERE*?!! CHECK THE HOUSE! *NOW!*

A QUICK SEARCH REVEALS EVIDENCE OF ANOTHER CHILD'S DEATH.

DAMMIT! THIS IS *ALL* WRONG.

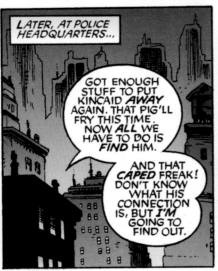

LATER, AT POLICE HEADQUARTERS...

GOT ENOUGH STUFF TO PUT KINCAID *AWAY* AGAIN. THAT PIG'LL FRY THIS TIME. NOW *ALL* WE HAVE TO DO IS *FIND* HIM!

AND THAT *CAPED* FREAK! DON'T KNOW WHAT HIS CONNECTION IS, BUT *I'M* GOING TO FIND OUT.

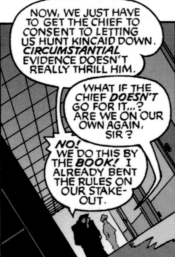

NOW, WE JUST HAVE TO GET THE CHIEF TO CONSENT TO LETTING US HUNT KINCAID DOWN. *CIRCUMSTANTIAL* EVIDENCE DOESN'T REALLY THRILL HIM.

WHAT IF THE CHIEF *DOESN'T* GO FOR IT...? ARE WE ON OUR OWN AGAIN, SIR?

NO! WE DO THIS BY THE *BOOK!* I ALREADY BENT THE RULES ON OUR STAKE-OUT.

I CAN'T MAKE ANY MORE EXCEPTIONS.

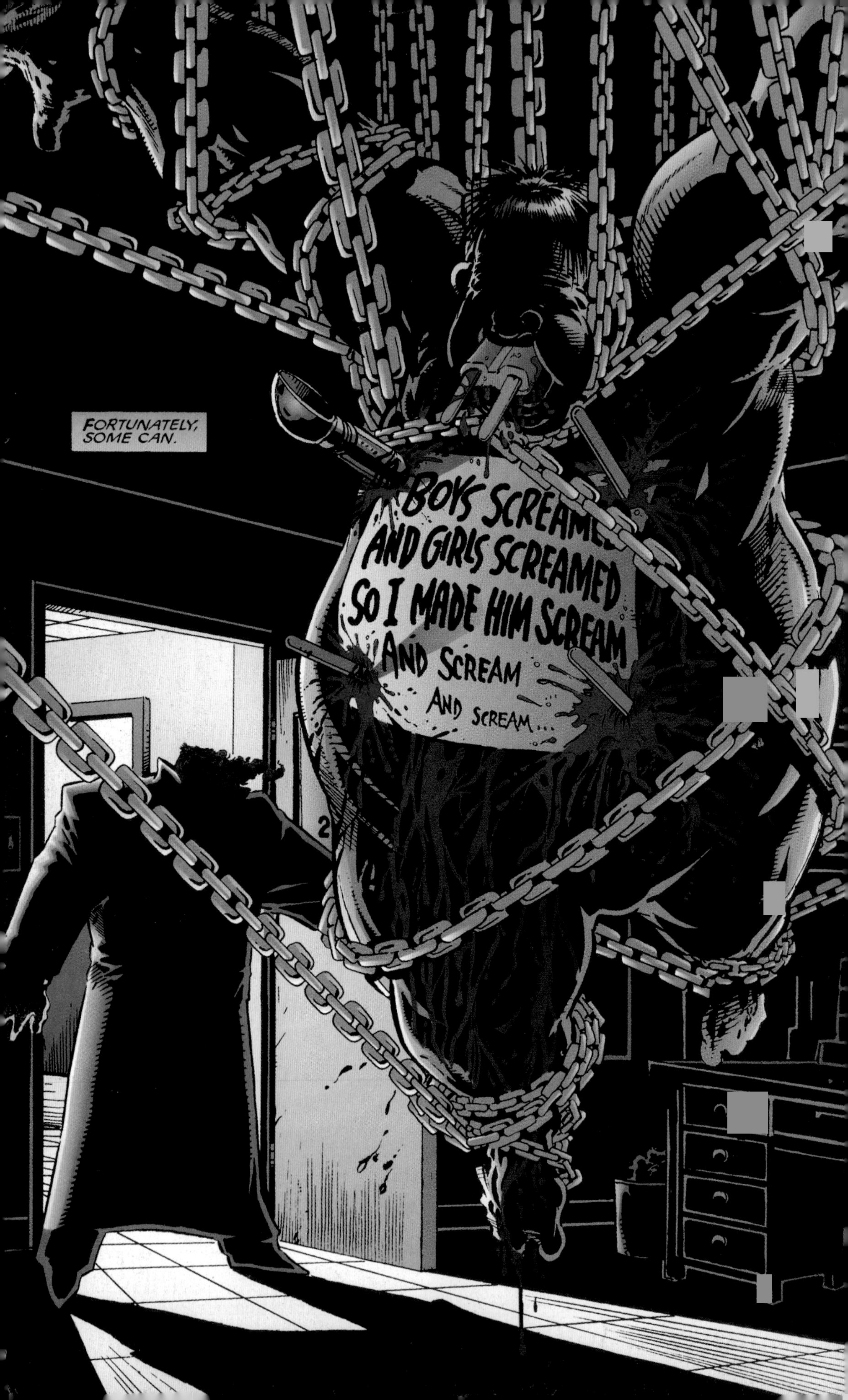
FORTUNATELY, SOME CAN.
BOYS SCREAMED
AND GIRLS SCREAMED
SO I MADE HIM SCREAM
AND SCREAM
AND SCREAM...

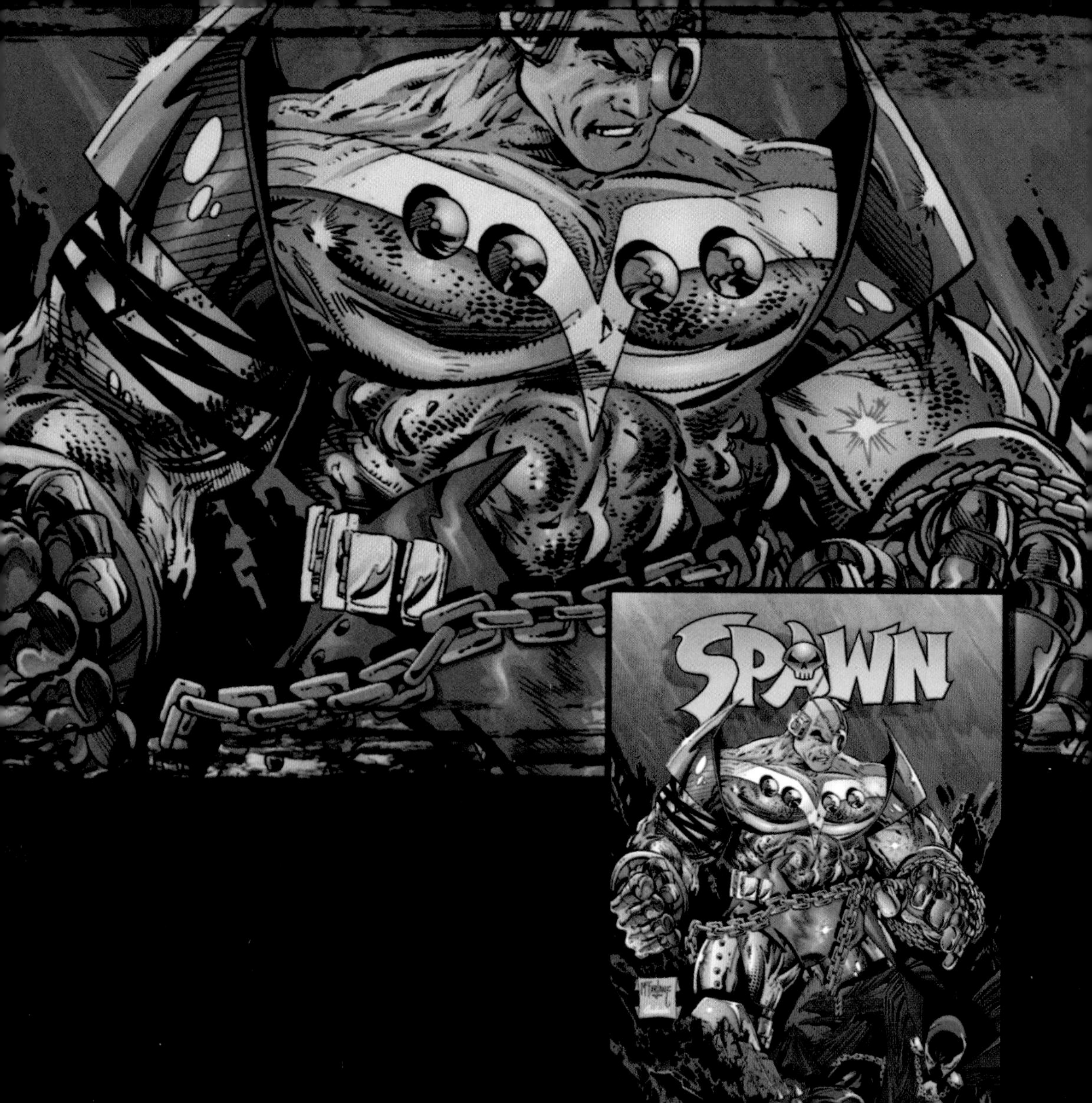
SPAWN

ISSUE SIX

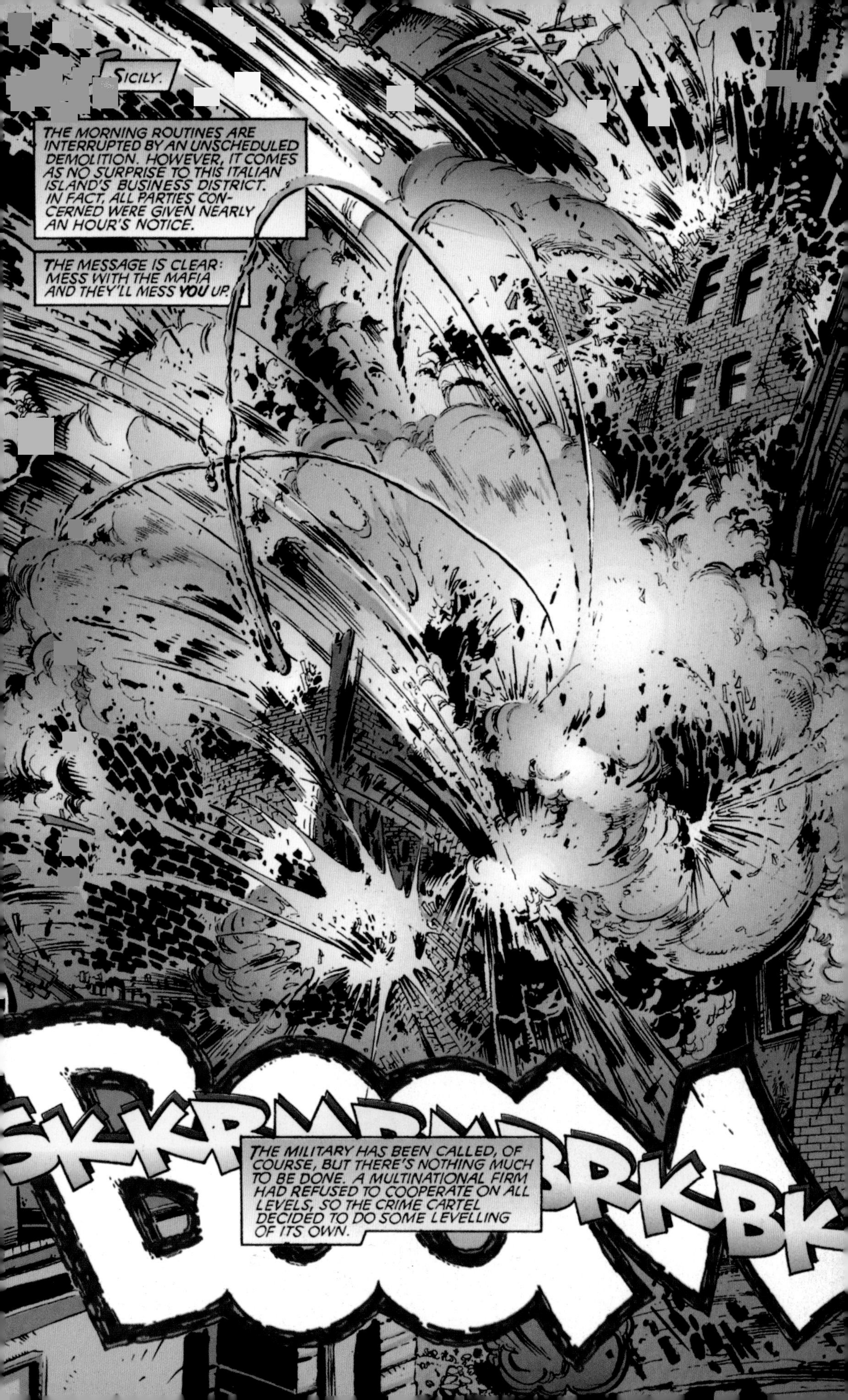
SICILY.
THE MORNING ROUTINES ARE INTERRUPTED BY AN UNSCHEDULED DEMOLITION. HOWEVER, IT COMES AS NO SURPRISE TO THIS ITALIAN ISLAND'S BUSINESS DISTRICT. IN FACT, ALL PARTIES CONCERNED WERE GIVEN NEARLY AN HOUR'S NOTICE.
THE MESSAGE IS CLEAR: MESS WITH THE MAFIA AND THEY'LL MESS **YOU** UP.
THE MILITARY HAS BEEN CALLED, OF COURSE, BUT THERE'S NOTHING MUCH TO BE DONE. A MULTINATIONAL FIRM HAD REFUSED TO COOPERATE ON ALL LEVELS, SO THE CRIME CARTEL DECIDED TO DO SOME LEVELLING OF ITS OWN.

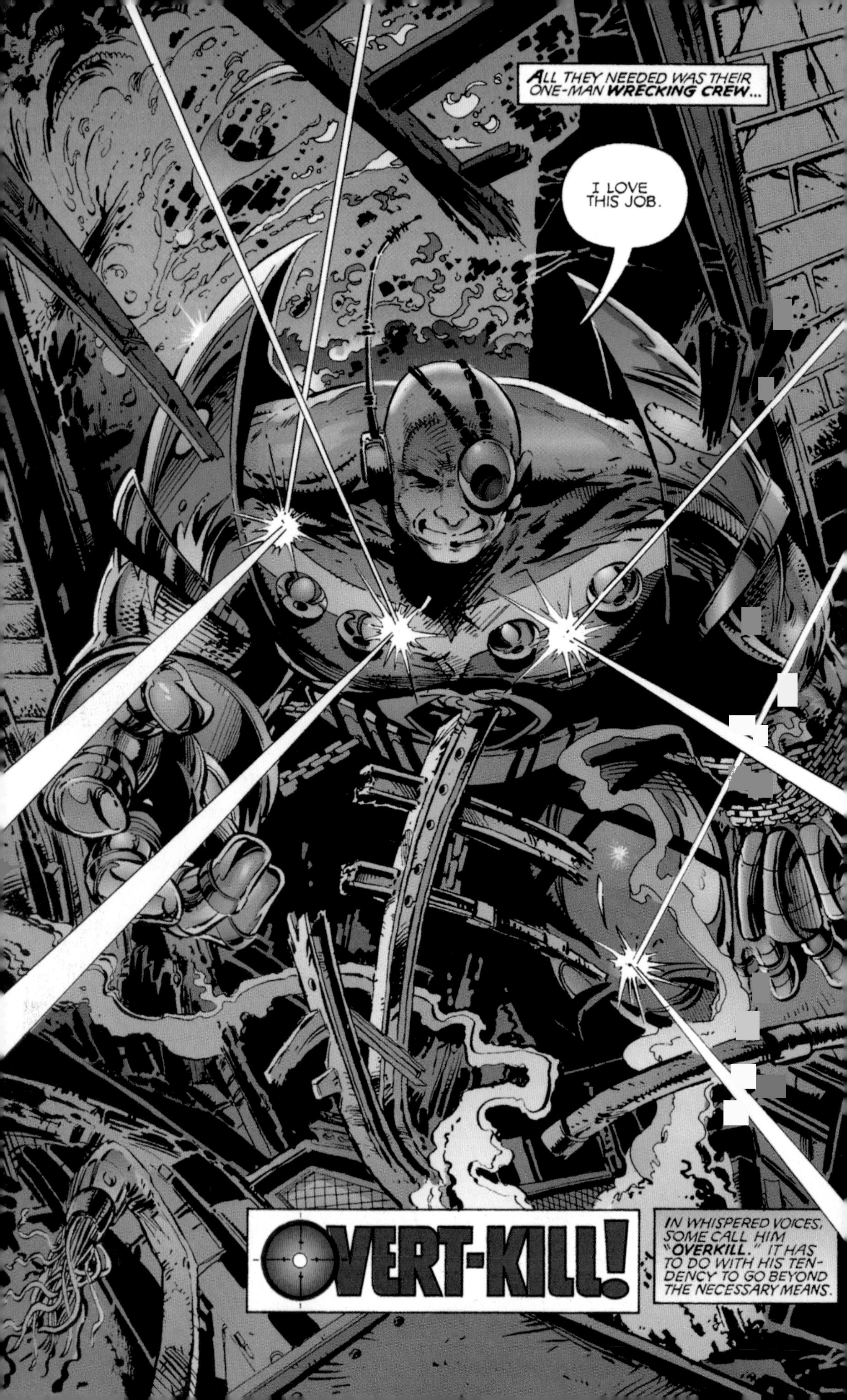
ALL THEY NEEDED WAS THEIR ONE-MAN WRECKING CREW...
I LOVE THIS JOB.
OVERT-KILL!
IN WHISPERED VOICES, SOME CALL HIM "OVERKILL." IT HAS TO DO WITH HIS TENDENCY TO GO BEYOND THE NECESSARY MEANS.

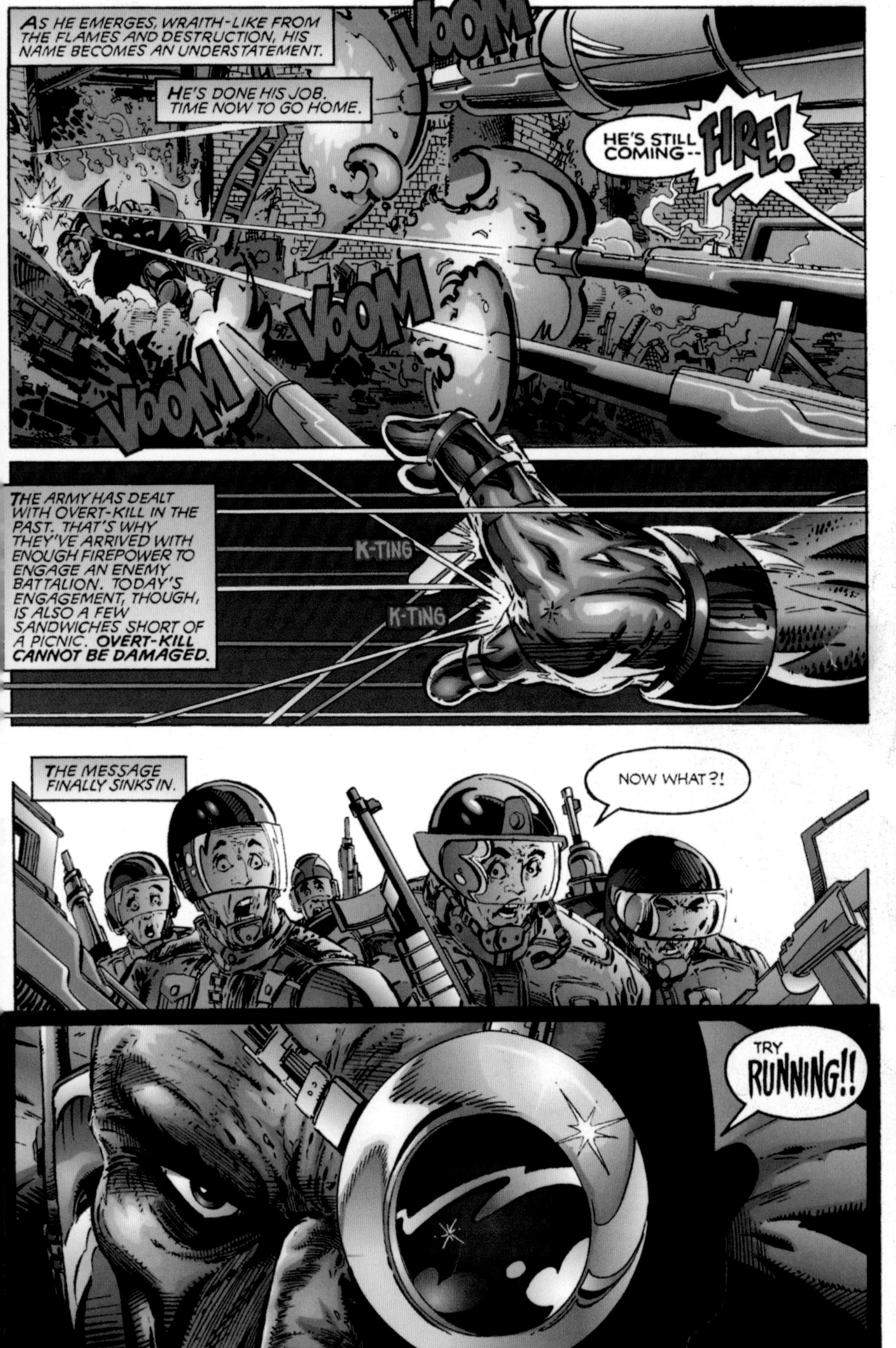

AS HE EMERGES, WRAITH-LIKE FROM THE FLAMES AND DESTRUCTION, HIS NAME BECOMES AN UNDERSTATEMENT.
VOOM
HE'S DONE HIS JOB. TIME NOW TO GO HOME.
HE'S STILL COMING-- FIRE!
VOOM
VOOM
THE ARMY HAS DEALT WITH OVERT-KILL IN THE PAST. THAT'S WHY THEY'VE ARRIVED WITH ENOUGH FIREPOWER TO ENGAGE AN ENEMY BATTALION. TODAY'S ENGAGEMENT, THOUGH, IS ALSO A FEW SANDWICHES SHORT OF A PICNIC. OVERT-KILL CANNOT BE DAMAGED.
K-TING
K-TING
THE MESSAGE FINALLY SINKS IN.
NOW WHAT?!
TRY RUNNING!!

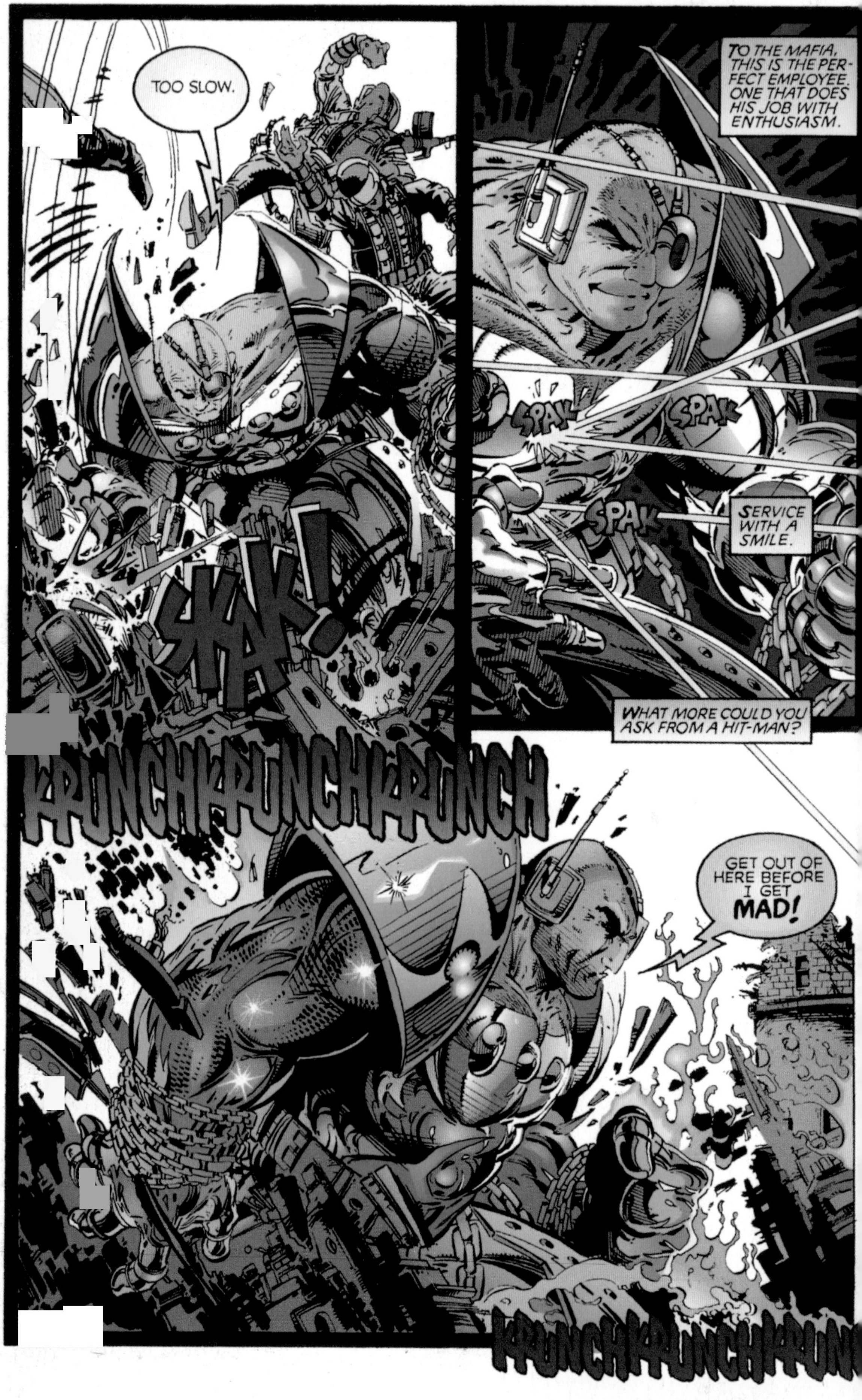

TOO SLOW.
SKAK!
TO THE MAFIA, THIS IS THE PERFECT EMPLOYEE. ONE THAT DOES HIS JOB WITH ENTHUSIASM.
SPAK
SPAK
SPAK
SERVICE WITH A SMILE.
WHAT MORE COULD YOU ASK FROM A HIT-MAN?
KRUNCHKRUNCHKRUNCH
GET OUT OF HERE BEFORE I GET MAD!

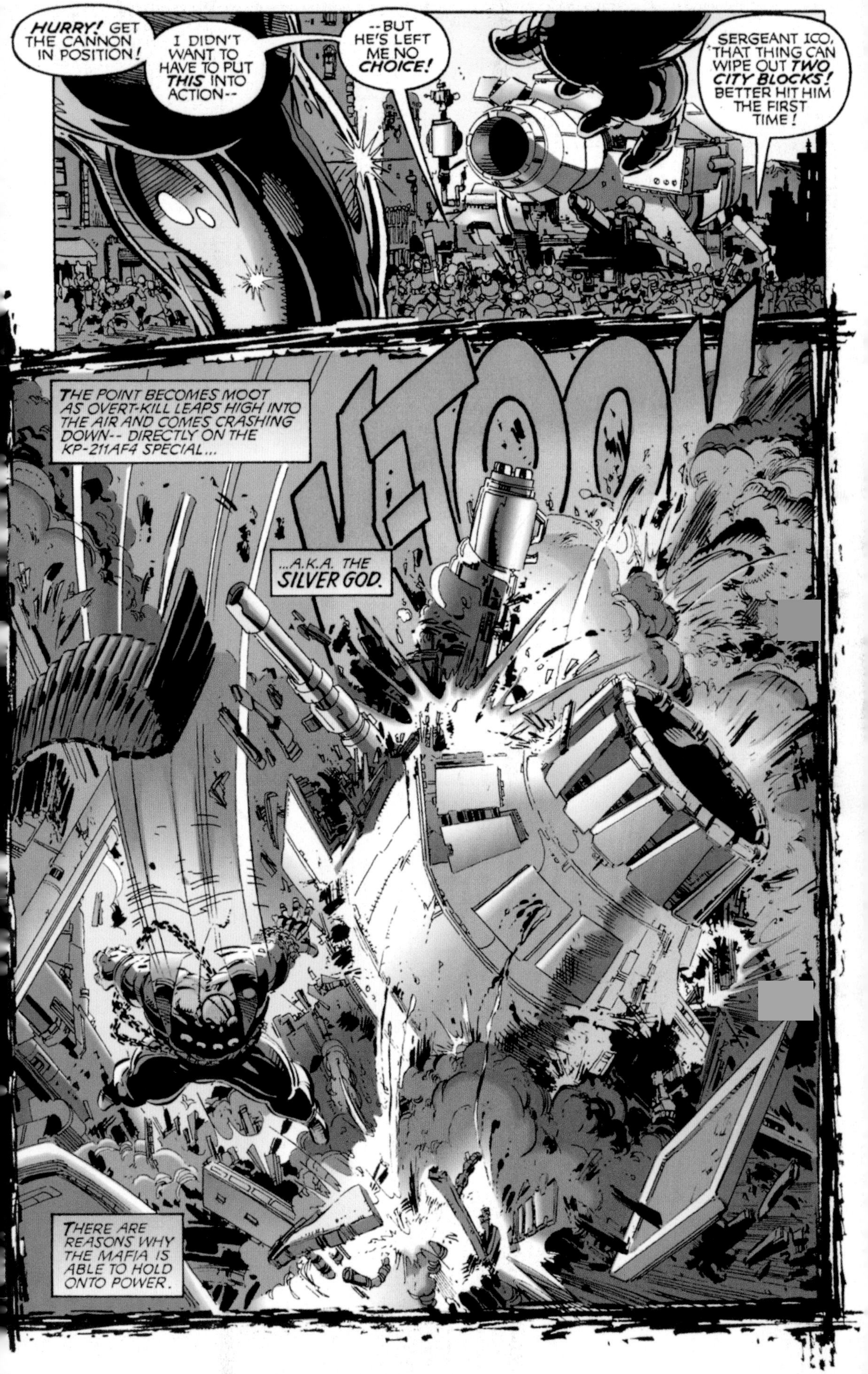
HURRY! GET THE CANNON IN POSITION!
I DIDN'T WANT TO HAVE TO PUT THIS INTO ACTION--
--BUT HE'S LEFT ME NO CHOICE!
SERGEANT ICO, THAT THING CAN WIPE OUT TWO CITY BLOCKS! BETTER HIT HIM THE FIRST TIME!
THE POINT BECOMES MOOT AS OVERT-KILL LEAPS HIGH INTO THE AIR AND COMES CRASHING DOWN-- DIRECTLY ON THE KP-211AF4 SPECIAL...
...A.K.A. THE SILVER GOD.
THERE ARE REASONS WHY THE MAFIA IS ABLE TO HOLD ONTO POWER.

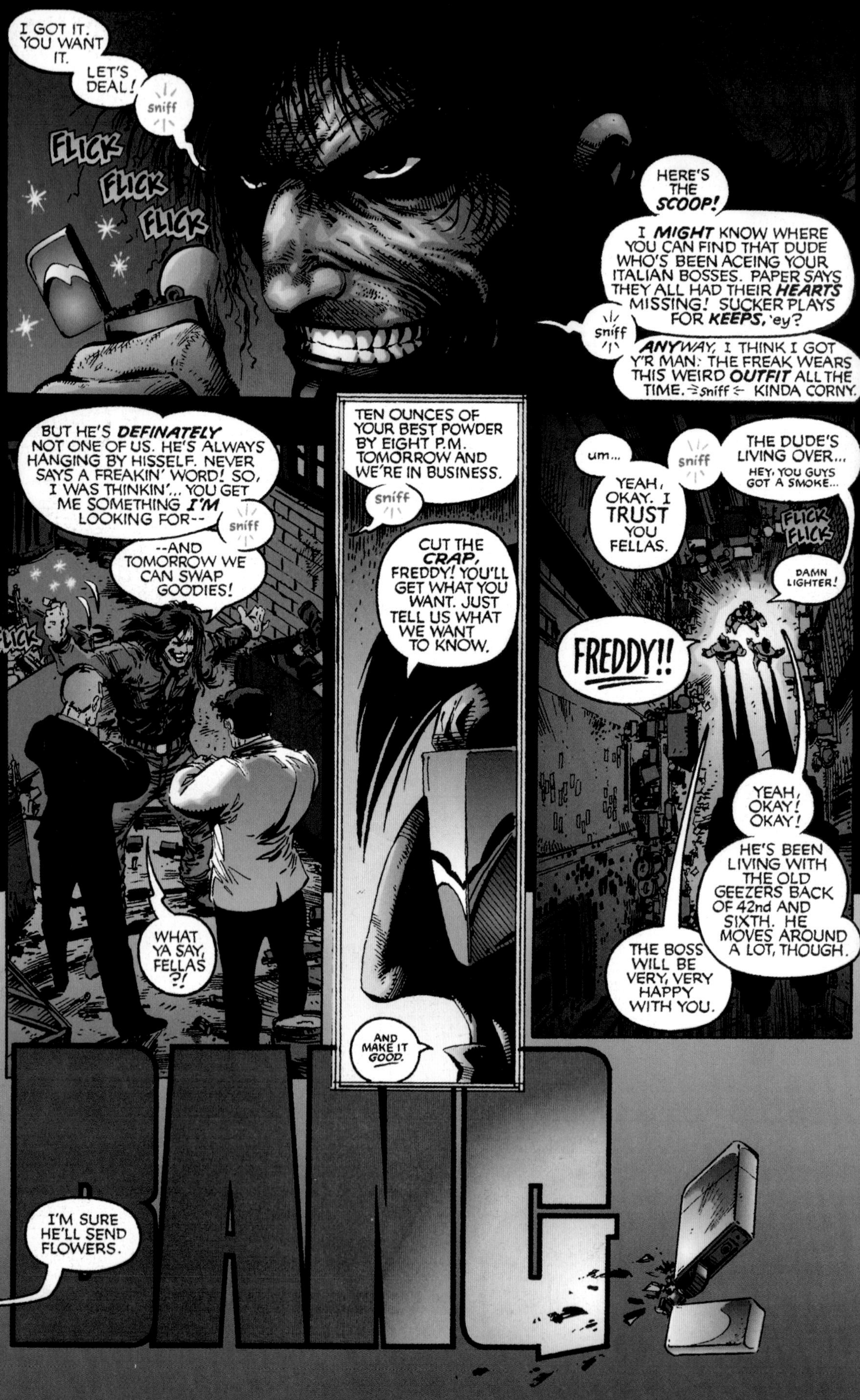

I GOT IT. YOU WANT IT.
LET'S DEAL!
sniff
FLICK
FLICK
FLICK
HERE'S THE SCOOP!
I MIGHT KNOW WHERE YOU CAN FIND THAT DUDE WHO'S BEEN ACEING YOUR ITALIAN BOSSES. PAPER SAYS THEY ALL HAD THEIR HEARTS MISSING! SUCKER PLAYS FOR KEEPS, 'ey?
sniff
ANYWAY, I THINK I GOT Y'R MAN: THE FREAK WEARS THIS WEIRD OUTFIT ALL THE TIME. sniff KINDA CORNY.
BUT HE'S DEFINATELY NOT ONE OF US. HE'S ALWAYS HANGING BY HISSELF. NEVER SAYS A FREAKIN' WORD! SO, I WAS THINKIN'... YOU GET ME SOMETHING I'M LOOKING FOR--
sniff
--AND TOMORROW WE CAN SWAP GOODIES!
FLICK
WHAT YA SAY, FELLAS ?!
TEN OUNCES OF YOUR BEST POWDER BY EIGHT P.M. TOMORROW AND WE'RE IN BUSINESS.
sniff
CUT THE CRAP, FREDDY! YOU'LL GET WHAT YOU WANT. JUST TELL US WHAT WE WANT TO KNOW.
AND MAKE IT GOOD.
um...
sniff
THE DUDE'S LIVING OVER...
HEY, YOU GUYS GOT A SMOKE...
YEAH, OKAY. I TRUST YOU FELLAS.
FLICK FLICK
DAMN LIGHTER!
FREDDY!!
YEAH, OKAY! OKAY!
HE'S BEEN LIVING WITH THE OLD GEEZERS BACK OF 42nd AND SIXTH. HE MOVES AROUND A LOT, THOUGH.
THE BOSS WILL BE VERY, VERY HAPPY WITH YOU.
BANG!
I'M SURE HE'LL SEND FLOWERS.

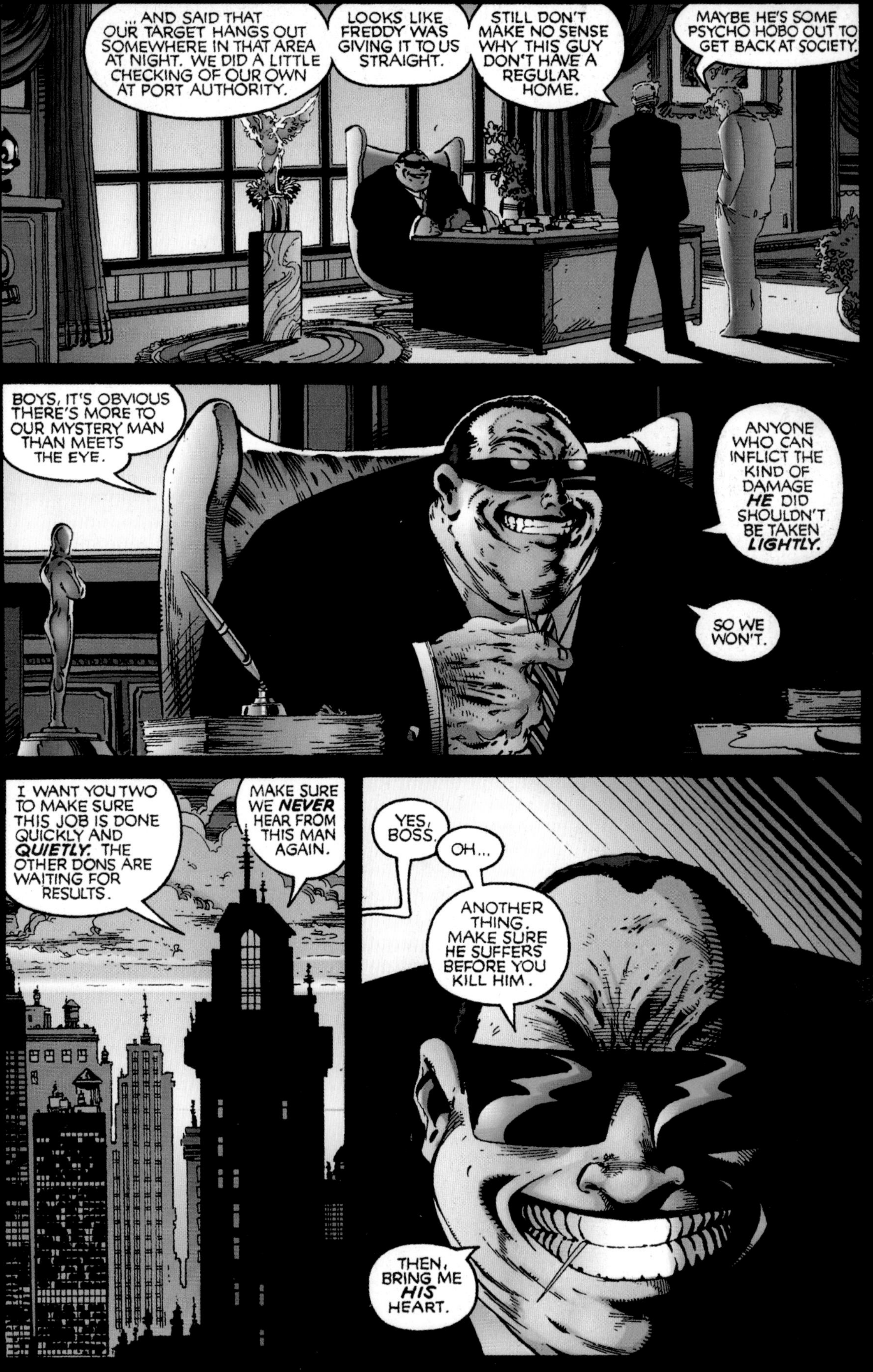
... AND SAID THAT OUR TARGET HANGS OUT SOMEWHERE IN THAT AREA AT NIGHT. WE DID A LITTLE CHECKING OF OUR OWN AT PORT AUTHORITY.
LOOKS LIKE FREDDY WAS GIVING IT TO US STRAIGHT.
STILL DON'T MAKE NO SENSE WHY THIS GUY DON'T HAVE A REGULAR HOME.
MAYBE HE'S SOME PSYCHO HOBO OUT TO GET BACK AT SOCIETY.
BOYS, IT'S OBVIOUS THERE'S MORE TO OUR MYSTERY MAN THAN MEETS THE EYE.
ANYONE WHO CAN INFLICT THE KIND OF DAMAGE **HE** DID SHOULDN'T BE TAKEN ***LIGHTLY.***
SO WE WON'T.
I WANT YOU TWO TO MAKE SURE THIS JOB IS DONE QUICKLY AND ***QUIETLY.*** THE OTHER DONS ARE WAITING FOR RESULTS.
MAKE SURE WE ***NEVER*** HEAR FROM THIS MAN AGAIN.
YES, BOSS.
OH...
ANOTHER THING. MAKE SURE HE SUFFERS BEFORE YOU KILL HIM.
THEN, BRING ME ***HIS*** HEART.

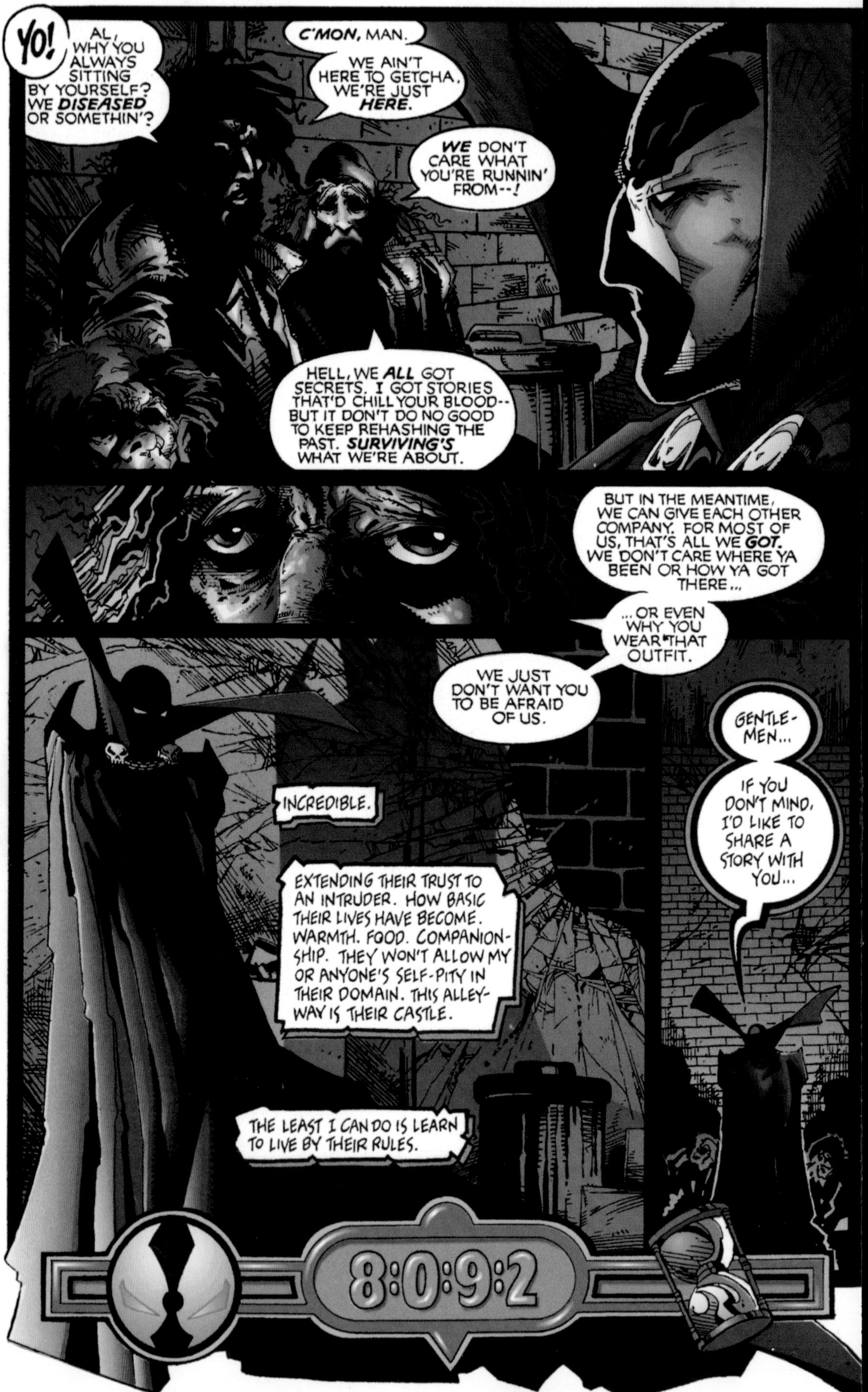
YO!
AL, WHY YOU ALWAYS SITTING BY YOURSELF? WE DISEASED OR SOMETHIN'?
C'MON, MAN.
WE AIN'T HERE TO GETCHA. WE'RE JUST HERE.
WE DON'T CARE WHAT YOU'RE RUNNIN' FROM--!
HELL, WE ALL GOT SECRETS. I GOT STORIES THAT'D CHILL YOUR BLOOD-- BUT IT DON'T DO NO GOOD TO KEEP REHASHING THE PAST. SURVIVING'S WHAT WE'RE ABOUT.
BUT IN THE MEANTIME, WE CAN GIVE EACH OTHER COMPANY. FOR MOST OF US, THAT'S ALL WE GOT. WE DON'T CARE WHERE YA BEEN OR HOW YA GOT THERE...
...OR EVEN WHY YOU WEAR THAT OUTFIT.
WE JUST DON'T WANT YOU TO BE AFRAID OF US.
INCREDIBLE.
EXTENDING THEIR TRUST TO AN INTRUDER. HOW BASIC THEIR LIVES HAVE BECOME. WARMTH. FOOD. COMPANIONSHIP. THEY WON'T ALLOW MY OR ANYONE'S SELF-PITY IN THEIR DOMAIN. THIS ALLEYWAY IS THEIR CASTLE.
THE LEAST I CAN DO IS LEARN TO LIVE BY THEIR RULES.
GENTLEMEN...
IF YOU DON'T MIND, I'D LIKE TO SHARE A STORY WITH YOU...
8:0:9:2

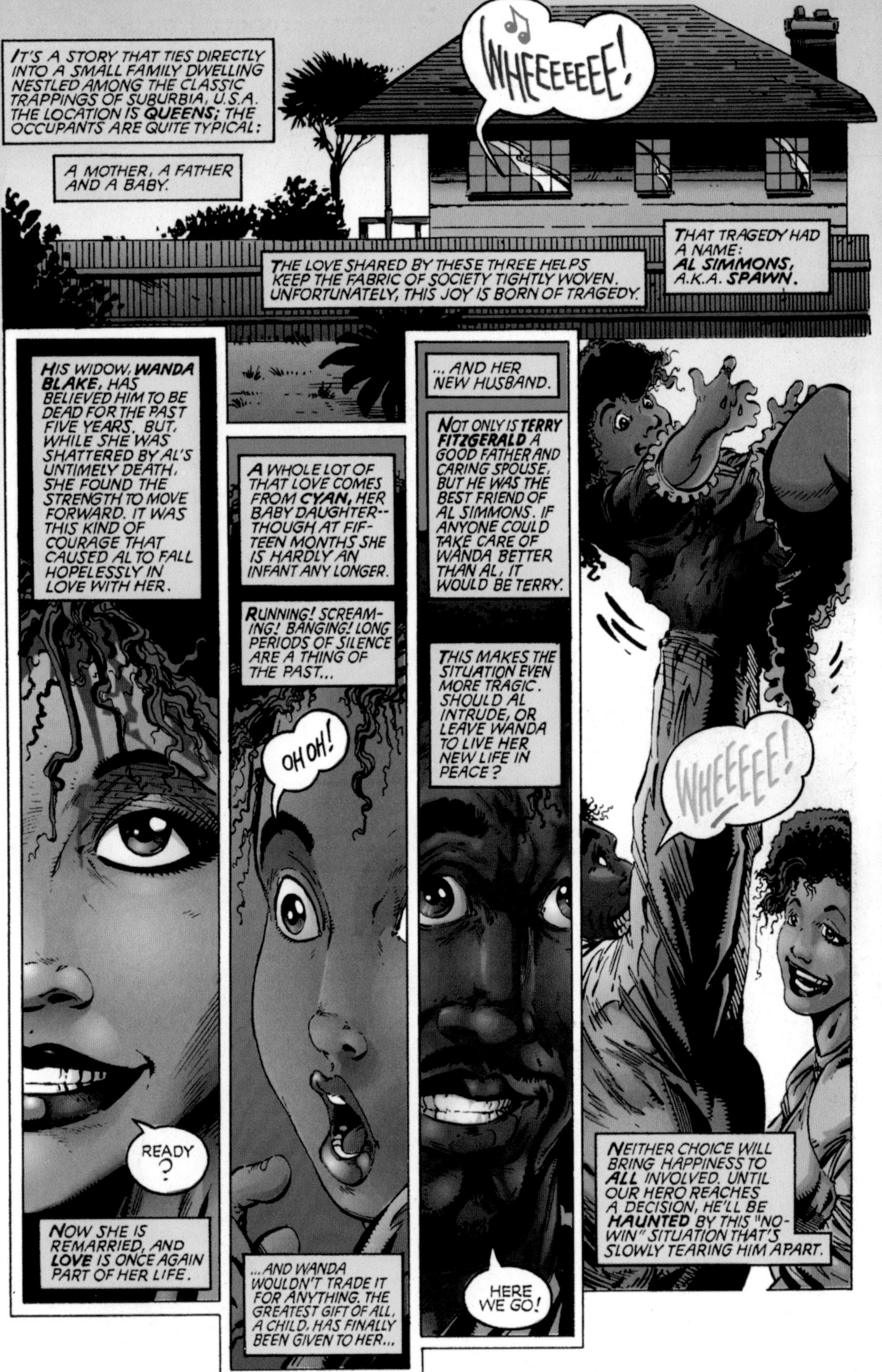
IT'S A STORY THAT TIES DIRECTLY INTO A SMALL FAMILY DWELLING NESTLED AMONG THE CLASSIC TRAPPINGS OF SUBURBIA, U.S.A. THE LOCATION IS QUEENS; THE OCCUPANTS ARE QUITE TYPICAL:
A MOTHER, A FATHER AND A BABY.
WHEEEEEEE!
THE LOVE SHARED BY THESE THREE HELPS KEEP THE FABRIC OF SOCIETY TIGHTLY WOVEN. UNFORTUNATELY, THIS JOY IS BORN OF TRAGEDY.
THAT TRAGEDY HAD A NAME: AL SIMMONS, A.K.A. SPAWN.
HIS WIDOW, WANDA BLAKE, HAS BELIEVED HIM TO BE DEAD FOR THE PAST FIVE YEARS. BUT, WHILE SHE WAS SHATTERED BY AL'S UNTIMELY DEATH, SHE FOUND THE STRENGTH TO MOVE FORWARD. IT WAS THIS KIND OF COURAGE THAT CAUSED AL TO FALL HOPELESSLY IN LOVE WITH HER.
READY?
NOW SHE IS REMARRIED, AND LOVE IS ONCE AGAIN PART OF HER LIFE.
A WHOLE LOT OF THAT LOVE COMES FROM CYAN, HER BABY DAUGHTER-- THOUGH AT FIFTEEN MONTHS SHE IS HARDLY AN INFANT ANY LONGER.
RUNNING! SCREAMING! BANGING! LONG PERIODS OF SILENCE ARE A THING OF THE PAST...
OH OH!
...AND WANDA WOULDN'T TRADE IT FOR ANYTHING. THE GREATEST GIFT OF ALL, A CHILD, HAS FINALLY BEEN GIVEN TO HER...
...AND HER NEW HUSBAND.
NOT ONLY IS TERRY FITZGERALD A GOOD FATHER AND CARING SPOUSE, BUT HE WAS THE BEST FRIEND OF AL SIMMONS. IF ANYONE COULD TAKE CARE OF WANDA BETTER THAN AL, IT WOULD BE TERRY.
THIS MAKES THE SITUATION EVEN MORE TRAGIC. SHOULD AL INTRUDE, OR LEAVE WANDA TO LIVE HER NEW LIFE IN PEACE?
HERE WE GO!
WHEEEEEE!
NEITHER CHOICE WILL BRING HAPPINESS TO ALL INVOLVED. UNTIL OUR HERO REACHES A DECISION, HE'LL BE HAUNTED BY THIS "NO-WIN" SITUATION THAT'S SLOWLY TEARING HIM APART.

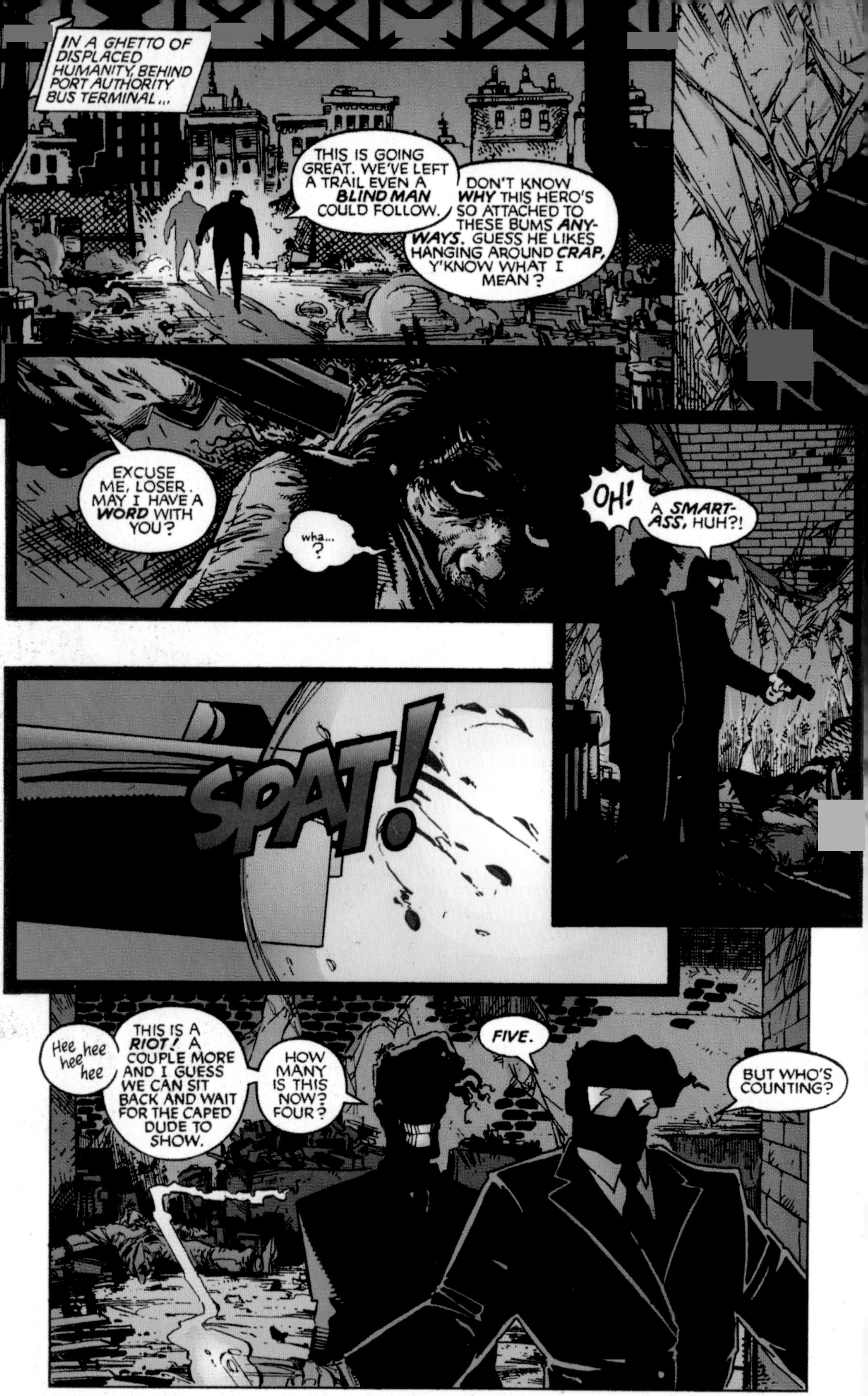
IN A GHETTO OF DISPLACED HUMANITY, BEHIND PORT AUTHORITY BUS TERMINAL...
THIS IS GOING GREAT. WE'VE LEFT A TRAIL EVEN A BLIND MAN COULD FOLLOW.
DON'T KNOW WHY THIS HERO'S SO ATTACHED TO THESE BUMS ANY-WAYS. GUESS HE LIKES HANGING AROUND CRAP, Y'KNOW WHAT I MEAN?
EXCUSE ME, LOSER. MAY I HAVE A WORD WITH YOU?
wha...?
OH!
A SMART-ASS, HUH?!
SPAT!
Hee hee hee hee
THIS IS A RIOT! A COUPLE MORE AND I GUESS WE CAN SIT BACK AND WAIT FOR THE CAPED DUDE TO SHOW.
HOW MANY IS THIS NOW? FOUR?
FIVE.
BUT WHO'S COUNTING?

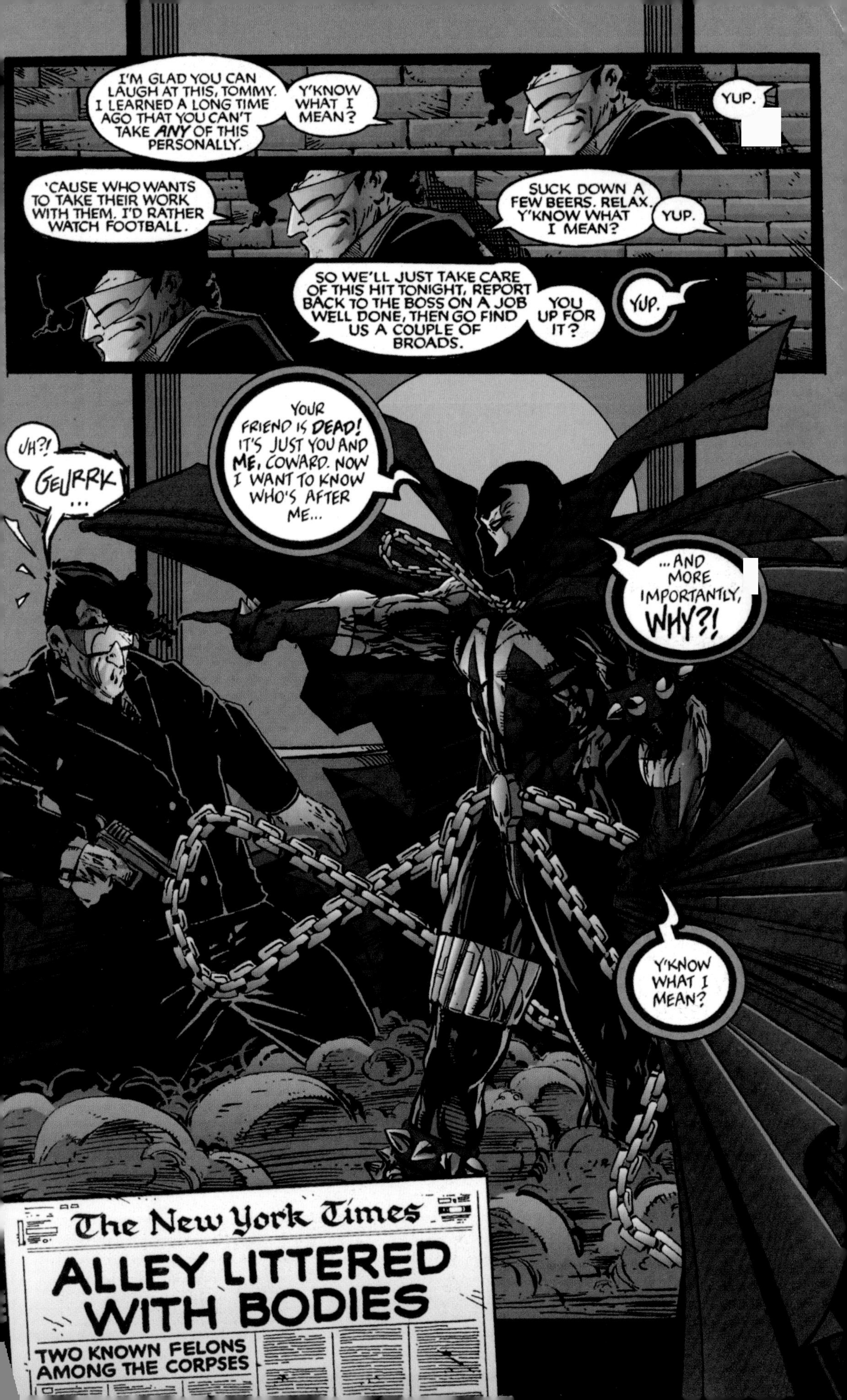

I'M GLAD YOU CAN LAUGH AT THIS, TOMMY. I LEARNED A LONG TIME AGO THAT YOU CAN'T TAKE ANY OF THIS PERSONALLY.
Y'KNOW WHAT I MEAN?
YUP.
'CAUSE WHO WANTS TO TAKE THEIR WORK WITH THEM. I'D RATHER WATCH FOOTBALL.
SUCK DOWN A FEW BEERS. RELAX. Y'KNOW WHAT I MEAN?
YUP.
SO WE'LL JUST TAKE CARE OF THIS HIT TONIGHT, REPORT BACK TO THE BOSS ON A JOB WELL DONE, THEN GO FIND US A COUPLE OF BROADS.
YOU UP FOR IT?
YUP.
UH?!
GEURRK...
YOUR FRIEND IS DEAD! IT'S JUST YOU AND ME, COWARD. NOW I WANT TO KNOW WHO'S AFTER ME...
...AND MORE IMPORTANTLY, WHY?!
Y'KNOW WHAT I MEAN?
The New York Times
ALLEY LITTERED WITH BODIES
TWO KNOWN FELONS AMONG THE CORPSES

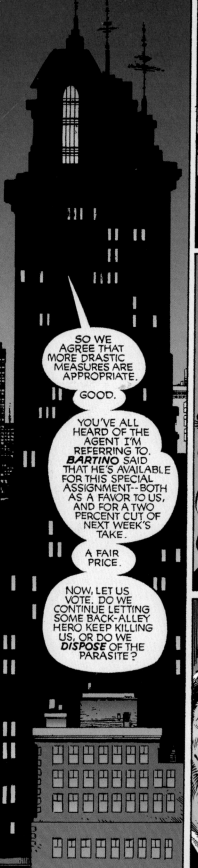

SO WE AGREE THAT MORE DRASTIC MEASURES ARE APPROPRIATE.

GOOD.

YOU'VE ALL HEARD OF THE AGENT I'M REFERRING TO. *BARTINO* SAID THAT HE'S AVAILABLE FOR THIS SPECIAL ASSIGNMENT--BOTH AS A FAVOR TO US, AND FOR A TWO PERCENT CUT OF NEXT WEEK'S TAKE.

A FAIR PRICE.

NOW, LET US VOTE. DO WE CONTINUE LETTING SOME BACK-ALLEY HERO KEEP KILLING US, OR DO WE *DISPOSE* OF THE PARASITE?

WHACK 'IM.

WHACK HIM.

WHACK HIM.

DISPOSE OF HIM.

HEE. HEE. **WHACK** HIM!

KILL HIM.

WHACK HIM, SIR.

LET HIM LIVE, I SAY!

-- JUST KIDDING. SLAUGHTER HIM!

VERY FUNNY, TONY. THEN IT'S UNANIMOUS.

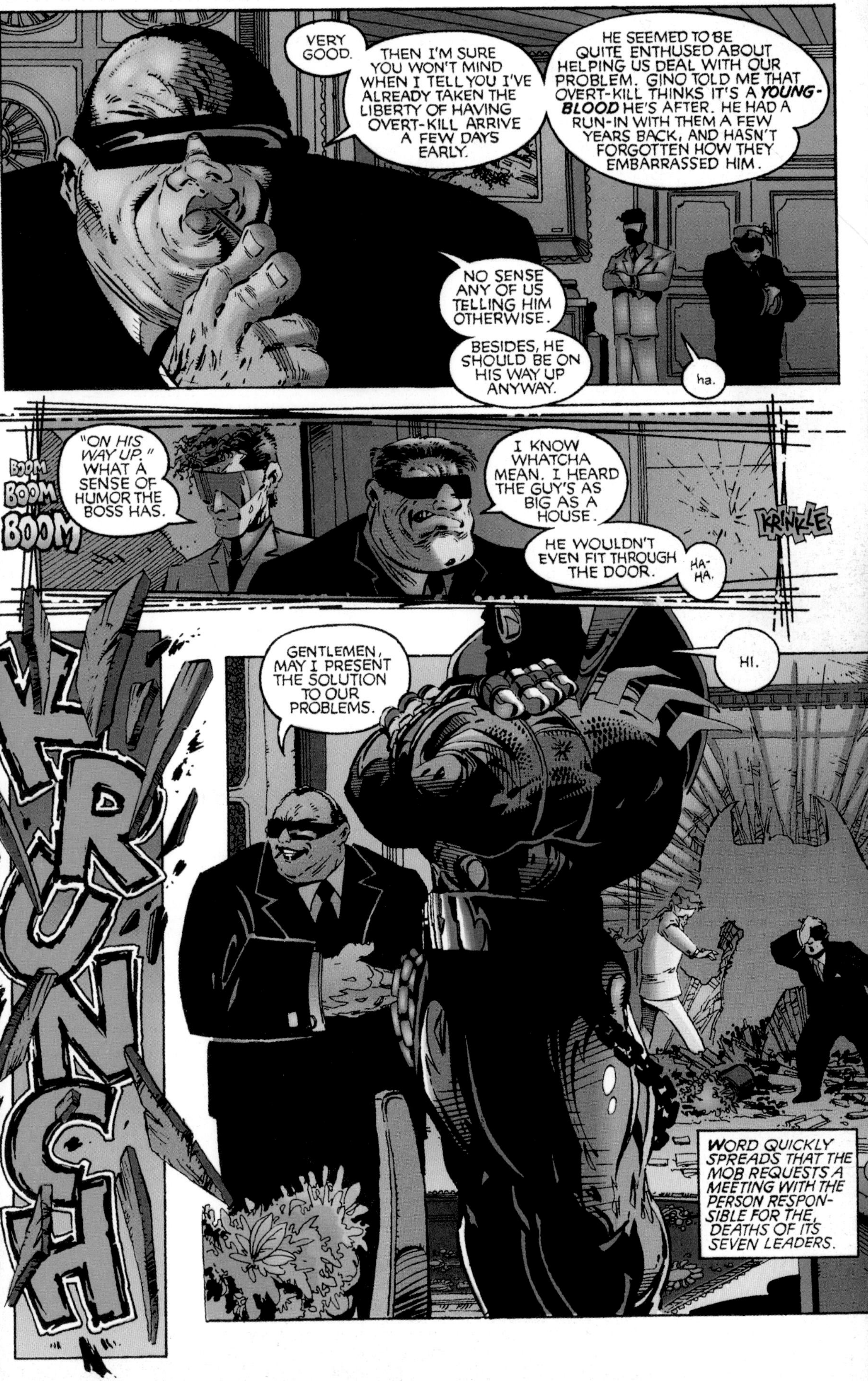
VERY GOOD.
THEN I'M SURE YOU WON'T MIND WHEN I TELL YOU I'VE ALREADY TAKEN THE LIBERTY OF HAVING OVERT-KILL ARRIVE A FEW DAYS EARLY.
HE SEEMED TO BE QUITE ENTHUSED ABOUT HELPING US DEAL WITH OUR PROBLEM. GINO TOLD ME THAT OVERT-KILL THINKS IT'S A YOUNGBLOOD HE'S AFTER. HE HAD A RUN-IN WITH THEM A FEW YEARS BACK, AND HASN'T FORGOTTEN HOW THEY EMBARRASSED HIM.
NO SENSE ANY OF US TELLING HIM OTHERWISE.
BESIDES, HE SHOULD BE ON HIS WAY UP ANYWAY.
ha.
BOOM BOOM BOOM
"ON HIS WAY UP." WHAT A SENSE OF HUMOR THE BOSS HAS.
I KNOW WHATCHA MEAN. I HEARD THE GUY'S AS BIG AS A HOUSE.
HE WOULDN'T EVEN FIT THROUGH THE DOOR.
HA-HA.
KRINKLE
KRUNCH
GENTLEMEN, MAY I PRESENT THE SOLUTION TO OUR PROBLEMS.
HI.
WORD QUICKLY SPREADS THAT THE MOB REQUESTS A MEETING WITH THE PERSON RESPONSIBLE FOR THE DEATHS OF ITS SEVEN LEADERS.

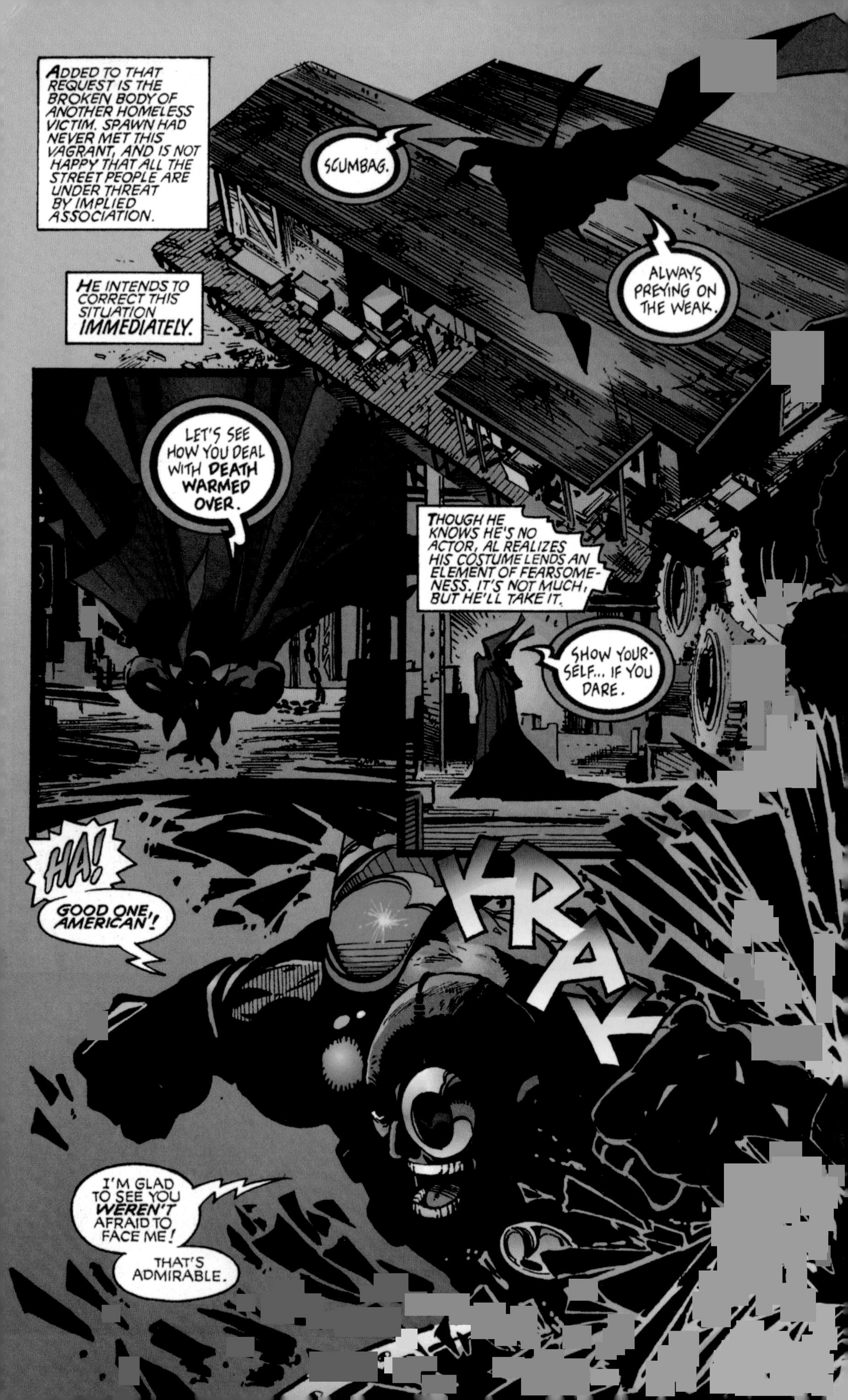
ADDED TO THAT REQUEST IS THE BROKEN BODY OF ANOTHER HOMELESS VICTIM. SPAWN HAD NEVER MET THIS VAGRANT, AND IS NOT HAPPY THAT ALL THE STREET PEOPLE ARE UNDER THREAT BY IMPLIED ASSOCIATION.
SCUMBAG.
ALWAYS PREYING ON THE WEAK.
HE INTENDS TO CORRECT THIS SITUATION IMMEDIATELY.
LET'S SEE HOW YOU DEAL WITH DEATH WARMED OVER.
THOUGH HE KNOWS HE'S NO ACTOR, AL REALIZES HIS COSTUME LENDS AN ELEMENT OF FEARSOME-NESS. IT'S NOT MUCH, BUT HE'LL TAKE IT.
SHOW YOUR-SELF... IF YOU DARE.
HA!
GOOD ONE, AMERICAN!
KRAK
I'M GLAD TO SEE YOU WEREN'T AFRAID TO FACE ME!
THAT'S ADMIRABLE.

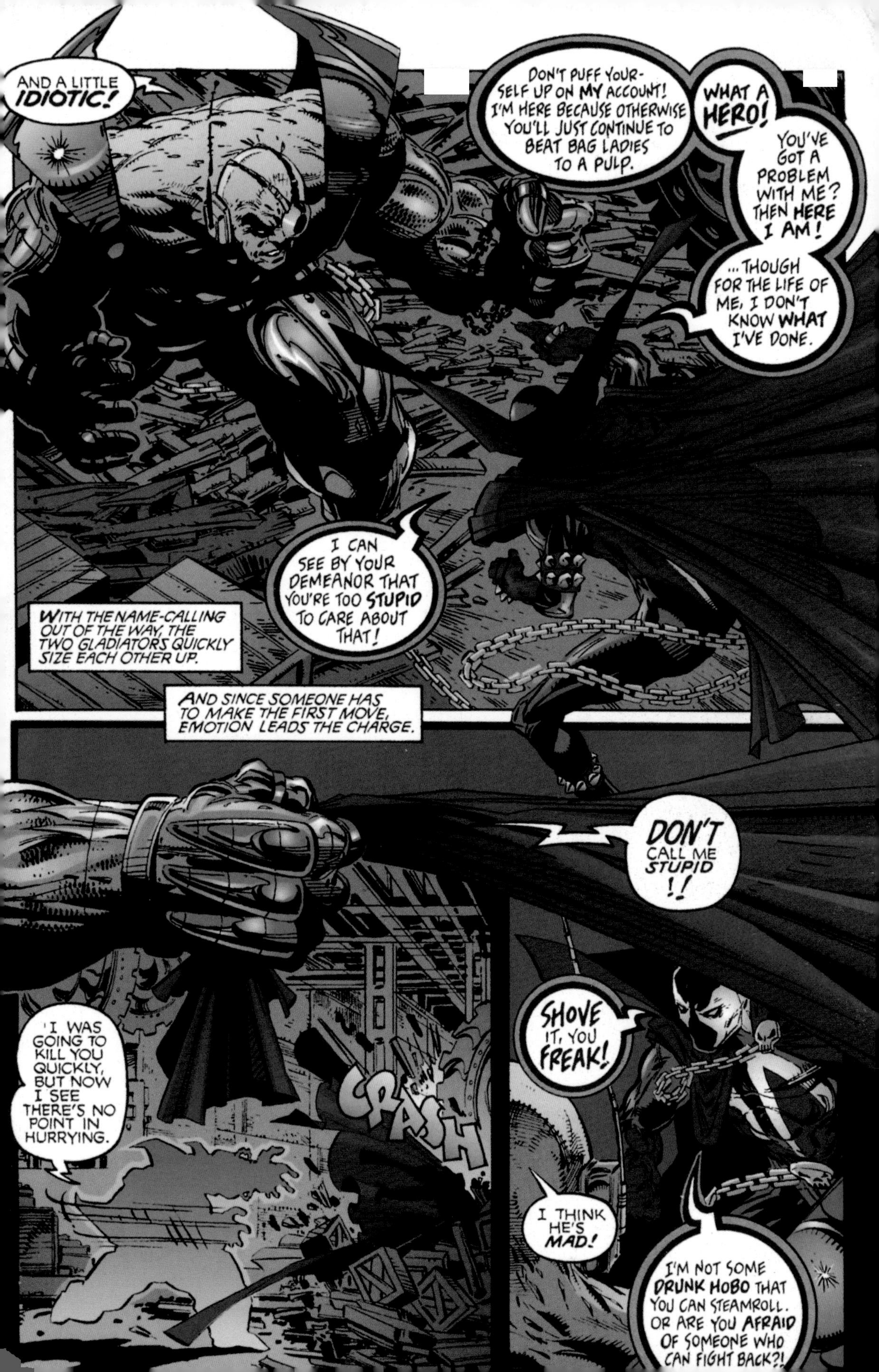
AND A LITTLE IDIOTIC!
DON'T PUFF YOURSELF UP ON MY ACCOUNT! I'M HERE BECAUSE OTHERWISE YOU'LL JUST CONTINUE TO BEAT BAG LADIES TO A PULP.
WHAT A HERO!
YOU'VE GOT A PROBLEM WITH ME? THEN HERE I AM!
...THOUGH FOR THE LIFE OF ME, I DON'T KNOW WHAT I'VE DONE.
I CAN SEE BY YOUR DEMEANOR THAT YOU'RE TOO STUPID TO CARE ABOUT THAT!
WITH THE NAME-CALLING OUT OF THE WAY, THE TWO GLADIATORS QUICKLY SIZE EACH OTHER UP.
AND SINCE SOMEONE HAS TO MAKE THE FIRST MOVE, EMOTION LEADS THE CHARGE.
DON'T CALL ME STUPID !!
I WAS GOING TO KILL YOU QUICKLY, BUT NOW I SEE THERE'S NO POINT IN HURRYING.
CRASH
SHOVE IT, YOU FREAK!
I THINK HE'S MAD!
I'M NOT SOME DRUNK HOBO THAT YOU CAN STEAMROLL. OR ARE YOU AFRAID OF SOMEONE WHO CAN FIGHT BACK?!

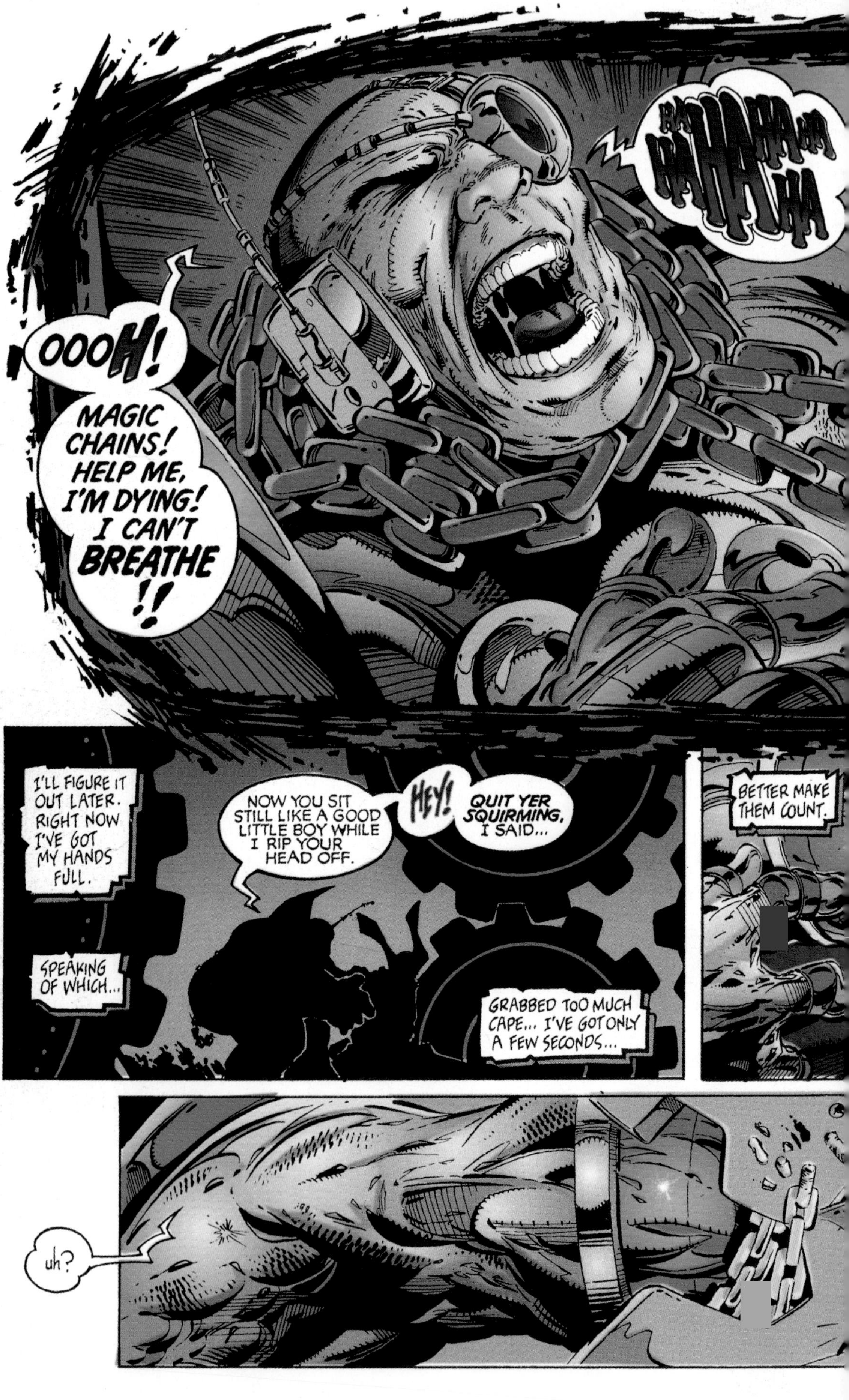
HA HAHAHA HA
HAHAHAHA
OOOH!
MAGIC CHAINS! HELP ME, I'M DYING! I CAN'T BREATHE !!
I'LL FIGURE IT OUT LATER. RIGHT NOW I'VE GOT MY HANDS FULL.
NOW YOU SIT STILL LIKE A GOOD LITTLE BOY WHILE I RIP YOUR HEAD OFF.
HEY!
QUIT YER SQUIRMING, I SAID...
SPEAKING OF WHICH...
GRABBED TOO MUCH CAPE... I'VE GOT ONLY A FEW SECONDS...
BETTER MAKE THEM COUNT.
uh?

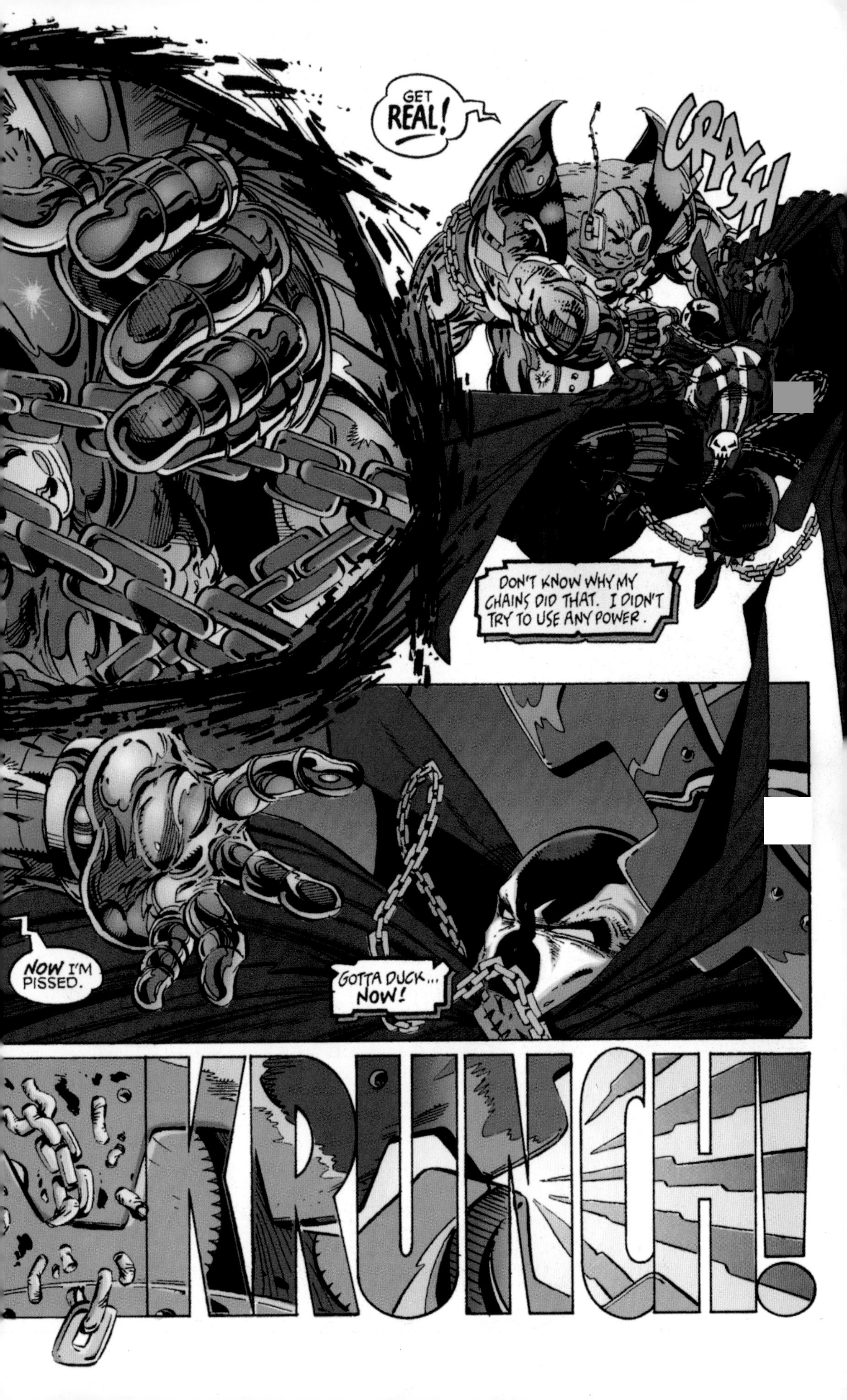
GET REAL!
CRASH
DON'T KNOW WHY MY CHAINS DID THAT. I DIDN'T TRY TO USE ANY POWER.
NOW I'M PISSED.
GOTTA DUCK... NOW!
KRUNCH!

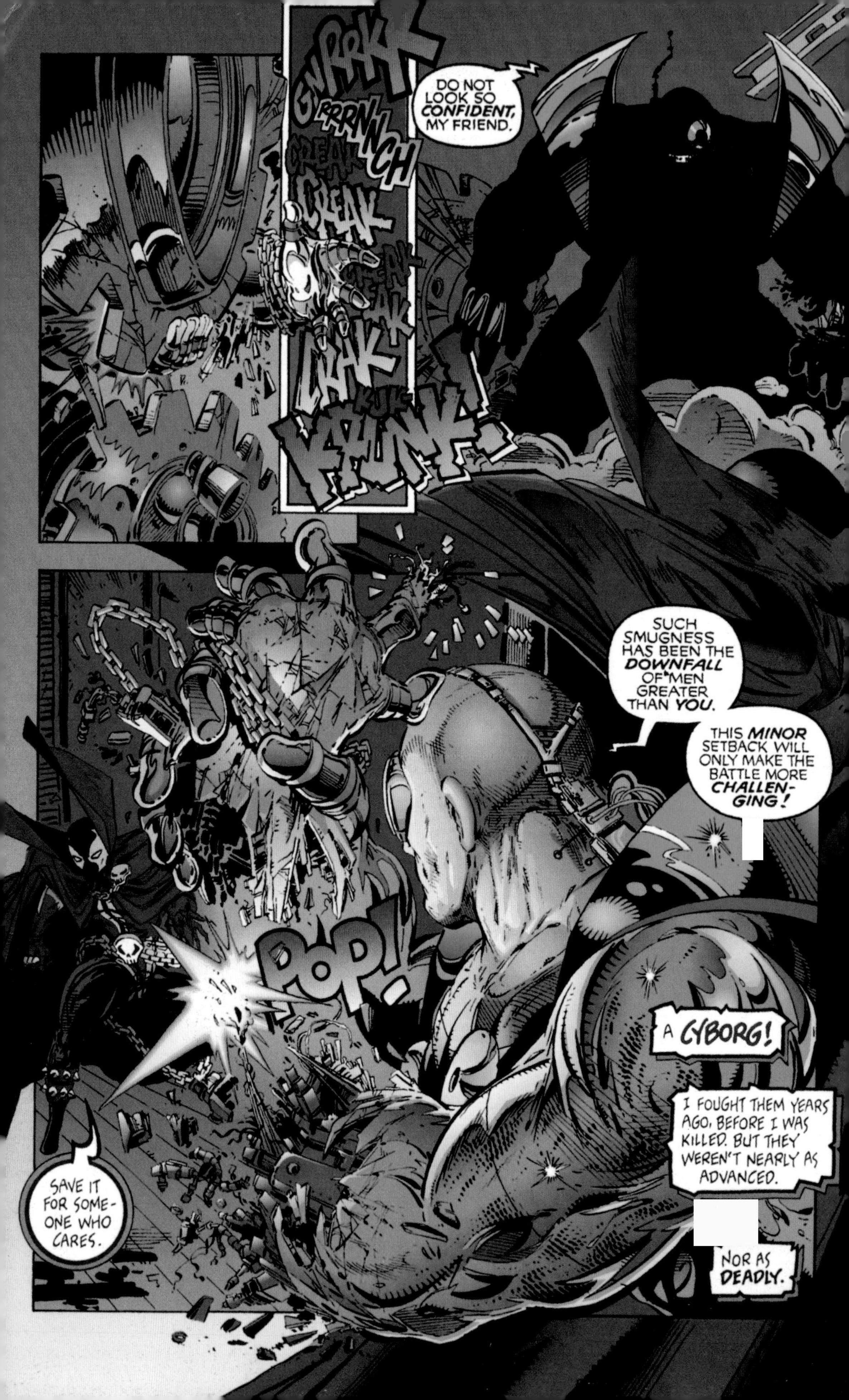

GNRRK
RRRNNCH
CREAK
CREAK
CREAK
CLAK
CLAK
KLIK
KRUNK
DO NOT LOOK SO CONFIDENT, MY FRIEND.
SUCH SMUGNESS HAS BEEN THE DOWNFALL OF MEN GREATER THAN YOU.
THIS MINOR SETBACK WILL ONLY MAKE THE BATTLE MORE CHALLENGING!
POP!
A CYBORG!
I FOUGHT THEM YEARS AGO, BEFORE I WAS KILLED. BUT THEY WEREN'T NEARLY AS ADVANCED.
NOR AS DEADLY.
SAVE IT FOR SOMEONE WHO CARES.

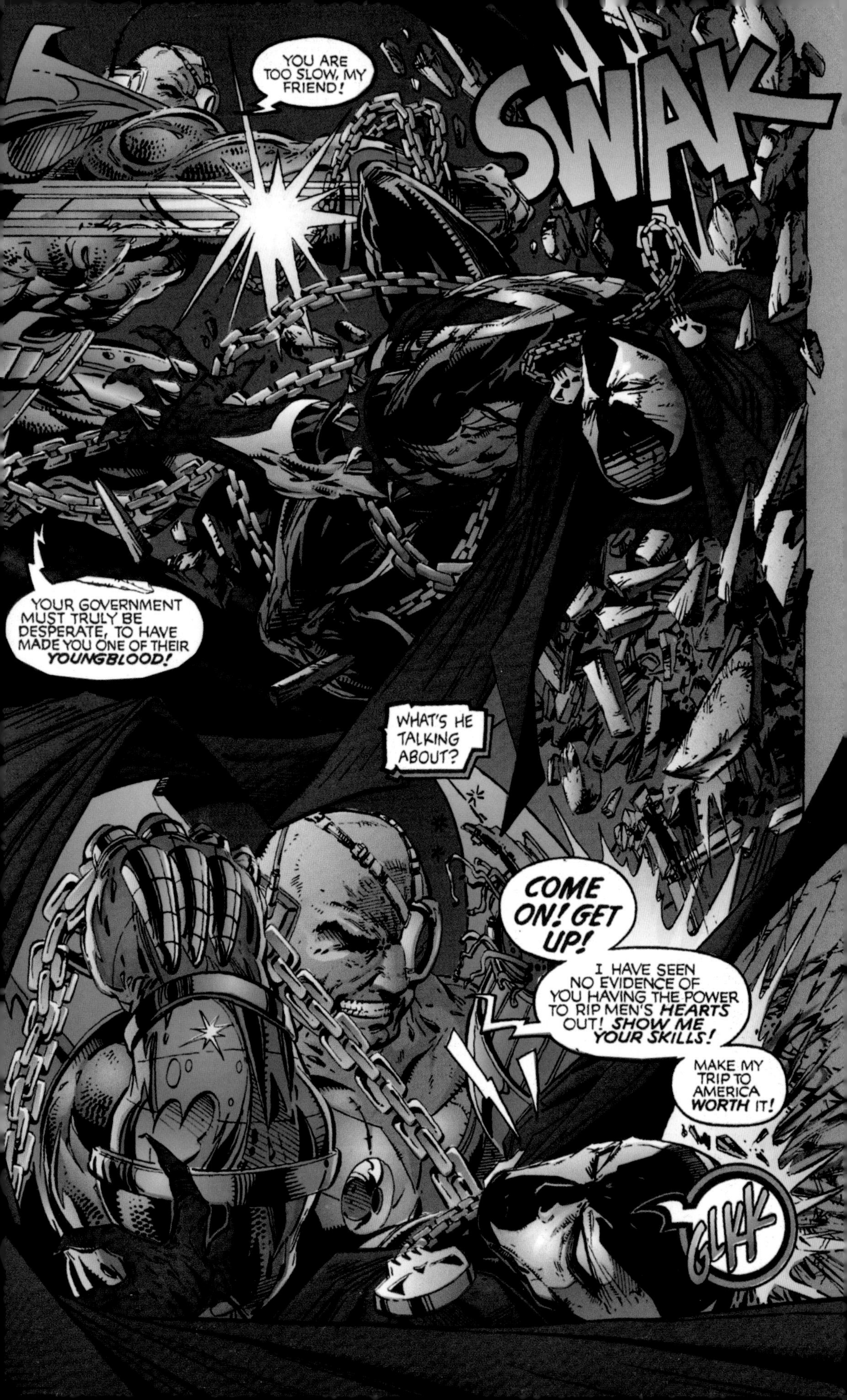
YOU ARE TOO SLOW, MY FRIEND!
SWAK
YOUR GOVERNMENT MUST TRULY BE DESPERATE, TO HAVE MADE YOU ONE OF THEIR *YOUNGBLOOD!*
WHAT'S HE TALKING ABOUT?
COME ON! GET UP!
I HAVE SEEN NO EVIDENCE OF YOU HAVING THE POWER TO RIP MEN'S *HEARTS* OUT! *SHOW ME YOUR SKILLS!*
MAKE MY TRIP TO AMERICA *WORTH* IT!
GLKK

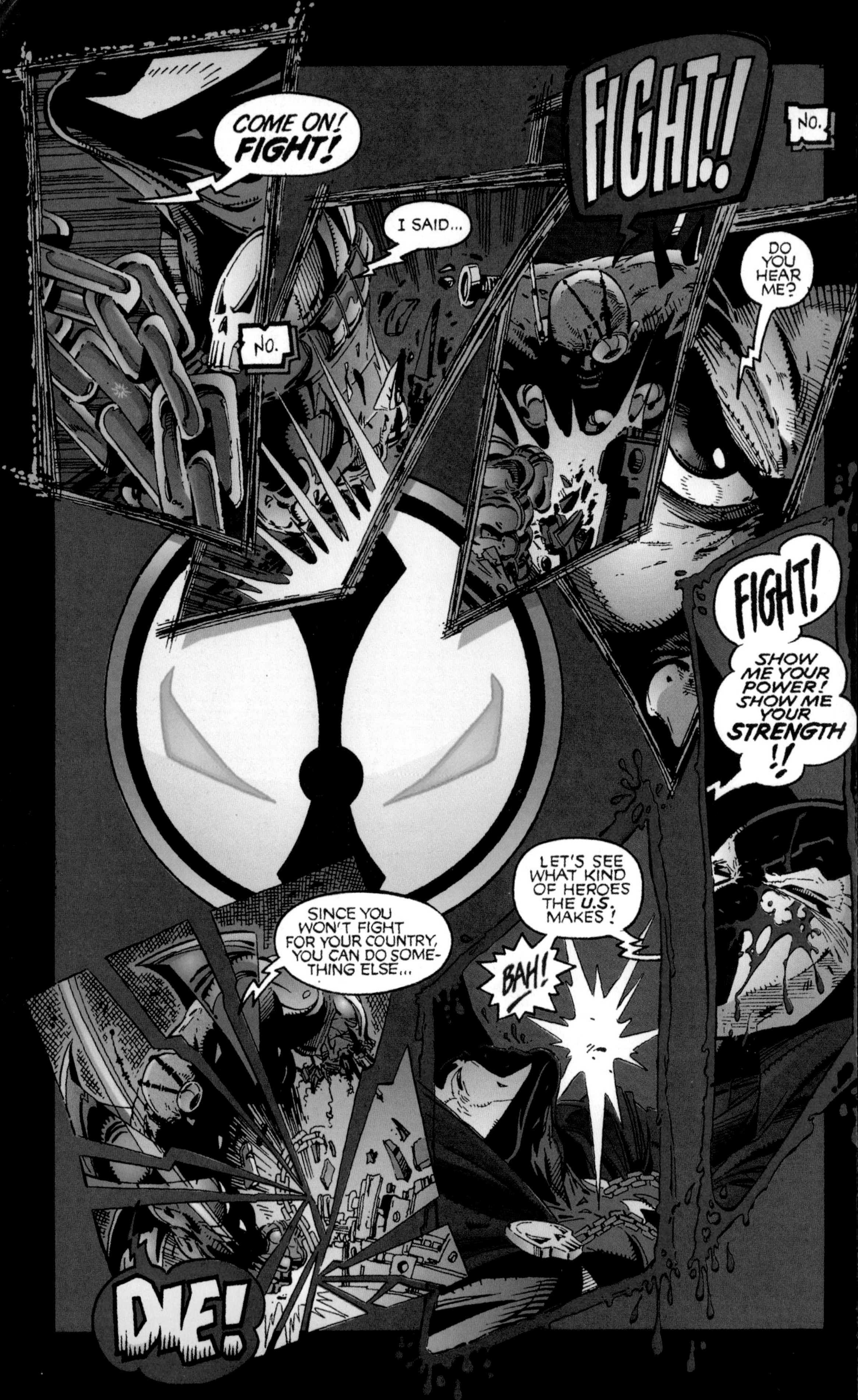
COME ON! FIGHT!
I SAID...
FIGHT!!
NO.
NO.
DO YOU HEAR ME?
FIGHT!
SHOW ME YOUR POWER! SHOW ME YOUR STRENGTH !!
SINCE YOU WON'T FIGHT FOR YOUR COUNTRY, YOU CAN DO SOMETHING ELSE...
LET'S SEE WHAT KIND OF HEROES THE U.S. MAKES!
BAH!
DIE!

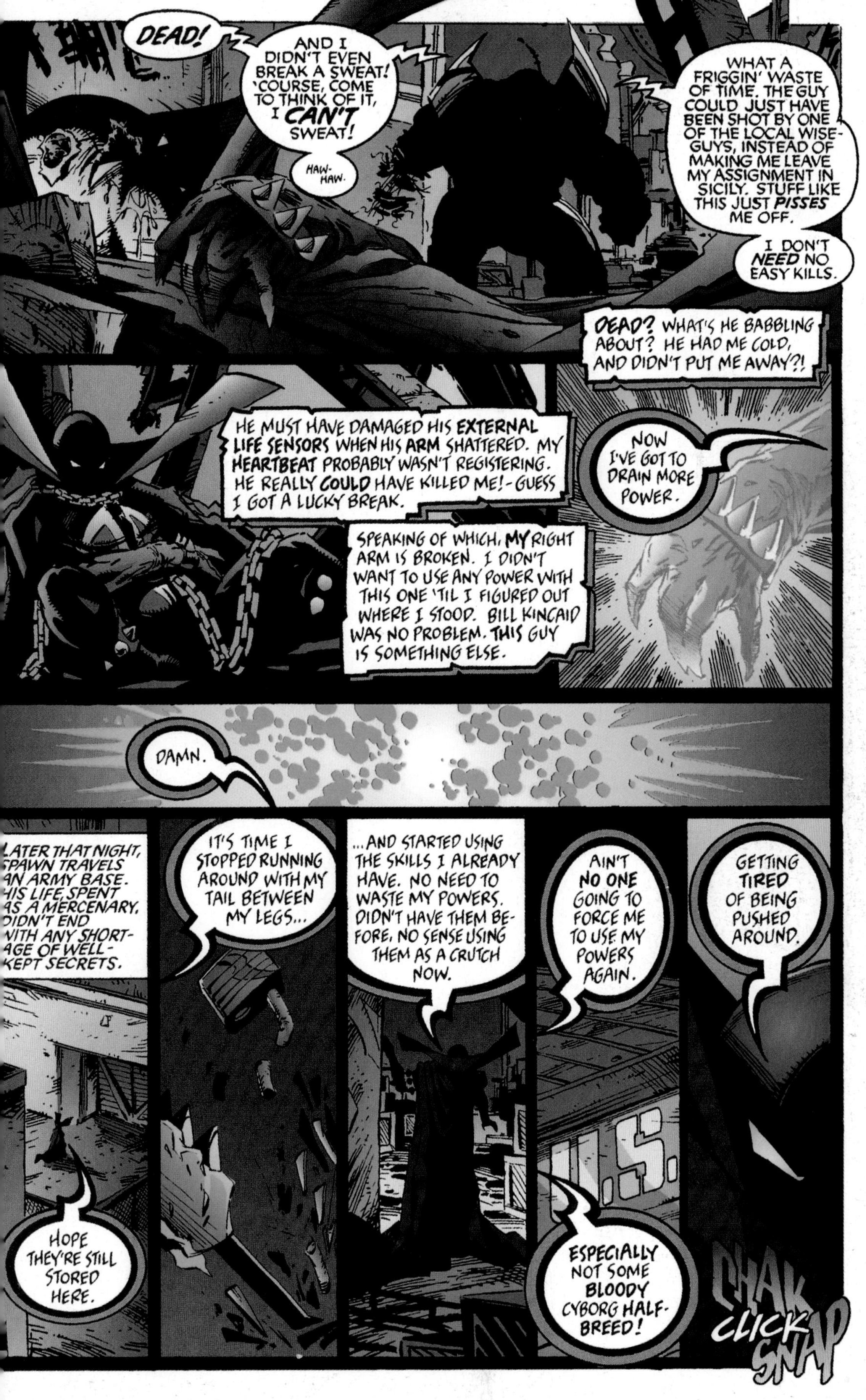
DEAD!
AND I DIDN'T EVEN BREAK A SWEAT! 'COURSE, COME TO THINK OF IT, I CAN'T SWEAT!
HAW-HAW.
WHAT A FRIGGIN' WASTE OF TIME. THE GUY COULD JUST HAVE BEEN SHOT BY ONE OF THE LOCAL WISE-GUYS, INSTEAD OF MAKING ME LEAVE MY ASSIGNMENT IN SICILY. STUFF LIKE THIS JUST PISSES ME OFF.
I DON'T NEED NO EASY KILLS.
DEAD? WHAT'S HE BABBLING ABOUT? HE HAD ME COLD, AND DIDN'T PUT ME AWAY?!
HE MUST HAVE DAMAGED HIS EXTERNAL LIFE SENSORS WHEN HIS ARM SHATTERED. MY HEARTBEAT PROBABLY WASN'T REGISTERING. HE REALLY COULD HAVE KILLED ME! - GUESS I GOT A LUCKY BREAK.
SPEAKING OF WHICH, MY RIGHT ARM IS BROKEN. I DIDN'T WANT TO USE ANY POWER WITH THIS ONE 'TIL I FIGURED OUT WHERE I STOOD. BILL KINCAID WAS NO PROBLEM. THIS GUY IS SOMETHING ELSE.
NOW I'VE GOT TO DRAIN MORE POWER.
DAMN.
LATER THAT NIGHT, SPAWN TRAVELS AN ARMY BASE. HIS LIFE SPENT AS A MERCENARY, DIDN'T END WITH ANY SHORTAGE OF WELL-KEPT SECRETS.
HOPE THEY'RE STILL STORED HERE.
IT'S TIME I STOPPED RUNNING AROUND WITH MY TAIL BETWEEN MY LEGS...
...AND STARTED USING THE SKILLS I ALREADY HAVE. NO NEED TO WASTE MY POWERS. DIDN'T HAVE THEM BEFORE, NO SENSE USING THEM AS A CRUTCH NOW.
AIN'T NO ONE GOING TO FORCE ME TO USE MY POWERS AGAIN.
ESPECIALLY NOT SOME BLOODY CYBORG HALF-BREED!
GETTING TIRED OF BEING PUSHED AROUND.
CHAK
CLICK
SNAP

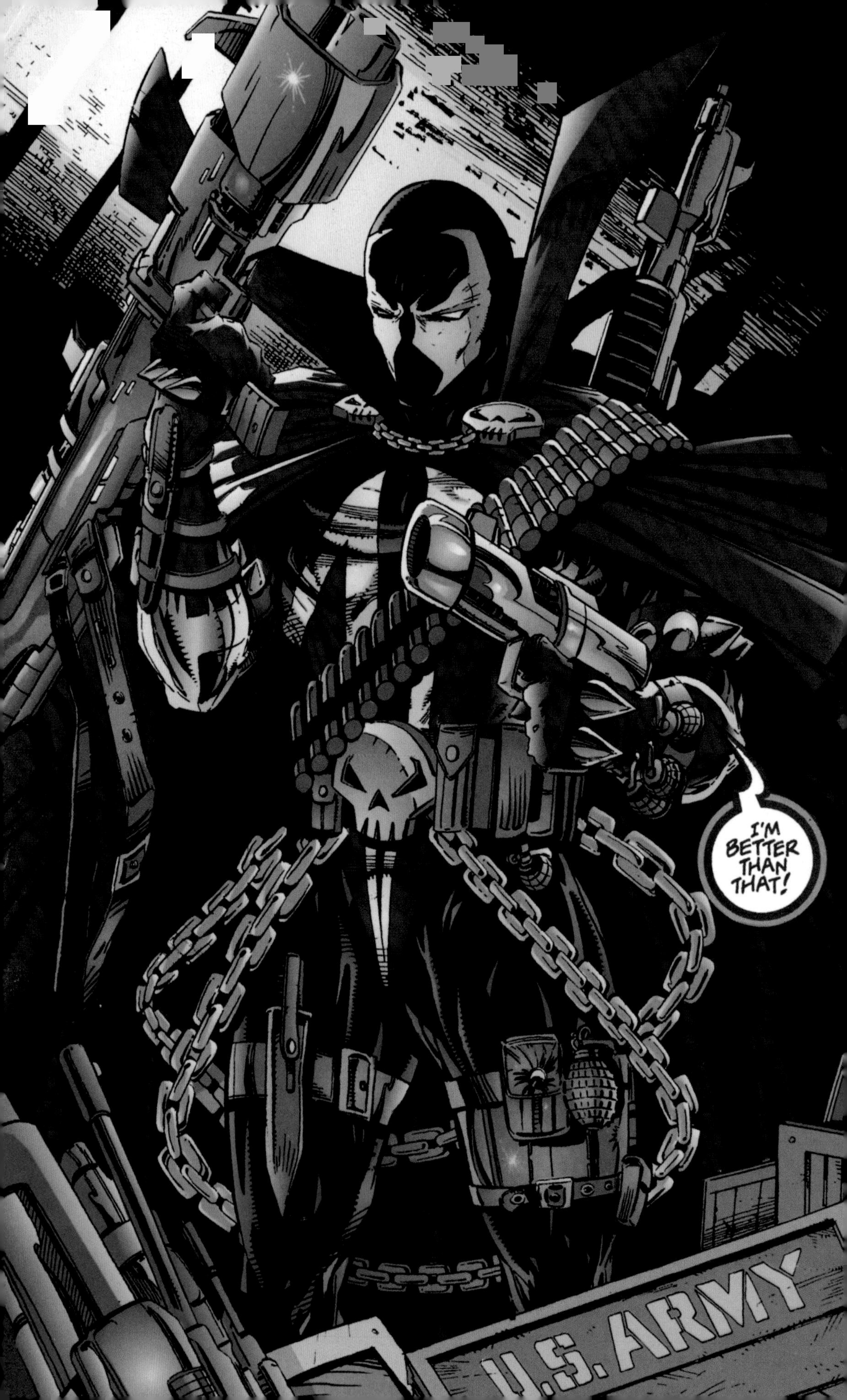
I'M BETTER THAN THAT!
U.S. ARMY

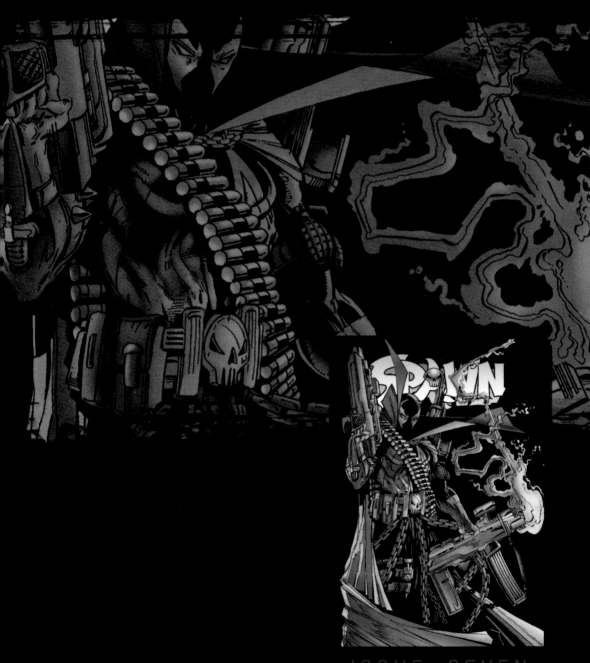

ISSUE SEVEN

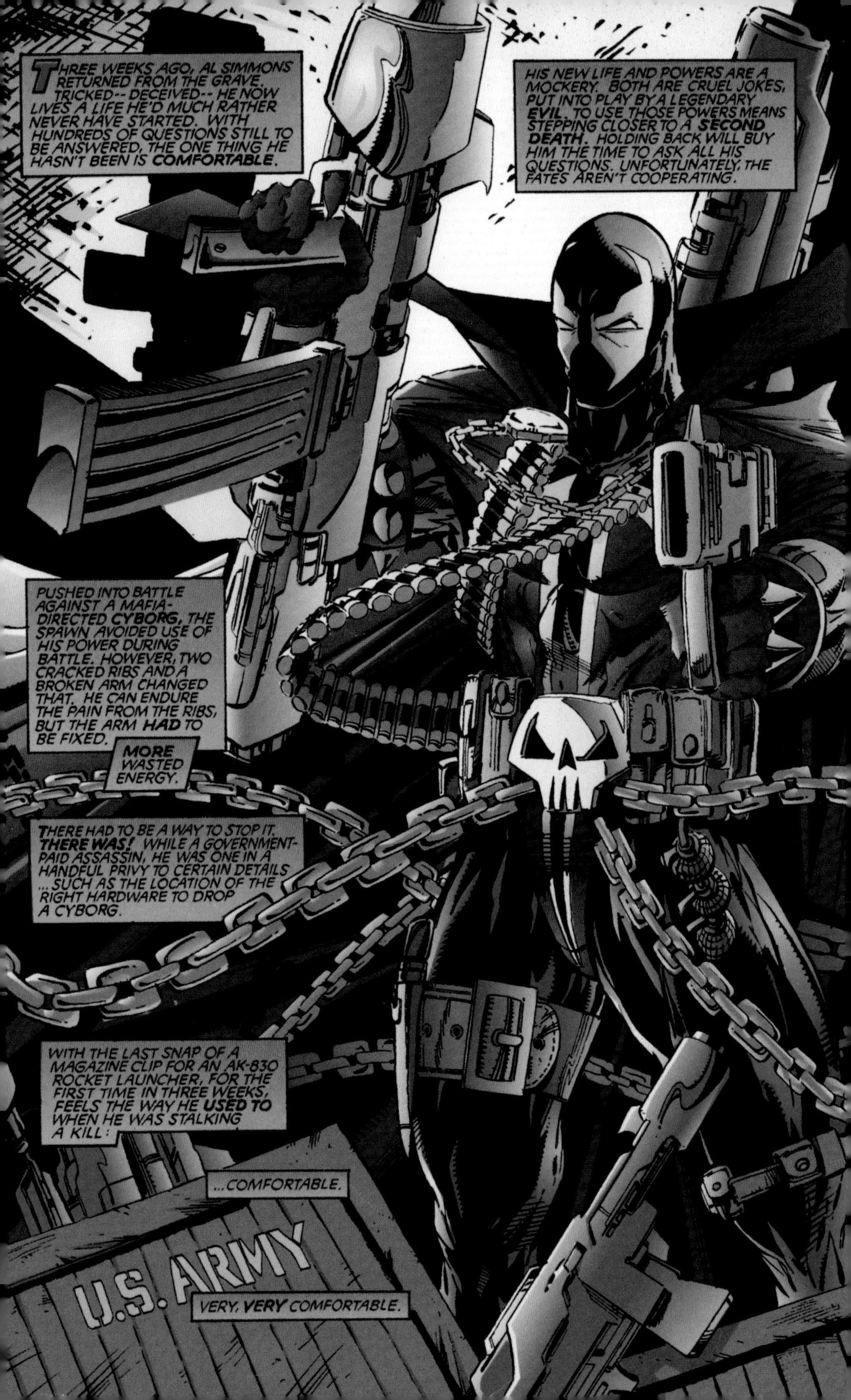
THREE WEEKS AGO, AL SIMMONS RETURNED FROM THE GRAVE. TRICKED-- DECEIVED-- HE NOW LIVES A LIFE HE'D MUCH RATHER NEVER HAVE STARTED. WITH HUNDREDS OF QUESTIONS STILL TO BE ANSWERED, THE ONE THING HE HASN'T BEEN IS COMFORTABLE.
HIS NEW LIFE AND POWERS ARE A MOCKERY. BOTH ARE CRUEL JOKES, PUT INTO PLAY BY A LEGENDARY EVIL. TO USE THOSE POWERS MEANS STEPPING CLOSER TO A SECOND DEATH. HOLDING BACK WILL BUY HIM THE TIME TO ASK ALL HIS QUESTIONS. UNFORTUNATELY, THE FATES AREN'T COOPERATING.
PUSHED INTO BATTLE AGAINST A MAFIA-DIRECTED CYBORG, THE SPAWN AVOIDED USE OF HIS POWER DURING BATTLE. HOWEVER, TWO CRACKED RIBS AND A BROKEN ARM CHANGED THAT. HE CAN ENDURE THE PAIN FROM THE RIBS, BUT THE ARM HAD TO BE FIXED.
MORE WASTED ENERGY.
THERE HAD TO BE A WAY TO STOP IT. THERE WAS! WHILE A GOVERNMENT-PAID ASSASSIN, HE WAS ONE IN A HANDFUL PRIVY TO CERTAIN DETAILS ... SUCH AS THE LOCATION OF THE RIGHT HARDWARE TO DROP A CYBORG.
WITH THE LAST SNAP OF A MAGAZINE CLIP FOR AN AK-830 ROCKET LAUNCHER, FOR THE FIRST TIME IN THREE WEEKS, FEELS THE WAY HE USED TO WHEN HE WAS STALKING A KILL:
...COMFORTABLE.
U.S. ARMY
VERY, VERY COMFORTABLE.

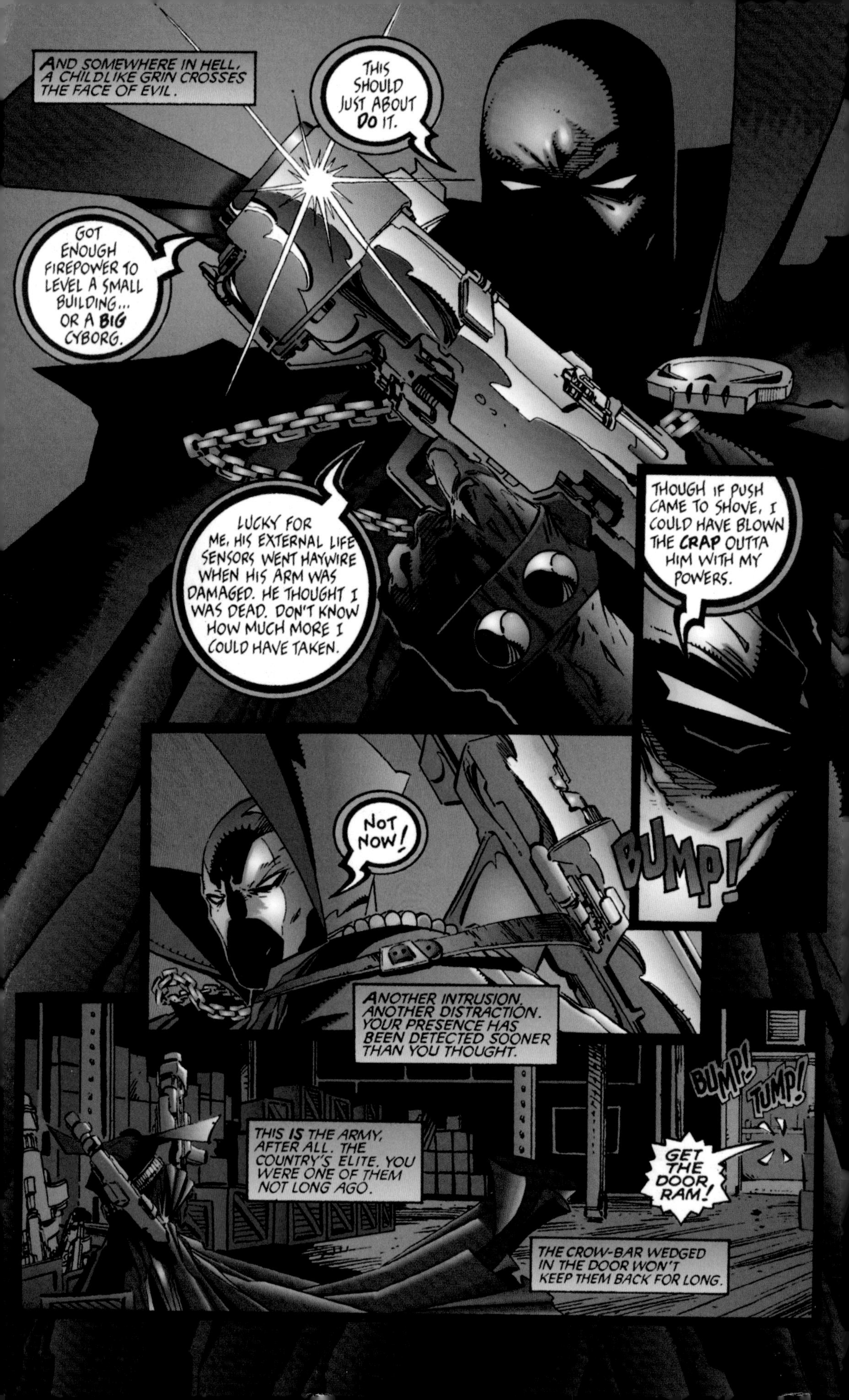

AND SOMEWHERE IN HELL, A CHILDLIKE GRIN CROSSES THE FACE OF EVIL.
THIS SHOULD JUST ABOUT DO IT.
GOT ENOUGH FIREPOWER TO LEVEL A SMALL BUILDING... OR A BIG CYBORG.
LUCKY FOR ME, HIS EXTERNAL LIFE SENSORS WENT HAYWIRE WHEN HIS ARM WAS DAMAGED. HE THOUGHT I WAS DEAD. DON'T KNOW HOW MUCH MORE I COULD HAVE TAKEN.
THOUGH IF PUSH CAME TO SHOVE, I COULD HAVE BLOWN THE CRAP OUTTA HIM WITH MY POWERS.
NOT NOW!
BUMP!
ANOTHER INTRUSION, ANOTHER DISTRACTION. YOUR PRESENCE HAS BEEN DETECTED SOONER THAN YOU THOUGHT.
BUMP! TUMP!
THIS IS THE ARMY, AFTER ALL. THE COUNTRY'S ELITE. YOU WERE ONE OF THEM NOT LONG AGO.
GET THE DOOR RAM!
THE CROW-BAR WEDGED IN THE DOOR WON'T KEEP THEM BACK FOR LONG.

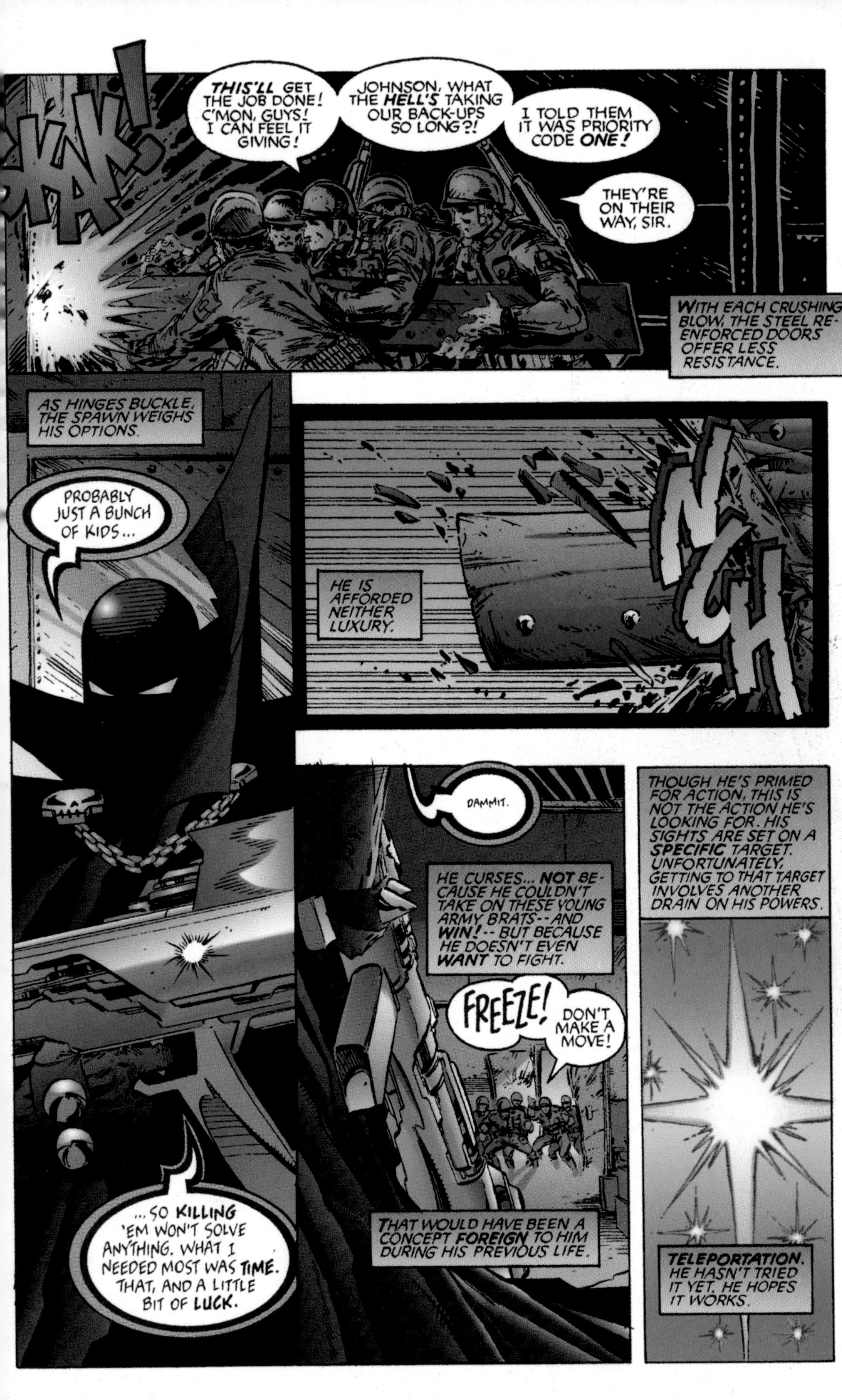
KAK!
THIS'LL GET THE JOB DONE! C'MON, GUYS! I CAN FEEL IT GIVING!
JOHNSON, WHAT THE HELL'S TAKING OUR BACK-UPS SO LONG?!
I TOLD THEM IT WAS PRIORITY CODE ONE!
THEY'RE ON THEIR WAY, SIR.
WITH EACH CRUSHING BLOW, THE STEEL RE-ENFORCED DOORS OFFER LESS RESISTANCE.
AS HINGES BUCKLE, THE SPAWN WEIGHS HIS OPTIONS.
PROBABLY JUST A BUNCH OF KIDS...
HE IS AFFORDED NEITHER LUXURY.
NCH
...SO KILLING 'EM WON'T SOLVE ANYTHING. WHAT I NEEDED MOST WAS TIME. THAT, AND A LITTLE BIT OF LUCK.
DAMMIT.
HE CURSES... NOT BECAUSE HE COULDN'T TAKE ON THESE YOUNG ARMY BRATS--AND WIN!--BUT BECAUSE HE DOESN'T EVEN WANT TO FIGHT.
FREEZE!
DON'T MAKE A MOVE!
THAT WOULD HAVE BEEN A CONCEPT FOREIGN TO HIM DURING HIS PREVIOUS LIFE.
THOUGH HE'S PRIMED FOR ACTION, THIS IS NOT THE ACTION HE'S LOOKING FOR. HIS SIGHTS ARE SET ON A SPECIFIC TARGET. UNFORTUNATELY, GETTING TO THAT TARGET INVOLVES ANOTHER DRAIN ON HIS POWERS.
TELEPORTATION. HE HASN'T TRIED IT YET. HE HOPES IT WORKS.

IT DOES, SORT OF.

HIS MOLECULES ARE RIPPED APART, ONE BY ONE, THEN MESHED TOGETHER WITH THE EXISTING MOLECULAR STRUCTURES PRESENT. THEY ARE THEN *VACUUMED*--SUCKED AT THE SPEED OF LIGHT--TO A PRE-ORDAINED LOCATION...

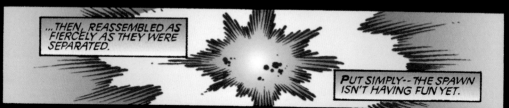

...THEN, REASSEMBLED AS FIERCELY AS THEY WERE SEPARATED.

PUT SIMPLY--THE SPAWN ISN'T HAVING FUN YET.

HOLY MOTHER!!

I THINK I'M GOING TO PUKE...

HE MELTS TO THE GROUND OF A DESERTED ALLEYWAY IN THE BOWERY, AN AREA THAT SOMEHOW DRAWS HIM BACK SINCE HIS RETURN TO EARTH.

THIS IS HIS NEW HOME. FULL OF GARBAGE AND CRAP AND DRUNKS, IT SERVES A PURPOSE: THAT OF A *CONSTANT*.

BESIDES, HE'S BEGINNING TO *BOND* WITH SOME OF HIS 'NEIGHBORS.'

HGKKHLKP

AS HE THRASHES, CRUMPLED ON THE CRACKED PAVEMENT, AN ADVANTAGE OF THIS ARRANGEMENT BECOMES APPARENT.

YO! RED MAN!

NEVER FEAR! *BOBBY'S* HERE!

YOU AIN'T *LOOKIN'* SO SOLID, I SAY TO MYSELF, IT'S TIME FOR GOOD OL' *UNCLE BOBBY* TO WEAVE SOME OF HIS STREET MAGIC.

hic_

oops!

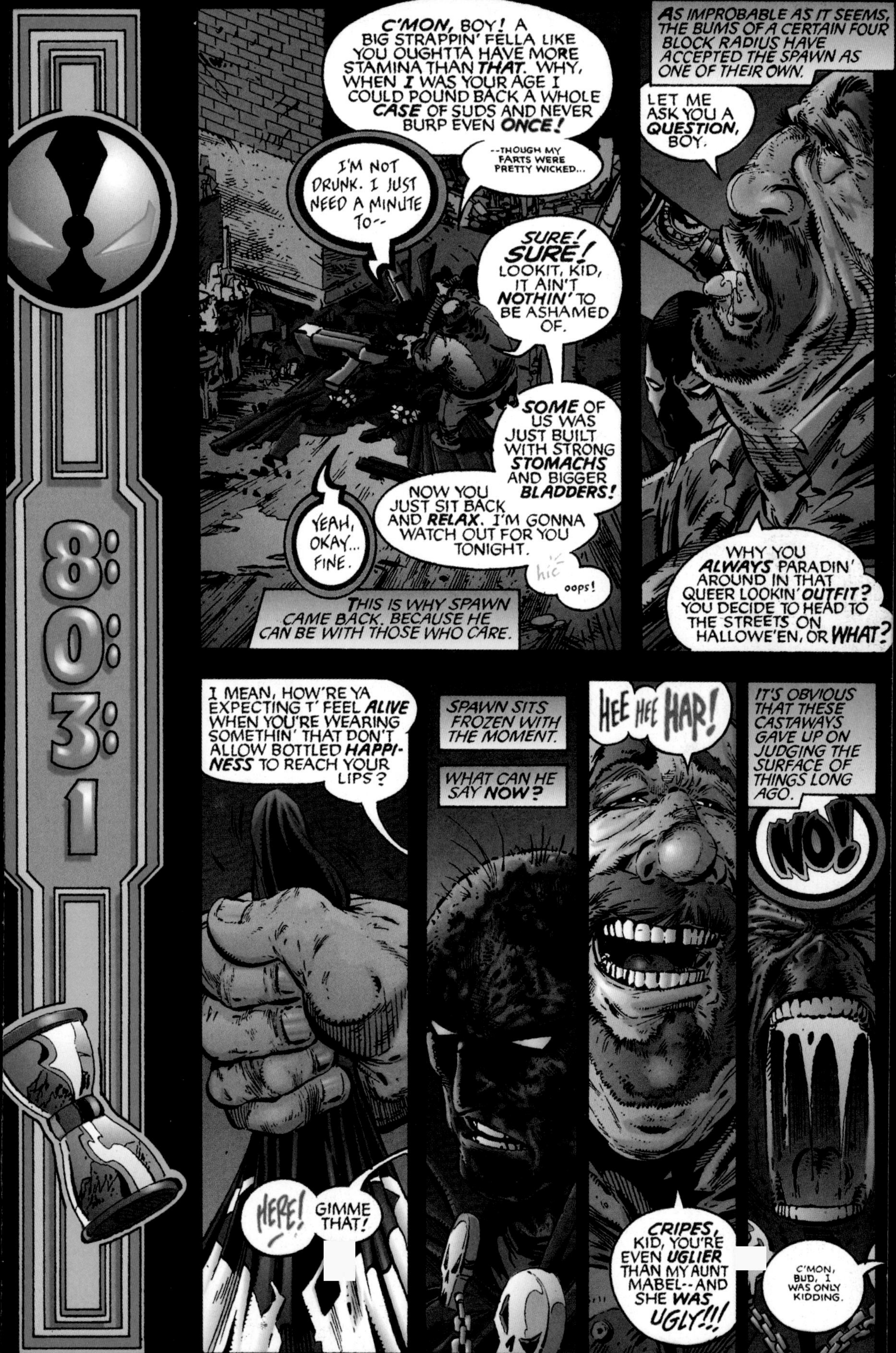
8:03:1
C'MON, BOY! A BIG STRAPPIN' FELLA LIKE YOU OUGHTTA HAVE MORE STAMINA THAN THAT. WHY, WHEN I WAS YOUR AGE I COULD POUND BACK A WHOLE CASE OF SUDS AND NEVER BURP EVEN ONCE!
--THOUGH MY FARTS WERE PRETTY WICKED...
I'M NOT DRUNK. I JUST NEED A MINUTE TO--
SURE! SURE! LOOKIT, KID, IT AIN'T NOTHIN' TO BE ASHAMED OF.
SOME OF US WAS JUST BUILT WITH STRONG STOMACHS AND BIGGER BLADDERS!
NOW YOU JUST SIT BACK AND RELAX. I'M GONNA WATCH OUT FOR YOU TONIGHT.
YEAH, OKAY... FINE.
hic
oops!
THIS IS WHY SPAWN CAME BACK. BECAUSE HE CAN BE WITH THOSE WHO CARE.
AS IMPROBABLE AS IT SEEMS, THE BUMS OF A CERTAIN FOUR BLOCK RADIUS HAVE ACCEPTED THE SPAWN AS ONE OF THEIR OWN.
LET ME ASK YOU A QUESTION, BOY.
WHY YOU ALWAYS PARADIN' AROUND IN THAT QUEER LOOKIN' OUTFIT? YOU DECIDE TO HEAD TO THE STREETS ON HALLOWE'EN, OR WHAT?
I MEAN, HOW'RE YA EXPECTING T' FEEL ALIVE WHEN YOU'RE WEARING SOMETHIN' THAT DON'T ALLOW BOTTLED HAPPI-NESS TO REACH YOUR LIPS?
HERE!
GIMME THAT!
SPAWN SITS FROZEN WITH THE MOMENT.
WHAT CAN HE SAY NOW?
HEE HEE HAR!
CRIPES, KID, YOU'RE EVEN UGLIER THAN MY AUNT MABEL--AND SHE WAS UGLY!!!
IT'S OBVIOUS THAT THESE CASTAWAYS GAVE UP ON JUDGING THE SURFACE OF THINGS LONG AGO.
NO!
C'MON, BUD, I WAS ONLY KIDDING.

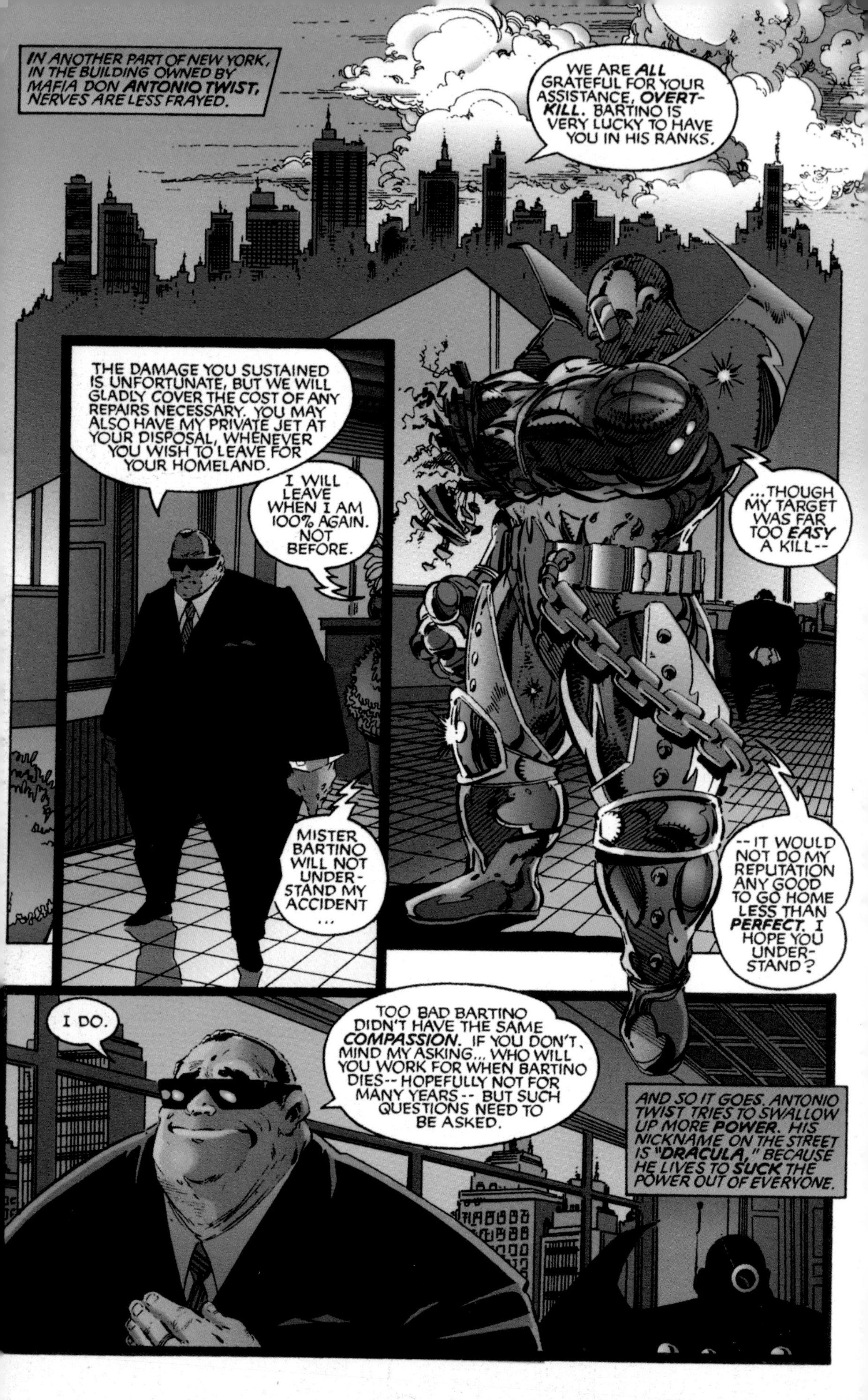
IN ANOTHER PART OF NEW YORK, IN THE BUILDING OWNED BY MAFIA DON ANTONIO TWIST, NERVES ARE LESS FRAYED.
WE ARE ALL GRATEFUL FOR YOUR ASSISTANCE, OVERT-KILL. BARTINO IS VERY LUCKY TO HAVE YOU IN HIS RANKS.
THE DAMAGE YOU SUSTAINED IS UNFORTUNATE, BUT WE WILL GLADLY COVER THE COST OF ANY REPAIRS NECESSARY. YOU MAY ALSO HAVE MY PRIVATE JET AT YOUR DISPOSAL, WHENEVER YOU WISH TO LEAVE FOR YOUR HOMELAND.
I WILL LEAVE WHEN I AM 100% AGAIN. NOT BEFORE.
...THOUGH MY TARGET WAS FAR TOO EASY A KILL--
MISTER BARTINO WILL NOT UNDER-STAND MY ACCIDENT ...
-- IT WOULD NOT DO MY REPUTATION ANY GOOD TO GO HOME LESS THAN PERFECT. I HOPE YOU UNDER-STAND?
I DO.
TOO BAD BARTINO DIDN'T HAVE THE SAME COMPASSION. IF YOU DON'T MIND MY ASKING... WHO WILL YOU WORK FOR WHEN BARTINO DIES-- HOPEFULLY NOT FOR MANY YEARS -- BUT SUCH QUESTIONS NEED TO BE ASKED.
AND SO IT GOES. ANTONIO TWIST TRIES TO SWALLOW UP MORE POWER. HIS NICKNAME ON THE STREET IS "DRACULA," BECAUSE HE LIVES TO SUCK THE POWER OUT OF EVERYONE.

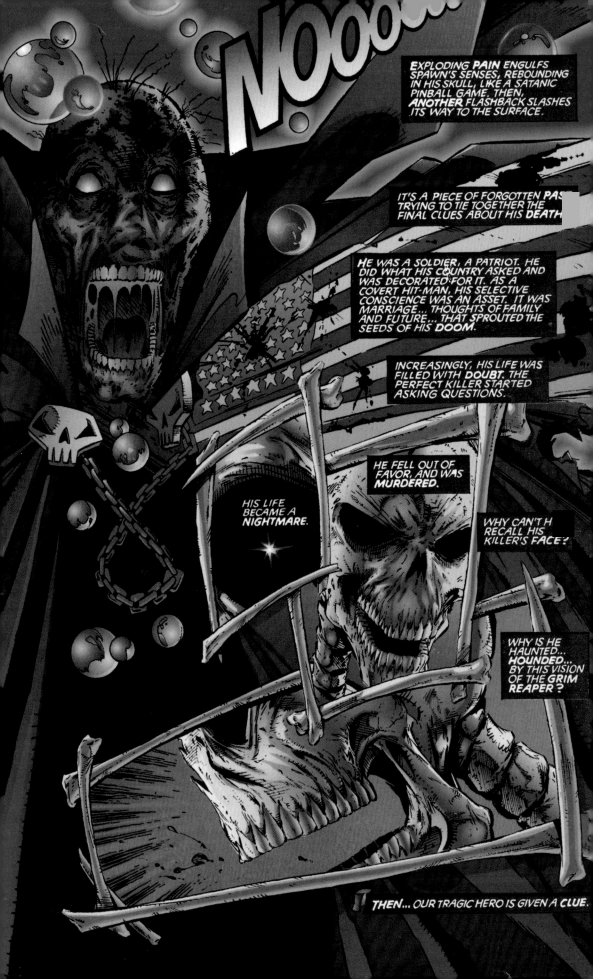

NOOo...

EXPLODING **PAIN** ENGULFS SPAWN'S SENSES, REBOUNDING IN HIS SKULL, LIKE A SATANIC PINBALL GAME. THEN, **ANOTHER** FLASHBACK SLASHES ITS WAY TO THE SURFACE.

IT'S A PIECE OF FORGOTTEN PAS TRYING TO TIE TOGETHER THE FINAL CLUES ABOUT HIS **DEATH**

HE WAS A SOLDIER, A PATRIOT. HE DID WHAT HIS COUNTRY ASKED AND WAS DECORATED FOR IT. AS A COVERT HIT-MAN, HIS SELECTIVE CONSCIENCE WAS AN ASSET. IT WAS MARRIAGE... THOUGHTS OF FAMILY AND FUTURE... THAT SPROUTED THE SEEDS OF HIS **DOOM**.

INCREASINGLY, HIS LIFE WAS FILLED WITH **DOUBT**. THE PERFECT KILLER STARTED ASKING QUESTIONS.

HE FELL OUT OF FAVOR, AND WAS **MURDERED**.

HIS LIFE BECAME A **NIGHTMARE**.

WHY CAN'T H RECALL HIS KILLER'S **FACE**?

WHY IS HE HAUNTED... **HOUNDED**... BY THIS VISION OF THE GRIM REAPER?

THEN... OUR TRAGIC HERO IS GIVEN A **CLUE**.

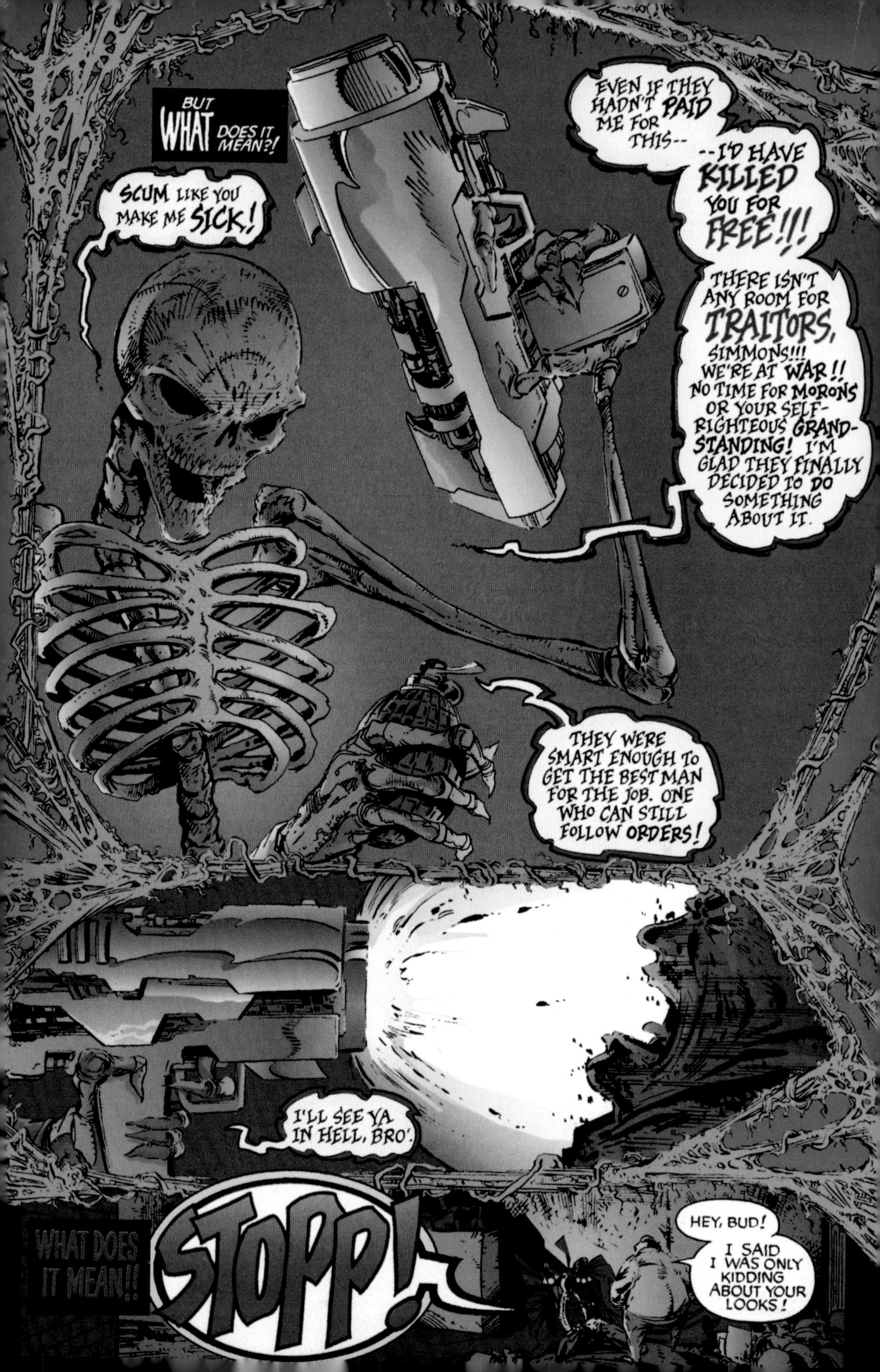
BUT WHAT DOES IT MEAN?!
SCUM LIKE YOU MAKE ME SICK!
EVEN IF THEY HADN'T PAID ME FOR THIS--
--I'D HAVE KILLED YOU FOR FREE!!!
THERE ISN'T ANY ROOM FOR TRAITORS, SIMMONS!!! WE'RE AT WAR!! NO TIME FOR MORONS OR YOUR SELF-RIGHTEOUS GRAND-STANDING! I'M GLAD THEY FINALLY DECIDED TO DO SOMETHING ABOUT IT.
THEY WERE SMART ENOUGH TO GET THE BEST MAN FOR THE JOB. ONE WHO CAN STILL FOLLOW ORDERS!
I'LL SEE YA IN HELL, BRO'.
WHAT DOES IT MEAN!!
STOPP!
HEY, BUD!
I SAID I WAS ONLY KIDDING ABOUT YOUR LOOKS!

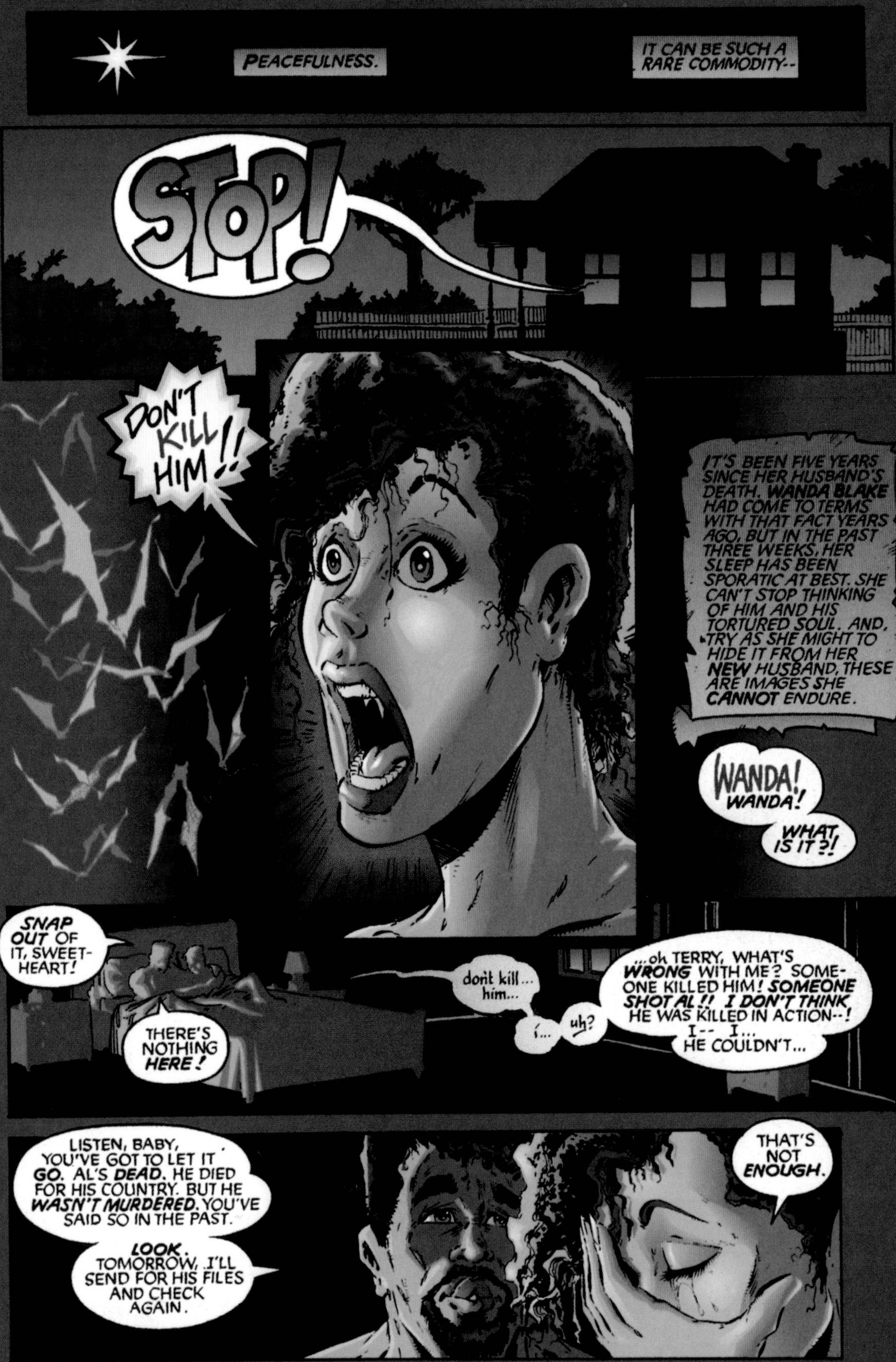
PEACEFULNESS.
IT CAN BE SUCH A RARE COMMODITY--
STOP!
DON'T KILL HIM!!
IT'S BEEN FIVE YEARS SINCE HER HUSBAND'S DEATH. WANDA BLAKE HAD COME TO TERMS WITH THAT FACT YEARS AGO, BUT IN THE PAST THREE WEEKS, HER SLEEP HAS BEEN SPORATIC AT BEST. SHE CAN'T STOP THINKING OF HIM AND HIS TORTURED SOUL. AND, TRY AS SHE MIGHT TO HIDE IT FROM HER NEW HUSBAND, THESE ARE IMAGES SHE CANNOT ENDURE.
WANDA! WANDA!
WHAT IS IT?!
SNAP OUT OF IT, SWEET-HEART!
THERE'S NOTHING HERE!
don't kill... him...
i... uh?
...oh TERRY, WHAT'S WRONG WITH ME? SOME-ONE KILLED HIM! SOMEONE SHOT AL!! I DON'T THINK HE WAS KILLED IN ACTION--! I-- I... HE COULDN'T...
LISTEN, BABY, YOU'VE GOT TO LET IT GO. AL'S DEAD. HE DIED FOR HIS COUNTRY. BUT HE WASN'T MURDERED. YOU'VE SAID SO IN THE PAST.
LOOK. TOMORROW, I'LL SEND FOR HIS FILES AND CHECK AGAIN.
THAT'S NOT ENOUGH.

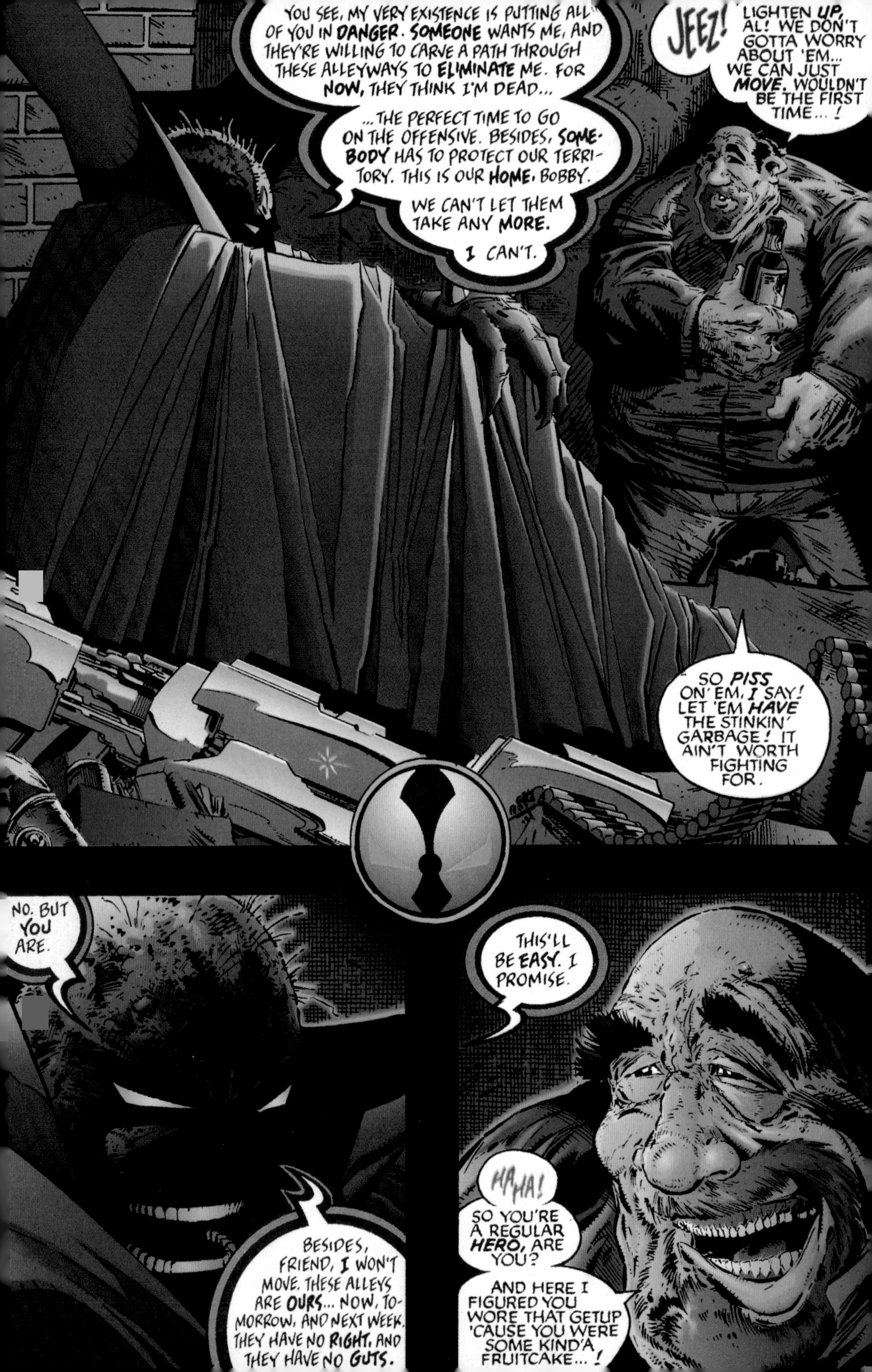
YOU SEE, MY VERY EXISTENCE IS PUTTING ALL OF YOU IN DANGER. SOMEONE WANTS ME, AND THEY'RE WILLING TO CARVE A PATH THROUGH THESE ALLEYWAYS TO ELIMINATE ME. FOR NOW, THEY THINK I'M DEAD...
...THE PERFECT TIME TO GO ON THE OFFENSIVE. BESIDES, SOMEBODY HAS TO PROTECT OUR TERRITORY. THIS IS OUR HOME, BOBBY.
WE CAN'T LET THEM TAKE ANY MORE.
I CAN'T.
JEEZ!
LIGHTEN UP, AL! WE DON'T GOTTA WORRY ABOUT 'EM... WE CAN JUST MOVE. WOULDN'T BE THE FIRST TIME... !
SO PISS ON 'EM, I SAY! LET 'EM HAVE THE STINKIN' GARBAGE! IT AIN'T WORTH FIGHTING FOR.
NO. BUT YOU ARE.
BESIDES, FRIEND, I WON'T MOVE. THESE ALLEYS ARE OURS... NOW, TOMORROW, AND NEXT WEEK. THEY HAVE NO RIGHT, AND THEY HAVE NO GUTS.
THIS'LL BE EASY. I PROMISE.
HA HA!
SO YOU'RE A REGULAR HERO, ARE YOU?
AND HERE I FIGURED YOU WORE THAT GETUP 'CAUSE YOU WERE SOME KIND'A FRUITCAKE... !

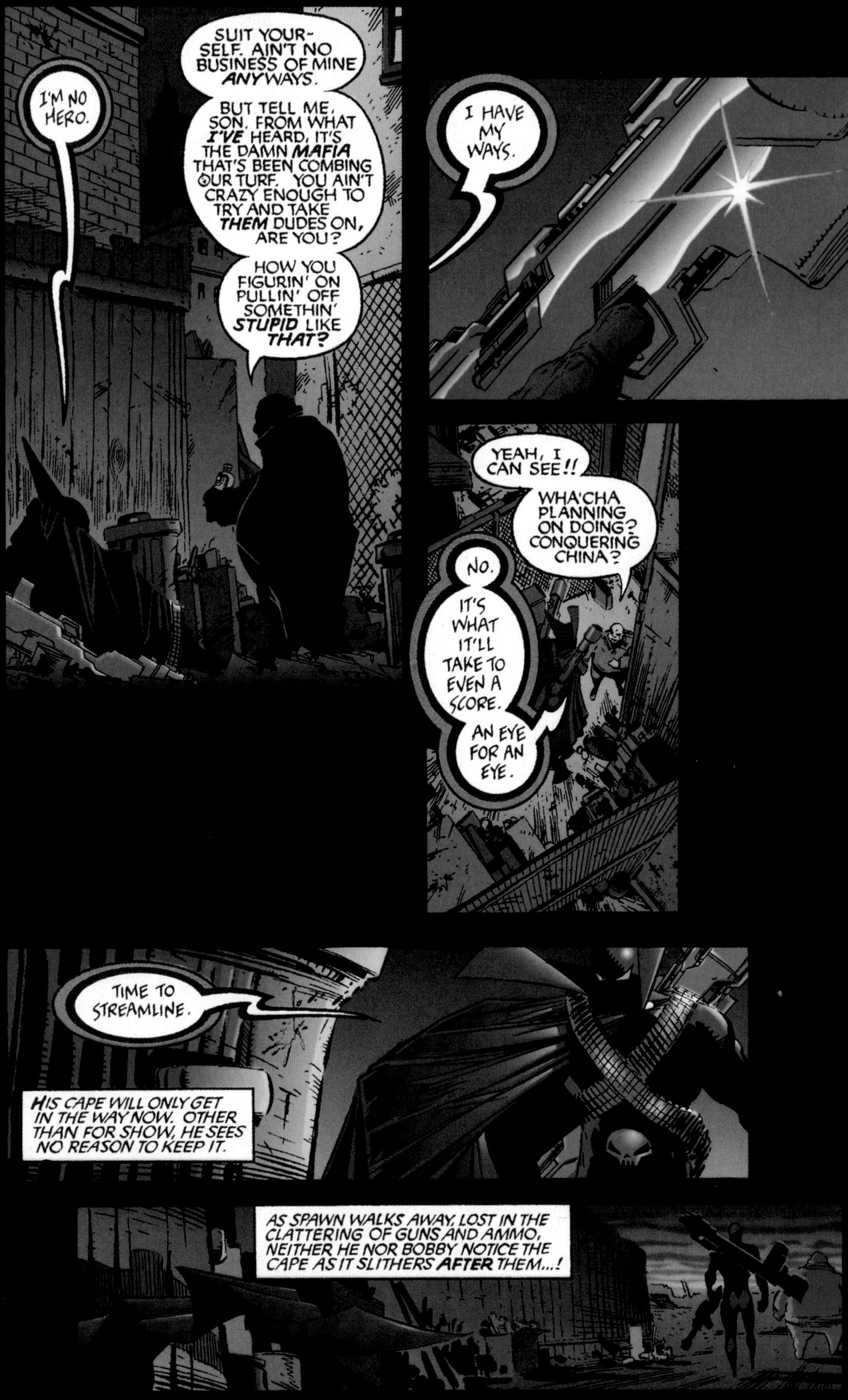
SUIT YOUR-SELF. AIN'T NO BUSINESS OF MINE ANYWAYS.
BUT TELL ME, SON. FROM WHAT I'VE HEARD, IT'S THE DAMN MAFIA THAT'S BEEN COMBING OUR TURF. YOU AIN'T CRAZY ENOUGH TO TRY AND TAKE THEM DUDES ON, ARE YOU?
HOW YOU FIGURIN' ON PULLIN' OFF SOMETHIN' STUPID LIKE THAT?
I'M NO HERO.
I HAVE MY WAYS.
YEAH, I CAN SEE!!
WHA'CHA PLANNING ON DOING? CONQUERING CHINA?
NO.
IT'S WHAT IT'LL TAKE TO EVEN A SCORE.
AN EYE FOR AN EYE.
TIME TO STREAMLINE.
HIS CAPE WILL ONLY GET IN THE WAY NOW. OTHER THAN FOR SHOW, HE SEES NO REASON TO KEEP IT.
AS SPAWN WALKS AWAY, LOST IN THE CLATTERING OF GUNS AND AMMO, NEITHER HE NOR BOBBY NOTICE THE CAPE AS IT SLITHERS AFTER THEM...!

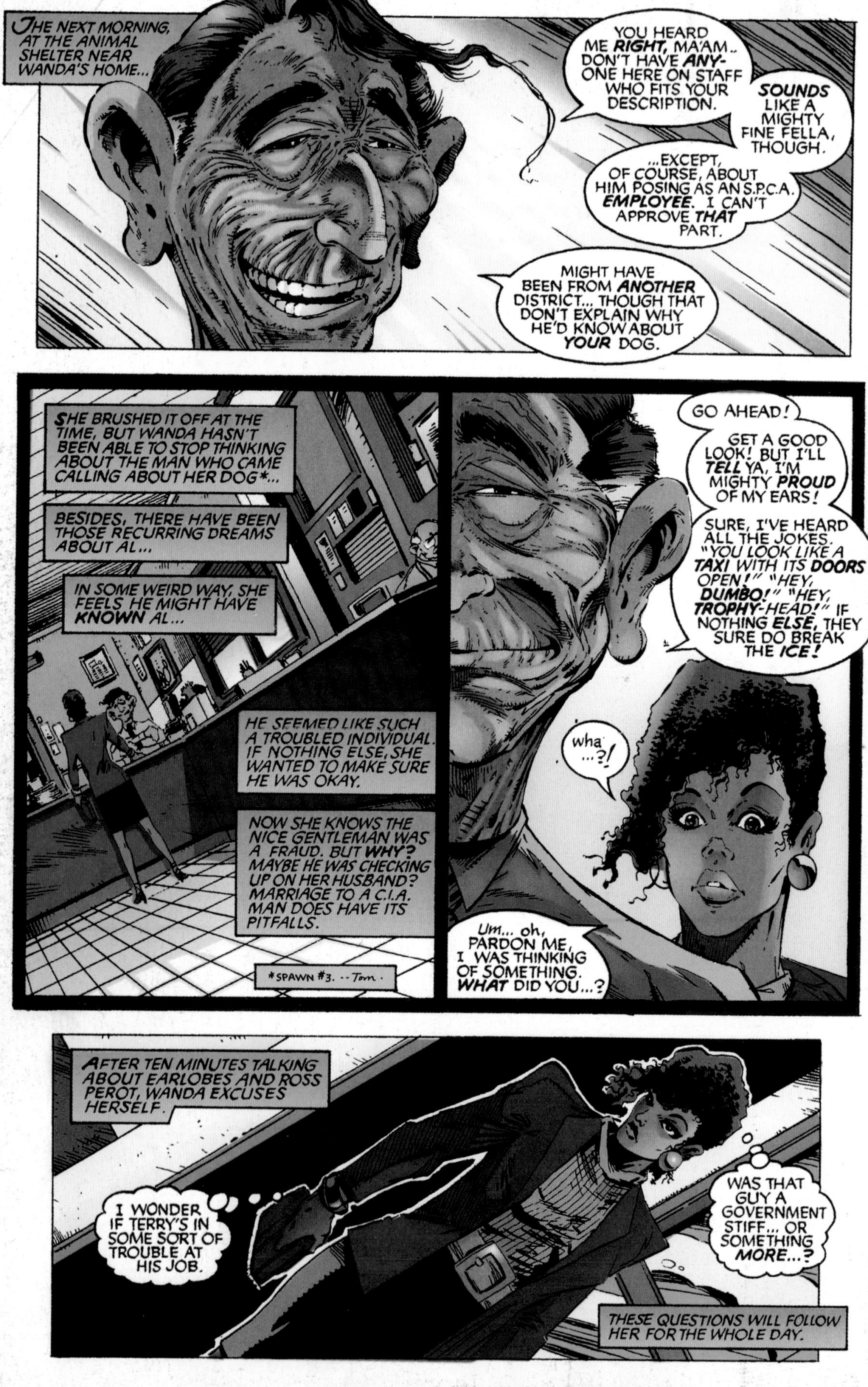
THE NEXT MORNING, AT THE ANIMAL SHELTER NEAR WANDA'S HOME...
YOU HEARD ME RIGHT, MA'AM.. DON'T HAVE ANY-ONE HERE ON STAFF WHO FITS YOUR DESCRIPTION.
SOUNDS LIKE A MIGHTY FINE FELLA, THOUGH.
...EXCEPT, OF COURSE, ABOUT HIM POSING AS AN S.P.C.A. EMPLOYEE. I CAN'T APPROVE THAT PART.
MIGHT HAVE BEEN FROM ANOTHER DISTRICT... THOUGH THAT DON'T EXPLAIN WHY HE'D KNOW ABOUT YOUR DOG.
SHE BRUSHED IT OFF AT THE TIME, BUT WANDA HASN'T BEEN ABLE TO STOP THINKING ABOUT THE MAN WHO CAME CALLING ABOUT HER DOG*...
BESIDES, THERE HAVE BEEN THOSE RECURRING DREAMS ABOUT AL...
IN SOME WEIRD WAY, SHE FEELS HE MIGHT HAVE KNOWN AL...
HE SEEMED LIKE SUCH A TROUBLED INDIVIDUAL. IF NOTHING ELSE, SHE WANTED TO MAKE SURE HE WAS OKAY.
NOW SHE KNOWS THE NICE GENTLEMAN WAS A FRAUD. BUT WHY? MAYBE HE WAS CHECKING UP ON HER HUSBAND? MARRIAGE TO A C.I.A. MAN DOES HAVE ITS PITFALLS.
*SPAWN #3. --Tom.
GO AHEAD!
GET A GOOD LOOK! BUT I'LL TELL YA, I'M MIGHTY PROUD OF MY EARS!
SURE, I'VE HEARD ALL THE JOKES. "YOU LOOK LIKE A TAXI WITH ITS DOORS OPEN!" "HEY, DUMBO!" "HEY, TROPHY-HEAD!" IF NOTHING ELSE, THEY SURE DO BREAK THE ICE!
wha ...?!
Um... oh, PARDON ME, I WAS THINKING OF SOMETHING. WHAT DID YOU...?
AFTER TEN MINUTES TALKING ABOUT EARLOBES AND ROSS PEROT, WANDA EXCUSES HERSELF.
I WONDER IF TERRY'S IN SOME SORT OF TROUBLE AT HIS JOB.
WAS THAT GUY A GOVERNMENT STIFF... OR SOMETHING MORE...?
THESE QUESTIONS WILL FOLLOW HER FOR THE WHOLE DAY.

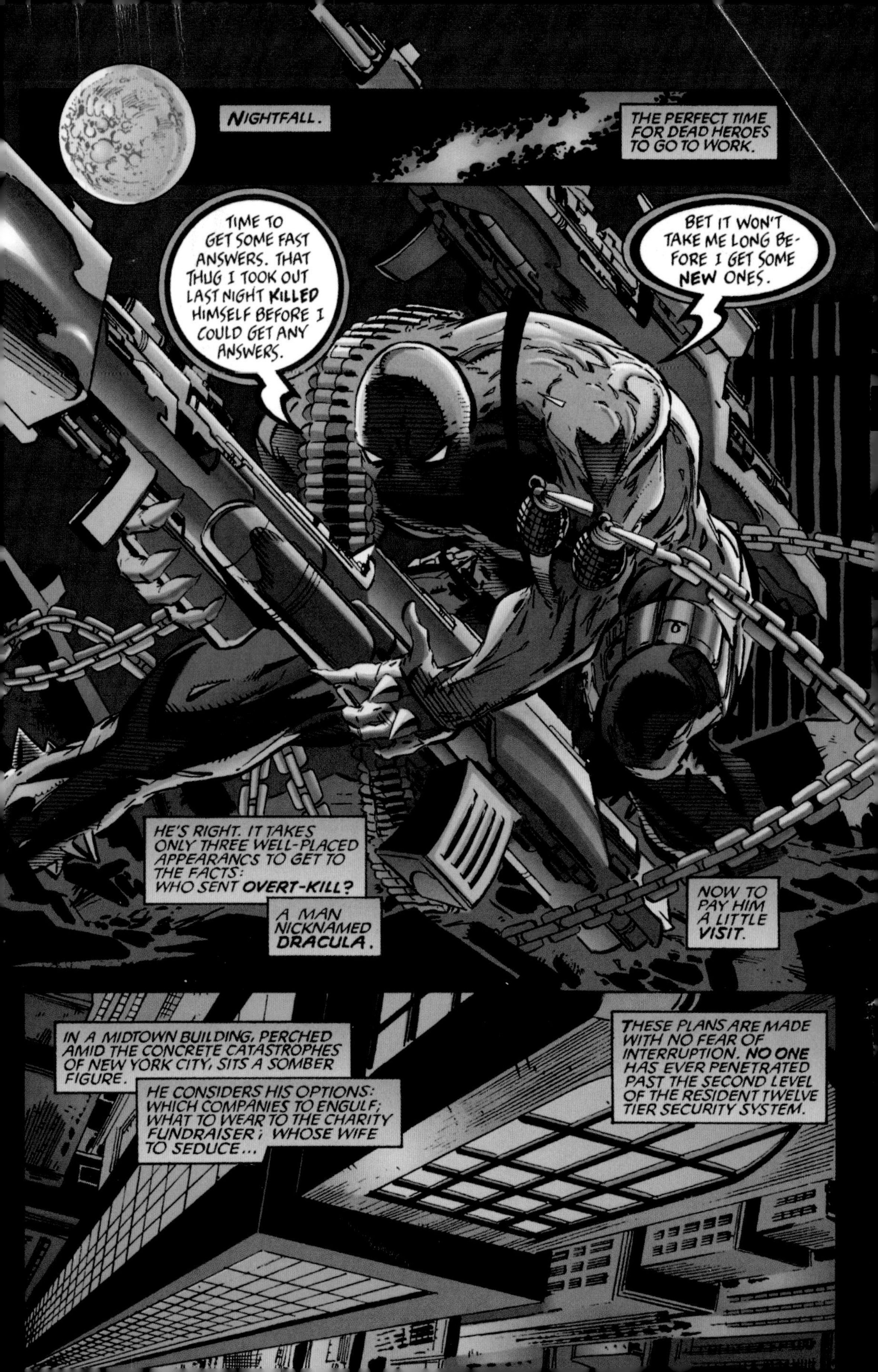
NIGHTFALL.
THE PERFECT TIME FOR DEAD HEROES TO GO TO WORK.
TIME TO GET SOME FAST ANSWERS. THAT THUG I TOOK OUT LAST NIGHT KILLED HIMSELF BEFORE I COULD GET ANY ANSWERS.
BET IT WON'T TAKE ME LONG BE-FORE I GET SOME NEW ONES.
HE'S RIGHT. IT TAKES ONLY THREE WELL-PLACED APPEARANCS TO GET TO THE FACTS: WHO SENT OVERT-KILL?
A MAN NICKNAMED DRACULA.
NOW TO PAY HIM A LITTLE VISIT.
IN A MIDTOWN BUILDING, PERCHED AMID THE CONCRETE CATASTROPHES OF NEW YORK CITY, SITS A SOMBER FIGURE.
HE CONSIDERS HIS OPTIONS: WHICH COMPANIES TO ENGULF; WHAT TO WEAR TO THE CHARITY FUNDRAISER; WHOSE WIFE TO SEDUCE...
THESE PLANS ARE MADE WITH NO FEAR OF INTERRUPTION. NO ONE HAS EVER PENETRATED PAST THE SECOND LEVEL OF THE RESIDENT TWELVE TIER SECURITY SYSTEM.

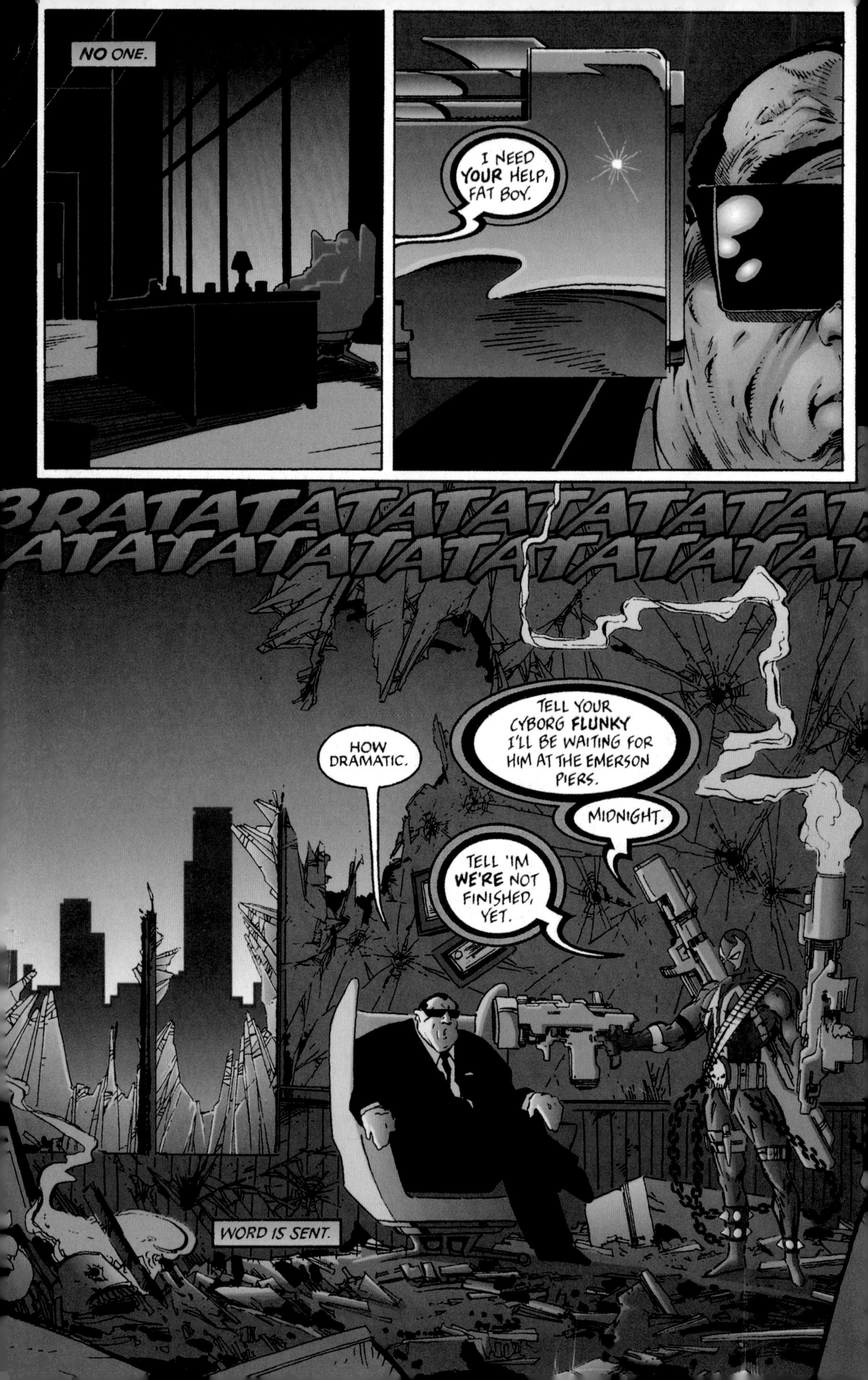
NO ONE.
I NEED YOUR HELP, FAT BOY.
BRATATATATATATATATATAT ATATATATATATATATATATAT
HOW DRAMATIC.
TELL YOUR CYBORG FLUNKY I'LL BE WAITING FOR HIM AT THE EMERSON PIERS.
MIDNIGHT.
TELL 'IM WE'RE NOT FINISHED, YET.
WORD IS SENT.

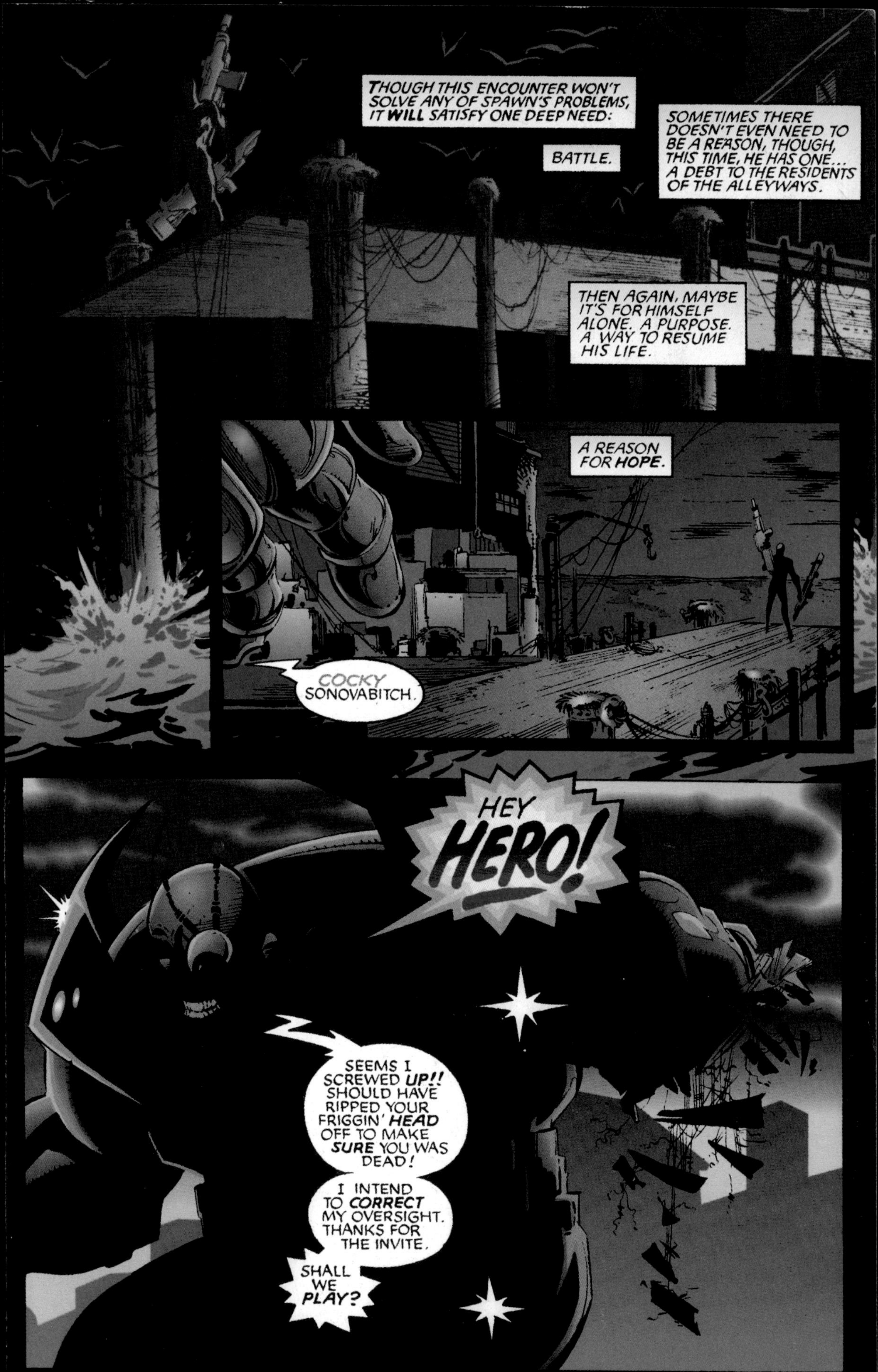
THOUGH THIS ENCOUNTER WON'T SOLVE ANY OF SPAWN'S PROBLEMS, IT WILL SATISFY ONE DEEP NEED:
BATTLE.
SOMETIMES THERE DOESN'T EVEN NEED TO BE A REASON, THOUGH, THIS TIME, HE HAS ONE... A DEBT TO THE RESIDENTS OF THE ALLEYWAYS.
THEN AGAIN, MAYBE IT'S FOR HIMSELF ALONE. A PURPOSE. A WAY TO RESUME HIS LIFE.
A REASON FOR HOPE.
COCKY SONOVABITCH.
HEY HERO!
SEEMS I SCREWED UP!! SHOULD HAVE RIPPED YOUR FRIGGIN' HEAD OFF TO MAKE SURE YOU WAS DEAD!
I INTEND TO CORRECT MY OVERSIGHT. THANKS FOR THE INVITE.
SHALL WE PLAY?

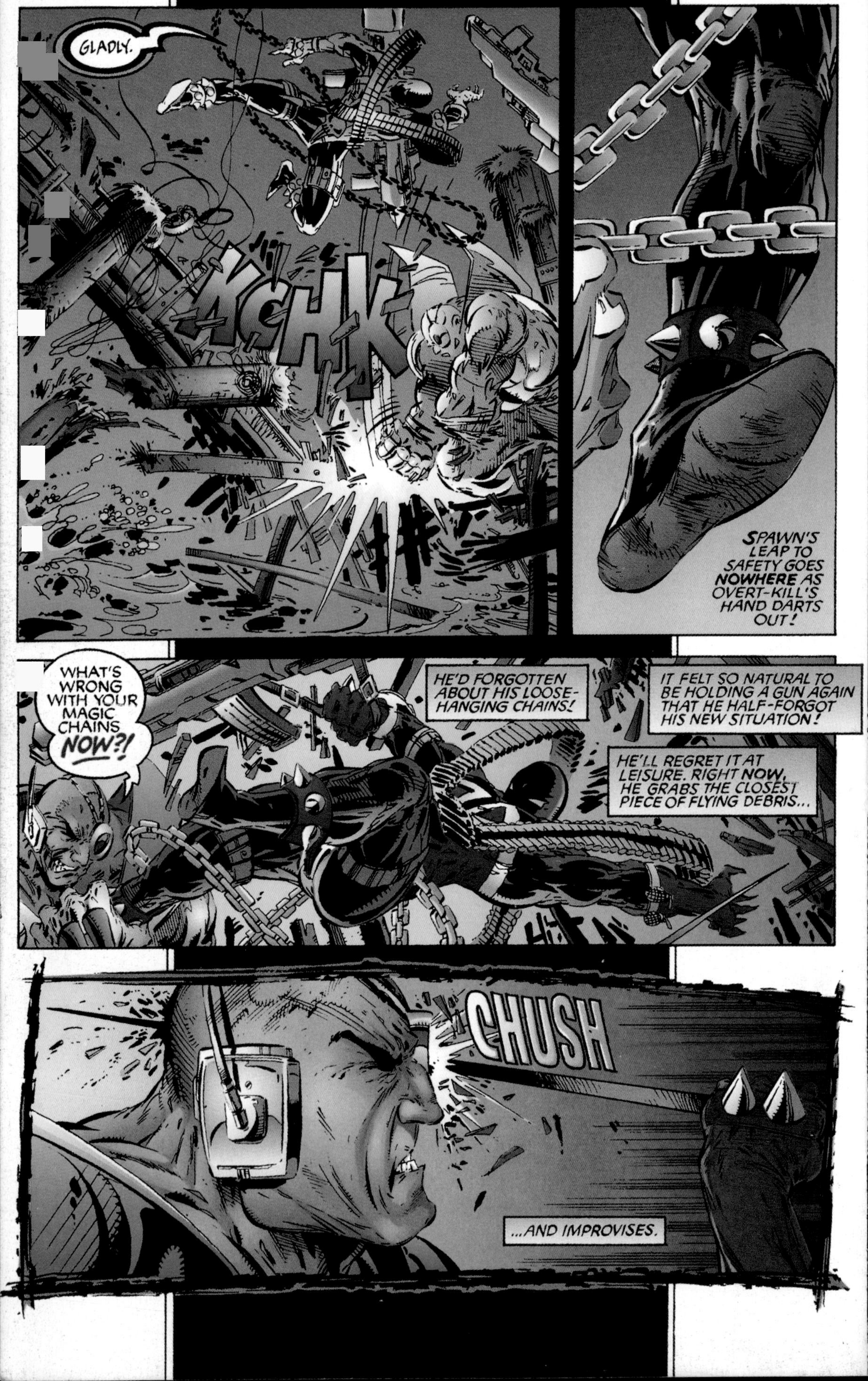
GLADLY.
KCHK
SPAWN'S LEAP TO SAFETY GOES NOWHERE AS OVERT-KILL'S HAND DARTS OUT!
WHAT'S WRONG WITH YOUR MAGIC CHAINS NOW?!
HE'D FORGOTTEN ABOUT HIS LOOSE-HANGING CHAINS!
IT FELT SO NATURAL TO BE HOLDING A GUN AGAIN THAT HE HALF-FORGOT HIS NEW SITUATION!
HE'LL REGRET IT AT LEISURE. RIGHT NOW, HE GRABS THE CLOSEST PIECE OF FLYING DEBRIS...
CHUSH
...AND IMPROVISES.

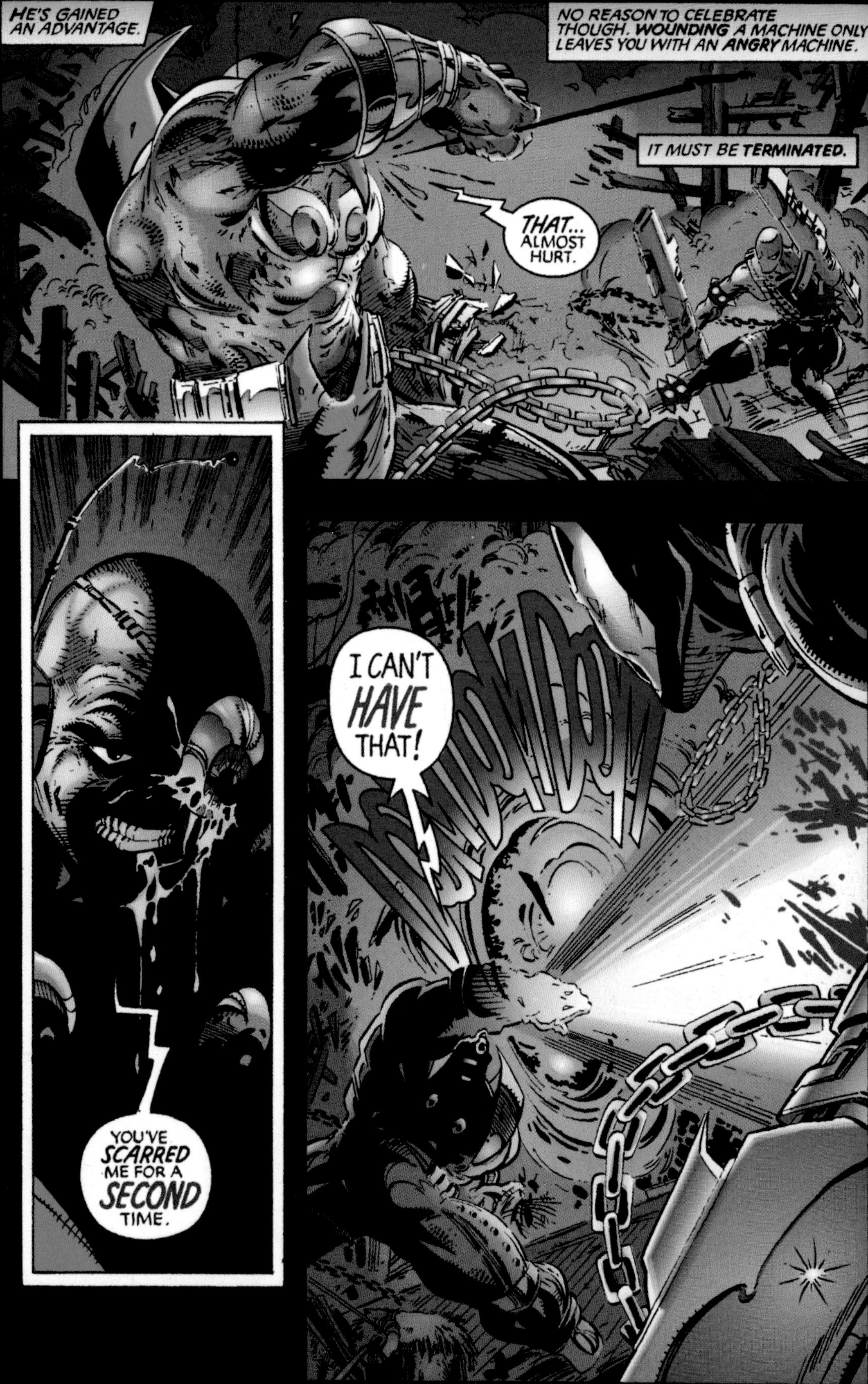
HE'S GAINED AN ADVANTAGE.
NO REASON TO CELEBRATE THOUGH. WOUNDING A MACHINE ONLY LEAVES YOU WITH AN ANGRY MACHINE.
IT MUST BE TERMINATED.
THAT... ALMOST HURT.
YOU'VE SCARRED ME FOR A SECOND TIME.
I CAN'T HAVE THAT!

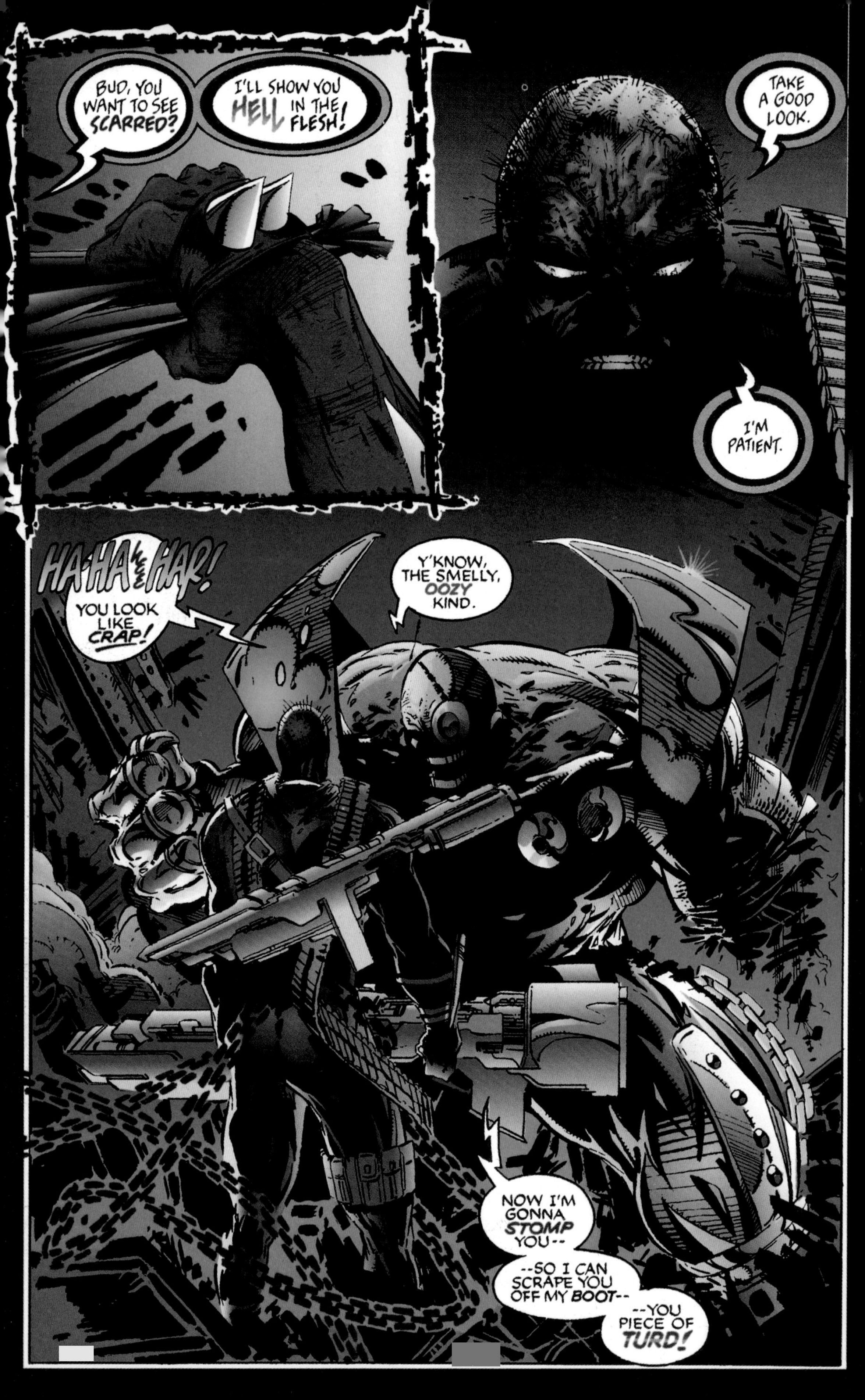
BUD, YOU WANT TO SEE SCARRED?
I'LL SHOW YOU HELL IN THE FLESH!
TAKE A GOOD LOOK.
I'M PATIENT.
HA-HA-HEE-HAR!
YOU LOOK LIKE CRAP!
Y'KNOW, THE SMELLY, OOZY KIND.
NOW I'M GONNA STOMP YOU--
--SO I CAN SCRAPE YOU OFF MY BOOT--
--YOU PIECE OF TURD!

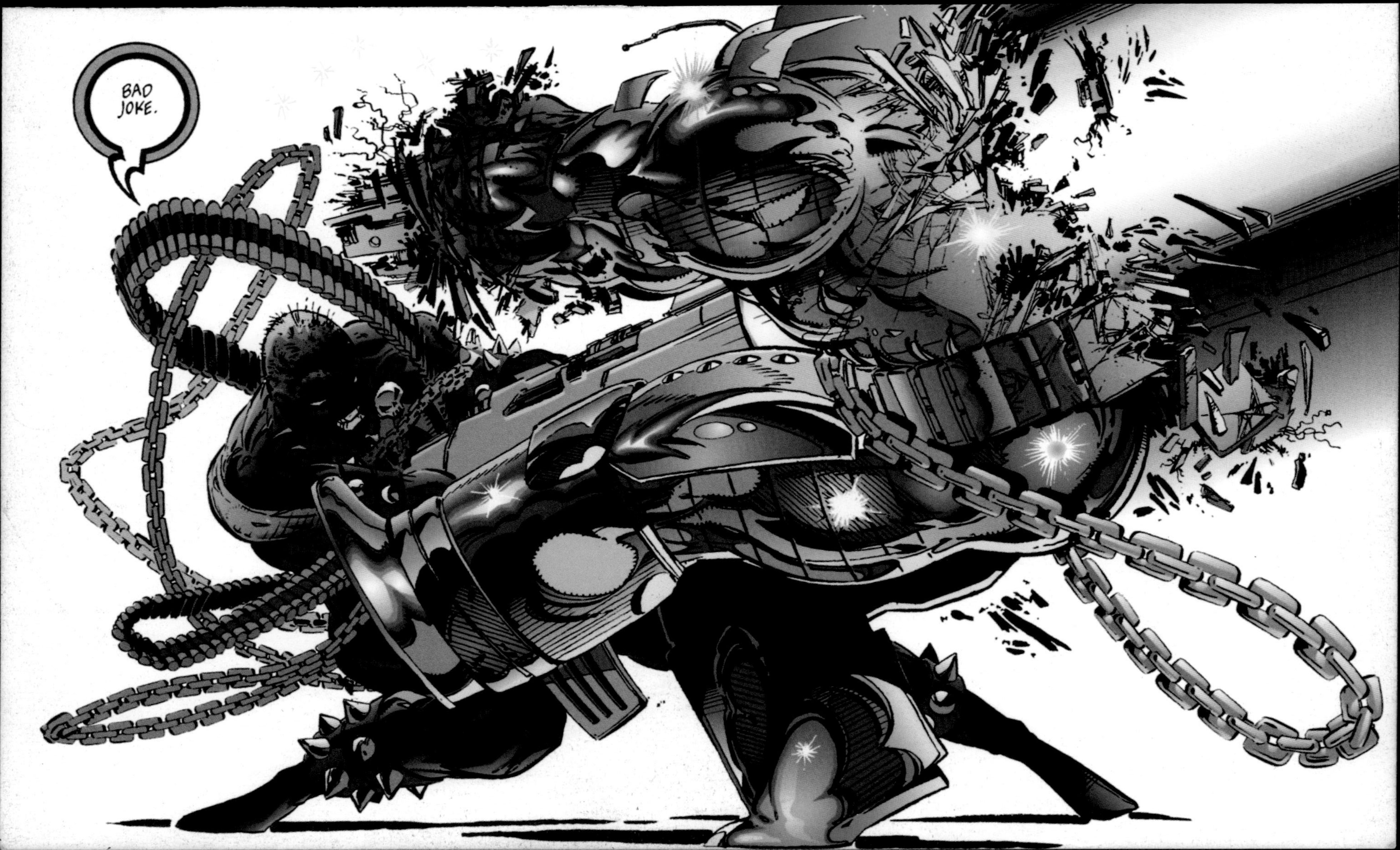
BAD JOKE.

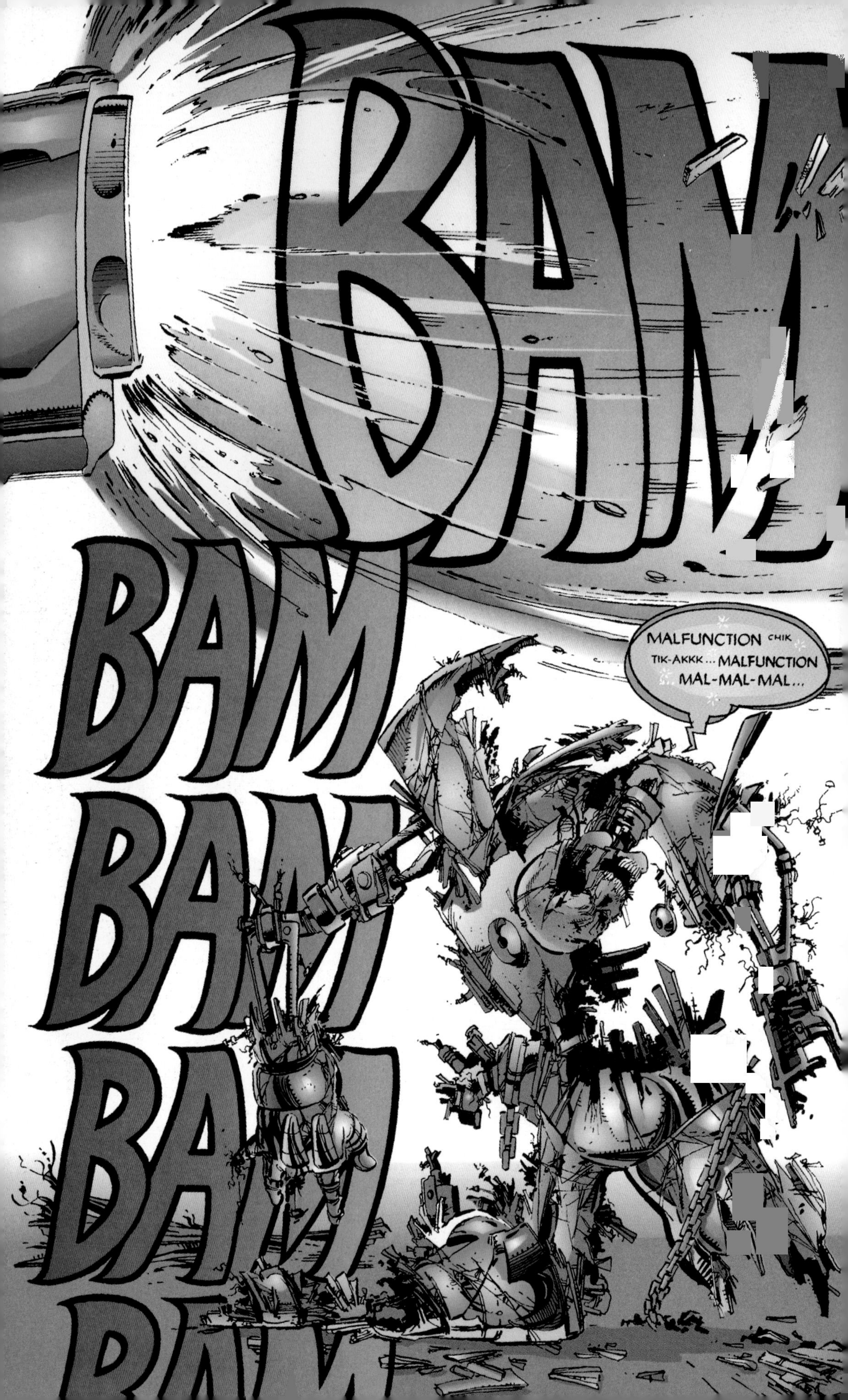
BAM
BAM
BAM
BAM
MALFUNCTION CHIK TIK-AKKK... MALFUNCTION MAL-MAL-MAL...

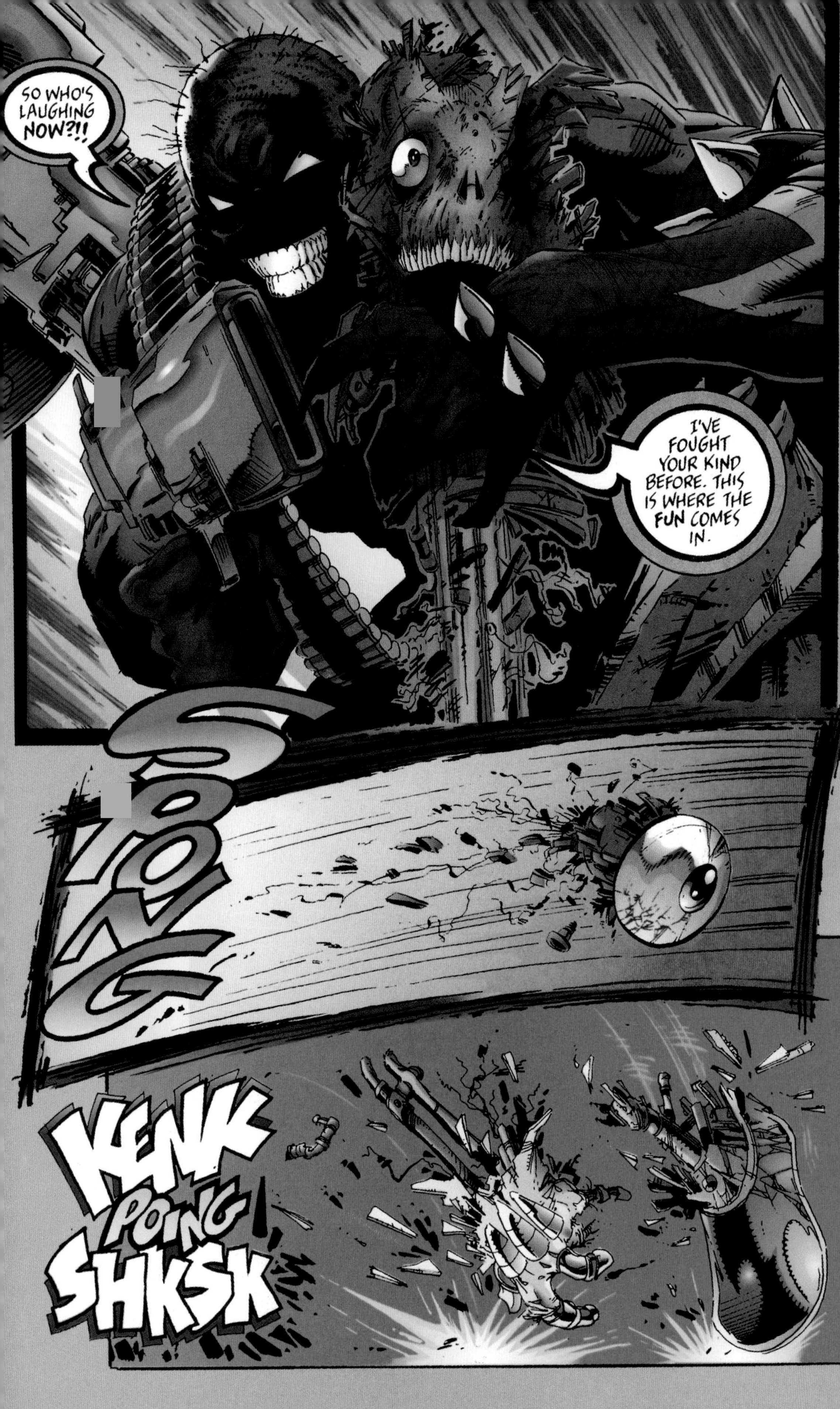
SO WHO'S LAUGHING NOW?!!
I'VE FOUGHT YOUR KIND BEFORE. THIS IS WHERE THE FUN COMES IN.
SPOONG
KENK
POING
SHKSK

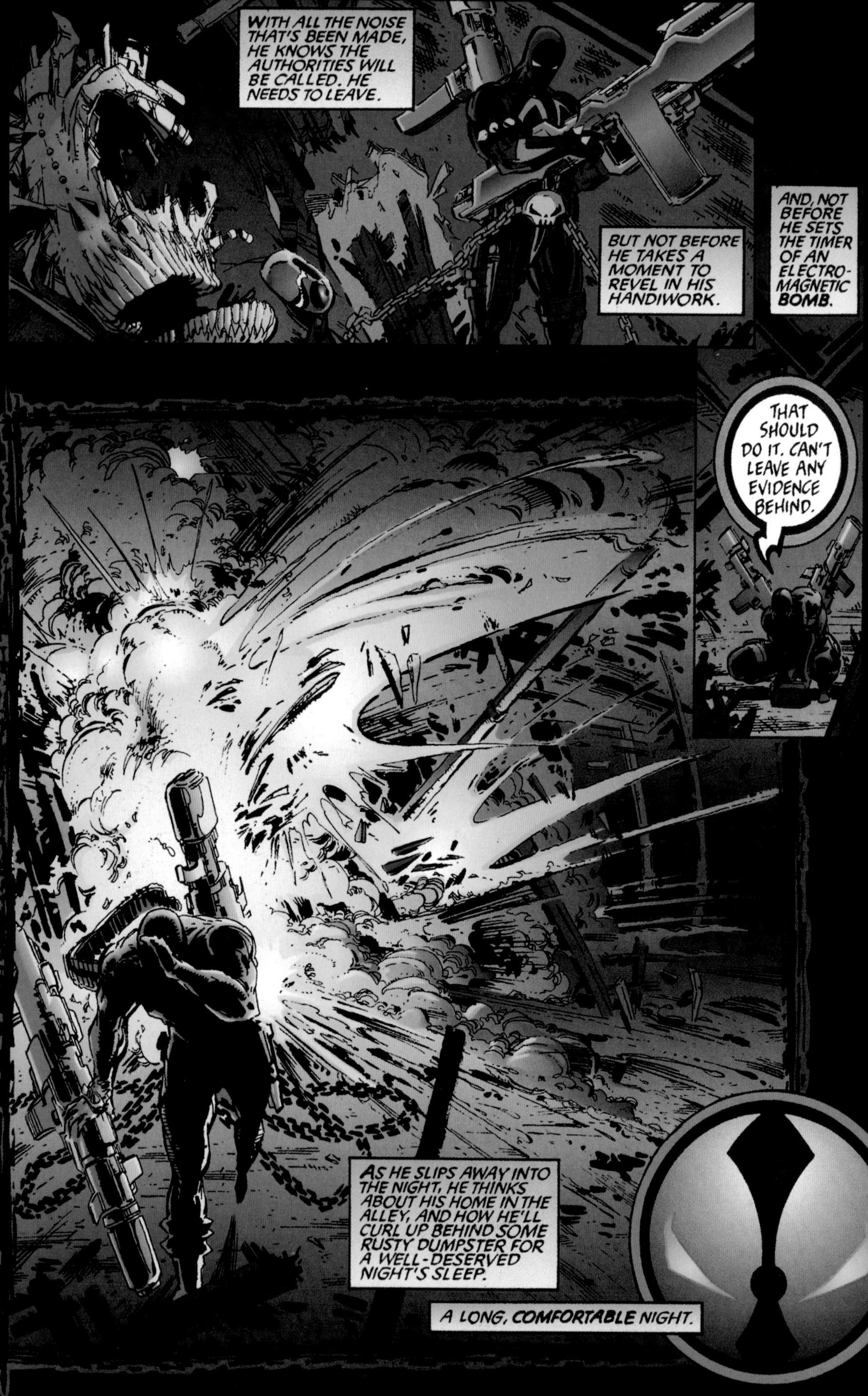
WITH ALL THE NOISE THAT'S BEEN MADE, HE KNOWS THE AUTHORITIES WILL BE CALLED. HE NEEDS TO LEAVE.
BUT NOT BEFORE HE TAKES A MOMENT TO REVEL IN HIS HANDIWORK.
AND, NOT BEFORE HE SETS THE TIMER OF AN ELECTRO-MAGNETIC BOMB.
THAT SHOULD DO IT. CAN'T LEAVE ANY EVIDENCE BEHIND.
AS HE SLIPS AWAY INTO THE NIGHT, HE THINKS ABOUT HIS HOME IN THE ALLEY, AND HOW HE'LL CURL UP BEHIND SOME RUSTY DUMPSTER FOR A WELL-DESERVED NIGHT'S SLEEP.
A LONG, COMFORTABLE NIGHT.

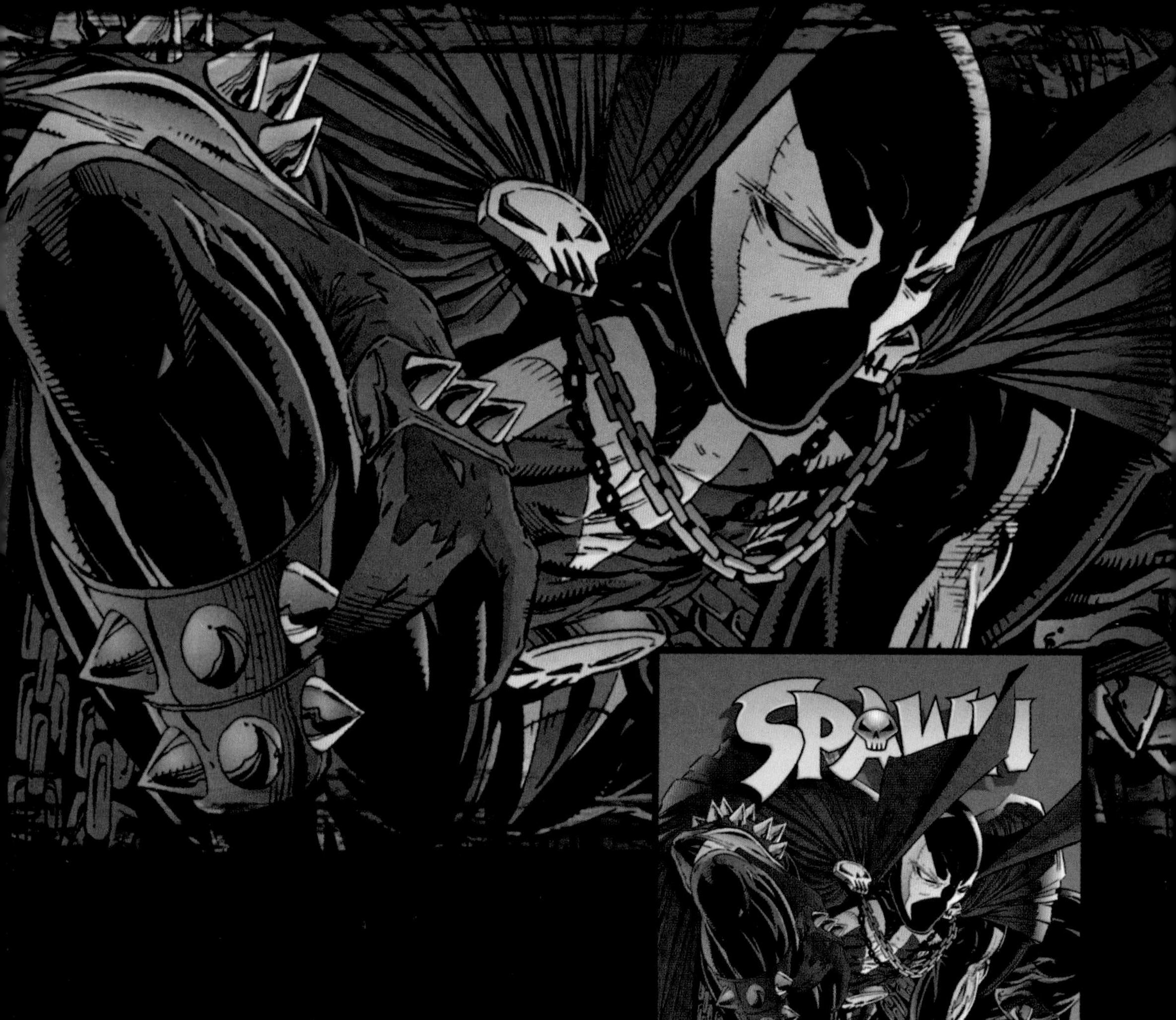
SPAWN

ISSUE EIGHT

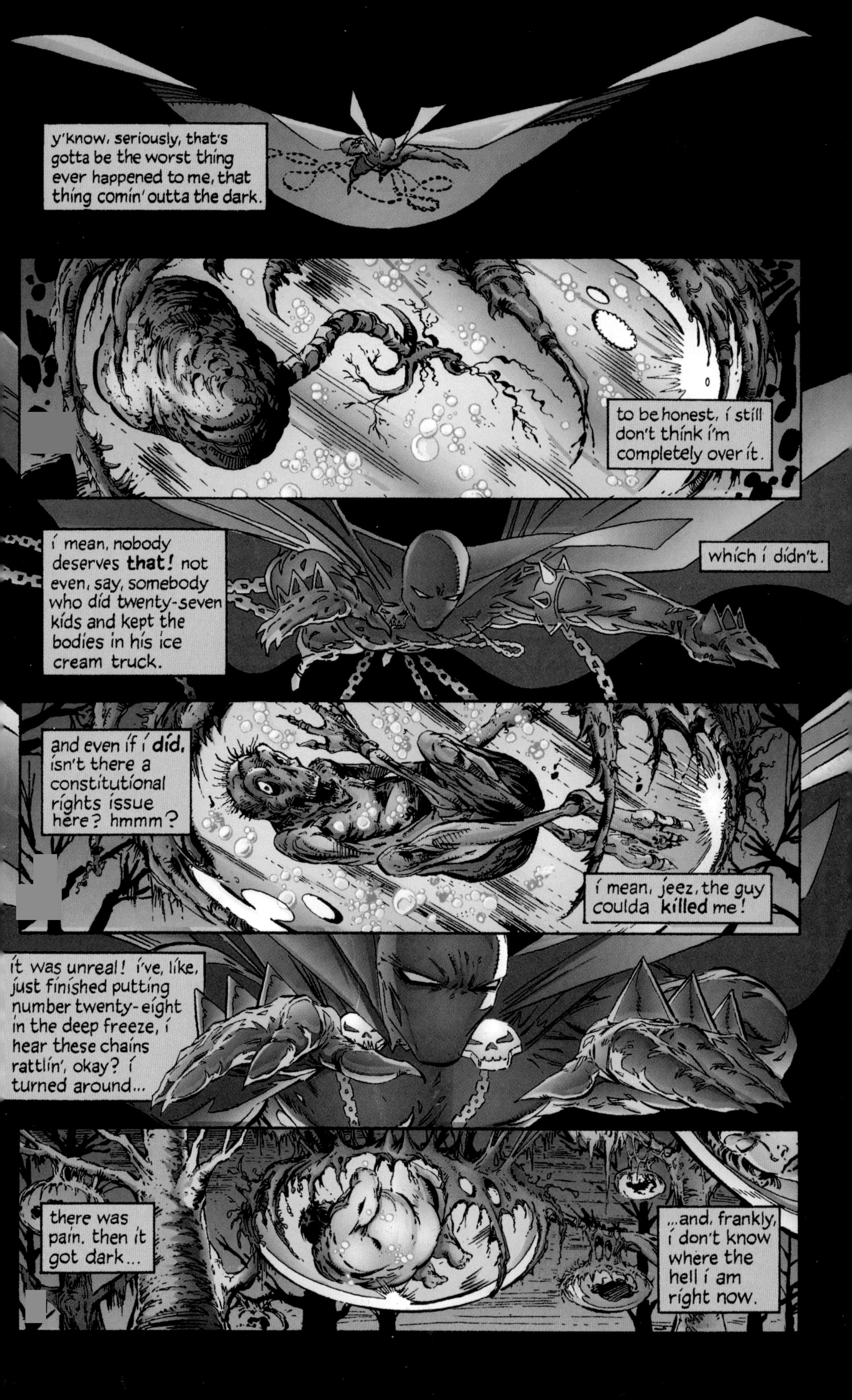
y'know, seriously, that's gotta be the worst thing ever happened to me, that thing comin' outta the dark.
to be honest, i still don't think i'm completely over it.
i mean, nobody deserves **that!** not even, say, somebody who did twenty-seven kids and kept the bodies in his ice cream truck.
which i didn't.
and even if i **did,** isn't there a constitutional rights issue here? hmmm?
i mean, jeez, the guy coulda **killed** me!
it was unreal! i've, like, just finished putting number twenty-eight in the deep freeze, i hear these chains rattlin', okay? i turned around...
there was pain. then it got dark...
...and, frankly, i don't know where the hell i am right now.

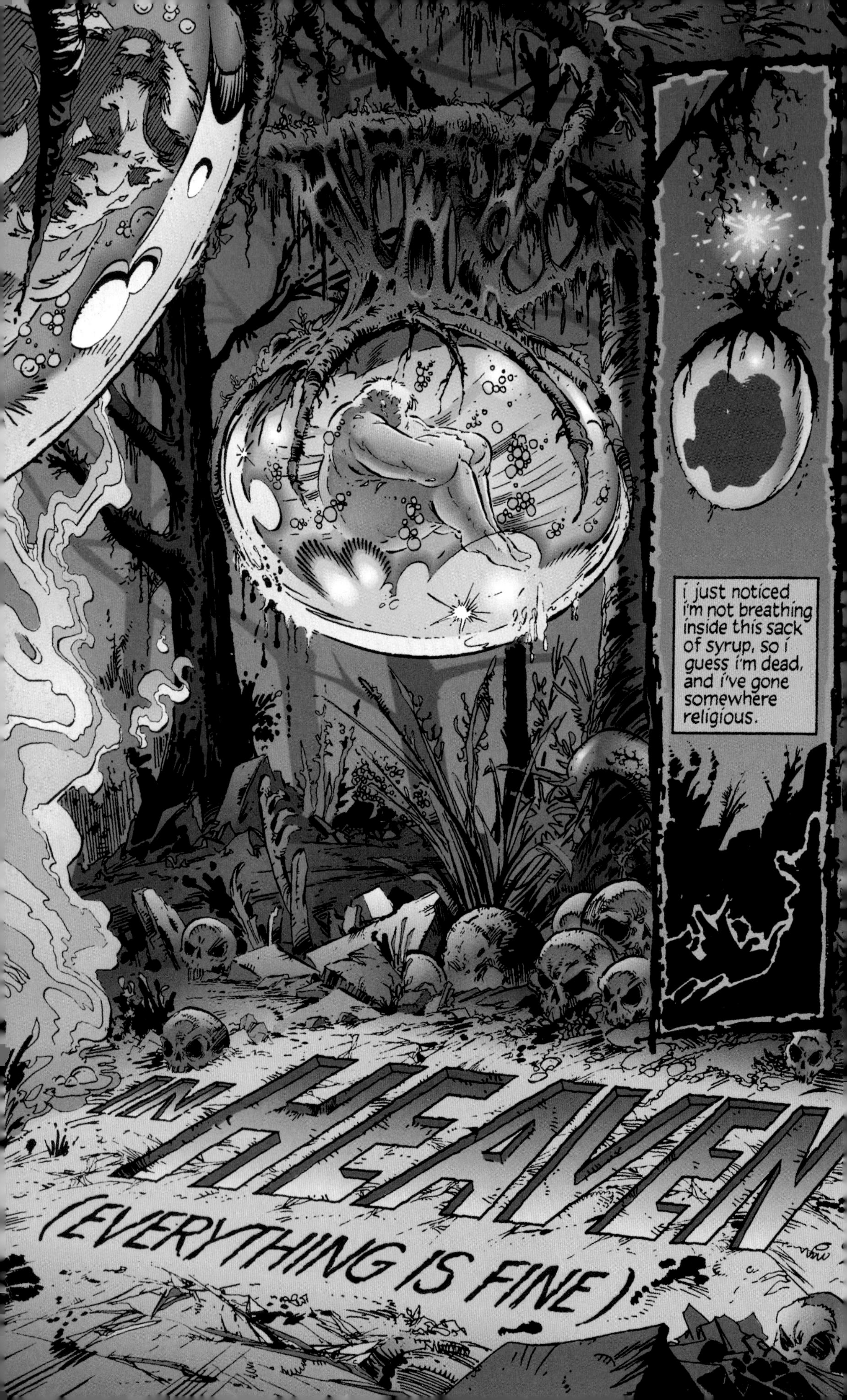
i just noticed i'm not breathing inside this sack of syrup, so i guess i'm dead, and i've gone somewhere religious.
IN HEAVEN
(EVERYTHING IS FINE)

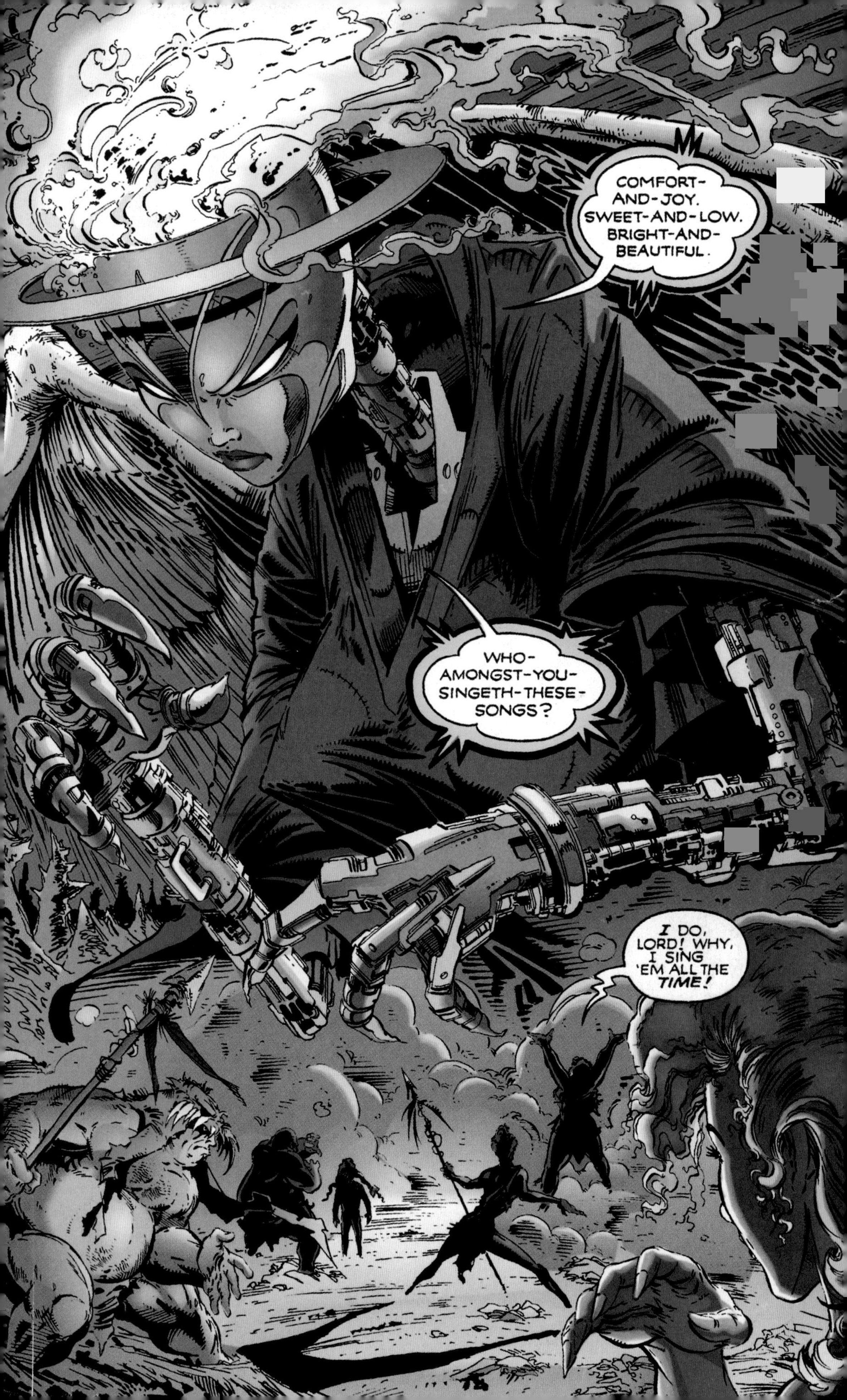
COMFORT-AND-JOY. SWEET-AND-LOW. BRIGHT-AND-BEAUTIFUL.
WHO-AMONGST-YOU-SINGETH-THESE-SONGS?
I DO, LORD! WHY, I SING 'EM ALL THE TIME!

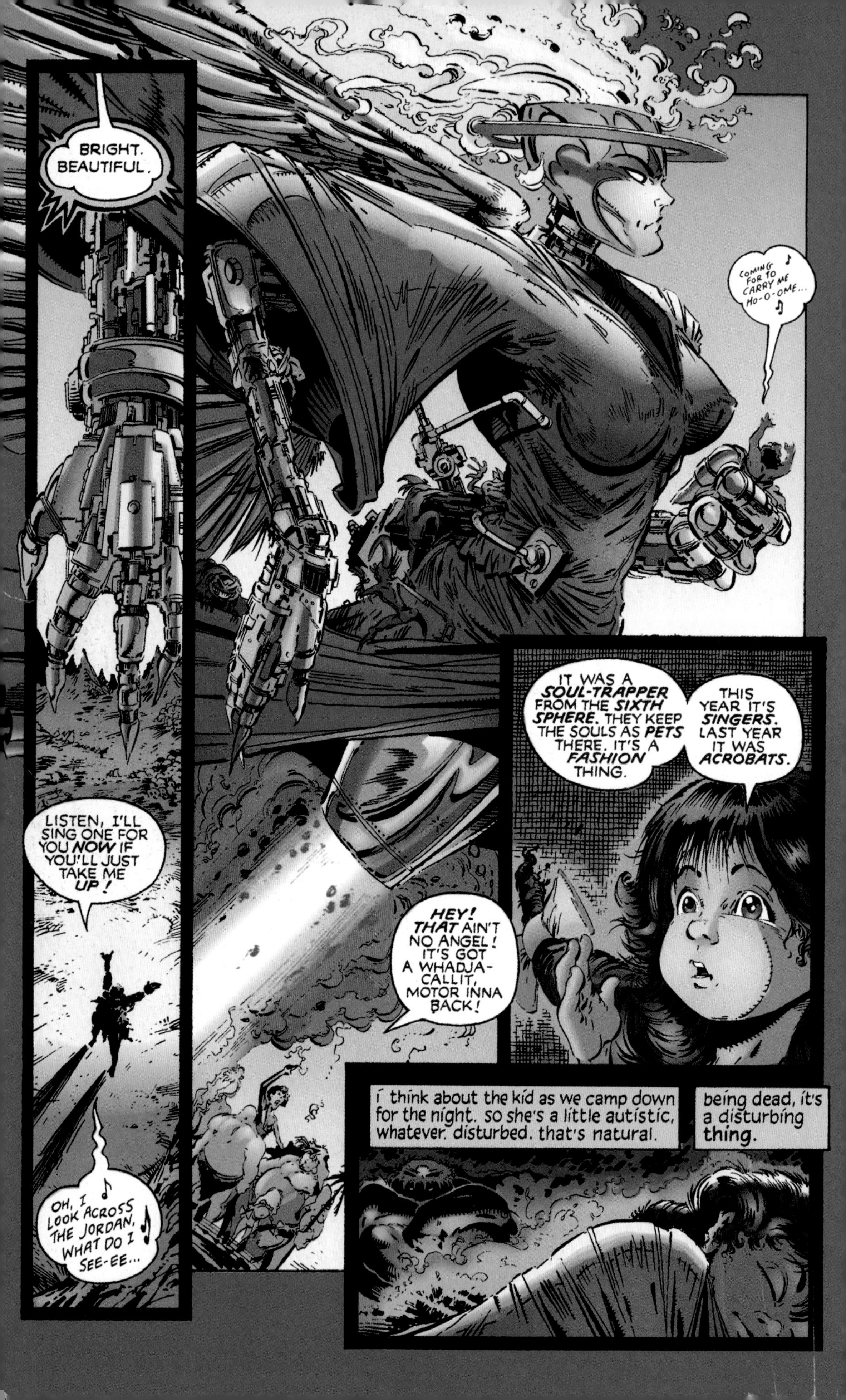
BRIGHT. BEAUTIFUL.
COMING FOR TO CARRY ME HO-O-OME...
LISTEN, I'LL SING ONE FOR YOU NOW IF YOU'LL JUST TAKE ME UP!
HEY! THAT AIN'T NO ANGEL! IT'S GOT A WHADJA-CALLIT, MOTOR INNA BACK!
OH, I LOOK ACROSS THE JORDAN, WHAT DO I SEE-EE...
IT WAS A SOUL-TRAPPER FROM THE SIXTH SPHERE. THEY KEEP THE SOULS AS PETS THERE. IT'S A FASHION THING.
THIS YEAR IT'S SINGERS. LAST YEAR IT WAS ACROBATS.
i think about the kid as we camp down for the night. so she's a little autistic, whatever. disturbed. that's natural.
being dead, it's a disturbing thing.

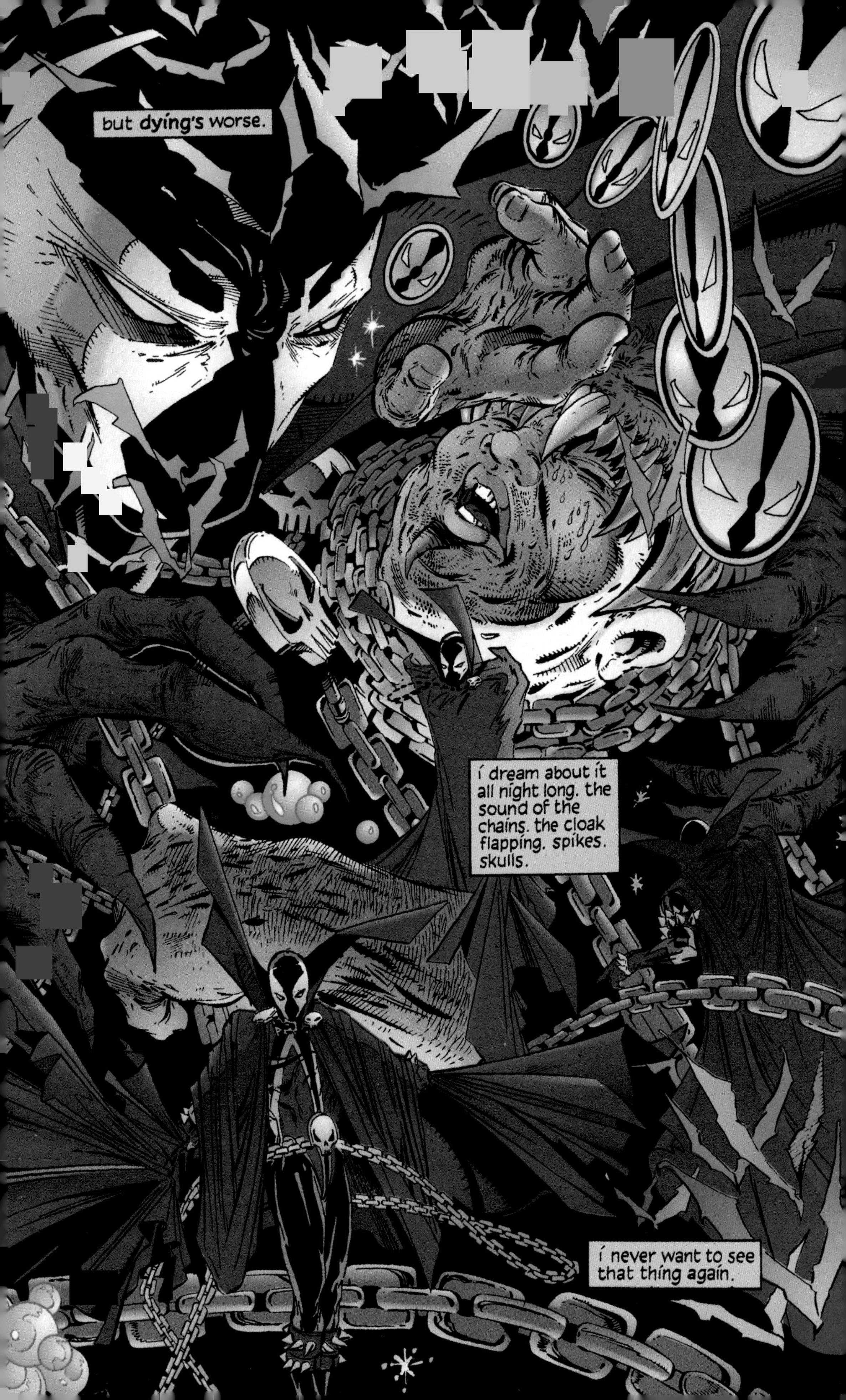
but dying's worse.
i dream about it all night long. the sound of the chains. the cloak flapping. spikes. skulls.
i never want to see that thing again.

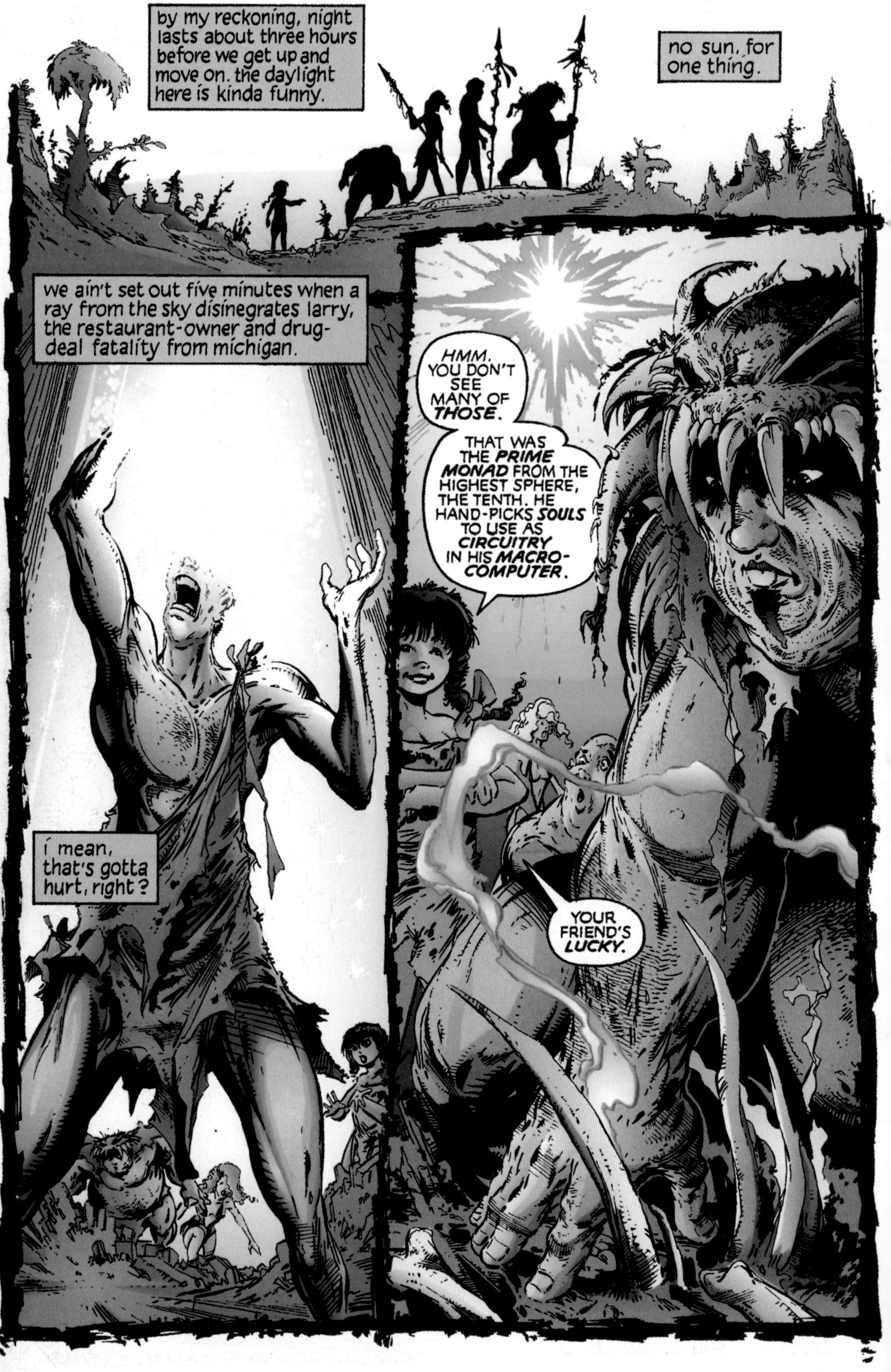
by my reckoning, night lasts about three hours before we get up and move on. the daylight here is kinda funny.
no sun, for one thing.
we ain't set out five minutes when a ray from the sky disinegrates larry, the restaurant-owner and drug-deal fatality from michigan.
i mean, that's gotta hurt, right?
HMM. YOU DON'T SEE MANY OF THOSE.
THAT WAS THE PRIME MONAD FROM THE HIGHEST SPHERE, THE TENTH. HE HAND-PICKS SOULS TO USE AS CIRCUITRY IN HIS MACRO-COMPUTER.
YOUR FRIEND'S LUCKY.

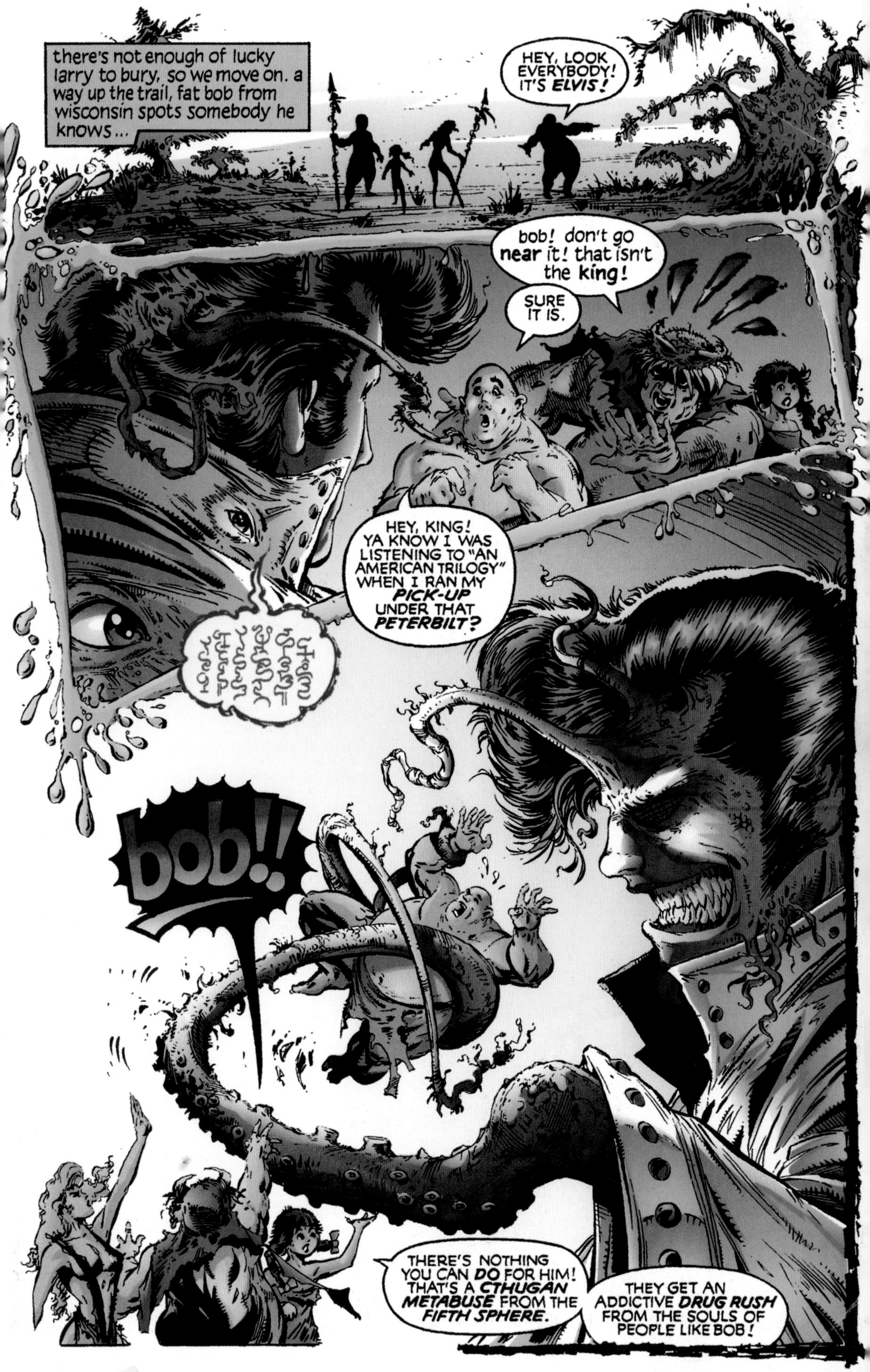

there's not enough of lucky larry to bury, so we move on. a way up the trail, fat bob from wisconsin spots somebody he knows...
HEY, LOOK EVERYBODY! IT'S ELVIS!
bob! don't go near it! that isn't the king!
SURE IT IS.
HEY, KING! YA KNOW I WAS LISTENING TO "AN AMERICAN TRILOGY" WHEN I RAN MY PICK-UP UNDER THAT PETERBILT?
bob!!
THERE'S NOTHING YOU CAN DO FOR HIM! THAT'S A CTHUGAN METABUSE FROM THE FIFTH SPHERE.
THEY GET AN ADDICTIVE DRUG RUSH FROM THE SOULS OF PEOPLE LIKE BOB!

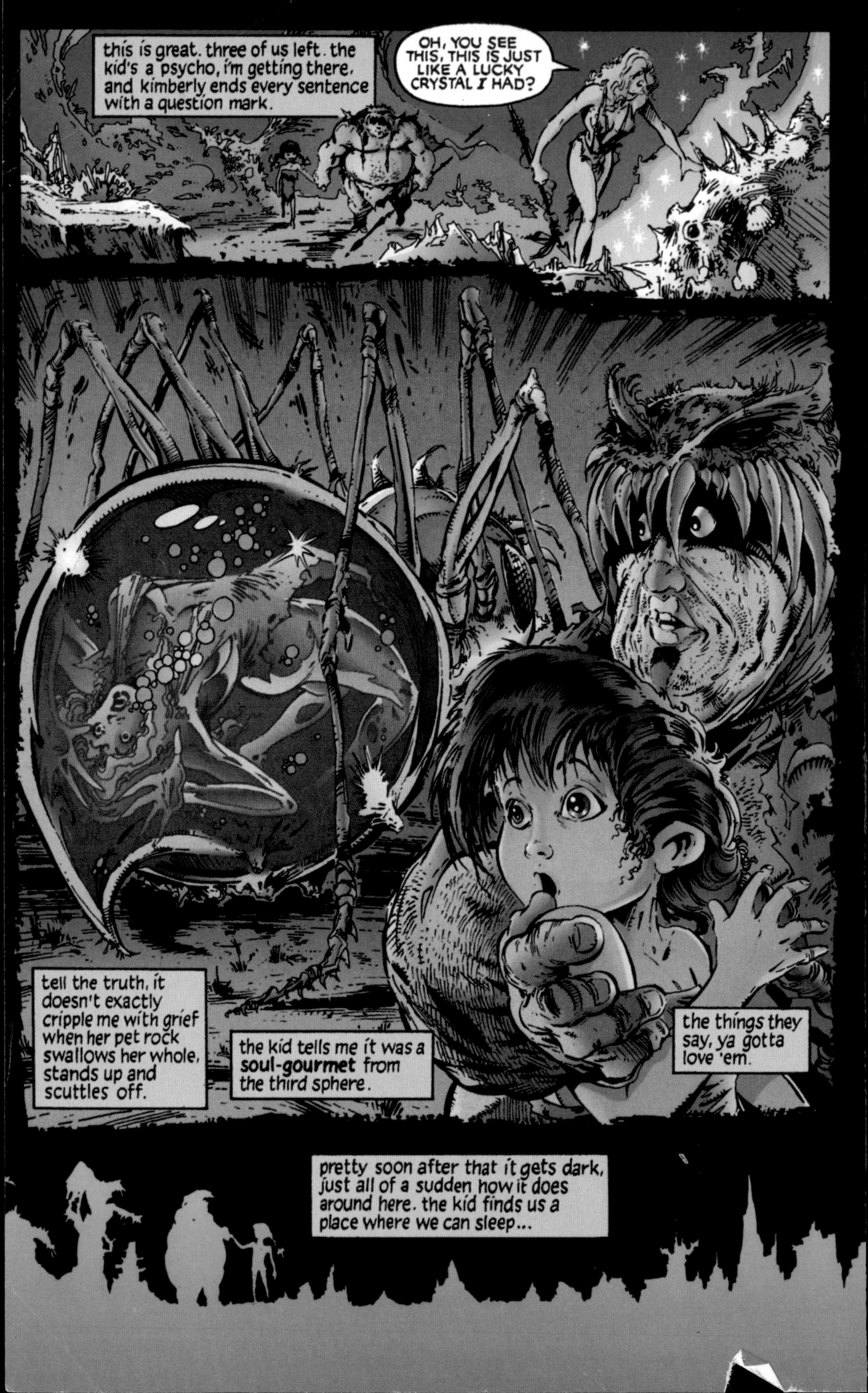
this is great. three of us left. the kid's a psycho, i'm getting there, and kimberly ends every sentence with a question mark.
OH, YOU SEE THIS, THIS IS JUST LIKE A LUCKY CRYSTAL I HAD?
tell the truth, it doesn't exactly cripple me with grief when her pet rock swallows her whole, stands up and scuttles off.
the kid tells me it was a soul-gourmet from the third sphere.
the things they say, ya gotta love 'em.
pretty soon after that it gets dark, just all of a sudden how it does around here. the kid finds us a place where we can sleep...

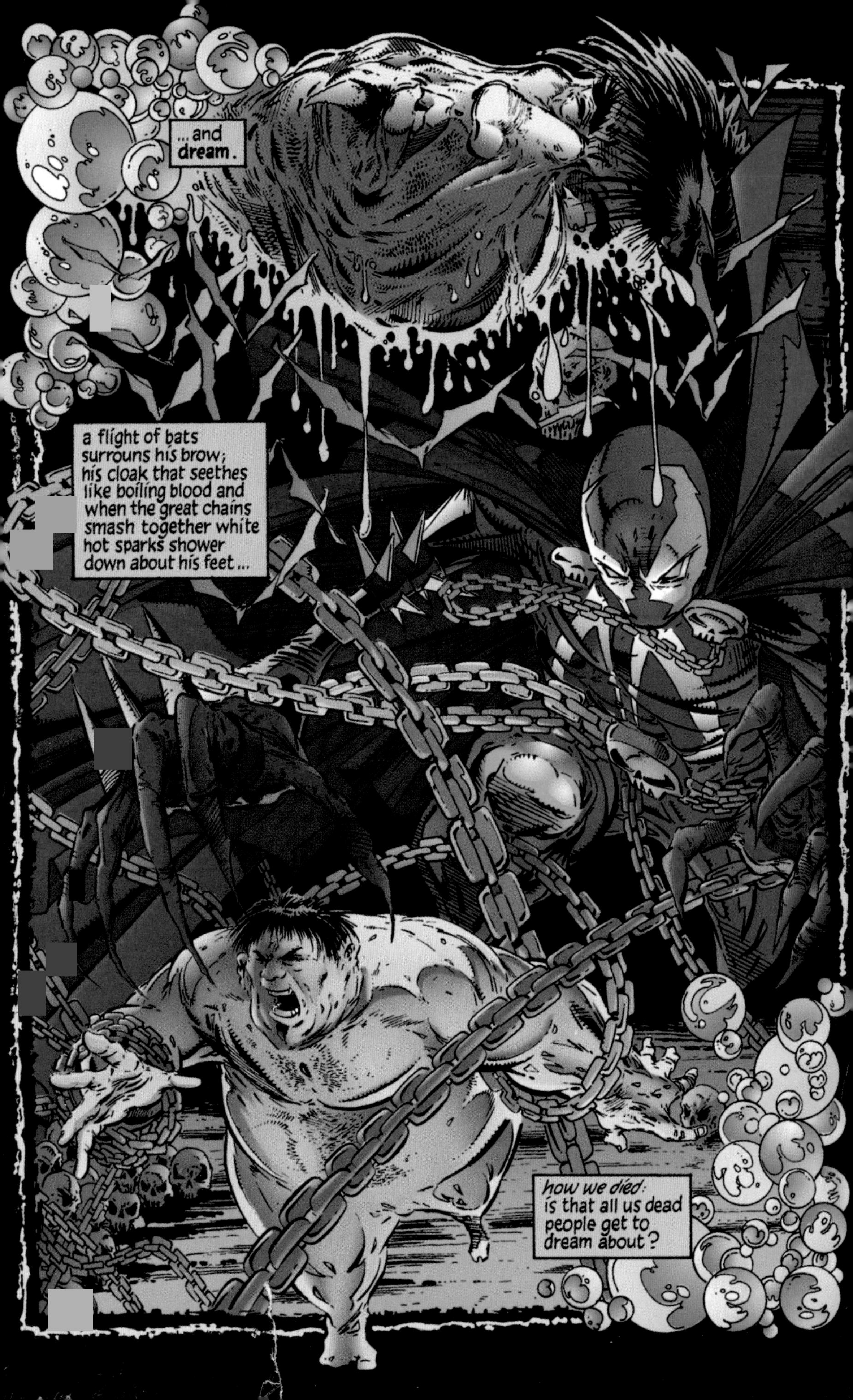
...and dream.
a flight of bats surrouns his brow; his cloak that seethes like boiling blood and when the great chains smash together white hot sparks shower down about his feet...
how we died: is that all us dead people get to dream about?

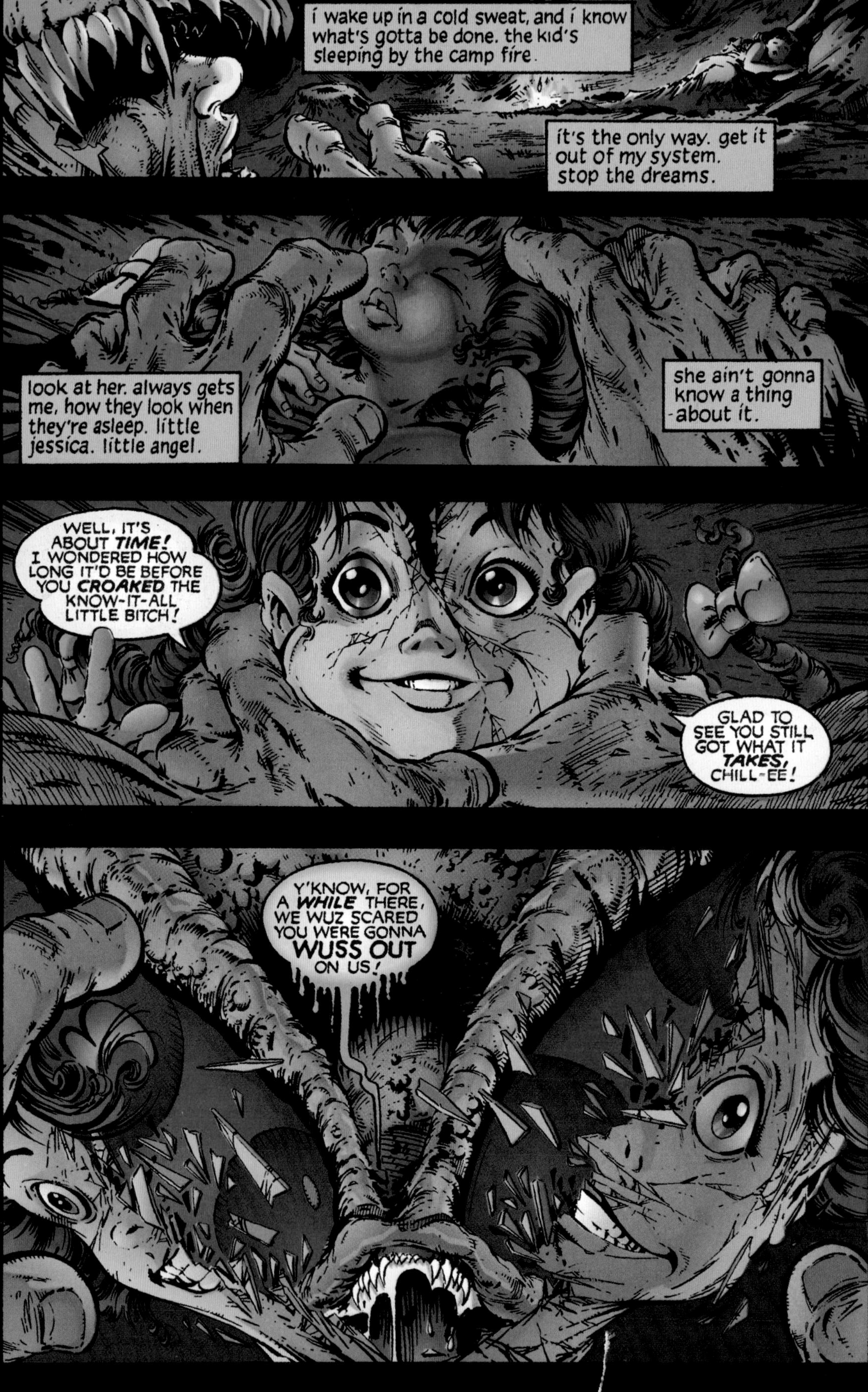

i wake up in a cold sweat, and i know what's gotta be done. the kid's sleeping by the camp fire.
it's the only way. get it out of my system. stop the dreams.
look at her. always gets me, how they look when they're asleep. little jessica. little angel.
she ain't gonna know a thing about it.
WELL, IT'S ABOUT TIME! I WONDERED HOW LONG IT'D BE BEFORE YOU CROAKED THE KNOW-IT-ALL LITTLE BITCH!
GLAD TO SEE YOU STILL GOT WHAT IT TAKES, CHILL-EE!
Y'KNOW, FOR A WHILE THERE, WE WUZ SCARED YOU WERE GONNA WUSS OUT ON US!

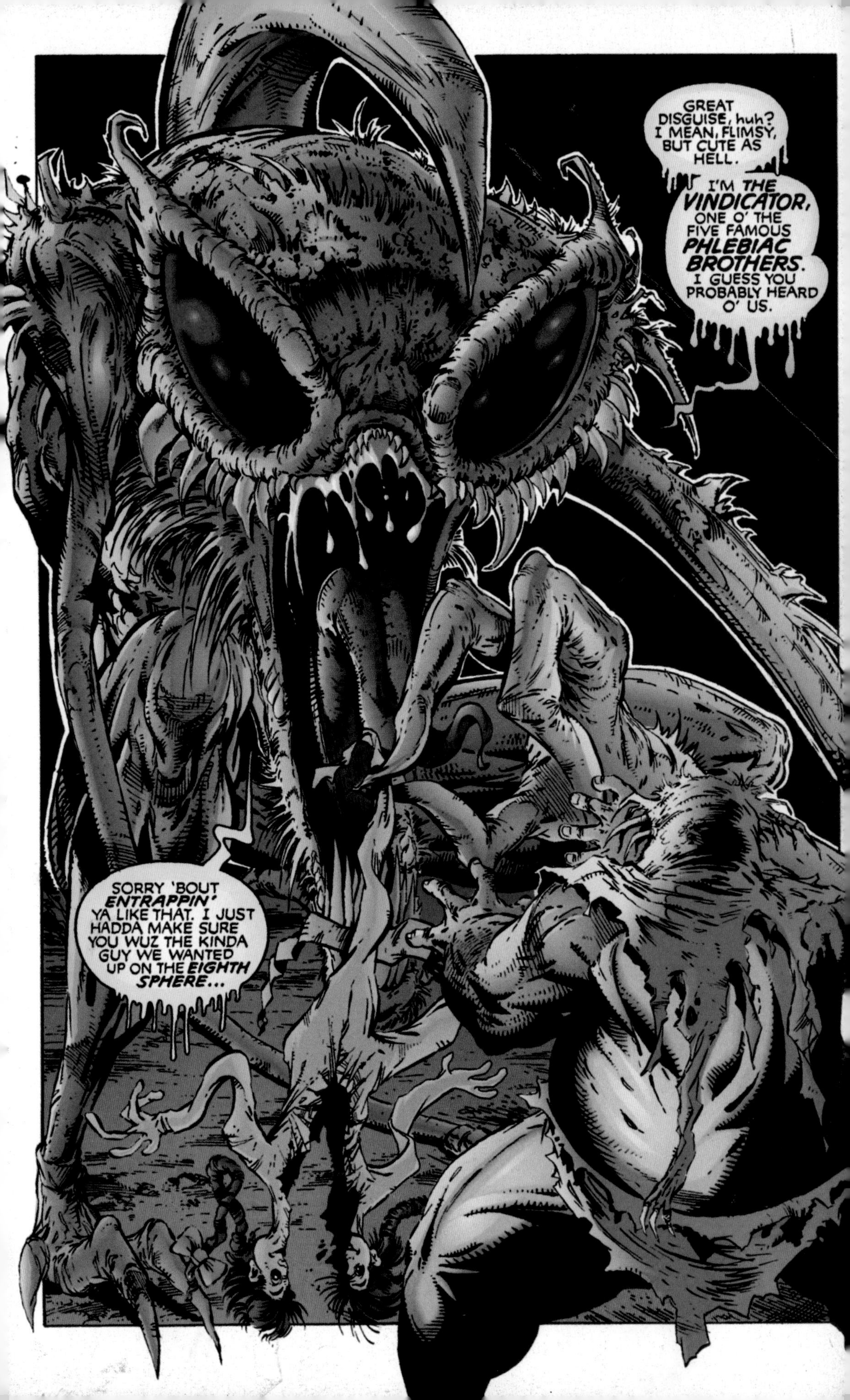
GREAT DISGUISE, huh? I MEAN, FLIMSY, BUT CUTE AS HELL.
I'M *THE VINDICATOR*, ONE O' THE FIVE FAMOUS *PHLEBIAC BROTHERS*. I GUESS YOU PROBABLY HEARD O' US.
SORRY 'BOUT *ENTRAPPIN'* YA LIKE THAT. I JUST HADDA MAKE SURE YOU WUZ THE KINDA GUY WE WANTED UP ON THE *EIGHTH SPHERE*...

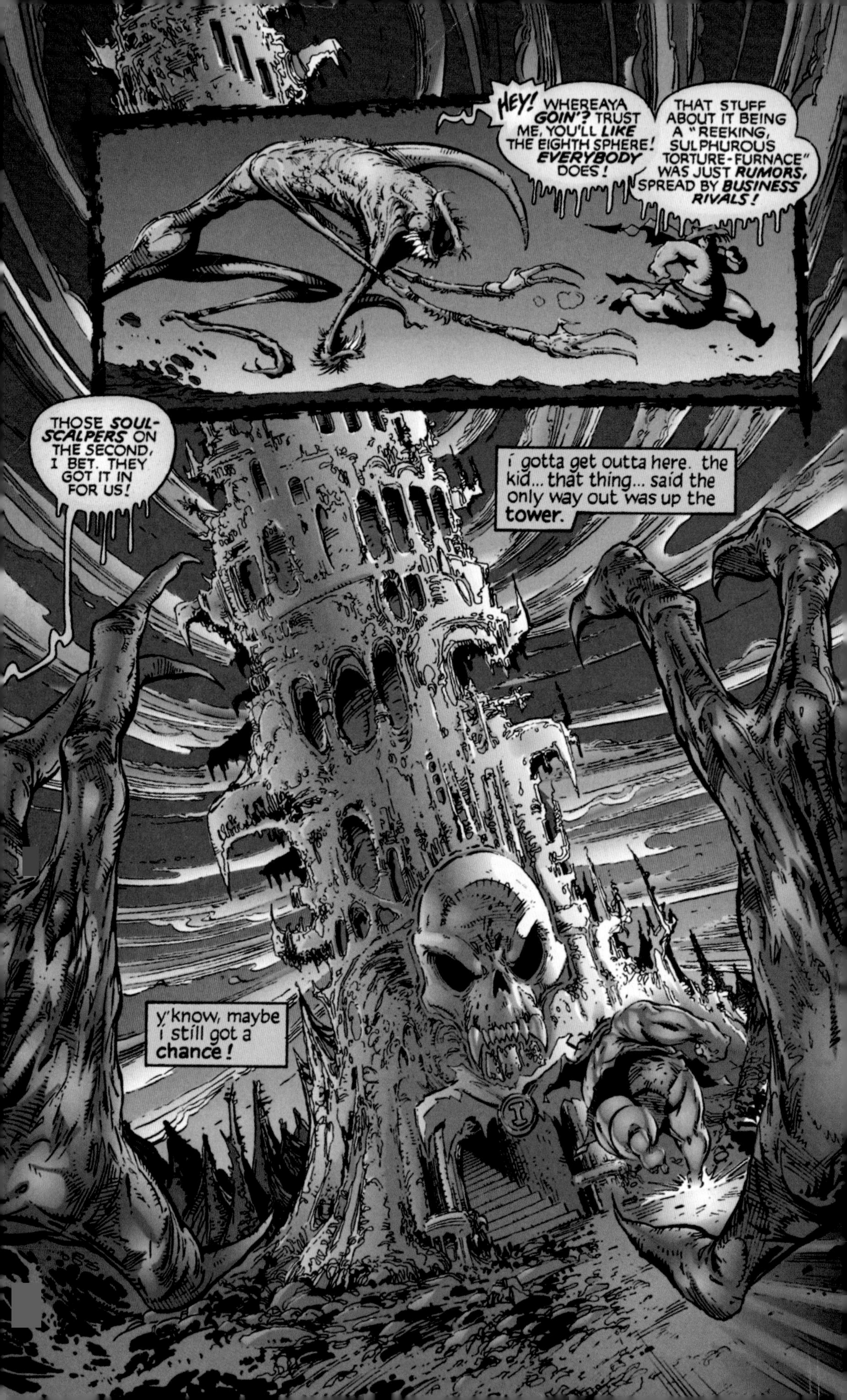

HEY! WHEREAYA GOIN'? TRUST ME, YOU'LL LIKE THE EIGHTH SPHERE! EVERYBODY DOES!
THAT STUFF ABOUT IT BEING A "REEKING, SULPHUROUS TORTURE-FURNACE" WAS JUST RUMORS, SPREAD BY BUSINESS RIVALS!
THOSE SOUL-SCALPERS ON THE SECOND, I BET. THEY GOT IT IN FOR US!
i gotta get outta here. the kid... that thing... said the only way out was up the tower.
y'know, maybe i still got a chance!

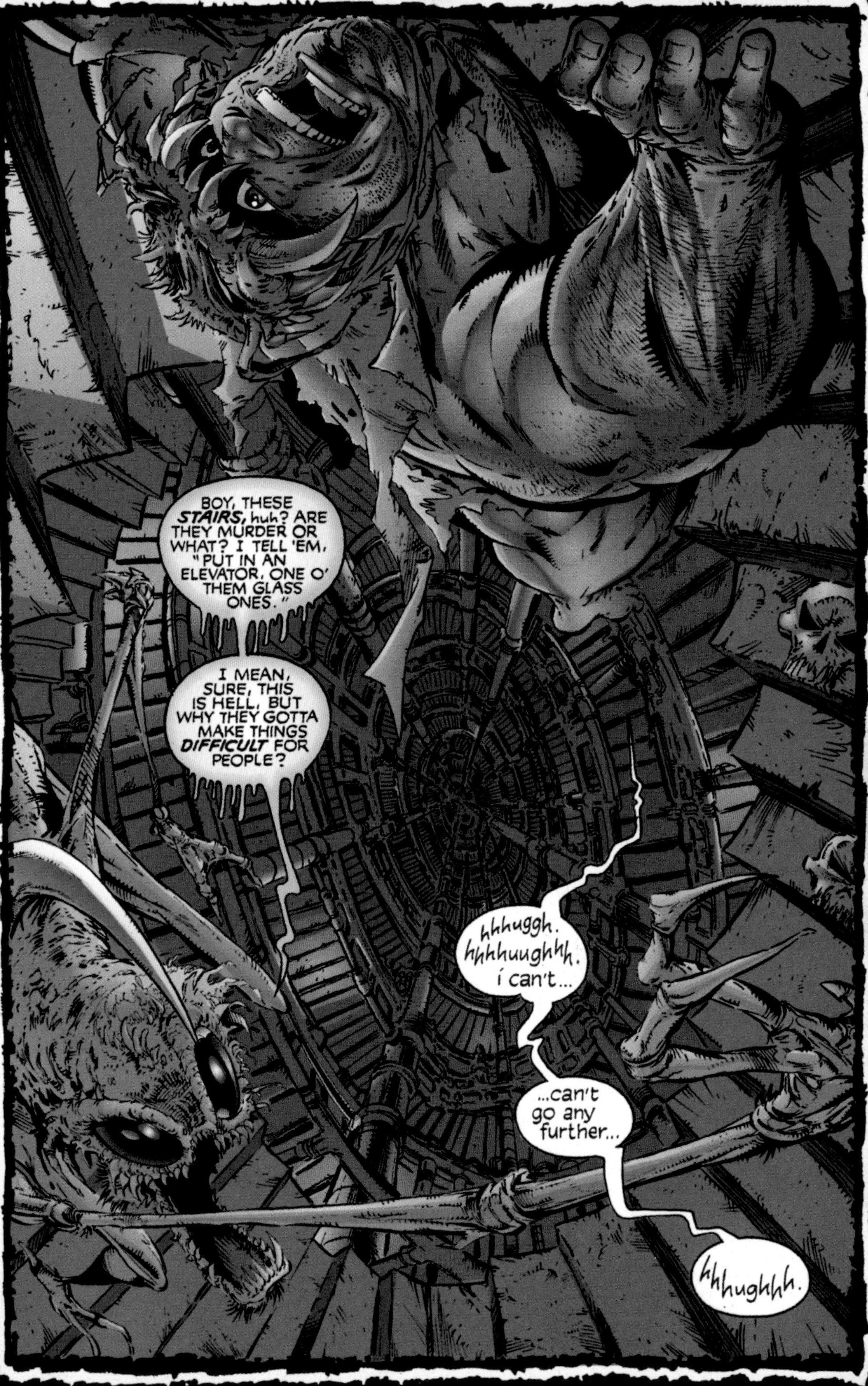
BOY, THESE STAIRS, huh? ARE THEY MURDER OR WHAT? I TELL 'EM, "PUT IN AN ELEVATOR. ONE O' THEM GLASS ONES."
I MEAN, SURE, THIS IS HELL, BUT WHY THEY GOTTA MAKE THINGS DIFFICULT FOR PEOPLE?
hhhuggh. hhhhuughhh. i can't...
...can't go any further...
hhhughhh.

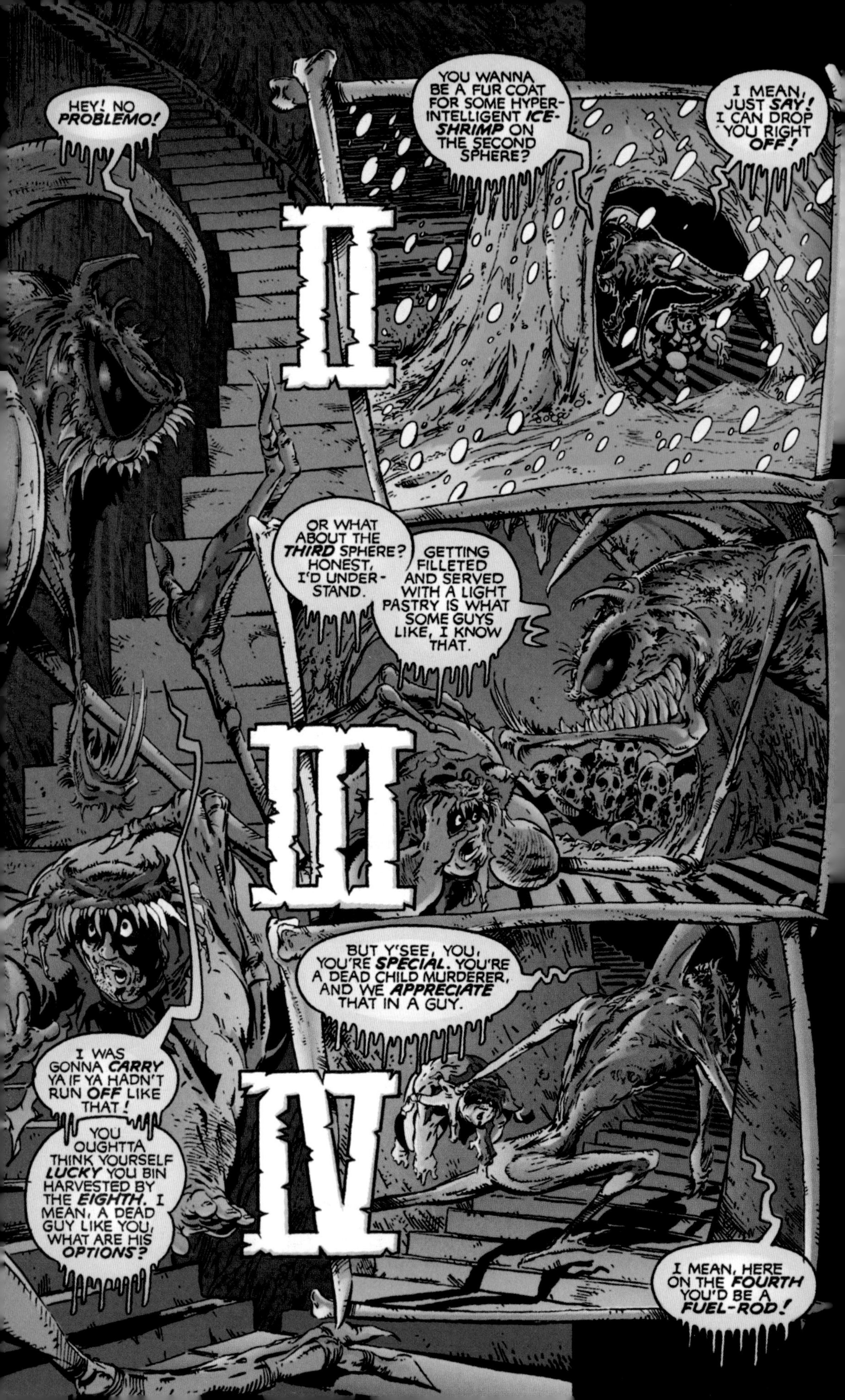
HEY! NO PROBLEMO!
II
YOU WANNA BE A FUR COAT FOR SOME HYPER-INTELLIGENT ICE-SHRIMP ON THE SECOND SPHERE?
I MEAN, JUST SAY! I CAN DROP YOU RIGHT OFF!
OR WHAT ABOUT THE THIRD SPHERE? HONEST, I'D UNDER-STAND.
GETTING FILLETED AND SERVED WITH A LIGHT PASTRY IS WHAT SOME GUYS LIKE, I KNOW THAT.
III
BUT Y'SEE, YOU, YOU'RE SPECIAL. YOU'RE A DEAD CHILD MURDERER, AND WE APPRECIATE THAT IN A GUY.
IV
I WAS GONNA CARRY YA IF YA HADN'T RUN OFF LIKE THAT!
YOU OUGHTTA THINK YOURSELF LUCKY YOU BIN HARVESTED BY THE EIGHTH. I MEAN, A DEAD GUY LIKE YOU, WHAT ARE HIS OPTIONS?
I MEAN, HERE ON THE FOURTH YOU'D BE A FUEL-ROD!

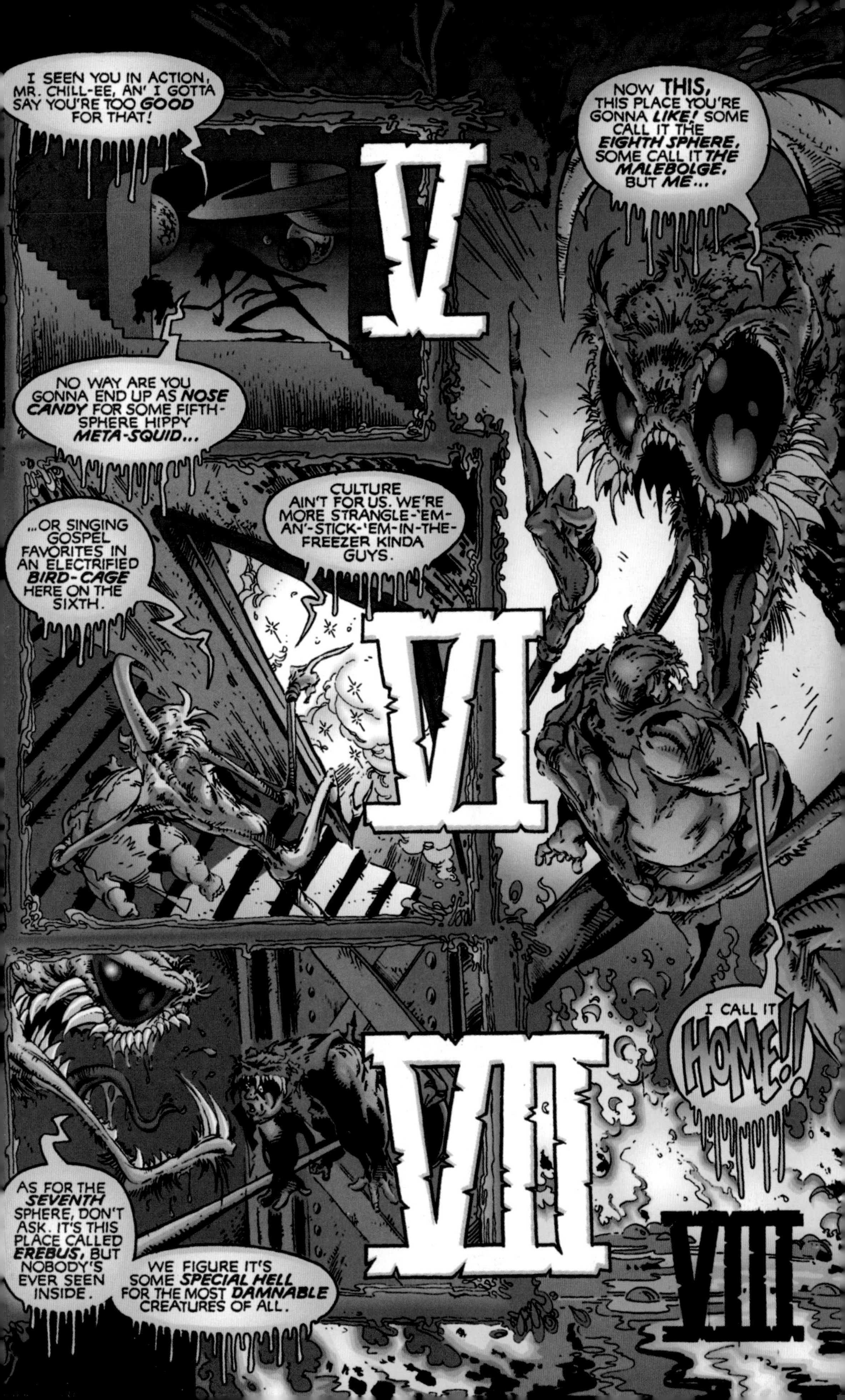
I SEEN YOU IN ACTION, MR. CHILL-EE, AN' I GOTTA SAY YOU'RE TOO GOOD FOR THAT!
V
NO WAY ARE YOU GONNA END UP AS NOSE CANDY FOR SOME FIFTH-SPHERE HIPPY META-SQUID...
...OR SINGING GOSPEL FAVORITES IN AN ELECTRIFIED BIRD-CAGE HERE ON THE SIXTH.
CULTURE AIN'T FOR US. WE'RE MORE STRANGLE-'EM-AN'-STICK-'EM-IN-THE-FREEZER KINDA GUYS.
VI
AS FOR THE SEVENTH SPHERE, DON'T ASK. IT'S THIS PLACE CALLED EREBUS, BUT NOBODY'S EVER SEEN INSIDE.
WE FIGURE IT'S SOME SPECIAL HELL FOR THE MOST DAMNABLE CREATURES OF ALL.
VII
NOW THIS, THIS PLACE YOU'RE GONNA LIKE! SOME CALL IT THE EIGHTH SPHERE, SOME CALL IT THE MALEBOLGE, BUT ME...
I CALL IT HOME!!
VIII

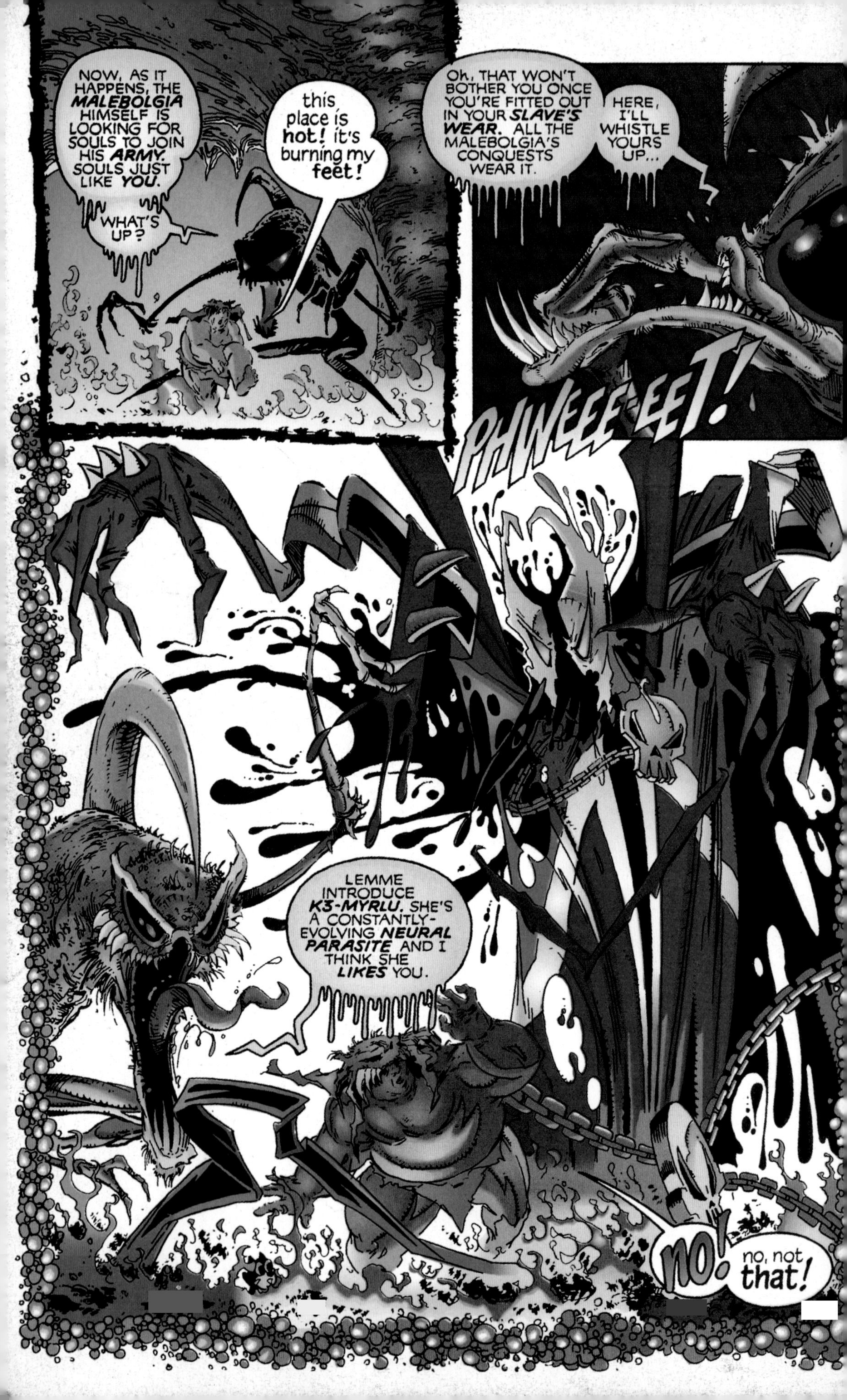
NOW, AS IT HAPPENS, THE MALEBOLGIA HIMSELF IS LOOKING FOR SOULS TO JOIN HIS ARMY. SOULS JUST LIKE YOU.
WHAT'S UP?
this place is not! it's burning my feet!
Oh, THAT WON'T BOTHER YOU ONCE YOU'RE FITTED OUT IN YOUR SLAVE'S WEAR. ALL THE MALEBOLGIA'S CONQUESTS WEAR IT.
HERE, I'LL WHISTLE YOURS UP...
PHWEEE-EET!
LEMME INTRODUCE K3-MYRLU. SHE'S A CONSTANTLY-EVOLVING NEURAL PARASITE AND I THINK SHE LIKES YOU.
no!
no, not that!

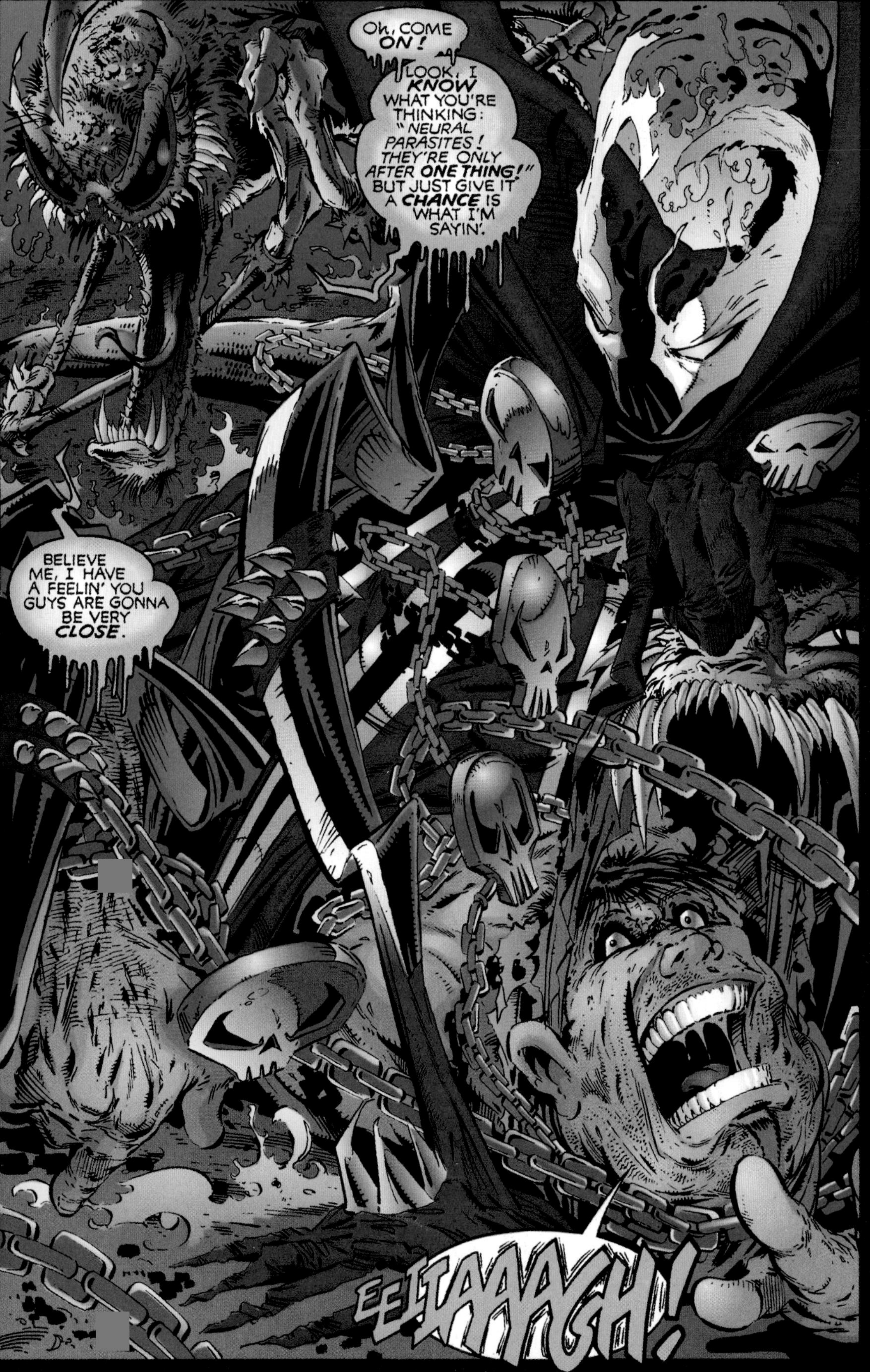
Oh, COME ON!
LOOK, I KNOW WHAT YOU'RE THINKING: "NEURAL PARASITES! THEY'RE ONLY AFTER ONE THING!" BUT JUST GIVE IT A CHANCE IS WHAT I'M SAYIN'.
BELIEVE ME, I HAVE A FEELIN' YOU GUYS ARE GONNA BE VERY CLOSE.
EEIAAAGH!

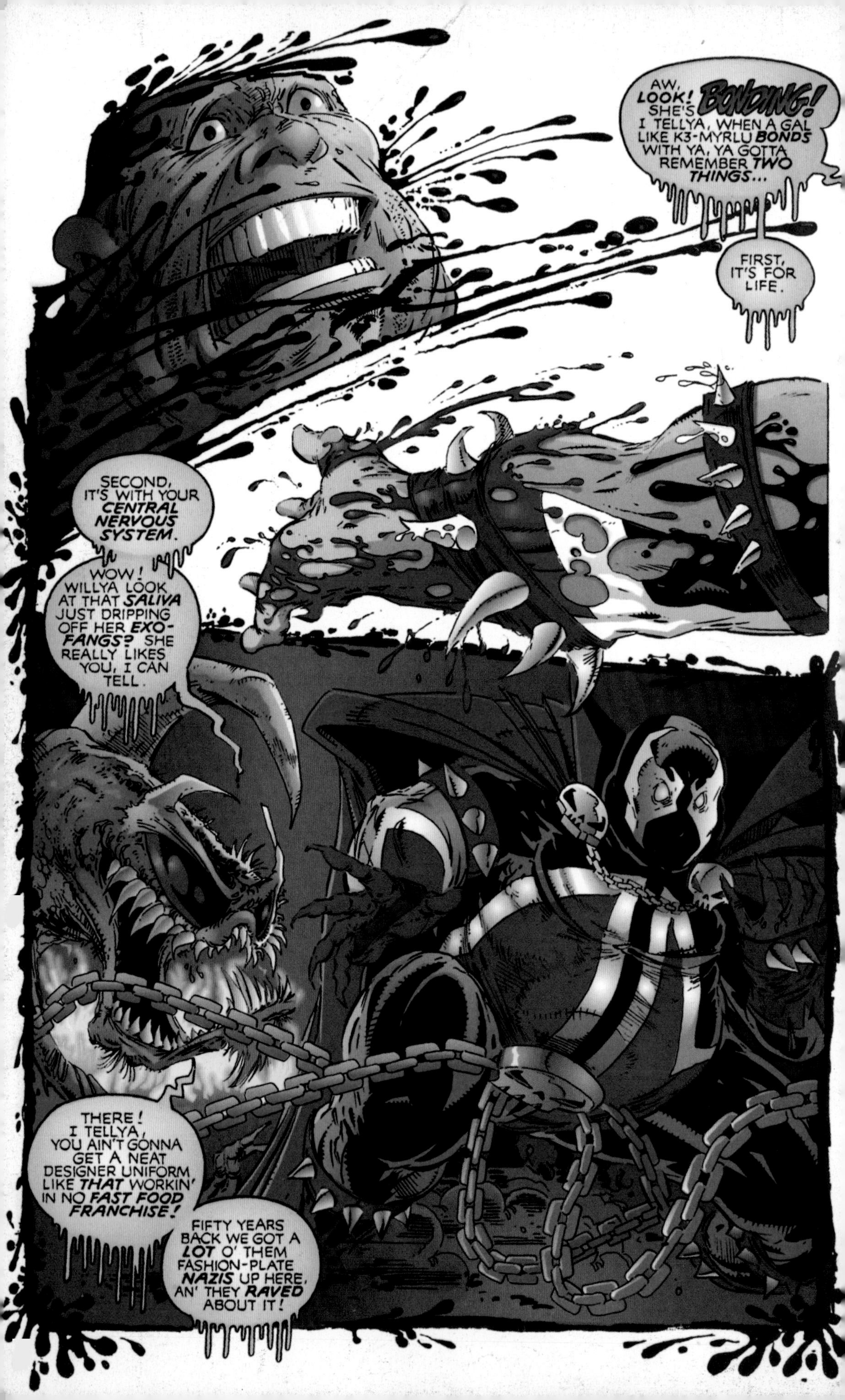
AW, LOOK! SHE'S BONDING! I TELLYA, WHEN A GAL LIKE K3-MYRLU BONDS WITH YA, YA GOTTA REMEMBER TWO THINGS...
FIRST, IT'S FOR LIFE.
SECOND, IT'S WITH YOUR CENTRAL NERVOUS SYSTEM.
WOW! WILLYA LOOK AT THAT SALIVA JUST DRIPPING OFF HER EXO-FANGS? SHE REALLY LIKES YOU, I CAN TELL.
THERE! I TELLYA, YOU AIN'T GONNA GET A NEAT DESIGNER UNIFORM LIKE THAT WORKIN' IN NO FAST FOOD FRANCHISE!
FIFTY YEARS BACK WE GOT A LOT O' THEM FASHION-PLATE NAZIS UP HERE, AN' THEY RAVED ABOUT IT!

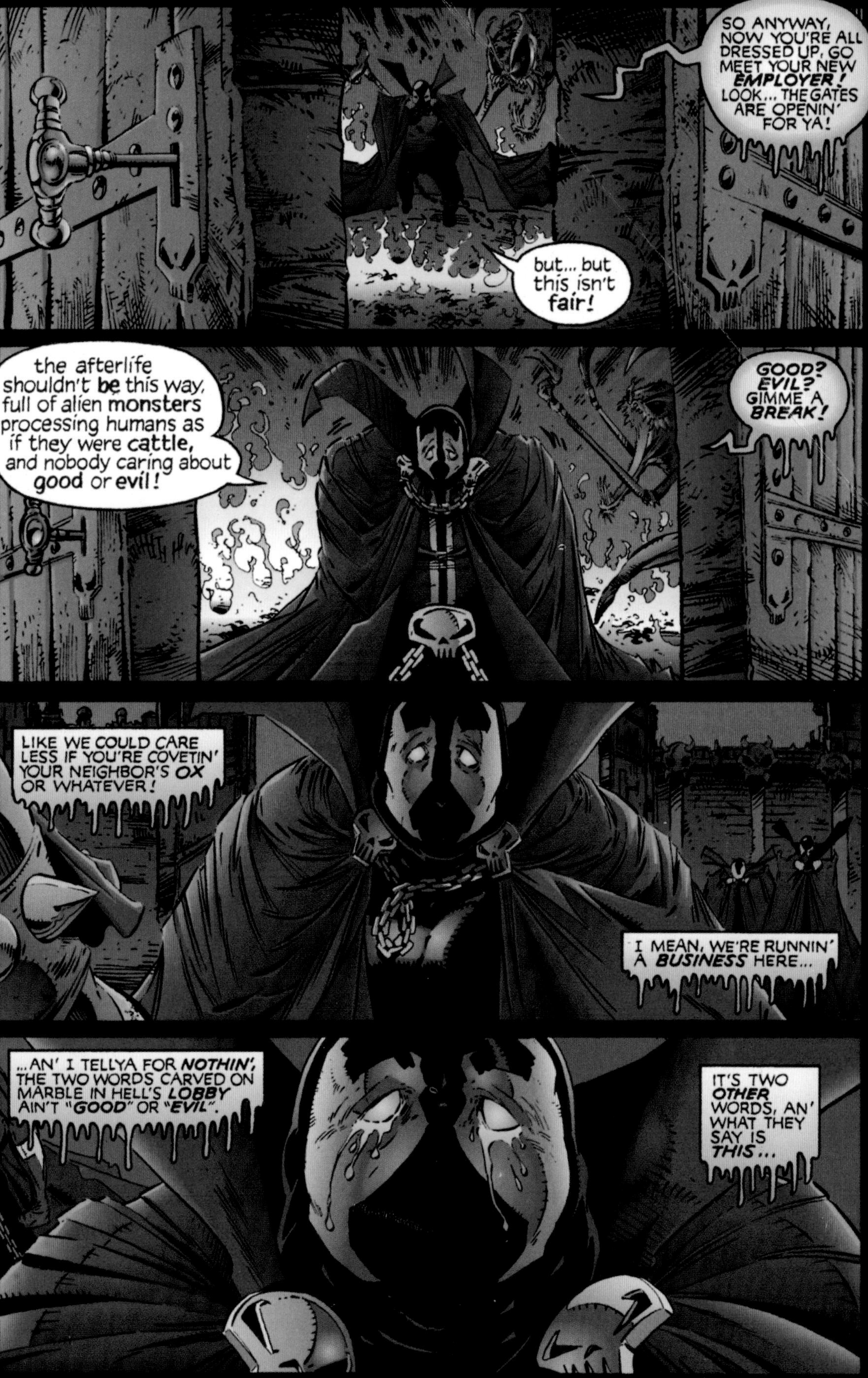
SO ANYWAY, NOW YOU'RE ALL DRESSED UP, GO MEET YOUR NEW EMPLOYER! LOOK... THE GATES ARE OPENIN' FOR YA!
but... but this isn't fair!
the afterlife shouldn't be this way, full of alien monsters processing humans as if they were cattle, and nobody caring about good or evil!
GOOD? EVIL? GIMME A BREAK!
LIKE WE COULD CARE LESS IF YOU'RE COVETIN' YOUR NEIGHBOR'S OX OR WHATEVER!
I MEAN, WE'RE RUNNIN' A BUSINESS HERE...
...AN' I TELLYA FOR NOTHIN', THE TWO WORDS CARVED ON MARBLE IN HELL'S LOBBY AIN'T "GOOD" OR "EVIL".
IT'S TWO OTHER WORDS, AN' WHAT THEY SAY IS THIS...

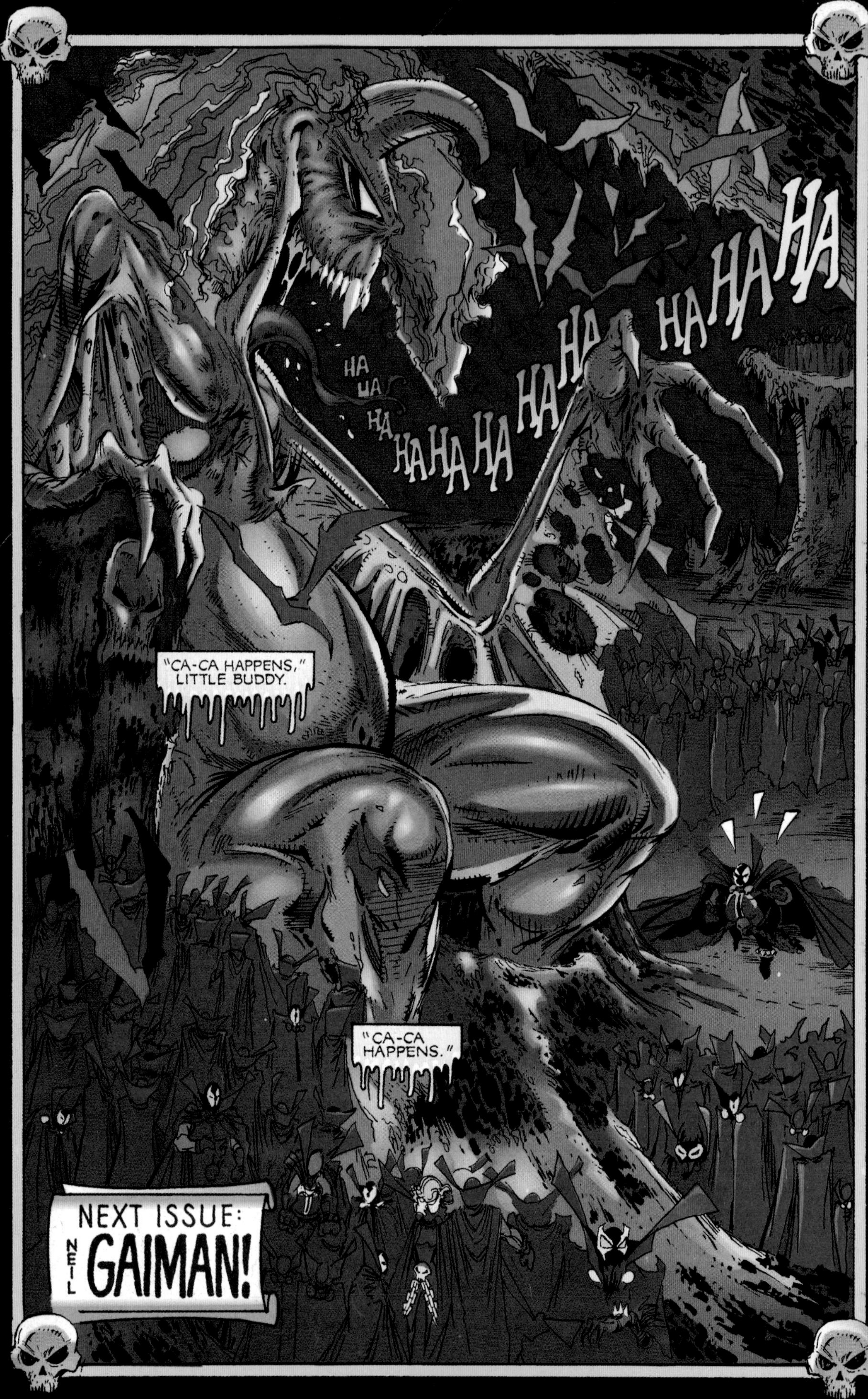
HA HA HA HAHAHA HA HA HA HA HAHAHAHA
"CA-CA HAPPENS," LITTLE BUDDY.
"CA-CA HAPPENS."
NEXT ISSUE: NEIL GAIMAN!

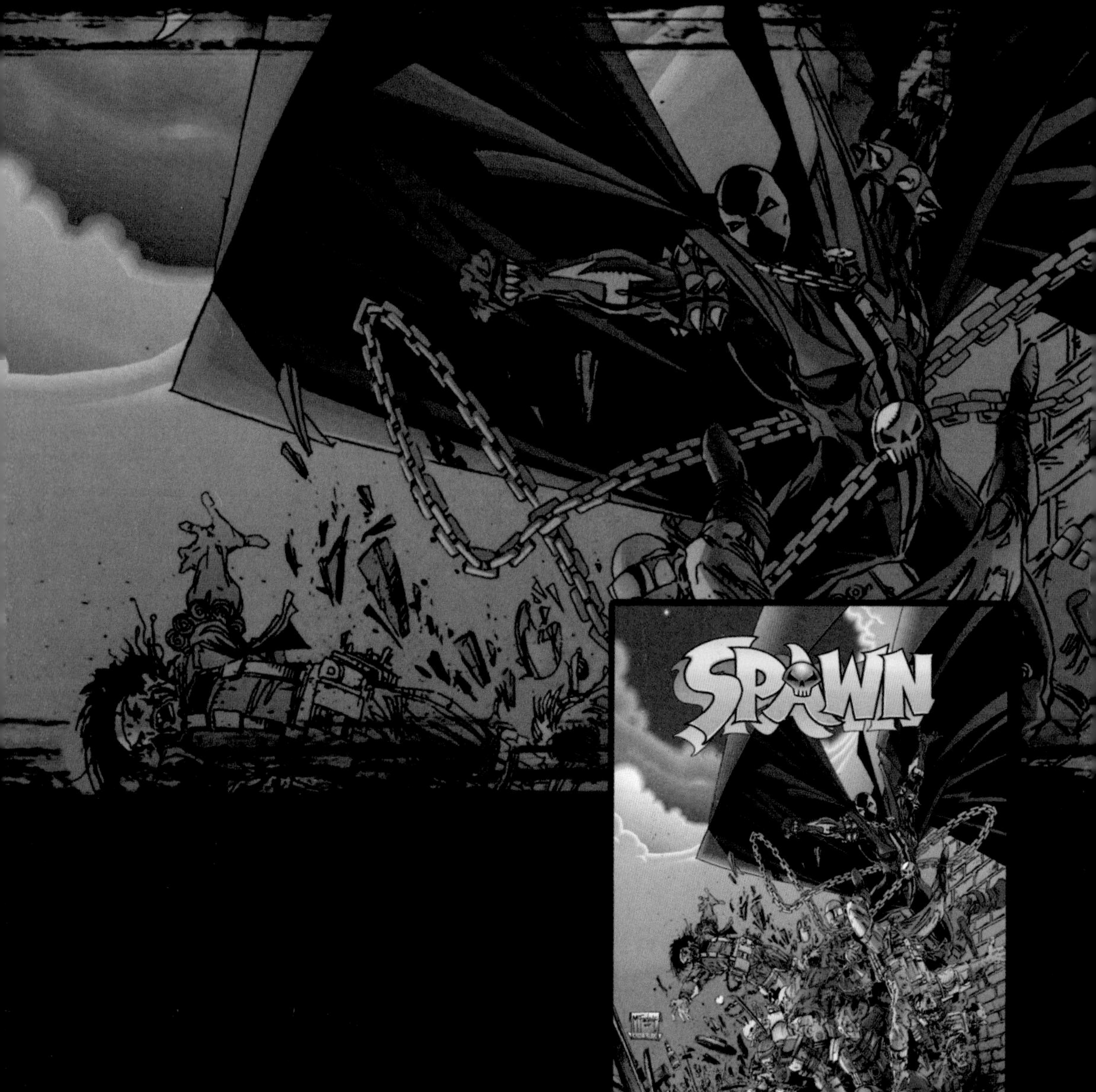
SPAWN

ISSUE ELEVEN

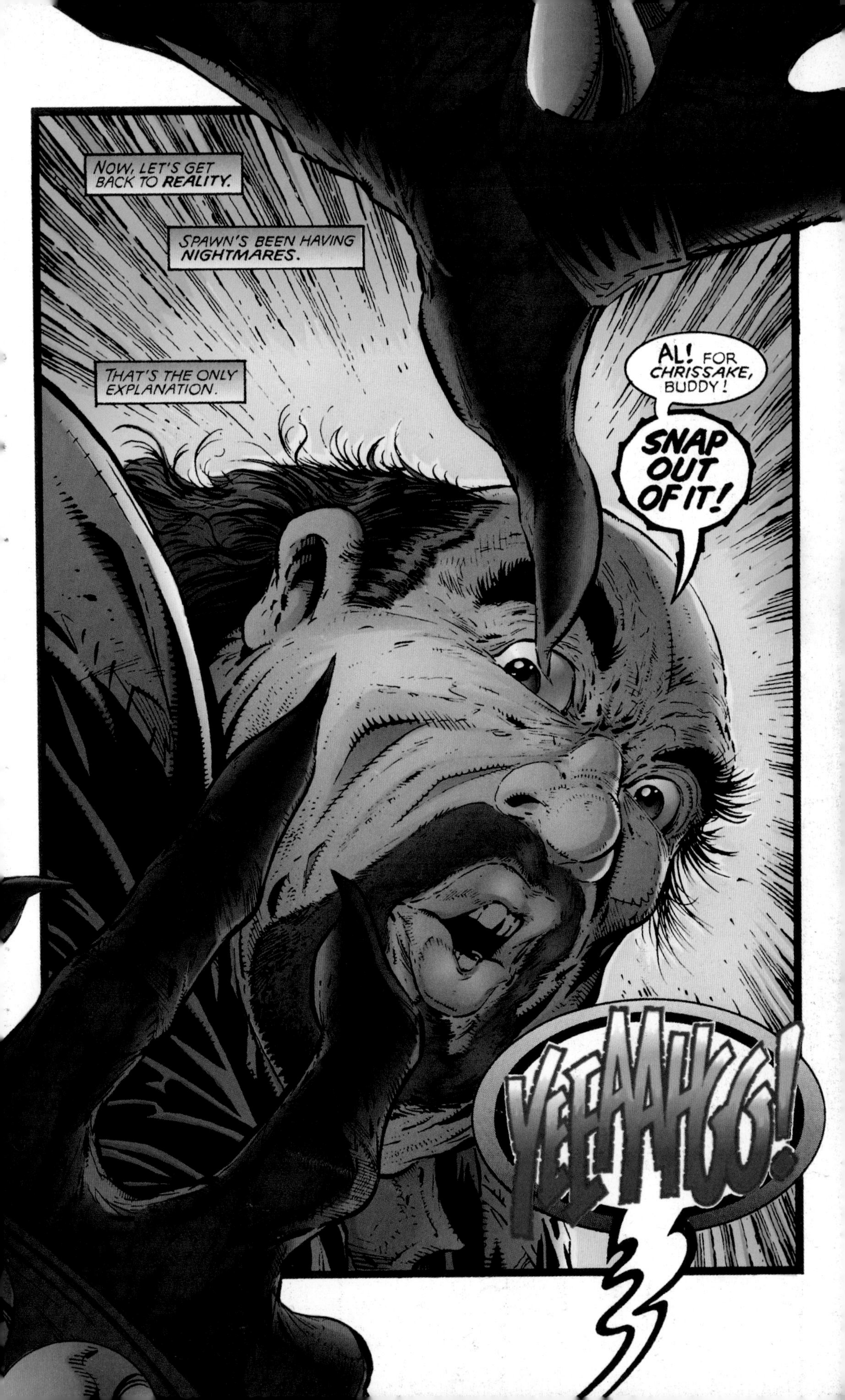
NOW, LET'S GET BACK TO REALITY.
SPAWN'S BEEN HAVING NIGHTMARES.
THAT'S THE ONLY EXPLANATION.
AL! FOR CHRISSAKE, BUDDY!
SNAP OUT OF IT!
YEEAAHGG!

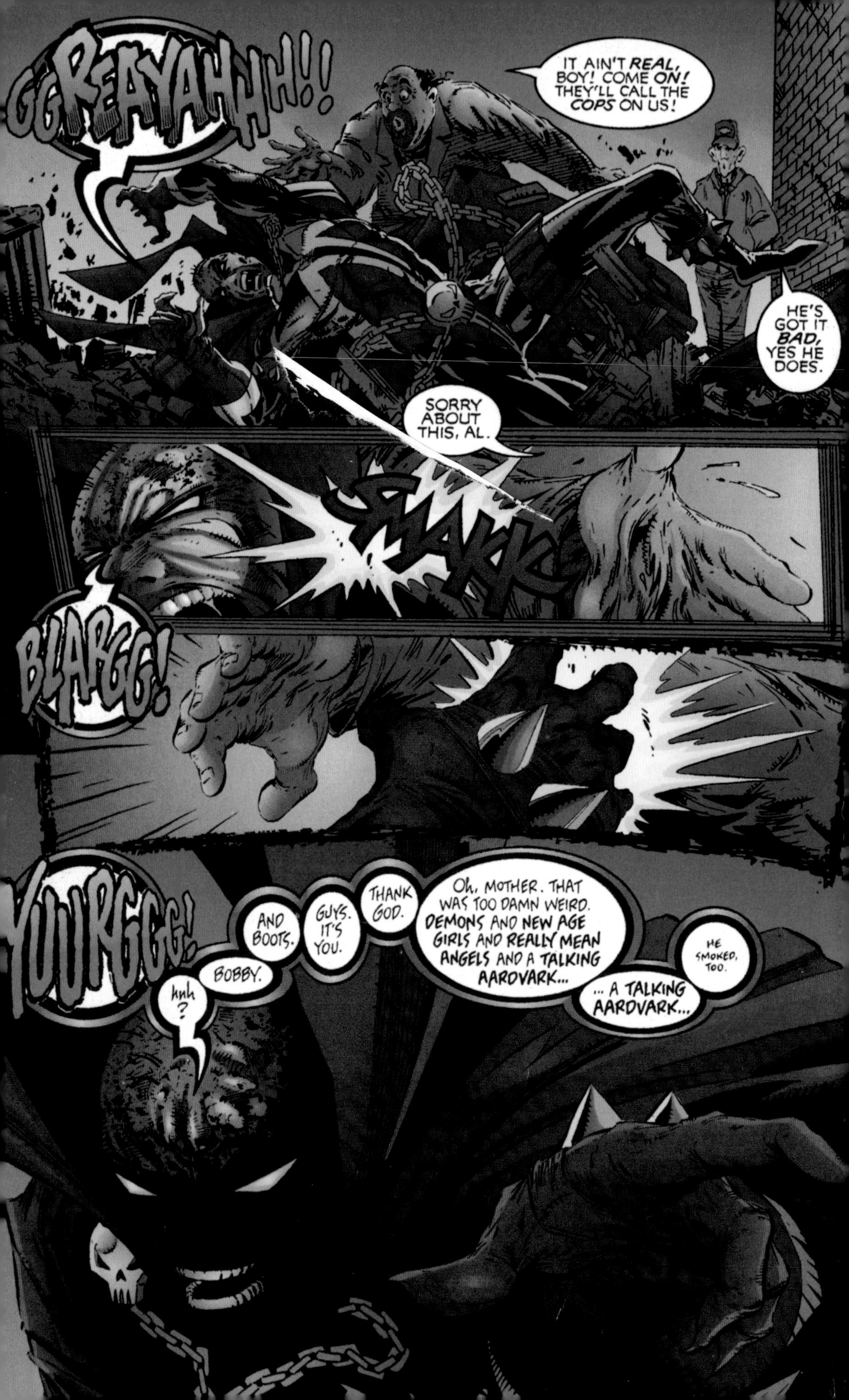
GGREAYAHHH!!
IT AIN'T REAL, BOY! COME ON! THEY'LL CALL THE COPS ON US!
HE'S GOT IT BAD, YES HE DOES.
SORRY ABOUT THIS, AL.
SMAKK
BLARGG!
YUURGGG!
hnh?
BOBBY.
AND BOOTS.
GUYS. IT'S YOU.
THANK GOD.
Oh, MOTHER. THAT WAS TOO DAMN WEIRD. DEMONS AND NEW AGE GIRLS AND REALLY MEAN ANGELS AND A TALKING AARDVARK...
... A TALKING AARDVARK...
HE SMOKED, TOO.

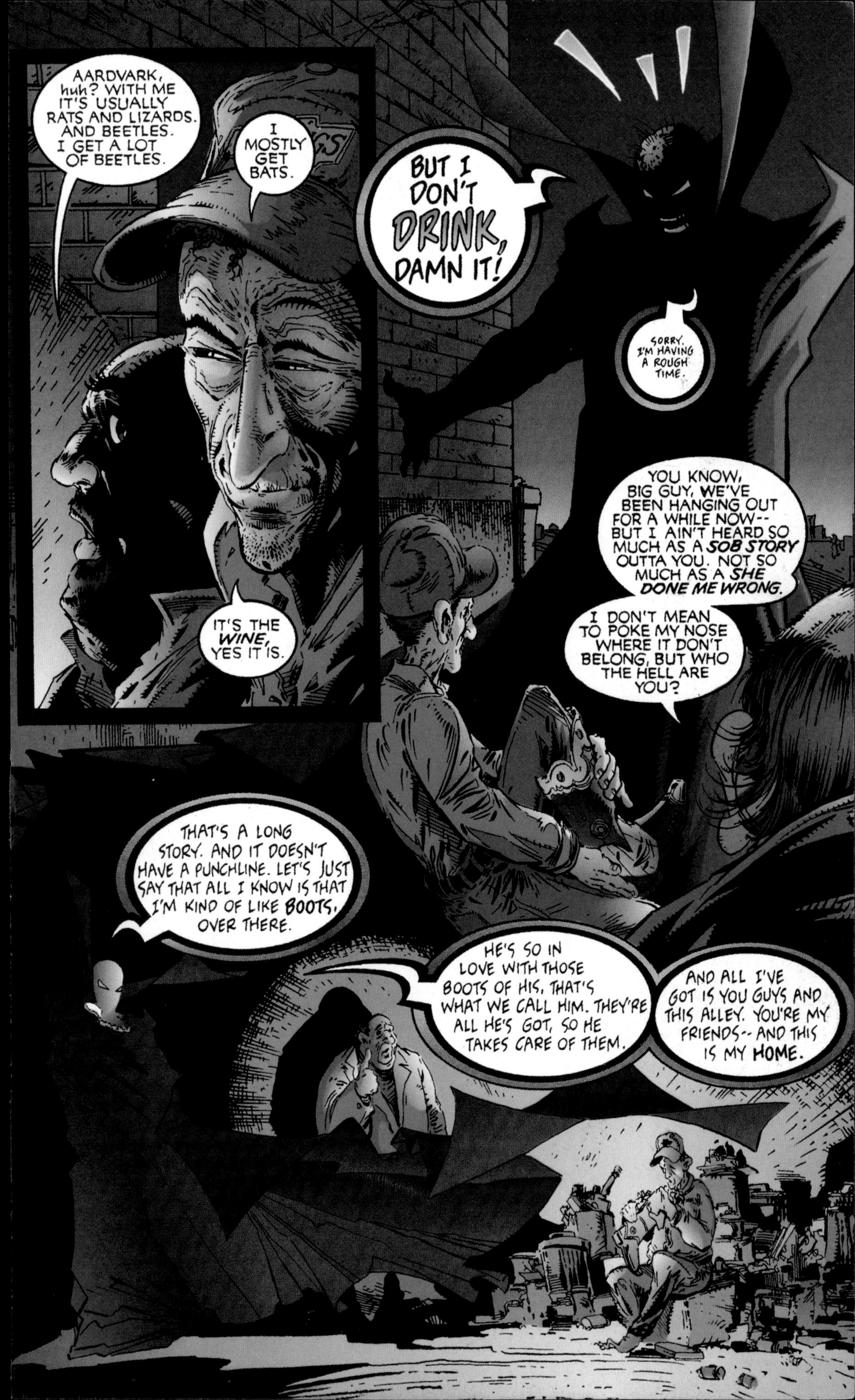
AARDVARK, huh? WITH ME IT'S USUALLY RATS AND LIZARDS. AND BEETLES. I GET A LOT OF BEETLES.
I MOSTLY GET BATS.
IT'S THE WINE, YES IT IS.
BUT I DON'T DRINK, DAMN IT!
SORRY. I'M HAVING A ROUGH TIME.
YOU KNOW, BIG GUY, WE'VE BEEN HANGING OUT FOR A WHILE NOW-- BUT I AIN'T HEARD SO MUCH AS A SOB STORY OUTTA YOU. NOT SO MUCH AS A SHE DONE ME WRONG.
I DON'T MEAN TO POKE MY NOSE WHERE IT DON'T BELONG, BUT WHO THE HELL ARE YOU?
THAT'S A LONG STORY. AND IT DOESN'T HAVE A PUNCHLINE. LET'S JUST SAY THAT ALL I KNOW IS THAT I'M KIND OF LIKE BOOTS, OVER THERE.
HE'S SO IN LOVE WITH THOSE BOOTS OF HIS, THAT'S WHAT WE CALL HIM. THEY'RE ALL HE'S GOT, SO HE TAKES CARE OF THEM.
AND ALL I'VE GOT IS YOU GUYS AND THIS ALLEY. YOU'RE MY FRIENDS-- AND THIS IS MY HOME.

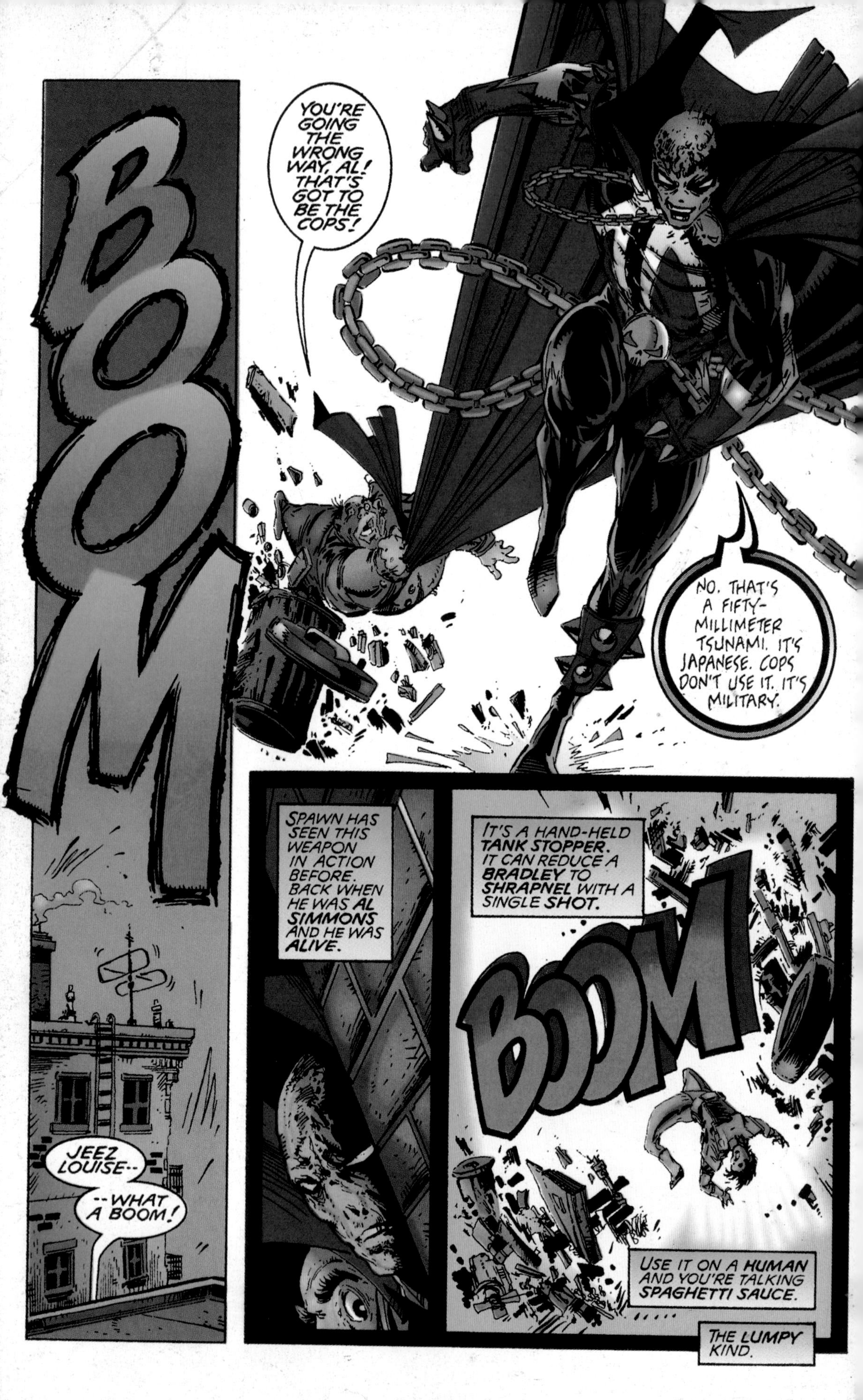
BOOM
YOU'RE GOING THE WRONG WAY, AL! THAT'S GOT TO BE THE COPS!
NO. THAT'S A FIFTY-MILLIMETER TSUNAMI. IT'S JAPANESE. COPS DON'T USE IT. IT'S MILITARY.
JEEZ LOUISE--
--WHAT A BOOM!
SPAWN HAS SEEN THIS WEAPON IN ACTION BEFORE. BACK WHEN HE WAS AL SIMMONS AND HE WAS ALIVE.
IT'S A HAND-HELD TANK STOPPER. IT CAN REDUCE A BRADLEY TO SHRAPNEL WITH A SINGLE SHOT.
BOOM
USE IT ON A HUMAN AND YOU'RE TALKING SPAGHETTI SAUCE.
......
THE LUMPY KIND.

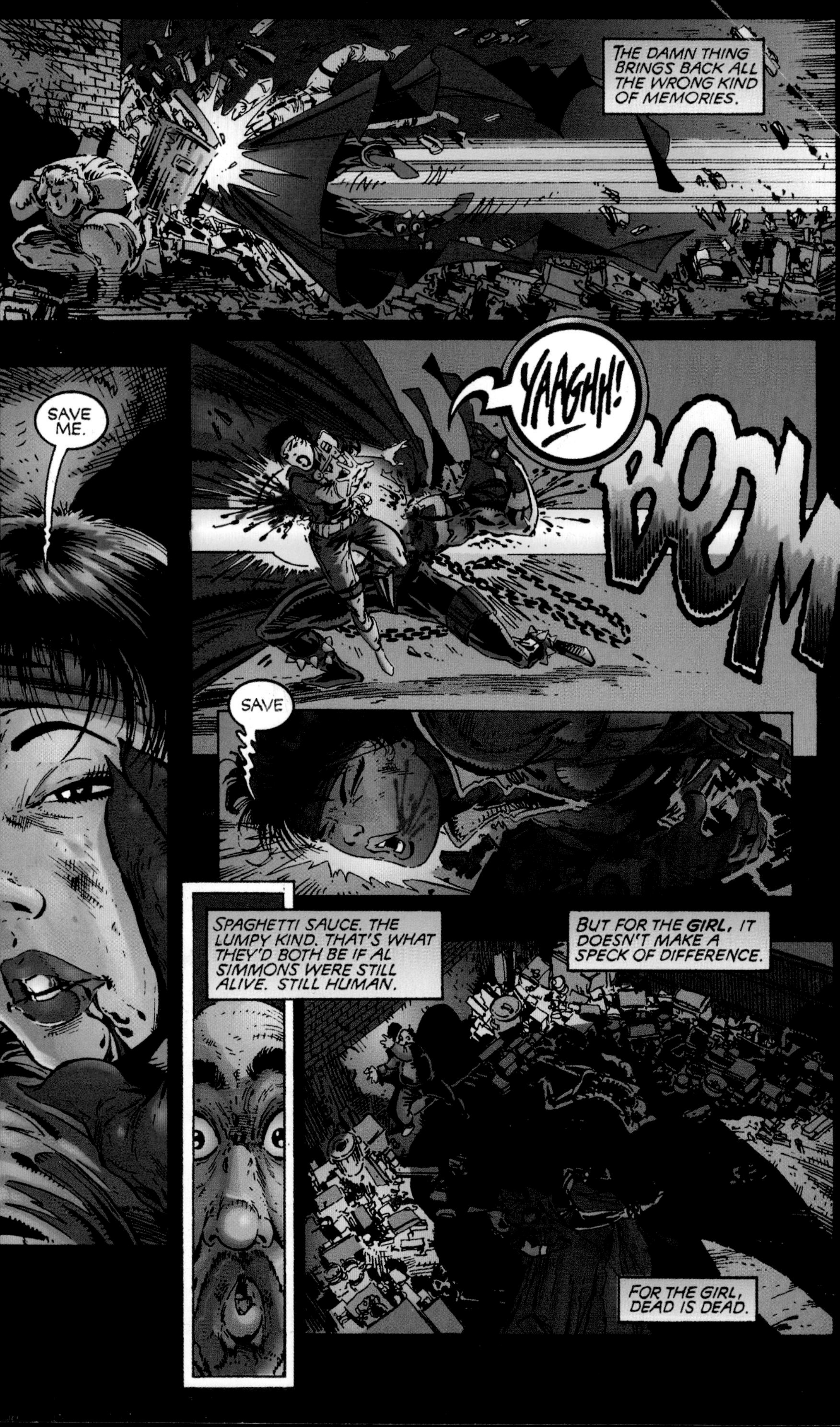

THE DAMN THING BRINGS BACK ALL THE WRONG KIND OF MEMORIES.
SAVE ME.
YAAGHH!
BOOM
SAVE
SPAGHETTI SAUCE. THE LUMPY KIND. THAT'S WHAT THEY'D BOTH BE IF AL SIMMONS WERE STILL ALIVE. STILL HUMAN.
BUT FOR THE GIRL, IT DOESN'T MAKE A SPECK OF DIFFERENCE.
FOR THE GIRL, DEAD IS DEAD.

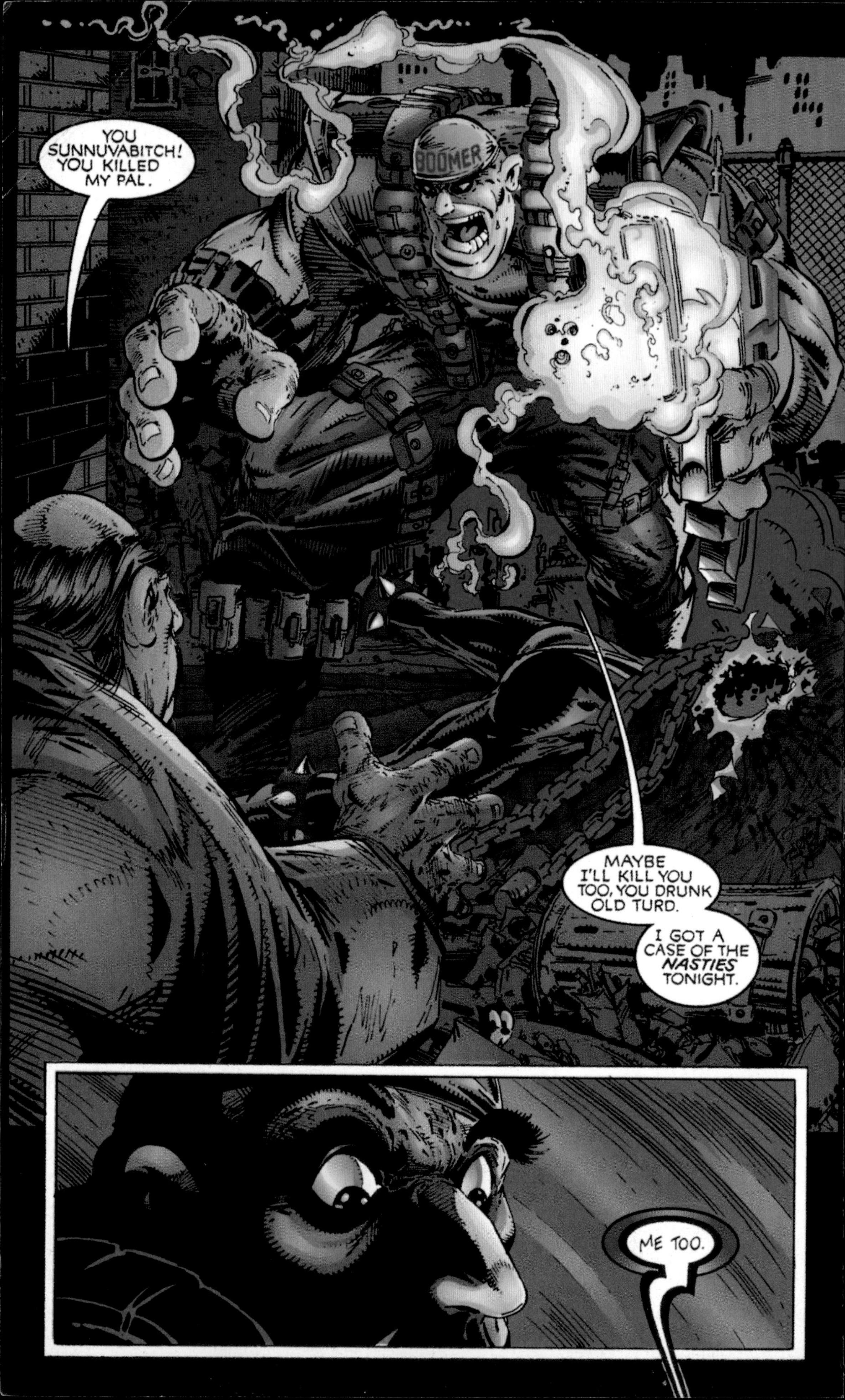
YOU SUNNUVABITCH! YOU KILLED MY PAL.
BOOMER
MAYBE I'LL KILL YOU TOO, YOU DRUNK OLD TURD.
I GOT A CASE OF THE *NASTIES* TONIGHT.
ME TOO.

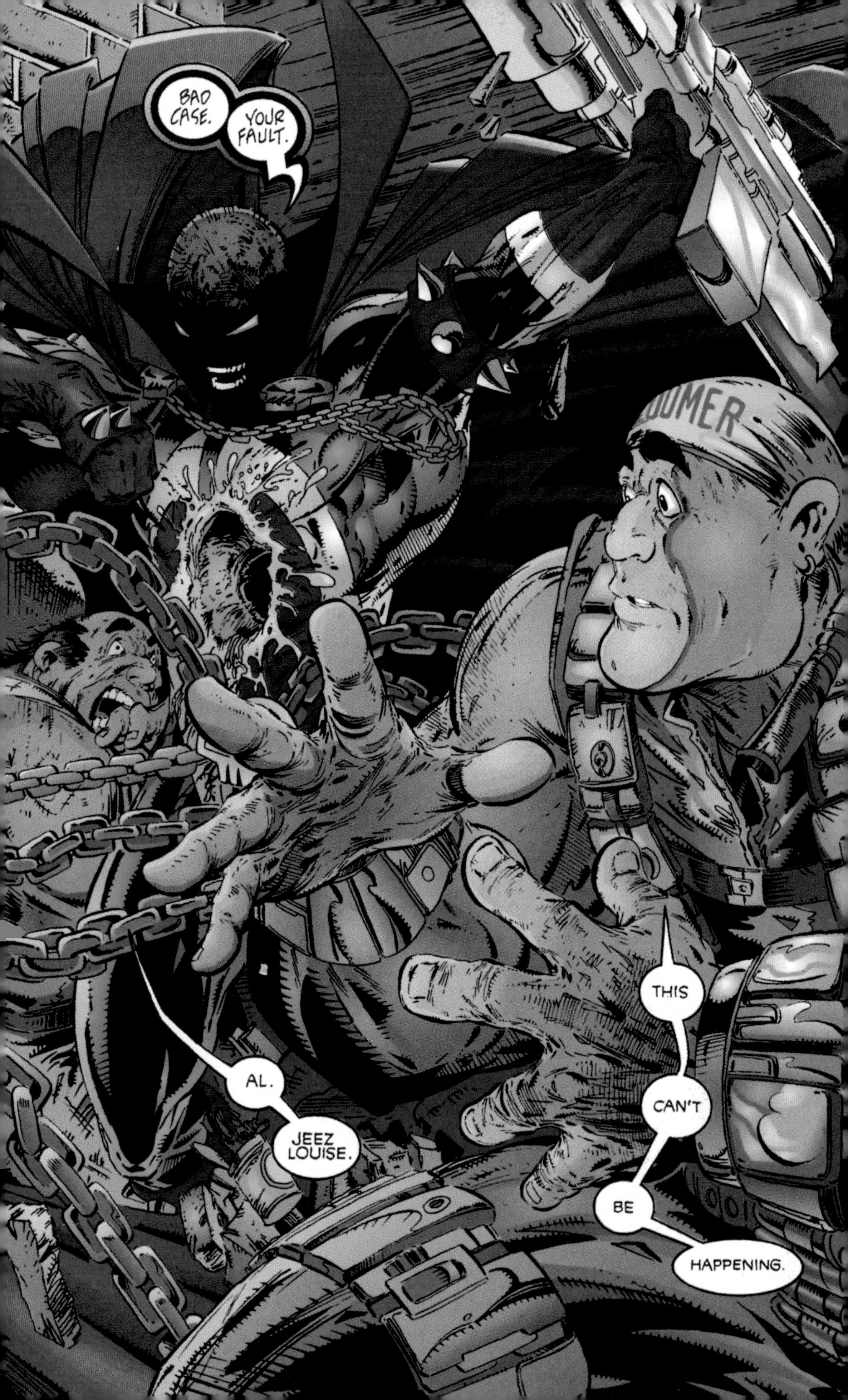
BAD CASE.
YOUR FAULT.
AL.
JEEZ LOUISE.
THIS
CAN'T
BE
HAPPENING.

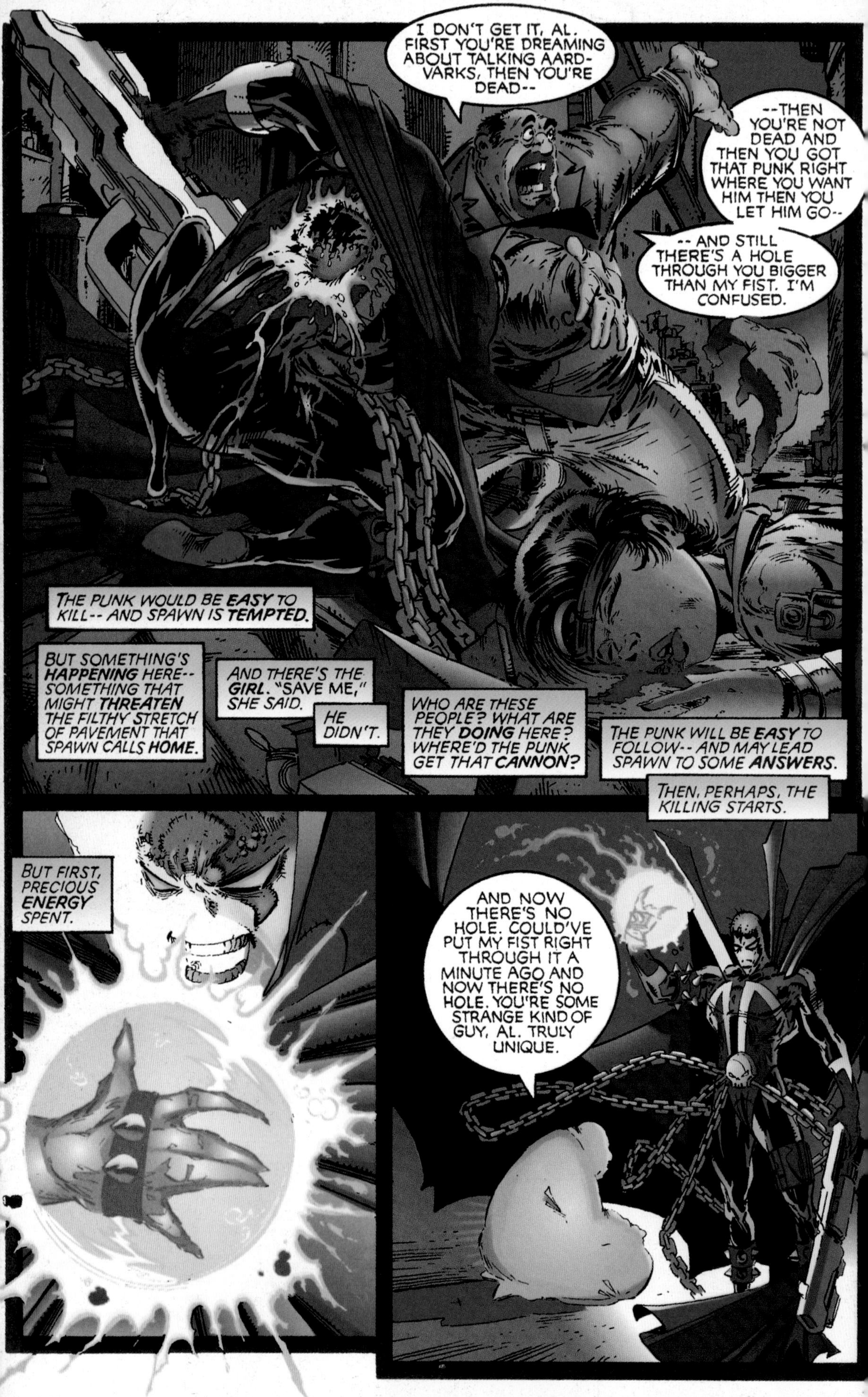
I DON'T GET IT, AL. FIRST YOU'RE DREAMING ABOUT TALKING AARD-VARKS, THEN YOU'RE DEAD--
--THEN YOU'RE NOT DEAD AND THEN YOU GOT THAT PUNK RIGHT WHERE YOU WANT HIM THEN YOU LET HIM GO--
-- AND STILL THERE'S A HOLE THROUGH YOU BIGGER THAN MY FIST. I'M CONFUSED.
THE PUNK WOULD BE EASY TO KILL-- AND SPAWN IS TEMPTED.
BUT SOMETHING'S HAPPENING HERE-- SOMETHING THAT MIGHT THREATEN THE FILTHY STRETCH OF PAVEMENT THAT SPAWN CALLS HOME.
AND THERE'S THE GIRL. "SAVE ME," SHE SAID.
HE DIDN'T.
WHO ARE THESE PEOPLE? WHAT ARE THEY DOING HERE? WHERE'D THE PUNK GET THAT CANNON?
THE PUNK WILL BE EASY TO FOLLOW-- AND MAY LEAD SPAWN TO SOME ANSWERS.
THEN, PERHAPS, THE KILLING STARTS.
BUT FIRST, PRECIOUS ENERGY SPENT.
AND NOW THERE'S NO HOLE. COULD'VE PUT MY FIST RIGHT THROUGH IT A MINUTE AGO AND NOW THERE'S NO HOLE. YOU'RE SOME STRANGE KIND OF GUY, AL. TRULY UNIQUE.

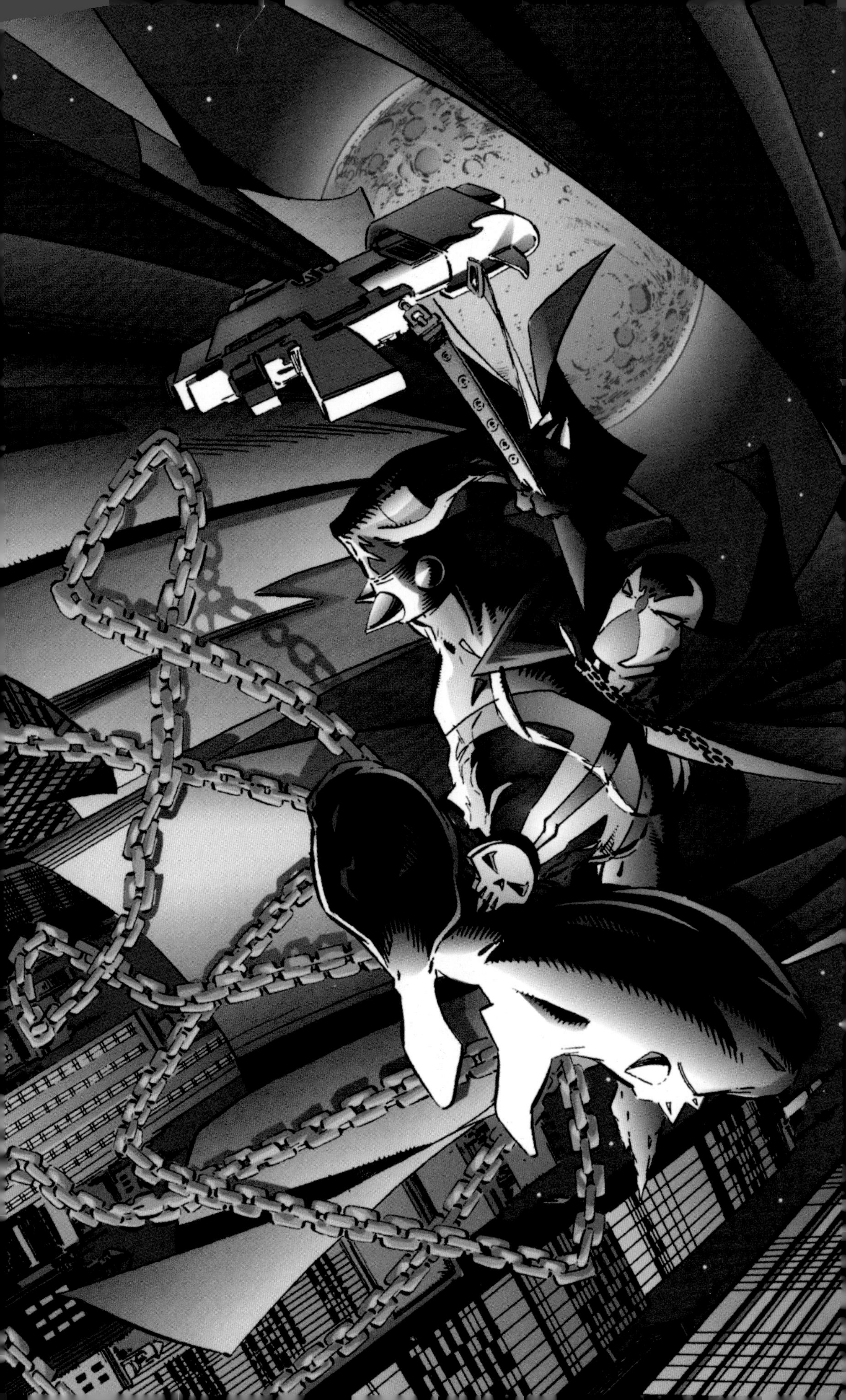

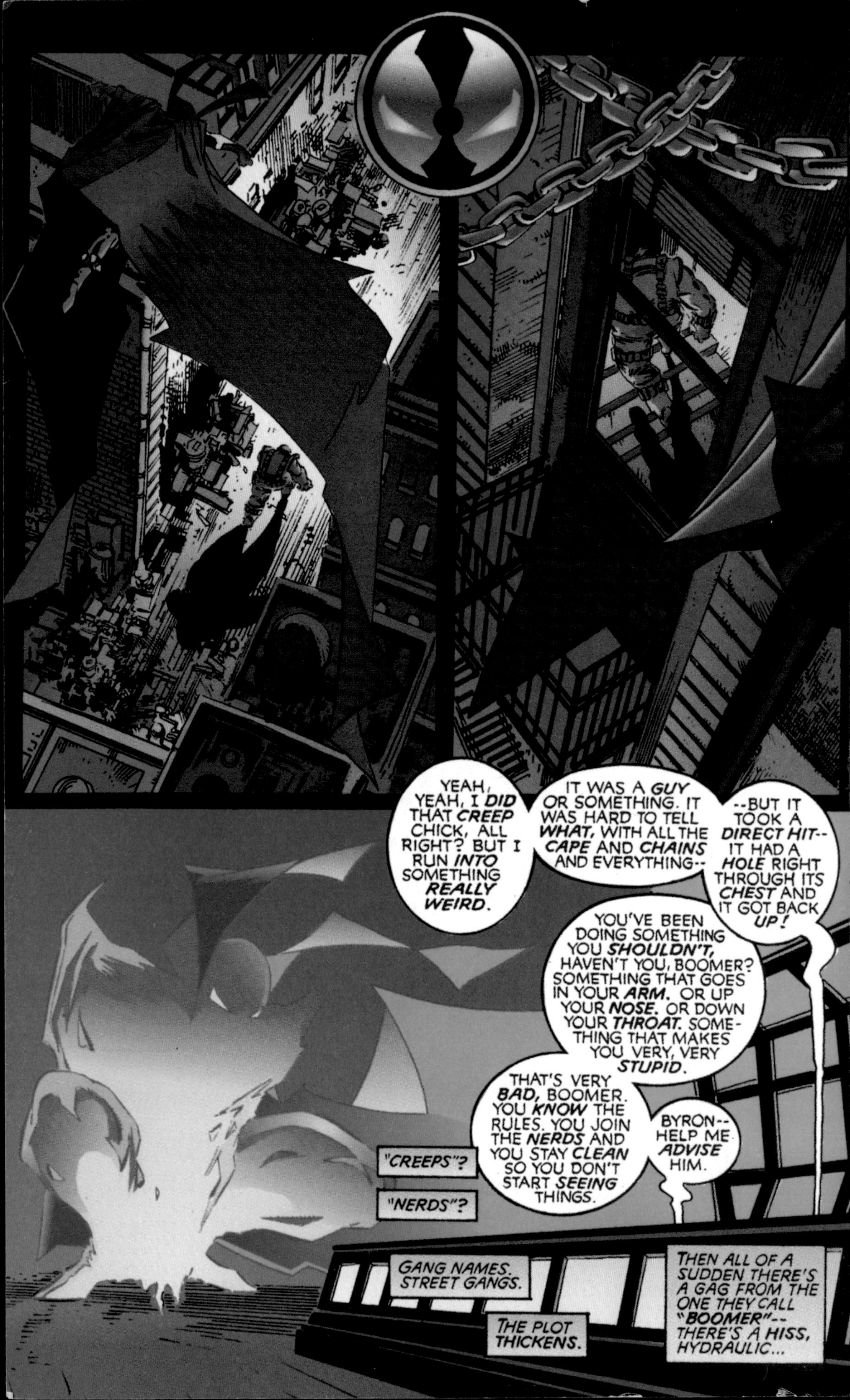
YEAH, YEAH, I DID THAT CREEP CHICK, ALL RIGHT? BUT I RUN INTO SOMETHING REALLY WEIRD.
IT WAS A GUY OR SOMETHING. IT WAS HARD TO TELL WHAT, WITH ALL THE CAPE AND CHAINS AND EVERYTHING--
--BUT IT TOOK A DIRECT HIT-- IT HAD A HOLE RIGHT THROUGH ITS CHEST AND IT GOT BACK UP!
YOU'VE BEEN DOING SOMETHING YOU SHOULDN'T, HAVEN'T YOU, BOOMER? SOMETHING THAT GOES IN YOUR ARM. OR UP YOUR NOSE. OR DOWN YOUR THROAT. SOMETHING THAT MAKES YOU VERY, VERY STUPID.
THAT'S VERY BAD, BOOMER. YOU KNOW THE RULES. YOU JOIN THE NERDS AND YOU STAY CLEAN SO YOU DON'T START SEEING THINGS.
BYRON-- HELP ME ADVISE HIM.
"CREEPS"?
"NERDS"?
GANG NAMES. STREET GANGS.
THE PLOT THICKENS.
THEN ALL OF A SUDDEN THERE'S A GAG FROM THE ONE THEY CALL "BOOMER"-- THERE'S A HISS, HYDRAULIC...

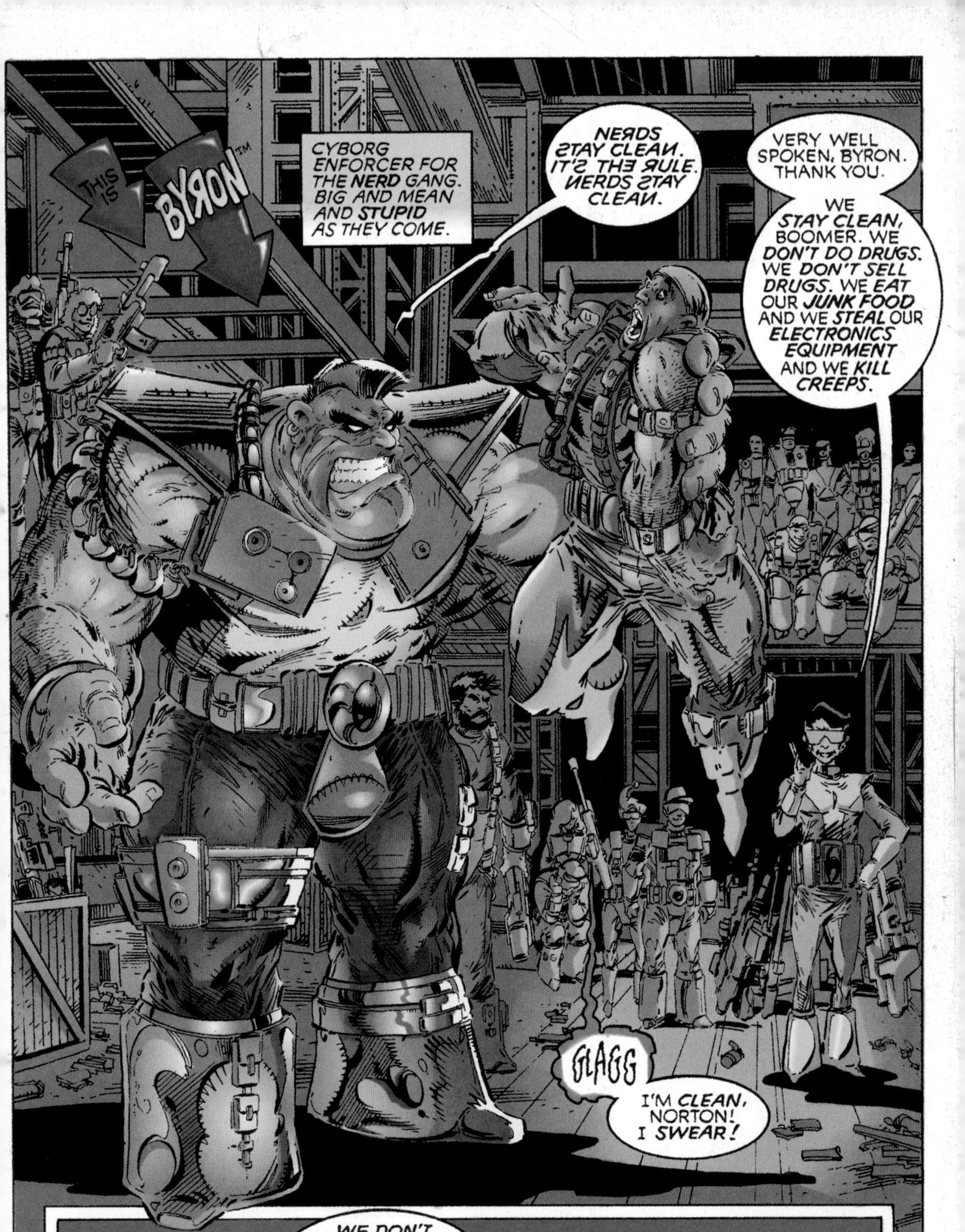
THIS IS BYRON™
CYBORG ENFORCER FOR THE NERD GANG. BIG AND MEAN AND STUPID AS THEY COME.
NERDS STAY CLEAN. IT'S THE RULE. NERDS STAY CLEAN.
VERY WELL SPOKEN, BYRON. THANK YOU.
WE STAY CLEAN, BOOMER. WE DON'T DO DRUGS. WE DON'T SELL DRUGS. WE EAT OUR JUNK FOOD AND WE STEAL OUR ELECTRONICS EQUIPMENT AND WE KILL CREEPS.
GLAGG
I'M CLEAN, NORTON! I SWEAR!

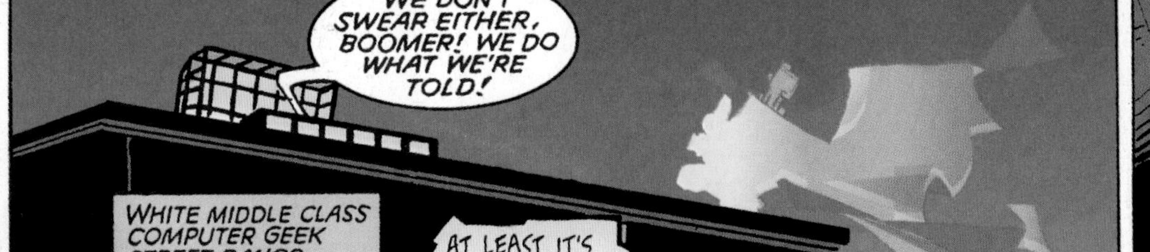
WE DON'T SWEAR EITHER, BOOMER! WE DO WHAT WE'RE TOLD!
WHITE MIDDLE CLASS COMPUTER GEEK STREET GANGS.
AT LEAST IT'S NOT A TALKING AARDVARK...

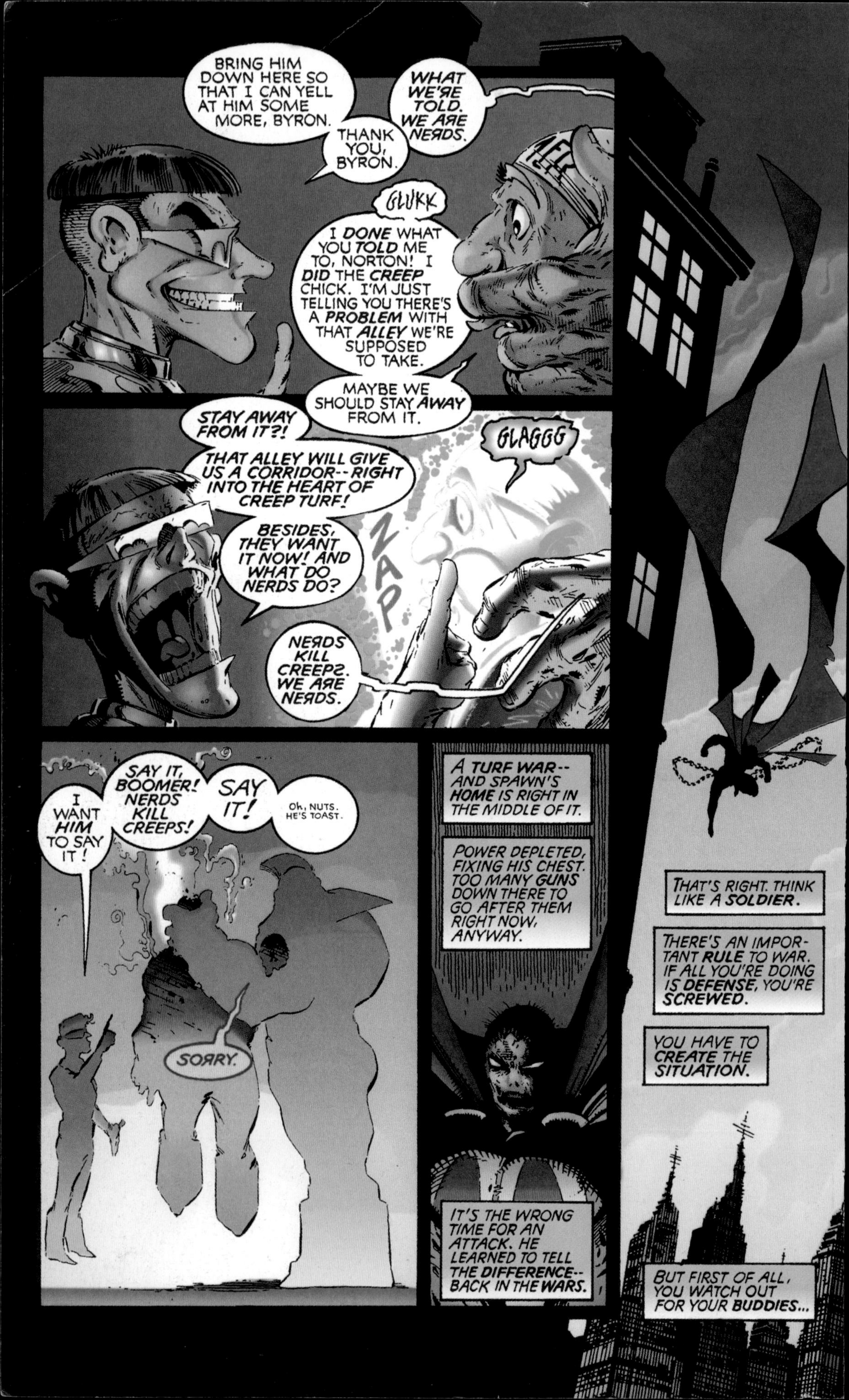

BRING HIM DOWN HERE SO THAT I CAN YELL AT HIM SOME MORE, BYRON.
THANK YOU, BYRON.
WHAT WE'RE TOLD. WE ARE NERDS.
GLUKK
I DONE WHAT YOU TOLD ME TO, NORTON! I DID THE CREEP CHICK. I'M JUST TELLING YOU THERE'S A PROBLEM WITH THAT ALLEY WE'RE SUPPOSED TO TAKE.
MAYBE WE SHOULD STAY AWAY FROM IT.
STAY AWAY FROM IT?!
THAT ALLEY WILL GIVE US A CORRIDOR--RIGHT INTO THE HEART OF CREEP TURF!
GLAGGG
BESIDES, THEY WANT IT NOW! AND WHAT DO NERDS DO?
ZAP
NERDS KILL CREEPS. WE ARE NERDS.
I WANT HIM TO SAY IT!
SAY IT, BOOMER! NERDS KILL CREEPS!
SAY IT!
Oh, NUTS. HE'S TOAST.
SORRY.
A TURF WAR--AND SPAWN'S HOME IS RIGHT IN THE MIDDLE OF IT.
POWER DEPLETED, FIXING HIS CHEST. TOO MANY GUNS DOWN THERE TO GO AFTER THEM RIGHT NOW, ANYWAY.
IT'S THE WRONG TIME FOR AN ATTACK. HE LEARNED TO TELL THE DIFFERENCE--BACK IN THE WARS.
THAT'S RIGHT. THINK LIKE A SOLDIER.
THERE'S AN IMPORTANT RULE TO WAR. IF ALL YOU'RE DOING IS DEFENSE, YOU'RE SCREWED.
YOU HAVE TO CREATE THE SITUATION.
BUT FIRST OF ALL, YOU WATCH OUT FOR YOUR BUDDIES...

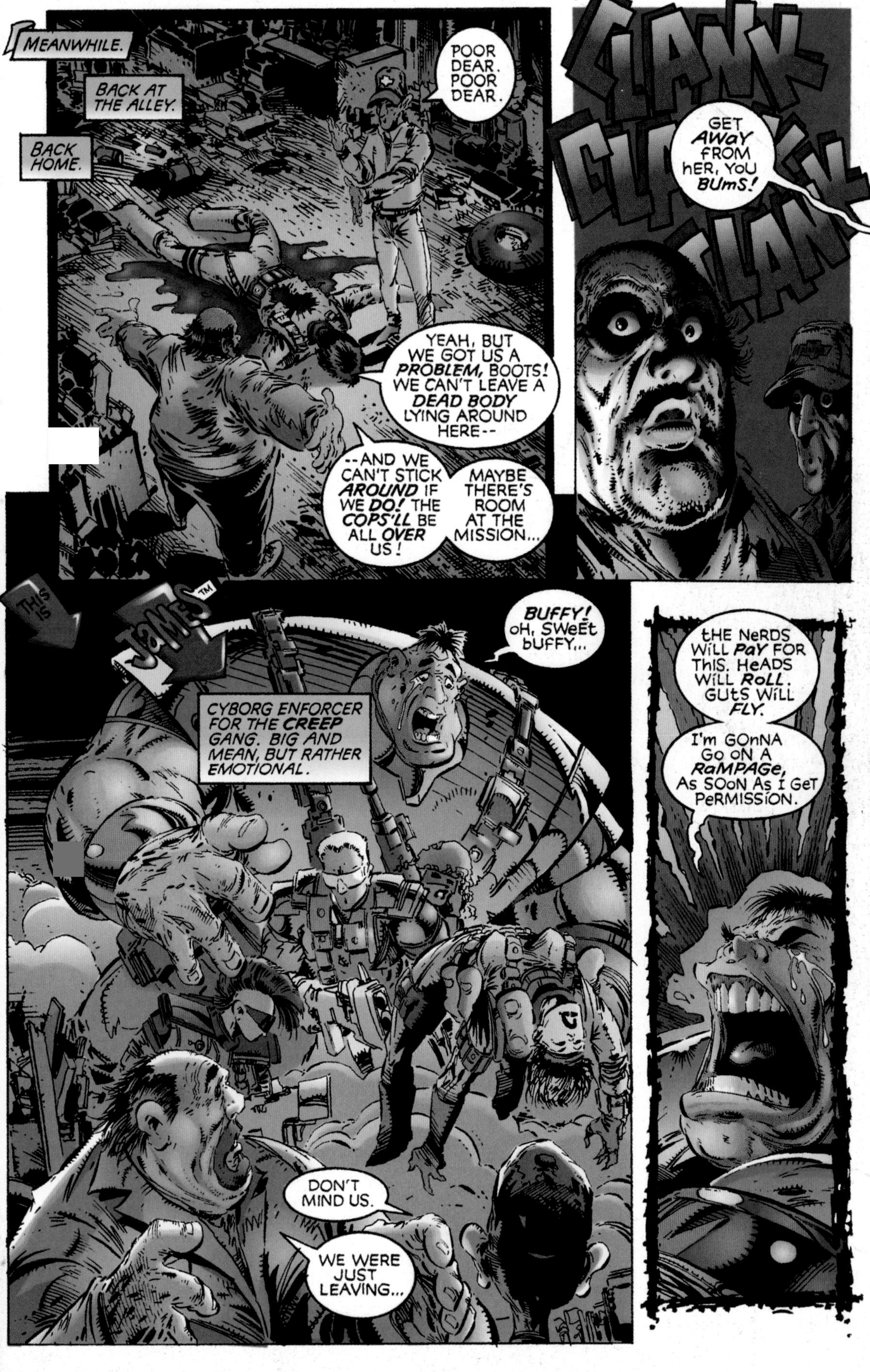
MEANWHILE.
BACK AT THE ALLEY.
BACK HOME.
POOR DEAR. POOR DEAR.
YEAH, BUT WE GOT US A PROBLEM, BOOTS! WE CAN'T LEAVE A DEAD BODY LYING AROUND HERE--
--AND WE CAN'T STICK AROUND IF WE DO! THE COPS'LL BE ALL OVER US!
MAYBE THERE'S ROOM AT THE MISSION...
CLANK
GET AWAY FROM HER, YOU BUMS!
THIS IS JAMES™
BUFFY! OH, SWEET BUFFY...
CYBORG ENFORCER FOR THE CREEP GANG. BIG AND MEAN, BUT RATHER EMOTIONAL.
THE NERDS WILL PAY FOR THIS. HEADS WILL ROLL. GUTS WILL FLY.
I'M GONNA GO ON A RAMPAGE, AS SOON AS I GET PERMISSION.
DON'T MIND US.
WE WERE JUST LEAVING...

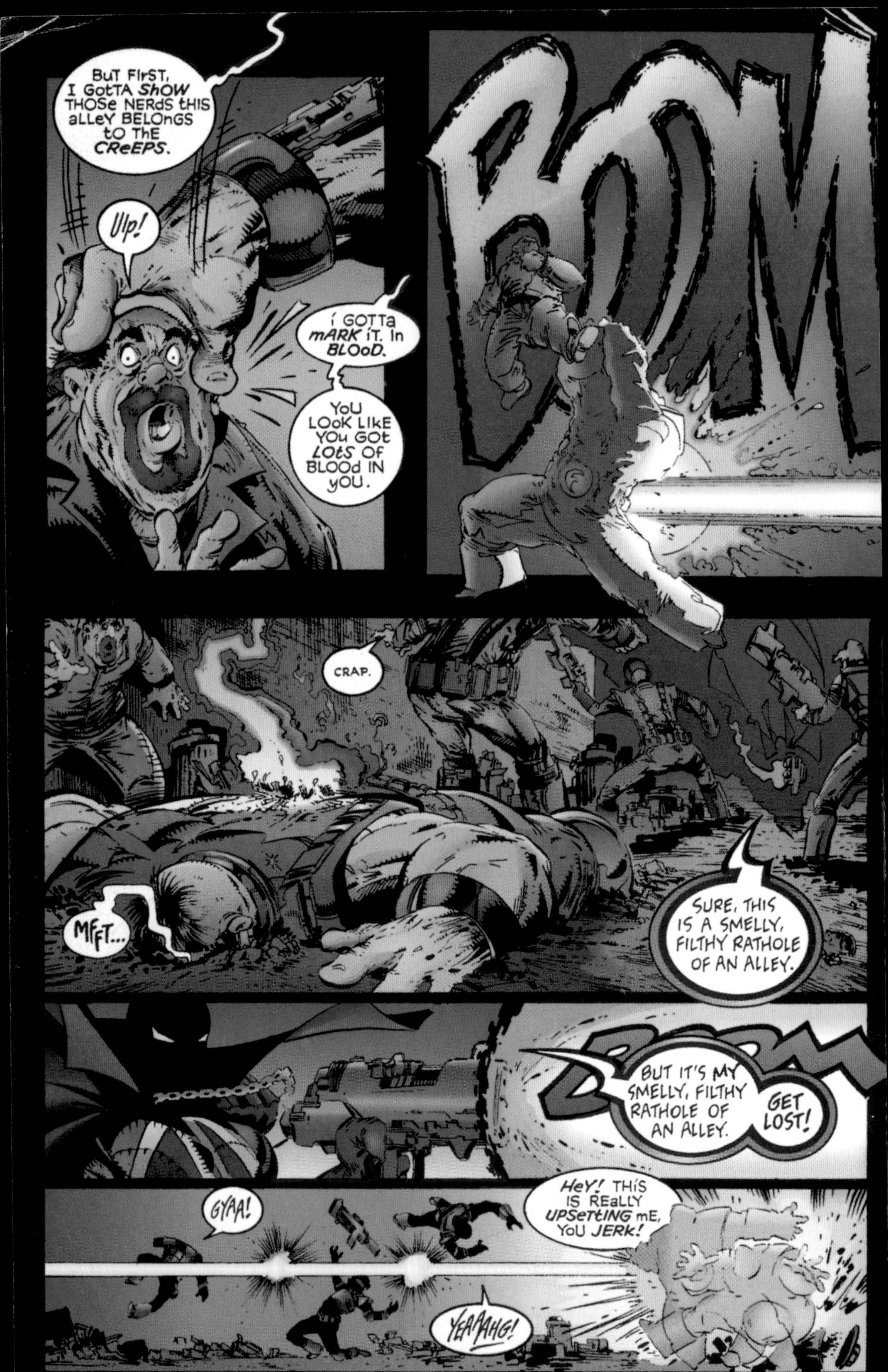
BUT FIRST, I GOTTA SHOW THOSE NERDS THIS ALLEY BELONGS TO THE CREEPS.
ULP!
I GOTTA MARK IT. IN BLOOD.
YOU LOOK LIKE YOU GOT LOTS OF BLOOD IN YOU.
BOOM
CRAP.
MFFT...
SURE, THIS IS A SMELLY, FILTHY RATHOLE OF AN ALLEY.
BUT IT'S MY SMELLY, FILTHY RATHOLE OF AN ALLEY.
GET LOST!
GYAA!
HEY! THIS IS REALLY UPSETTING ME, YOU JERK!
YEAAAHG!

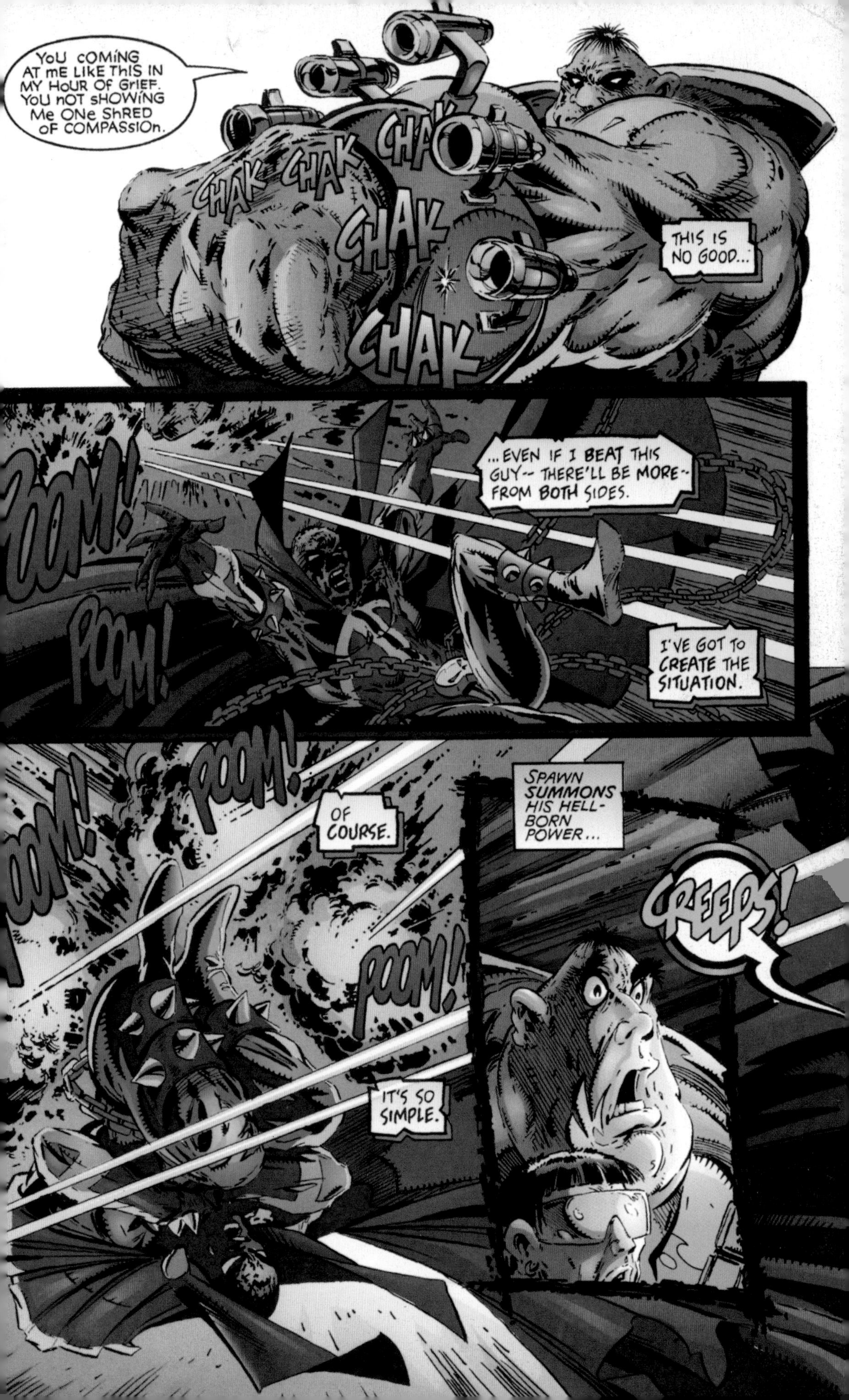
YOU COMING AT ME LIKE THIS IN MY HOUR OF GRIEF. YOU NOT SHOWING ME ONE SHRED OF COMPASSION.
CHAK CHAK CHAK
CHAK
CHAK
THIS IS NO GOOD...
...EVEN IF I BEAT THIS GUY-- THERE'LL BE MORE-- FROM BOTH SIDES.
POOM!
POOM!
I'VE GOT TO CREATE THE SITUATION.
POOM!
OF COURSE.
SPAWN SUMMONS HIS HELL-BORN POWER...
CREEPS!
POOM!
IT'S SO SIMPLE.

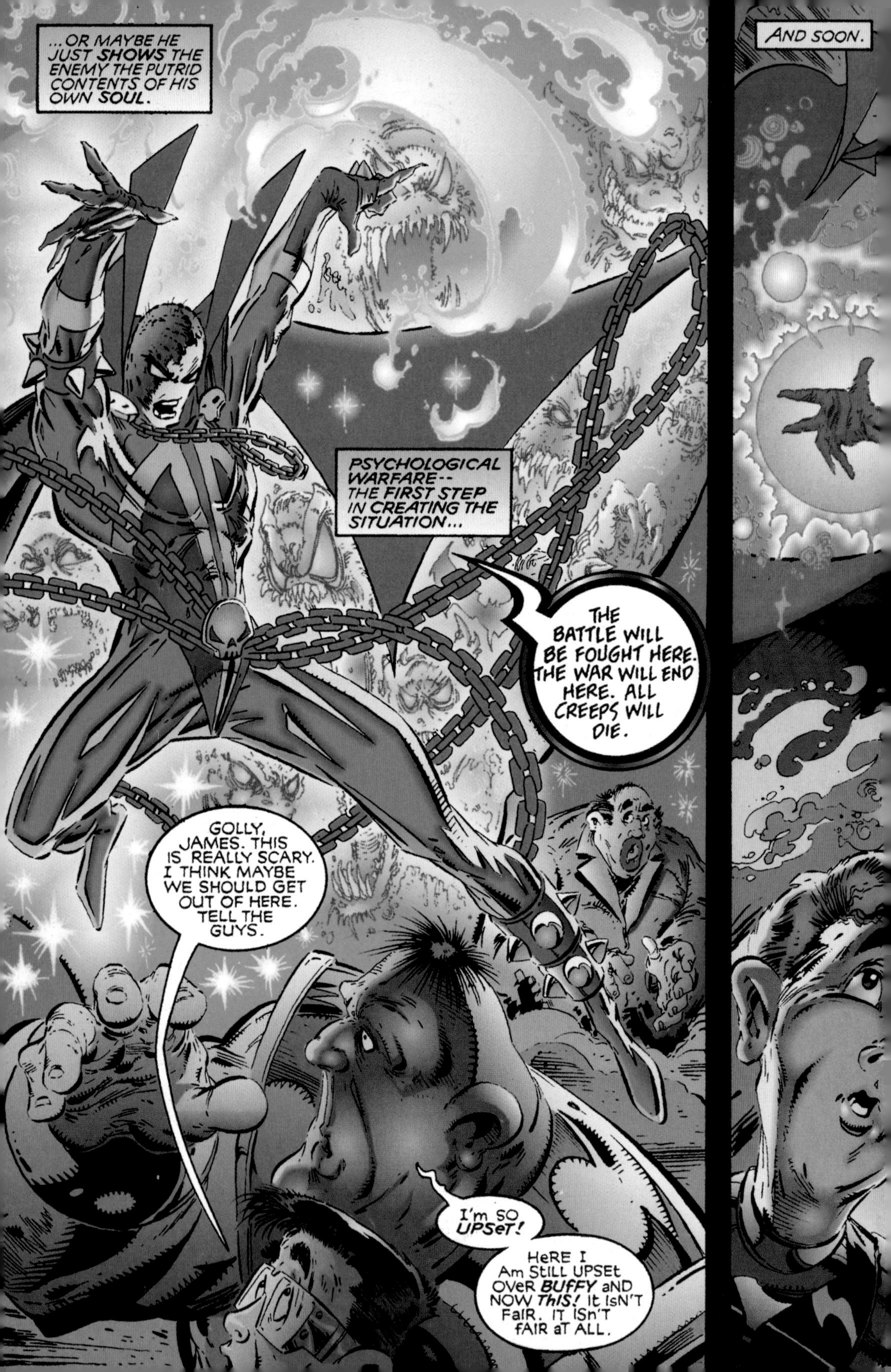
...OR MAYBE HE JUST SHOWS THE ENEMY THE PUTRID CONTENTS OF HIS OWN SOUL.
PSYCHOLOGICAL WARFARE-- THE FIRST STEP IN CREATING THE SITUATION...
THE BATTLE WILL BE FOUGHT HERE. THE WAR WILL END HERE. ALL CREEPS WILL DIE.
GOLLY, JAMES. THIS IS REALLY SCARY. I THINK MAYBE WE SHOULD GET OUT OF HERE. TELL THE GUYS.
I'm SO UPSeT!
HeRE I Am StILL UPSEt OVeR BUFFY aND NOW THIS! It ISN'T FaIR. IT ISn'T FAIR aT ALL.
AND SOON.

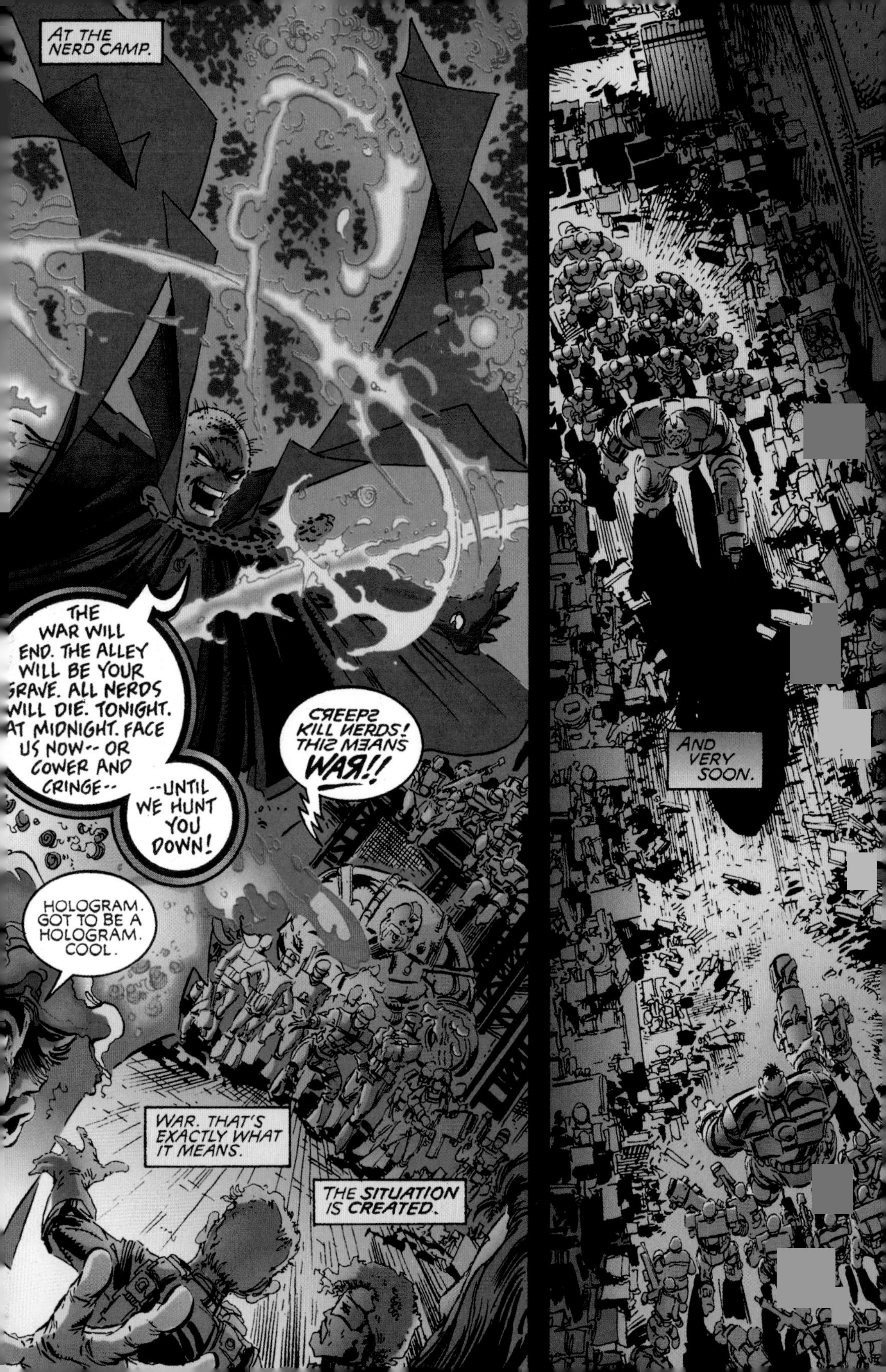
AT THE NERD CAMP.
THE WAR WILL END. THE ALLEY WILL BE YOUR GRAVE. ALL NERDS WILL DIE. TONIGHT. AT MIDNIGHT. FACE US NOW-- OR COWER AND CRINGE--
--UNTIL WE HUNT YOU DOWN!
CREEPS KILL NERDS! THIS MEANS WAR!!
HOLOGRAM. GOT TO BE A HOLOGRAM. COOL.
WAR. THAT'S EXACTLY WHAT IT MEANS.
THE SITUATION IS CREATED.
AND VERY SOON.

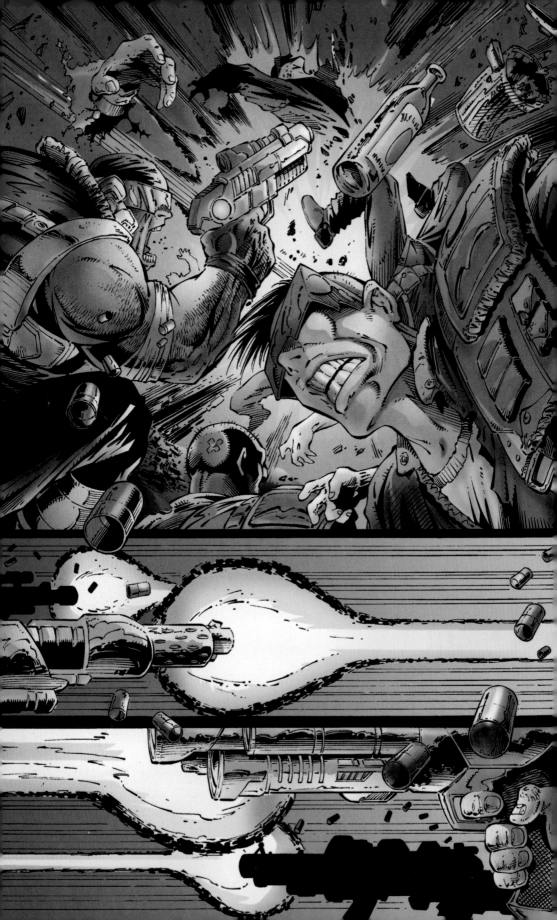

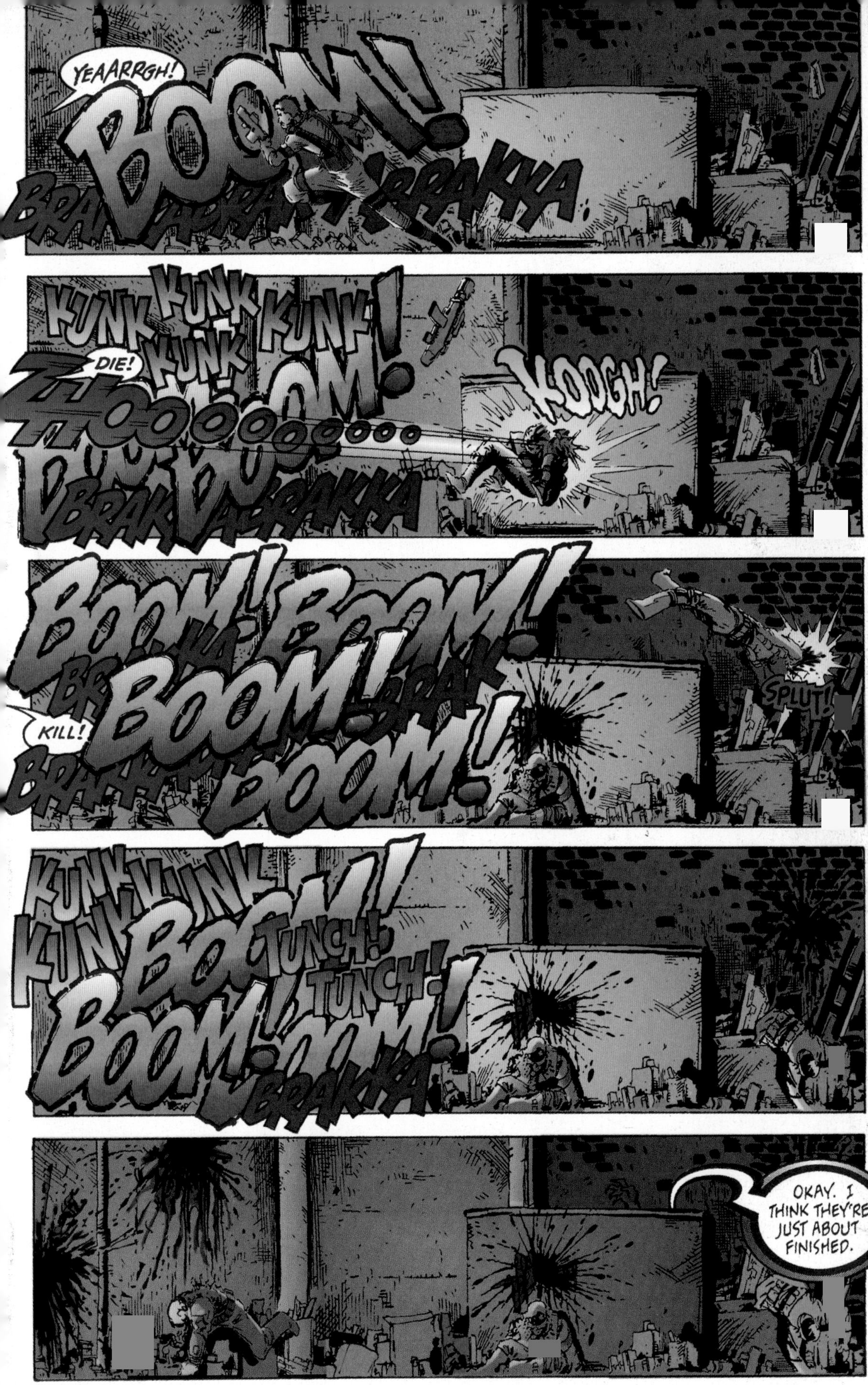
YEAARRGH!
BOOM!
KUNK KUNK KUNK KUNK!
DIE!
BOOM!
VOOGH!
BRAKKA
BOOM! BOOM!
BOOM!
KILL!
SPLUT!
BOOM!
TUNCH! TUNCH!
BOOM!
BRAKKA
OKAY. I THINK THEY'RE JUST ABOUT FINISHED.

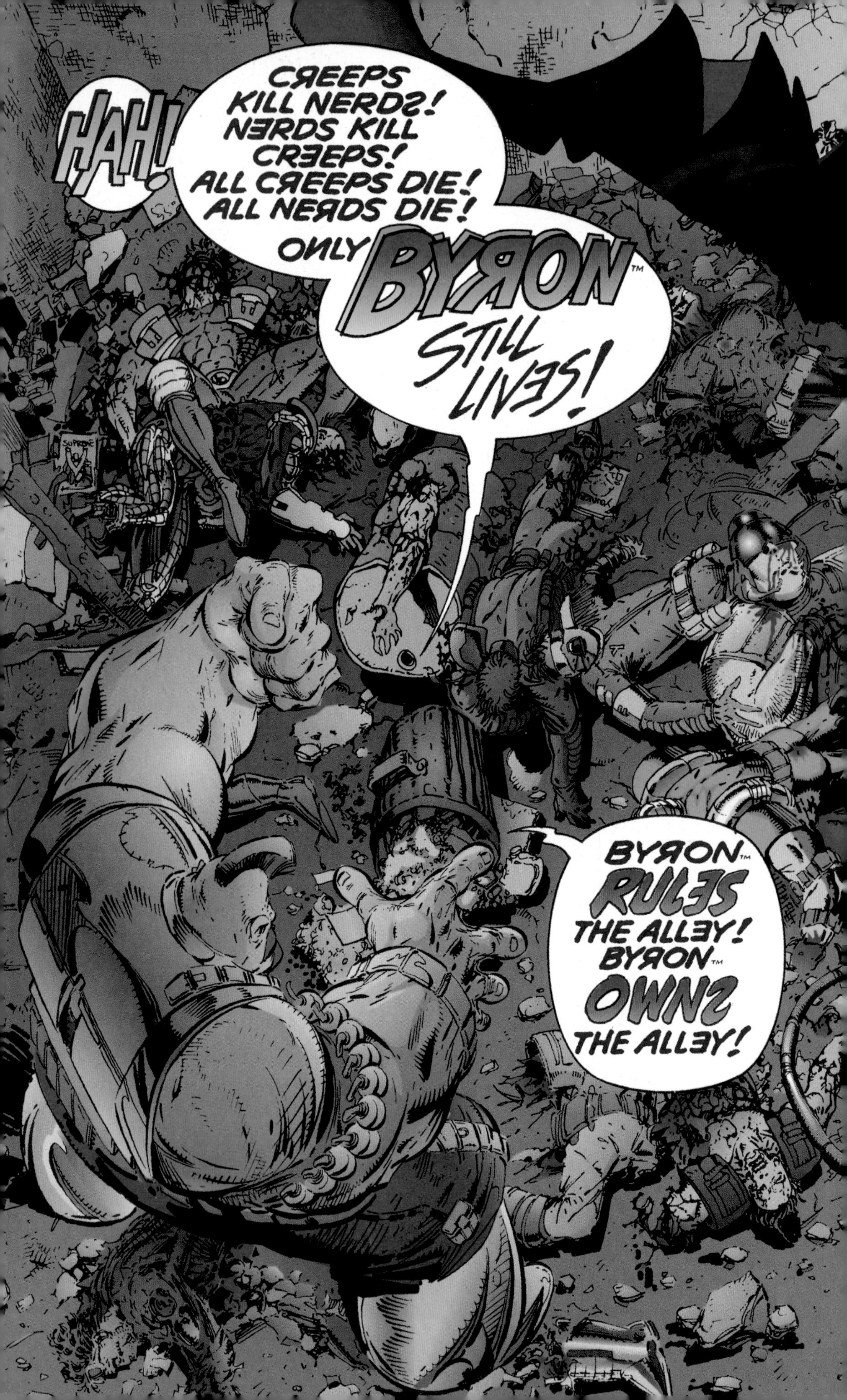
HAH!
CREEPS KILL NERDS! NERDS KILL CREEPS! ALL CREEPS DIE! ALL NERDS DIE! ONLY BYRON™ STILL LIVES!
BYRON™ RULES THE ALLEY! BYRON™ OWNS THE ALLEY!

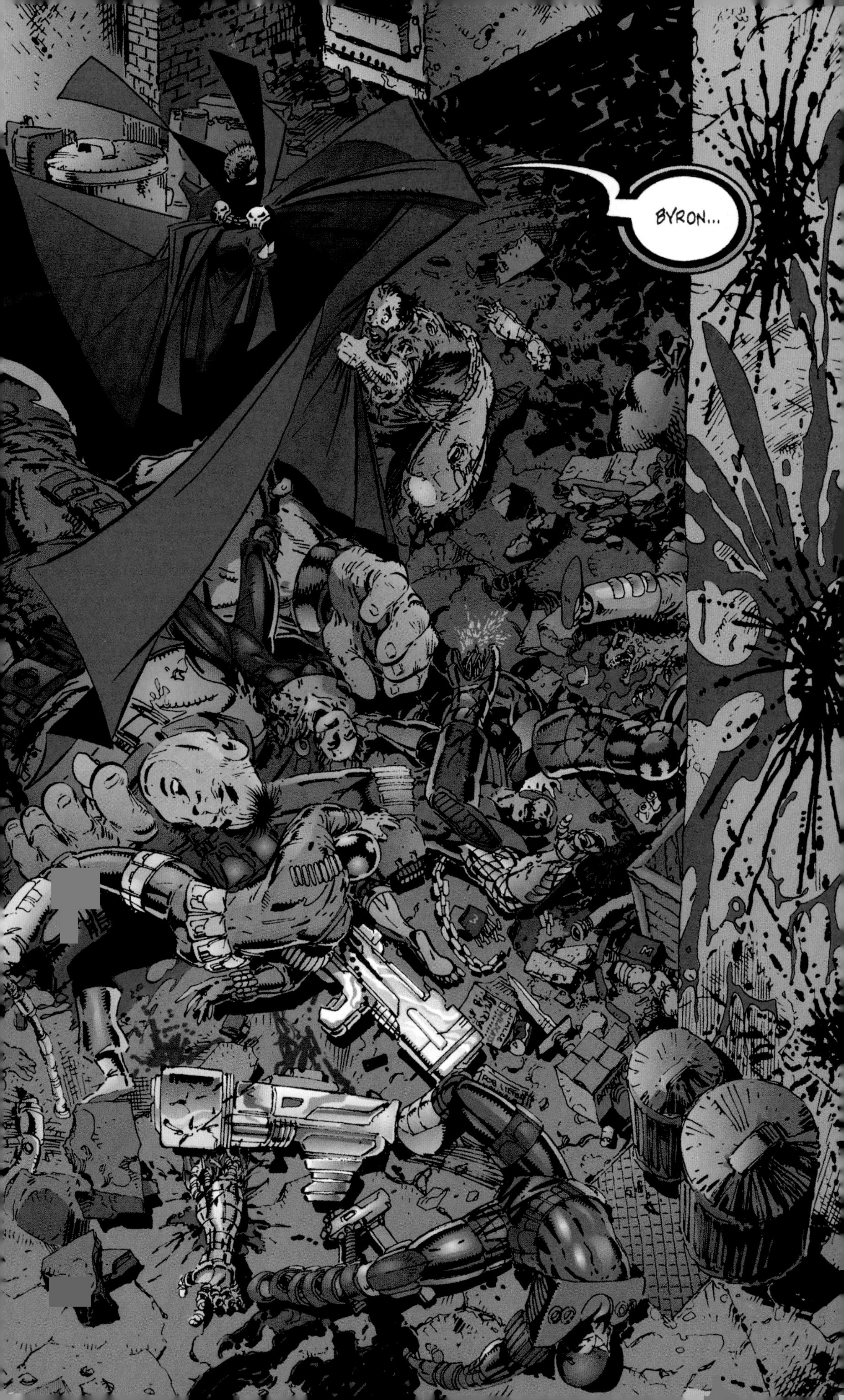
BYRON...

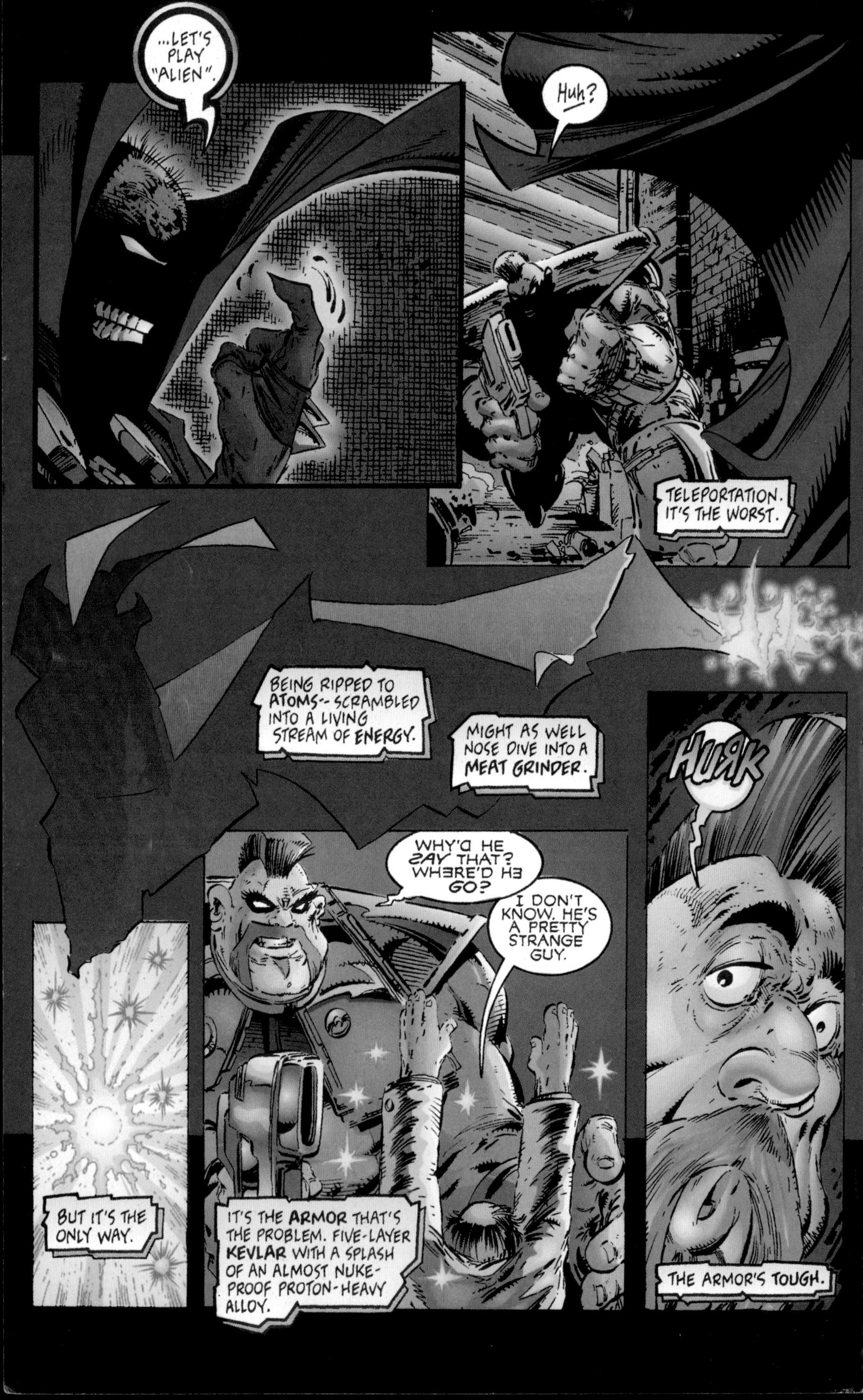
...LET'S PLAY "ALIEN".
Huh?
TELEPORTATION. IT'S THE WORST.
BEING RIPPED TO ATOMS-- SCRAMBLED INTO A LIVING STREAM OF ENERGY.
MIGHT AS WELL NOSE DIVE INTO A MEAT GRINDER.
HURK
WHY'D HE SAY THAT? WHERE'D HE GO?
I DON'T KNOW. HE'S A PRETTY STRANGE GUY.
BUT IT'S THE ONLY WAY.
IT'S THE ARMOR THAT'S THE PROBLEM. FIVE-LAYER KEVLAR WITH A SPLASH OF AN ALMOST NUKE-PROOF PROTON-HEAVY ALLOY.
THE ARMOR'S TOUGH.

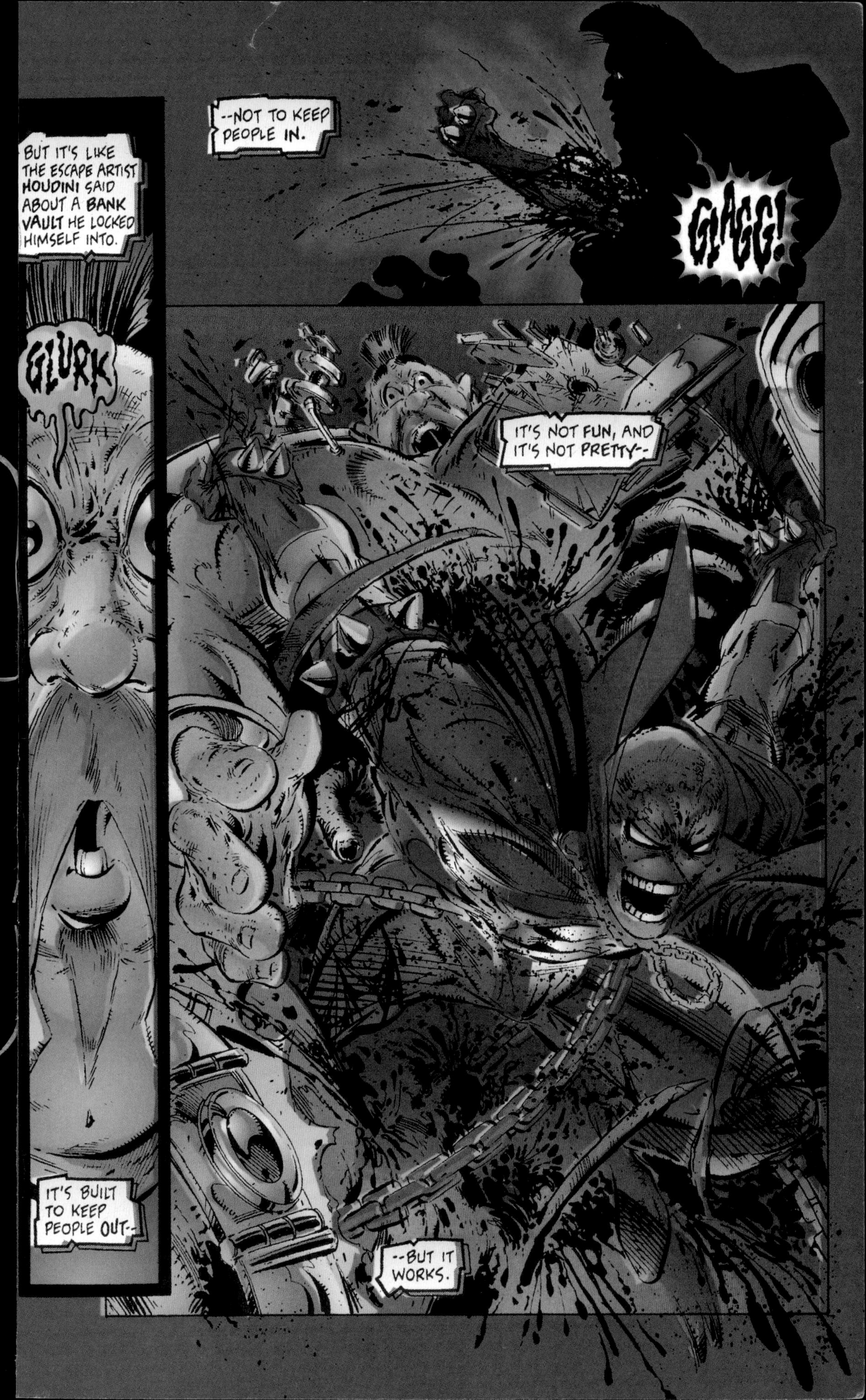
BUT IT'S LIKE THE ESCAPE ARTIST HOUDINI SAID ABOUT A BANK VAULT HE LOCKED HIMSELF INTO.
IT'S BUILT TO KEEP PEOPLE OUT-
--NOT TO KEEP PEOPLE IN.
GLAGG!
GLURK
IT'S NOT FUN, AND IT'S NOT PRETTY--
--BUT IT WORKS.

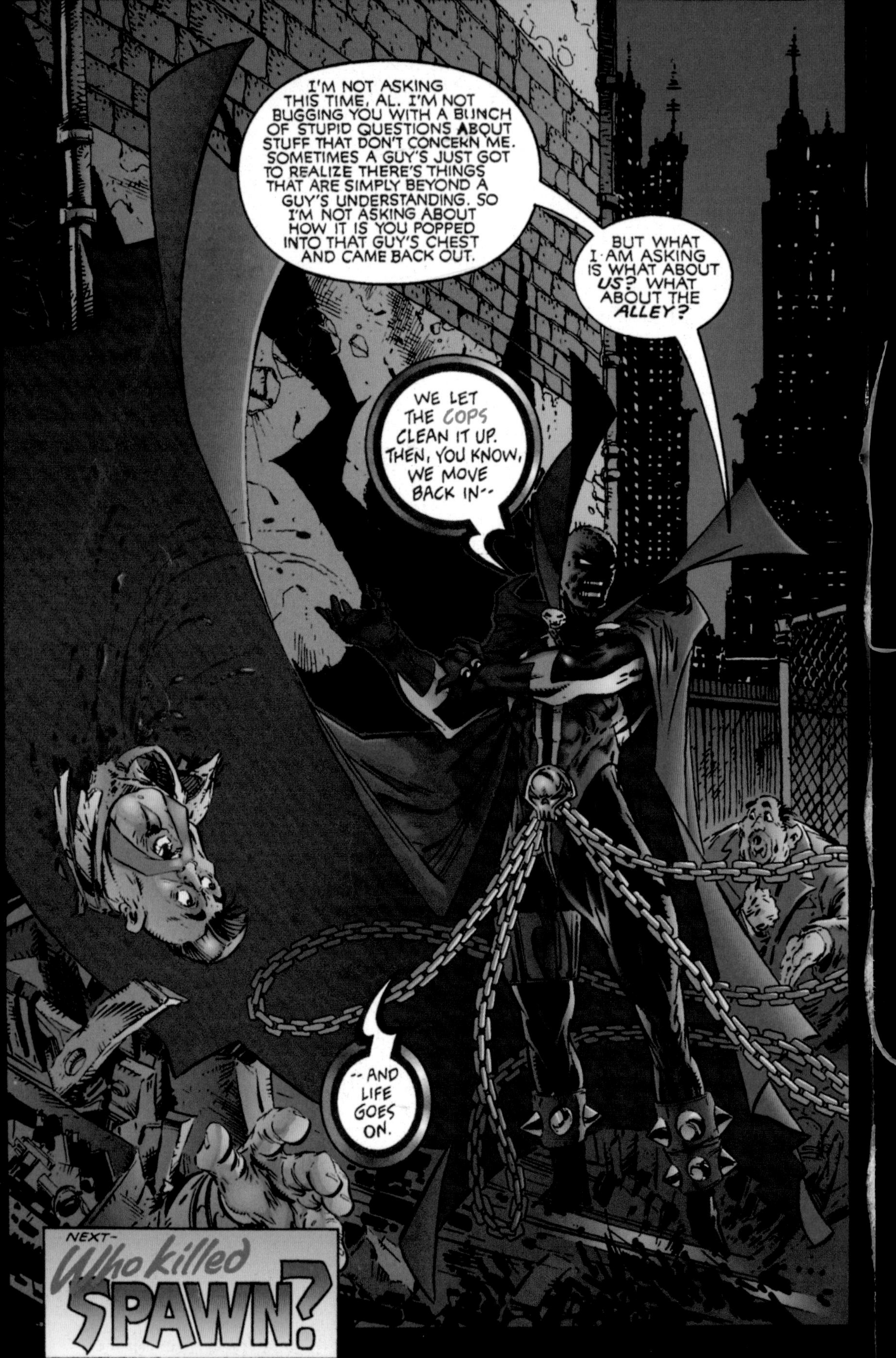
I'M NOT ASKING THIS TIME, AL. I'M NOT BUGGING YOU WITH A BUNCH OF STUPID QUESTIONS ABOUT STUFF THAT DON'T CONCERN ME. SOMETIMES A GUY'S JUST GOT TO REALIZE THERE'S THINGS THAT ARE SIMPLY BEYOND A GUY'S UNDERSTANDING. SO I'M NOT ASKING ABOUT HOW IT IS YOU POPPED INTO THAT GUY'S CHEST AND CAME BACK OUT.
BUT WHAT I AM ASKING IS WHAT ABOUT US? WHAT ABOUT THE ALLEY?
WE LET THE COPS CLEAN IT UP. THEN, YOU KNOW, WE MOVE BACK IN--
--AND LIFE GOES ON.
NEXT-
Who killed SPAWN?

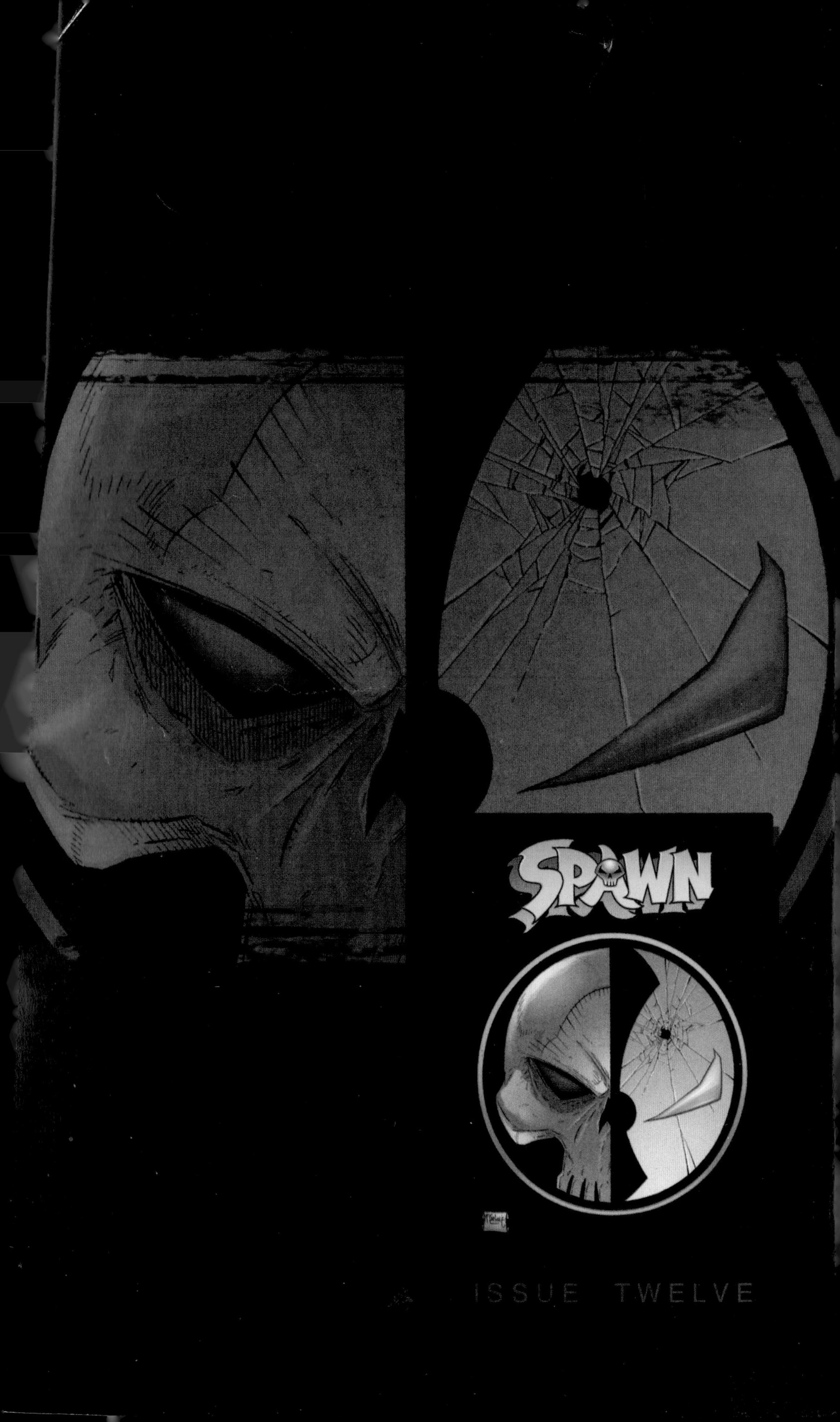
SPAWN
ISSUE TWELVE

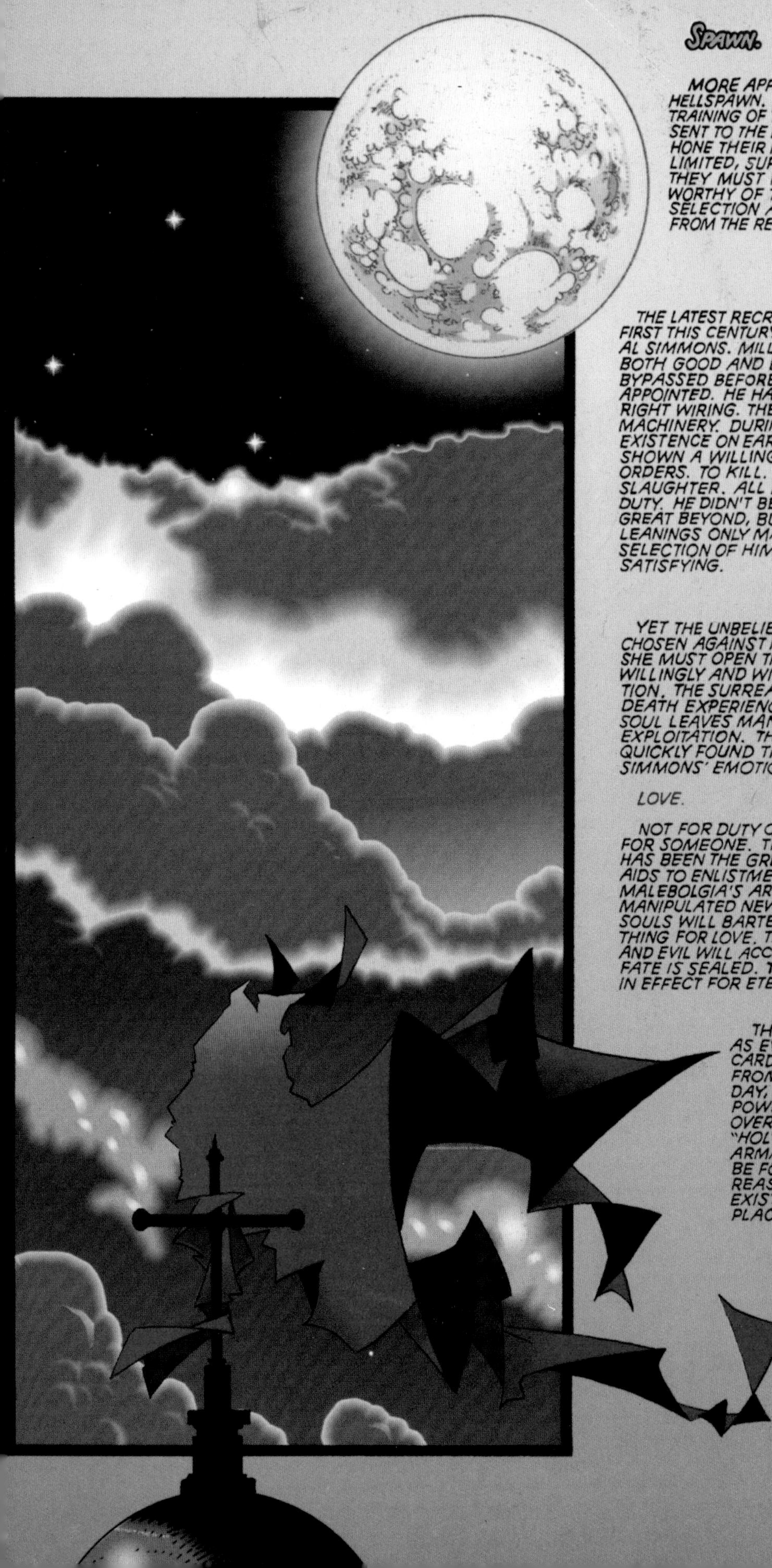

SPAWN.

MORE APPROPRIATELY, HELLSPAWN. THE OFFICERS-IN-TRAINING OF THE MALEBOLGIA, SENT TO THE LIVING WORLD TO HONE THEIR POTENT, YET LIMITED, SUPPLY OF POWER. THEY MUST FIRST PROVE WORTHY OF THEIR RARE SELECTION AS A WARRIOR FROM THE REALMS BEYOND.

THE LATEST RECRUIT, AND THE FIRST THIS CENTURY, IS LT. COLONEL AL SIMMONS. MILLIONS OF SOULS, BOTH GOOD AND EVIL, WERE BYPASSED BEFORE SIMMONS WAS APPOINTED. HE HAD THE GIFT. THE RIGHT WIRING. THE WELL-TOOLED MACHINERY. DURING HIS FIRST EXISTENCE ON EARTH, HE HAD SHOWN A WILLINGNESS TO FOLLOW ORDERS. TO KILL. TO MURDER. TO SLAUGHTER. ALL IN THE NAME OF DUTY. HE DIDN'T BELIEVE IN THE GREAT BEYOND, BUT HIS ATHEISTIC LEANINGS ONLY MADE HELL'S SELECTION OF HIM EVEN MORE SATISFYING.

YET THE UNBELIEVER CANNOT BE CHOSEN AGAINST HIS WILL. HE OR SHE MUST OPEN THE DOOR TO EVIL WILLINGLY AND WITHOUT HESITATION. THE SURREAL TRAUMA OF DEATH EXPERIENCED BY EACH SOUL LEAVES MANY OPEN TO EXPLOITATION. THE EVIL ONE QUICKLY FOUND THE **CHINK** IN SIMMONS' EMOTIONAL ARMOR:

LOVE.

NOT FOR DUTY OR COUNTRY, BUT FOR SOMEONE. THIS WEAKNESS HAS BEEN THE GREATEST OF ALL AIDS TO ENLISTMENT FOR THE MALEBOLGIA'S ARMY. EASILY-MANIPULATED NEWLY-ARRIVED SOULS WILL BARTER NEARLY ANYTHING FOR LOVE. THEY WILL PROMISE, AND EVIL WILL ACCEPT. THUS, THEIR FATE IS SEALED. THE PACT WILL BE IN EFFECT FOR ETERNITY.

THIS IRONY-- LOVE AS EVIL'S TRUMP CARD-- IS NOT HIDDEN FROM GOD. SOME DAY, THESE TWO POWERS WILL CLASH OVER THIS COSMIC "HOLY GRAIL"-- ARMAGEDDON WILL BE FOUGHT FOR THE REASON HUMANS EXIST IN THE FIRST PLACE...

LOVE.

AL SIMMONS TRADED HIS SOUL FOR IT.

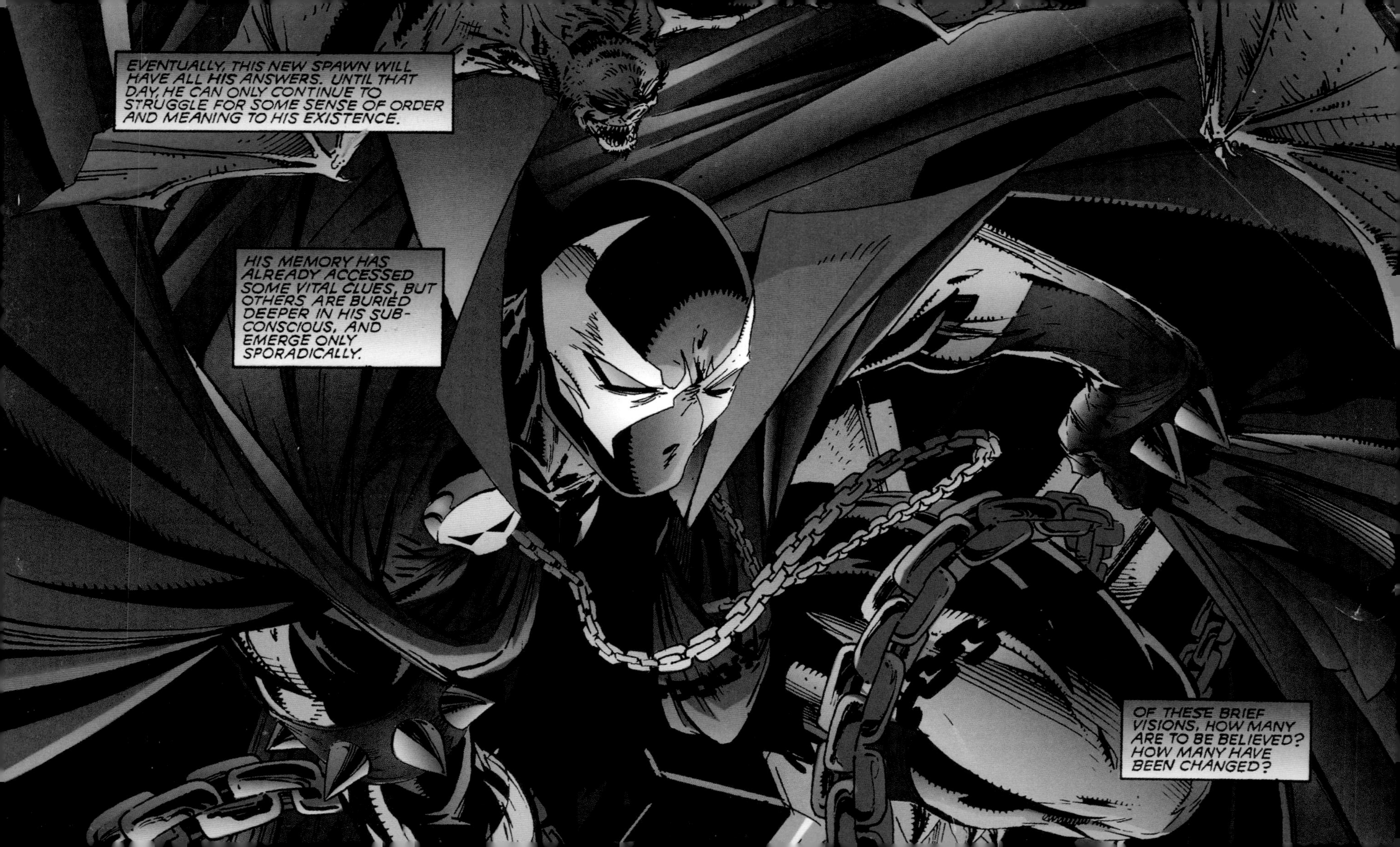
EVENTUALLY, THIS NEW SPAWN WILL HAVE ALL HIS ANSWERS. UNTIL THAT DAY, HE CAN ONLY CONTINUE TO STRUGGLE FOR SOME SENSE OF ORDER AND MEANING TO HIS EXISTENCE.
HIS MEMORY HAS ALREADY ACCESSED SOME VITAL CLUES, BUT OTHERS ARE BURIED DEEPER IN HIS SUB-CONSCIOUS, AND EMERGE ONLY SPORADICALLY.
OF THESE BRIEF VISIONS, HOW MANY ARE TO BE BELIEVED? HOW MANY HAVE BEEN CHANGED?

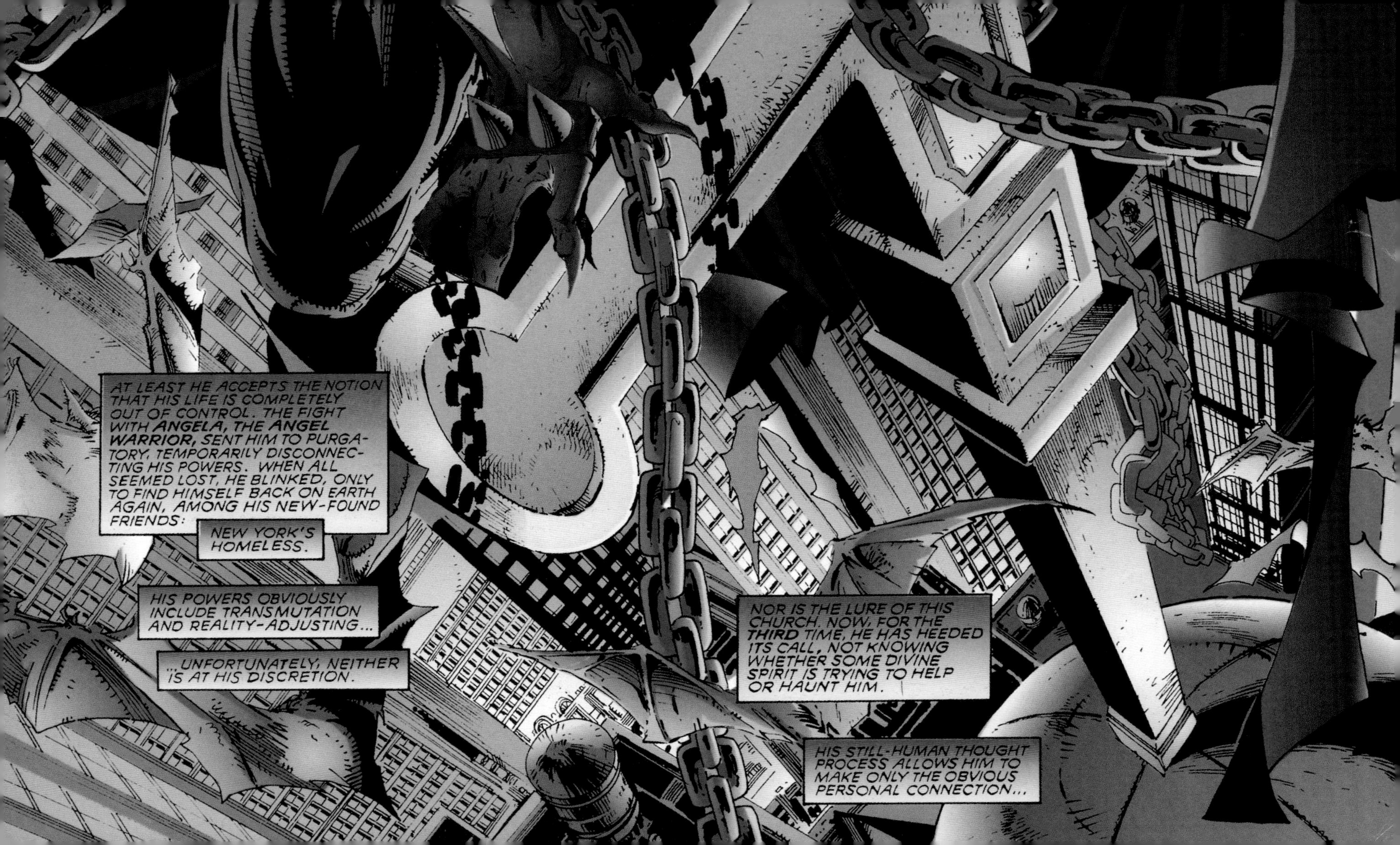
AT LEAST HE ACCEPTS THE NOTION THAT HIS LIFE IS COMPLETELY OUT OF CONTROL. THE FIGHT WITH ANGELA, THE ANGEL WARRIOR, SENT HIM TO PURGATORY, TEMPORARILY DISCONNECTING HIS POWERS. WHEN ALL SEEMED LOST, HE BLINKED, ONLY TO FIND HIMSELF BACK ON EARTH AGAIN, AMONG HIS NEW-FOUND FRIENDS:
NEW YORK'S HOMELESS.
HIS POWERS OBVIOUSLY INCLUDE TRANSMUTATION AND REALITY-ADJUSTING...
...UNFORTUNATELY, NEITHER IS AT HIS DISCRETION.
NOR IS THE LURE OF THIS CHURCH. NOW, FOR THE THIRD TIME, HE HAS HEEDED ITS CALL, NOT KNOWING WHETHER SOME DIVINE SPIRIT IS TRYING TO HELP OR HAUNT HIM.
HIS STILL-HUMAN THOUGHT PROCESS ALLOWS HIM TO MAKE ONLY THE OBVIOUS PERSONAL CONNECTION...

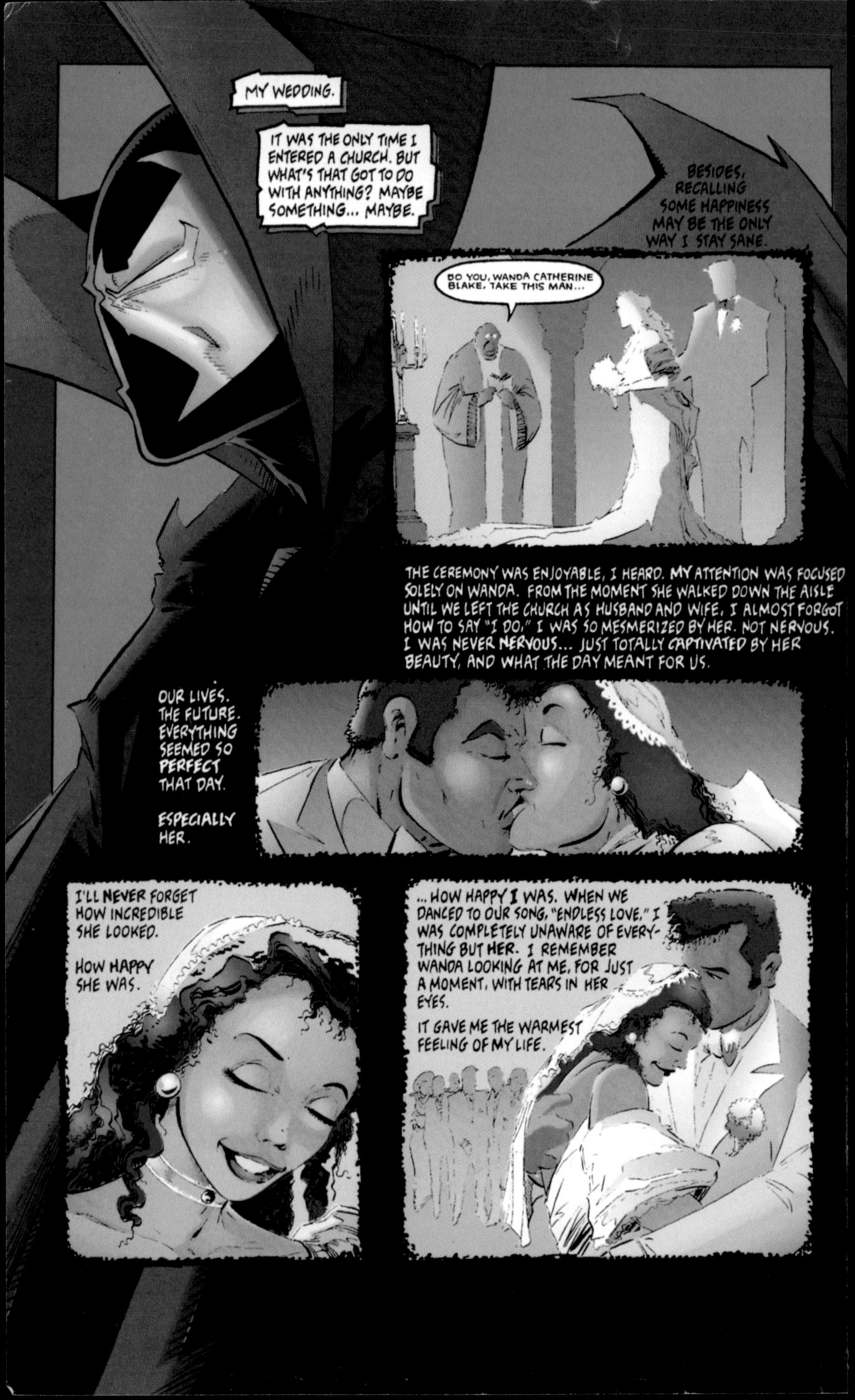
MY WEDDING.
IT WAS THE ONLY TIME I ENTERED A CHURCH. BUT WHAT'S THAT GOT TO DO WITH ANYTHING? MAYBE SOMETHING... MAYBE.
BESIDES, RECALLING SOME HAPPINESS MAY BE THE ONLY WAY I STAY SANE.
DO YOU, WANDA CATHERINE BLAKE, TAKE THIS MAN...
THE CEREMONY WAS ENJOYABLE, I HEARD. MY ATTENTION WAS FOCUSED SOLELY ON WANDA. FROM THE MOMENT SHE WALKED DOWN THE AISLE UNTIL WE LEFT THE CHURCH AS HUSBAND AND WIFE, I ALMOST FORGOT HOW TO SAY "I DO," I WAS SO MESMERIZED BY HER. NOT NERVOUS. I WAS NEVER NERVOUS... JUST TOTALLY CAPTIVATED BY HER BEAUTY, AND WHAT THE DAY MEANT FOR US.
OUR LIVES. THE FUTURE. EVERYTHING SEEMED SO PERFECT THAT DAY.
ESPECIALLY HER.
I'LL NEVER FORGET HOW INCREDIBLE SHE LOOKED.
HOW HAPPY SHE WAS.
...HOW HAPPY I WAS. WHEN WE DANCED TO OUR SONG, "ENDLESS LOVE," I WAS COMPLETELY UNAWARE OF EVERY-THING BUT HER. I REMEMBER WANDA LOOKING AT ME, FOR JUST A MOMENT, WITH TEARS IN HER EYES.
IT GAVE ME THE WARMEST FEELING OF MY LIFE.

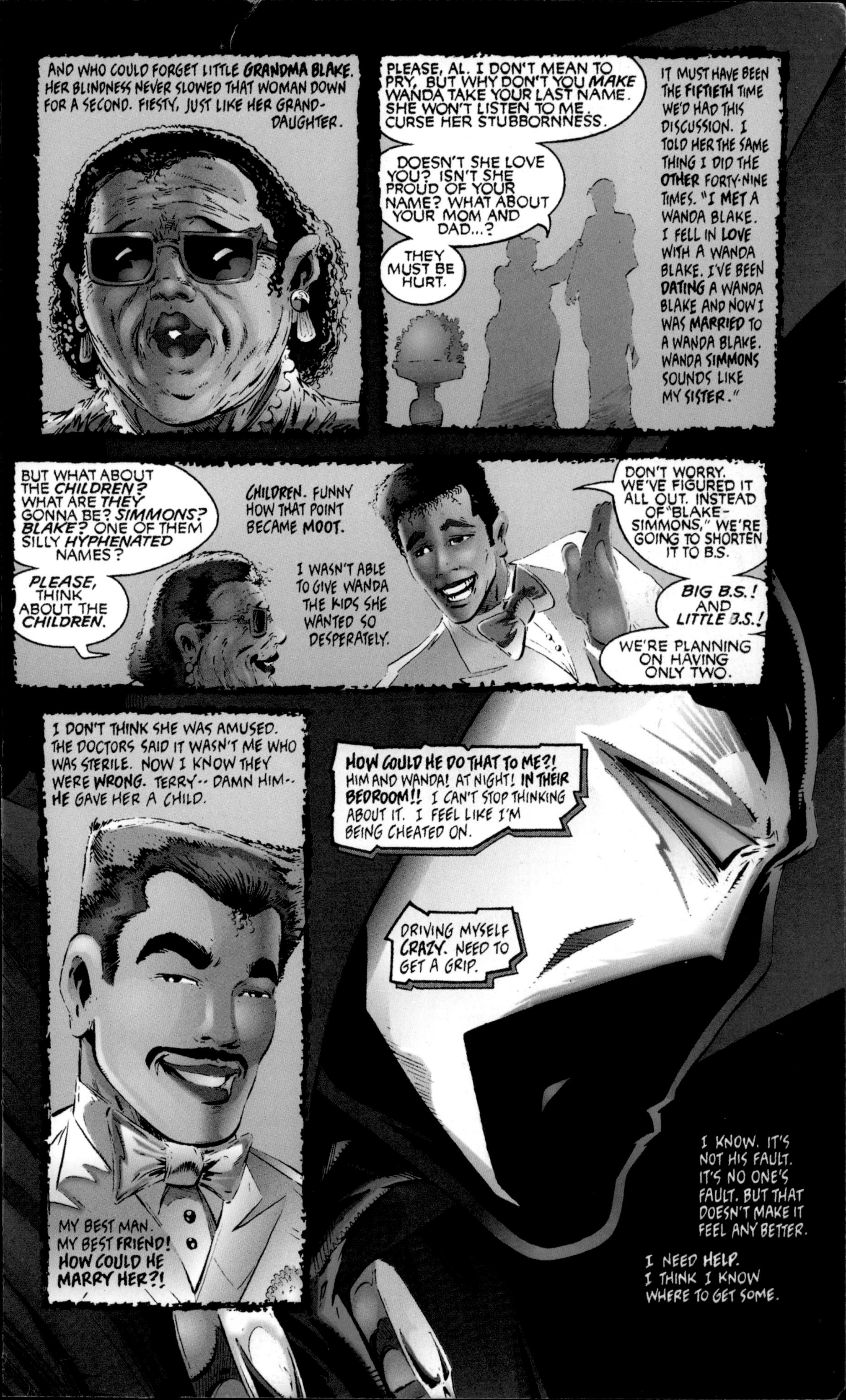
AND WHO COULD FORGET LITTLE GRANDMA BLAKE. HER BLINDNESS NEVER SLOWED THAT WOMAN DOWN FOR A SECOND. FIESTY, JUST LIKE HER GRAND-DAUGHTER.
PLEASE, AL. I DON'T MEAN TO PRY, BUT WHY DON'T YOU MAKE WANDA TAKE YOUR LAST NAME. SHE WON'T LISTEN TO ME. CURSE HER STUBBORNNESS.
DOESN'T SHE LOVE YOU? ISN'T SHE PROUD OF YOUR NAME? WHAT ABOUT YOUR MOM AND DAD...?
THEY MUST BE HURT.
IT MUST HAVE BEEN THE FIFTIETH TIME WE'D HAD THIS DISCUSSION. I TOLD HER THE SAME THING I DID THE OTHER FORTY-NINE TIMES. "I MET A WANDA BLAKE. I FELL IN LOVE WITH A WANDA BLAKE. I'VE BEEN DATING A WANDA BLAKE AND NOW I WAS MARRIED TO A WANDA BLAKE. WANDA SIMMONS SOUNDS LIKE MY SISTER."
BUT WHAT ABOUT THE CHILDREN? WHAT ARE THEY GONNA BE? SIMMONS? BLAKE? ONE OF THEM SILLY HYPHENATED NAMES?
PLEASE, THINK ABOUT THE CHILDREN.
CHILDREN. FUNNY HOW THAT POINT BECAME MOOT.
I WASN'T ABLE TO GIVE WANDA THE KIDS SHE WANTED SO DESPERATELY.
DON'T WORRY. WE'VE FIGURED IT ALL OUT. INSTEAD OF "BLAKE-SIMMONS," WE'RE GOING TO SHORTEN IT TO B.S.
BIG B.S.! AND LITTLE B.S.!
WE'RE PLANNING ON HAVING ONLY TWO.
I DON'T THINK SHE WAS AMUSED. THE DOCTORS SAID IT WASN'T ME WHO WAS STERILE. NOW I KNOW THEY WERE WRONG. TERRY-- DAMN HIM-- HE GAVE HER A CHILD.
HOW COULD HE DO THAT TO ME?! HIM AND WANDA! AT NIGHT! IN THEIR BEDROOM!! I CAN'T STOP THINKING ABOUT IT. I FEEL LIKE I'M BEING CHEATED ON.
DRIVING MYSELF CRAZY. NEED TO GET A GRIP.
MY BEST MAN. MY BEST FRIEND! HOW COULD HE MARRY HER?!
I KNOW. IT'S NOT HIS FAULT. IT'S NO ONE'S FAULT. BUT THAT DOESN'T MAKE IT FEEL ANY BETTER.
I NEED HELP. I THINK I KNOW WHERE TO GET SOME.

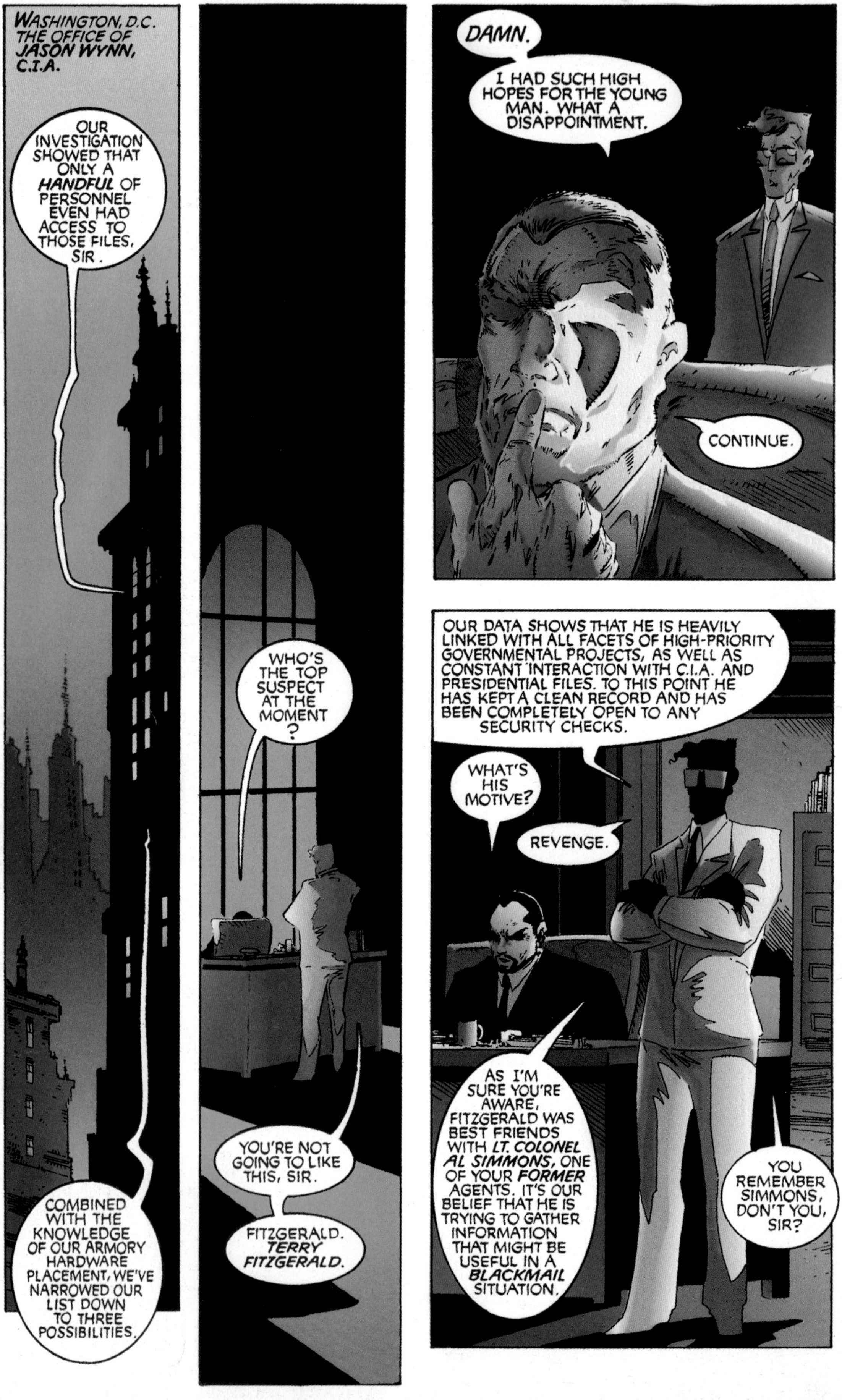
WASHINGTON, D.C. THE OFFICE OF JASON WYNN, C.I.A.
OUR INVESTIGATION SHOWED THAT ONLY A HANDFUL OF PERSONNEL EVEN HAD ACCESS TO THOSE FILES, SIR.
COMBINED WITH THE KNOWLEDGE OF OUR ARMORY HARDWARE PLACEMENT, WE'VE NARROWED OUR LIST DOWN TO THREE POSSIBILITIES.
WHO'S THE TOP SUSPECT AT THE MOMENT?
YOU'RE NOT GOING TO LIKE THIS, SIR.
FITZGERALD. TERRY FITZGERALD.
DAMN.
I HAD SUCH HIGH HOPES FOR THE YOUNG MAN. WHAT A DISAPPOINTMENT.
CONTINUE.
OUR DATA SHOWS THAT HE IS HEAVILY LINKED WITH ALL FACETS OF HIGH-PRIORITY GOVERNMENTAL PROJECTS, AS WELL AS CONSTANT INTERACTION WITH C.I.A. AND PRESIDENTIAL FILES. TO THIS POINT HE HAS KEPT A CLEAN RECORD AND HAS BEEN COMPLETELY OPEN TO ANY SECURITY CHECKS.
WHAT'S HIS MOTIVE?
REVENGE.
AS I'M SURE YOU'RE AWARE, FITZGERALD WAS BEST FRIENDS WITH LT. COLONEL AL SIMMONS, ONE OF YOUR FORMER AGENTS. IT'S OUR BELIEF THAT HE IS TRYING TO GATHER INFORMATION THAT MIGHT BE USEFUL IN A BLACKMAIL SITUATION.
YOU REMEMBER SIMMONS, DON'T YOU, SIR?

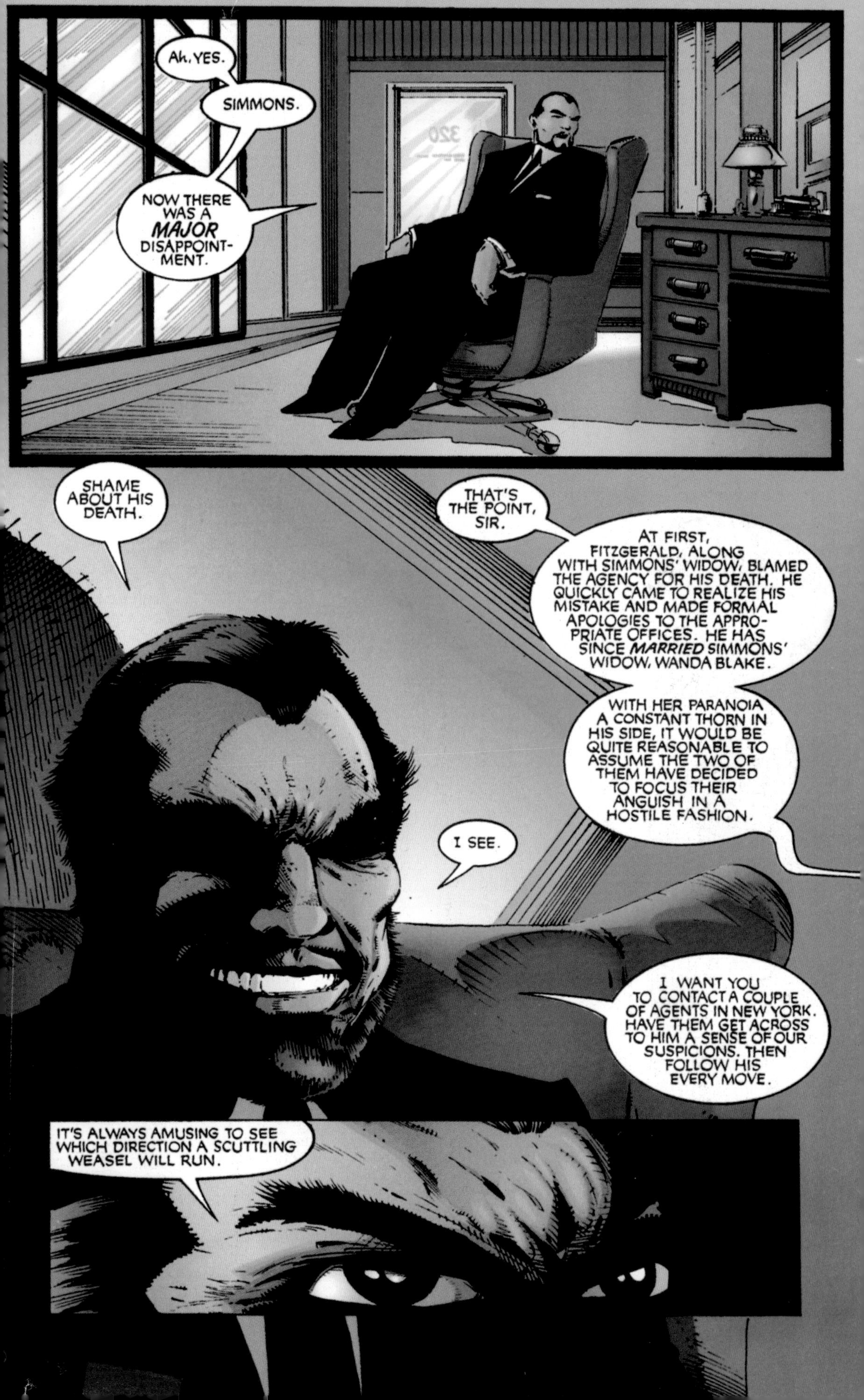
Ah, YES.
SIMMONS.
NOW THERE WAS A *MAJOR* DISAPPOINT-MENT.
SHAME ABOUT HIS DEATH.
THAT'S THE POINT, SIR.
AT FIRST, FITZGERALD, ALONG WITH SIMMONS' WIDOW, BLAMED THE AGENCY FOR HIS DEATH. HE QUICKLY CAME TO REALIZE HIS MISTAKE AND MADE FORMAL APOLOGIES TO THE APPRO-PRIATE OFFICES. HE HAS SINCE *MARRIED* SIMMONS' WIDOW, WANDA BLAKE.
WITH HER PARANOIA A CONSTANT THORN IN HIS SIDE, IT WOULD BE QUITE REASONABLE TO ASSUME THE TWO OF THEM HAVE DECIDED TO FOCUS THEIR ANGUISH IN A HOSTILE FASHION.
I SEE.
I WANT YOU TO CONTACT A COUPLE OF AGENTS IN NEW YORK. HAVE THEM GET ACROSS TO HIM A SENSE OF OUR SUSPICIONS. THEN FOLLOW HIS EVERY MOVE.
IT'S ALWAYS AMUSING TO SEE WHICH DIRECTION A SCUTTLING WEASEL WILL RUN.

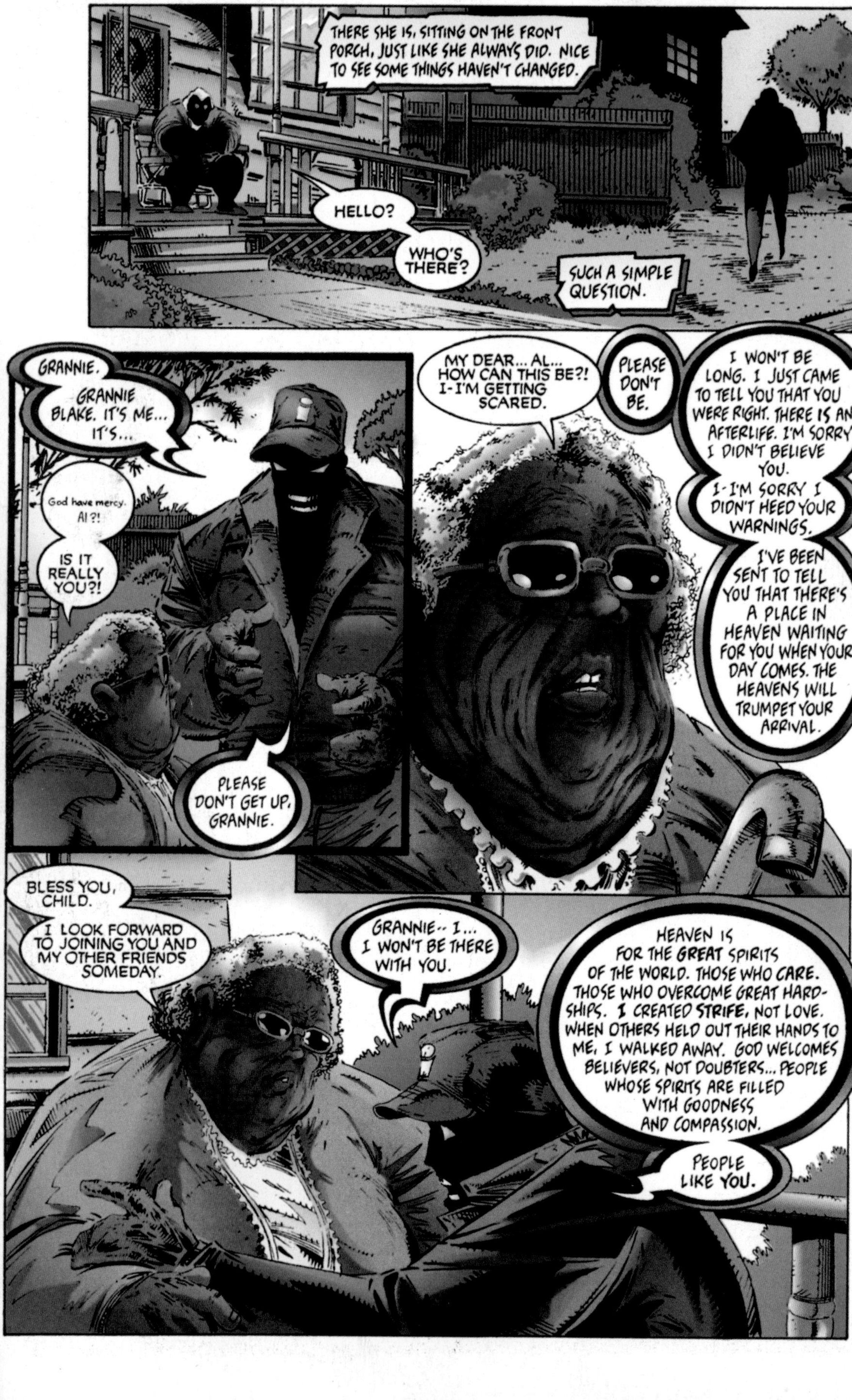
THERE SHE IS, SITTING ON THE FRONT PORCH, JUST LIKE SHE ALWAYS DID. NICE TO SEE SOME THINGS HAVEN'T CHANGED.
HELLO?
WHO'S THERE?
SUCH A SIMPLE QUESTION.
GRANNIE.
GRANNIE BLAKE. IT'S ME... IT'S...
God have mercy. Al?!
IS IT REALLY YOU?!
PLEASE DON'T GET UP, GRANNIE.
MY DEAR... AL... HOW CAN THIS BE?! I-I'M GETTING SCARED.
PLEASE DON'T BE.
I WON'T BE LONG. I JUST CAME TO TELL YOU THAT YOU WERE RIGHT. THERE IS AN AFTERLIFE. I'M SORRY I DIDN'T BELIEVE YOU.
I-I'M SORRY I DIDN'T HEED YOUR WARNINGS.
I'VE BEEN SENT TO TELL YOU THAT THERE'S A PLACE IN HEAVEN WAITING FOR YOU WHEN YOUR DAY COMES. THE HEAVENS WILL TRUMPET YOUR ARRIVAL.
BLESS YOU, CHILD.
I LOOK FORWARD TO JOINING YOU AND MY OTHER FRIENDS SOMEDAY.
GRANNIE.. I... I WON'T BE THERE WITH YOU.
HEAVEN IS FOR THE GREAT SPIRITS OF THE WORLD. THOSE WHO CARE. THOSE WHO OVERCOME GREAT HARDSHIPS. I CREATED STRIFE, NOT LOVE. WHEN OTHERS HELD OUT THEIR HANDS TO ME, I WALKED AWAY. GOD WELCOMES BELIEVERS, NOT DOUBTERS... PEOPLE WHOSE SPIRITS ARE FILLED WITH GOODNESS AND COMPASSION.
PEOPLE LIKE YOU.

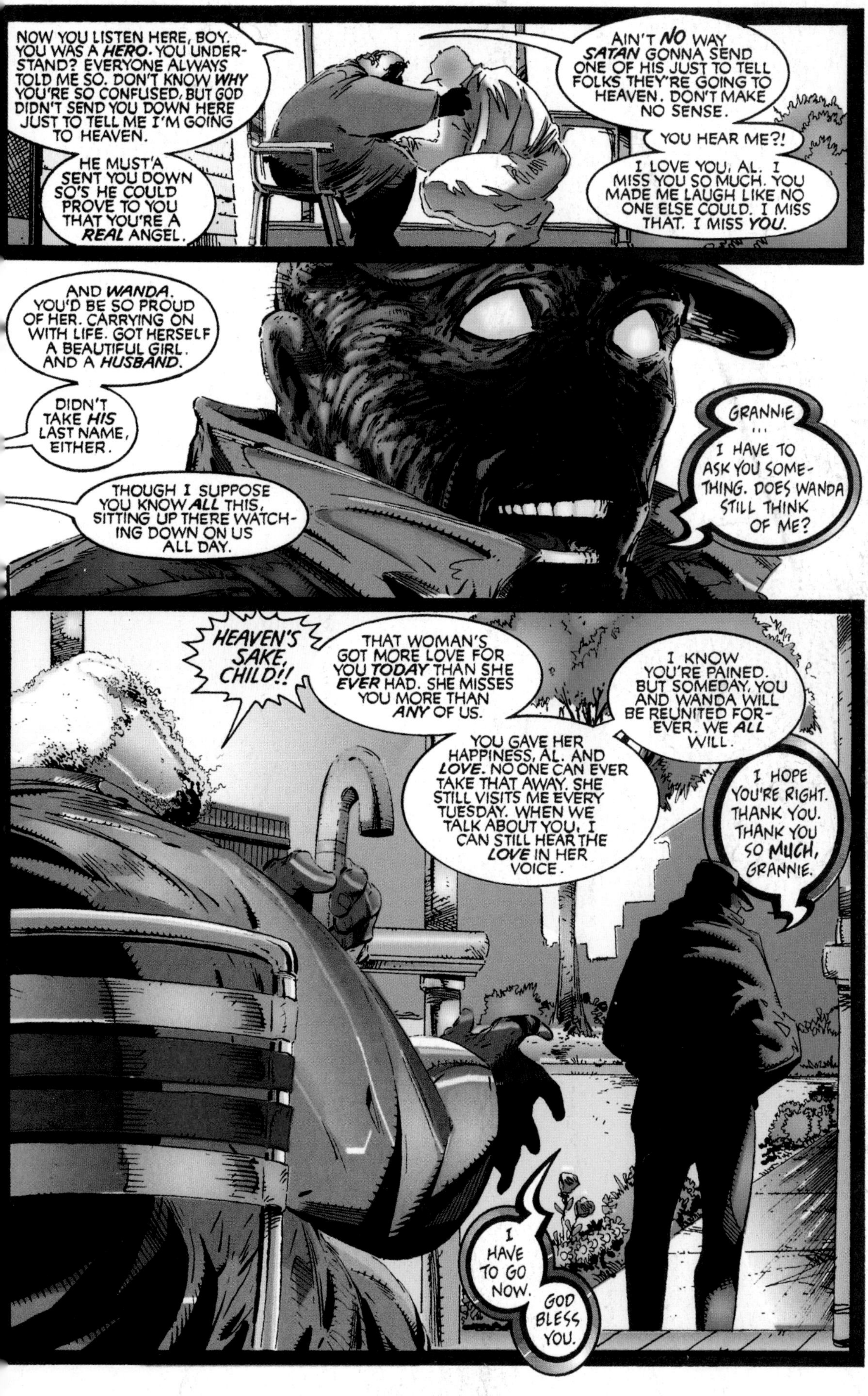
NOW YOU LISTEN HERE, BOY. YOU WAS A HERO. YOU UNDERSTAND? EVERYONE ALWAYS TOLD ME SO. DON'T KNOW WHY YOU'RE SO CONFUSED, BUT GOD DIDN'T SEND YOU DOWN HERE JUST TO TELL ME I'M GOING TO HEAVEN.
HE MUST'A SENT YOU DOWN SO'S HE COULD PROVE TO YOU THAT YOU'RE A REAL ANGEL.
AIN'T NO WAY SATAN GONNA SEND ONE OF HIS JUST TO TELL FOLKS THEY'RE GOING TO HEAVEN. DON'T MAKE NO SENSE.
YOU HEAR ME?!
I LOVE YOU, AL. I MISS YOU SO MUCH. YOU MADE ME LAUGH LIKE NO ONE ELSE COULD. I MISS THAT. I MISS YOU.
AND WANDA. YOU'D BE SO PROUD OF HER. CARRYING ON WITH LIFE. GOT HERSELF A BEAUTIFUL GIRL. AND A HUSBAND.
DIDN'T TAKE HIS LAST NAME, EITHER.
THOUGH I SUPPOSE YOU KNOW ALL THIS, SITTING UP THERE WATCHING DOWN ON US ALL DAY.
GRANNIE ... I HAVE TO ASK YOU SOMETHING. DOES WANDA STILL THINK OF ME?
HEAVEN'S SAKE, CHILD!!
THAT WOMAN'S GOT MORE LOVE FOR YOU TODAY THAN SHE EVER HAD. SHE MISSES YOU MORE THAN ANY OF US.
YOU GAVE HER HAPPINESS, AL. AND LOVE. NO ONE CAN EVER TAKE THAT AWAY. SHE STILL VISITS ME EVERY TUESDAY. WHEN WE TALK ABOUT YOU, I CAN STILL HEAR THE LOVE IN HER VOICE.
I KNOW YOU'RE PAINED. BUT SOMEDAY, YOU AND WANDA WILL BE REUNITED FOREVER. WE ALL WILL.
I HOPE YOU'RE RIGHT. THANK YOU. THANK YOU SO MUCH, GRANNIE.
I HAVE TO GO NOW.
GOD BLESS YOU.

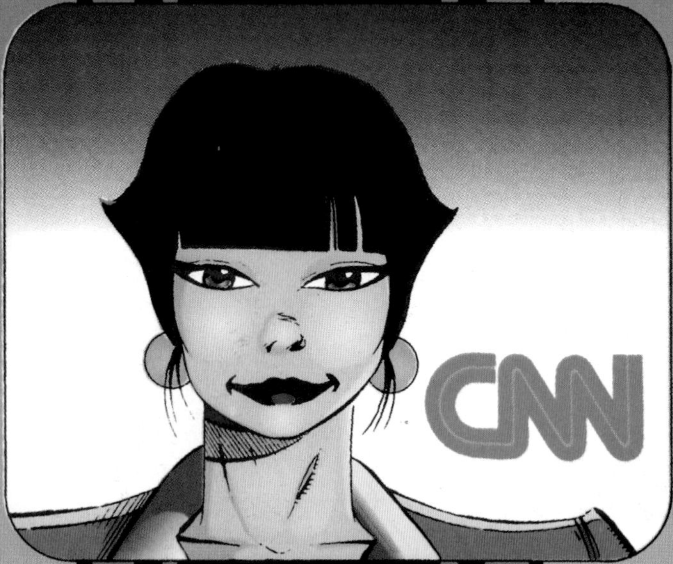
CNN

NEW YORK CITY OFFICIALS CONFIRMED THEIR INTENT TO BEEF UP POLICE PRESENCE IN MANHATTAN'S LOWER WEST IN RESPONSE TO THE SUDDEN RASH OF ***VIOLENCE*** IN THAT CITY'S BACK STREETS. BESIDES EARLIER REPORTS OF NONSANCTIONED ***YOUNGBLOOD*** ACTIVITY, THERE REMAINS THE QUESTION OF WHY SO MANY OF THE VICTIMS ARE SUSPECTE OF CONNECTIONS TO THE ***MAFIA***.

WITH THIS NEW DEVELOPMENT, IT COMES AS NO SURPRISE TO ORGANIZED CRIME WATCHER THAT SICILIAN BODYGUARD ***OVERT-KILL*** WAS REPORTEDLY SEEN IN NEW YORK LAST WEEK. HOWEVER, OUR REPORTERS HAVE HAD NO LUCK IN DETERMINING HIS WHEREABOUTS.

ACCORDING TO SOURCES CLOSE TO THE MAYOR'S OFFICE, MANHATTAN IS FACING THE GRIM POSSIBILITY OF A ***WAR***, SEEMINGLY BETWEEN THOSE MAFIA GANGS AND THE MOBS OF DISENFRANCHISED YOUTH WHO PATTERN THEMSELVES AFTER THE GOVERNMENT'S ***YOUNGBLOOD*** PROGRAM.

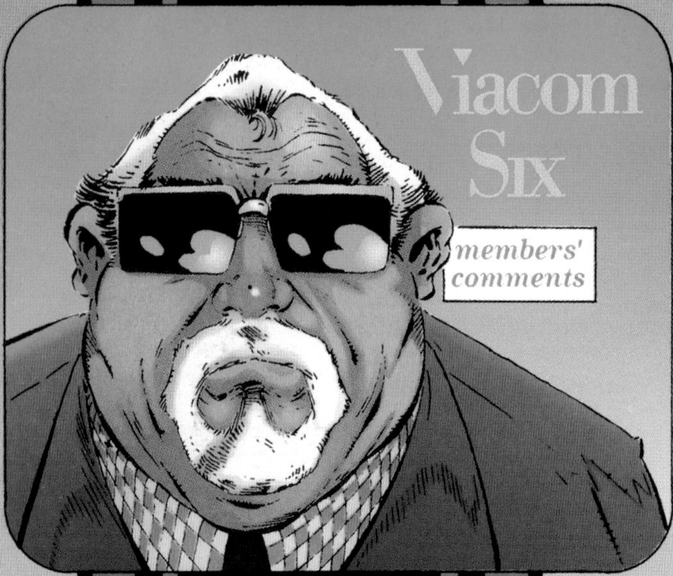
Viacom
Six
members' comments

SPINELESS WHELPS!!

THAT'S RIGHT, YOU PUNKS, ***YOU HEARD ME!*** IN MY DAY, WE DIDN'T RESORT TO SUCH ***COWARDLY*** STUNTS AS SHOOTING ONE ANOTHER! MIND YOU, I DON'T GIVE A ***HOOT*** IF YOU WANT TO LITTER THE ALLEYS WITH EACH OTHERS' ***INTESTINES!***

FACT ***IS***, THAT'D MAKE ME RATHER ***GIDDY.*** WHAT GETS MY GOAT, THOUGH, IS THAT YOU HAVE TO SHOOT AT ***ALL***. YOU WANT TO EMULATE THE GOVERNMENT WHIZ KIDS, FINE! I THINK THAT'S ***MORONIC***, BUT WHAT CAN I EXPECT FROM A BUNCH OF TEENAGE ***TECHNO-NERDS?!***

CERTAINLY ***NOT*** INTELLIGENCE.

WHEN ***I*** BELONGED TO GANGS, WE SETTLED THINGS WITH OUR ***FISTS!*** YOU COULD SEE THE ENEMY'S EYES. NOW ***YOU*** USE YOUNGBLOOD-TYPE MILITARY ***HARDWARE*** THAT CAN LEVEL A ***CITY BLOCK*** IN ONE SHOT.

OH YEAH, WHAT A BUNCHA ***FRIGGIN'*** HEROES

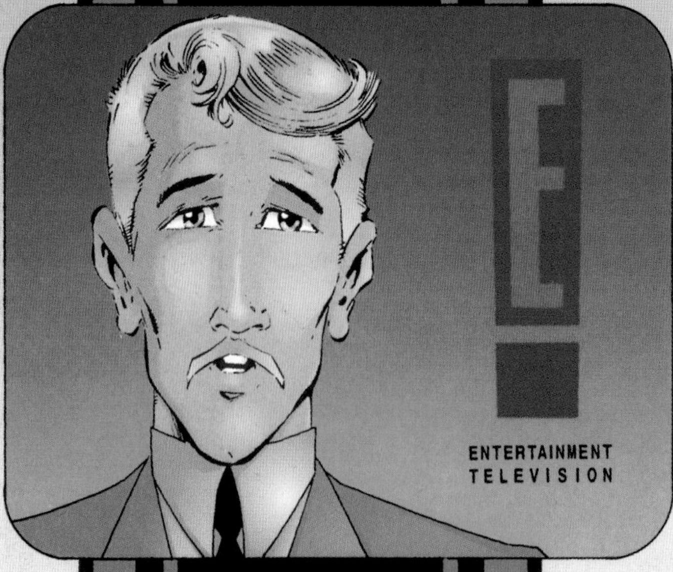
E!
ENTERTAINMENT
TELEVISION

IN A MAJOR COUP FOR ***PARAMOUNT***, STUDIO EXECUTIVES HAVE PURCHASED THE FILM RIGHTS TO MARK CURTIS' BEST-SELLER, ***"COURAGEOUS AMBITIONS: THE AL SIMMONS STORY."*** THIS UNOFFICIAL BIOGRAPHY DELVES INTO THE POLITICAL ARENA TO SHOW US JUST HOW DEMANDING IT CAN BE, WORKING AS ONE OF THE PRESIDENT'S ***ERRAND BOYS***.

FOLLOWING THE HUGE SUCCESS OF CLINT EASTWOOD'S NEW FILM *"IN THE LINE OF FIRE,"* AS WELL AS PRIOR FASCINATION WITH COLONEL OLIVER NORTH AND GENERAL "STORMIN'" NORMAN SCHWARTZ-KOPF, IT LOOKS AS IF HOLLYWOOD IS DETERMINED TO RUN THIS NEW GENRE INTO THE GROUND.

THIS JUST IN...

WE'VE RECEIVED WORD THAT THE AGENCY HANDLING YOUNGBLOODS' VERY OWN ***BEDROCK*** HAS RUN INTO SOME LEGAL SNAGS WITH ANIMATORS ***HANNA-BARBARA*** OVER NAME-USE RIGHTS.

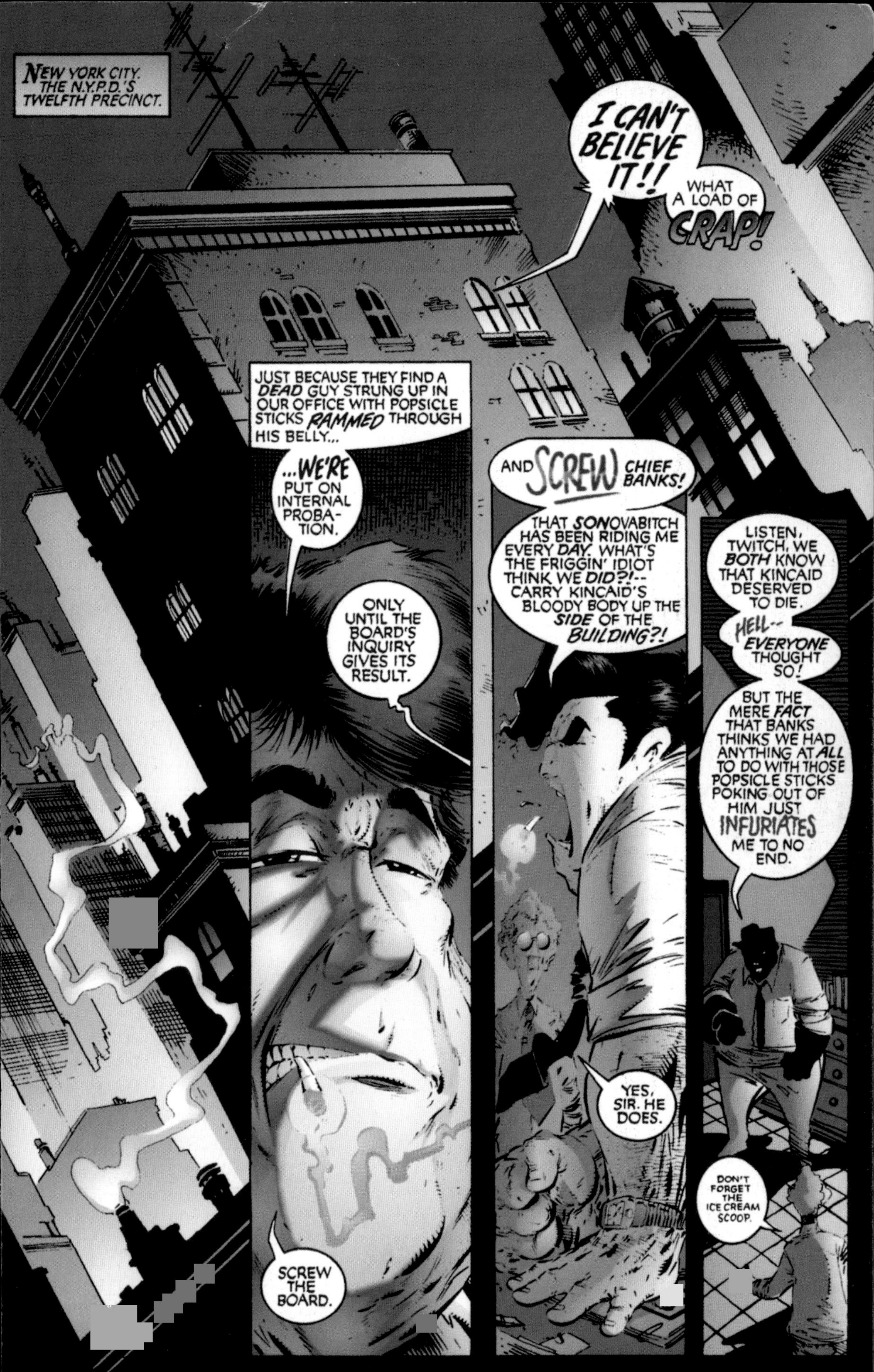
NEW YORK CITY. THE N.Y.P.D.'S TWELFTH PRECINCT.
I CAN'T BELIEVE IT!!
WHAT A LOAD OF CRAP!
JUST BECAUSE THEY FIND A DEAD GUY STRUNG UP IN OUR OFFICE WITH POPSICLE STICKS RAMMED THROUGH HIS BELLY...
...WE'RE PUT ON INTERNAL PROBA-TION.
ONLY UNTIL THE BOARD'S INQUIRY GIVES ITS RESULT.
SCREW THE BOARD.
AND SCREW CHIEF BANKS!
THAT SONOVABITCH HAS BEEN RIDING ME EVERY DAY. WHAT'S THE FRIGGIN' IDIOT THINK WE DID?!-- CARRY KINCAID'S BLOODY BODY UP THE SIDE OF THE BUILDING?!
YES, SIR. HE DOES.
LISTEN, TWITCH, WE BOTH KNOW THAT KINCAID DESERVED TO DIE.
HELL-- EVERYONE THOUGHT SO!
BUT THE MERE FACT THAT BANKS THINKS WE HAD ANYTHING AT ALL TO DO WITH THOSE POPSICLE STICKS POKING OUT OF HIM JUST INFURIATES ME TO NO END.
DON'T FORGET THE ICE CREAM SCOOP.

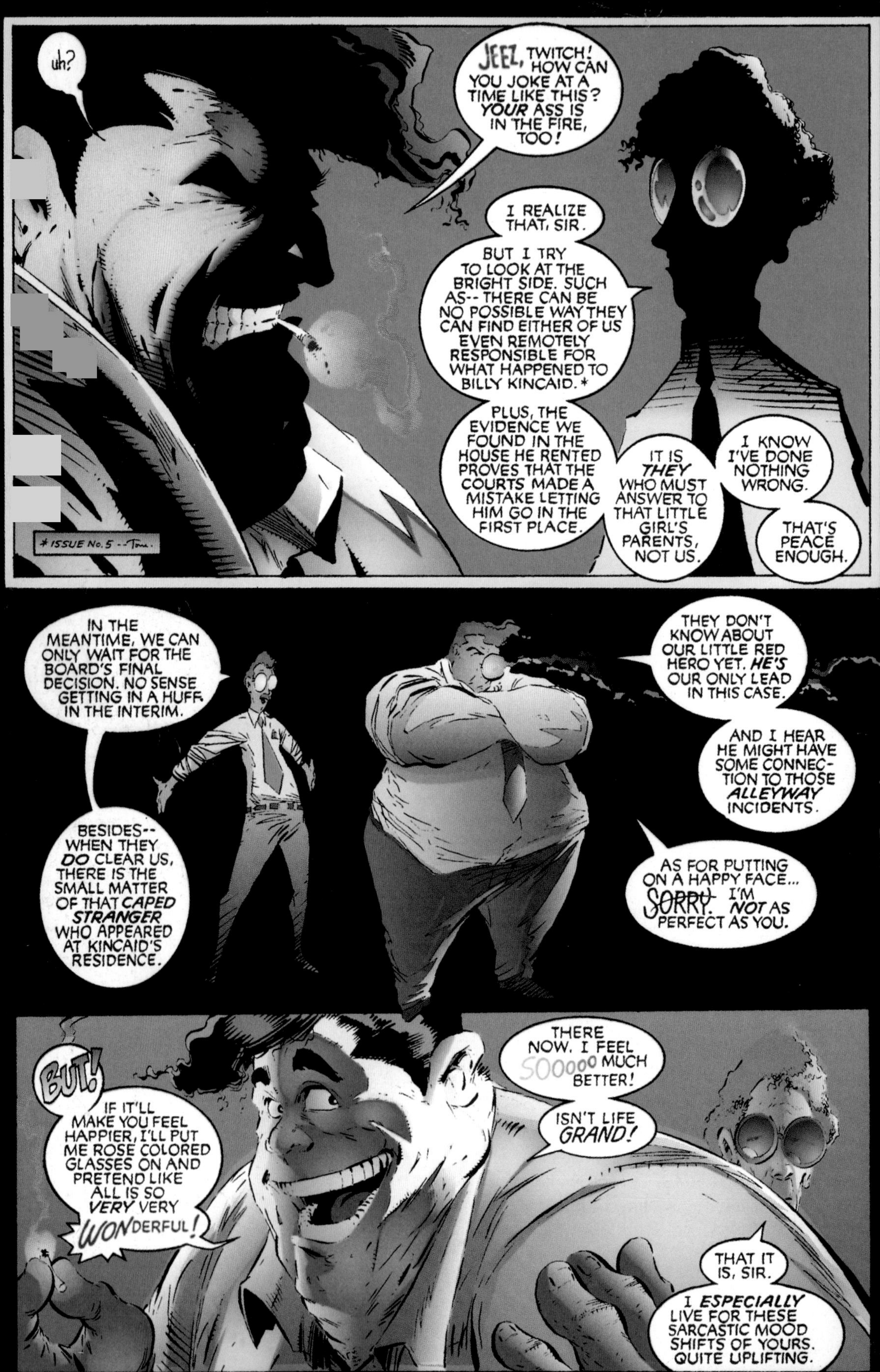
uh?
JEEZ, TWITCH! HOW CAN YOU JOKE AT A TIME LIKE THIS? YOUR ASS IS IN THE FIRE, TOO!
I REALIZE THAT, SIR.
BUT I TRY TO LOOK AT THE BRIGHT SIDE. SUCH AS-- THERE CAN BE NO POSSIBLE WAY THEY CAN FIND EITHER OF US EVEN REMOTELY RESPONSIBLE FOR WHAT HAPPENED TO BILLY KINCAID.*
PLUS, THE EVIDENCE WE FOUND IN THE HOUSE HE RENTED PROVES THAT THE COURTS MADE A MISTAKE LETTING HIM GO IN THE FIRST PLACE.
IT IS THEY WHO MUST ANSWER TO THAT LITTLE GIRL'S PARENTS, NOT US.
I KNOW I'VE DONE NOTHING WRONG.
THAT'S PEACE ENOUGH.
*ISSUE No.5 --Tom.
IN THE MEANTIME, WE CAN ONLY WAIT FOR THE BOARD'S FINAL DECISION. NO SENSE GETTING IN A HUFF IN THE INTERIM.
BESIDES-- WHEN THEY DO CLEAR US, THERE IS THE SMALL MATTER OF THAT CAPED STRANGER WHO APPEARED AT KINCAID'S RESIDENCE.
THEY DON'T KNOW ABOUT OUR LITTLE RED HERO YET. HE'S OUR ONLY LEAD IN THIS CASE.
AND I HEAR HE MIGHT HAVE SOME CONNECTION TO THOSE ALLEYWAY INCIDENTS.
AS FOR PUTTING ON A HAPPY FACE... SORRY. I'M NOT AS PERFECT AS YOU.
BUT!
IF IT'LL MAKE YOU FEEL HAPPIER, I'LL PUT ME ROSE COLORED GLASSES ON AND PRETEND LIKE ALL IS SO VERY VERY WONDERFUL!
THERE NOW. I FEEL SOOOOO MUCH BETTER!
ISN'T LIFE GRAND!
THAT IT IS, SIR.
I ESPECIALLY LIVE FOR THESE SARCASTIC MOOD SHIFTS OF YOURS. QUITE UPLIFTING.

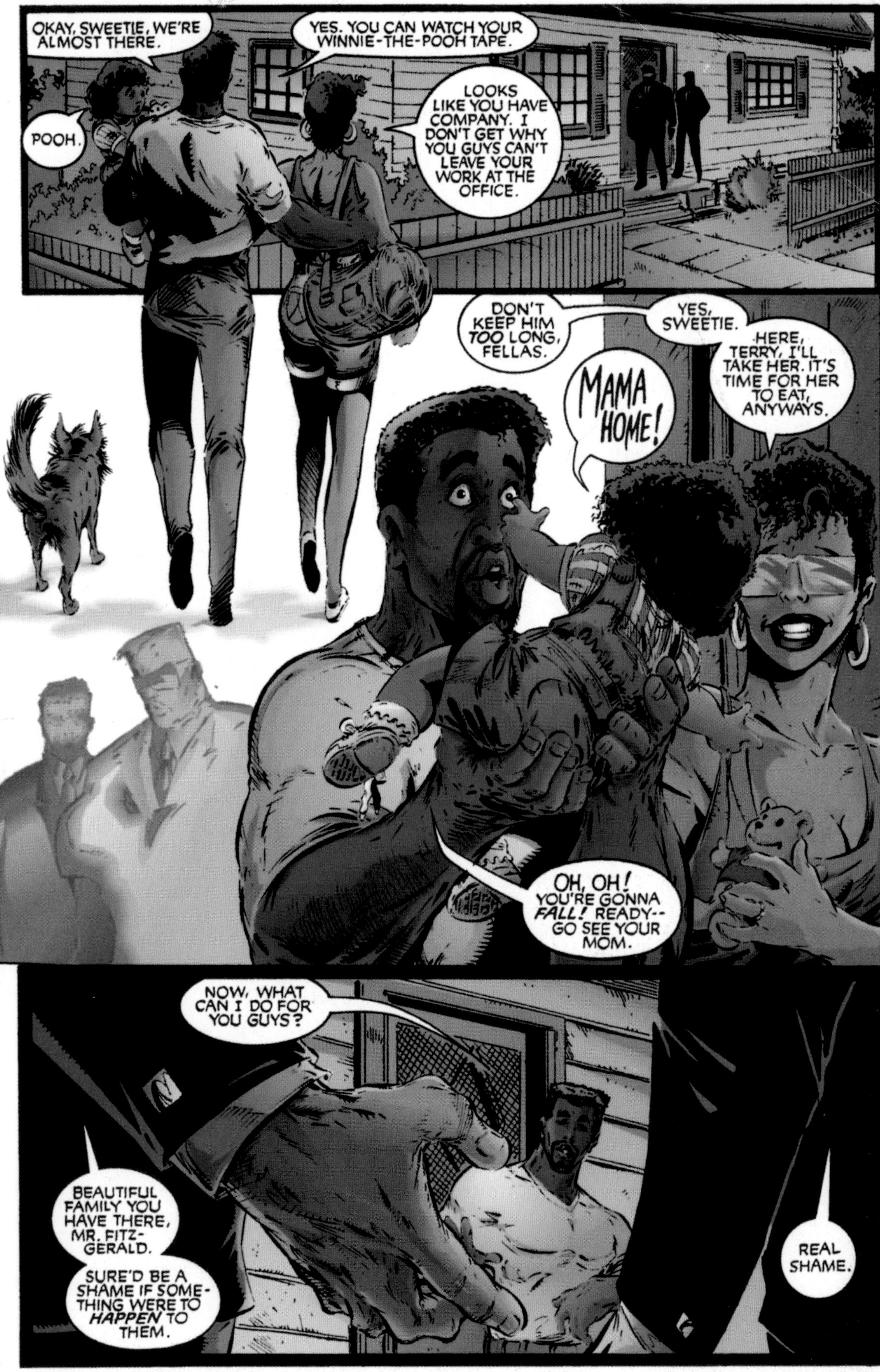

OKAY, SWEETIE, WE'RE ALMOST THERE.
POOH.
YES. YOU CAN WATCH YOUR WINNIE-THE-POOH TAPE.
LOOKS LIKE YOU HAVE COMPANY. I DON'T GET WHY YOU GUYS CAN'T LEAVE YOUR WORK AT THE OFFICE.
DON'T KEEP HIM TOO LONG, FELLAS.
YES, SWEETIE.
MAMA HOME!
HERE, TERRY, I'LL TAKE HER. IT'S TIME FOR HER TO EAT, ANYWAYS.
OH, OH! YOU'RE GONNA FALL! READY-- GO SEE YOUR MOM.
NOW, WHAT CAN I DO FOR YOU GUYS?
BEAUTIFUL FAMILY YOU HAVE THERE, MR. FITZ-GERALD.
SURE'D BE A SHAME IF SOMETHING WERE TO HAPPEN TO THEM.
REAL SHAME.

EXCELLENT! EXCELLENT!

FITZGERALD HAS BEEN PROPERLY ADVISED?!

YES, SIR.

WE'VE ALSO STARTED AROUND-THE-CLOCK SURVEILLANCE ON BOTH HE AND HIS WIFE.

PERFECT.

MIDNIGHT. THE BACK STREETS OF MANHATTAN'S LOWER EAST SIDE.

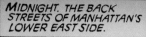

FRIENDS SHARE THEIR BOTTLES AND STORIES WITH EACH OTHER.

THEY ALSO SHARE ANYTHING ELSE THEY MIGHT HAVE IN COMMON WITH ONE ANOTHER.

WILMA!

glug-glug-

♪ FLINTST✲NES! MEET THE FLINTST✲NES! THEY'RE A MOD-uh STONE-AGE FA-uh-LY. FROM THE TO-uh OF BEDR✲CK— THEY'RE A PAGE RI-uh OUT OF HIS-TO-RY. WHEN uh— MEET THE FLINTST✲NES— YOU'LL HAVE A YABBA-uh-BA-D✲O TIME! A uh-BA-D✲O TIME! YOU'LL HAVE A GAY uh'TIME! ♪

WHOA!! TAKE IT EASY THERE, AL. SAVE SOME FOR US.

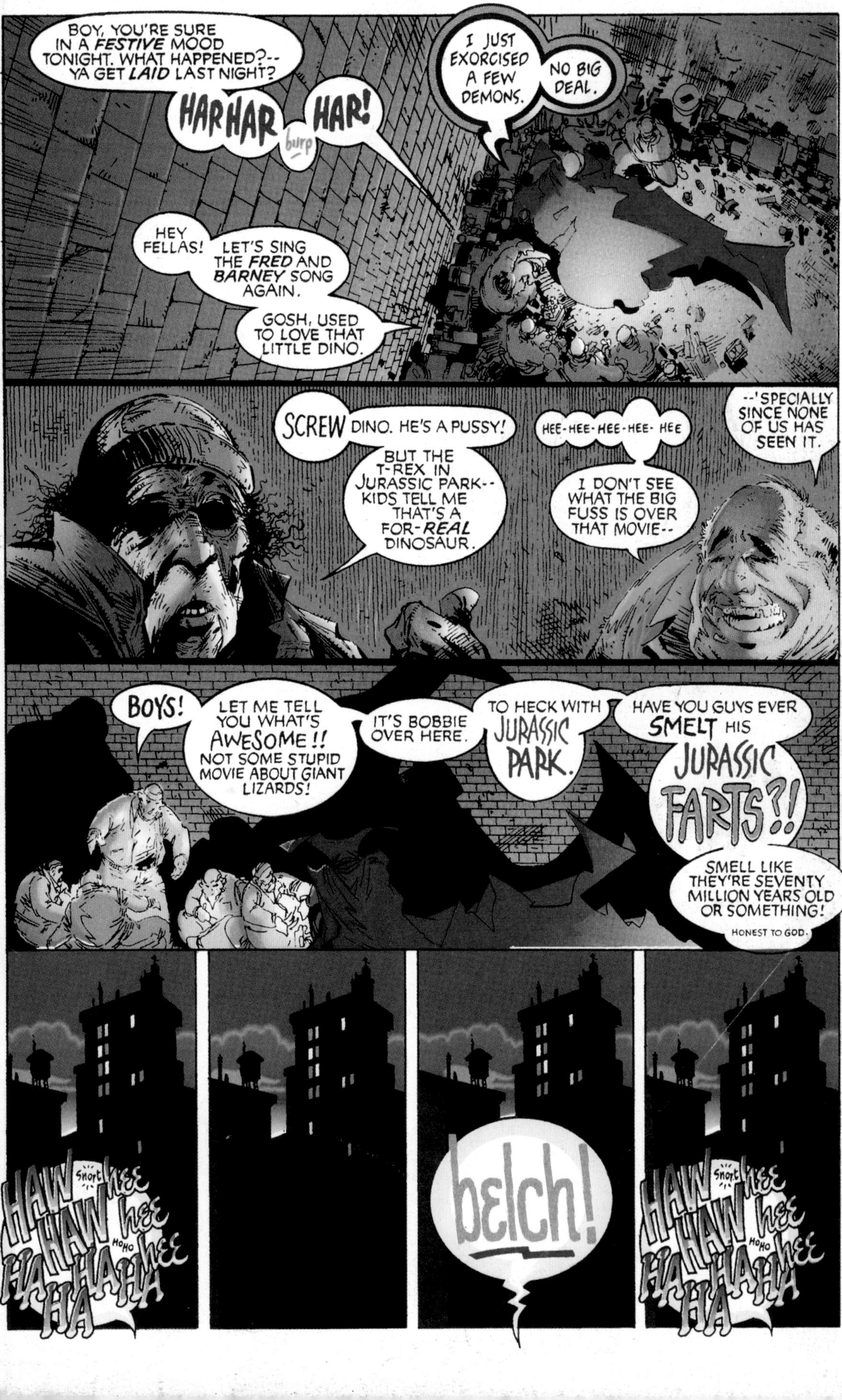

BOY, YOU'RE SURE IN A FESTIVE MOOD TONIGHT. WHAT HAPPENED?-- YA GET LAID LAST NIGHT?
HAR HAR burp HAR!
I JUST EXORCISED A FEW DEMONS.
NO BIG DEAL.
HEY FELLAS!
LET'S SING THE FRED AND BARNEY SONG AGAIN.
GOSH, USED TO LOVE THAT LITTLE DINO.
SCREW DINO. HE'S A PUSSY!
BUT THE T-REX IN JURASSIC PARK-- KIDS TELL ME THAT'S A FOR-REAL DINOSAUR.
HEE-HEE-HEE-HEE-HEE
I DON'T SEE WHAT THE BIG FUSS IS OVER THAT MOVIE--
--'SPECIALLY SINCE NONE OF US HAS SEEN IT.
BOYS!
LET ME TELL YOU WHAT'S AWESOME!! NOT SOME STUPID MOVIE ABOUT GIANT LIZARDS!
IT'S BOBBIE OVER HERE.
TO HECK WITH JURASSIC PARK.
HAVE YOU GUYS EVER SMELT HIS JURASSIC FARTS?!
SMELL LIKE THEY'RE SEVENTY MILLION YEARS OLD OR SOMETHING!
HONEST TO GOD.
HAW snort hee HAW hee HOHO hee HA HA HA HA HA
belch!
HAW snort hee HAW hee HOHO hee HA HA HA HA HA

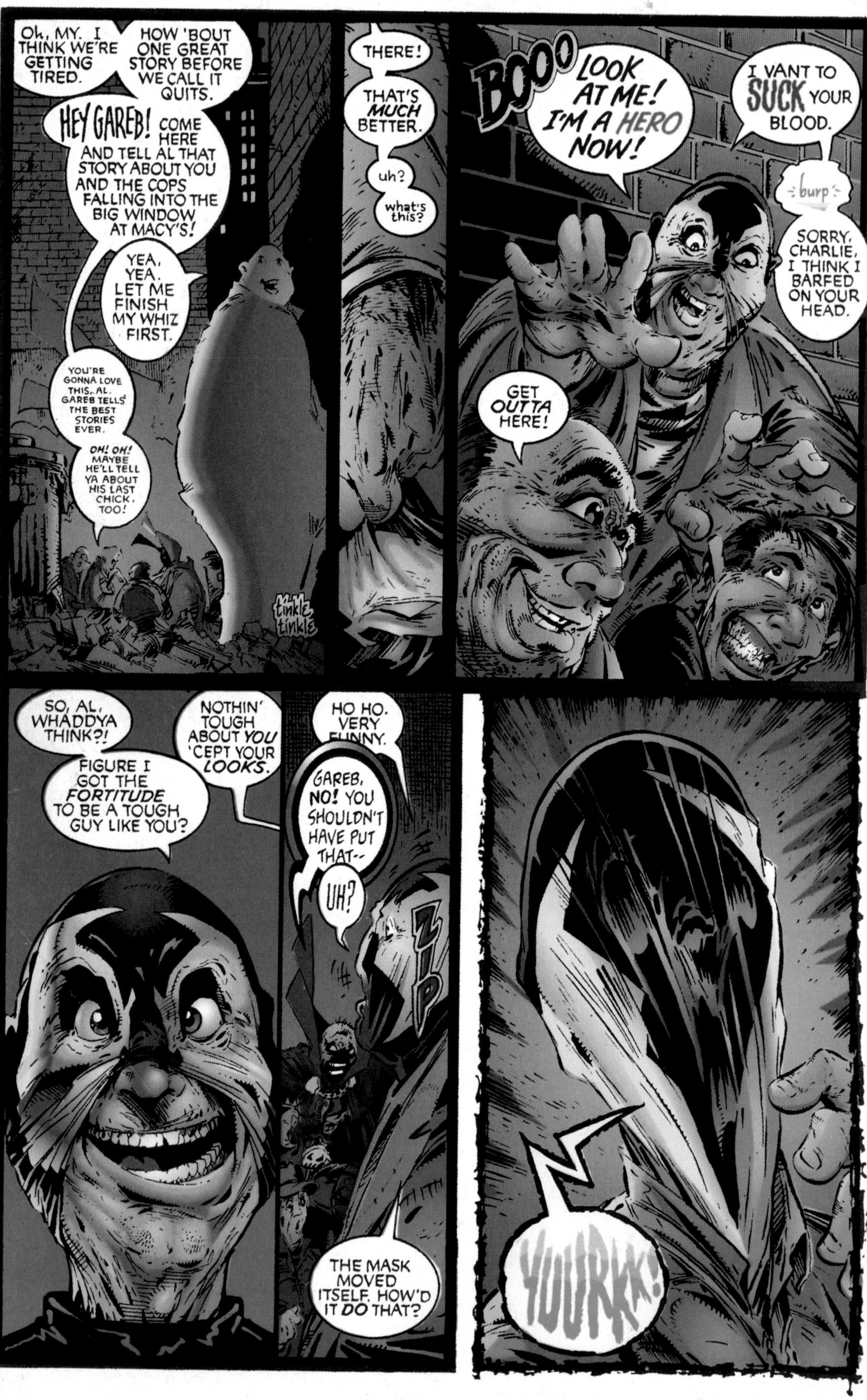

Oh, MY. I THINK WE'RE GETTING TIRED.
HOW 'BOUT ONE GREAT STORY BEFORE WE CALL IT QUITS.
HEY GAREB! COME HERE AND TELL AL THAT STORY ABOUT YOU AND THE COPS FALLING INTO THE BIG WINDOW AT MACY'S!
YEA, YEA. LET ME FINISH MY WHIZ FIRST.
YOU'RE GONNA LOVE THIS, AL. GAREB TELLS THE BEST STORIES EVER.
OH! OH! MAYBE HE'LL TELL YA ABOUT HIS LAST CHICK, TOO!
tinkle tinkle
THERE!
THAT'S MUCH BETTER.
uh?
what's this?
BOOO
LOOK AT ME! I'M A HERO NOW!
I VANT TO SUCK YOUR BLOOD.
burp
SORRY, CHARLIE, I THINK I BARFED ON YOUR HEAD.
GET OUTTA HERE!
SO, AL, WHADDYA THINK?!
FIGURE I GOT THE FORTITUDE TO BE A TOUGH GUY LIKE YOU?
NOTHIN' TOUGH ABOUT YOU 'CEPT YOUR LOOKS.
HO HO. VERY FUNNY.
GAREB, NO! YOU SHOULDN'T HAVE PUT THAT--
UH?
ZIP
THE MASK MOVED ITSELF. HOW'D IT DO THAT?
YUURKK!

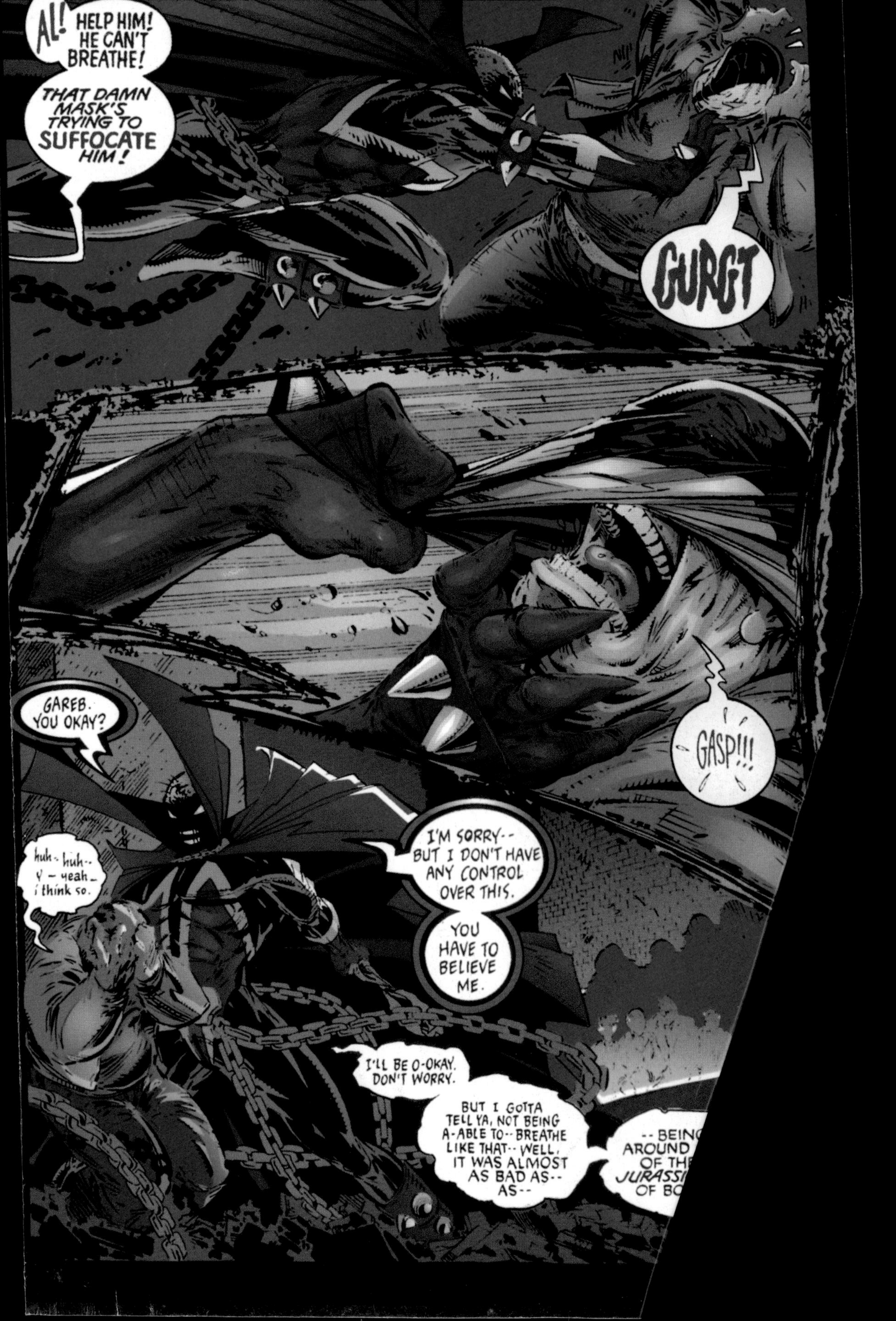
AL! HELP HIM! HE CAN'T BREATHE!
THAT DAMN MASK'S TRYING TO SUFFOCATE HIM!
GURGT
GAREB. YOU OKAY?
GASP!!!
huh-huh-y-yeah-i think so.
I'M SORRY-- BUT I DON'T HAVE ANY CONTROL OVER THIS.
YOU HAVE TO BELIEVE ME.
I'LL BE O-OKAY. DON'T WORRY.
BUT I GOTTA TELL YA, NOT BEING A-ABLE TO--BREATHE LIKE THAT--WELL, IT WAS ALMOST AS BAD AS-- AS--

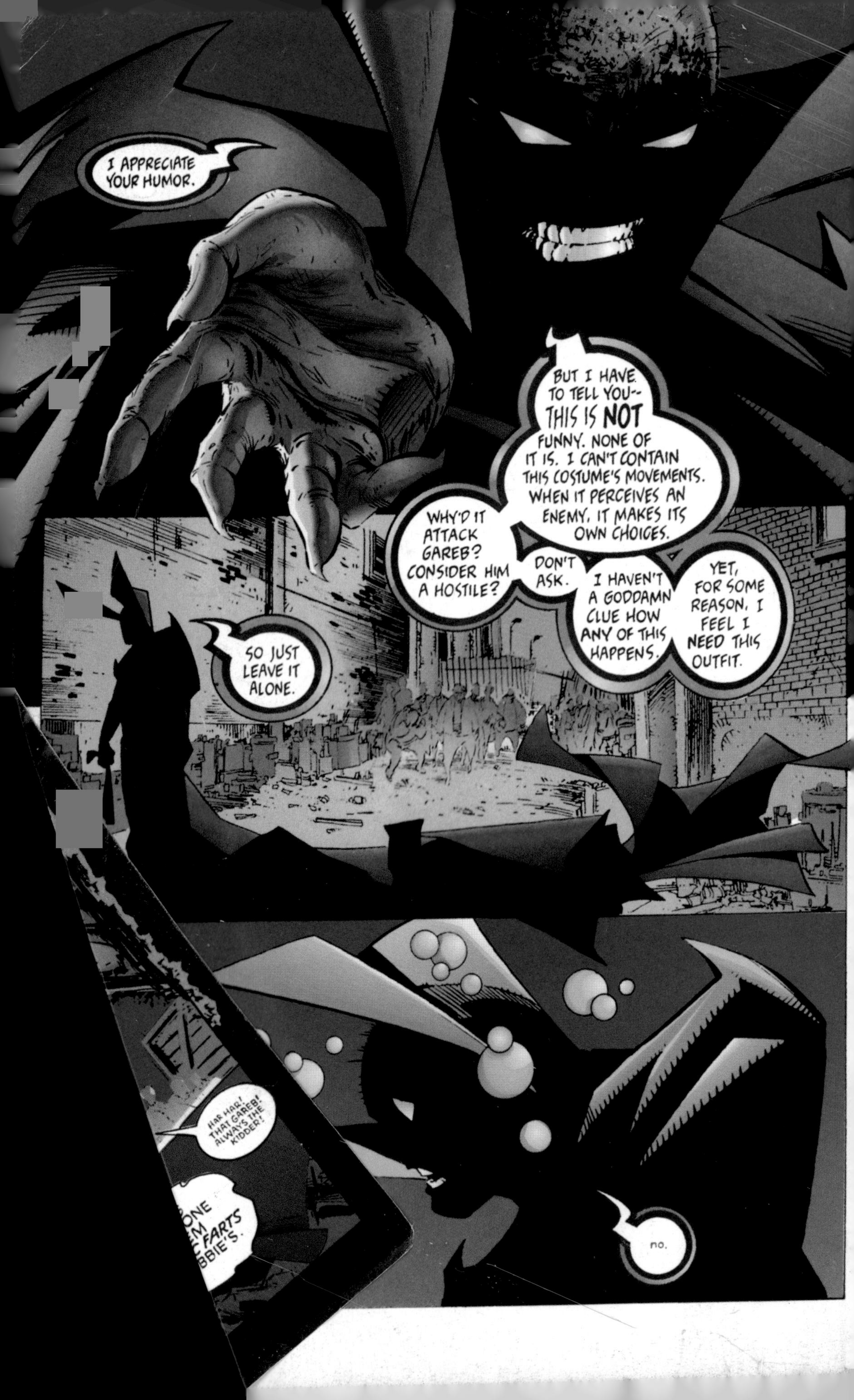
I APPRECIATE YOUR HUMOR.
BUT I HAVE TO TELL YOU-- THIS IS **NOT** FUNNY. NONE OF IT IS. I CAN'T CONTAIN THIS COSTUME'S MOVEMENTS. WHEN IT PERCEIVES AN ENEMY, IT MAKES ITS OWN CHOICES.
WHY'D IT ATTACK GAREB? CONSIDER HIM A HOSTILE?
DON'T ASK.
I HAVEN'T A GODDAMN CLUE HOW ANY OF THIS HAPPENS.
YET, FOR SOME REASON, I FEEL I NEED THIS OUTFIT.
SO JUST LEAVE IT ALONE.
HAR HAR! THAT GAREB! ALWAYS THE KIDDER!
ONE M FARTS BBIE'S.
no.

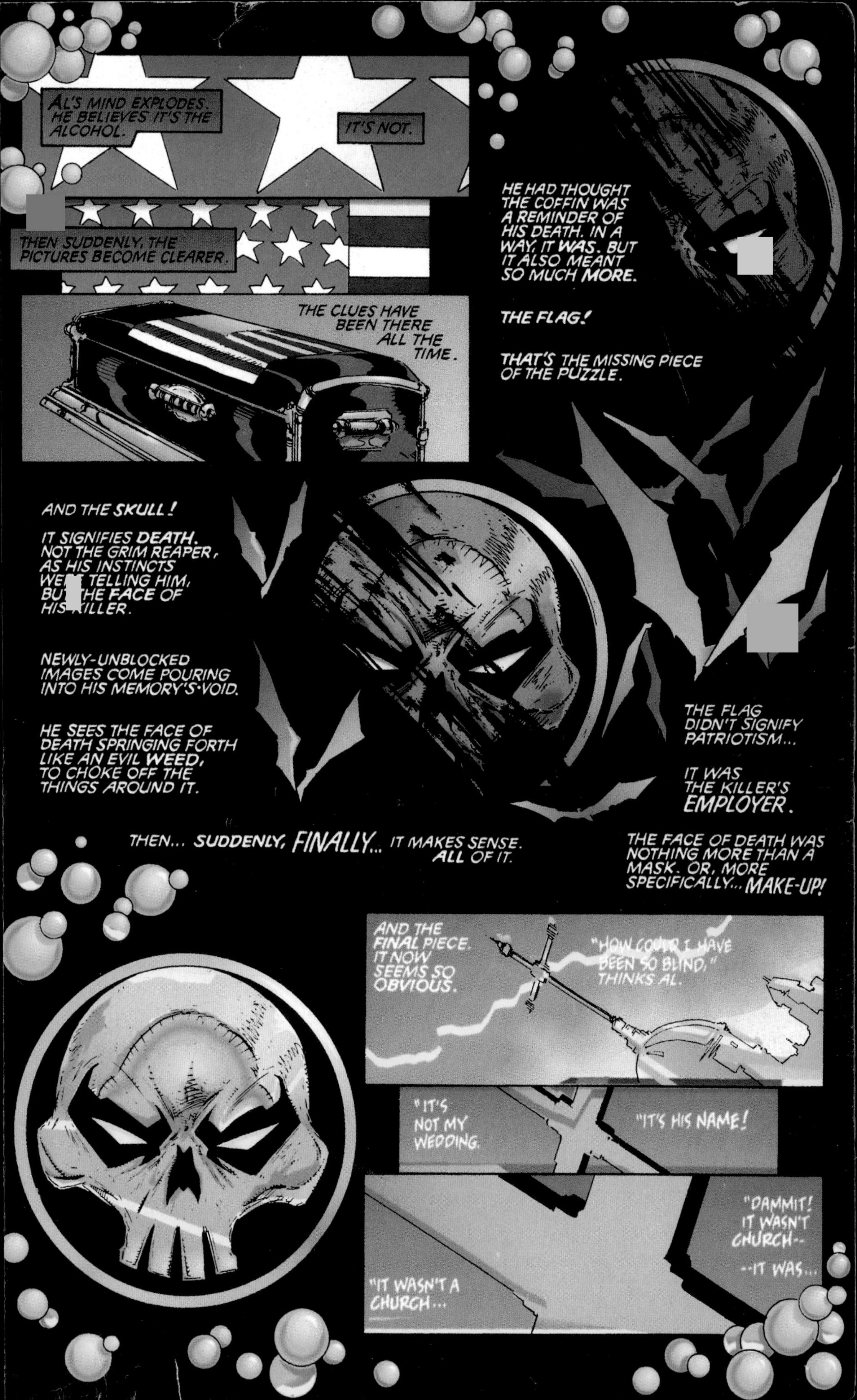
AL'S MIND EXPLODES. HE BELIEVES IT'S THE ALCOHOL.
IT'S NOT.
THEN SUDDENLY, THE PICTURES BECOME CLEARER.
THE CLUES HAVE BEEN THERE ALL THE TIME.
HE HAD THOUGHT THE COFFIN WAS A REMINDER OF HIS DEATH. IN A WAY, IT WAS. BUT IT ALSO MEANT SO MUCH MORE.
THE FLAG!
THAT'S THE MISSING PIECE OF THE PUZZLE.
AND THE SKULL!
IT SIGNIFIES DEATH. NOT THE GRIM REAPER, AS HIS INSTINCTS WERE TELLING HIM, BUT THE FACE OF HIS KILLER.
NEWLY-UNBLOCKED IMAGES COME POURING INTO HIS MEMORY'S VOID.
HE SEES THE FACE OF DEATH SPRINGING FORTH LIKE AN EVIL WEED, TO CHOKE OFF THE THINGS AROUND IT.
THE FLAG DIDN'T SIGNIFY PATRIOTISM...
IT WAS THE KILLER'S EMPLOYER.
THEN... SUDDENLY, FINALLY... IT MAKES SENSE. ALL OF IT.
THE FACE OF DEATH WAS NOTHING MORE THAN A MASK. OR, MORE SPECIFICALLY... MAKE-UP!
AND THE FINAL PIECE. IT NOW SEEMS SO OBVIOUS.
"HOW COULD I HAVE BEEN SO BLIND," THINKS AL.
"IT'S NOT MY WEDDING.
"IT'S HIS NAME!
"IT WASN'T A CHURCH...
"DAMMIT! IT WASN'T CHURCH--
--IT WAS...

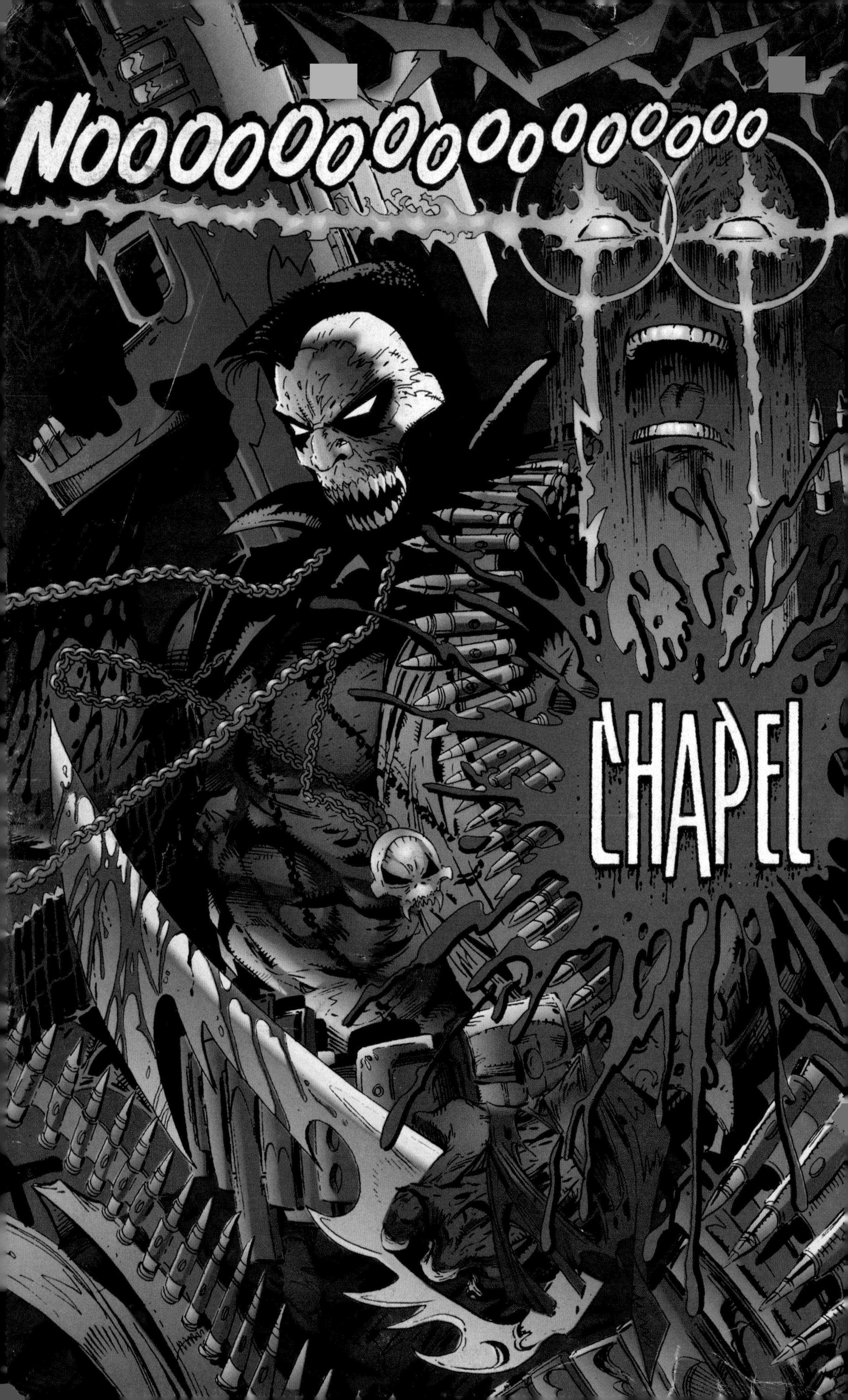
NOOOOOOOOOOOOOOOO
CHAPEL